MW00442736

EDITORIAL BOARD

SAUL LEVMORE
DIRECTING EDITOR
William B. Graham Distinguished Service Professor of Law and
Former Dean of the Law School
University of Chicago

DANIEL A. FARBER
Sho Sato Professor of Law
University of California at Berkeley

HEATHER K. GERKEN
Dean and the Sol & Lillian Goldman Professor of Law
Yale University

SAMUEL ISSACHAROFF
Bonnie and Richard Reiss Professor of Constitutional Law
New York University

HAROLD HONGJU KOH
Sterling Professor of International Law and
Former Dean of the Law School
Yale University

THOMAS W. MERRILL
Charles Evans Hughes Professor of Law
Columbia University

ROBERT L. RABIN
Calder Mackay Professor of Law
Stanford University

HILLARY A. SALE
Professor of Law and Affiliated Faculty
McDonough School of Business, Georgetown University

UNITED STATES CONSTITUTIONAL LAW

DANIEL FARBER
Sho Sato Professor of Law
University of California at Berkeley

NEIL S. SIEGEL
David W. Ichel Professor of Law
Professor of Political Science
Duke Law School

CONCEPTS AND INSIGHTS SERIES®

The publisher is not engaged in rendering legal or other professional advice, and this publication is not a substitute for the advice of an attorney. If you require legal or other expert advice, you should seek the services of a competent attorney or other professional.

Concepts and Insights Series is a trademark registered in the U.S. Patent and Trademark Office.

© 2019 LEG, Inc. d/b/a West Academic
    444 Cedar Street, Suite 700
    St. Paul, MN 55101
    1-877-888-1330

Printed in the United States of America

ISBN: 978-1-64020-801-8

To my brother Mike and my sisters Jackie and Lisa.

– DAF

For my parents, Sharon and Steven Siegel, for loving me and teaching me to value learning so that I might hope to lead a good, examined life.

– NSS

PREFACE

We approached this project with two goals in mind. First and foremost, for the benefit of students in law and political science and interested members of the public, we wanted to provide a clear, accessible, balanced, and intellectually sophisticated introduction to the field of U.S. constitutional law. In our view, providing such an introduction requires close attention *both* to the legal doctrine that is developed by the U.S. Supreme Court *and* to the ideas about the Constitution that circulate in constitutional politics—especially within social movements, political parties, and governmental institutions.

Second, by carefully documenting the interaction between judge-made constitutional law and constitutional politics in almost every area of constitutional law that is covered in the basic course in law school, we sought to make an intellectual contribution of our own. We wanted to document not just "dialogue" between the Constitution inside and outside the courts, but also the extent to which each is shaped by the other. In addition, we wished to offer theoretical ideas, historical examples, and citations to various literatures that scholars and instructors in law and political science might benefit from consulting as they pursue their own research and teaching. Among many other things, readers will find discussions within these pages of the main theories of constitutional interpretation; collective action federalism and more formalist approaches to constitutional federalism; the debate over the theory of the unitary executive; the benefits and costs of abandoning robust judicial protection of economic liberty; the three main mediating principles of constitutional equality, which model disagreements over race within both the Court and American society; the ideology of the separate spheres for men and women, which the women's movement sought—with substantial but incomplete success—to disestablish; and the modern Court's efforts to vindicate equality values in addition to liberty values under substantive due process.

We are satisfied that this first edition makes substantial progress in achieving these two goals. In future editions, we plan to fix any mistakes and omissions, as well as to refine and extend our analyses. We therefore encourage all readers—whether students, professors, or citizens—to contact us if they have corrections, criticisms, or comments they wish to share. Dan Farber can be reached at dfarber@berkeley.edu. Neil Siegel can be reached at siegel@law.duke.edu.

Dan Farber thanks the co-authors in previous writings about constitutional law from whom he has learned so much: Bill Eskridge, the late Phil Frickey, John Nowak, Jane Schacter, and Suzanna Sherry. And he also thanks Dianne Farber for her patience during an intense writing process.

Neil Siegel thanks the many law students, undergraduates, and judges he has had the privilege of teaching—and learning from—over the past fifteen years. He also recognizes the strong support of Kate Bartlett and David Levi, his Deans at Duke Law School. He is indebted as well to his co-authors over the years—especially Curt Bradley, Bob Cooter, and Reva Siegel—whose work with him is partially reflected in these pages. Most of all, he is grateful to his spouse and daughters—Maria, Sydney, and Dylan—for their love, enthusiasm, and encouragement while he worked on this book.

DANIEL FARBER

NEIL S. SIEGEL

February 2019

SUMMARY OF CONTENTS

PREFACE V

Chapter 1. Introduction 1
I.   Our Approach 1
II.   A Catalogue of Constitutional Arguments 6
III. How to Use This Book 9
IV.   Audiences for the Book 10
V.   Roadmap 11

Chapter 2. The Role (and Regulation) of the Courts 17
I.   Judicial Review 17
II.   The Regulation of Courts 31

Chapter 3. Implementing Judicial Review 43
I.   Limits on Federal Jurisdiction 43
II.   Theories of Constitutional Interpretation 60

**Chapter 4. Defining the Nature of the Union: The Federal
Structure and the Necessary and Proper Clause** 79
I.   From the Articles to the Constitution 81
II.   Nationalism and the Marshall Court: The Constitutional
Politics and Law of the Bank 85
III. The Necessary and Proper Clause Today 102

Chapter 5. Interstate Commerce Clause 107
I.   Introduction 107
II.   The Marshall Court 110
III. The Republican Era 115
IV.   The Crisis of 1937 and Constitutional Change 126
V.   From 1937 to the 1990s 129
VI.   The Current Era 134
VII. The Dormant Commerce Principle 159

Chapter 6. Taxing and Spending Powers 163
I.   The Purposes for Which Congress May Tax and Spend 164
II.   The Difference Between a Tax and a Penalty 167
III. The Limits on Conditional Federal Spending 176

Chapter 7. Presidential Power 183
I.   The President's Constitutional Role 183
II.   The *Steel Seizure Case* and Theories of the Presidency 186
III. The President as Chief Executive 194
IV.   Foreign Affairs and Military Powers 205
V.   Checks on Presidential Power 220

Chapter 8. Constitutional Rights and the States **231**
I.   The Bill of Rights and Civil War Amendments 233
II.   Incorporation 239
III. State Action Doctrine 245

Chapter 9. Economic Regulation and Constitutional Rights **255**
I.   The Nineteenth Century and the *Lochner* Era 255
II.   Rational Basis Review and *Carolene Products* 260
III. The Takings Clause 267
IV.   Procedural Due Process 273

Chapter 10. "The Equal Protection of the Laws": Race and Gender **279**
I.   Race and the Constitution 280
II.   Gender and the Constitution 324

Chapter 11. Fundamental Rights Protected Under Equal Protection **347**
I.   Legislative Districting 348
II.   Access to Redress 362
III. The Right to Travel 366
IV.   Education 369

Chapter 12. Fundamental Rights: Substantive Due Process **377**
I.   Family Autonomy and Marriage 378
II.   Reproductive Rights 381
III. Gay Rights and the Constitution 410
IV.   Privacy Rights at the End of Life 421

Chapter 13. Where Structure Meet Rights: The Reconstruction Powers **427**
I.   May Congress Regulate Private Conduct? 429
II.   What Is the Nature of Section 5 of the Fourteenth Amendment? 434
III. Enforcement of the Fifteenth Amendment 443

Appendix. The Constitution of the United States **455**

TABLE OF CASES 475

INDEX 481

TABLE OF CONTENTS

PREFACE V

Chapter 1. Introduction 1
I.   Our Approach.. 1
II.   A Catalogue of Constitutional Arguments............................. 6
III. How to Use This Book 9
IV.   Audiences for the Book.. 10
V.   Roadmap... 11

Chapter 2. The Role (and Regulation) of the Courts 17
I.   Judicial Review.. 17
      A.   A New Hope for Federalists 18
      B.   The Democratic Republicans Strike Back.................... 20
      C.   Return of the Federalists 20
      D.   Marshall's Case for Judicial Review............................ 23
      E.   The Importance of Critiquing Marshall's Arguments 27
II.   The Regulation of Courts 31
      A.   Size of Supreme Court (and Organization of Lower
           Federal Courts) 31
      B.   Congressional Control of Federal Court Jurisdiction....... 34
      C.   Nomination and Confirmation of Federal Judges 37
      D.   Impeachment of Federal Judges.................................. 38
      E.   Constitutional Amendment.. 39
      F.   Presidential Rhetoric, Social Movement Advocacy,
           and Litigation... 40

Chapter 3. Implementing Judicial Review 43
I.   Limits on Federal Jurisdiction 43
      A.   Political Question Doctrine 45
      B.   Standing 48
      C.   Ripeness, Mootness, and Other Limitations................. 55
II.   Theories of Constitutional Interpretation............................ 60
      A.   The *Carolene Products* Approach................................. 62
      B.   Originalism 64
      C.   Evolutionary Theories 70

**Chapter 4. Defining the Nature of the Union: The
Federal Structure and the Necessary and Proper
Clause**.. 79
I.   From the Articles to the Constitution 81
      A.   The Articles of Confederation and the Critical
           Period.. 81
      B.   The Constitutional Convention.................................... 83
      C.   The Constitution and Collective Action 84
II.   Nationalism and the Marshall Court: The Constitutional
      Politics and Law of the Bank.. 85
      A.   The Constitutional Convention.................................... 86
      B.   The Political Branches 87

C.   *McCulloch v. Maryland* 90
D.   Constitutional Politics, Again 99
III. The Necessary and Proper Clause Today 102

Chapter 5. Interstate Commerce Clause 107
I.   Introduction 107
II.   The Marshall Court 110
A.   *Gibbons v. Ogden* 110
B.   Collective Action Federalism 114
C.   Putting *Gibbons* in Perspective 115
III. The Republican Era 115
A.   Economic Changes and Constitutional Politics 116
B.   What Is "Commerce"? 118
C.   When Is Commerce "Among the Several States"? 122
D.   The Big Picture 125
IV.   The Crisis of 1937 and Constitutional Change 126
V.   From 1937 to the 1990s 129
A.   A New Era 129
B.   The Constitutionality of the Civil Rights Act of
      1964 132
VI.   The Current Era 134
A.   Changes in Constitutional Politics 135
B.   Changes in Commerce Clause Doctrine 136
C.   Applying Current Commerce Clause Doctrine 144
D.   The Constitutionality of the "Individual Mandate" 146
E.   The Anti-Commandeering Principle 149
VII. The Dormant Commerce Principle 159

Chapter 6. Taxing and Spending Powers 163
I.   The Purposes for Which Congress May Tax and Spend 164
A.   The Constitutional Politics of the "General
      Welfare" 164
B.   The Constitutional Law of the "General Welfare" 166
II.   The Difference Between a Tax and a Penalty 167
A.   The Distinction Before *NFIB* 167
B.   *NFIB* 173
III. The Limits on Conditional Federal Spending 176
A.   *Dole* and the Relatedness Requirement 177
B.   *NFIB* and Coercion 178

Chapter 7. Presidential Power 183
I.   The President's Constitutional Role 183
II.   The *Steel Seizure Case* and Theories of the Presidency 186
A.   Presidential Power in the Founding Era 186
B.   Theoretical Perspectives 189
C.   The *Steel Seizure Case* 190
III. The President as Chief Executive 194
A.   The Appointments Power 195
B.   The Implied Removal Power 198
C.   The Unitary Executive Theory and Its Critics 202

IV. Foreign Affairs and Military Powers... 205
    A. Inherent Foreign Affairs Powers 206
    B. Executive Agreements.. 209
    C. The President as Commander in Chief 212
    D. Executive Power and Individual Rights........................ 214
V. Checks on Presidential Power 220
    A. Congressional Appropriations and Investigations 220
    B. Legislative Control of Statutory Implementation 221
    C. Judicial Oversight... 225

Chapter 8. Constitutional Rights and the States................ 231
I. The Bill of Rights and Civil War Amendments..................... 233
    A. Individual Rights and the Original Constitution 233
    B. The Reconstruction Amendments................................ 235
II. Incorporation.. 239
    A. The (Near) Demise of the Privileges or Immunities
       Clause 239
    B. The Incorporation Debates... 241
    C. Incorporation Today 244
III. State Action Doctrine 245
    A. *The Civil Rights Cases*... 246
    B. *Shelley v. Kramer* and the Civil Rights Era.................. 247
    C. Modern State Action Doctrine 250

**Chapter 9. Economic Regulation and Constitutional
    Rights 255**
I. The Nineteenth Century and the *Lochner* Era...................... 255
    A. Pre-*Lochner*-Era Restrictions on Economic
       Regulation 256
    B. *Lochner* and Related Cases 257
II. Rational Basis Review and *Carolene Products*...................... 260
    A. The Death of Substantive Due Process 260
    B. Equal Protection and Economic Regulation................... 262
    C. Understanding the Retreat from *Lochner*..................... 264
III. The Takings Clause... 267
    A. Foundations of Regulatory Takings Doctrine 267
    B. Physical Takings.. 269
    C. Total Takings 270
IV. Procedural Due Process.. 273

**Chapter 10. "The Equal Protection of the Laws": Race
    and Gender 279**
I. Race and the Constitution 280
    A. The Constitutional Law and Politics of Slavery 280
    B. Adoption of the Reconstruction Amendments 285
    C. The Republican Era 289
    D. *Brown v. Board of Education* 295
    E. The Emergence of the Suspect Classification
       Doctrine 305
    F. Disparate Impact 308

    G.   Affirmative Action 313
II. Gender and the Constitution 324
    A.   History... 324
    B.   The Race-Sex Analogy 329
    C.   The Road to Intermediate Scrutiny............................... 330
    D.   The Meaning of Intermediate Scrutiny...................... 334
    E.   Pregnancy as Justification for Different
        Treatment.. 336
    F.   Establishing a Sex Classification 340

**Chapter 11. Fundamental Rights Protected Under
Equal Protection 347**
I.   Legislative Districting... 348
    A.   One Person, One Vote... 349
    B.   Racial Discrimination and Racial
        Gerrymandering 355
    C.   Political Gerrymandering... 359
II. Access to Redress.. 362
    A.   Access to Courts.. 362
    B.   Access to the Ballot.. 365
III. The Right to Travel 366
IV. Education 369

**Chapter 12. Fundamental Rights: Substantive Due
Process... 377**
I.   Family Autonomy and Marriage 378
    A.   Parental Rights and Family Relationships.................... 378
    B.   Marriage... 380
II. Reproductive Rights 381
    A.   Sterilization.. 382
    B.   Contraception.. 384
    C.   *Roe v. Wade* and Strict Scrutiny 392
    D.   *Casey* and the Undue Burden Test 401
    E.   Beyond *Casey* 405
III. Gay Rights and the Constitution.............................. 410
    A.   Sodomy Laws 411
    B.   *Obergefell* and Beyond.. 416
IV. Privacy Rights at the End of Life 421
    A.   Refusals of Medical Treatment 422
    B.   Physician-Assisted Suicide....................................... 423

**Chapter 13. Where Structure Meet Rights: The
Reconstruction Powers 427**
I.   May Congress Regulate Private Conduct?............................ 429
    A.   *The Civil Rights Cases*... 429
    B.   Current Law... 432
II. What Is the Nature of Section 5 of the Fourteenth
    Amendment? 434
    A.   The Nationalist View.. 435
    B.   The States' Rights View 438

III. Enforcement of the Fifteenth Amendment 443
    A.   The Nationalist View 445
    B.   The States' Rights View 446

Appendix. The Constitution of the United States 455

TABLE OF CASES 475

INDEX 481

UNITED STATES CONSTITUTIONAL LAW

Chapter 1

INTRODUCTION

As anyone who reads a newspaper or a blog, watches cable TV, or follows Twitter knows, debates about the Constitution are a central part of public life in the United States. When the Supreme Court upholds a health care "mandate" as a tax but gives states discretion over expanding Medicaid, one-sixth of the U.S. economy is affected, along with a multitude of individual lives. So the practical importance of constitutional law should need no argument.

U.S. constitutional law is also an intellectually exciting and dynamic field of study. It combines the analytical rigor of the best legal reasoning with the theoretical, historical, political, and cultural insights of scholarship in a number of academic disciplines. Constitutional law is the basic course in the law school curriculum that is most closely tied to changes in national politics. As Americans continue to work out how they define their community and what they owe one another, their resolutions of these issues affect, and are affected by, the legal doctrine that is developed by the U.S. Supreme Court. This book offers law students, political science students, scholars, teachers, and engaged citizens an accessible introduction to the concepts and insights that are most central to the field of U.S. constitutional law.

In this introductory chapter, we will first explain our approach to the subject, which seeks to draw on learning from both law and political science. We will then introduce the kinds of constitutional arguments that participants in constitutional debates routinely make. After that, we will suggest how to use this book and we will identify the multiple audiences for the book. Finally, we will provide a roadmap to the remainder of the book. The roadmap is not only a glimpse at coming attractions; it also gives the opportunity to illustrate our approach and to offer an overview of the major areas of doctrine.

I. Our Approach

There are different ways in which a book can attempt to illuminate constitutional law for students and citizens. The most traditional approach, and still the dominant one in law schools, is to focus on the decisions and doctrines of the U.S. Supreme Court. Some experts on constitutional law, following Professor Alexander Bickel, regard the Court as so powerful and so independent an institution that they believe judge-made constitutional law presents a "countermajoritarian difficulty."[1] On this view, the prominent role of judicial decisions in limiting what popular majorities can do is not easily reconciled with the American commitment to majoritarian democracy. Bickel emphasized "the essential reality that judicial review is a deviant institution in American democracy," and he identified as "[t]he root difficulty" the fact that "judicial review is a counter-majoritarian force in our system."[2]

In support of this perspective on constitutional law, one might invoke the commitments of advocates of gun control in debates over the Second Amendment. The Court's leading decisions protecting gun rights, *District of Columbia v. Heller* in 2008[3] and *McDonald v. City of Chicago* in 2010,[4] render unconstitutional at least some gun control measures that democratic majorities may seek to enact in order to combat gun violence. From the point of view of gun control advocates, then, the Court stands in the path of democracy. Yet the contrary perspective of gun rights advocates also supports the idea that the Court enjoys substantial independence from democratic politics. The National Rifle Association (NRA) views the Second Amendment as far more sweeping than the Court's opinions to date plausibly support. From the NRA's point of view, the Court is lagging behind important political actors. Both sides view the Court as an independent actor, not just a reflection of politics.

An alternative approach to introducing the field of constitutional law, and one that predominates among political scientists and law professors who study the political determinants of judicial decisionmaking, is to focus on constitutional politics instead of constitutional law. Constitutional politics can be thought of as the beliefs about the Constitution of non-judicial actors such as politicians, political elites, social movements, interest groups, and the media. Experts who emphasize the importance of constitutional politics believe that Supreme Court doctrine *reflects* the constitutional commitments and ideas circulating outside the courts far more often than the doctrine *shapes* these commitments and ideas.

For example, Professor Barry Friedman wrote in response to Bickel and the many experts who followed Bickel's lead that "the classic complaint about judicial review—that it interferes with the

---

[1] ALEXANDER M. BICKEL, THE LEAST DANGEROUS BRANCH: THE SUPREME COURT AT THE BAR OF POLITICS 18 (1962).

[2]   *Id.* at 16.

[3]   554 U.S. 570 (2008).

[4]   561 U.S. 742 (2010).

will of the people to govern themselves—is radically overstated."[5] In Friedman's view, Bickel's concern misses the reality that "[t]he accountability of the justices . . . to the popular will has been established time and time again."[6] Friedman carefully qualifies his claim, however, to apply only to salient issues gaining broad public attention, only to most (not all) of these decisions, and only over the long run. Thus, even on Friedman's view, many consequential decisions of the Supreme Court may impact society despite being out of tune with popular beliefs.[7]

This approach to introducing the field of constitutional law also finds support in the example of the Second Amendment. After decades of failed legal advocacy but much greater political success, the NRA and other supporters of gun rights eventually succeeded in influencing Supreme Court decisionmaking to a substantial (if far-from-complete) extent. The same could be said of the social movement for gay rights that eventually resulted in the Court's declaration in *Obergefell v. Hodges* in 2015 that the fundamental right to marry includes same-sex marriage.[8] Although the majority opinions in *Heller* and *Obergefell* emphasized different approaches to constitutional interpretation (originalism and living constitutionalism, respectively), both opinions partially reflected the influence of social movements on the path of Supreme Court doctrine and the success of these movements in persuading large segments of the public.

Animating this book is the conviction that each of the two approaches to teaching constitutional law identified above captures a partial truth but misses the partial truth captured by the other. In our view (which was actually Bickel's as well), the Court both acts and is acted upon. There is an interactive relationship between constitutional politics and judge-made constitutional law, not simply a one-way direction of influence from the Court to the country or from the country to the Court. Abortion is a good example. Over the decades since the Court decided *Roe v. Wade* in 1973,[9] the issues of whether and when governments may restrict women's access to abortion have profoundly influenced judicial appointments. Pro-life forces have constantly pushed back against the Court, testing the limits of what it will allow. Yet so far, although the Court has

---

[5]   BARRY FRIEDMAN, THE WILL OF THE PEOPLE: HOW PUBLIC OPINION HAS INFLUENCED THE SUPREME COURT AND SHAPED THE MEANING OF THE CONSTITUTION 9 (2009).

[6]   *Id.* at 370.

[7]   For a discussion of the significance of these important qualifications on Friedman's argument, see Neil S. Siegel, *A Coase Theorem for Constitutional Theory*, 2010 MICH. ST. L. REV. 583, 594 (symposium on FRIEDMAN, *supra* note 5).

[8]   135 S. Ct. 2584 (2015).

[9]   410 U.S. 113 (1973).

tempered its position, it has not given in, with Republican appointees Sandra Day O'Connor, David Souter, and Anthony Kennedy illustrating how Justices and other judges can be somewhat independent of the political coalitions primarily responsible for their presence on the Court.[10]

This book therefore takes a third, middle approach to introducing the subject of U.S. constitutional law. In our view, Supreme Court decisions are worthy of close examination in their own right for a number of reasons: they are widely recognized as binding; the executive branch feels an obligation to comply with or enforce them even when it strongly disagrees with their reasoning or results; the Court in deciding cases relies in part on precedent—on its own prior decisions—in a way that makes legal doctrine important; the Justices enjoy life tenure and are somewhat insulated from public opinion; and pivotal Justices have at critical times shown fierce independent streaks. As a result, Supreme Court decisions can have large social consequences that are meaningfully independent of developments in constitutional politics or politics more generally.

It matters, for example, that the Court has the capacity to obtain compliance with its decisions in an institutional struggle with the President. President Richard Nixon turned over secret recordings of his Oval Office conversations after the Court held in *United States v. Nixon* in 1974 that a President's attempt to keep communications with advisors secret (called an invocation of "executive privilege") can be overcome by the judiciary's need for evidence in a criminal trial.[11] The Court also obtained compliance with its 1988 decision in *Morrison v. Olson*, which upheld the constitutionality of a federal statute that restricted the President's authority to remove the independent counsel.[12] The job of the independent counsel is to investigate and potentially prosecute criminality within the executive branch of government, including wrongdoing by the President or other high-ranking executive branch officials. As a result, the Court emphasized, the independent counsel should possess some independence from presidential control.

Because the Court can obtain compliance even at the expense of presidential power and enjoys other forms of independence, this book provides careful descriptions of the most important aspects of U.S. Supreme Court doctrine in areas of constitutional law that are most typically covered in the basic course in law school. Thus, readers will find analysis of leading Supreme Court cases from *Marbury v. Madison* to the present, and we will explain the applicable legal

---

[10]   *See* Planned Parenthood of Se. Pa. v. Casey, 505 U.S. 833 (1992).

[11]   418 U.S. 683 (1974).

[12]   487 U.S. 654 (1988).

standards on issues ranging from Congress's power to regulate interstate commerce to affirmative action. These doctrines matter not only to lawyers, but also to anyone who wants to understand contemporary debates about federal power, presidential authority, and individual rights.

While the Court is an independent institutional force, it is also true that, over time, Supreme Court decisions tend to reflect the dominant ideas and values circulating in constitutional politics during the eras in which these decisions take place. There are at least three reasons for this. The first has to do with the nature of the constitutional text and the practice of constitutional interpretation in the United States. Although some of the language in the text of the Constitution is stated as rules that permit little judicial discretion in interpreting the language, much of the text articulates value-laden standards and principles,[13] which different judges will interpret differently using the various approaches to constitutional interpretation discussed below that mainstream judges employ.

The second reason why the Court's jurisprudence tends to track constitutional politics over the long run has to do with the nomination and confirmation process for Supreme Court Justices and other federal judges. The Constitution expressly makes this process a political one: nomination by the President and confirmation by the Senate.[14] The political nature of the process enables constitutional politics to shape—and not just be shaped by—judge-made constitutional law. As illustrated recently by the partisan fight over when to fill Justice Antonin Scalia's seat on the Court (that is, before or after the 2016 elections), politicians, interest groups, and engaged citizens care passionately about which political party will get to appoint the next Justice. They care because the issue genuinely matters.

The third reason the Court's decisions tend to reflect changes in constitutional politics has to do with the Justices themselves. They have learned from hard experience the potential hazards for the Court of deciding cases in ways that are outside the political mainstream of the period. An example is the constitutional crisis of 1937 discussed in these pages.

Courts are not only shaped by politics; they also provide a key forum in which societal conflicts about values and ideas play themselves out in the United States. A case in point is the fight during the presidency of Barack Obama over whether Congress

---

[13]   *See* JACK M. BALKIN, LIVING ORIGINALISM 14–16 (2011) (distinguishing among the rules, standards, and principles that are set forth in the text of the Constitution).

[14]   *See* U.S. CONST. art. II, § 2, cl. 2.

possessed the constitutional authority to enact healthcare reform, which the Court decided in *NFIB v. Sebelius* in 2012.[15] Accordingly, this book also emphasizes the role of social movements, political parties, and other groups in influencing the course of Supreme Court doctrine.

Constitutional doctrine has become increasingly complex. Law school casebooks on the subject have been known to exceed 2000 pages. This makes it difficult even for law students to understand the forest for the trees. One of our main goals in this book is to explain the general themes and the most critical doctrines. Subsidiary nuances can more easily be understood once the overall pattern is clear. Similarly, the historical and political science literatures about constitutional law have become vast and complex. We would not purport to cover all the nuances and areas of controversy, but it is impossible to truly grasp constitutional controversies without understanding how institutions, political parties, and social movements, not just doctrinal logic, have shaped legal outcomes.

The risk is either falling to one extreme by viewing constitutional law as simply a matter of legal logic correctly or incorrectly applied by the courts, or falling to the other extreme by viewing constitutional law as a political football to achieve desired outcomes. But savvy constitutional lawyers know that judicial decisions reflect not only purely "legal" arguments but also political philosophies, while politicians know that the courts have significant power to have their own views enforced. Our hope is to provide a balanced treatment, so that readers will have some ability to understand how the law came to be what it is today and how it might change in the future. The two of us have our own views about current doctrine and about where and how we would like to see it change, but as much as possible we have tried to exclude such advocacy from the book.

II. A Catalogue of Constitutional Arguments

We turn now to the kinds of arguments that participants in constitutional debates typically make.[16] It is not the case that "anything goes" in American constitutional law and politics when Americans make claims on the Constitution. For example, it is not viewed as persuasive in court or in mainstream political discourse to argue that the guiding principle of constitutional interpretation should be whatever interpretation advances the fortunes of one political party over another, or one religion over another, or one advocacy group over another. Nor is it persuasive in these settings to

---

[15]   567 U.S. 519 (2012).

[16]   The paragraphs that follow draw in part from Curtis A. Bradley & Neil S. Siegel, *Constructed Constraint and the Constitutional Text*, 64 DUKE L.J. 1213 (2015).

argue that clear constitutional text may simply be ignored in settling constitutional disputes, or that the Bible or Marx's theory of the classless society trumps the Constitution in cases of conflict between them.

Professor Philip Bobbitt, in his 1982 book *Constitutional Fate*, identified six "modalities" of constitutional argument that participants in American constitutional practice—from the time of the Marshall Court to the present—have invoked as authority to support their favored interpretations of the Constitution.[17] Bobbitt's list has proven enormously influential. For example, it has been taught in American law schools, either explicitly or implicitly, to generations of law students.[18] You will also find these arguments in opinion editorials, blog posts, and commentaries on TV and radio.

The first two type of arguments refer directly to the written document adopted in 1789 and its amendments. In Bobbitt's telling, *textual* arguments rely on the language of the text of the Constitution, as well as the rules for interpreting constitutional texts (as opposed to other kinds of legal texts, especially statutes). An example would be the argument that the reference to a "well regulated Militia" in the Second Amendment implies that there is no individual right to bear arms for self-defense. *Structural* arguments examine the constitutional text (or a part of the constitutional text) as a whole, drawing inferences from the theory and institutions of government that are asserted to be created by the Constitution in order to discern how the constitutional system is supposed to function in practice. (These inferences go beyond the written text and often take into account some of the historical and prudential considerations discussed below.) Arguments based on the concept of the separation of powers are a classic example.

The next two arguments are backward looking, seeking guidance in past events. *Historical* arguments appeal either to preratification history (such as debates over whether to ratify the Constitution) or to postratification history (such as arguments from tradition or against tradition). Arguments based on the "original intent" of the Constitution's Framers or ratifiers, or the "original meaning" of a constitutional provision, are the most common form of this mode. *Precedential* arguments offer the existence of previous decisions, either of past political practice or past judicial rulings, as

---

[17]   For discussions of various so-called modalities of constitutional interpretation, see generally PHILIP BOBBITT, CONSTITUTIONAL INTERPRETATION (1993); PHILIP BOBBITT, CONSTITUTIONAL FATE: THEORY OF THE CONSTITUTION (1982); *see also* BALKIN, *supra* note 13, at 4–6, 341–42 n.2.

[18]   *See, e.g.*, PAUL BREST ET AL., PROCESSES OF CONSTITUTIONAL DECISIONMAKING 53–59 (5th ed. 2006) (using Bobbitt's typology to identify the kinds of constitutional arguments invoked by Chief Justice Marshall in *McCulloch v. Maryland*, discussed in Chapter 4).

justifications for a certain outcome in a later case. The Supreme Court rarely overrules its previous decisions (although it often distinguishes them), and its opinions are replete with citations to precedent.

The final two types of arguments are less directly tied to the specifics of text or history and are more addressed to the present. *Ethos* arguments tell a story about national identity; they typically take a narrative or historical form and ask whether a given interpretation of the Constitution exhibits fidelity to the meaning or destiny of the country, its deepest cultural commitments, or its national character, such as our general commitments to equality or to respect for institutions such as the family. Unlike other arguments invoking history, however, arguments based on ethos are ultimately about the people we are today, not simply what happened in the past. *Prudential* or consequentialist arguments identify the good or bad social consequences of an interpretation—for example, the possibility that a restrictive interpretation of presidential powers might endanger national security. These arguments focus on the present but will often appeal to history for evidence.

In addition to Bobbitt's catalogue of modalities, participants in constitutional debates sometimes assert the purpose of a constitutional provision. *Purposive* arguments deserve separate treatment because purposive interpretation is distinguishable from both the textual modality and the structural approach. Purposivism shares with textual interpretation a focus on particular constitutional provisions, but there can be tensions between "plain meaning" arguments and purposive arguments, as textualists are quick to point out.[19] In addition, purposivism shares with structural interpretation a concern with the proper functioning of the constitutional system, either in whole or in part, but purposivism is clause-bound (i.e., clause-focused) in a way that structural argument is not.

Advocates, judges, commentators, and citizens may rely most heavily on a single form of argument, but they commonly invoke several types. There are vigorous debates over the validity and weight of these various forms of argument. For example, originalists often argue that text and history are decisive except to the extent that certain issues are considered settled by precedent. Some originalists do not concede that precedent should be valued when it conflicts with text and history. Many originalists are resistant to arguments based on prudentialism, but few would be willing to hew

---

[19]   *See generally, e.g.,* John F. Manning, *The Eleventh Amendment and the Reading of Precise Constitutional Texts,* 113 YALE L.J. 1663 (2004); John F. Manning, *What Divides Textualists from Purposivists?,* 106 COLUM. L. REV. 70 (2006).

solely to text and history if the consequence was disaster, and originalist judges often seem implicitly to consider consequences in less extreme cases. Proponents of the "living Constitution" generally concede the relevance of text and history, but they put significant weight on purpose, recent historical practice, evolving traditions, and ethos arguments.

We also note that Bobbitt groups together certain kinds of constitutional arguments that may warrant being separated. Political precedent and judicial precedent are both forms of precedential reasoning, but they are different forms. With customary political branch practice (also called historical governmental practice or just historical practice), unlike U.S. Supreme Court precedent, a single prior action or decision generally does not warrant deference in constitutional interpretation. Instead, the search is typically for longstanding patterns of behavior by the political branches.[20] Similarly, it is not obvious that preratification and postratification history are best considered together as forms of historical interpretation and distinguished from textual argument. Originalists, for example, focus on preratification history but not most postratification history as relevant to textual interpretation, especially when the postratification history occurs long after the Founding.

Be on the lookout throughout this book for examples of the different modalities of interpretation: text, purpose, structure, pre-ratification history (i.e., originalism), post-ratification history, judicial precedent, historical governmental practice, ethos, and prudence. We will have much to say about each of these modalities of interpretation as they appear in different areas of constitutional law. Again, some judges and experts emphasize certain modalities over others, and different modalities can push an interpreter in different directions with respect to a particular constitutional question. Typically, however, interpreters invoke multiple modalities in support of a given interpretation, and they present them as mutually supporting, like strands in a rope.[21]

III. How to Use This Book

Readers can use this book in several ways. One is simply to read it through as an accessible introduction to the field or as a way of pulling together all of the confusing threads in more detailed accounts. Students often find themselves able to explain specifics

---

[20]   *See, e.g.*, Curtis A. Bradley & Trevor W. Morrison, *Historical Gloss and the Separation of Powers*, 126 HARV. L. REV. 411 (2012).

[21]   For a theoretical defense of this practice, see Richard H. Fallon, Jr., *A Constructivist Coherence Theory of Constitutional Interpretation*, 100 HARV. L. REV. 1189 (1987).

such as the current legal standard for scrutinizing gender discrimination or the post-New Deal test for the constitutionality of Commerce Clause legislation, but without much sense of how all of the pieces fit together.

The book can also be used one chapter at a time as an introductory and non-exhaustive reference while enrolled in a course. Even within a single area of constitutional law, such as the Commerce Clause or voting rights, the complexities of the law may seem overwhelming. This book should help, whether before, during, or after studying a subject, to highlight the overall structure and provide a framework into which students can fit additional nuances and complexities.

IV. Audiences for the Book

We have several audiences in mind for the book. One consists of students soon to begin law school, who are looking for what to read. Like some classic short histories of the Supreme Court, we want to give the context that makes the field come alive, while also teaching doctrine that students can use later.

In addition, and central to our purposes, the book should provide "usable knowledge" to students enrolled in a law school course on constitutional law. Again, our goal is not to cover all doctrines in exhaustive detail. Instead, we aim to provide a deeper understanding of key issues and to help students learn how to make convincing arguments in both the law school setting and practice. A good constitutional lawyer knows more than just the doctrinal takeaways. And the same is true of successful law students.

We also intend the book to be useful for students enrolled in undergraduate or graduate courses in U.S. constitutional law or constitutional politics—classes taught by one of the authors in addition to law school courses. The book will provide some insight into how political scientists and historians view the development of constitutional law, while giving students enough knowledge of legal doctrine to make constitutional litigation intelligible.

Moreover, we also hope the book will be of benefit to law professors and political scientists who specialize in constitutional law or constitutional politics. Although we have prioritized the clarity of our presentation in order to make the book fully accessible to students, this is not a textbook. Scholars and teachers will find in these pages fresh theoretical ideas, political dynamics, historical examples, and citations to relevant literatures what may enhance their own writing and teaching.

Last but not least are members of the public who want to understand more about constitutional law than they can glean from the headlines. People who are neither future lawyers nor students of political science want to know how the federal government came to have such sweeping powers, from where Presidents derive the power to make important policy decisions, or why the Supreme Court vindicates some individual rights claims but not others. And these days, engaged citizens may want to understand the meaning of debates over originalism or living constitutionalism, and how different constitutional methodologies have been used historically. At a time when civic education is sorely needed but frequently slighted, this book contributes to a rebalancing of the instructional scales that is overdue.

V. Roadmap

This book will discuss the major areas of Supreme Court doctrine covered in introductory constitutional law courses, along with some of the major historical developments that are central to political science courses. Due to space limitations, we exclude some significant constitutional issues. Criminal procedure has become its own, highly complex area of law stemming from judicial interpretation of the Fourth, Fifth, and Sixth Amendments. We do not cover it here. The First Amendment has also become too doctrinally complex to for us to cover effectively. Readers with an interest in freedom of speech and religion should consult a companion volume written by one of the authors of this one.[22]

The book begins by considering the role of constitutional law in the courts and beyond. The Constitution does not explicitly give courts the power to declare laws or presidential actions unconstitutional. This is a power that the Court itself claimed ownership of in the early Nineteenth Century. In Chapter 2, we discuss this crucial legal development and how Congress and the President have in turn made efforts to structure and sometimes revamp judicial authority.

Chapter 3 considers how the Supreme Court has expanded or contracted judicial authority over time, in response to concerns about either the need for vigorous judicial review or the potential dangers of judicial assertiveness. These concerns are not limited to the Court itself. Rather, they stem from political controversy over the role of the federal courts more generally in American society. Although the relevant "justiciability" doctrines trace back earlier, they have become increasingly elaborate since the 1950s as conservatives and liberals have contested the proper extent of judicial power. One of these doctrines, standing, should be part of the toolkit of any lawyer. And not just lawyers, but also ordinary citizens, need to understand

---

[22]   DANIEL A. FARBER, THE FIRST AMENDMENT (4th ed., 2014).

the ongoing debate over methods of constitutional interpretation, which figure both in court decisions and in political discourse.

With chapter 4, we begin a chunk of materials involving the structure of government. Chapter 4 discusses the debate, even older than the Constitution itself, between advocates of states' rights and advocates of national power. Key Supreme Court decisions during the early Nineteenth Century, under the leadership of Chief Justice John Marshall, form the foundation of present doctrine. But key issues were still hotly debated in the political arena until they were settled substantially, but far from entirely, by the Civil War.

Much of the struggle over federal power has involved the Commerce Clause, which grants Congress authority to regulate interstate commerce. Chapter 5 traces this history. The issues first surfaced in the first half of the Nineteenth Century, but Congress began to flex its legislative muscle only after the Civil War. For the next seventy years, the Supreme Court attempted to hold the line against federal power. But the Court also recognized a suite of justifications for Congress to regulate activities that did not themselves cross state lines. This period culminated in the 1930s, when the Court struck down major initiatives of the New Deal Congress. In the ensuing controversy—the constitutional crisis of 1937—the Court beat a retreat, and from the late 1930s to the early 1990s, the Court interpreted the Commerce Clause to place few, if any, restrictions on Congress. In the conservative reaction that began during the late Twentieth Century, however, the Supreme Court began to place some restrictions on further expansion of congressional power, although without attempting to roll back the regulatory state that had emerged since the New Deal. Chapter 5 closes by turning from federalism-based limits on federal power to federalism-based limits on state power. We discuss the ways in which the Court has inferred from the Commerce Clause a structural principle of federalism, called the dormant commerce doctrine, that limits the regulatory power of state governments to burden interstate commerce even when Congress has not acted—that is, when its commerce power lies dormant.

Chapter 6 fills out the story of federal power with a discussion of other congressional powers. We focus in particular on the highly consequential authorities of Congress to tax and spend. Debates about these powers also trace back to the early Republic. Such debates played a major role in the controversy over the constitutionality of health care reform during the Obama presidency.

With Chapter 7, we switch our attention from Congress to the President. Whether or not the Framers foresaw this development, the presidency has emerged as the focal point of American government and politics. There is general agreement about the President's authority—in fact, general duty—to implement laws passed by Congress.[23] But debate has raged for two centuries about the extent of presidential power beyond this core. As famously explained by Justice Robert Jackson in the *Steel Seizure* case, where the Court declared unconstitutional President Truman's seizure of the steel mills to keep them running in the face of a planned nationwide strike during the Korean War, the Court has recognized but limited presidential authority to act in domestic matters when Congress has not spoken.[24] Presidential authority over foreign affairs and the military are also ongoing controversies; probably every modern President has been accused of usurping congressional powers by the political party out of power. With the tremendous growth in the size and power of the executive branch, the courts have increasingly found themselves arbitrating disputes about the boundaries between presidential and congressional authority over the appointment and tenure of government officials.

Chapter 8 turns the focus from government structure to individual rights. As the Constitution was originally ratified, it had little to say about individual rights. One outgrowth of the arguments of anti-Federalists (who opposed ratification of the Constitution) about the dangers of a strong federal government was the creation of the Bill of Rights, which consists of the first ten amendments to the Constitution. But many people are unaware that the Bill of Rights applied only to the federal government for much of American history; as far as the U.S. Constitution was concerned, states remained free to limit free speech or religion, take private property without compensation, eliminate jury trials, and so forth. And of course, nothing in the original Constitution challenged state laws recognizing slavery. The crisis of federalism in the Civil War era led to the passage of the Thirteenth Amendment (abolishing slavery), the Fourteenth Amendment (establishing birthright citizenship and requiring states to observe due process and equal protection), and the Fifteenth Amendment (prohibiting racial discrimination in voting). It was not until a century later, however, that the Supreme Court concluded during the Civil Rights era of the 1950s and 1960s that nearly all of the provisions of the Bill of Rights were "incorporated" in the Due Process Clause of the Fourteenth Amendment and therefore were applicable against the states. In so concluding, the

---

[23]   *See* U.S. CONST. art. II, § 3 (providing that the President "shall take Care that the Laws be faithfully executed").

[24]   *See* Youngstown Sheet & Tube Co. v. Sawyer, 343 U.S. 579, 637 (1952) (Jackson, J., concurring) ("When the President acts in the absence of either a congressional grant or denial of authority, he can only rely upon his own independent powers, but there is a zone of twilight in which he and Congress may have concurrent authority, or in which its distribution is uncertain.").

Court completed a development that began in the late Nineteenth and early Twentieth centuries.

From the Nineteenth Century onward, a major bone of contention has been the extent to which the Constitution protects economic rights, an issue we discuss in Chapter 9. The development here roughly parallels the history of the Commerce Clause, with courts using what lawyers call "economic substantive due process" to strike down state laws (such as those specifying minimum wages and maximum hours) until the New Deal, then retreating almost entirely, and more recently engaging somewhat gingerly in addressing some perceived regulatory excesses by labeling them either takings of property or First Amendment violations. This chapter also addresses the other aspect of due process, called procedural due process, which is the requirement that the government use fair procedures before depriving a person of life, liberty, or property.

Chapter 10 turns to issues of racial and gender equality. As we explain, the institution of chattel slavery long pre-existed the Constitution, and race was central to the passage of the Reconstruction Amendments. We also discuss how the Court came to use the Equal Protection Clause to further racially liberal views of civil rights in the 1950s and 1960s. We then turn to how an increasingly conservative Court used equal protection jurisprudence to advance racially conservative views on the subjects of disparate impact and affirmative action, although the constitutionality of affirmative action in higher education has produced something of an awkward compromise between racially liberal and conservative commitments. There was also a long history of discrimination against, and subordination of, women tolerated under the Constitution, and it was not until the rise of the women's movement in the 1970s that the Court began to take claims of gender discrimination seriously. In more recent years, courts have also taken increasing notice of discrimination on the basis of sexual orientation, a development we cover in Chapter 12.

As Chapter 11 shows, concerns about whether the Court was stepping too far into the "political thicket" have surrounded its efforts to use the Equal Protection Clause to adjust voting rights.[25] Of course, the Fifteenth Amendment prohibits racial discrimination in voting, but it says nothing about other issues such as unequal voting power between different regions of a state. In the 1960s, amidst concerns that urban voters had substantially less political voice than rural voters, the Supreme Court intervened in a series of cases by

---

[25]   Colegrove v. Greene, 328 U.S. 549, 556 (1946) (admonishing that "[c]ourts ought not to enter this political thicket" of legislative reapportionment).

announcing its principle of "one person, one vote."[26] It then found itself immersed in issues about ballot access, racial gerrymandering, and, most recently, political gerrymandering.

Chapter 12 brings us to perhaps the most controversial area of current constitutional doctrine. Building on a handful of earlier decisions dealing with family autonomy and procreation, the Supreme Court began in the 1960s to provide protection for the reproductive rights of contraception and abortion. The Court's abortion decisions eventually triggered a revolt led by religious conservatives, leading to a moderation of judicial doctrine in a jurisprudential compromise that failed to satisfy critics and past supporters alike. The Court then participated in a national debate about same-sex intimacy and same-sex marriage, issues on which public views changed very rapidly in the early Twenty-First Century. And other issues, such as right to refuse medical care and physician-assisted suicide, have been subject to social controversy, although the Court so far has avoided any dramatic interventions.

Chapter 13, our finale, brings together the issues of governmental powers and individual rights. The Reconstruction Amendments contain direct prohibitions on state action that apply without implementation by Congress, but the amendments also grant Congress the power to enforce these prohibitions. Congress used these enforcement powers to pass sweeping legislation in the aftermath of the Civil War and again in the modern Civil Rights era. A racially conservative Supreme Court intervened after the Civil War to severely retrench this legislation. The modern legislation had greater judicial success in the Twentieth Century, but the Court in recent decades has limited the scope of congressional power under the Fourteenth Amendment and has more recently declared a major provision of voting rights legislation unconstitutional. Thus, as readers of this book will learn, the struggle between advocates of states' rights and advocates of national power remains ongoing, with implications both for federal power and for individual rights.

Further Readings

AKHIL REED AMAR, AMERICA'S UNWRITTEN CONSTITUTION: THE PRECEDENTS AND PRINCIPLES WE LIVE BY (2012).

JACK M. BALKIN, LIVING ORIGINALISM (2011).

ALEXANDER BICKEL, THE LEAST DANGEROUS BRANCH: THE SUPREME COURT AT THE BAR OF POLITICS (1962).

---

[26] *See, e.g.,* Gray v. Sanders, 372 U.S. 368, 381 (1963) ("The conception of political equality from the Declaration of Independence, to Lincoln's Gettysburg Address, to the Fifteenth, Seventeenth, and Nineteenth Amendments can mean only one thing—one person, one vote.").

DANIEL A. FARBER & SUZANNA SHERRY, JUDGMENT CALLS: PRINCIPLE AND POLITICS IN CONSTITUTIONAL LAW (2008).

BARRY FRIEDMAN, THE WILL OF THE PEOPLE: HOW PUBLIC OPINION HAS INFLUENCED THE SUPREME COURT AND SHAPED THE MEANING OF THE CONSTITUTION (2009).

ROBERT G. MCCLOSKEY & SANFORD LEVINSON, THE AMERICAN SUPREME COURT (6th ed. 2016).

Keith E. Whittington, *Originalism: A Critical Introduction*, 82 FORDHAM L. REV. 375 (2013).

Chapter 2

THE ROLE (AND REGULATION)
OF THE COURTS

Judicial review is the authority of judges to declare federal laws, presidential actions, or state laws unconstitutional in cases properly before them. Although judicial review is the foundation of modern constitutional law, the U.S. Constitution does not explicitly give courts the power of judicial review, a feature of many modern constitutions. But a number of the Framers of the Constitution contemplated some form of judicial review;[1] the Supreme Court claimed this authority for itself in the 1790s;[2] and the practice was increasingly accepted in 1803, when the Court for the first time exercised the power of judicial review to invalidate an act of Congress.[3]

This chapter first discusses that critical legal development by focusing on the constitutional politics and constitutional law of *Marbury v. Madison*,[4] the most famous judicial decision in all of American constitutional law. No decision better illustrates the reality that constitutional law not only disciplines constitutional politics, but also is shaped by constitutional politics. As we will see, Chief Justice John Marshall justified judicial review by positing a sharp distinction between constitutional law and politics in a case in which this very distinction was significantly undermined by Marshall's own debatable and politically motivated reasoning. After discussing the courts' power of judicial review, this chapter next considers how Congress, the President, and the citizenry can turn the tables and exercise their own considerable authority to structure and sometimes limit judicial authority.

I.   Judicial Review

In 1800, for the first time in history, a nation's existing set of political leaders was voted out of office in popular elections and replaced by their political opponents. The peaceful transfer of power that followed the pivotal presidential and congressional elections of 1800 was all the more remarkable by historical standards given how the two sides felt about each other. The victorious Democratic-

---

[1]   *See, e.g.*, THE FEDERALIST NO. 78 (Alexander Hamilton) (Clinton Rossiter ed., 1961).

[2]   *See, e.g.*, Hylton v. United States, 3 U.S. 171 (1796); United States v. La Vengeance, 3 U.S. 297 (1796); Calder v. Bull, 3 U.S. 386 (1798).

[3]   *See* Marbury v. Madison, 5 U.S. 137 (1803).

[4]   *Id.*

Republican Party (of Thomas Jefferson and James Madison) and the previously dominant Federalist Party (of John Adams and Alexander Hamilton) were not ordinary political adversaries. Rather than regard one another as legitimate rivals that would alternate in power, each viewed the other as being aligned with foreign powers (either England or France) and as posing an existential threat to the Constitution.[5]

The degree of partisan animosity was reflected in how long it took to determine the outcome of the presidential election. The Federalist incumbent President Adams was the clear loser. But Jefferson and his would-be running mate, Aaron Burr, tied in the Electoral College because the Democratic Republicans incompetently failed to hold back one vote for Burr at a time when the candidate with the second-most votes in the Electoral College became Vice President.[6] (In a crucial lapse of foresight, the Framers did not anticipate political parties; the Twelfth Amendment, ratified in 1804, fixed this problem by expressly requiring separate ballots for the candidates for President and Vice-President.) Because both Jefferson and Burr had received a majority of electoral votes, the choice between them was thrown into the lame-duck, Federalist-controlled House of Representatives under Article II, Section 1, Clause 3. The Federalists generally preferred Burr because he was anti-slavery, although Hamilton (who was also anti-slavery) despised him.[7] Only after several months and 36 ballots did enough Federalists in the House acquiesce and, consistent with the popular will, enable Jefferson to become President.

A.   A New Hope for Federalists[8]

The Federalists nonetheless continued to view the Democratic Republicans as illegitimate. For this reason, and also because the Founders lacked the norms and conventions that later restrained partisanship in order to manage political transitions, the Federalists were not content simply to hand over the keys to the White House and Congress.[9] Instead, President Adams and his defeated party members sought to strengthen their control of the federal courts. In

---

[5]   For a discussion of the competing constitutional visions of the Federalists and Democratic Republicans, see Michael W. McConnell, *The Story of* Marbury v. Madison: *Making Defeat Look Like Victory, in* CONSTITUTIONAL LAW STORIES 13–31 (Michael C. Dorf ed., 2004).

[6]   *See* U.S. CONST. art. II, § 1, cl. 3.

[7]   *See, e.g.*, Lin-Manuel Miranda, Hamilton: A Musical (2015).

[8]   The Star Wars headings that follow are intended to help students remember the events. They are not intended to take sides in the partisan fight between Federalists and Democratic Republicans.

[9]   For discussion of the crisis of 1800–1803, see generally BRUCE ACKERMAN, THE FAILURE OF THE FOUNDING FATHERS: JEFFERSON, MARSHALL, AND THE RISE OF PRESIDENTIAL DEMOCRACY (2007).

late January 1801, Adams successfully nominated John Marshall as Chief Justice of the United States. For the remaining weeks of the Adams Administration, Marshall would serve both in this role and as Acting Secretary of State. (In case you are wondering, that would never happen today!)

Then, on February 13, the lame-duck Federalist Congress passed, and Adams signed into law, the Judiciary Act of 1801. Among other things, the law ended the onerous practice of circuit riding by Supreme Court Justices and instead created six new circuit courts with sixteen new federal judges.[10] All of these new judgeships went to devoted Federalists. The statute also expanded the scope of federal jurisdiction and reduced the size of the Supreme Court from six to five, denying the next President his first appointment. The Democratic-Republicans were furious. As Jefferson wrote in personal correspondence using military imagery that revealed intense partisan animosity, "[the Federalists] have retired into the Judiciary as a stronghold . . . and from that battery all the works of Republicanism are to be beaten down and erased."[11]

On February 27, a week before the end of his Presidency, Adams and the Federalist Congress acted on a relatively minor part of their judicial strategy by passing and signing into law the Organic Act for the District of Columbia. The statute created the office of justice of the peace in the new District of Columbia. Justices of the peace would serve for five-year terms and be responsible for maintaining public order in the District. Adams submitted forty-two names to the Senate, one of whom was William Marbury, a 38-year old businessman from Georgetown. By the end of the work-day on March 3, the day before Jefferson's inauguration, all of Adams' nominees were rapidly confirmed by the Senate. Adams signed the commissions into the evening, and his aides transported them to the State Department, where none other than John Marshall himself, in his capacity as Acting Secretary of State, affixed the Great Seal of the President of the United States to them. Some of the commissions were delivered, including by Marshall's younger brother James. But some were not, including the one for Marbury; they were discovered at the State Department when Jefferson took office the following day.

---

[10]   The Judiciary Act of 1789 provided for six Supreme Court Justices, three Circuit Courts of Appeals composed of two Supreme Court justices and a district judge, and thirteen District Courts, one per state, each with one judge. Justices would "ride circuit" twice a year, hearing appeals from District Courts, and the Supreme Court would hear appeals of the Justices' Circuit Court decisions. The system was "slow, inefficient, and arguably unfair." McConnell, *supra* note 5, at 15.

[11]   Letter from Thomas Jefferson to John Dickinson, Dec. 19, 1801, *in* THE WRITINGS OF THOMAS JEFFERSON 302, 302 (Albert E. Bergh ed., 1907).

B.   The Democratic Republicans Strike Back

Jefferson ordered that these commissions not be delivered. He also reduced the number of justices of the peace (as the law permitted him to do), and he nominated Democratic Republicans in place of many of Adams' Federalist appointees. With these measures, Jefferson and his party were just getting started.

Democratic Republicans in Congress repealed the Judiciary Act of 1801, restoring circuit riding by the Justices and removing the sixteen new circuit judges from office notwithstanding Article III's provision of life tenure (that is, service during "good Behaviour") for federal judges.[12] Then, in order to delay and discourage any Supreme Court decision striking down the Repeal Act, Congress passed a law canceling the Supreme Court's June Term, thereby postponing the next meeting of the Court for more than a year—until the second Monday in February 1803. The House of Representatives also initiated impeachment proceedings against a Federalist judge (John Pickering of New Hampshire) and was known to be contemplating the impeachment of Federalist Supreme Court Justices, starting with the highly partisan Samuel Chase.

C.   Return of the Federalists

The great issue of the day was whether the Justices would risk impeachment by arguably defying the results of the 1800 elections and holding that the Repeal Act violated Article III. Neither Federalists nor Democratic Republicans cared much about whether the Adams appointees received their commissions to serve as justices of the peace in the District of Columbia. Nonetheless, litigation over this matter began in December 1801, when Charles Lee, a Virginia Federalist who had been Attorney General during both the Washington and Adams Administrations, showed up at the Supreme Court. Lee asked the Justices to issue a writ of mandamus to compel Jefferson's Secretary of State, Madison, to deliver copies of their commissions to Marbury and three other Adams appointees. A writ of mandamus is an order issued by a court to a government official or a lower court requiring the performance of a non-discretionary duty pertaining to the office held by the official or judge. Marshall set the case for argument during the Court's next Term, which (as noted above) did not occur until February 1803.

Also on the Court's docket was the substantially more significant case of *Stuart v. Laird*,[13] which involved a direct attack on the constitutionality of the Repeal Act. The Court in this case unanimously and meekly upheld the Repeal Act in a short opinion

---

12   *See* U.S. CONST. art. III, § 1.

13   5 U.S. 299 (1803).

that did not explain how terminating federal judgeships was consistent with Article III's guarantee of life tenure for federal judges. The Court so held almost certainly because the Justices had no realistic choice but to bow to political pressure. The Jefferson Administration would have refused to enforce or comply with any decision invalidating the Repeal Act, and such a decision might have provoked Congress to impeach and remove Federalist Justices.

Likewise, a good way to understand Marshall's strangely organized opinion for a unanimous Court in *Marbury* is to begin with this point: given the Court's highly vulnerable institutional position, Marbury *had* to lose.[14] The issue facing Marshall and his Federalist colleagues was whether to hand the Jefferson administration a complete victory, or whether there was a way to have Marbury lose while still offering some consolation to fellow Federalists and the federal judiciary. Marshall's offered consolation in two ways.

First, Marshall decided the merits of the case in a way that was favorable to Marbury *before* deciding that the Court lacked subject matter jurisdiction to decide the merits.[15] Because the Court held that it lacked jurisdiction, there could be no order issued by the Court for the Jefferson Administration to ignore and no provocation for impeachment proceedings. This attempt at consolation, like much of the Court's analysis discussed below, came at the expense of sound legal reasoning. Jurisdiction concerns the power of a court to decide a case; a court without jurisdiction has no business deciding the merits. For example, if we tell our own children to put on sunscreen while at the beach, there is no question of parental jurisdiction; we get to decide the merits. But if we walk up to someone else's children on the beach and tell them to put on sunscreen, we should expect to be told to buzz off, meaning in effect that we lack jurisdiction to decide the merits.

Marshall offered consolation in a second way. He planted seeds of judicial power for the future by claiming for the Court the power of judicial review of federal statutes and presidential actions. Moreover, and critically, the Court invalidated an act of Congress in a case whose disposition left the political branches with no opportunity to reject this assertion of judicial power by defying the Court's decision.

---

[14]   For a classic analysis of Marshall's opinion, see generally William W. Van Alstyne, *A Critical Guide to* Marbury v. Madison, 18 DUKE L.J. 1 (1969).

[15]   As law students learn in Civil Procedure, subject matter jurisdiction concerns the authority of a court to decide the type of case brought to the court. It is based on either the subject matter of the dispute (e.g., whether a federal question is present) or the identity of the parties (e.g., whether the plaintiff and defendant are from different states). Subject matter jurisdiction is distinct from personal jurisdiction, which concerns whether a court has power over the party being sued.

Turning to specifics, Marshall's opinion was as legally vulnerable as it was politically skillful. On the merits, Marshall held first that Marbury was legally entitled to his commission and second that he was further entitled to a writ of mandamus as a remedy for being denied his commission. It was not clear that Marbury was legally entitled to his commission, however, given that the statute gave the President discretion to determine the number of justices of the peace, and Jefferson had elected to reduce the number.[16] In addition, it was unsettled at the time whether courts possessed the power to issue affirmative orders to officials in the Executive Branch.[17]

At least as importantly, the Court's legal reasoning in support of its holding that it lacked jurisdiction ranged from dubious to questionable. Marshall held that the Court lacked jurisdiction to decide the case because Section 13 of the Judiciary Act of 1789, which he read as granting the Court original jurisdiction to hear suits for a writ of mandamus, violated Article III and so was unconstitutional because Congress is not permitted to enlarge the original jurisdiction of the Court. Original jurisdiction refers to the Supreme Court's power to hear cases as an initial (or original) matter. Appellate jurisdiction refers to the Court's authority to hear appeals from lower courts. Because Lee initially filed suit on Marbury's behalf in the Supreme Court, *Marbury* was an original jurisdiction case.

As a matter of statutory interpretation, there are two basic problems with Marshall's reasoning. First, the relevant portion of Section 13 probably referred only to the Court's appellate jurisdiction, not to its original jurisdiction.[18] Second, and in any event, statutory authority to grant a writ of mandamus is not best thought of as itself creating jurisdiction, original or appellate. Rather, a writ of mandamus is a remedy (like money damages or injunctive relief) that courts may be permitted to order if they independently possess jurisdiction. In other words, Marshall confused the distinction between jurisdiction and remedies.

---

[16]   *See* McConnell, *supra* note 5, at 28.

[17]   *Id.* at 28–29.

[18]   After discussing in previous sentences the circumstances in which the Court would have exclusive jurisdiction and original but not exclusive jurisdiction, the next sentence in § 13 stated:

> The Supreme Court shall also have appellate jurisdiction from the circuit courts and courts of the several states, in the cases herein after specially provided for; and shall have power to issue writs of prohibition to the district courts, when proceeding as courts of admiralty and maritime jurisdiction, and writs of mandamus, in cases warranted by the principles and usages of law, to any courts appointed, or persons holding office, under the authority of the United States.

Turning from statutory interpretation to constitutional interpretation, Marshall was no doubt correct that Marbury's case did not fall within the three categories of original jurisdiction listed in Section 2 of Article III: "all Cases affecting Ambassadors, other public Ministers and Consuls, and those in which a State shall be Party."[19] But Marshall did not convincingly explain why the Constitution's division of the Court's authority to hear cases between original and appellate jurisdiction would be irrelevant—"mere surplasage," in his words[20]—if Congress could add to the Court's original jurisdiction by statute. Marshall read Article III as imposing a *ceiling* on the Court's original jurisdiction, but Article III could at least as persuasively be read as identifying a *starting point* that Congress could later adjust by statute. Indeed, the Exceptions Clause of Article III, Section 2, seems to authorize Congress to "make" "Exceptions" to the textual allocation of jurisdiction between original and appellate jurisdiction.[21]

Note, however, that this particular legal question has long been settled by *Marbury* and subsequent precedent. The Court's holding in *Marbury* that Congress may not expand the Court's original jurisdiction remains the law to this day. By contrast, Marshall's unnecessary statement—which lawyers call "dictum"—that Congress may not confer appellate jurisdiction in the three categories of cases listed as within the Court's original jurisdiction has not been followed by subsequent Congresses and Courts and is not the law.

D. Marshall's Case for Judicial Review

Marshall was an extraordinarily gifted lawyer whose interpretive moves in *Marbury* likely reflected not only an attempt to console fellow Federalists, but also an intention to tee up the issue of judicial review. Rather than practicing *constitutional avoidance*, which counsels judges to show restraint by interpreting a statute in a way that avoids a constitutional question if the statute can reasonably be so read, Marshall—like a heat-seeking missile—read Section 13 in a way that required the Court to answer a constitutional question. Construing Section 13 and Article III as he did, the question for which *Marbury v. Madison* later became famous was squarely presented: even if the Court concludes that Section 13 violates Article III, does the Court have the authority to declare the

---

[19]   Based on the constitutional text alone, one might be tempted to argue that Madison, as Secretary of State, qualifies as a "public Minister[ ]." The historical context of Article III makes clear, however, that the text here refers to foreign dignitaries, not U.S. government officials.

[20]   *Marbury*, 5 U.S. at 174.

[21]   *See* U.S. CONST. art. III, § 2, cl. 2 ("In all the other Cases before mentioned, the supreme Court shall have appellate Jurisdiction, both as to Law and Fact, with such Exceptions, and under such Regulations as the Congress shall make.").

provision unconstitutional, thereby refusing to apply it? To reiterate, no provision in the Constitution expressly gives the federal courts the power of judicial review, although key Framers and Founders anticipated some form of it and the Court had claimed the power in *upholding* federal statutes in the 1790s.[22] There was not similar authority for judicial review of executive actions, however, and in this regard Marshall's claims in *Marbury* were more assertive.[23]

In defending judicial review, Marshall made matters easy on himself by asking "whether an act repugnant to the Constitution can become be the law of the land."[24] Boy is that a loaded framing of the issue presented! It begs the relevant question by conflating the Court's view of the Constitution with the Constitution itself. Hamilton made the same debater's move in his defense of judicial review during the ratification debate over the Constitution,[25] and in this and other key ways Marshall borrowed from Hamilton. Again, the actual, more difficult question presented is how the Court should respond when the Justices disagree with Congress and the President about the meaning of the Constitution. This question was especially pressing in *Marbury* itself, given that many of the drafters of Section 13 in Congress were also present at the Constitutional Convention.

Moving beyond rhetoric, Marshall's key substantive claim in support of judicial review was that "[i]t is emphatically the duty of the Judicial Department to say what the law is."[26] This claim requires some unpacking. Marshall was saying in essence that: (1) law and politics are distinct realms; (2) the political branches govern in the political realm; and (3) the judicial branch controls interpretation in the legal realm because it is the responsibility of judges to interpret the law, including the Constitution, which is a kind of law.

Of course, the power of judicial review is so deeply established in the United States that it is not going away whatever one thinks of Marshall's reasoning. Even so, it is worth asking whether his arguments in support of the third claim are persuasive. If they are less than fully persuasive, then it is worth asking whether there are better arguments for judicial review than the ones Marshall offered. It is also worth asking why the institution of judicial review eventually flourished in the United States notwithstanding the vulnerabilities of Marshall's arguments on behalf of the institution.

---

[22]   *See supra* notes 1–2 and accompanying text.

[23]   McConnell, *supra* note 5, at 29.

[24]   5 U.S. at 176.

[25]   *See* Hamilton, *supra* note 1.

[26]   5 U.S. at 177.

As in *McCulloch v. Maryland*,[27] another famous Marshall Court decision that we will examine in Chapter 4, Marshall began with theoretical, structural reasoning and then turned to provisions of the text of the Constitution to confirm his reasoning. First, he described the Constitution as imposing written limits on the exercise of governmental power, and he asserted that these limits would be meaningless without judicial review. Although there is some force to this reasoning, without judicial review there would still be electoral checks (i.e., "vote the bums out of office") and political checks (i.e., pushback from other branches or the states), as there are in some modern countries that have written constitutions but lack judicial review. Moreover, Marshall's argument may prove too much because it would also seem to apply to the Court itself, which after all was determining the constitutional limits of its own authority in *Marbury*.

Marshall's second structural argument was that those who apply the law must determine the law's validity; in other words, judicial review is inherent to judicial role. It is not clear, however, why courts cannot apply a law such as Section 13 without determining its validity; that is what statutory interpretation is all about. Alternatively or additionally, courts could review whether a law was passed using the proper procedures (e.g., passage by both Houses of Congress and signature by the President[28]) without determining the substantive constitutionality of the law.

Turning from the constitutional structure to the constitutional text, Marshall observed that Article III gives the federal judiciary jurisdiction to hear "Cases . . . arising under this Constitution."[29] Marshall rhetorically asked why the Constitution would give the federal courts such jurisdiction if they were not supposed to examine the consistency of a law with the Constitution. It turns out, however, that a grant of jurisdiction does not invariably imply authority to interpret the law in a case. For example, federal courts exercising diversity jurisdiction almost always defer to state-court interpretations of state law even when federal courts disagree with these interpretations.

That said, Marshall made an important point here; this grant of jurisdiction makes little sense if federal courts may not examine *any* constitutional questions in cases properly before them. In contrast, the grant of diversity jurisdiction is based on the identity of the parties, rather than the basis of the legal claim. It would seem odd to say that a case "arises" under the Constitution if the court is not

---

[27]   17 U.S. 316 (1819).

[28]   *See* U.S. CONST. art. I, § 7, cl. 2.

[29]   *See* U.S. CONST. art. III, § 2, cl. 1.

allowed to consider any constitutional issues. But Marshall's point did not get him all the way to where he wanted to go because it does not follow that federal courts can examine *all* constitutional questions, especially judicial review of acts of Congress and the President. There is a very strong historical and functional argument for vertical judicial review—that is, for federal court review of state legislatures, state executive officials, and state courts. Vertical judicial review is necessary both to ensure the *supremacy* of federal law, which the Supremacy Clause of Article VI mandates, and to ensure *uniformity* in the interpretation of federal law, which is highly valuable even if not constitutionally mandatory. Yet there would be no federal jurisdiction in many such cases without the "arising under" provision invoked by Marshall.

Marshall next argued that because the Constitution requires judges to take an oath of fidelity to the Constitution, they must have the authority to consult the Constitution in deciding cases. This is not a particularly good argument for at least two reasons. First, Presidents and members of Congress take an oath as well, so it is not clear which way the argument cuts. Second, Marshall's invocation of the judicial oath is question-begging: if judges lack the power of judicial review, then they do not violate their oaths when they decline to strike down laws on constitutional grounds.

Finally, Marshall references the Supremacy Clause, which mentions the Constitution first and deems supreme only those law made in pursuance of the Constitution. It is difficult to see how these observations advance Marshall's case. That the Constitution is supreme does not determine who gets to determine its meaning in the face of disagreement about its meaning. Marshall might instead have observed that the Supremacy Clause does contemplate some form of judicial review by providing that "the Judges in every State shall be bound" to the Constitution.[30] And given the plausible structural inference (and widely held assumption at the Constitutional Convention) that the Supreme Court has the power to review the decisions of state courts on questions of federal law,[31] there is a pretty good argument for judicial review by the Supreme Court as well.[32] But even this formal argument does not fully justify judicial review by the federal courts of acts of Congress and presidential actions. Federal courts may have the same power of judicial review as state courts possess, but state courts may lack the

---

[30]   *See* U.S. CONST. art. VI.

[31]   In the debate in Philadelphia over whether the Constitution should provide for lower federal courts in addition to the Supreme Court, *see infra* note 64 and accompanying text, both sides assumed that U.S. Supreme Court review of state court decisions would be available.

[32]   For development of this argument, see Herbert Wechsler, *Toward Neutral Principles of Constitutional Law*, 73 HARV. L. REV. 1 (1959).

power to invalidate federal laws and presidential conduct. Establishing that they have such power requires a separate argument that neither the text of the Constitution nor obvious structural inferences provide.

On the other hand, perhaps one reason for Marshall's success is that he skillfully maneuvered his argument so that opponents would have to take a particularly extreme position in order to reject it. Given the general understanding that state laws were subject to judicial review, opponents could not argue that the Constitution was a purely political document, not a legal document that could be applied by courts. Nor, in the context of *Marbury* itself, could opponents rely on "departmentalism," which is the theory that each branch of government has the power to apply its own interpretation of the Constitution to its own actions. Because Section 13, as interpreted by Marshall, required the courts themselves to violate the Constitution by taking jurisdiction over cases forbidden to them by the Constitution, departmentalism would have allowed the Supreme Court to decline to comply with Congress's instructions. Thus, to argue that *Marbury* was wrongly decided on the issue of judicial review, opponents would have had to argue either that Congress's interpretations of the Constitution were supreme over the interpretations of the other two branches (as well as over the interpretations of the states), or that departmentalism applied only to the interpretations of these other two branches. Neither position is easily defended.

E.   The Importance of Critiquing Marshall's Arguments

To be clear, the point of the foregoing exercise is not that judicial review is unjustified. Our purposes, rather, are three-fold. First, students of constitutional law are challenged to analyze legal arguments rigorously. The vulnerability of Marshall's arguments in *Marbury* offers us an opportunity to model early in the book what this practice of critical engagement looks like.

Second, the vulnerability of Marshall's structural inferences and textual interpretations suggests the advisability of looking elsewhere for a stronger justification of judicial review. Perhaps we ought to supplement or supplant Marshall's relatively *formal* arguments, which are grounded in the asserted requirements of the text, structure, or original understanding of the Constitution, with *functional* arguments—that is, with arguments that justify judicial review in terms of its tendency to promote a certain attractive conception of American governance, society, or democracy. Our own view is that judicial review can be done in a variety of ways; that each way has real costs and benefits; and that any persuasive justification of judicial review ultimately involves an all-things-considered judgment that the benefits of the institution outweigh the costs over the long run.

Experts on constitutional law, whether judges or professors, have offered a variety of functional justifications for judicial review. For example, some experts have justified judicial review as helping to sustain the system of separation of powers and checks and balances among the three branches of the national government created by the Constitution.[33] Other experts have emphasized the necessity of judicial review for supervising the relationship between the federal government and the states: judicial review can help protect the states when the federal government overreaches, but (as discussed below) its primary role historically has been to help ensure the supremacy and uniform interpretation of federal law.[34] Still other experts have viewed the Justices, who possess both insulation from electoral politics and the power of judicial review, as best situated to preserve fundamental values of American society—values that can temporarily be forgotten in the heat of the political moment.[35] Finally, process-oriented scholars have justified judicial review insofar as it helps perfect American democracy, which politicians may seek to undermine in order to stay in power (for example, by punishing criticism of them in violation of the First Amendment or by violating the fundamental right to vote of their opponents).[36]

Third, we hope that an understanding of the vulnerabilities of Marshall's arguments in *Marbury* will inspire students to ask why the institution of judicial review nonetheless eventually flourished in the United States. If the answer is not that the Constitution's text, structure, or pre-ratification history somehow compels the existence of the institution, why, then, is judicial review widely and deeply (if

---

[33] *See, e.g.*, Youngstown Sheet & Tube Co. v. Sawyer, 343 U.S. 579, 637–38 (1952) (Jackson, J., concurring) ("When the President takes measures incompatible with the expressed or implied will of Congress, his power is at its lowest ebb, for then he can rely only upon his own constitutional powers minus any constitutional powers of Congress over the matter. Courts can sustain exclusive presidential control in such a case only by disabling the Congress from acting upon the subject. Presidential claim to a power at once so conclusive and preclusive must be scrutinized with caution, for what is at stake is the equilibrium established by our constitutional system.").

[34] *See, e.g.*, Oliver Wendell Holmes, Jr., *Law and the Court: Speech at a Dinner of the Harvard Law School Association of New York, in* THE ESSENTIAL HOLMES 145, 147 (Richard A. Posner ed., 1992) (Feb. 15, 1913) ("I do not think the United States would come to an end if we lost our power to declare an Act of Congress void. I do think the Union would be imperiled if we could not make that declaration as to the laws of the several States. For one in my place sees how often a local policy prevails with those who are not trained to national views and how often action is taken that embodies what the Commerce Clause was meant to end.").

[35] *See* ALEXANDER BICKEL, THE LEAST DANGEROUS BRANCH: THE SUPREME COURT AT THE BAR OF POLITICS 24–27 (1962).

[36] *See generally* JOHN HART ELY, DEMOCRACY AND DISTRUST: A THEORY OF JUDICIAL REVIEW (1980).

not unanimously[37]) accepted in America today? Like many questions in law and life, there are likely several answers, each of which possesses some validity. Judicial review is an institution that has developed in history and that has come to be regarded as more legitimate over time for particular reasons. This development was not inevitable.

Part of the answer may be that, because of Marshall's political skill and attunement to the constitutional politics of his time, *Marbury* was more ignored than attacked when it was handed down. Marshall's political enemies got what they wanted—Marbury was denied his commission. If Marshall had exposed the Court's institutional vulnerability by ordering Madison to deliver the commission, the story of judicial review in America might have taken a different course.

A second part of the answer may be that judicial review of federal legislation or presidential action was used very sparingly until the legitimacy of judicial review was more widely accepted. After *Marbury*, the Supreme Court did not declare unconstitutional another federal law until its infamous decision in *Dred Scott v. Sanford* in 1857,[38] which we will encounter in Chapter 10. The Court did, however, vigorously exercise judicial review against state legislation. By the time the Court began aggressively employing judicial review against the other two branches, the general practice was an accepted part of American government. In other words, *Marbury*'s invalidation of a provision of *federal* law was the exception during the first half of the 19th Century, not the rule.

Third, between *Marbury* and *Dred Scott*, it was in the political interest of Congress and the President to support the Court's assertions of authority to ensure the supremacy of the federal government and federal law over the states. An example is *Martin v. Hunter's Lessee* in 1816, in which the Supreme Court asserted the power of judicial review to invalidate state laws on federal constitutional grounds, and also asserted the power to review state court decisions interpreting federal law.[39] Justice Joseph Story's opinion for the Court emphasized the need for *uniformity* in the interpretation of the Constitution and federal law. Back in 1787, an Anti-Federalist writing under the pseudonym Brutus had accurately predicted that the Supreme Court would not be a neutral umpire between the federal government and the states; rather, it would use judicial review to increase the power of the federal government at the

---

[37]   For arguments against judicial review, see generally MARK TUSHNET, TAKING THE CONSTITUTION AWAY FROM THE COURTS (1999); Jeremy Waldron, *The Core of the Case Against Judicial Review*, 115 YALE L.J. 1346 (2006).

[38]   60 U.S. 393 (1857).

[39]   14 U.S. 304 (1816).

expense of the states.[40] With some very important exceptions, Brutus has largely been proven right.

A fourth part of the answer is likely the explosion of judicially protected constitutional rights in the United States, first through the judicial practice of incorporation in the early-to-mid Twentieth Century, which we will study in Chapter 8, and also after *Brown v. Board of Education* in 1954,[41] which we will analyze in Chapter 10. There eventually arose a strong public expectation that it is the role of the Supreme Court and courts more generally to protect vulnerable minorities, even as disagreements endure about which minorities are worthy of constitutional protection.

Fifth, for the most part, Justices subsequent to Marshall have followed his lead and had the good sense to register that the Court depends on the support of the very politicians and Americans whose conduct the Justices purport to police in the name of the Constitution. *Marbury* illustrates in dramatic fashion some basic facts about how the American constitutional system operates in practice. The Supreme Court does not just act; it is also acted upon. The Court, if it is to succeed in vindicating its understanding of the Constitution, must work to secure its legitimacy not only in the eyes of legal professionals (that is, other judges, lawyers, and law professors), but also in the eyes of the political branches and the general public.[42] The Court must account for the conditions of its own public legitimacy, which may require it to balance its fidelity to sound legal reasoning with shrewd political judgment and responsiveness to changing popular beliefs about the values protected by the Constitution. One of us has called this balancing act the virtue of judicial statesmanship.[43] Judge-made constitutional law disciplines constitutional politics, but it continues to possess this power only by retaining its public legitimacy—and, therefore, only by partially reflecting constitutional politics.

Notably, Marshall made space for constitutional politics to influence judge-made constitutional law by not over-claiming with respect to the practice of judicial review. As former federal judge and Professor Michael McConnell has observed, nothing in his opinion "went beyond the well-accepted middle ground."[44] Marshall did not

---

[40]   Brutus, *Essay XI, in* 2 THE COMPLETE ANTI-FEDERALIST 417–22 (Herbert J. Storing ed., 1981).

[41]   347 U.S. 483 (1954).

[42]   *See generally* Robert C. Post & Neil S. Siegel, *Theorizing the Law/Politics Distinction: Neutral Principles, Affirmative Action, and the Enduring Insight of Paul Mishkin*, 95 CAL. L. REV. 1473 (2007) (distinguishing the internal perspective of the lawyer from the external perspective of the public).

[43]   *See generally* Neil S. Siegel, *The Virtue of Judicial Statesmanship*, 86 TEX. L. REV. 959 (2008).

[44]   McConnell, *supra* note 5, at 30.

assert that the power of judges to interpret the Constitution was exclusive of the authority of the political branches and the people to interpret the Constitution. Nor did he espouse *judicial supremacy*, which is the view that Supreme Court opinions (as opposed to outcomes in specific cases) must be accepted as authoritative by the political branches and the states in all contexts and for all purposes. He did not even assert the finality of judicial decisions outside of "particular cases."[45]

II. The Regulation of Courts

Judicial review involves the power of courts to regulate the political branches. The next part of this chapter details some of the ways in which the political branches, as well as the citizenry, have the power to regulate the federal courts. Such regulation helps enables constitutional politics to influence the course of judge-made constitutional law.

A. Size of Supreme Court (and Organization of Lower Federal Courts)

The Constitution requires the existence of "one supreme Court,"[46] so Congress lacks authority to legislate the Court out of existence. But the Constitution does not specify the size of the Court, and this determination is left to Congress exercising its authority under the Necessary and Proper Clause, which we will study in Chapter 4.[47] For most of the Constitution's first century, the size of the Court was related to how Congress chose to organize the lower federal courts. Although the size of the Court is no longer connected to the organization of the lower federal courts, Congress continues to control their organization today.

In the Judiciary Act of 1789, Congress provided that the Court would have six Justices.[48] This number was related to the circuit court system established by the Act: in addition to creating thirteen district courts, the Act created three judicial circuits, and it directed that these circuits were to hold two sessions per year and would be staffed by two Supreme Court Justices and one district court judge.[49] (To reduce the burden of circuit-riding, Congress changed the law in 1793 to require that only one Supreme Court Justice would have to sit with a district court judge in a given circuit session, which meant

---

[45]   *Marbury*, 5 U.S. at 177.

[46]   U.S. CONST. art. III, § 1.

[47]   *See* U.S. CONST. art. I, § 8, cl. 18.

[48]   Judiciary Act of 1789, ch. 20, § 1, 1 Stat. 73, 73. The following paragraphs draw in part from Curtis A. Bradley & Neil S. Siegel, *Historical Gloss, Constitutional Conventions, and the Judicial Separation of Powers*, 105 GEO. L.J. 255, 271–72 (2017).

[49]   Judiciary Act of 1789, ch. 20, § 4.

that each Justice would have to ride circuit only once per year.[50]) Except for the brief interruption in 1801 discussed above, the close connection between the size of the Court and the structure of the circuit court system persisted until 1869, which is also the last time that Congress altered the size of the Court.[51]

In 1801, as we have seen, the lame-duck Federalist Congress directed that upon the next vacancy on the Court, its size would be reduced to five in order to deny incoming President Jefferson an appointment.[52] Congress also provided in this statute for separate staffing of the circuit courts.[53] The incoming Democratic-Republican Congress, however, quickly restored the number to six (before a vacancy arose) and reestablished the connection between the size of the Court and the circuit court system.[54] In 1807, Congress established a seventh judicial circuit consisting of the new states Ohio, Kentucky, and Tennessee, and, as contemplated by the statutory scheme, increased the size of the Court to seven, giving Jefferson another appointment.[55]

In 1837, when the Democratic Party finally gained full control over both political branches, Congress reorganized the judiciary, creating nine judicial circuits and increasing the size of the Court to nine.[56] Because by design a majority of the resulting circuits were composed entirely of slave states, and because of the convention of having one Justice reside in each circuit, these changes had the effect of ensuring that a majority of Justices resided in slave states, a pattern that continued throughout the rest of the antebellum period (which helps account for the pro-slavery decisions rendered by the Court, which we will study in Chapter 10).

During the Civil War, a Republican Congress added another judicial circuit to accommodate the admission of California into the Union and increased the number of Justices to ten, giving Republican President Abraham Lincoln another appointment.[57] After Lincoln was assassinated and his Vice President, Andrew Johnson, became President, Congress decreased the size of the Court to seven, arguably in an effort to block Johnson, a Democrat who sympathized with the South, from making appointments. Relations between Congress and Johnson were so fraught that the House of

---

[50]   See Act of Mar. 2, 1793, ch. 22, § 1, 1 Stat. 333.

[51]   See JOHN V. ORTH, HOW MANY JUDGES DOES IT TAKE TO MAKE A SUPREME COURT? 5 (2006).

[52]   See Act of Feb. 13, 1801, ch. 4, § 3, 2 Stat. 89, 89.

[53]   Id. § 7.

[54]   See Act of Mar. 8, 1802, ch. 8, 2 Stat. 132.

[55]   Act. of Feb. 24, 1807, ch. 16, 2 Stat. 420.

[56]   See Act of Mar. 3, 1837, ch. 34, 5 Stat. 176.

[57]   Act of Mar. 3, 1863, ch. 100, 12 Stat. 794.

Representatives subsequently impeached Johnson, although he was not convicted in the Senate. After Ulysses Grant was elected, Congress passed the 1869 Judiciary Act, which increased the number of Justices back to nine (matching the number of circuits at that time), a number that has since remained unchanged.[58]

Some of these changes in the size of the Court over the course of the Constitution's first century appeared politically motivated. This might suggest that Congress has extensive authority to alter the size of the Court not only for considerations relating to judicial efficiency and workload, but also for the purpose of changing its ideological composition. Indeed, the Constitution is not generally thought by experts to prohibit a political party in control of Congress from expanding the size of the U.S. Supreme Court in order to pack it with partisan Justices.[59]

It is noteworthy, however, that any such plan to increase the size of the Court today would risk intense bipartisan opposition. This is what happened in 1937, when Democratic President Franklin Delano Roosevelt (FDR) tried to pack the Court in response to conservative Supreme Court decisions that were thwarting his New Deal economic recovery plans, which sought to move the country out of the Great Depression. (We will study these decisions in Chapter 5.) The Democrat-controlled Senate Judiciary Committee vigorously opposed FDR's Court-packing plan on the ground that it was an attack on judicial independence.[60]

Soon, however, the Court's personnel changed decisively. The four conservatives (Pierce Butler, James Clark McReynolds, George Sutherland, and Willis Van Devanter), whom critics called the Four Horsemen of the Apocalypse, were replaced by New Dealers. By 1942, FDR had made eight consecutive appointments to the Court—all New Dealers—with a view to changing the Court's decisions. Using his power to nominate Justices, he accomplished the very doctrinal change that he had wanted to secure through Court-packing. Yet most experts, then and now, regarded his use of judicial nominations

---

[58] *See* Act of Apr. 10, 1869, ch. 22, 16 Stat. 44. The current version is at 28 U.S.C. § 1.

[59] *See, e.g.*, Michael C. Dorf, *How the Written Constitution Crowds Out the Extraconstitutional Rule of Recognition*, *in* THE RULE OF RECOGNITION AND THE U.S. CONSTITUTION 69, 79 (Matthew D. Adler & Kenneth Einar Himma eds. 2009) ("If, say, Congress were to increase the size of the Supreme Court to eleven Justices, neither the Court itself, nor any member of Congress, could plausibly claim that in so doing it was acting unconstitutionally. Nonetheless, if, in increasing the Court's size, the President and Congress were principally motivated by a desire to shape judicial outcomes, it would be engaged in Court packing in violation of a strong customary norm.").

[60] For discussion of FDR's Court-packing plan and the response of the Senate Judiciary Committee (among other actors), see Bradley Siegel, *supra* note 48, at 269–87.

for ideological purposes as appropriate but his attempt at Court packing as illegitimate. It is worth pausing to think about why this might be.

Among other things, the historical practice of the political branches with respect to judicial appointments and Court packing is different, perhaps because of the different degrees of immediate political control over the Court that each entails. Whereas Court packing can be done without any sitting Justice retiring or dying in office, judicial appointments cannot be accomplished without vacancies on the Court arising. There may also be virtues associated with slowing down the processes of personnel change. Whereas Court packing can entail adding a number of seats all at once, FDR made so many appointments because he and his party won so many elections, and so he arguably earned the democratic legitimacy necessary to make these appointments. For these reasons, Court packing likely poses a greater threat to judicial independence.

Accordingly, adjusting the size of the Supreme Court is no ordinary way in which the political branches can regulate the federal judiciary. In the modern American constitutional tradition, changing the size of the Court for ideological reasons would constitute an extraordinary act. Such a move, while generally viewed as constitutionally permissible, would end a 150-year-old tradition of restraint. It may be telling in this regard that, even in current, polarized times, no serious proposal to pack the Supreme Court has emerged in Congress—although certain liberal legal scholars have been urging Democratic politicians to seriously consider adding two or four seats to the Court when they are in a position to do so, in response to (among other things) the refusal by Republicans to consider President Barack Obama's nominee to replace Justice Antonin Scalia.[61] Such an effort would require control of both houses of Congress as well as the White House, and probably a filibuster-proof majority in the Senate or a willingness to eliminate the filibuster.

B.   Congressional Control of Federal Court Jurisdiction

A more common way in which the political branches may seek to regulate the exercise of judicial power is by limiting the jurisdiction of the federal courts. The issues involved are varied, interdependent,

---

[61]   *See, e.g.*, Michael Klarman, *Why Democrats Should Pack the Supreme Court*, TAKE CARE (Oct. 15, 2018), https://takecareblog.com/blog/why-democrats-should-pack-the-supreme-court ("Democrats must seize the earliest opportunity to offset those [two Trump] appointments [to the Court] with some of their own."); Mark Tushnet, *Expanding the Judiciary, the Senate Rules, and the Small-c Constitution*, BALKINIZATION (Nov. 25, 2017), https://balkin.blogspot.com/2017/11/expanding-judiciary-senate-rules-and.html ("I think—really, I do think this—that Democrats should be thinking about the possibility of expanding the Court's size to 11 as soon as they get the chance (if they ever do).").

and highly complex, and the general subject is covered in the law school curriculum far more often in the course on Federal Courts than in the basic course on Constitutional Law. We will therefore limit ourselves to a few observations. It is widely agreed that Congress enjoys significant authority to define and restrict the jurisdiction of the federal courts.[62] The constitutional limits on Congress's exercise of this authority, however, are deeply contested.

Article III begins by declaring that "[t]he judicial Power of the United States, shall be vested" not only "in one supreme Court," but also "in such inferior Courts as the Congress may from time to time ordain and establish."[63] (Delegates at the Constitutional Convention could not agree on whether to create lower federal courts, so they punted the question to future Congresses in what came to be known as the Madisonian Compromise.[64]) The discretion possessed by Congress in deciding whether to create a lower federal court at all is understood to imply the power to create it and then limit its jurisdiction. But when and how far Congress may go in limiting the jurisdiction of the lower federal courts remains a subject of substantial dispute.

As for the Supreme Court, the first clause of Article III, Section 2, extends the federal judicial power to nine categories of cases and controversies, including "all Cases . . . arising under" federal law. Clause 2 grants the Supreme Court original jurisdiction in certain cases, and provides—in what has come to be known as the Exceptions Clause—that "[i]n all the other Cases before mentioned, the supreme Court shall have appellate Jurisdiction, both as to Law and Fact, with such Exceptions, and under such Regulations as the Congress shall make."[65] Experts have long debated whether the plain text of the Exceptions Clause authorizes a congressional restriction on the appellate jurisdiction of the Supreme Court that reflects a substantive disagreement with how the Court has decided, or is expected to decide, a constitutional question. Experts have further debated whether the original understanding of Article III, the constitutional structure, and Supreme Court precedent authorize such an act of jurisdiction stripping as an "Exception" to the general rule of Supreme Court appellate jurisdiction.[66]

In our view, the debate remains unresolved because the text sends mixed messages, the original understanding is disputed,

---

[62]   RICHARD H. FALLON, JR. ET AL., HART AND WECHSLER'S THE FEDERAL COURTS AND THE FEDERAL SYSTEM 30–33 (7th ed. 2015).

[63]   U.S. CONST. art. III, § 1.

[64]   FALLON ET AL., *supra* note 62, at 7–9.

[65]   U.S. CONST. art. III, § 2, cl. 2.

[66]   For discussion of these debates, see Bradley & Siegel, *supra* note 48, at 287–312.

general structural reasoning turns on contestable visions of the fundamental role of the Supreme Court in the federal system, and the most relevant Supreme Court decision offers something for everyone.[67] It seems fair to say that Congress possesses greater authority to restrict the jurisdiction of the lower federal courts based on actual or anticipated disagreement with their decisionmaking than it does to strip the appellate jurisdiction of the Supreme Court. But much else remains disputed.

Recently, experts have inspected the relevant historical practice of the political branches with respect to stripping the appellate jurisdiction of the Supreme Court. The history shows that, although Congress has long regulated the Court's appellate jurisdiction, it has almost never engaged in jurisdiction stripping, despite many calls over the years for it to do so in cases involving such controversial issues as alleged subversive activities, school prayer, busing, and abortion. This history has been of relatively limited importance to legal scholars, but it has been of great importance to members of Congress and Executive Branch officials when they have considered the permissibility of limiting the Court's appellate jurisdiction based on substantive disagreements with its decisionmaking. Although there is enduring disagreement about the constitutionality of stripping the Court's appellate jurisdiction, there is arguably a convention against it that members of both political parties in Congress have long respected.[68]

Although jurisdiction stripping is extremely rare, the issue is profoundly important. The greater is Congress's authority in this area, the greater is its ability to wrestle control from the Supreme Court over the substantive content of constitutional law. Moreover, given that there are relatively few cases each year that the Supreme Court can accept for review, the greater the extent to which Congress withdraws lower federal court jurisdiction, the more acute becomes the question of whether state courts can be trusted to effectively have the final word on important questions of federal constitutional law.

Although a full discussion of the topic is outside the scope of this book, it is worth adding a few words about how the Court has approached exercises of congressional control over jurisdiction. First, the Court has generally recognized the power of Congress to control lower court jurisdiction, with one major exception concerning Congress's effort to partially strip judicial authority to issue writs of habeas corpus.[69] Second, the Court has distinguished between congressional control over jurisdiction and congressional dictates to

---

[67]   For elaboration of this view, see *id.*

[68]   For development of this position, see *id.*

[69]   *See* Boumediene v. Bush, 553 U.S. 723 (2008).

the courts regarding how they must decide individual cases.[70] Although this distinction has proved slippery, it remains good law.

C. Nomination and Confirmation of Federal Judges

Any process for installing judges will face a tradeoff between securing judicial independence on the one hand, and ensuring the democratic accountability of judges on the other hand. Different systems address this tradeoff differently. In many states, judges are elected and/or re-elected, which reflects a concern to prioritize accountability over independence. In a number of constitutional democracies around the world, judges on constitutional courts are appointed for a limited term of, say, twelve to eighteen years, which can be thought of as seeking a middle ground between independence and accountability. And as we have already seen, federal judges in the United States enjoy life tenure, which arguably places greater emphasis on independence over accountability.

The first section of Article III provides that "[t]he Judges, both of the supreme and inferior Courts, shall hold their Offices during good Behaviour, and shall at stated Times, receive for their Services, a Compensation, which shall not be diminished during their Continuance in Office."[71] The tenure and salary protections of Article III help establish a system in which federal judges enjoy very substantial independence once they are confirmed. Moreover, the effective term of federal judges has only increased as Americans live longer on average. A justice appointed in her forties today could remain on the Court for nearly half a century.

With federal judges enjoying so much independence *after* they are appointed, the Constitution specifies ways to ensure the democratic accountability of the federal judiciary *before* they are appointed. Article II, Section, 2, provides that the President "shall nominate, and by and with the Advice and Consent of the Senate, shall appoint . . . Judges of the supreme Court, and all other Officers of the United States, whose Appointments are not herein otherwise provided for, and which shall be established by Law."[72] The President's power to nominate federal judges, and the Senate's power either to confirm them or to deny them confirmation, together constitute a profoundly important way in which the political branches regulate the federal courts.

---

[70]   See Patchak v. Zinke, 138 S. Ct. 897, 200 L. Ed. 2d 92 (2018), in which a divided Court upheld a law requiring federal courts to dismiss any case involving a particular parcel of land, with four Justices upholding it as a form of jurisdiction stripping rather than dictating the outcome in cases, two upholding it as a repeal of a waiver of sovereign immunity, and the remaining Justices dissenting.

[71]   U.S. CONST. art. III, § 1.

[72]   U.S. CONST. art. II, § 2, cl. 2.

For example, Professors Jack Balkin and Sanford Levinson have articulated a descriptive theory of "partisan entrenchment" to explain routine, gradual changes in constitutional law that they believe are characteristic of how the American constitutional system functions.[73] According to their theory, the President's power to nominate Justices and other federal judges means that the party controlling the White House can, if it chooses, appoint federal judges with roughly similar ideological orientations on issues of greatest significance to the party (subject to a potential check from the Senate). Over time, this process can produce substantial changes in constitutional law. The theory of partisan entrenchment helps explain why political parties, engaged citizens, social movements, and advocacy groups care profoundly about which President of which party gets to decide who sits on the federal courts, especially the Supreme Court. They all care because the future of constitutional law in key areas may be at stake.

D.   Impeachment of Federal Judges

Based on both the "good Behaviour" Clause and historical governmental practice,[74] it has long been understood that federal judges can be removed from office only through impeachment, and that impeachment cannot be used merely because of a disagreement with a judge's decisions. To be sure, as we have seen, Federalists had reason to fear that a Democratic Republican Congress would impeach and remove Federalist judges and Justices for partisan reasons: the Democratic Republicans did impeach and remove a Federalist district court judge (John Pickering), albeit one who was an alcoholic and possibly mentally ill; they also impeached but failed to remove the partisan Federalist Justice Samuel Chase.[75] But the early national period was a time in which the country lacked conventions regarding the circumstances in which judicial impeachments would be appropriate. There subsequently developed an understanding that the impeachment power may not be wielded just because the party in control of both houses of Congress disagrees with a judge's rulings. The constitutional text likely helped this norm to develop: although impeachment requires only a majority vote in the House, removal requires two-thirds support in the Senate.[76] This means that there will ordinarily not be enough votes to remove a federal judge without at least some bipartisan support.

---

[73]   *See* Jack M. Balkin & Sanford Levinson, *Understanding the Constitutional Revolution*, 87 VA. L REV. 1045 (2001).

[74]   *See* U.S. CONST. art. III, § 1.

[75]   *See* McConnell, *supra* note 5, at 22.

[76]   *See* U.S. CONST. art. I, § II, cl. 6; *id.* § III, cl. 6.

The norm against judicial impeachments based upon interpretive disagreements has significantly limited use of the impeachment power to discipline federal judges. In all likelihood, this tradition is for the best. As we will see (and have already seen), Americans routinely disagree on matters of constitutional interpretation. If such disagreements sufficed to impeach federal judges, judicial impeachment might become a routine affair and federal judges would not be able to do their jobs without constantly looking over their shoulders.

Impeachment remains available, however, to remove federal judges when they behave egregiously, including by committing crimes or engaging in otherwise disqualifying or highly unethical behavior. For example, the 1993 case of *Nixon v. United States* involved a federal district court judge who had been impeached by the House and removed by the Senate after he was convicted of making false statements to a grand jury but refused to resign from the bench and continued to collect his judicial salary while in prison.[77] Non-criminal examples have historically included intoxication on the bench, mental illness, failure to hold court, and improper business relationships with litigants.[78]

E.   Constitutional Amendment

Article V makes the U.S. Constitution extraordinarily difficult to amend, whether through the traditional method (initial proposal by two-thirds of each House of Congress), or through the method that has never before been used (a convention of the fifty states called for by two-thirds of the state legislatures).[79] Either way, three-quarters of the states must approve, meaning that it requires only thirteen states to defeat a proposed amendment. Accordingly, constitutional amendment is not even an occasional, let alone a routine, method of regulating the federal courts by "overruling" their decisions.

Still, constitutional amendment remains a possibility to undo the work of a runaway Supreme Court, and the existence of this possibility may help keep the Justices within the political mainstream of American society. This is not only a theoretical possibility. Over the course of American history, several consequential amendments repudiated Supreme Court decisions. They include the Eleventh Amendment, which protects state sovereign immunity from lawsuits filed by certain private parties for

---

[77]   506 U.S. 224 (1993).

[78]   *See* List of Individuals Impeached by the House of Representatives, UNITED STATES HOUSE OF REPRESENTATIVES, https://history.house.gov/Institution/Impeachment/Impeachment-List/.

[79]   U.S. CONST. art. V.

money damages without the consent of the state being sued.[80] Another example is Section One of the Fourteenth Amendment, which confers birthright citizenship and so rejects the pre-Civil War holding of the Court in *Dred Scott* that even free blacks could under no circumstances be U.S. citizens.[81] A third example, is the Sixteenth Amendment, which permits a federal income tax.[82] A final example is the Twenty-Fourth Amendment, which prohibits denying citizens the right to vote in federal elections for failure to pay a poll tax or other tax.[83]

F. Presidential Rhetoric, Social Movement Advocacy, and Litigation

Last but certainly not least are "softer" forms of influence that the public and the political branches may exert on the federal courts. Federal judges are, after all, human beings who are often open to persuasion, and some of their values and views change over time. The public may engage in efforts to alter social norms, whether through social movement advocacy, litigation, or both. As we will see in subsequent chapters, over the course of American history, social movements—for women's suffrage, civil rights, sex equality, gay rights, and gun rights—have had a profound impact on the course of judge-made constitutional law.

Norm contestation may also occur through the rhetoric of Presidents and other influential politicians, as well as through the litigation priorities of the current presidential administration.[84] "To succeed in changing social norms," Professor Jack Balkin observes, "may be as powerful as changing judges and politicians, for it alters the underlying sense of what is reasonable and unreasonable for governments to do. It shifts political and professional discourse about what is off-the-wall and on-the-wall in making claims on the Constitution."[85]

Further Readings

BRUCE ACKERMAN, THE FAILURE OF THE FOUNDING FATHERS: JEFFERSON, MARSHALL, AND THE RISE OF PRESIDENTIAL DEMOCRACY (2007).

---

[80]   The Eleventh Amendment, ratified in 1795, overruled *Chisholm v. Georgia*, 2 U.S. 419 (1793).

[81]   The Citizenship Clause of Section One of the Fourteenth Amendment, ratified in 1868, overruled *Dred Scott v. Sandford*, 60 U.S. 393 (1857).

[82]   The Sixteenth Amendment, ratified in 1913, overruled *Pollock v. Farmers' Loan and Trust Company*, 157 U.S. 429 (1894).

[83]   The Twenty-Fourth Amendment, ratified in 1964, overruled *Breedlove v. Suttles*, 302 U.S. 277 (1937).

[84]   *See, e.g.,* JACK M. BALKIN, LIVING ORIGINALISM 70–71 (2011).

[85]   *Id.* at 71.

Curtis A. Bradley & Neil S. Siegel, *Historical Gloss, Constitutional Conventions, and the Judicial Separation of Powers*, 105 GEO. L.J. 255 (2017).

THE FEDERALIST NO. 78 (Alexander Hamilton) (Clinton Rossiter ed., 1961).

Michael W. McConnell, *The Story of* Marbury v. Madison*: Making Defeat Look Like Victory, in* CONSTITUTIONAL LAW STORIES 13–31 (Michael C. Dorf ed., 2004).

William W. Van Alstyne, *A Critical Guide to* Marbury v. Madison, 18 DUKE L.J. 1 (1969).

KEITH E. WHITTINGTON, POLITICAL FOUNDATIONS OF JUDICIAL SUPREMACY: THE PRESIDENCY, THE SUPREME COURT, AND CONSTITUTIONAL LEADERSHIP IN U.S. HISTORY (2007).

Chapter 3

IMPLEMENTING JUDICIAL REVIEW

Marbury and its counterparts involving the constitutionality of state laws made courts responsible for deciding constitutional cases. But once it is accepted that the Court has the power of judicial review, two further sets of questions arise.

First, who can bring constitutional cases and under what circumstances? Is every constitutional question appropriate for courts to decide? (No.) Can the President simply ask the Court to provide its views about the constitutionality of a proposed action? (No, such "advisory opinions" are not allowed in the federal courts.) Can individuals bring such cases? (Yes, as we will see—but not always.)

Second, in cases where the meaning of the Constitution is subject to dispute, how should a court go about resolving the question? Should it be guided by the text, the original understanding of the text, and past judicial precedent? (Yes, according to almost everyone). What about traditions of the American people, established practices of government, and current social values? (More controversial.)

In Part I of this chapter, we address the first question and explore the limits on a federal court's authority to decide constitutional issues. We will ask which constitutional issues a court has the authority to decide, as well as who can be bring suit and when. These issues make up much of the subject matter of an advanced law school course on federal jurisdiction (typically called Federal Courts), and we will attempt to cover only the basics. Part II turns to the second issue and discusses theories of constitutional interpretation. Many trees have been sacrificed to print books, scholarly articles, and judicial opinions on this subject, and the issue is also a frequent subject of discussion in the press and by politicians. It would take a book, or perhaps a series of books, to fully explore the subject. Our goal is only to highlight some of the key theories and explain a bit of the surrounding debate.

I. Limits on Federal Jurisdiction

In the Nineteenth Century, when the nation was not at war, the federal government's main functions were collecting tariffs, governing and then selling public lands, and paying military pensions. Constitutional issues generally arose in the context of traditional litigation—criminal cases, or cases of trespass, breach of contract, or personal injury.

In the Twentieth Century, the role of government shifted. State and federal regulation expanded exponentially, particularly during the New Deal period of the 1930s. With this changed role came litigation seeking to expand or defeat regulatory protections. These cases might involve economic loss, or threats of economic loss, but not any traditional property or contract right. This development caused courts to expand their views of appropriate litigation. In addition, the civil rights cases of the second half of the Twentieth Century transformed the Court's justiciability doctrines—that is, the doctrines that define what cases are suitable for judicial resolution. Matters that judges had traditionally left to state and local administrators—voting practices, public education, management of state institutions (e.g., prisons)—came under the ever-closer scrutiny of federal judges. Moreover, litigation under a new set of environmental laws brought lawsuits involving broad interests in clean air or protection of nature. Courts were then pressed to revamp their views about who can sue, when, and for what remedy.

It had long been clear that federal courts could hear cases only when something was at stake between the parties beyond their disagreement over the correct answer to an abstract legal issue. Courts are limited to hearing cases in which the plaintiff has some more definite personal connection with an alleged violation of law. The easiest cases are those in which the government action directly deprives the plaintiff of some specific legal right—the kinds of cases that courts customarily heard in the Nineteenth Century. In *Marbury*, for example, the plaintiff claimed to have the right to a specific government job (and salary) that was being illegally withheld by the defendant. *Marbury* indicates the traditional willingness of courts to intervene in such situations. But today, government actions often affect the interests of millions of people with varying degrees of directness and tangibility, and courts have struggled to draw a line between purely partisan or ideological disputes and concrete legal controversies.

Ultimately, the effort to draw this line is rooted in the language of Article III of the Constitution itself. According to Article III, the power of the federal courts is "judicial"—it is not "legislative," as is Congress's (Article I, § 1), nor is it "executive," as is the President's (Article II, § 1). If courts go beyond the "judicial" function, they invade the provinces of Congress and the President. But what is the judicial function? Article III defines it in terms of hearing "Cases" or "Controversies." These terms—which are essentially synonymous except that perhaps the latter refers only to civil cases—seem to encompass only adversarial litigation.

Limiting the power of federal judges to hearing only adversarial lawsuits has at least two complementary justifications, one functional and the other formal. As a functional matter, judges have experience and training in handling a live controversy between adverse parties, but have no special expertise in considering abstract policy questions. Moreover, an adversarial dispute ensures that the courts will have a full basis for making a decision. As a formal matter, when judges reach beyond the adversarial situation and consider abstract policy questions, they arguably violate the separation of powers—they invade the legislative or executive domains. It was for such reasons that, very early in its history, the Court decided that it would not issue advisory opinions at the request of the President or Congress. Thus, when Washington asked the Court's advice about the interpretation of treaties with France during an international crisis, the Justices politely declined to answer.[1] But what makes a lawsuit sufficiently "judicial" is far from obvious.

Over the past two centuries—and increasingly so in the past few decades—the Court has filled this gap with a set of elaborate doctrines about federal jurisdiction. We will discuss four of these doctrines in this section. The first doctrine, the political question doctrine, excludes federal courts from deciding certain constitutional issues. The other three (standing, ripeness, and mootness) exclude cases on the basis of the identity of the plaintiff or the timing of the suit.

A.   Political Question Doctrine

The "political question doctrine" posits that some constitutional issues are not justiciable because the issue is committed to the political branches of government (Congress and the President). In *Marbury*, Chief Justice John Marshall acknowledged that, where the President or another executive branch official had "legal discretion," the judiciary would not grant relief.[2] This distinction was also implicit in Marshall's insistence that the role of courts is to say what the law is,[3] which assumes a defined domain of legal questions distinct from policy ones.

Although the contours of the political question doctrine are different, it reflects a similar effort to define the line between the "legal" and the "political." The modern way of making this distinction is to say that the Constitution delegates resolution of the issue to the

---

[1]   The Justices' response to Washington's request can be found in 3 HENRY P. JOHNSTON, CORRESPONDENCE AND PUBLIC PAPERS OF JOHN JAY 486–89 (1801).

[2]   5 U.S. 137, 166 (1803).

[3]   *See id.* at 177.

other branches of the government, or that there are "no judicially cognizable standards" that a court could apply.

The foundational case on the political question doctrine was *Luther v. Borden*.[4] Rhode Island was in a condition amounting to civil war: Some citizens who were disenfranchised under the original colonial charter went into rebellion, seeking a new and more democratic state constitution. The government organized under the colonial charter imposed martial law and gave its soldiers various police powers. The issue in the case was whether the soldiers had committed a trespass when breaking into a private home. The trespass issue turned in part on whether the original charter government was still in power, or whether the insurgents had created a legitimate new government, thereby revoking any authority the old one had to impose martial law. The President had treated the old government as the legitimate authority. But the trespass victim argued that the old government, because of its undemocratic features, violated the guarantee of a "republican form of government" in the Guarantee Clause.[5] Thus, in the end, the case turned on which of the contending "governments" had been legitimate.

The Court ducked the issue. It held that a federal court could not determine which of two competing state governments was legally authorized or whether a state government was "republican" in nature. The Court argued that a court was not well equipped to consider this problem. It also took solace in the language of the Constitution, which suggested that Congress (not the courts) has the authority to decide what governments are "republican." The Court contended that any congressional resolution should not be subject to judicial second-guessing. This holding turned out to be very important after the Civil War, when it gave the Reconstruction Congress the final authority to decide which southern states had reestablished lawful governments and could therefore return their representatives to Congress.

The leading modern decision interpreting the political question doctrine is *Baker v. Carr*.[6] The case involved legislative districting in Tennessee. Legislative districts had not changed since 1901 and by the 1960s were badly out of alignment with the state's population. As in many parts of the country, there had been a dramatic shift of population from rural areas to cities, but the legislature remained dominated by the dwindling number of rural voters. The Court assumed that any challenge under the Guarantee Clause was

---

[4]   48 U.S. 1 (1849).

[5]   U.S. CONST. art. IV, § 4 ("The United States shall guarantee to every State in this Union a Republican Form of Government . . . .").

[6]   369 U.S. 186 (1962).

foreclosed by *Luther*, but it allowed a challenge based on the Equal Protection Clause. Justice William Brennan clustered most of the prior political question cases into three categories: foreign relations cases, cases dealing with the official start and end dates of wars, and cases dealing with the procedural validity of constitutional amendments. He distilled from his analysis a set of guiding principles governing application of the doctrine: (1) whether the Constitution assigned an issue to another branch of government, (2) whether there were judicially manageable standards for deciding an issue, (3) the need for the government to speak with a single voice (as in foreign affairs), and (4) whether courts could provide an effective remedy.[7] As we will see in Chapter 11, *Baker v. Carr* opened the door for the Court's far-reaching "one-person, one-vote" decisions.

In recent decades, the political question doctrine has been in decline as the Court's institutional self-confidence has increased. With one exception, the Court has not held the political question doctrine applicable since *Baker v. Carr*. For example, in *Powell v. McCormick*,[8] the Court held that it had the power to review a decision by the House of Representatives to deny a seat to a Congressman based on allegations of misconduct. The Court concluded that the House could consider only the qualifications set out in the Constitution itself for holding a seat (such as age). Given this interpretation, there were judicially manageable standards to apply and hence no political question. The Court distinguished the decision to seat a member of Congress, which was limited to the constitutionally specified factors, from the decision to expel a member who had already been seated, which might well be a political question.[9]

One of the areas flagged for application of the political question doctrine in *Baker v. Carr* was foreign affairs, but there too the Court has whittled away at the doctrine. In *Zivotofsky v. Clinton*,[10] the issue before the Court was the constitutionality of a statute allowing Americans born in Jerusalem to have Israel listed as their place of birth on their passports. This was contrary to a longstanding executive branch decision by presidents of both political parties (prior to President Trump) to avoid taking a stand on the controversial issue of the political status of the city, which Palestinians also claim as their capitol. Consequently, the Secretary of State refused to comply with the statute and argued that it infringed the President's constitutionality authority over foreign affairs—specifically, the President's exclusive authority to recognize foreign governments.

---

[7]   *See id.* at 217.
[8]   395 U.S. 486 (1969).
[9]   *See id.* at 522–23.
[10] 566 U.S. 189 (2012).

The Court held that there was no political question because the only issue before it was a purely legal one regarding the constitutionality of the statute, giving it clear standards to apply.[11]

The one case in the past fifty years in which the Court has actually found a political question is *Nixon v. United States*.[12] The case involved Judge Walter Nixon, not President Richard Nixon. Judge Nixon had been impeached and removed from office for perjury to a grand jury. He claimed that the Senate had used an unconstitutional procedure in trying him, allowing him a full hearing only before a committee rather before the Senate as a whole, although the entire Senate did vote on the basis of the hearing transcript. The Court held this issue to be a political question because the Constitution gives the Senate the "sole Power" to try cases of impeachment.[13] The court viewed this language as a textual commitment of the issue to the Senate, and it also perceived a lack of judicial standards for determining the applicable procedures. Among the other factors articulated in *Baker v. Carr*, the Court also pointed to the need to respect a final determination rather than leaving the validity of impeachments open during litigation—an especially important factor, the Court pointed out, in cases of presidential impeachment.

As things stand today, the political question doctrine is still alive but has very limited scope. Yet the underlying concerns about the appropriate scope of the judicial role, such as respecting the proper roles of other branches of government, remain on the Justices' minds. So is the need to avoid the "political thicket,"[14] including political controversies that might damage the Court's institutional position. Today, however, the Court is likely to implement these concerns through its use of justiciability doctrines such as standing and mootness, to which we turn now.

B. Standing

Although the political question doctrine has narrow scope today, the enterprise of defining the limits of the judicial role remains very much alive. Standing doctrine is the primary vehicle for resolving these issues. In principle, standing involves a very different issue than the political question doctrine: not whether an *issue* is appropriate for judicial resolution, but whether a specific *plaintiff*

---

[11]   *See id.* at 196–98.

[12]   506 U.S. 225 (1993).

[13]   U.S. CONST. art. I, § 3, cl. 6.

[14]   In modern times, this phrase has been used primarily in cases involving partisan gerrymandering. Vieth v. Jubelirer, 541 U.S. 267, 319 (2004) (Kennedy, J., concurring in the judgment); Davis v. Bandemer, 478 U.S. 109, 147 (1986) (O'Connor, J., concurring in the judgment). The concern about overexposing the Court to divisive political issues, however, is much broader.

has the ability to sue. In many cases, however, rejection of standing may mean that no plaintiff can raise a claim, in effect placing the underlying issue outside of judicial purview. Standing doctrine acts as a gatekeeper into the courthouse, with large implications for the ability of social movements, advocacy groups, and political partisans to pursue their goals through the courts. Narrowing federal standing law moves more decisions to the states, Congress, and the President, while expanding standing shifts authority to the courts. Thus, standing doctrine has implications for federalism and the separation of powers.

Many observers also think that the Court sometimes uses standing doctrine to dodge contentious issues that might result in political conflicts damaging to the Court or to American society. Alternatively, many commentators suggest that the Court uses standing as a way to dispose of litigation when it disapproves of the substance of the litigation but would prefer not to say so.

The legal test for standing is deceptively simple. Even twenty years ago, a leading scholar on the subject (now a federal judge) described the doctrine as "numbingly familiar."[15] Put simply, standing under Article III of the Constitution involves a three-part test: a plaintiff must demonstrate the existence of an "injury in fact" that is "legally cognizable," "fairly traceable" to the defendant, and capable of being "redressed" by the court.[16]

This definition more or less captures most ordinary litigation. If Phil hits Jane's car and she sues him for damages, she has clearly suffered harm, which was directly caused by Phil, and the damages will compensate her for the injury. In the post-Civil Rights era, however, much important litigation does not involve tangible injuries with easily assigned causes and clear-cut remedies. Plaintiffs may also bring claims based on harm to the environment, invasions of privacy, psychological harm, infringements of state authority, and other less tangible factors. And the defendant's conduct may not be the direct cause of the harm, or the court's ability to remedy the situation may be in doubt. Thus, it is not surprising that courts have struggled to apply the test to the complexities of modern litigation. At the very least, however, the three factors of injury-causation-remedy do provide a framework for lawyers and judges.

The degree to which this test is supported by either the original understanding of the Constitution or pre-1970s precedent is unclear.

---

[15]   William A. Fletcher, *The Structure of Standing*, 98 YALE L.J. 221, 222 (1988).

[16]   *See, e.g.*, Lujan v. Defenders of Wildlife, 504 U.S. 555, 560 (1992); Gene R. Nichol, Jr., *Rethinking Standing*, 72 CAL. L. REV. 68, 71–73 (1984). Judge Fletcher referred to "the apparent lawlessness of many standing cases when the wildly vacillating results in those cases are explained in the analytic terms made available by current doctrine." Fletcher, *supra* note 15, at 223.

Professor Cass Sunstein contends that the injury-in-fact test is a "revisionist view of Article III, with no textual or historical support."[17] He musters considerable historical evidence, showing that a number of common law writs were available to citizens generally, without any need to show special injury, in both English law and early American law. Nevertheless, no Justice on the current Supreme Court has expressed any doubts about the validity of the test, and there is no reason to expect the Court to reconsider it.

Each part of the test seems clear enough on the surface, yet each has proved remarkably tricky in practice, to the dismay of judges, litigants, law professors, and law students. Here we will discuss some illustrative cases and the general evolution of the doctrine.

The first part of the test—the injury-in-fact requirement—was first articulated in the foundational case of *Sierra Club v. Morton*.[18] The Sierra Club, an environmental group, challenged a plan by Walt Disney Enterprises to build a $35 million resort in the Mineral King Valley, which the Court described as "an area of great natural beauty nestled in the Sierra Nevada Mountains."[19] The Sierra Club challenged the plan but did not claim that its members would be directly injured by the construction of the resort. Instead, it invoked its status as a public interest group with a longstanding focus on preservation of the environment.

The Supreme Court held that the Sierra Club lacked standing. In order to establish standing, the Court said, a plaintiff seeking judicial review of agency action must show an "injury in fact." The Sierra Club, the Court held, had failed to show the necessary injury in fact to it or its members. But the Court defined injury in broad terms. According to the Court, the Sierra Club could establish the existence of an injury by alleging that some of its members would not be able to continue hiking through an unspoiled wilderness. As the Court said, "[a]esthetic and environmental well-being, like economic well-being, are important ingredients of the quality of life in our society, and the fact that particular environmental interests are shared by the many rather than the few does not make them less deserving of legal protection through the judicial process."[20]

In the years after *Sierra Club*, the Court continued to define standing broadly. But after the appointment of more conservative

---

[17]   Cass R. Sunstein, *What's Standing After* Lujan? *Of Citizen Suits, "Injuries," and Article III*, 91 MICH. L. REV. 163, 167 (1992).

[18]   405 U.S. 727 (1972).

[19]   *Id.* at 728.

[20]   *Id.* at 734. For an incisive contemporary critique of the Court's insistence on a showing of interference with the interests of users of the resource, see Joseph L. Sax, *Standing to Sue: A Critical Review of the Mineral King Decision*, 12 NAT. RES. J. 76 (1973).

Justices by President Reagan, a strong judicial reaction set in. The turning point may have been Justice Sandra Day O'Connor's majority opinion in *Allen v. Wright*.[21] A group of African American parents alleged that the Internal Revenue Service (IRS) was giving charitable tax exemptions to racially discriminatory private schools, contrary to federal tax laws. The parents claimed that these schools were pulling white children out of the public schools, limiting school integration. In holding for the Court that they lacked standing, Justice O'Connor first articulated the current three-part test. The problem, she said, was not the type of injury suffered by the plaintiffs; the Court conceded that the loss of the opportunity to attend integrated schools would be an "injury in fact." The problem, rather, she then held for the Court, was that the alleged injury was not fairly traceable to the IRS grant of tax exemptions. It was speculative, she reasoned, whether denying the exemptions would actually decrease the flight of white children to private schools.[22] The Court ignored Justice John Paul Stevens' economic argument that tax exemptions allowed private schools to offer lower prices (tuition), in turn increasing demand for their product.[23] Justice O'Connor also emphasized the concern that allowing suits such as this one would open up the courts to suits based on generalized grievances about government programs and requests to restructure these programs.

After his appointment to the Court, Justice Antonin Scalia emerged as the strongest advocate on the Court for narrowing standing. The high point of Justice Scalia's campaign to restrict standing came in his majority opinion in *Lujan v. Defenders of Wildlife*.[24] The plaintiffs alleged that they would be harmed in various ways by federally supported actions taking place in Egypt and Sri Lanka, actions that would allegedly violate the Endangered Species Act (ESA). The Court held that they lacked standing, in the process holding the ESA's provision authorizing citizen suits unconstitutional as applied to the case. Without any injury in fact, the Court said, the plaintiffs could be suing only to vindicate an abstract interest in administrative compliance with the law—but this interest is properly the concern not of the courts but of the President, who is constitutionally obligated to " 'take care that the laws be faithfully executed.' "[25]

Defenders of Wildlife, an environmental organization, had unsuccessfully alleged several forms of injury. Two members alleged that they had visited the relevant areas of Egypt and Sri Lanka in

---

[21]   468 U.S. 737 (1984).

[22]   *Id.* at 758.

[23]   *Id.* at 788 (Stevens, J., dissenting).

[24]   504 U.S. 555 (1992).

[25]   *Id.* at 577 (quoting Article II of the Constitution).

the past, were unable to do so currently because of conditions there, but hoped to do so again in the future. "Such 'some day intentions' without any description of concrete plans, or indeed even any specification of when the some day will be," Justice Scalia wrote, were not enough to support standing.[26] Justice Scalia was no more impressed with the plaintiffs' other "novel" standing theories.[27] Although the ESA is aimed in part at the protection of entire ecosystems, Justice Scalia found no basis for concluding that it created a cause of action on behalf of people who use parts of the ecosystem "not perceptibly affected" by the government's action.[28] The caustic tone of Justice Scalia's opinion, even more than its content, heralded a more skeptical attitude toward environmental standing.

A concurrence by Justice Anthony Kennedy, who was joined by Justice David Souter, attempted to stake out a middle ground. It received less attention at the time, probably because its rhetoric was so much more subdued and less arresting. But he and Justice Souter were the swing voters in *Defenders of Wildlife*, and their concurrence added significant caveats to the holding in the case. Justice Scalia's opinion may never actually have represented a majority of the Court, even in those sections that were not formally designated as joined by only a plurality.

Indeed, Justice Kennedy set forth such significant qualifications to the central arguments in the majority opinion that, as far as the future was concerned, he might almost as well have written a dissent. He agreed that the record in the case was inadequate to support the plaintiff's nexus theories, but he was not willing to foreclose them as a matter of law in some future case. He also saw a greater role for Congress in defining the perimeter of injury in fact. In his view, Congress had the "power to define injuries and articulate chains of causation that will give rise to a case or controversy where none existed before," but to exercise this power, "Congress must at the very least identify the injury it seeks to vindicate and relate the injury to the class of persons entitled to bring suit."[29] In contrast, Justice Scalia's majority opinion had seemed to give Congress no power to modify the application of the injury-in-fact test.

---

[26]   *Id.* at 564.

[27]   Justice Scalia described these theories as "novel." *Id.* at 565. Adjectives such as "novel" and "creative" are seldom compliments when judges use them to refer to legal theories.

[28]   *Id.* at 564.

[29]   *Id.* at 580 (Kennedy, J., concurring).

As it turned out, Justice Kennedy really was not on board with Justice Scalia's approach to standing.[30] This disagreement resulted in one of the most expansive applications of standing doctrine in recent years, *Massachusetts v. EPA*.[31] The case involved a challenge to the Environmental Protection Agency's refusal during the second Bush Administration to regulate greenhouse gases emitted by vehicles. The state of Massachusetts claimed to be injured by this failure in a number of respects, including the prospect that sea level change would erode its coastlines. The arguments against standing were that significant harm was likely to occur only decades in the future, so that the harm was not imminent; that regulation of U.S. vehicle pollution would cause only a small decrease in global emissions anyway; and that the harm caused by climate change is global, not unique to any one individual or group. Nevertheless, the Court held that the state had standing. Summarizing its application of the three-part test, the Court said:

> In sum—at least according to petitioners' uncontested affidavits—the rise in sea levels associated with global warming has already harmed and will continue to harm Massachusetts. The risk of catastrophic harm, though remote, is nevertheless real. That risk would be reduced to some extent if petitioners received the relief they seek. We therefore hold that petitioners have standing to challenge the EPA's denial of their rulemaking petition.[32]

Earlier in the opinion, the Court had pointed to some additional factors that favored a generous application of standing in the case: Congress had explicitly made the agency's rejection of rulemaking petitions reviewable; the plaintiffs were seeking to protect a procedural right (their right to demand a rulemaking); and the state was trying to protect its quasi-sovereign interest in the integrity of its own territory.[33]

The modern Court is far from finding consensus on how to apply the three-part standing test. Typical of standing cases, *Massachusetts v. EPA* was a 5–4 decision. Two other recent 5–4 splits further illustrate the perplexities of the doctrine. In *Clapper v. Amnesty International*,[34] a human rights organization challenged the legality of an electronic surveillance program, alleging that the

---

[30]   This became clear from subsequent cases such as *Friends of the Earth, Inc. et al. v. Laidlaw Environmental Services, Inc.*, 528 U.S. 167 (2000), and *Federal Election Commission v. Akins*, 524 U.S. 11 (1998), both cases in which Justice Kennedy voted to find standing while Justice Scalia strongly dissented.

[31]   549 U.S. 497 (2007).

[32]   *Id*. at 526.

[33]   *See id*. at 518–20.

[34]   568 U.S. 398 (2013).

program had interfered with its ability to communicate with foreign witnesses and give confidential information to its clients, many of whom feared being surveillance targets. In an opinion by Justice Samuel Alito, the Court rejected their claim of standing on the ground that they had failed to prove that the harm was sufficiently imminent. In fact, Justice Alito wrote, it was impossible for them to prove that they were currently under surveillance, since the government's wiretapping efforts were top secret.

The typical pattern in standing cases has been that the liberals on the Court favor expansive standing while the conservatives resist. This is understandable since liberals are generally more interested in empowering groups such as public interest organizations to challenge government or corporate actions. But this pattern does not always hold. In *Hollingsworth v. Perry*,[35] the issue was whether the sponsor of a ballot referendum banning same-sex marriage had standing to defend the referendum on appeal when the state government declined to do so. The Court refused to permit standing, over the objections of an unusual coalition of dissenters: Justices Kennedy, Clarence Thomas, Alito, and Sonia Sotomayor. The majority, in an opinion by Chief Justice John Roberts and joined by Justices Scalia, Ruth Bader Ginsburg, Stephen Breyer, and Elena Kagan, concluded that the referendum sponsors could not speak for the state government and did not have a judicially recognizable interest of their own to protect. Rather, the Chief Justice wrote, they were like any other citizen who felt strongly about their own view of the permissibility of banning same-sex marriage.

Although the three-part test for standing seems clear enough in its wording, its application requires judgment calls about when an injury is concrete enough, whether it is "fairly traceable" to the defendant (which obviously calls for a value judgment in addition to an empirical one), and the appropriateness and utility of judicial remedies. Judges' votes are likely to be shaped by their general views about the institutional role of the courts, which are not easily separated from their views about the urgency of judicial intervention in a particular situation—that is to say, of their views of the merits of a case. It is not hard to speculate that the liberals in *Massachusetts v. EPA* and *Clapper v. Amnesty International* viewed climate change and government surveillance programs as more in need of judicial oversight than did the conservatives on the Court—or that the split in *Hollingsworth v. Perry* at least partially reflected differences of opinion about the desirability of deciding the merits at that time. Invocation of the separation of powers seems to provide little assistance given the vagueness of the concept.

---

[35]   570 U.S. 693 (2013).

Justice Kennedy's concurring opinion in *Defenders of Wildlife*, where he was the swing voter and the majority opinion in *Massachusetts v. EPA*, which he joined, seem to give Congress some power to clarify the outer boundaries of standing. The extent of this power, however, remains unclear. Congress has considerable power to limit the jurisdiction of the federal courts. Thus, Congress can narrow standing fairly easily. But how much can it expand standing? The Court was confronted with this question in *Spokeo, Inc. v. Robins*.[36] At issue was a federal statute that allows individuals to sue credit agencies for inaccurate information and receive some damages even without proof of economic injury. In this case, the credit agency had overstated the plaintiff's job qualifications, which the plaintiff thought might lead employers to view him as overqualified. The Court held that the mere existence of a statutory violation involving an individual's information was too intangible to be a basis for standing under Article III. What is needed, the Court said, is a showing that in some sense the violation adversely affected the individual, although Congress can base standing on an injury that the Court might otherwise consider too intangible. The Court remanded the case to the lower court to consider whether the plaintiff's injury claim was enough to provide a basis for standing.

The meaning of the *Spokeo* opinion seems elusive, but perhaps the implication is that Congress can lower the thresholds for standing, so long as it does not entirely eliminate them. If so, perhaps Congress could provide standing to individuals who have a plausible claim of being impacted by a surveillance program, without having to show that an invasion of their own privacy was imminent. For instance, like the plaintiff in *Clapper*, the plaintiff might show that the program increased their expenses by requiring them to forgo electronic communications and deterred others from communicating candidly with them. The Court found these effects insufficient in *Clapper,* but perhaps Congress could grant standing to such plaintiffs under *Spokeo*.

C. Ripeness, Mootness, and Other Limitations

The ripeness and mootness doctrines are relatives of standing doctrine that tend to focus on matters of timing. In very rough terms, ripeness means that a plaintiff does not yet have standing because the injury is still too speculative or remote (think green bananas, which are not ripe), while mootness means that the plaintiff has lost standing because the injury has disappeared or has become irreversible (think black bananas, which are overripe). But there are subtle twists to ripeness and mootness that make a separate discussion necessary. In addition, this section will also address

---

[36]   136 S. Ct. 1540 (2016).

"prudential" extensions of justiciability doctrines, although the validity of these extensions is now in some question.

Modern ripeness doctrine stems from the foundational case of *Abbott Laboratories v. Gardner*.[37] This was a challenge by drug manufacturers to new regulations by the Food and Drug Administration (FDA). The question was whether they could challenge the regulations immediately or whether they would have to wait for enforcement actions to be taken against them. Compliance would require significant investments on their part, but as a practical matter, they would be under heavy pressure to comply rather than risk enforcement proceedings and the attendant bad publicity. The Court began its analysis of ripeness by noting that the "injunctive and declaratory judgment remedies are discretionary, and courts traditionally have been reluctant to apply them to administrative determinations unless these arise in the context of a controversy 'ripe' for judicial resolution."[38] The Court saw ripeness doctrine as performing duel purposes: "to prevent the courts, through avoidance of premature adjudication, from entangling themselves in abstract disagreements over administrative policies, and also to protect the agencies from judicial interference until an administrative decision has been formalized and its effects felt in a concrete way by the challenging parties."[39] Correspondingly, the Court announced a two-part test for ripeness, involving "the fitness of the issues for judicial decision" and "the hardship to the parties of withholding court consideration."[40]

Notably, the Court rooted this doctrine in remedies law, not in Article III. One possible implication is that Congress may be able to dispense with any separate requirement of ripeness, as it has attempted to do in many later regulatory statutes by authorizing immediate judicial review of newly issued regulations.

A ripeness claim is based on a contention that a case has been brought prematurely. A mootness claim alleges that the case has been brought too late or has lost its vitality in the course of litigation. An example of mootness would be a criminal case where the defendant dies before a conviction is final. Essentially, any case or controversy has died along with the defendant, since there is no longer anything at stake in the case. Thus, in general, a case is over when the plaintiff (the state, in a criminal case) no longer has an injury that could be remedied by a court, or more simply, when the

---

[37]   387 U.S. 136 (1967).

[38]   *Id.* at 148–49.

[39]   *Id.*

[40]   *Id.*

plaintiff has lost standing. But there are several exceptions to this rule.[41]

First, the requirement of imminence may be relaxed in the context of mootness as compared with standing to sue in the first place. Suppose that the defendant is sued for impending, threatened conduct, but then meekly proclaims that it will no longer take the threatened action. For instance, a prosecutor may threaten to enforce a law in a way that would violate the First Amendment, but then back down when someone actually went to court over the issue. If this tactic were enough to make the suit moot, and if the prosecutor repeated it whenever she was sued, the tactic might allow the law to remain on the books indefinitely. In this setting, rather than the plaintiff's having the burden of showing an imminent risk that the defendant will again change its mind, the defendant has the burden of showing the permanence of its current position. Voluntary cessation by the defendant of the activity in question does not by itself moot a case.

Second, a class action does not die merely because the named plaintiff's claim has become moot. For example, a class action on behalf of all students over an unconstitutional school practice does not become moot when the lead plaintiff graduates. A class action is a case brought by one or more named individuals in the name of all others similarly situated. The remedy in such a case applies to every member of the class, and every member of the class is bound by the court's judgment in the case even if they never personally participate. When the named plaintiff's case becomes moot, the other members of the class have a continuing stake in the action, and their continuing stake is enough for a live case or controversy. Under a contrary rule, class members would lose their rights even though the case was brought on behalf of every member of the class and the lawyers were ethically obligated to represent the interests of the entire class.

Third, even in the absence of a class action or imminent harm, a case may avoid mootness based on the likelihood that deciding it would avoid repetition of the issue while continuing to escape review. An example might be a challenge to the constitutionality of an abortion restriction by a woman who gives birth before the Supreme Court can decide the issue. If such a case is dismissed as moot, the Court might never have the opportunity to rule on the validity of the statute, since litigation typically proceeds much more slowly than

---

[41] For discussion of these exceptions and citations to the leading cases, see generally Matthew I. Hall, *The Partially Prudential Doctrine of Mootness*, 77 GEO. WASH L. REV. 562 (2009).

gestation.[42] It is often said that cases are not moot when they are capable of repetition yet evade review.

Finally, the Supreme Court has sometimes declined to find a case moot when it has been fully litigated and there is a strong public interest in resolving the issue before it. This branch of the doctrine most clearly highlights the difference between standing and mootness, since no amount of public interest or legal clarity would allow dispensing with the requirement of an injury-in-fact, which the Court deems grounded in Article III.

Thus, mootness doctrine explicitly embodies practical considerations of a kind different than the factors announced by the Court in its test for Article III standing. The Court has also applied such "prudential" considerations to impose standing restrictions beyond those stemming from Article III. For instance, the Court generally does not allow a third party to bring a claim based on another person's constitutional rights. To take one example, the proper party to challenge a criminal conviction, even an unconstitutional one, is the defendant, not some family member (e.g., a financial dependent of the defendant) who will suffer economic loss due to the conviction. Here, too, the Court has recognized exceptions, such as allowing a doctor to challenge an abortion restriction applying to her even though the claim is that the statute violates the constitutional rights of her patients, not of herself.[43]

The validity of such prudential doctrines was thrown into doubt by the Supreme Court's opinion in *Lexmark International, Inc. v. Static Control Components, Inc.*[44] The defendant in this false-advertising case basically argued that the plaintiff was only incidentally harmed and that suit could be brought only by the direct victims, its competitors. The Court rejected the idea that any special standing requirement applied beyond the Article III requirements and those of the false-advertising statute itself. In one passage, Justice Scalia's opinion for the Court expressed skepticism about the whole idea of prudential standing:

> Lexmark urges that we should decline to adjudicate Static Control's claim on grounds that are "prudential," rather than constitutional. That request is in some tension with our recent reaffirmation of the principle that "a federal court's 'obligation' to hear and decide" cases within its jurisdiction "is 'virtually unflagging.'" In recent decades, however, we have adverted to a "prudential" branch of standing, a doctrine not derived from Article III and "not

---

[42]   Roe v. Wade, 410 U.S. 113, 125 (1973) (holding such as case not to be moot).

[43]   *See id.*

[44]   572 U.S. 118 (2014).

exhaustively defined" but encompassing (we have said) at least three broad principles: " 'the general prohibition on a litigant's raising another person's legal rights, the rule barring adjudication of generalized grievances more appropriately addressed in the representative branches, and the requirement that a plaintiff's complaint fall within the zone of interests protected by the law invoked.' "[45]

But the Court did not expressly repudiate any of these prudential doctrines. Moreover, the passage was dictum—that is, language not necessary to resolve the case—because the Court almost immediately noted that the defendant's argument was really statutory rather than involving any special judicial doctrine of prudential standing.[46]

At this point, it is unclear whether the Court is prepared to follow through on this dictum and purge all of the prudential elements in justiciability doctrine.[47] These prudential considerations are aimed at genuine problems, such as strategic litigation behavior that would interfere with the use of the federal courts to vindicate rights. We suspect that the Court will ultimately find that the practical advantages of these doctrines outweigh the appeal of theoretical consistency and the desire to limit judicial discretion.

Even outside of these prudential doctrines, most observers believe that doctrines such as standing are too open-ended to truly constrain the courts. To underscore an earlier point, deciding what harms a court will count as genuine injuries, when these harms can be fairly traced to a defendant who did contribute to their occurrence, or whether a plaintiff's desire for a remedy is sufficiently related to the harms—all of these questions are value-laden. It is not surprising that Supreme Court cases on standing so often result in 5–4 votes or that divisions on standing often follow ideological lines.

One possible use of justiciability doctrines is to dodge merits rulings that might involve the Court in direct confrontations with the Congress or the President, or might result in too much of a public backlash. Some observers applaud the prudent use of these doctrines to preserve the Court's political capital from unnecessary harm.[48]

---

[45]   *Id.* at 126 (citations omitted). The Court blunted the force of these observations by stating in a footnote that the generalized grievance rule stemmed from Article III, the zone-of-interests rule was statutory, and (Justice Scalia admitted) the third-party standing rule was hard to classify. The Court added that "[t]his case does not present any issue of third-party standing, and consideration of that doctrine's proper place in the standing firmament can await another day." *Id.* at 1387 n. 3.

[46]   *See id.*

[47]   *See* Ernest A. Young, *Prudential Standing After* Lexmark International, Inc. v. Static Control Components, Inc.*, 10 DUKE J. CONST. L. & PUB. POL'Y 149 (2014).

[48]   For the classic articulation of this view, see ALEXANDER M. BICKEL, THE LEAST DANGEROUS BRANCH: THE SUPREME COURT AT THE BAR OF POLITICS 111–98 (1962).

Others argue that the Court should apply neutral legal principles and let the chips fall where they may.[49]

II. Theories of Constitutional Interpretation

The doctrines in the preceding section operate as threshold requirements that may prevent a court from deciding a constitutional issue. But what happens when a case surmounts these obstacles and the court turns to the merits of a constitutional claim? Some issue are too clear to require any interpretation of the Constitution—a thirty-year-old cannot be president because Article II sets a minimum age of 35.[50] But when this kind of laser-like quality is absent (lawyers call it a clear, determinate rule), how should courts decide disputes about the meaning of the Constitution?

Scholars—and a few judges themselves—have not shied away from offering theories about how to determine the meaning of the Constitution. In this section, we will focus on three main approaches. The first approach, which is both a theory of judicial review and a theory of constitutional interpretation because it focuses on how judges in particular should interpret the Constitution, was dominant from the late 1930s into the early 1980s. It stresses the role that courts can play in improving American democratic rule by reforming the political process and ensuring equal treatment for politically powerless minorities. The second approach, which has displaced the first approach at least among many conservatives, argues that courts are bound by the original meaning of the Constitution and should decide cases accordingly. A third approach, called living constitutionalism, embraces the idea that the meaning of the Constitution changes over time and attempts to explain how this process both does and should operate. We will discuss these approaches in that order.

Before turning to the individual approaches, it is worth noting some commonalities that cut across these categories. First, advocates of each of the above approaches feel compelled to address the "dead hand" problem, which concerns the authority of constitutional provisions ratified long ago to bind current generations. Second, in all three categories, constitutional theorists feel the need to respond to the counter-majoritarian difficulty, which concerns the democratic legitimacy of having unelected judges override the choices of today's majorities based on judicial interpretations of these provisions. Third, nearly everyone agrees that the constitutional text and its original meaning are significant factors in constitutional interpretation; the only debate is over *how* significant. Finally, nearly

---

[49]   For the canonical statement of this position, see Herbert Wechsler, *Toward Neutral Principles of Constitutional Law*, 73 HARV. L. REV. 1, 5–9 (1959).

[50]   *See* U.S. CONST. art. II, § 5.

all constitutional theorists and judges accept what lawyers call "stare decisis," the doctrine under which courts normally follow precedent. This means that many constitutional cases will be decided based on prior decisions rather than by application of any constitutional theory. Indeed, the reader of Supreme Court opinions will find far more discussions of past judicial rulings than of historical documents like the *Federalist Papers*. Thus, despite what can be rather bitter debates among theorists and judges, they share a great deal of common ground.

On another dimension, there has been considerable discussion of whether the Supreme Court should be cautious in taking on controversial issues and diffident about overturning the views of coordinate branches of government. The argument for cautious, deferential judicial review traces back at least to William Thayer in the late Nineteenth Century. He argued that judges should strike down federal legislation only when its unconstitutionality was clear beyond a reasonable doubt.[51] As Thayer put it, "having regard to the great, complex, ever-unfolding exigencies of government, much which will seem unconstitutional to one man, or body of men, may reasonably not seem so to another."[52] Within this range of reasonable interpretation, he contended, "the constitution does not impose upon the legislature any one specific opinion, but leaves open this range of choice," so that "whatever choice is rational is constitutional."[53] Like with respect to the use of justiciability doctrines, moreover, other commentators have argued for judicial avoidance to prevent the loss of the Court's political capital and to avoid a political backlash against controversial judicial interventions.

These forms of judicial modesty could be combined with any of the theories we will be discussing, raising the burden of proof to be placed on a law's challengers. (This is why a theory of judicial review—of the proper role of courts—is not the same thing as a theory of constitutional interpretation, which need not be specific to how *judges* should interpret the Constitution.) For instance, an originalist following Thayer would argue that statutes should be declared unconstitutional only when it is clear beyond a reasonable doubt that they violate the Constitution's original meaning, but a politician need not be similarly constrained in voting against a bill on originalist grounds. Whether or not they apply a theory or simply make atheoretical strategic judgments, judges are clearly selective about

---

[51] *See* William Thayer, *The Origin and Scope of the American Doctrine of Constitutional Law*, 7 HARV. L. REV. 129 (1893).

[52] *Id.* at 144.

[53] *Id.*

when and how they take on controversial constitutional issues, behavior of great interest to political scientists.

A.   The *Carolene Products* Approach

Until the rise of originalism in the 1980s, the dominant approach to judicial review was encapsulated in a famous footnote in *United States v. Carolene Products Co.*[54] Justice Harlan Fiske Stone's opinion for the Court was one of a cluster of post-1937 cases that, as we discuss in Chapter 9, abandoned a tradition of skeptical judicial scrutiny of economic regulations. As *Carolene Products* reduced the degree of judicial scrutiny applicable to economic regulations, it suggested, in its since-famous footnote 4, a new set of roles for the Supreme Court. The Court announced a general presumption that legislation is constitutional, but then articulated some important exceptions:

> [1] There may be narrower scope for operation of the presumption of constitutionality when legislation appears on its face to be within a specific prohibition of the Constitution. . . .

> [2] It is unnecessary to consider now whether legislation which restricts those political processes which can ordinarily be expected to bring about repeal of undesirable legislation, is to be subjected to more exacting judicial scrutiny under the general prohibitions of the Fourteenth Amendment than are most other types of legislation. [The Court cited cases involving the rights to vote, to disseminate information, to organize politically, and to assemble peaceably.]

> [3] Nor need we enquire whether similar considerations enter into the review of statutes directed at particular religious . . . or national . . . or racial minorities[;] whether prejudice against discrete and insular minorities may be a special condition, which tends seriously to curtail the operation of those political processes ordinarily to be relied upon to protect minorities, and which may call for a correspondingly more searching judicial inquiry. . . .[55]

The first paragraph of the footnote seems uncontroversial after *Marbury*: the Court should apply meaningful scrutiny and strike down legislation that violates express constitutional prohibitions. But *Carolene Products* assumed that these prohibitions also apply to

---

[54]   304 U.S. 144 (1938).

[55]   *Id.* at 152 (citations omitted).

the states through the Fourteenth Amendment, a topic we discuss in Chapter 8.

The second paragraph suggests that judicial deference to economic regulations is based on a judicial presumption of a fair political playing field. If there is reason to doubt this presumption, the Court reasoned, then there is also less reason to defer to the political process. This approach to constitutional law can be criticized because it does not rely on explicit constitutional text, although it may be defended as an inference from the many provisions relating to political representation and voting rights. (And besides, the *Caroline Products* Court might have retorted, there is no explicit textual support for judicial review in the first place, let alone directions on how to exercise it.) A narrower objection points out the difficulty in defining what structural defects in democracy are important enough to warrant higher judicial scrutiny.

The third paragraph of footnote 4 has also been controversial. It suggests that the strategy of the second paragraph is insufficient, standing alone, to promote fair politics. For example, even if the formal political rules about voting and so on are fair, a "discrete and insular minority" against which the majority is prejudiced is still likely to lose. The key to the third paragraph is "prejudice," an asserted distortion of the political process under which certain minorities are rendered politically powerless.

As with paragraph 2, paragraph 3's theory supporting stringent judicial scrutiny can find no constitutional text specifically supporting it. Moreover, note the difficult definitional questions posed by paragraph 3: what is a "discrete and insular minority," and what is "prejudice"? Is prejudice different from a sincerely held moral belief, such as opposition to same-sex intimacy or marriage? A related problem is where to draw the line on political fairness; for example, should consumers be heard about their inability to prevent the adoption of special interest legislation?[56]

Carolene Products fell out of favor for a variety of reasons, including the above difficulties and the resurgence of conservatism after 1980, but also because the nature of the issues changed. *Carolene Products* worked reasonably well in an era when the Court was primarily focused on protecting politically powerless minorities. But it seemed to provide less insight when the focus shifted to other issues such as discrimination against women, a majority of the

---

[56] For the most influential scholarly theory of judicial review that builds out Footnote 4, see generally JOHN HART ELY, DEMOCRACY AND DISTRUST: A THEORY OF JUDICIAL REVIEW (1980). For criticism of Ely's theory as making many more substantive value choices than he lets on, see generally Paul Brest, *The Substance of Process*, 42 OHIO ST. L.J. 131 (1981); Laurence H. Tribe, *The Puzzling Persistence of Process-Based Constitutional Theories*, 89 YALE L.J. 1063 (1980).

population (see Chapter 10), reproductive rights issues such as birth control and abortion (see Chapter 12), and the "imperial presidency" (see Chapter 7).

B. Originalism

In response to liberal Supreme Court decisions of the 1960s and 1970s, conservative commentators began to demand a return to the vision of the Framers, as these conservatives understood it. Liberals counterattacked in defense of a "living Constitution" that adapts to changes in American society and its contemporary values. This section and the following one will discuss the longstanding, and still ongoing, debate between these two schools of constitutional thought.

In broad terms, originalism holds that constitutional interpretation should be based solely on the meaning of a textual provision when it was adopted; thus, the primary task of judges and other interpreters is historical inquiry. First-generation originalists, and some still today, think that constitutional interpretations should be based on the original intentions of Framers such as James Madison or of the delegates at the state ratifying conventions (since ratification is what made the Constitution governing law). Most originalists today (called second-generation originalists) focus on how a reasonable reader at the time of ratification would have understood the language of the text; this is called the original semantic meaning of a constitutional provision. What all originalists share is the belief that the meaning of a constitutional provision is fixed the instant it is adopted, with no room for further evolution as long as the originalist inquiry yields decisive answers to interpretive questions.[57]

To see the contrast between originalism and *Carolene Products*, consider the issue of racial gerrymandering—that is, the design of legislative districts to minimize the number of legislators representing racial minorities. From a *Carolene Products* perspective, it seems obvious that racial gerrymandering should be unconstitutional since it unfairly limits the ability of members of the minority group to participate in the political process. But answering this question from a originalist perspective requires significant historical inquiry. The Fourteenth Amendment guarantees "equal protection of the laws" and the Fifteenth Amendment prohibits racial restrictions on voting.[58] But neither by its terms says anything about racial gerrymandering, and it would take historical research to

---

[57]   For a discussion of the evolution of originalism over the past several decades, see generally Keith E. Whittington, *Originalism: A Critical Introduction*, 82 FORDHAM L. REV. 375 (2013).

[58]   *See* U.S. CONST. amend. XIV, § 1; amend. XV, § 1.

determine the original understanding as to whether these terms applied to legislative districting.

Another example would be whether the Second Amendment protects private ownership of firearms for purposes of self-defense or whether it is limited to protecting state militias from interference by the federal government. The historical evidence is bitterly contested.[59] But since gun owners are far from being unrepresented in the political process (the National Rifle Association is a very powerful lobbying force), *Carolene Products* would suggest leaving the issue of gun control to the legislature.

At a more theoretical level, originalism and *Carolene Products* have two different responses to the counter-majoritarian difficulty. *Carolene Products* points to flaws in the democratic process as the basis for invalidating specific kinds of laws. Originalism points to the super-majority that ratified the constitutional provision as being entitled to more respect than the momentary majority that has passed legislation. On this view, judges who carry out the views of this supermajority can claim democratic legitimacy even for rulings contrary to the views of current majorities, but any interpretation contrary to the views of this supermajority lacks this legitimizing foundation.

The debate over originalism has raged for more than forty years and shows no signs of abating. We will try to give a quick overview of the arguments on both sides of this debate. Rather than cluttering the text with dozens of footnotes, we simply provide some of the main sources in the accompanying note.[60] This strategy is feasible because originalists tend to present a united front, with only secondary disagreements among themselves. As we will see in the next section, evolutionary constitutional theories are too diverse to be discussed as a collective unit.

Originalists contend that their approach provides a principled basis for constitutional interpretation, eliminating or at least curtailing judicial discretion. They view non-originalist theories as too formless to restrain judges from simply imposing their own policy

---

[59]   *See* District of Columbia v. Heller, 554 U.S. 570 (2008).

[60]   *See generally* JACK M. BALKIN, LIVING ORIGINALISM (2011); RAOUL BERGER, GOVERNMENT BY JUDICIARY: THE TRANSFORMATION OF THE FOURTEENTH AMENDMENT (1977); Mitchell Berman, *Originalism Is Bunk*, 84 N.Y.U. L. REV. 1 (2009); ROBERT H. BORK, THE TEMPTING OF AMERICA: THE POLITICAL SEDUCTION OF LAW (1990); FRANK B. CROSS, THE FAILED PROMISE OF ORIGINALISM (2013); Daniel A. Farber, *Historical Versus Iconic Meaning: The Declaration, the Constitution, and the Interpreter's Dilemma*, 89 U. SO. CAL. L. REV. 457 (2016); H. Jefferson Powell, *The Original Understanding of Original Intent*, 98 HARV. L. REV. 885 (1984); ANTONIN SCALIA, A MATTER OF INTERPRETATION: FEDERAL COURTS AND THE LAW (1997); KEITH E. WHITTINGTON, CONSTITUTIONAL INTERPRETATION: TEXTUAL MEANING, ORIGINAL INTENT, AND JUDICIAL REVIEW (1999).

positions and normative commitments at the expense of the democratic process. In the view of originalists, such judicial policymaking happened all too often during the mid-Twentieth Century in cases involving the rights of criminal defendants, religious freedom, abortion, and federal power. They view these opinions as generally lacking any foundation in historical evidence of the Framers' understanding of the Constitution. Justice Scalia was especially insistent about the need for originalism to curb judicial activism. In his view, only originalism had any prospect of keeping judges on the correct side of the law/politics divide.

There are also some well-known arguments against originalism. One relates to the difficulty of determining the original intent. There are significant gaps in the historical record, and different historians tend to interpret the record differently. In addition, there is no reason to think that all of the supporters of the Constitution had the same expectations about how it would be applied. As we will see in the next few chapters, Madison and Hamilton famously disagreed about the scope of congressional and executive power in the original Constitution. The same can be said about the original intent behind the provisions of the Reconstruction Amendments.

In response to these concerns about the difficulty of reconstructing the original intent, many originalists switched their focus from original expectations or intentions to original understandings or objective meaning. Put another way, they deemphasized the authors of the Constitution in favor of its contemporary audience, seeking to identify constitutional meaning with the interpretation of a reasonable reader of the time. This move to audience understandings opens an array of questions about the background knowledge of the reasonable reader and the methods of interpretation this reader would have applied. There might be a temptation to attribute to this hypothetical reasonable reader the judge's own views of the issue. There is also the concern that the distinction in principle between original intent and original meaning tends to collapse in practice given the tendency of originalists to offer up the views of especially prominent Founders (such as Madison, Hamilton, and Jefferson) as evidence of the original meaning.

Thus, originalists agree that interpretation should be based on the "original ____," but they disagree about precisely how to fill in the blank. Originalists also differ in the degree of generality they seek in interpreting constitutional provisions. For instance, the Eighth Amendment bans "cruel and unusual" punishments. One might interpret this provision on the basis of the specific punishments that were (and were not) deemed cruel and unusual in 1791, when the amendment was ratified. Or one might find evidence of a broader desire to ban rarely imposed punishments that violate norms against cruelty at the time of interpretation, given that what is regarded as cruel and unusual obviously changes over time.

As the "level of generality" increases, the line between originalism and evolutionary theories begins to blur; at the extreme, it is hard to tell the difference. For instance, Jack Balkin (one of the few liberal originalists) views the open-ended phrases of the Constitution such as "equal protection of the laws" as having been framed with the understanding that they delegate to future generations the task of defining their scope.[61] On this view, the Equal Protection Clause does not set forth a clear, determinate rule or even a relatively constraining, fixed standard; instead, it states a general principle of equality whose application can change over time.

Although Balkin's version of originalism claims the sanction of original meaning, his theory does bear more than a passing resemblance to living constitutionalism. He argues that "[e]ach generation is charged with the obligation to flesh out and implement text and principle in their own time," and thus his version of originalism "views living constitutionalism as a process of permissible constitutional construction."[62] Although Balkin defends this approach as a legitimate variant of originalism, it clearly incorporates non-originalist methods of decisionmaking. Indeed, his objective is to overcome the apparent opposition between these two general interpretive approaches.[63]

Despite their differences, originalists are in agreement that the original intent or meaning trumps other approaches to constitutional interpretation (except, perhaps, firmly settled precedent) whenever the original history can be discerned with sufficient specificity to resolve the question at issue. As Justice Scalia once wrote, the "Great Divide with regard to constitutional interpretation is not that between framers' intent and objective meaning, but rather that between *original meaning* (whether derived from framers' intent or not) and *current meaning*."[64]

Regardless of its particular form, originalism has received a barrage of criticism. To begin with, critics have argued that originalism failed as an effort to root judicial review in the prior democratic adoption of the Constitution. After all, when the Constitution was adopted, women could not vote and a substantial portion of the population consisted of slaves. Even apart from

---

[61]   *See* BALKIN, *supra* note 60, at 7.

[62]   *Id.* at 23.

[63]   For a sympathetic critique of Balkinian originalism as more living constitutionalist than originalist, see generally Neil S. Siegel, *Jack Balkin's Rich Historicism and Diet Originalism: Health Benefits and Risks for the Constitutional System*, 111 MICH. L. REV. 931 (2013).

[64]   SCALIA, *supra* note 60, at 38.

questions that arise because of limitations on the franchise during the Framing period, it remains unclear that a restriction on the current democratic majority can gain legitimacy *solely* from the fact of its enactment by a much earlier, long-dead majority that purported to insulate its own values and preferences from simple majoritarian change. (This, to repeat, is often called the "dead hand" objection.) One pillar of support for a legal regime can be the legitimacy of the process of adoption, but it is less clear that this can function effectively as the *only* support without taking into account other motivations for public acceptance.

Critics have also challenged the originalist claim of reducing judicial discretion and thereby depoliticizing constitutional law. These critics question whether historical events yield readily ascertainable interpretations or whether original meanings of constitutional texts were clear-cut. They also question whether lawyers and judges possess the training and historical knowledge needed for expert judgment about long-ago periods of time.[65] Meanwhile, critics argue that originalism is indeterminate on the critical question of the level of generality; for instance, in cases involving government-mandated racial segregation (which we will encounter in Chapter 10), it is unclear whether judges should be seeking the original understanding about whether segregated schools violate the Equal Protection Clause or the original understanding of the general concept of equality embedded in the clause.

Finally, critics have argued that originalism fails to accurately describe the American constitutional tradition. Modern non-originalists opinions by the Supreme Court have banned racial segregation, provided legal protection to advocacy by dissidents, limited discrimination against women and sexual orientation minorities, and allowed federal regulation of matters such as employment discrimination, environmental pollution, and organized crime. Critics have portrayed originalism as a threat to re-impose an archaic legal order to the detriment of equality values, civil liberties, and a modern, integrated economy and society.

In response, some conservative scholars have attempted to demonstrate that these decisions actually are consistent with the original understanding. Resort to higher levels of generality is one way to square originalism with modern-day decisions that have established principles with deep normative appeal. For instance, Professor Steven Calabresi and Julia Rickert argue that modern

---

[65] As Judge Richard Posner put this criticism, "[t]he decisive objection to the quest for original meaning, even when conducted in good faith, is that judicial historiography rarely dispels ambiguity. Judges are not competent historians. Even real historiography is frequently indeterminate, as real historians acknowledge." RICHARD A. POSNER, REFLECTIONS ON JUDGING 185 (2013).

decisions requiring heightened scrutiny in gender discrimination cases are consistent with original meaning.[66] The core of their argument is that Fourteenth Amendment reaches "all special or partial laws that single out certain persons or classes for special benefits or burdens."[67] In a departure from standard originalist methodology, they also rely on the later-enacted Nineteenth Amendment to support their interpretation of the Fourteenth Amendment. In their view, the modern "change in our understanding of women's abilities has been constitutionalized by a monumental Article V amendment—the Nineteenth Amendment, which in 1920 gave women the right to vote."[68]

A tension between constitutional meaning and present-day understanding is inherent in the nature of originalism, and it limits the ability of Professor Calabresi and like-minded originalist scholars to collapse the distance between the two. Without some distinction between current-day understanding and original meaning, originalism would be indistinguishable from the "living Constitution" approach that it rejects. Judge Bork, for example, made the connection between originalism and historical fixity clear:

> When we speak of "law," we ordinarily refer to a rule that we have no right to change except through prescribed procedures. That statement assumes that the rule has a meaning independent of our own desires. . . .
>
> What is the meaning of a rule that judges should not change? It is the meaning understood at the time of the law's enactment.[69]

In the same vein, a Supreme Court opinion from a century ago maintains that "[t]he Constitution is a written instrument. As such its meaning does not alter. That which it meant when adopted it means now."[70] And yet variants of the "new originalism" emphasize the idea of "constitutional construction" as an enterprise distinct from constitutional interpretation.[71] According to new originalists,

---

[66]   Steven G. Calabresi & Julia T. Rickert, *Originalism and Sex Discrimination*, 90 TEX. L. REV. 1 (2011).

[67]   *Id.* at 7.

[68]   *Id.* at 9. This argument originated with Professor Akhil Amar, whose views are described in the section on evolutionary theories, although he straddles the line between the two categories.

[69]   BORK, *supra* note 60, at 144.

[70]   South Carolina v. United States, 199 U.S. 437, 448 (1905); McIntyre v. Ohio Elections Comm'n, 514 U.S. 334, 359 (1995).

[71]   *See generally, e.g.,* KEITH E. WHITTINGTON, CONSTITUTIONAL CONSTRUCTION: DIVIDED POWERS AND CONSTITUTIONAL MEANING (1999); Randy E. Barnett, *Interpretation and Construction*, 34 HARV. J.L. & PUB. POL'Y 65, 67 (2011); Lawrence B. Solum, *Originalism and Constitutional Construction*, 82 FORDHAM L. REV. 453 (2013).

interpretation focuses on the original meaning of the constitutional text, but construction does not; construction kicks in when original meaning runs out. The so-called construction zone of these new originalists is a space dominated by the interpretive methods of evolutionary theories, to which we now turn.

C.   Evolutionary Theories

Evolutionary theories of constitutional interpretation, which are on the other side of the "great divide" described by Justice Scalia, are highly diverse. Some evolutionary theorists view constitutional evolution as properly centered on the courts; others have doubts about judicial review and embrace some form of populism. The theorists do have in common a firm rejection of the originalist premise that the meaning of a constitutional provision is fixed at the moment of ratification. In their view, the meaning of the Constitution changes over time. Thus, in one way or another, they all make room for changes in constitutional meaning. They all regard this evolutionary process as both desirable and descriptively accurate of how the constitutional system actually functions in practice. But they are otherwise very diverse.

All these theories not only reject originalism, but also are in tension with *Carolene Products*. Evolutionary theorists agree that reinforcing the democratic process is an important function of judicial review. But they also think that constitutional interpretation must make room for protection of other social values—for instance, evolving concepts of human dignity or liberty, and equality for members of groups that may not qualify as "discrete and insular minorities"—thus going beyond representation-reinforcement as a goal.

Evolutionary theories have a readily available answer to the "dead hand" problem—past supermajorities do not in principle rule the current generation of Americans. But evolutionary theories must contend with the counter-majoritarian difficulty to a greater extent than the theories of constitutional interpretation that we have already discussed. If law must change with the times, as evolutionary theorists believe, why should it be courts rather than the political process that make this change? As we see it, evolutionary theorists have two lines of response. The first is to emphasize ways in which non-originalist judicial review can be seen as part of democracy rather than a limit on democracy. One such argument is that judicial review enhances public deliberation about fundamental issues by making them more salient. Another is that the American public broadly supports the institution of judicial review, in no small part because the Court tends to track public opinion over the long run on issues that Americans care about. Indeed, most political scientists and many law professors doubt that judicial review presents much of a counter-majoritarian difficulty at all.[72]

Yet another such argument is that the federal electoral process and the national policymaking process are shot-through with counter-majoritarian characteristics.[73] For example, from a majoritarian perspective, legislatures may not do very well in deciding some crucial issues because they are apt to reflect the views of only the most energized or wealthiest or politically most powerful voters or interests, while the judiciary may actually be more representatives because it contains judges appointed over time by a diverse group of presidents who are insulated from the inequalities of access to the political process.

The second line of defense is that protecting certain human rights is more important than the presumptive entitlement of a popular majority to rule. This prioritization makes some decisions illegitimate however majoritarian democratic their pedigree. Or to put it another way, one might argue that the case for majority rule fails morally unless it is coupled with certain forms of protection for human rights.

---

[72] *See generally, e.g.,* ROBERT BENNETT & LAWRENCE B. SOLUM, CONSTITUTIONAL ORIGINALISM: A DEBATE (2011); BARRY FRIEDMAN, THE WILL OF THE PEOPLE: HOW PUBLIC OPINION HAS INFLUENCED THE SUPREME COURT AND SHAPED THE MEANING OF THE CONSTITUTION (2009); THOMAS R. MARSHALL, PUBLIC OPINION AND THE REHNQUIST COURT (2008); KEITH E. WHITTINGTON, POLITICAL FOUNDATIONS OF JUDICIAL SUPREMACY: THE PRESIDENCY, THE SUPREME COURT, AND CONSTITUTIONAL LEADERSHIP IN U.S. HISTORY (2007); THOMAS R. MARSHALL, PUBLIC OPINION AND THE SUPREME COURT (1989); MARTIN SHAPIRO, FREEDOM OF SPEECH: THE SUPREME COURT AND JUDICIAL REVIEW (1966); Kevin T. McGuire & James A. Stimson, *The Least Dangerous Branch Revisited: New Evidence on Supreme Court Responsiveness to Public Preferences,* 66 J. POL. 1018 (2004); Jack M. Balkin & Sanford Levinson, *Understanding the Constitutional Revolution,* 87 VA. L. REV. 1045 (2001); Robert A. Dahl, *Decision-Making in a Democracy: The Supreme as a National Policy-Maker,* 6 J. PUB. L. 279 (1957).

[73] Consider each state's allocation of two Senators regardless of state population, the Electoral College method of electing the president (which reproduces the malapportionment of the Senate), partisan gerrymandering aided by computer technology, the more efficient distribution of Republican voters around the nation because Democrats tend to live in urban areas, and a federal statute that requires single-member congressional districts. Consider also the bicameralism and presentment requirements, the latter of which grants veto power to the president. U.S. CONST. art. I, § 7, cl. 2. Congressional rules and practices such as the filibuster and the unrepresentative committee system, as well as political dynamics including the disproportionate access granted to wealthy donors and lobbyists, also add to the counter-majoritarian characteristics of the federal policymaking process. For discussions of political branch counter-majoritarianism, see generally SANFORD LEVINSON, OUR UNDEMOCRATIC CONSTITUTION: WHERE THE CONSTITUTION GOES WRONG (AND HOW WE THE PEOPLE CAN CORRECT IT) (2006); PAUL BREST ET AL., PROCESSES OF CONSTITUTIONAL DECISIONMAKING: CASES AND MATERIALS 147–51 (6th ed. 2015); Corinna Barrett Lain, *Upside-Down Judicial Review,* 101 GEO. L.J. 113, 144–157 (2012).

Many of the arguments for evolutionary constitutionalism are simply the flipside of the arguments against originalism. But evolutionary theories also rest on an argument that many political scientists embrace. Looking back over constitutional history, as we will do in the remainder of this book, it is plain that constitutional law has evolved over time in dramatic ways to reflect the changes in the larger society—and these changes in constitutional law have occurred largely outside the amendment process specified in Article V, which is the pathway of constitutional change emphasized by originalists. If constitutional evolution is inevitable anyway, it may be more important to think about how to do evolutionary constitutionalism better, rather than simply decrying it.

Below, we will describe four theories of constitutional evolution, which we will divide into two groups. One set of theories emphasizes the role of courts in the evolutionary process. The other set of theories views the public as the critical actors, with courts and other institutions reflecting popular sentiments.

Court-Focused Theories

David Strauss's theory of common law constitutionalism analogizes constitutional law to such common law subjects as contract law and property law. As non-lawyers may be surprised to learn, even today the legal rules governing contracts and property are often the outcome of decades of judicial precedent rather than legislative enactments. Strauss argues that, despite the significance accorded the written Constitution, in reality the most important parts of constitutional law are the outcome of two centuries of judicial rulings rather than of the text itself, let alone its original meaning.

Strauss views "emphasis on text, or on the original understanding" as reflecting "an implicit adherence to the postulate that law must ultimately be connected to some authoritative source" such as the Framers, whereas "the common law has been the great opponent of this authoritative approach" and locates the source of law in "understandings that evolve over time."[74] And in his view, "it is the common law approach, not the approach that connects law to an authoritative text, or an authoritative decision by the Framers or by 'we the people,' that best explains, and best justifies, American constitutional law today."[75] Nor is Strauss troubled by the counter-majoritarian critique as applied to common law judges. Among other responses, he argues that this critique is factually unfounded because "the principles developed through the common law method are not

---

[74] David A. Strauss, *Common Law Constitutionalism*, 63 U. CHI. L. REV. 877 (1996).

[75] *Id.*

likely to stay out of line for long with views that are widely and durably held in the society."[76]

Strauss's common law constitutionalism can be considered part of a broader family of theories that political theorists call Burkeanism, which is the belief that legal change is essential but should be achieved incrementally and deliberatively, with due regard for longstanding societal arrangements that have worked at least tolerably well. This philosophy is named after Edmund Burke, an Eighteenth Century British political thinker and member of Parliament. He also believed that legislators should exercise independent judgment about what is in the best interests of the whole society rather than simply reflecting the potentially parochial views of their constituents on every issue.[77] Burkeans emphasize that change should be organic and evolutionary rather than revolutionary.[78] This approach is related to other theories of constitutional law that urge caution on judges. For instance, Professor Cass Sunstein has argued for judicial minimalism, which is a theory of judicial opinion writing that urges judges to rest their decisions on narrow and shallow grounds to allow room for additional deliberation, to maintain social solidarity, and to avoid mistakes before proceeding further in any particular direction.[79]

In concrete terms, Burkeanism also requires respect for long-established rules and historical governmental practices.[80] For instance, in a separation of powers case, a Burkean would tend to accept an exercise of presidential power that had taken place over a long period of time and seemed to be accepted by Congress.[81] Likewise, in a federalism case, a Burkean would think it wrong to challenge the constitutionality of paper money or the federal minimum wage or the Social Security system, regardless of the original understanding, because of how deeply entrenched all of them are. An earlier Burkean was Professor Alexander Bickel, who argued

---

[76]   *Id.* at 929. For the most recent articulation of this theory, which incorporates additional work by Strauss, see generally DAVID A. STRAUSS, THE LIVING CONSTITUTION (2010).

[77]   For a discussion of this implications of Burke's thought for legislators, see generally Neil S. Siegel, *After the Trump Era: A Constitutional Role Morality for Presidents and Members of Congress*, 107 GEO. L.J. 109 (2018).

[78]   *See generally* Ernest A. Young, *Rediscovering Conservatism: Burkean Political Theory and Constitutional Interpretation*, 72 N.C. L. REV. 619 (1994).

[79]   *See generally* Cass R. Sunstein, *Burkean Minimalism*, 105 MICH. L. REV. 353 (2006). *See also* CASS R. SUNSTEIN, ONE CASE AT A TIME: JUDICIAL MINIMALISM ON THE SUPREME COURT (1999).

[80]   Burkeanism tends to garner greater support in cases involving the constitutional structure than in cases involving constitutional rights. This is because many judges and commentators believe that most constitutional rights exist to discipline or eliminate certain harmful traditions, not to perpetuate them.

[81]   *See generally* Curtis A. Bradley & Trevor W. Morrison, *Historical Gloss and the Separation of Powers*, 126 HARV. L. REV. 411 (2012).

for a combination of principle and prudence in the Court's decisionmaking in the book that coined the phrase the "counter-majoritarian difficulty" and inspired more than a half-century of constitutional theorizing about how to meet it.[82] The doctrine of stare decisis, under which courts follow their own prior decisions much of the time even when arguably wrong, is the most Burkean aspect of constitutional law. Even most originalists concede that judicial precedents deserve respect and should not be reexamined every time an issue comes before the Court again.

Public-Focused Theories

Some constitutional theorists have argued in favor of constitutional change via super-majoritarian action. For instance, a new constitutional amendment such as the Nineteenth Amendment (giving women the right to vote) clearly changes the law within its domain. But Akhil Amar argues that the Constitution must be interpreted as a whole, including amendments, so that a new amendment can require reinterpretation of other provisions of the Constitution. In his view, for example, the Nineteenth Amendment, reflecting a super-majoritarian recognition of gender equality, could require a reinterpretation of the Fourteenth Amendment's Equal Protection Clause to make gender discrimination in other contexts unconstitutional.[83] Professor Reva Siegel has made a similar argument in identifying the foundation in constitutional history of the Court's equal protection, sex discrimination jurisprudence; she canvasses the debates over woman suffrage that began with the framing of the Fourteenth Amendment and culminated with the ratification of the Nineteenth Amendment.[84]

But not every super-majoritarian consensus results in a constitutional amendment, in part because the Court may hasten to adopt such widespread views, making an amendment unnecessary. Perhaps it could be argued that not just constitutional amendments, but other types of uncommonly significant political events as well, should be considered to have modified the constitutional order. Professor Bruce Ackerman has expanded upon this idea and has sought to give it a formal grounding.[85] Ackerman initially suggested that there have been three big "Constitutional Moments"—the Founding, Reconstruction, and the New Deal—each of which resulted in a dramatic expansion in the role of the federal government and shifts in constitutional doctrine. Ackerman saw a similar process

---

[82]   BICKEL, *supra* note 48, at 18.

[83]   *See* Akhil Reed Amar, *Women and the Constitution*, 18 HARV. J.L. & PUB. POL'Y 465 (1995).

[84]   *See* Reva B. Siegel, *She the People: The Nineteenth Amendment, Sex Equality, Federalism, and the Family*, 115 HARV. L. REV. 947 (2002).

[85]   BRUCE ACKERMAN, WE THE PEOPLE, VOLUME 1: FOUNDATIONS (1991).

unfold in each case: a political crisis, followed by an intense period of political debate over constitutional issues, followed by a strong popular electoral ratification of a new order of governance. Note how this theory sidesteps Article V, which most constitutional theorists consider the only formal mechanism by which the Constitution can be amended. In later work, he expanded the number of constitutional moments to eight.[86] Ackerman is a living constitutionalist in the sense that his theory of legitimate constitutional change is not bound by the original meaning of a constitutional provision. But he is also an originalist of sorts; he just identifies more Founding moments than other originalists do.

Other constitutional theorists seek in varying degrees to displace the courts as sources of legitimate constitutional change, joining hands with critics of *Marbury*.[87] Larry Kramer is a prominent example:

> Rather than worry about what judges do solely from concern for the domain of ordinary politics, the Court's new critics worry as much or more about judicial usurpation of the people's role as constitutional interpreters. This shift in perspective, in turn, has changed the grounds of debate by raising different arguments against judicial supremacy, arguments that rest on different conceptions of the Constitution and its relationship to democratic citizenship.[88]

Kramer is scathing in discussing the idea of judicial primacy in interpreting the Constitution:

> Somehow, Americans have been pacified, lulled into believing that the meaning of their Constitution is something beyond their compass, something that should be left to others. Somehow, constitutional history has been recast as a story of judicial triumphalism. A judicial monopoly on constitutional interpretation is depicted as inexorable and inevitable, as something that was meant to be and that saved us from ourselves. The historical voice of judicial authority is privileged while opposition to the

---

[86]   Bruce Ackerman, *The Living Constitution*, 120 HARV. L. REV. 1737 (2007) (delivered as the Oliver Wendell Holmes, Jr. Lectures); Bruce Ackerman & Jennifer Nou, *Canonizing the Civil Rights Revolution: The People and the Poll Tax*, 103 NW. U.L. REV. (2009).

[87]   *See, e.g.*, MARK TUSHNET, TAKING THE CONSTITUTION AWAY FROM THE COURTS (1999).

[88]   Lary D. Kramer, *Popular Constitutionalism, Circa 2004*, 92 CALIF. L. REV. 959, 960 (2004).

Court's self-aggrandizing tendencies is ignored, muted, or discredited.[89]

Kramer's theory of popular constitutionalism seems inconsistent with all of the other theories we have discussed. It inverts originalism, since popular constitutionalism privileges present-day constitutional understandings over past ones, and it is at least in severe tension with representation reinforcement, since popular constitutionalism seems willing to countenance discrimination against minorities at the will of the majority. And of course it is the antithesis of such judge-oriented theories as Strauss's common-law constitutionalism.[90] Kramer and Strauss differ far more than first-generation and second-generation originalists.

We have primarily focused on constitutional theories that set up distinguishable approaches. But there are also theories that tend to bridge (or, some would say, paper over) the gaps between these approaches. Some theorists favor eclectic approaches that take into account all considerations—text, structure, pre-ratification and post-ratification history, precedent, historical practice, publicly held values, and practical effects.[91] Dialogic theories see the Court as playing an important role in constitutional decisions, but as participating in a dialogue with other institutions and the public rather than as issuing the final word.[92] As explained in Chapter 1, this book offers an interactive account of the relationship between constitutional politics and judge-made constitutional law.

The remainder of this book deals with the substance of constitutional issues, not the process of litigation or the methods used by judges or other interpreters. But cases involving substantive constitutional issues often involve disputes over whether the case is properly before the Court at all or the extent to which the Court should rely on the original meaning, judicial precedent, or other modalities. You will have to form your own judgment about how successfully the Court has decided only concrete disputes and applied principled methods of constitutional interpretation—and whether occasional deviations from these typical roles of the Court have been justified by other considerations.

---

[89]   *Id.* at 1010.

[90]   For Kramer's full exposition of his theory of popular constitutionalism, see generally LARRY D. KRAMER, THE PEOPLE THEMSELVES: POPULAR CONSTITUTIONALISM AND JUDICIAL REVIEW (2005).

[91]   *See, e.g.,* DANIEL A. FARBER & SUZANNA SHERRY, JUDGMENT CALLS: PRINCIPLE AND POLITICS IN CONSTITUTIONAL LAW (2008).

[92]   *See, e.g.,* Robert Post & Reva Siegel, Roe *Rage: Democratic Constitutionalism and Backlash,* 42 HARV. C.R.-C.L. L. REV. 373 (2007).

Further Readings

JACK M. BALKIN, LIVING ORIGINALISM (2011).

Mitchell Berman, *Originalism Is Bunk*, 84 N.Y.U. L. REV. 1 (2009).

ALEXANDER BICKEL, THE LEAST DANGEROUS BRANCH: THE SUPREME COURT AT THE BAR OF POLITICS (1962).

ROBERT H. BORK, THE TEMPTING OF AMERICA: THE POLITICAL SEDUCTION OF LAW (1990).

ERWIN CHEMERINSKY, FEDERAL JURISDICTION (7TH ED. 2016).

FRANK B. CROSS, THE FAILED PROMISE OF ORIGINALISM (2013).

Richard H. Fallon, Jr., *The Fragmentation of Standing*, 82 TEX. L. REV. 1061 (2015).

DANIEL A. FARBER & SUZANNA SHERRY, A HISTORY OF THE AMERICAN CONSTITUTION (3d ed. 2013).

DANIEL A. FARBER & SUZANNA SHERRY, JUDGMENT CALLS: PRINCIPLE AND POLITICS IN CONSTITUTIONAL LAW (2008).

LARRY KRAMER, THE PEOPLE THEMSELVES: POPULAR CONSTITUTIONALISM AND JUDICIAL REVIEW (2005).

ANTONIN SCALIA & BRYAN A. GARNER, READING LAW: THE INTERPRETATION OF LEGAL TEXTS (2012).

DAVID A. STRAUSS, THE LIVING CONSTITUTION (2010).

KEITH E. WHITTINGTON, CONSTITUTIONAL INTERPRETATION: TEXTUAL MEANING, ORIGINAL INTENT, AND JUDICIAL REVIEW (1999).

Chapter 4

DEFINING THE NATURE OF THE UNION: THE FEDERAL STRUCTURE AND THE NECESSARY AND PROPER CLAUSE

Unlike state governments, which are governments of *general* or *plenary* powers, the federal government is a government of *limited* or *enumerated* powers. This means that, in order to act, the federal government requires a source of authority in the Constitution (or, more colloquially, a constitutional "hook") that permits the action. State governments, by contrast, do not require permission from the Constitution in order to act. State governments need only respect independent limits on their authority that are set forth in the Constitution, most notably individual rights protections and the supremacy of valid federal laws over conflicting state laws. This distinction between state governments of general powers and a national government of enumerated powers is reflected in various places in the constitutional text: the opening line of Article I,[1] the Tenth Amendment,[2] and the enumeration of many of the legislative powers of Congress in Article I, Section 8. As Chief Justice John Marshall wrote in *Gibbons v. Ogden*, a seminal Commerce Clause decision that we will encounter in Chapter 5, "[t]he enumeration presupposes something not enumerated."[3]

The legislative powers listed in Section 8 include the authority to tax,[4] to regulate interstate and international commerce,[5] and to raise and support a military.[6] Not included in the enumeration, however, are many additional powers that most Americans—both today and when the Constitution was ratified in 1788—would expect Congress to exercise. For example, the Constitution plainly assumes that there will be federal departments, federal offices, and federal officers,[7] but no provision explicitly gives Congress the authority to

---

[1]   *See* U.S. CONST. art. I, § 1 ("All legislative Powers herein granted . . . .").

[2]   *See* U.S. CONST. amend. 10 ("The powers not delegated to the United States by the Constitution, nor prohibited by it to the States, are reserved to the States respectively, or to the people.").

[3]   Gibbons v. Ogden, 22 U.S. 1, 195 (1824).

[4]   *See* U.S. CONST. art. I, § 8, cl. 1.

[5]   *See* U.S. CONST. art. I, § 8, cl. 3.

[6]   *See* U.S. CONST. art. I, § 8, cl. 11–16.

[7]   *See, e.g.*, U.S. CONST. art. I, § 8, cl. 18 (referring to "any Department or Officer" of "the Government of the United States"); art. II, § 2, cl. 1–2 (referring to "the principal Officer in each of the executive Departments," "Ambassadors, other public

79

establish them. The Constitution gives Congress the specific power to punish certain crimes (namely, counterfeiting and piracy),[8] but no provision expressly gives Congress the general power to impose criminal (or civil) penalties for violating federal law. Several constitutional provisions give Congress extensive powers over the nation's finances,[9] but no provision explicitly gives Congress the power to create a national bank or charter federal corporations.

One way to justify many of these federal activities is through an expansive interpretation of the individual powers. For instance, the power to regulate interstate commerce can be construed to include the power to punish violations of Commerce Clause regulations. Alternatively, these unspecified but unquestionable congressional powers, and many others, are conferred textually by the eighteenth and final Clause of Article I, Section 8.[10] It gives Congress the authority "[t]o make all Laws which shall be necessary and proper for carrying into Execution" the other federal powers granted by the Constitution.[11] This residual clause—called at various times in American history the "Elastic Clause," the "Sweeping Clause," and (from the Twentieth Century onward) the "Necessary and Proper Clause"—is the constitutional hook for the vast majority of federal laws. Virtually every federal statute creating the machinery of government is enacted under the authority of the Necessary and Proper Clause. It also provides support for a wide range of substantive statutes, including national security laws, antidiscrimination laws, labor laws, criminal laws, securities laws, and environmental laws. Because the nature of the Union created by the Constitution turns first and foremost on its interpretation, some authors consider the Necessary and Proper Clause the single most important provision in the Constitution.[12]

This chapter introduces the constitutional politics and constitutional law of the Necessary and Proper Clause. We begin by discussing the general problems of governance in the United States during the 1780s that eventually resulted in the movement from the Articles of Confederation, the young nation's first constitutional

---

Ministers and Consuls, Judges of the supreme Court, and all other Officers of the United States," "inferior Officers," "the Courts of Law," "the Heads of Departments," and "Vacancies that may happen during the Recess of the Senate").

[8]   *See* U.S. CONST. art. I, § 8, cl. 6, 10.

[9]   *See, e.g.,* U.S. CONST. art. I, § 8, cl. 1–6.

[10]   There are also structural arguments in favor of certain implied powers, as Chief Justice Marshall reasons in *McCulloch v. Maryland,* 17 U.S. 316 (1819), discussed below.

[11]   *See* U.S. CONST. art. I, § 8, cl. 18.

[12]   *See* Gary Lawson & Neil S. Siegel, *Necessary and Proper Clause,* NATIONAL CONSTITUTION CENTER, INTERACTIVE CONSTITUTION (2016), https://constitution center.org/interactive-constitution/articles/article-i/necessary-and-proper-clause/ clause/.

arrangement, to the Constitution, including its Necessary and Proper Clause. We then tell the story of the constitutional debate over the scope of federal power to create a national bank, which persisted outside and inside the courts for most of the Constitution's first half-century. The Marshall Court's historic 1819 decision in *McCulloch v. Maryland* formed just one part of this story.[13] We close by examining the constitutional politics and law of the Necessary and Proper Clause today, including part of the Supreme Court's 2012 decision in the *Health Care Case, NFIB v. Sebelius*.[14]

In interpreting this clause, courts and political actors such as Hamilton and Jefferson have also found it necessary to address fundamental issues about national sovereignty, methods of constitutional interpretation, and the scope of federal power. In particular, as we will see, Chief Justice Marshall used the dispute of *McCulloch* as the occasion for cementing some fundamental principles of constitutional law.

I.   From the Articles to the Constitution

The first framework for American government was the Articles of Confederation. It created a structure of governance that frequently prevented the states from acting collectively to pursue their common interests. Solving these problems of "collective action" was a central reason for calling the Constitutional Convention. A collective action problem is one in which individually rational behavior produces collectively irrational results.[15] An example is the Prisoners' Dilemma game, in which each prisoner has a rational, self-interested incentive to rat out the other prisoner regardless of whether the other prisoner rats him out, but when each prisoner rats out the other both are worse off than they would have been had each kept quiet. The need to solve collective action problems facing the states, especially preventing (and preparing for) future wars with European powers and preventing them among the states, was also a primary reason why the Constitution was ratified notwithstanding substantial concerns about the extent of federal power licensed by the document that emerged from Philadelphia in 1787.[16]

A.   The Articles of Confederation and the Critical Period

The Articles of Confederation was introduced in Congress in 1776, not approved by Congress until 1777, and not ratified by the

---

[13]   17 U.S. 316 (1819).

[14]   567 U.S. 519 (2012).

[15]   For a discussion with examples, see generally Robert D. Cooter & Neil S. Siegel, *Collective Action Federalism: A General Theory of Article I, Section 8*, 63 STAN. L. REV. 115 (2010) [hereinafter "Cooter & Siegel, *Collective Action Federalism*"].

[16]   *See generally* DAVID C. HENDRICKSON, PEACE PACT: THE LOST WORLD OF THE AMERICAN FOUNDING (2003).

final state until 1781. The problems with this initial constitution were immediately apparent to political leaders with a nationalist sensibility and vision, including James Madison, Alexander Hamilton, and James Wilson, all of whom soon began pushing for reforms. The basic difficulty with the Articles was that it reflected Revolutionary America's extraordinary distrust of centralized power at the expense of effective government. "Each state retains its sovereignty, freedom, and independence," the Articles declared at the outset, "and every power, jurisdiction, and right, which is not by this Confederation *expressly* delegated to the United States, in Congress assembled."[17]

There were at least three more specific problems with the Articles. First, the Articles established no national executive and no national judiciary; it instead gave all national powers to the Confederation Congress. Without executive or judicial branches, it was very difficult for the national government to enforce federal commitments against the states. These commitments included peace and trade treaties, state noncompliance with which could cause wars and impede future negotiations.

Second, the Confederation Congress had great difficulty exercising the powers that were given to it. This was because each state had an equal vote in Congress, and most significant actions required supermajority or unanimous support among the states. In the early 1780s, for example, Rhode Island, Virginia, and New York each blocked proposals that would have given the Confederation Congress the power to raise critically needed revenue for the federal government by taxing imports.[18] These were states with prominent ports, and such self-interested actions by individual states were producing collectively harmful results.

Third, Congress's powers were sharply circumscribed in terms of both the ends it could achieve and the means it could use to achieve them. As for ends, Congress (among other things) lacked the authority to regulate interstate commerce, and so it was powerless to stop states from treating sister states in the commercial sphere in the way that nations treat one another today in the absence of effective free trade agreements. States erected tariff barriers and trade walls, seriously hampering economic development.

As for the means not available to Congress, most troubling was Congress's lack of authority to raise revenue directly through taxation of individuals and to raise a national military. Instead, Congress was limited to borrowing money and "requisitioning" the

---

[17]   ARTICLES OF CONFEDERATION OF 1781, art. II (emphasis added).

[18]   *See, e.g.,* Robert D. Cooter & Neil S. Siegel, *Not the Power to Destroy: An Effects Theory of the Tax Power,* 98 VA. L. REV. 1195, 1201 (2012).

states to contribute their fair share of taxes to the national treasury and troops to the national military. By the late 1780s, Congress had exhausted its credit, and the system of congressional requisitions to the states resulted in states refusing to send money to Congress and the nation being vulnerable to attack by European powers.[19]

The problems of collective action confronting America in 1787 "necessitated a government with many more powers than were possessed by Congress under the Articles—including the great powers to tax, to raise and support armies, and to regulate commerce."[20] Facing these problems also "necessitated conferring authority to exercise these powers by acting directly on individual citizens."[21]

B. The Constitutional Convention

In thinking through the scope of congressional powers that would eventually become Article I, Section 8, the delegates at the Philadelphia Convention of 1787 focused to a significant extent on the problems of collective action facing the states. The Convention instructed its Committee of Detail, which met in the middle of the summer and was charged with drafting constitutional text reflective of the decisions of the Convention, that Congress would be authorized "to legislate in all Cases for the *general Interests of the Union*, and also in those Cases to which *the States are separately incompetent*, or in which the Harmony of the United States may be interrupted by the Exercise of individual Legislation."[22] This language registers the need to empower Congress to solve the collective action problems facing the states that the states had proven incapable of solving on their own. The language was offered by Gunning Bedford of Delaware on July 17, 1787, in order to clarify the sixth resolution of the Virginia Plan, so named because it was drafted by the Virginia delegation (especially Madison) before the Convention was ready to proceed.[23] Notably, when the Committee of Detail made its report ten days later, "[i]t had changed the indefinite language of Resolution VI into an enumeration of the powers of Congress closely resembling Article I, Section 8 of the Constitution as it was finally adopted."[24]

This "radical change" wrought by the Committee of Detail was uncontroversial among the delegates; the Convention "accepted

---

[19]   *See, e.g.*, Cooter & Siegel, *Collective Action Federalism, supra* note 15, at 121.

[20]   Larry Kramer, *Madison's Audience*, 112 HARV. L. REV. 611, 619 (1999).

[21]   *Id.* at 619–20.

[22]   2 RECORDS OF THE FEDERAL CONVENTION OF 1787, at 131–32 (Max Farrand ed., rev. ed. 1966).

[23]   *See* JACK N. RAKOVE, ORIGINAL MEANINGS: POLITICS AND IDEAS IN THE MAKING OF THE CONSTITUTION 59 (1996).

[24]   Robert L. Stern, *That Commerce Which Concerns More States than One*, 47 HARV. L. REV. 1335, 1340 (1934).

without discussion the enumeration of powers made by a committee which had been directed . . . that the Federal Government was 'to legislate in all cases for the general interests of the Union . . . and in those to which the states are separately incompetent.' "[25] The delegates apparently perceived the connection between the general propositions in Resolution VI and the specific powers conferred in Article I, Section 8. "If the Convention had thought that the committee's enumeration was a departure from the general standard for the division of powers to which it had thrice agreed, there can be little doubt that the subject would have been thoroughly debated on the Convention floor."[26]

C.   The Constitution and Collective Action

To be sure, the Constitution as ultimately written and ratified did not include Resolution VI of the Virginia Plan. Even so, this history illuminates the order, content, and, perhaps, the appropriate interpretation of Article I, Section 8. For example, direct federal power to tax individuals is listed first for a reason: the initial clause solves the previously existing collective action problem by giving Congress the power to tax and, by implication, the power to spend federal tax revenue in order to "provide for the common Defence and general Welfare of the United States."[27] The third clause gives Congress the power to end state practices of economic protectionism and to create a national free trade zone by "regulat[ing] Commerce . . . among the several States."[28] Clauses 11–16 solve the collective action problem of defending the nation by giving Congress a variety of direct powers to raise, support, and regulate a national military.[29]

The final clause, in further contrast to the Articles, gives Congress unenumerated, implied powers "[t]o make all Laws which shall be necessary and proper for carrying into Execution" the other powers granted to the federal government by the Constitution.[30] What is more, the Tenth Amendment, in reminding the reader that "[t]he powers not delegated to the United States" nor prohibited to the states are reserved to the states, self-consciously omits the qualifier "expressly" that the Articles had placed before the phrase "delegated to the United States."[31] The Tenth Amendment's formulation implies the existence of implied legislative powers of Congress.

---

[25]   *Id.*

[26]   *Id.*

[27]   U.S. CONST. art. I, § 8, cl. 1.

[28]   U.S. CONST. art. I, § 8, cl. 3.

[29]   U.S. CONST. art. I, § 8, cl. 11–16.

[30]   U.S. CONST. art. I, § 8, cl. 18.

[31]   U.S. CONST. amend. X.

We will focus on the Necessary and Proper Clause for the duration of this chapter. The Clause advances Section 8's vision of effective collective action in three ways.[32] First, it underscores that Congress possesses the authority not just to directly solve collective action problems through use of its enumerated powers, but also to pass laws that do not themselves solve such problems but are convenient or useful to carrying into execution congressional powers that do. We will see a potential, controversial example when we turn to the constitutionality of healthcare reform at the end of the chapter. Second, as we will also see when we turn to recent decisions, the Clause may allow Congress to solve certain collective action problems when other federal powers are unavailable.

Third, and turning from the "federalism" component of the Clause (that is, its effect on the relationship between the federal government and the states) to the "separation of powers" component (that is, its effect on the relationship between Congress and the other branches), the part of the Clause that authorizes Congress "[t]o make all Laws which shall be necessary and proper for carrying into Execution . . . all other Powers vested by this Constitution in the Government of the United States, or in any Department or Officer thereof," grants Congress broad authority to structure the executive and judicial branches. Thus, Congress decided "how many cabinet departments would fill the executive branch; how [they] would be shaped and bounded; how many justices would compose the Supreme Court; [and] where and when the Court would sit."[33] As Americans learned through difficult experience under the Articles, the effective enforcement of federal laws requires an effective executive branch and federal judiciary.

II. Nationalism and the Marshall Court: The Constitutional Politics and Law of the Bank

It is widely agreed that the Necessary and Proper Clause gives Congress implied powers. Both historically and today, however, the scope of the Clause has been controversial. What kind or degree of connection with another enumerated power makes a federal law necessary and proper for carrying this other power into execution? In the 1790s during the Washington administration, and again nearly three decades later in the Supreme Court, attempts to create a national bank in order to aid the nation's finances generated competing understandings of the kind or degree of connection with

---

[32]   For development of these points, see generally Neil S. Siegel, *The Necessary and Proper Clause and the Collective Action Principle*, NATIONAL CONSTITUTION CENTER, INTERACTIVE CONSTITUTION (2016), https://constitutioncenter.org/interactive-constitution/articles/article-i/necessary-and-proper-clause-and-the-collective-action-principle-siegel/clause/.

[33]   AKHIL REED AMAR, AMERICA'S CONSTITUTION: A BIOGRAPHY 111 (2005).

another enumerated power that renders a federal law a permissible means of implementing this power. We begin the story at the Constitutional Convention, however, because the issue of federal power to charter corporations (including a national bank) arose during its proceedings.

A. The Constitutional Convention

The Continental Congress had chartered the Bank of North America to help manage the young nation's serious financial problems as it emerged from the American Revolution.[34] The Bank of North America did not ultimately succeed, but the issue of a national bank remained on the minds of the delegates during the Constitutional Convention. Madison proposed giving Congress the authority "to grant charters of incorporation where the interest of the U. S. might require & the legislative provisions of individual States may be incompetent."[35] Rufus King of Massachusetts was opposed. "In Philada. & New York," he said, "It will be referred to the establishment of a Bank, which has been a subject of contention in those Cities. In other places it will be referred to mercantile monopolies."[36]

James Wilson, whose nationalist vision during the Founding Era was second perhaps only to Madison's, disagreed. He had previously supported the Bank of North America on the ground that "[w]henever an object occurs, to the direction of which no particular state is competent, the management of it must, of necessity, belong to the United States in congress assembled."[37] Now Wilson simply replied that, "[a]s to Banks he did not think with Mr. King that the power in that point of view would excite the prejudices & parties apprehended."[38] George Mason of Virginia proposed giving Congress only the power to charter canal companies; he was "afraid of monopolies of every sort" and "did not think they were by any means already implied by the Constitution as supposed by Mr. Wilson."[39] Because delegates who favored Madison's proposal feared putting the matter to a vote lest it either be defeated or else be approved and jeopardize ratification,[40] the only vote that was taken was on a

---

[34]   *See* Daniel A. Farber, *The Story of* McCulloch: *Banking on National Power,* in CONSTITUTIONAL LAW STORIES 34–35 (Michael C. Dorf ed., 2004).

[35]   2 RECORDS OF THE FEDERAL CONVENTION OF 1787, *supra* note 22, at 615.

[36]   *Id.* at 616.

[37]   James Wilson, *Consideration on the Bank of North America* (1785), *in* CONTEXTS OF THE CONSTITUTION: A DOCUMENTARY COLLECTION ON PRINCIPLES OF AMERICAN CONSTITUTIONAL LAW 368, 373 (Neil H. Cogan ed., 1999).

[38]   2 RECORDS OF THE FEDERAL CONVENTION OF 1787, *supra* note 22, at 616.

[39]   *Id.*

[40]   *See* BRAY HAMMOND, BANKS AND POLITICS IN AMERICA FROM THE REVOLUTION TO THE CIVIL WAR 104–05 (1957).

modified motion to limit congressional power to charter canal companies, as Mason had suggested. The motion failed, which also doomed further consideration of Madison's broader proposal to give Congress the power to charter corporations.

B.   The Political Branches

As the first Secretary of the Treasury, Hamilton advocated a bold plan to stimulate a faltering national economy. He proposed having the federal government raise taxes through tariffs and refinance the Revolutionary War debts of both the federal government and the states.[41] A pivotal component of Hamilton's scheme was creating a national bank. As one of us has written, such a bank "would be the government's chief fiscal agent, making it easier to collect taxes, make payments, and obtain short-term loans. Its notes would provide a national currency, and it would provide a source of capital for financing businesses."[42] Opposition to the bank came from several directions, perhaps most notably from former opponents of the Constitution who sought to promote an agrarian America and to defend state autonomy, and who rejected the emphasis of Hamilton and other Federalists on the promotion of commerce and the construction of national financial institutions.[43]

In the House of Representatives, Madison, who by then had retreated from his earlier advocacy of national power, led the opposition to the bank bill. He condemned it as beyond the scope of Congress's enumerated powers, including the Necessary and Proper Clause. "The essential characteristic of the government, as composed of limited and enumerated powers, would be destroyed," he declared, "[i]f instead of direct and incidental means, any means could be used, which in the language of the preamble to the bill, 'might be conceived to be conducive to the successful conducting of the finances; or might be *conceived* to *tend* to give *facility* to the obtaining of loans.' "[44] In Madison's view, a law that was merely convenient to the implementation of an enumerated power was not necessary and proper to its implementation, which is what the Constitution required. Unpersuaded, Madison's colleagues in the House passed

---

[41]   *See* Farber, *supra* note 34, at 36–37.

[42]   *Id.* at 37.

[43]   *Id.*

[44]   James Madison, Opinion on the Constitutionality of the Bill to Establish a National Bank (Feb. 2, 1791), *in* CONTEXTS OF THE CONSTITUTION, *supra* note 37, at 527, 531. As the quotation in the text suggests, Madison believed that permissible means were not only "direct" but also "incidental" to an enumerated power. For a discussion of what was meant by "incidental" means, see *infra* notes 95, 129–137, and accompanying text.

the bank bill by a vote of 39 to 20 after it had unanimously passed the Senate.[45]

The debate now moved to the Executive Branch. President Washington asked his two cabinet secretaries not named Hamilton for their views on the constitutionality of bank bill. Secretary of State Jefferson, a Southern planter with an agrarian vision of America's future who was suspicious of manufacturing, commerce, and finance, condemned the bill as unconstitutional. His test for the Necessary and Proper Clause was even more demanding than Madison's. Jefferson would have required an essential or indispensable connection between the bill and the implementation of an enumerated power: only "those means without which the [implemented] grant of the power would be nugatory" were permissible.[46] Jefferson was calling for *strict construction* of Congress's enumerated powers. He added for good measure the originalist argument that "the very power now proposed *as a means*, was rejected *as an end*, by the Convention which formed the constitution."[47] Attorney General Edmund Randolph agreed that the bill was unconstitutional.[48]

Washington asked Hamilton to respond. His response was important not only because it persuaded Washington to sign the bill into law, but also because Chief Justice Marshall would subsequently draw from Hamilton's reasoning almost three decades later in *McCulloch*. Hamilton began with the general structural principle that every power of government includes "a right to employ all the *means* requisite, and fairly applicable to the attainment of the *ends* of such power."[49] He took strong exception to Jefferson's embrace of strict construction, arguing that Congress's enumerated powers (especially those concerning finances, trade, and defense) should be construed liberally. According to Hamilton, the "means by which national exigencies are to be provided for, national inconveniencies [sic] obviated, national prosperity promoted, are of such infinite variety, extent and complexity, that there must, of necessity, be great latitude of discretion in the selection & application of those means."[50]

---

[45]   *See* Farber, *supra* note 34, at 39.

[46]   Thomas Jefferson, Opinion on the Constitutionality of the Bill to Establish a National Bank (Feb. 15, 1791), *in* CONTEXTS OF THE CONSTITUTION, *supra* note 37, at 540, 542.

[47]   *Id.* at 542.

[48]   *See* H. JEFFERSON POWELL, THE CONSTITUTION AND THE ATTORNEYS GENERAL 3–9 (1999).

[49]   Alexander Hamilton, Opinion on the Constitutionality of the Bill to Establish a National Bank (Feb. 23, 1791), *in* CONTEXTS OF THE CONSTITUTION, *supra* note 37, at 544, 545.

[50]   *Id.* at 549.

Hamilton was calling for *broad construction* of Congress's enumerated powers, according to which federal laws were necessary and proper to implementing enumerated powers if they were convenient, useful, or—in the language of modern constitutional law—rationally related to carrying an enumerated power into execution. The bank bill easily passed this test. Regarding Congress's taxing power (discussed in detail in Chapter 6), a national bank would increase the circulation of money (in the form of bank notes), thus furnishing the means of paying taxes.[51] Regarding the power of borrowing money, a national bank would provide a means of loans, including emergency loans during wars or other emergencies.[52] Regarding the power to regulate interstate commerce (discussed in detail in the next chapter), expanding the money supply would provide a "convenient medium" for trade.[53] Washington was persuaded. Two days after receiving Hamilton's opinion, he signed the bank bill into law.

This debate between Hamilton and his Jeffersonian adversaries illustrates a number of important ways in which the American constitutional system functions in practice, and it is worth pausing for a moment to note them. First, from the very beginning of the Constitution's existence, there have been robust practices of constitutional interpretation outside the courts—what this book calls constitutional politics. Second, from the very beginning, there has been irreconcilable disagreement on some of the most basic constitutional questions. We will see this again when we examine disagreements between Madison and Hamilton on the scope of Congress's spending power in Chapter 6 and on the scope of executive power in Chapter 7. (It is controversial whether the fact of irreconcilable disagreement has implications for the viability of originalism as an interpretive project.) Third, constitutional theories partially reflect the hopes and fears of constitutional interpreters. Madison and Jefferson were worried about all of the bad things that the federal government could do with essentially unlimited power. Hamilton was concerned about all of the good things that needed doing that only the federal government was competent to perform.

The next part of the story occurred two decades later. The law chartering the National Bank had what lawyers call a sunset provisio: it expired after twenty years, in 1811. The Bank had become politically unpopular for a variety of reasons, including opposition by state banks, which competed with it for business.[54] Congress initially

---

[51]   *Id.* at 560.

[52]   *Id.* at 562.

[53]   *Id.* at 563.

[54]   *See* 1 CHARLES WARREN, THE SUPREME COURT IN UNITED STATES HISTORY 504 (rev. ed. 1926).

failed to renew it by a single vote in both chambers due to the strength of anti-national forces in Congress.[55] The War of 1812 with England, however, underscored the policy wisdom of a national bank, as did questionable practices by state banks, upon which the federal government had to rely to borrow money and pay debts.[56] In 1816, Congress issued a new twenty-year charter, and the Second National Bank was born.[57]

Notwithstanding his earlier constitutional objections, President Madison signed the second bank bill into law. By this time, he had "waiv[ed] the question of the constitutional authority of the Legislature to establish an incorporated bank, as being precluded, in my judgment, by the repeated recognitions under varied circumstances of the validity of such an institution, in acts of the Legislative, Executive, and Judicial branches of the Government, accompanied by indications, in different modes, of a concurrence of the general will of the nation."[58] This accretion of governmental practice changed Madison's view of the matter.

The Second Bank, like its predecessor, became politically unpopular, this time for mismanagement and its alleged responsibility for a post-war financial collapse. Numerous states outside the Northeast passed legislation reflecting hostility toward the Bank, including laws that taxed local branches of the Bank.

C. *McCulloch v. Maryland*

Maryland was one such state. *McCulloch v. Maryland* was a lawsuit filed by Maryland against James W. McCulloch, the cashier of the Maryland branch of the Second National Bank. Maryland sued in state court to collect a fine of $100, which was the penalty for circulating a bank note without the required Maryland stamp; the penalty could be avoided if the Bank paid a $15,000 annual tax to the state.[59] *McCulloch* became a test case for the constitutionality of the Bank. And, if the Bank were declared constitutional, *McCulloch* would also be a test case for the authority of a state to tax branches of the Bank within its borders.

An immediate question arises about the relationship between Maryland's arguments. If Maryland was intending to tax the Baltimore branch of the National Bank, why would it want to argue that the Bank was unconstitutional? Maryland argued first that the Bank was beyond Congress's power to charter, in which case the state

---

[55]   Hammond, *supra* note 40, at 210.

[56]   *See* PAUL BREST ET AL., PROCESSES OF CONSTITUTIONAL DECISIONMAKING: CASES AND MATERIALS 40 (6th ed. 2015).

[57]   *See* Farber, *supra* note 34, at 44.

[58]   Madison, *quoted in* HAMMOND, *supra* note 40, at 233.

[59]   *See* Farber, *supra* note 34, at 44.

law was simply imposing a tax on a private firm engaged de facto in the banking business within the state. Maryland went on to argue that if one concluded otherwise, states may tax a federal instrumentality because nothing in the Constitution prohibited them from doing so.

Unsurprisingly given the constitutional politics of the time period, the Maryland courts upheld the Maryland law providing for the tax on the Bank, and federal officials appealed to the U.S. Supreme Court. Unlike today, when oral arguments typically last an hour, oral arguments in *McCulloch* lasted nine days as the Justices heard from some of the best constitutional lawyers in the nation: Daniel Webster, Attorney General William Wirt, and William Pinkney for the Bank, and Luther Martin for Maryland.[60] Only three days after the arguments ended, Chief Justice Marshall handed down the opinion of a unanimous Court.[61] The Court upheld the constitutionality of the Bank as within the scope of Congress's enumerated powers, and the Court further held that states were categorically forbidden from taxing branches of the Bank within their borders.

Marshall began by standing on the shoulders of *Marbury*: "by this tribunal alone can the decision be made," he declared in emphasizing the practical implications of the questions presented for "the great operations of the government."[62] Also like in *Marbury*, Marshall's arguments were not especially novel; he again relied on Hamilton's prior reasoning, as well as on the oral arguments.[63] But Marshall's opinion for the Court in *McCulloch* was powerfully structured, written, and reasoned. It is a masterpiece of judicial writing that weaves together almost all of the modalities of constitutional interpretation.[64] His opinion can be divided into five parts (with the fifth addressing the state's power to tax a federal instrumentality).

First, Marshall observed that the initial question presented— the constitutionality of a national bank—was hardly novel. Like President Madison before him, he underscored that there were high-quality debates in Congress and in the Executive Branch concerning the constitutionality of a national bank, and that almost three decades of historical practice of the political branches reflecting and reinforcing the conviction that a national bank was within the scope of Congress's enumerated powers. He conceded "that a bold and

---

60   For a discussion of these Supreme Court advocates, see *id.* at 44–47.

61   *See* Farber, *supra* note 34, at 52.

62   *McCulloch*, 17 U.S. at 400–01.

63   *See* Farber, *supra* note 34, at 53.

64   For a discussion of the modalities of constitutional interpretation, see Chapter 1.

daring usurpation might be resisted, after an acquiescence still longer and more complete than this."[65] But he insisted that courts should accord such customary political branch practice significant weight, at least when questions of constitutional structure were at issue, as in *McCulloch*, as opposed to matters of individual rights.[66] It is noteworthy that Marshall viewed the political branches as worthy partners in the practice of constitutional interpretation. By contrast, the modern Supreme Court has sometimes viewed Congress as a threat to its interpretive supremacy, especially when Congress uses its legislative powers to enforce the Civil War Amendments.[67]

Second, Marshall weighed in on a dispute between the parties about whether the federal government or the states were truly "sovereign" in the system created by the Constitution. Maryland insisted that, in interpreting the Constitution, it was important to "consider that instrument, not as emanating from the people, but as an act of sovereign and independent states."[68] Because in Maryland's view Congress's enumerated powers were "delegated by the states who alone are truly sovereign," Congress must exercise its powers "in subordination to the states, who alone possess supreme dominion."[69]

It may not be obvious why the case turned on the outcome of this provocative question, and Marshall seemed not to be sure himself that it did.[70] After all, even if the states and not the people created the federal government, it does not follow that the states are supreme. Which level of government is supreme with respect to which matters depends on the terms of the "contract" that the states "signed" in ratifying the Constitution, and the Supremacy Clause makes emphatically clear that valid federal laws are supreme over conflicting state laws. Legally, the issue likely mattered because of what St. George Tucker—a Virginia judge, a law professor at William and Mary, and a states' rights Jeffersonian—in 1803 called the " 'maxim of political law' " that a sovereign can be deprived of its powers only if it gives its express consent, and this consent must be narrowly construed.[71] If the states were sovereign, as Maryland insisted, then the implication was that Article I, Section 8, should be

---

[65]   *McCulloch*, 17 U.S. at 401.

[66]   *Id.*

[67]   *See, e.g.*, City of Boerne v. Flores, 521 U.S. 507 (1997), discussed in Chapter 13.

[68]   *McCulloch*, 17 U.S. at 402.

[69]   *Id.*

[70]   *See id.* at 404 (using the qualifying phrase "whatever may be the influence of this fact on the case"). Marshall's language is quoted *infra* text accompanying note 73.

[71]   H. Jefferson Powell, *The Original Understanding of Original Intent*, 98 HARV. L. REV. 885, 931 (1984) (quoting Tucker).

given " 'the most strict construction that the instrument will bear' " in favor of the retention of power by the states.[72]

Marshall vehemently rejected Maryland's position on this issue. "The government of the Union," he insisted, "(whatever may be the influence of this fact on the case), is, emphatically, and truly, a government of the people. In form and in substance, it emanates from them. Its powers are granted by them, and are to be exercised directly on them, and for their benefit."[73] In Marshall's telling, the Constitution derived its binding authority from the state ratifying conventions, which represented the people, not from the states themselves or the state legislatures.[74] Marshall so argued even as he had just conceded that "[n]o political dreamer was ever wild enough to think of breaking down the lines which separate the states, and of compounding the American people into one common mass. Of consequence, when they act, they act in their states."[75] In truth, Marshall did not explain what, exactly, his theory of popular sovereignty was, although he was clear that he did not believe the states created the federal government.[76]

Marshall's answer to the question whether the states were sovereign nicely set up the third part of his opinion, which concerned the constitutional scope of federal power to create a national bank. Methodologically, this portion of the opinion was fundamentally structural, not textual. Marshall articulated two structural principles: (1) the federal government is "supreme within its sphere of action;"[77] and (2) if an end is within the federal government's sphere of action, then Congress may use whatever means are convenient or useful in achieving the end.[78] Only after arguing on behalf of these structural principles did Marshall turn to the Supremacy Clause and the Necessary and Proper Clause, and he turned to them only to confirm his structural reasoning.

It was to establish the first principle that Marshall deemed it so important to argue that the federal government derived its powers directly from the people. In contrast to each state, which derives its powers from only some of the people, the federal government derives its powers from the whole people. As a consequence, Marshall reasoned, the federal government enjoyed superior democratic legitimacy. And because "[i]t is the government of all," and not just

---

[72]   *Id.* (quoting Tucker).

[73]   *McCulloch*, 17 U.S. at 404–05.

[74]   *See id.* at 403–04.

[75]   *Id.* at 403.

[76]   For a discussion, see Farber, *supra* note 34, at 54.

[77]   *McCulloch*, 17 U.S. at 405.

[78]   *See id.* at 406–09.

of a "component part[ ]," the federal government is supreme over the states—it "must necessarily bind its component parts" when acting within the scope of its authority.[79]

As for his second structural principle (regarding the means available to Congress), Marshall noted the omission of the word "expressly" from the Tenth Amendment,[80] and he defended the necessity of liberal construction in terms of the nature of a written constitution. "A constitution, to contain an accurate detail of all the subdivisions of which its great powers will admit, and of all the means by which they may be carried into execution, would partake of the complexity of a legal code, and could scarcely be embraced by the human mind."[81] As a result, he reasoned, the nature of a constitution necessitated "that only its great outlines should be marked, its important objects designated, and the minor ingredients which compose those objects, be deduced from the nature of the objects themselves."[82] In examining the constitutional scope of Congress's enumerated powers, he therefore insisted, "we must never forget it is a *constitution* we are expounding."[83]

As is characteristic of structural reasoning, Marshall's structural argument was informed by consequentialist considerations. "[A] government entrusted with such ample powers," he wrote, "on the due execution of which the happiness and prosperity of the nation so vitally depends, must also be entrusted with ample means for their execution."[84] "The power being given," he continued, "it is in the interest of the nation to facilitate its execution."[85] Marshall did not articulate why such prudential reasoning was relevant to the meaning of the Constitution, but it is noteworthy how frequently such reasoning shows up in judicial opinions in constitutional cases.

Marshall's structural and consequentialist reasoning also reflected a contestable (and contested) conception of the American ethos:

> Throughout this vast republic, from the St. Croix to the Gulf of Mexico, from the Atlantic to the Pacific, revenue is to be collected and expended, armies are to be marched and supported. The exigencies of the nation may require that

---

[79]   *Id.* at 405.

[80]   *Id.* at 406. *See id.* ("[T]here is no phrase in the instrument which, like the Articles of Confederation, excludes incidental or implied powers and which requires that everything granted shall be expressly and minutely described.").

[81]   *Id.* at 407.

[82]   *Id.*

[83]   *Id.*

[84]   *Id.* at 408.

[85]   *Id.*

the treasure raised in the north should be transported to the south, *that* raised in the east conveyed to the west, or that this order should be reversed. Is that construction of the constitution to be preferred which would render these operations difficult, hazardous, and expensive?[86]

This is not best understood as further consequentialist reasoning, because Marshall was describing national borders that did not (yet) fully exist. He was, in essence, arguing for robust federal power so that the nation could fulfill its (manifest) destiny.[87] For these reasons of structure, prudence, and ethos, Marshall concluded, congressional power to create a bank or other corporation was just a means, and only a means, like any other means.

In the fourth part of his opinion, Marshall turned to the constitutional text—specifically, the Necessary and Proper Clause—for "the constitution of the United States has not left the right of Congress to employ the necessary means, for the execution of the powers conferred on the government, to general reasoning."[88] He rejected Maryland's submission that the term "necessary" in this Clause withdrew from Congress the broad discretion over its choice of means that Marshall had just concluded it would otherwise derive directly from its enumerated powers. Marshall observed that the word "necessary" means different things depending on the context, and that it "frequently imports no more than that one thing is convenient, or useful, or essential to another."[89] He pointed out that the Constitution elsewhere (in Article I, Section 10) uses the term "absolutely necessary," which means something different from "necessary."[90] He argued that the meaning of the word "proper" has a qualifying effect on the meaning of the word "necessary."[91] He noted that the text places and phrases the Clause as an additional source of power, not (like Article I, Section 9) as a limitation of powers already granted.[92] Interweaving consequentialist reasoning, he added that strict construction would defeat "the execution of those great powers on which the welfare of a nation essentially depends," and that, in a constitution "intended to endure for ages to come, and consequently, to be adapted to the various *crises* of human affairs," it would have made scant sense to "provide, by immutable rules, for

---

86   *Id.*

87   For discussions, see LEWIS HENRY LARUE, CONSTITUTIONAL LAW AS FICTION: NARRATIVE IN THE RHETORIC OF AUTHORITY 88–90 (1995); J.M. Balkin & Sanford Levinson, *The Canons of Constitutional Law*, 111 HARV. L. REV. 963, 987–88 (1998).

88   *McCulloch*, 17 U.S. at 411.

89   *Id.* at 413.

90   *Id.* at 414–15.

91   *Id.* at 418–19.

92   *Id.* at 419–20.

exigencies which, if foreseen at all, must have been seen dimly, and must be best provided for as they occur."[93]

In language that subsequently became famous, Marshall laid down a rule of law—governing to this day—regarding the constitutional scope of congressional power under the Necessary and Proper Clause: "Let the end be legitimate, let it be within the scope of the constitution, and all means which are appropriate, which are plainly adapted to the end, which are not prohibited, but consist with the letter and spirit of the constitution, are constitutional."[94] Marshall concluded that the Second National Bank easily met this test; it was simply a means to several constitutional ends (for example, taxing, borrowing money, and regulating interstate commerce) listed in Section 8. Earlier in the opinion, he implied that there were constitutional limits on the scope of the Necessary and Proper Clause that the Bank respected. Using words that would reappear almost two centuries later in the *Health Care Case*, he stated that "[t]he power of creating a corporation . . . is not, like the power of making war or levying taxes or of regulating commerce, a great substantive and independent power which cannot be implied as incidental to other powers or used as a means of executing them. It is never the end for which other powers are exercised, but a means by which other objects are accomplished."[95]

In the fifth and final part of his opinion for the Court, Marshall turned to the second question presented in the case: if the Bank is within the scope of congressional power to create, may states nonetheless tax branches of the Bank within its borders? Marshall answered this question emphatically in the negative, and he offered two rationales in support of his conclusion.

Before turning to Marshall's analysis, it is worth noting that this part of his opinion is even less textual than the first part. Taxation is universally regarded as a concurrent power, meaning that both the federal government and the states may raise revenue through taxation. (No government can long exist without revenue.) As Marshall himself noted in his opinion, Article I, Section 10, imposes certain limits on the power of states to tax: they may not tax imports or exports without the consent of Congress except when doing so is absolutely necessary for executing their inspection laws.[96] Section 10 does not prohibit states from taxing institutions of the federal government within their borders. As a result, Maryland argued, states may tax the Baltimore branch of the National Bank. As a

---

93   *Id.* at 415.

94   *Id.* at 421.

95   *Id.* at 411.

96   U.S. CONST. art. I, § 10.

strictly textual matter, this argument has a lot going for it. Marshall conceded that the constitutional text was unhelpful to him when he noted that "[t]here is no express provision for the case."[97]

Marshall responded instead with a syllogism and a structural argument. The premises of the syllogism are that: (1) the power to create is the power to preserve; (2) the power to destroy is incompatible with the power to preserve; and (3) the power to tax is the power to destroy. The conclusion that follows from these premises is that state power to tax the Bank is incompatible with federal power to create it, which was established in the first part of the opinion. And given principles of federal supremacy (as well as the Supremacy Clause) that were also established in the first part of the opinion, the ultimate conclusion is that federal power to create the Bank trumps state power to tax its branches.[98]

It is unlikely, however, that a constitutional question of this magnitude can be soundly resolved simply through logic chopping. Marshall's conclusion follows from his premises, but one of his premises is questionable: the power to tax is not necessarily the power to destroy, especially given the possibility of judicial review of exercises of the tax power. Despite Maryland's obvious hostility to the Bank, Maryland's particular tax was not destructive of the Bank, and a little more than a century later, Justice Oliver Wendel Holmes, Jr., would write that "[t]he power to tax is not the power to destroy while this Court sits."[99] Given the different time period in which *McCulloch* arose, Marshall was understandably concerned that states hostile to the Bank could not be trusted to exercise their tax power in non-destructive ways, and this concern may have justified the Court's nipping the problem in the bud.[100] Marshall was also concerned that it would be inappropriate for courts to try to determine when particular uses of the tax power went too far,[101] although we will soon see that the modern Court in the *Health Care Case* did just that. Whoever is right about these matters, they are not reducible to a logic game.

---

[97]   *McCulloch*, 17 U.S. at 426.

[98]   *Id.* at 426–27, 431.

[99]   Penhandle Oil Co. v. Mississippi ex rel. Knox, 277 U.S. 218, 223 (1928) (Holmes, J., dissenting).

[100]   *See McCulloch*, 17 U.S. at 431 ("But is this a case of confidence? Would the people of any one State trust those of another with a power to control the most insignificant operations of their State Government? We know they would not. Why, then, should we suppose that the people of any one State should be willing to trust those of another with a power to control the operations of a Government to which they have confided their most important and most valuable interests?").

[101]   *Id.* at 430 ("We are not driven to the perplexing inquiry, so unfit for the judicial department, what degree of taxation is the legitimate use and what degree may amount to the abuse of the power").

Marshall's second, structural argument was more promising. He began by observing that "[t]he only security against the abuse of [the tax] power is found in the structure of the Government itself," for "[i]n imposing a tax, the legislature acts upon its constituents," who can hold their representatives accountable for the taxes they impose.[102] Because Americans outside a state are not represented within the state's legislature, however, "the means employed by the Government of the Union have no such security, nor is the right of a State to tax them sustained by the same theory."[103]

Later in the opinion, Marshall explained the difference between the whole taxing each part of the whole, and the part taxing the whole:

> The people of all the States have created the General Government, and have conferred upon it the general power of taxation. The people of all the States, and the States themselves, are represented in Congress, and, by their representatives, exercise this power. When they tax the chartered institutions of the States, they tax their constituents, and these taxes must be uniform. But when a State taxes the operations of the Government of the United States, it acts upon institutions created not by their own constituents, but by people over whom they claim no control. It acts upon the measures of a Government created by others as well as themselves, for the benefit of others in common with themselves. The difference is that which always exists, and always must exist, between the action of the whole on a part, and the action of a part on the whole— between the laws of a Government declared to be supreme, and those of a Government which, when in opposition to those laws, is not supreme.[104]

Marshall was saying that states are only part of the whole, and a part may not tax the whole, even non-destructively. This is because, as a matter of basic democratic principle, no legislature in America may tax individuals who are not represented within the political process that elects the legislators who impose the tax. Marshall was thus brilliantly, if only implicitly, invoking a part of the Founding American ethos, born of the colonists' protests to the Crown: "no taxation without representation."

Marshall's "intelligible standard," which anticipates the process theory of judicial review discussed in the previous chapter by well

---

[102]   *Id.* at 428.

[103]   *Id.*

[104]   *Id.* at 435–36.

more than a century,[105] was that the power of taxation extends only to "all subjects over which the sovereign power of a State extends."[106] Supporting this principle, and Marshall's structural analysis more generally, is a multi-state collective action problem. Every state has an incentive to overtax federal institutions because each state internalizes all of the benefits of such taxation (i.e., the tax revenue) and externalizes much of the costs (i.e., the impaired functioning of the institutions) onto sister states. If all states engage in this behavior, however, all are worse off than if none of them did so. A similar logic helps justify the dormant commerce principle, which we will encounter at the end of the next chapter. The dormant commerce principle prohibits state laws—typically, protectionist measures— that impose an undue burden on interstate commerce.[107]

D.   Constitutional Politics, Again

The Court's opinion in *McCulloch* caused an immediate, strong reaction, especially in the South and (what is today the) Midwest. For example, Virginia Judge Spencer Roane insisted in anonymous essays that the Constitution "is a *compact* between the people of each state, and those of all the states, and it is nothing more than a compact."[108] He further insisted that "[t]hat man must be a deplorable idiot who does not see that there is no earthly difference between an *unlimited* grant of power, and a grant limited in its terms, but accompanied with *unlimited* means of carrying it into execution."[109] Roane's response reflected what critics of the Court found so troubling about *McCulloch*, and it was not primarily the holdings. Although some states would continue to resist these holdings after the Court handed down its decision,[110] by this time period few Americans of national prominence doubted the constitutionality of a national bank. Most troubling to critics, rather, was that Marshall went well beyond the questions presented. He articulated a vision of one American people governed by a federal government with robust powers, supported by a Court eager to defer to Congress. Some found this vision alarming, particularly in its

---

[105]   See United States v. Carolene Products Co., 304 U.S. 144, 152 n.4, (1938), which is discussed in Chapter 9. For the most influential scholarly development of the process theory, see generally JOHN HART ELY, DEMOCRACY AND DISTRUST: A THEORY OF JUDICIAL REVIEW (1980).

[106]   *McCulloch*, 17 U.S. at 429.

[107]   *See, e.g.*, Granholm v. Heald, 544 U.S. 460 (2005).

[108]   *Roane's "Hampden" Essays*, RICH. ENQUIRER, June 11–22, 1819, *reprinted in* JOHN MARSHALL'S DEFENSE OF *MCCULLOCH V. MARYLAND* 127 (Gerald Gunther ed., 1969).

[109]   *Id.* at 110.

[110]   *See, e.g.*, Osborn v. Bank of the United States, 22 U.S. 738 (1824) (involving Ohio's imposition of a $50,000 tax on each of the branches of the Bank in the state).

implications for federal interference with slavery, which we will discuss in Chapter 10.

There was no dissenting opinion in *McCulloch*, and so no Justice took exception to Marshall's nationalist vision. The country, however, was not united. A de facto dissent from Marshall's vision was issued continuously over the course of many decades by adherents of Southern constitutionalism. As one of us has written, *McCulloch* "must be seen as part of the battle over states' rights that began with the Virginia and Kentucky Resolutions."[111] The Resolutions were enacted in 1798 in opposition to the controversial and constitutionally problematic Alien and Sedition Acts of 1798, which essentially made it a crime to criticize the Federalist Adams Administration. Democratic Republican Congressman Madison, in secretly drafting the Virginia Resolutions for adoption by the Virginia legislature, and Vice President Jefferson, in secretly drafting the Kentucky Resolutions for adoption by the Kentucky legislature, endorsed the state-compact theory of the Constitution that Maryland would later espouse in *McCulloch*. Madison and Jefferson, each in their own way, also seemed to flirt with state nullification of federal laws deemed unconstitutional by the state.[112]

Roane too was squarely within this tradition. He had earlier used the same theories to argue that the judgments of state courts were not subject to appellate review by the U.S. Supreme Court on the ground that one sovereign could not direct the actions of another. The Supreme Court emphatically rejected Roane's claims in decisions that remains good law to this day.[113] A little later, the compact theory formed the basis for the theory of state nullification of federal laws articulated by John C. Calhoun of South Carolina, and after that, for the theory of Southern secession.[114]

And so, the most profound issue raised in *McCulloch*—how to conceptualize the Union—was not resolved in *McCulloch* itself because it could not be decided by any judicial opinion. As we will see, it was initially decided by the Civil War, which effectively ended at Appomattox Courthouse on April 9, 1865, when Confederate General Robert E. Lee surrendered to Union General Ulysses S. Grant. The issue was more fully (although far from completely) decided a century later by the Civil Rights Movement of the 1950s and 60s, when

---

[111]   Farber, *supra* note 34, at 63.

[112]   *See* Virginia Resolution (Dec. 24, 1798), The Avalon Project, Yale Law School, http://avalon.law.yale.edu/18th_century/virres.asp; Kentucky Resolution (Dec. 3, 1799), The Avalon Project, Yale Law School, http://avalon.law.yale.edu/18th_century/kenres.asp.

[113]   *See* Martin v. Hunter's Lessee, 14 U.S. 304 (1816); Cohens v. Virginia, 19 U.S. 264 (1821).

[114]   *See* Farber, *supra* note 34, at 63.

Southern states finally complied with federal court orders to desegregate their public schools.

As for the Bank, the political consensus that had supported it in 1816 was gone by the time Congress passed a bill extending its charter in 1832. President Andrew Jackson, another Southerner and a departmentalist on matters of constitutional interpretation,[115] had the last word. (Note that the Supreme Court does not have the last word on constitutional questions when it *upholds* government action, whether a national bank or an affirmative action program.) Jackson vetoed the bill, and his veto message engaged both the constitutional merits of the issue and the allocation of authority to interpret the Constitution among the three branches:

> If the opinion of the Supreme Court covered the whole ground of this act, it ought not to control the coordinate authorities of this Government. The Congress, the Executive, and the Court must each for itself be guided by its own opinion of the Constitution. Each public officer who takes an oath to support the Constitution swears that he will support it as he understands it, and not as it is understood by others.[116]

Congress did not override the veto, Jackson withdrew all federal deposits from the Bank, and it expired in 1836.[117] The Bank did not rise a third time, but today's Federal Reserve and national banking system perform many of the functions that Hamilton had wanted the first Bank to perform.

Looking beyond the Bank, Marshall's iconic opinion in *McCulloch* has proven very influential in the post-New Deal world of robust federal power. The Supreme Court has tended to perform what scholars call a legitimating function.[118] The historical role of the Court has been to legitimate the actions of the federal government far more often than it has been to invalidate them. *McCulloch* exactly exemplifies this point. The historic relationship between the Court and the states has been far different. *McCulloch* illustrates this point too. The Court has tended to interpret the Constitution to defend federal power at the expense of state power. This is a key reason why the President and Congress have tended to defend the Court's exercise of judicial review, even when they loathe specific decisions.

As the next two chapters will explore, however, the meaning and significance of *McCulloch* are increasingly contested on the modern

---

[115]   For a discussion of departmentalism, see Chapter 2.

[116]   Andrew Jackson, Veto Message (July 10, 1832), The Avalon Project, Yale Law School, http://avalon.law.yale.edu/19th_century/ajveto01.asp.

[117]   *See* Farber, *supra* note 34, at 63.

[118]   *See* BREST ET AL., *supra* note 56, at 135.

Supreme Court. Its "states' rights" majority, a product of the "Reagan Revolution" of the 1980s and early 1990s—beginning with a President who declared in his First Inaugural Address that "the Federal Government did not create the States; the States created the Federal Government[119]—has imposed a variety of judicially enforceable limits on the scope of federal power. Although to date these limits have been relatively modest, Americans on and off the Court are still debating the nature of the Union that the Constitution brought into being. This, too, Marshall anticipated: "the question respecting the extent of the powers actually granted is perpetually arising, and will probably continue to arise so long as our system shall exist."[120]

III. The Necessary and Proper Clause Today

For the most part, Chief Justice Marshall's expansive view of the meaning of the Necessary and Proper Clause remains governing constitutional law. As noted at the beginning of this chapter, the Necessary and Proper Clause provides the textual hook for a large and diverse number of federal laws. It would not be possible for the Clause to do so much work without a very broad understanding of its scope.

For example, the Court's 2010 decision in *United States v. Comstock* reaffirms the Marshall Court's understanding of the Necessary and Proper Clause.[121] The question presented in the case was whether Congress has the power under this clause to authorize the Attorney General of the United States to civilly commit mentally ill, sexually dangerous federal prisoners after the completion of their federal sentences if no state will accept custody of them. The Court held 7–2 that Congress has such authority under the Necessary and Proper Clause. Quoting extensively from Marshall's opinion in *McCulloch*,[122] Justice Stephen Breyer reaffirmed for the Court that, "in determining whether the Necessary and Proper Clause grants Congress the legislative authority to enact a particular federal statute, we look to see whether the statute constitutes a means that is rationally related to the implementation of a constitutionally enumerated power."[123] "[T]he relevant inquiry," he continued, "is simply whether the means chosen are reasonably adapted to the attainment of a legitimate end under the commerce power or under

---

[119] Ronald Reagan, First Inaugural Address (Jan. 20, 1981), The Avalon Project, Yale Law School, http://avalon.law.yale.edu/20th_century/reagan1.asp.

[120] *McCulloch*, 17 U.S. at 405.

[121] 560 U.S. 126 (2010).

[122] *See id.* at 133–35.

[123] *Id.* at 134 (citing Sabri v. United States, 541 U.S. 600, 605 (2004)). Joining Justice Breyer's majority opinion were Chief Justice John Roberts and Justices John Paul Stevens, Ruth Bader Ginsburg, and Sonia Sotomayor.

other powers that the Constitution grants Congress the authority to implement."[124]

Notably in light of the discussion of collective action problems at the beginning of this chapter, the Court and individual Justices relied in part on the fact that the case implicated a collective action problem involving multiple states.[125] The Court recognized the "NIMBY" dilemma ("not in my backyard"). After the sentence of a sexually dangerous prisoner has expired, the federal government might release him for civil commitment in any number of states, including the state where he had been tried or the state where he is presently housed. A state that agrees to assume custody of the prisoner must pay all of the financial costs associated with indefinite civil commitment while other states potentially enjoy all of the benefits from committing the individual, who might otherwise move out of state. If not committed, he might move out of state upon release in part because the federal government had severed the prisoner's ties to the state by incarcerating him for a long time. Rather than dwelling on the fact that the federal government had helped to create the problem that it now sought to solve, the Court underscored evidence that states often refuse to assume custody, potentially hoping to free ride on some other state's decision to do so.[126] Both the Court and Justices Anthony Kennedy and Samuel Alito, who concurred in the judgment, stressed the relationship between the federal statute at issue and a multi-state collective action problem, which the federal government is better situated to address than the states.[127]

In contrast to the Marshall Court, however, the modern Court has understood the words "necessary" and "proper" in the Necessary and Proper Clause to impose independent constitutional limits on the scope of congressional authority. In *NFIB v. Sebelius*, Chief Justice John Roberts, in his controlling plurality opinion, appeared to concede that the term "necessary" in the Clause requires only a rational relationship between a federal statutory means and the implementation of an enumerated power.[128] But he interpreted the word "proper" in terms of Marshall's distinction between (1) "the

---

[124]   *Id.* at 135 (quotation marks omitted). By contrast, Justice Anthony Kennedy would insist on "a demonstrated link in fact, based on empirical demonstration." *Id.* at 152 (Kennedy, J., concurring in judgment). Justice Samuel Alito seemed to endorse Justice Kennedy's more demanding standard. *See id.* at 155 (Alito, J., concurring in judgment).

[125]   This paragraph draws from Neil S. Siegel, *Collective Action Federalism and the Minimum Coverage Provision*, 75 LAW & CONTEMP. PROBS. 29 (2012) (no. 3).

[126]   *Comstock*, 560 U.S. at 139, 143.

[127]   *See id.* at 154 (Kennedy, J., concurring in judgment); *id.* at 156, 158 (Alito, J., concurring in judgment).

[128]   567 U.S. 519, 559–60 (2012) (opinion of Roberts, C.J.).

power of making war or levying taxes or of regulating commerce, a great substantive and independent power," and (2) a power that can "be implied as incidental to other powers or used as a means of executing them."[129]

As we will discuss in the next two chapters, *NFIB* was a case in which ideas about individual liberty and limits on federal power circulating in constitutional politics were translated into constitutional law in perhaps record time.[130] The litigation concerned the constitutionality of the Patient Protection and Affordable Care Act of 2010 (ACA), which was first derisively and later colloquially known as "Obamacare." A key provision of the law was the minimum coverage provision, dubbed the "individual mandate" by its opponents. This provision required many Americans either to purchase a minimum level of health insurance coverage required by the ACA, or else to pay the federal government a sum of money each year for foregoing insurance. Those challenging the provision argued that it was beyond the scope of Congress's powers under the Commerce Clause, the Taxing Clause, and the Necessary and Proper Clause. (The commerce and taxing power challenges are discussed in the next two chapters, respectively.)

The potential justification for the minimum coverage provision under the Necessary and Proper Clause reflects the policy rationale for the provision. It is a convenient (and arguably essential) means for carrying into execution—that is, making more effective—the ACA's clearly valid (we will see why in the next chapter) Commerce Clause regulations of health insurance companies. These regulations include the ACA's prohibitions on denying coverage to people with pre-existing conditions, charging them higher premiums based on their medical history, or imposing yearly or lifetime limits on coverage. Such prohibitions solve collective action problems by, for example, dis-incentivizing insurance companies from moving to states that allow them to deny coverage to people with pre-existing conditions or to control costs in the other ways noted above. Without federal intervention, a destructive "race to the bottom" might ensue, in which even states that preferred to protect residents with pre-existing conditions nonetheless allowed insurers to deny them coverage.[131]

A requirement to purchase insurance is convenient for carrying these valid Commerce Clause regulations into effect because it

---

[129]   *McCulloch*, 17 U.S. at 411.

[130]   *See, e.g.*, Jack M. Balkin, *From Off the Wall to On the Wall: How the Mandate Challenge Went Mainstream*, THE ATLANTIC, June 4, 2012, https://www.theatlantic.com/national/archive/2012/06/from-off-the-wall-to-on-the-wall-how-the-mandate-challenge-went-mainstream/258040/.

[131]   *See* Siegel, *supra* note 125, at 61–73.

combats the perverse incentive people would otherwise have to wait until they became sick to purchase insurance. They would have such an incentive because the ACA guarantees them access to health insurance even after sickness arises. With healthy people staying out of insurance markets and sick people filing claims, insurance premiums would increase substantially. The Necessary and Proper Clause rationale for the minimum coverage provision emphasizes Congress's power to ensure that its regulations will accomplish their objective of expanding—not reducing—access to affordable health insurance.[132] The four *dissenters* in *NFIB* (Justice Ruth Bader Ginsburg, joined by Justices Breyer, Sonia Sotomayor, and Elena Kagan) emphasized this rationale.[133]

As noted above, Chief Justice Roberts did not deny that, for the foregoing reasons, the minimum coverage provision was "necessary" in the *McCulloch* sense. He instead insisted that a purchase requirement was not "proper" because it was not " 'incidental' to the exercise of the commerce power."[134] And a purchase mandate was not "derivative of, and in service to, a granted power," in his view, because it "vests Congress with the extraordinary ability to create the necessary predicate to the exercise of an enumerated power."[135]

The Chief Justice appeared to conclude that a purchase requirement was a great power like taxing, regulating commerce, and declaring and waging war, not a power derivative of these great powers. Unfortunately, it is not clear to us why this is so, nor did he offer much guidance regarding how to distinguish great powers from incidental ones. And given all of the exercises of congressional power that heretofore have been considered incidental by the Court—for example, creating a national bank, deporting people, enacting criminal laws, and putting people in prison or to death—a great deal will turn on how, if at all, this recently operationalized distinction will used by the Court in the years ahead.[136] Only time will tell whether this ruling will spawn a significant limit on national power or will be dismissed as dictum (since the Court did uphold the "mandate" on other grounds, as we discuss in Chapter 6).[137]

---

[132]   *See id.*

[133]   *See NFIB*, 567 U.S. at 589, 618–22 (Ginsburg, J., concurring in part, concurring in judgment in part, and dissenting in part).

[134]   *NFIB*, 567 U.S. at 560 (opinion of Roberts, C.J.) (quoting *McCulloch*, 17 U.S. at 418).

[135]   *Id.*

[136]   For a discussion, see Neil S. Siegel, *More Law than Politics: The Chief, the "Mandate," Legality, and Statesmanship, in* THE HEALTH CARE CASE: THE SUPREME COURT'S DECISION AND ITS IMPLICATIONS 192, 192–214 (Nathaniel Persily et al. eds., 2013).

[137]   For the first subsequent decision interpreting the Necessary and Proper Clause, see *United States v. Kebodeaux*, 570 U.S. 387 (2014) (holding that, as applied

Further Readings

PAUL BREST ET AL., PROCESSES OF CONSTITUTIONAL DECISIONMAKING: CASES AND MATERIALS 29–85 (6th ed. 2015) (Chapter 1—The Bank of the United States: A Case Study).

Daniel A. Farber, *The Story of* McCulloch*: Banking on National Power*, *in* CONSTITUTIONAL LAW STORIES 33–67 (Michael C. Dorf ed., 2004).

DANIEL A. FARBER & SUZANNA SHERRY, A HISTORY OF THE AMERICAN CONSTITUTION 165–220 (3d ed. 2014).

Gary Lawson & Neil S. Siegel, *Necessary and Proper Clause*, NATIONAL CONSTITUTION CENTER, INTERACTIVE CONSTITUTION (2016), https://constitutioncenter.org/interactive-constitution/articles/article-i/necessary-and-proper-clause/clause/.

Gary Lawson, *The Necessary and Proper Clause and the Law of Agency*, NATIONAL CONSTITUTION CENTER, INTERACTIVE CONSTITUTION (2016), https://constitutioncenter.org/interactive-constitution/articles/article-i/the-necessary-and-proper-clause-and-the-law-of-agency-lawson/clause/.

Jack N. Rakove, ORIGINAL MEANINGS: POLITICS AND IDEAS IN THE MAKING OF THE CONSTITUTION (1996).

Neil S. Siegel, *The Necessary and Proper Clause and the Collective Action Principle*, NATIONAL CONSTITUTION CENTER, INTERACTIVE CONSTITUTION (2016), https://constitutioncenter.org/interactive-constitution/articles/article-i/necessary-and-proper-clause-and-the-collective-action-principle-siegel/clause/.

---

to respondent, the registration requirements of the Sex Offender Registration and Notification Act fall within the scope of congressional power under the Necessary and Proper Clause).

Chapter 5

INTERSTATE COMMERCE CLAUSE

I. Introduction

This chapter considers the scope of Congress's power to regulate "commerce . . . among the several States," which is the third clause of Article I, Section 8. As noted at the beginning of Chapter 3, concern over interstate commerce played a key role in leading to the Constitutional Convention of 1787. During the 1780s, states discriminated against goods from other states by imposing tariff barriers and trade walls. Sister states retaliated, leaving most states worse off than they would have been if no state had engaged in protectionist behavior. This was a collective action problem, and Madison decried it in the memorandum he wrote while preparing for the Constitutional Convention. Madison there expressed concern, among other things, about "want of concert in matters where common interest requires it," a "defect . . . strongly illustrated in the state of our commercial affairs."[1] "How much," he asked rhetorically, "has the national dignity, interest, and revenue suffered from this cause?"[2]

The material in this chapter is very important as a practical matter. Numerous areas of federal law rest on the Interstate Commerce Clause (or Commerce Clause, for short), either alone or in combination with the Necessary and Proper Clause. These include federal statutes regulating the economy, civil rights, labor and employment, the environment, criminality, securities, and health care, among others.

The material on the Commerce Clause is also significant theoretically and intellectually. The modern scope of congressional power under the Commerce Clause puts great pressure on the idea of a national government of limited, enumerated powers. As a result, Commerce Clause cases have historically served as important vehicles for the Supreme Court to consider questions of constitutional federalism.

We begin with the Marshall Court's decision in *Gibbons v. Ogden*.[3] In this seminal case, the Court offered relatively broad understandings of which kinds of conduct constitute "Commerce" and

---

[1]   James Madison, *Vices of the Political System of the United States* (Apr. 1787), *at* NATIONAL ARCHIVES, FOUNDERS ONLINE, https://founders.archives.gov/documents/Madison/01-09-02-0187.

[2]   *Id.*

[3]   22 U.S. 1 (1824).

when such commerce exists "among the several States."[4] For most of the Nineteenth Century, however, the Commerce Clause was rarely used by Congress and so was rarely interpreted by the Court.

We turn next to the so-called Republican Era (or *Lochner* Era), which lasted from the late 1800s to 1937. As the nation increasingly industrialized, Congress increasingly used the Commerce Clause to regulate the interstate economic system that was developing at a rapid pace. The Court, which was ideologically resistant to government regulation of business and the economy, constricted the scope of the commerce power, invalidating a good number of federal laws for the first time in history. These federal laws sought, among other things, to regulate monopolies, guarantee minimum wages to workers, limit the number of hours they could work, ensure the safety of dangerous workplaces, and protect unions. As we will see in Chapter 9, the Court during this period also invalidated many similar state laws as violating what lawyers call "economic substantive due process" or "freedom of contract."[5]

As discussed below, constitutional law in this area turned on a dime after the constitutional crisis of 1937. Surrendering to political pressure (and, its critics would add, to economic reality and intellectual assault), the Court finally stopped invalidating President Franklin Delano Roosevelt's New Deal economic recovery plans, which sought to move the country out of the Great Depression. From 1937 to 1995, the Supreme Court construed the Commerce Clause so expansively that it did not invalidate a single federal law as beyond its scope, even as Congress aggressively used its authority under the Clause.

Finally, we examine the current era of Commerce Clause jurisprudence. It began with President Reagan's Supreme Court appointments in the 1980s and the Court's invalidations of a few federal statutes on federalism grounds in the 1990s. During this time period, the Court has modestly narrowed the scope of the Commerce Clause, and it has imposed an additional structural limit—called the anti-commandeering principle—on the scope of Congress's commerce power.

We close this chapter by describing the dormant (or negative) commerce doctrine. This doctrine is best thought of as a structural principle of constitutional law that limits *state* power (but not federal power) to discriminate against, or otherwise burden, interstate commerce. The Supreme Court during the Nineteenth Century inferred the dormant commerce principle from both the history of

---

4   U.S. CONST. art. I, § 8, cl. 3.

5   *See, e.g.*, Lochner v. New York, 198 U.S. 45 (1905) (invalidating a state maximum hours law for bakers).

state protectionism that helped inspire the Constitutional Convention and the grant of affirmative power to Congress to regulate interstate commerce. The Court continues to robustly enforce the dormant commerce principle today, even as certain Justices criticize it for lacking a firm basis in the text of the Constitution.

Before we begin this journey, it is worth explaining why this chapter takes an historical approach to the Commerce Clause. We do so for three main reasons.

First, an historical approach vividly illustrates how American "[c]onstitutional law is historically conditioned and politically shaped," as constitutional historian H. Jefferson Powell has written.[6] In approaching the material historically, one can see Supreme Court doctrine change significantly over time in response to economic, political, and social changes in American society, including changes in values and ideas outside the courts about what the Constitution prohibits and permits.

Second, the Court's vacillations over the scope of Congress's commerce power illuminate the difficulty of the federalism dilemma that the original Constitution brought into being. One horn of the dilemma is to ensure that the federal government is powerful enough to address effectively the numerous problems that require government intervention and that the states cannot address effectively on their own.[7] The other, simultaneous horn of the dilemma is to ensure that the federal government remains one of limited, enumerated powers.

Third, although much of the historical material that we will encounter (especially during the Republican Era) has been superseded, it is difficult to understand the shape of current Supreme Court doctrine without understanding what came before it. Likewise, it is difficult to assess current doctrine intelligently without understanding what came before it. The end of the Republican Era after the constitutional crisis of 1937 casts a long shadow over the contemporary debate about the scope of the Commerce Clause. Critics of the Court's current conservative majority charge it with restricting federal power in arbitrary ways by imposing formal

---

[6] H. JEFFERSON POWELL, A COMMUNITY BUILT ON WORDS: THE CONSTITUTION IN HISTORY AND POLITICS 6 (2002).

[7] Note that American federalism also includes the Reconstruction Amendments (numbers 13–15). The structural logic of the federal government's role in protecting civil rights is very different from the logic of collective action. *See* Neil S. Siegel, *Collective Action Federalism and Its Discontents*, 91 TEX. L. REV. 1937, 1948 (2013) ("[T]he enforcement clauses [of the Civil War Amendments] give Congress authority to regulate the internal policy choices of state governments concerning certain subject matters regardless of collective action problems facing the states.") (footnotes omitted). We discuss the Reconstruction Amendments in Chapters 10–13.

distinctions reminiscent of the distinctions that characterized and eventually doomed the doctrine during the Republican Era. By contrast, defenders of the modern Court applaud it for restoring a measure of structural balance by limiting the role of functional tests that in their view fail to meaningfully limit federal power.

There are also important normative arguments in favor of federalism as opposed to a more centralized system of government. Centralization may be more efficient when problems spill across state borders, and it gives national majorities more leeway in implementing their values. Centralization can also safeguard against rights violations by local majorities. As a practical matter, some problems can be addressed adequately only at the national level. But federalism serves other values: allowing the tailoring of policies to the preferences and commitments of communities (sometimes called value pluralism); limiting the risk of abuse of power at the national level (sometimes called tyranny prevention); providing individuals the opportunity to participate in democratic governance and hold elected officials accountable at a scale where they may be more likely to have a voice and effective vote; facilitating experiments in different states when the best solution to a problem is uncertain (sometimes called the states as laboratories of democracy); and achieving efficiency when problems are local in scope, as opposed to interstate or national. As we will see, the Court has struggled over time to strike the proper balance among these competing values.

II. The Marshall Court

Like *McCulloch* five years earlier, *Gibbons v. Ogden* was another historic Marshall Court decision.[8] It was the principal case that defined the scope of the Interstate Commerce Clause during the Constitution's first half-century. The Court in this case interpreted the Clause relatively broadly. As discussed further below, however, Congress did not use its commerce power much before the late 1800s. As a result, subsequent Courts had few occasions to interpret (or reinterpret) Congress's power to regulate interstate commerce.

A.   *Gibbons v. Ogden*

The New York legislature gave Robert Fulton and Robert Livingston the exclusive right (that is, a monopoly) to operate steamboats in the waters of New York. They in turn granted Aaron Ogden a license to operate a steamboat between New York City and spots in New Jersey. Thomas Gibbons operated steamboats between New York and Elizabethtown, New Jersey, and so he was violating the exclusive right granted by New York to Fulton and Livingston. Ogden brought suit in New York state court to enjoin Gibbons from

---

[8]   22 U.S. 1 (1824).

operating his steamboats in contravention of New York law. Gibbons responded that his steamboats were licensed pursuant to a 1793 federal statute, and that the federal license entitled him to navigate between New York and New Jersey notwithstanding the monopoly that New York granted to Fulton and Livingston.

Although Ogden prevailed in the New York courts (just as Maryland had prevailed in the Maryland courts in *McCulloch*), the U.S. Supreme Court reversed in a unanimous opinion written by Chief Justice John Marshall (also as in *McCulloch*). Marshall focused his opinion on whether Congress had the power to regulate navigation of the steamboats. It is important at the outset to understand how this constitutional issue arose in light of the three questions presented in the case.

The first question presented was an issue of statutory interpretation: did the 1793 federal statute license Gibbons to navigate between New York and New Jersey? Marshall read the statute as granting such a license to Gibbons. We will not focus on the language of the statute, which the New York appellate court read not to grant Gibbons such a license. More important for our purposes is the analytical point that the Court would have had no occasion to consider the constitutionality of the New York law had it answered this threshold question of statutory interpretation in the negative. In constitutional litigation, the presence or absence of an important constitutional question often turns on how a court initially interprets the language of a statute. Law school courses in Legislation (sometimes called Statutory Interpretation) focus on how to apply statutory language.

The second question presented was one of "preemption." Preemption is the constitutional principle, grounded in the Supremacy Clause of Article VI, that constitutionally valid federal laws trump conflicting state laws. Preemption analysis requires a court to examine: (i) whether federal law conflicts with state law, a question of statutory interpretation; and, if so, (ii) whether the federal law is valid, a question of constitutional interpretation. Given how Marshall read the federal statute in *Gibbons*, there was a clear conflict between federal law and state law; the federal license conflicted with the state-granted monopoly.

The second question under preemption analysis was therefore teed up: was the federal law that created the federal license constitutionally valid? Because no constitutional rights were at stake and no other enumerated power was available to Congress, the answer to this question turned on whether the federal law was within the scope of the Commerce Clause.

The third question presented in *Gibbons* implicated what has come to be known as the dormant commerce principle. Dormant commerce analysis asks whether, even if there were no federal law that granted Gibbons a federal license to operate his steamboats in violation of New York law (so that the federal commerce power lay dormant), the New York law granting the monopoly was still invalid because it placed an undue burden on interstate commerce. This is how courts would ask the question today. In *Gibbons*, Justice William Johnson wrote a concurring opinion in which he argued that Congress's power to regulate interstate commerce was exclusive,[9] an issue that Marshall did not decide for the Court even as he perceived "great force" in this argument.[10] Congress's commerce power has not been viewed as exclusive either historically or today,[11] but there is a robust dormant commerce principle according to which state laws that discriminate against interstate commerce or unduly burden interstate commerce are presumptively unconstitutional. We will have more to say about the dormant commerce principle at the end of this chapter.

For now, we will focus on the issue of the scope of Congress's commerce power in *Gibbons*. To avoid confusion, one should always remind oneself that the Commerce Clause is a grant of power to Congress, not (like the dormant commerce principle) an implied constitutional limit on regulatory power of states.

Marshall first asked into the meaning of the word "Commerce" in the Commerce Clause. As would be expected, counsel for Ogden interpreted the word narrowly, arguing that it should be restricted "to traffic, to buying and selling, or the interchange of commodities."[12] (To this day, Justice Clarence Thomas and certain scholars embrace the "trade" theory of the Commerce Clause, which views the original meaning of the word "commerce" as limited to trade or exchange of goods.[13]) Because navigation is not buying and selling, it follows from this position that the federal license was unconstitutional. And, counsel for Ogden added, because there was no conflict between New York law and a *valid* federal law, the state of New York was constitutionally permitted to regulate navigation, including by conferring a steamboat monopoly.

---

[9]   *Id.* at 227, 231–32 (Johnson, J., concurring).

[10]   *Id.* at 209 (opinion of the Court).

[11]   *See* Cooley v. Board of Wardens, 53 U.S. 299 (1852) (settling the exclusivity issue in the negative by holding that the states have the authority to regulate certain aspects of interstate commerce).

[12]   *Gibbons*, 22 U.S. at 189.

[13]   *See, e.g.*, United States v. Lopez, 514 U.S. 549, 584, 585–86 (Thomas, J., concurring); RANDY E. BARNETT, RESTORING THE LOST CONSTITUTION: THE PRESUMPTION OF LIBERTY 291–93 (2004).

Marshall rejected this definition of commerce as too narrow; it "would restrict a general term, applicable to many objects, to one of its significations."[14] In his view, commerce includes navigation in addition to trade, and it further includes more than navigation. "Commerce undoubtedly is traffic," he acknowledged, "but it is something more: it is intercourse. It describes the commercial intercourse between nations, and parts of nations, in all its branches, and is regulated by prescribing rules for carrying on that intercourse."[15] Marshall did not define the term "intercourse" beyond concluding that it definitely includes navigation. Experts today debate whether intercourse is limited to trade,[16] or also includes all economic conduct,[17] or also includes the exchange of people and ideas, meaning that networks of transportation and communication fall within the scope of the commerce power.[18]

Marshall next turned to the meaning of the phrase "among the several States" in the Commerce Clause. He did not endorse the narrow view that the word "among" means "between," so that Congress may regulate only commerce that is literally crossing state boundary lines. Instead, he insisted that "[t]he word 'among' means intermingled with. A thing which is among others, is intermingled with them. Commerce among the States, cannot stop at the external boundary line of each State, but may be introduced into the interior."[19]

At the same time, Marshall emphasized that the word "among" was not limitless in its meaning; it did not extend to "that commerce which is completely internal, which is carried on between man and man in a state, or between different parts of the same state, and which does not extend to or affect other states."[20] "Comprehensive as the word 'among' is," he continued, "it may very properly be restricted to that commerce which concerns more States than one."[21] He thus made clear that "[t]he completely internal commerce of a State" was beyond the scope of federal commerce power.[22] Generalizing, he

---

[14]   *Gibbons*, 22 U.S. at 189.

[15]   *Id.* at 189–90.

[16]   *See supra* note 13 (citing examples of proponents of the trade theory).

[17]   *See generally, e.g.*, Grant S. Nelson & Robert J. Pushaw Jr., *Rethinking the Commerce Clause: Applying First Principles to Uphold Federal Commercial Regulations but Preserve State Control over Social Issues*, 85 IOWA L. REV. 1 (1999).

[18]   *See* JACK M. BALKIN, LIVING ORIGINALISM 138–59 (2011); *see also* AKHIL REED AMAR, AMERICA'S CONSTITUTION: A BIOGRAPHY 107–108 (2005).

[19]   *Gibbons*, 22 U.S. at 194.

[20]   *Id.*

[21]   *Id.*

[22]   *Id.* at 195.

memorably described the rationale behind the Constitution's division of powers between the federal government and the states:

> The genius and character of the whole government seem to be, that its action is to be applied to all the external concerns of the nation, and to those internal concerns which affect the states generally; but not to those which are completely within a particular state, which do not affect other states, and with which it is not necessary to interfere, for the purpose of executing some of the general powers of the government.[23]

By rejecting extreme positions, Marshall's approach created the challenge of determining what commerce is purely internal to a state and what commerce concerns more than one state. For example, it may not be clear that any commerce is purely internal (especially as the country develops and integrates economically) if the actual, empirical effects of such commerce in other states are considered. The risk is that constitutional analysis will then become an arbitrary line-drawing exercise of determining how much, or what kind, of an effect is sufficient to conclude that the commerce is interstate. The Court has struggled with this problem ever since, and it has offered different solutions at different times.

B. Collective Action Federalism

The theory of *collective action federalism*, which has been developed by legal scholars (including one of us), is intended to help distinguish interstate from intrastate commerce.[24] As discussed in the previous chapter, Article VI of the Virginia Plan proposed to give Congress the power to act where the states are "separately incompetent."[25] The theory of collective action federalism interprets the Commerce Clause in light of the Virginia plan by distinguishing problems whose solution warrants collective action by states, and problems regarding which individual action by states is sufficient.

On this view, the original purpose of the Commerce Clause was to empower Congress to address collective action problems involving two or more states in their commercial relations with one another—for example, to prohibit states from discriminating against goods coming from out of state. Thus, the phrase "among the Several States" means a collective action problem involving more than one state—a problem that the states cannot solve effectively on their own

---

[23]   *Id.*

[24]   *See generally* Robert D. Cooter & Neil S. Siegel, *Collective Action Federalism: A General Theory of Article I, Section 8*, 63 STAN. L. REV. 115 (2010); BALKIN, *supra* note 18, at 160–77; AMAR, *supra* note 18, at 108.

[25]   2 RECORDS OF THE FEDERAL CONVENTION OF 1787, at 131–32 (Max Farrand ed., rev. ed. 1966).

because of interstate externalities (also called spillover effects). Although the Court has *not* adopted this theory as governing constitutional law, we will see many examples of collective action problems and collective action reasoning by the Court in its decisions after 1937, just as we saw some examples in the previous chapter. By contrast, the Court during the Republican Era, to which we will soon turn, expressly rejected the logic of collective action.

C. Putting *Gibbons* in Perspective

Like *McCulloch*, *Gibbons* has wielded great influence in the post-New Deal eras of federalism jurisprudence. The Court since 1937 has given Congress very broad authority to regulate using the Commerce Clause, including in recent decades during the heyday of the more conservative Rehnquist and Roberts Courts. It is worth bearing in mind, however, that Congress enacted very few federal laws purporting to regulate interstate commerce before the late Nineteenth Century.[26] One reason was opposition by Southerners to the use of this power. Like many other issues in the pre-Civil War era, questions about the scope of the Commerce Clause were tangled up with the problem of slavery, for a broadly interpreted Commerce Clause might also have given the federal government authority over much of the slave trade. Thus, there were few important regulations of commerce and few significant cases. For decades following *Gibbons*, the constitutionality of federal laws under the Commerce Clause was not a major question before the Supreme Court; the main issue, rather, was the dormant commerce question raised in *Gibbons*—namely, the power of states to regulate interstate commerce (or matters affecting it) in the absence of any congressional legislation.[27] It was not until Congress began legislating in response to industrialization in the late 1800s, long after slavery was gone, that the scope of the commerce power became an issue of major concern.

III. The Republican Era

The Republican Era lasted from the late 1800s to 1937. Lawyers also refer to it as the *Lochner* Era after the most (in)famous Supreme Court decision invalidating a state law during this period.[28] It was the first era in which the Supreme Court used its power of judicial review with some frequency both to limit federal power under the

---

26   *See* PAUL BREST ET AL., PROCESSES OF CONSTITUTIONAL DECISIONMAKING: CASES AND MATERIALS 197 (6th ed. 2015).

27   *See, e.g.*, Willson v. Black-Bird Creek Marsh Co., 27 U.S. 245 (1829) (rejecting a dormant commerce challenge to the state-authorized construction of a dam across a navigable waterway, apparently because the Court viewed the dam as a health measure and the waterway as minor).

28   *See, e.g.*, Lochner v. New York, 198 U.S. 45 (1905) (invalidating a state maximum hours law for bakers).

Commerce Clause and to restrict state authority under the Due Process Clause of Section One of the Fourteenth Amendment.[29] We will discuss the constitutional restrictions on state laws in Chapter 9. Here we present the Court's Commerce Clause jurisprudence, which was characterized by a series of formal distinctions that were defended as limiting federal power and were criticized as arbitrary and ideologically biased.[30]

A.   Economic Changes and Constitutional Politics

Although the process had begun before the Civil War, the American economy was industrializing and nationalizing at a rapid clip in the late 1800s. Railroads spread around the country, bringing different regions closer together. Networks and methods of communication—the telephone, the telegraph, and the mail—followed the railroads, whose growth fueled ever more industrialization and economic specialization.[31] The gross national product grew at the astonishing rate of nearly 15 percent a year from 1870 to 1900; steel became the material of choice in building machinery; immigration to the United States increased substantially; and Americans moved from rural areas to cities as "[t]he agrarian economy gave way to an urban and industrial one."[32] The 1870 census was the last one recording a majority of Americans engaged in agriculture,[33] and 1920 was the last one showing a majority of Americans living in rural America.[34]

With rapid economic development came huge concentrations of wealth (and, at times, monopoly power) in American corporations and individual leaders of the business community. With economic growth also came social dislocations for the ever-increasing number of Americans (including children) who now lived in urban areas and toiled in industrial settings like mines and factories, often for long hours and low wages in unsafe working conditions. Popular protests and social movements demanded government intervention to

---

[29]   See U.S. CONST. amend. XIV, § 1.

[30]   As Professor Jack Balkin has observed, one of these distinctions (between commerce and other stages of business) actually began somewhat earlier in the Nineteenth Century. See BALKIN, *supra* note 18, at 180, 396 (discussing decisions from 1852 and 1877 that distinguished commerce from manufacturing and agricultural production).

[31]   See BARRY FRIEDMAN, THE WILL OF THE PEOPLE: HOW PUBLIC OPINION HAS INFLUENCED THE SUPREME COURT AND SHAPED THE MEANING OF THE CONSTITUTION 150 (2009).

[32]   *Id.*

[33]   See *id.*

[34]   See U.S. DEP'T OF COMMERCE, BUREAU OF THE CENSUS, HISTORICAL STATISTICS OF THE UNITED STATES: COLONIAL TIMES TO 1957 9, 14 (1960) (recording that 1920 was the first census year in which more Americans lived in urban territory than rural territory).

moderate the negative effects of industrialization and render somewhat less unequal the distribution of its financial rewards.[35] The federal government, as well as many state governments, began to respond. For example, the Interstate Commerce Act of 1877 authorized federal regulation of railroads, and the Sherman Antitrust Act of 1890 authorized federal regulation of monopolies and other restraints on trade.

This period is called the Republican Era because it was largely dominated nationally by the Republican Party, which had tired by this time of trying to guarantee racial equality to African Americans in the face of stiff Southern resistance and Northern indifference, as we will discuss in Chapter 10. The GOP reigned supreme more often than not in no small part due to the financial support of Corporate America, which made clear that its generosity was contingent on the appointment of Supreme Court Justices and other federal judges who were sympathetic to the financial interests and constitutional convictions of the business community. The Republican Party obliged (as did Democratic President Grover Cleveland), and the result was a Court that was ideologically committed to a relatively unregulated American economy until 1937.[36]

Again, it was not just federal laws that the Court invalidated for invading the regulatory spheres of the states; more often, it was state laws that the Court struck down for violating the economic liberty of individuals, as we will explore in Chapter 9. The result was an economic sphere little touched by significant government regulation. Whether or not the Justices thought they were simply following the law of the Constitution, the term *laissez faire* best captures the economic system that they deemed required by the Constitution.

For example, Justice David Brewer, who had been appointed to the Court by Republican President Benjamin Harrison in 1890, gave a speech in 1893 entitled *The Nation's Safeguard*, which he delivered to the annual meeting of the New York Bar Association in Albany.[37] He stressed the moral evils of economic redistribution and the need for robust judicial review to protect the property rights of the wealthy from being violated by the poor. He decried those who "seeing that which a man has attempts to wrest it from him and transfer it to those who have not," even though "[i]t is the unwavering law, that the wealth of the community will be in the hands of a few."[38] "[T]he salvation of the nation," he concluded, "the permanence of

---

[35]   *See* FRIEDMAN, *supra* note 31, at 150–55.

[36]   *See id.* at 155–205.

[37]   David J. Brewer, *The Nation's Safeguard, in* PROCEEDINGS OF THE NEW YORK STATE BAR ASSOCIATION, SIXTEENTH ANNUAL MEETING 37–47 (1893).

[38]   *Id.* at 39.

government of and by the people, rests upon the independence and vigor of the judiciary," which exist "[t]o stay the waves of popular feeling, to restrain the greedy hand of the many from filching from the few that which they have honestly acquired, and to protect in every man's possession and enjoyment, be he rich or poor, that which he hath."[39]

The foregoing account is brief and somewhat oversimplified; a half-century is a long time, and a lot happened that cannot be neatly packaged together and presented, including the economic downturn of 1873, the Progressive movement, World War I, and the Great Depression. The era was marked by discontinuities as well as continuities in the Court's federalism jurisprudence, and the Court was sympathetic to certain government regulations at certain times. But as a general matter, Justice Brewer's blunt speech captures well both the constitutional politics of the Republican Party during most of this period and the Commerce Clause jurisprudence of the Court.

B.   What Is "Commerce"?

The Court sought to limit federal commerce power by articulating a series of formal, binary distinctions. The first was its opposition between production and commerce, the former of which was beyond the scope of federal commerce power. For example, in *United States v. E.C. Knight Company*,[40] the federal government invoked the Sherman Act to block the acquisition by the American Sugar Refining Company of several competing sugar refineries, which would have given it control over more than 98 percent of the industry. The Court held by a margin of 8 to 1 that application of the federal antitrust law to the company was beyond the scope of the Commerce Clause. It reasoned that commerce was one stage of business distinct from the stage that came before it: production, manufacturing, or mining. "Commerce succeeds to manufacture," the Court instructed, "and is not a part of it."[41] Congress, the Court explained, may regulate only the commerce stage when relying on the Commerce Clause. The Court made clear that it was distinguishing commerce and manufacturing in order to prevent an unlimited federal commerce power, which might leave nothing left for the states to regulate. "[T]he preservation of the autonomy of the States," the Court wrote, is "required by our dual form of government."[42]

Although the case law over the next half-century was not a model of clarity or consistency, this restrictive definition of commerce

---

[39]   *Id.* at 47.
[40]   156 U.S. 1 (1895).
[41]   *Id.* at 12.
[42]   *Id.* at 13.

lasted until 1937. In 1936, for example, the Court in *Carter v. Carter Coal Company* held that the Commerce Clause could not support the Bituminous Coal Conservation Act of 1935, which authorized local coal boards to determine coal prices and, after collective bargaining, the wages and hours of employees of coal companies.[43] The law was one of President Franklin Delano Roosevelt's New Deal economic recovery programs, which sought to end the Great Depression through a mix of bold experimentation and government regulation. As the *Wall Street Journal* explained at the time, the purpose of the 1935 Act was to secure labor peace in "the country's most important 'sick industry,'" in which excessive coal production had resulted in heated competition over wages and prices, as well as labor conflict in the coalfields that required frequent resort to U.S. soldiers.[44]

The Court responded to the Act by warning that "[e]very journey to a forbidden end begins with the first step."[45] It defined commerce as "intercourse for the purposes of trade" (note the restrictive riff on *Gibbons*), and it insisted that "the incidents leading up to and culminating in the mining of coal do not constitute such intercourse."[46] Rather, "[t]he employment of men, the fixing of their wages, hours of labor and working conditions, the bargaining in respect of these things . . . each and all constitute intercourse for the purposes of production, not trade."[47] In the Court's view, "[m]ining brings the subject matter of commerce into existence," while "[c]ommerce disposes of it."[48]

Indeed, the Court had earlier gone farther by holding that Congress may not regulate even what literally constitutes interstate commerce if the effect is to control production. The federal law invalidated by the Court in 1918, in *The Child Labor Case* (*Hammer v. Dagenhart*), did not actually prohibit child labor.[49] Rather, it prohibited the *shipment in interstate commerce* of goods made by child labor. The Carolinas were the nation's leading users of child labor, and in this case, a North Carolina father sought to enjoin enforcement of the federal law on behalf of himself and his two minor sons, who worked in a cotton mill in Charlotte. The Court reasoned that the states had exclusive authority to regulate child labor,[50] and that "if Congress can . . . regulate matters entrusted to local

---

[43]   298 U.S. 238 (1936).

[44]   *See* FRIEDMAN, *supra* note 31, at 203–04 (quoting Editorial, *Coal and Regulation*, WALL ST. J., May 19, 1936, at 4).

[45]   *Carter Coal Co.*, 298 U.S. at 295.

[46]   *Id.* at 298, 303.

[47]   *Id.* at 303.

[48]   *Id.* at 304.

[49]   247 U.S. 251 (1918).

[50]   *See id.* at 275–76.

authority by prohibition on the movement of commodities in interstate commerce," then "the power of the States over local matters may be eliminated, and thus our system of government be practically destroyed."[51]

Critics of the Court's distinction between production and commerce made several points. Although the doctrine that gave rise to these criticisms has long passed away, the criticisms have continued to have resonance. These criticisms help explain why the post-New Deal swung so far in the opposite direction. They also explain why the current Court, which has revived some limits on the Commerce Clause, did not choose to revive the pre-New Deal doctrines.

To begin with, critics of the pre-New Deal jurisprudence contended that it made no sense to allow Congress to regulate only the commerce stage of an integrated business. The business *purpose* of acquiring a monopoly in production in an industry is to earn greater profits in sales (which was the Court's definition of "commerce") by increasing prices to consumers. As a matter of empirical, economic reality, in other words, production is intimately related to commerce. As the dissenters emphasized in *Carter Coal*, "[m]ining and agriculture and manufacture are not interstate commerce considered by themselves, yet their relation to that commerce may be such that, for the protection of the one, there is need to regulate the other."[52]

Second, critics charged that the Court did not adequately justify its assumption that there must be some defined sphere of economic activity, like production, reserved to the states. To hold that congressional regulation of production takes too much (or the wrong kind of) authority away from the states requires a substantive account of the proper scope of federal and state power—some view of what each should be doing (and not doing) in the American federal system. The Court during the Republican Era did not offer such an account. Nor did it confront the collective action problem that crippled state regulation in their supposed sphere of exclusive authority. As the first Justice John Marshall Harlan emphasized in his lone dissent in *E.C. Knight*, a monopoly operating in multiple states "cannot by adequately controlled by any one State," and "[t]he common government of all the people is the only one that can adequately deal with a matter which directly and injuriously affects

---

[51]   *Id.* at 276.

[52]   *Id.* at 327 (Cardozo, J., joined by Brandeis and Stone, JJ., dissenting).

the entire commerce of the country, [and] which concerns equally all the people of the Union."[53]

Third, critics charged the Court with inconsistency borne of ideological bias. They argued, for example, that *The Child Labor Case* could not be reconciled with the Court's prior decision in *The Lottery Case, Champion v. Ames*.[54] In 1895, Congress passed the Federal Lottery Act, which banned sending lottery tickets through the mails or from one state to another by any other means. The law was challenged on the ground that Congress may not use to Commerce Clause to regulate morals, which is left to the states. The Court disagreed, holding by a vote of 5 to 4 that Congress may use its commerce power to protect people from the "widespread pestilence of lotteries" and "an evil of such appalling character,[55] and to ensure that interstate commerce "shall not be polluted by the carrying of lottery tickets from one State to another."[56]

The Court's defenders reconciled this ruling with *The Child Labor Case* by arguing that, in *The Child Labor Case*, federal law had the effect (and perhaps the purpose) of controlling production and production is left to the states. In *The Lottery Case*, by contrast, the law did not have the effect or purpose of controlling production.

Critics were unpersuaded. For one thing, eliminating the interstate market inevitably decreased production, and such an effect might very well have been Congress's purpose. For another thing, critics argued that the need for federal regulation might actually have been stronger in *The Child Labor Case* given what we would now call a collective action problem facing the states. Because some states regulated child labor while others did not, businesses in states that did not regulate child labor had a competitive advantage over businesses in states that did, pressuring states to compete in a deregulatory "race to the bottom." Only federal intervention could equalize the playing field and thereby address the collective action problem.[57] Solicitor General John Davis argued on behalf of the federal government in *The Child Labor Case* that the existence of sister states and a national market meant states acting individually could not regulate the problem effectively. But the Court explicitly rejected the unfair competition argument in the *Child Labor Case*.[58]

---

[53]   United States v. E.C. Knight Co., 156 U.S. 1, 45 (1895) (Harlan, J., dissenting).

[54]   188 U.S. 321 (1903).

[55]   *Id.* at 357–58.

[56]   *Id.* at 356.

[57]   *See* Cooter & Siegel, *supra* note 24, at 160–61 (articulating this rationale).

[58]   *See* Hammer v. Dagenhart, 247 U.S. 251, 273 (1918).

That the Justices in the majority likely did not themselves regard the competition as unfair may have helped them reach this conclusion. This suspicion caused critics to accuse the Court of ideological bias. On this cynical view, a Court that was both economically and religiously conservative should be expected to invalidate federal regulations of the market economy but to uphold federal morals legislation, which is what the Court often (although not always) did.[59]

C.   When Is Commerce "Among the Several States"?

The Court during the Republican Era did not adopt a single, consistent approach to the question of how to distinguish interstate commerce from intrastate commerce. It instead used several formal distinctions to define the phrase "among the several States."[60] These distinctions were difficult to apply consistently, but they shared a purpose that was easy enough to identify: preventing unlimited federal commerce power.

Most significantly, the Court distinguished "direct" effects on interstate commerce, which justified use of the Commerce Clause, from "indirect" effects, which did not. The distinction was hard to draw. As we will see below, the Court made clear that the distinction turned on the perceived *nature* of the effects, not on their *size*.

The Court also distinguished goods "in the flow" (or "stream" or "current") of commerce, which were within the scope of the Commerce Clause, from goods "out of the flow" (or "stream" or "current"), which were beyond federal commerce power.[61] Goods could be out of the flow of commerce either because interstate shipment had not yet begun when congressional regulations applied, or because interstate shipment had ended by the time congressional regulations applied.

Still another distinction was between inherently dangerous goods, which Congress was permitted to regulate using the Commerce Clause, and goods that were not inherently dangerous, which Congress could not regulate. The Court upheld federal bans on the interstate shipment of unsafe food and drugs, diseased cattle,

---

[59]   *See, e.g.*, Caminetti v. United States, 242 U.S. 470 (1917) (holding that the Commerce Clause justified the Mann Act, which criminalized taking a woman across state lines for "immoral purposes").

[60]   U.S. CONST. art. I, § 8, cl. 3.

[61]   *See, e.g.*, Stafford v. Wallace, 258 U.S. 495, 516 (1922) (upholding federal regulation of stockyards, where livestock was held, on the ground that "stockyards are but a throat through which the current [of commerce] flows, and the transactions which occur therein are only incident to this current from the West to the East, and from one State to another").

materials deemed obscene, and (as we have seen) lottery tickets, which were thought to be immoral.[62]

The Court's approach is exemplified by *Schechter Poultry Corporation v. United States*, often called the "sick chicken" case.[63] This 1935 case involved the National Industrial Recovery Act (NIRA), another piece of New Deal legislation. The statute sought to address the collapse of the American economy—including a precipitous decline in wages, prices, and employment, as well as associated labor unrest—by allowing the President to approve cooperative codes of fair competition developed by boards of different industries. President Roosevelt approved the Live Poultry Code for New York City. Among other things, the Code prohibited child labor, established a forty-hour workweek, and required a minimum wage. The question presented in the case was whether the Commerce Clause supported the application of this Live Poultry Code to a New York slaughterhouse.

A key argument in favor of federal power was that almost all of the chickens received by the New York slaughterhouses were purchased from out of state. Because the wages and hours of employees at the slaughterhouses impacted the business costs borne by the owners of the slaughterhouses, the wages and hours provisions of the Code significantly affected the owners' demand for out-of-state chickens and so the purchase price of these chickens. In addition, individual action by states might be ineffective in addressing low wages and long hours because of a collective action problem—once again, a race to the bottom.

The Court rejected these arguments, holding that the Commerce Clause does not allow Congress to regulate the wages and hours of New York butchers. It reasoned that wages and hours at the slaughterhouses had no "direct" effect on interstate commerce; rather, the effect, no matter how large in degree, was indirect in nature.[64] The Court also deemed irrelevant to the Commerce Clause inquiry the concern about a race to the bottom, dismissing the federal government's "point that efforts to enact state legislation establishing high labor standards have been impeded by the belief that, unless similar action is taken generally, commerce will be diverted from the States adopting such standards, and that this fear

---

[62]　　*See, e.g.*, Hammer v. Dagenhart, 247 U.S. 251, 270–72 (1918) (stating that "the facility of interstate transportation can be taken away from the demoralization of lotteries, the debasement of obscene literature, the contagion of diseased cattle or persons, the impurity of food and drugs" because "the use of interstate transportation was necessary to the accomplishment of harmful results," unlike in the case of child labor, for "[t]he goods shipped are, of themselves, harmless").

[63]　　295 U.S. 495 (1935).

[64]　　*See id.* at 546, 548–49.

of diversion has led to demands for federal legislation on the subject of wages and hours."[65] Likewise, in *Carter Coal* the following year, the Court went out of its way to reject the "proposition, often advanced and as often discredited, that the power of the federal government inherently extends to purposes affecting the nation as a whole with which the states severally cannot deal or cannot adequately deal."[66]

Finally, the Court in *Schechter Poultry* held that the "flow" or "stream of commerce" theory it had applied in other cases was unavailable to the federal government here because the chickens were no longer in the stream by the time they arrived in New York; interstate commerce was over by then. "So far as the poultry here in question is concerned," the Court stated, "the flow in interstate commerce had ceased."[67] The problem in *Carter Coal*, by contrast, was that the Coal Act "deals with commodities at rest before interstate commerce has begun."[68]

As was the case with the Court's distinction between production and commerce, the main analytical problem with the Court's distinction between direct and indirect effects was how to draw a defensible line between the two kinds of effects—that is, one that is not arbitrary, ad hoc, or results-oriented. A good way to see the problem is to compare *Schechter Poultry* to one of the Court's railroad cases, the *Shreveport Rate Cases* of 1914.[69] In this case, Congress was regulating intrastate railroad rates—that is, the rates charged by railroads operating entirely within Texas. The Court nonetheless held that the Commerce Clause authorized Congress to empower the Interstate Commerce Commission (ICC) to prohibit railroads from charging rates for transportation within Texas that were lower than the rates set by the ICC for identical distances between Texas and Louisiana. The Court reasoned that Congress "does possess the power to foster and protect interstate commerce, and to take all measures necessary or appropriate to that end, although intrastate transactions of interstate carriers may thereby be controlled."[70]

To be sure, the Court had a sensible rationale for allowing the federal government to regulate the intrastate rates. An intrastate railroad could charge a lower price and undersell the interstate railroad, thereby threatening its survival or forcing price increases for interstate travel to compensate. Because Congress had a

---

[65]   *Id.* at 549.

[66]   Carter v. Carter Coal Co., 298 U.S. 238, 291 (1936).

[67]   *Schechter Poultry Corp.*, 295 U.S. at 543.

[68]   *Carter Coal Co.*, 298 U.S. at 309.

[69]   Houston, E. & W. Tex. Ry. Co. v. United States, 234 U.S. 342 (1914).

[70]   *Id.* at 353.

legitimate interest in ensuring the survival of the interstate railroad that was subject to federal regulation, it could regulate the intrastate railroad in order to protect the interstate railroad.

The key analytical question, however, is why this effect was direct while the effect in *Schechter Poultry* was indirect. In one case, low intrastate railroad rates undermined the price set by the ICC for interstate railroad rates. In the other case, low wages and long hours within a state significantly affected the price of chickens in the interstate market. In both cases, there were significant *quantitative* effects on interstate commerce. The Court never persuasively explained what it was about the *qualitative* nature of the effects that led to different outcomes in the two cases.

As for the "stream of commerce" approach that the Court sometimes invoked, *Schechter Poultry* can perhaps be distinguished from other "stream of commerce" cases on the ground that federal regulations were triggered after the chickens had already been in interstate commerce, not before. The problem with this distinction from a federalism perspective, however, is that federal regulations in effect at the place of delivery affect interstate commerce just as much as the regulations in effect at the place of origin or along the way.

D. The Big Picture

Before turning to the events of 1937 and the ensuing period of virtually unlimited federal commerce power, it is worth taking a step back and asking whether and why the Court's decisions during this era imposed sound or unsound limits on the scope of the Commerce Clause. The Court did succeed in preventing this enumerated power from becoming a grant of unlimited federal authority. As a practical matter, moreover, it is plausible to believe—as the Court did, and as some experts continue to argue today—that the most effective way to limit federal power through judicial review is for judges to articulate relatively crisp, formal distinctions, even if they leave something to be desired from the functional perspective of vindicating the underlying federalism values.[71]

To the extent that the Court's commerce jurisprudence failed during the Republican Era, which is the prevailing (although not the unanimous) view on and off the modern Court, it is worth asking why. One oft-given answer is that the formalistic distinctions drawn by the Court could not be applied consistently, and/or were subject to ideological manipulation in order to partially constitutionalize laissez faire. Another criticism, this one from the theory of collective action federalism, is that the Court's distinctions did not relate to the

---

[71]   For an argument to this effect, see Lawrence Lessig, *Translating Federalism: United States v. Lopez,* 1995 SUP. CT. REV. 125, 197.

regulatory advantages of the federal government and the states—that the Court was wrong to reject the existence of collective action problems facing the states as irrelevant to the scope of federal commerce power.

The Court abandoned all of these distinctions in the post-1937 transformations of Commerce Clause doctrine. But the issue of the soundness of limiting federal power through formal restraints became very important again after certain federalism decisions of the Rehnquist and Roberts Courts. As we will see, these decisions have imposed modest limits on the scope of federal commerce power through a different set of formal distinctions.

IV. The Crisis of 1937 and Constitutional Change

If ever U.S. constitutional law did an about face, it was in 1937. The Republican Era ended suddenly, and it did not end well for the Court. Explaining why his party lost seats in the House of Representatives during the 1934 elections when the party out of power (then and now) typically gains seats in such elections, the outspoken progressive Republican Senator William E. Borah of Idaho explained that the people "are offered the Constitution—but the people can't eat the Constitution."[72] Economic and political pressures on the Court would continue to mount in the following years.

Professor Barry Friedman has nicely captured the enormous economic pressures for constitutional change caused by the collapse of the American economy—and how oblivious the "old Court" was to the national crisis:

> It is difficult to overstate the depth of misery of the Great Depression. Between the crash of the stock market in 1929 and the 1932 election, unemployment in the United States rose to fully 25 percent, while industrial output and prices both dropped by roughly a third. Steel mills were running at 12 percent of capacity. The mortgage default rate among urbanites was about 20 percent, though that number doubled in some cities; by 1933, fully 40 percent of farm owners had lost their land. The economic downturn spared few.[73]

With unemployment reaching astonishing heights, public assistance virtually nonexistent, and individual states obviously incapable of meeting the economic emergency on their own, public support for a

---

[72]   William Borah, *quoted in* FRIEDMAN, *supra* note 31, at 209.

[73]   *Id.* at 196–97.

national policy response grew strong.[74] The result was a political transformation.

The 1936 presidential and congressional elections are regarded by political scientists as pivotal ones in American history; they "put squarely to the voters the question of whether government in general, and the federal government in particular, should have broad economic authority."[75] President Roosevelt was resoundingly re-elected, which he interpreted as a mandate to continue pursuing bold experiments and plans for national economic recovery. In addition, Democrats dominated both Houses of Congress to an extent that neither party dreams of today: the Democrats held more than three-fourths of the seats in the House and seventy-five of the Senate's ninety-six seats.[76] As noted in the previous section, FDR's various proposals to move the country out of the Depression in the 1930s were known as the New Deal, which was more than just a set of policy recommendations. It was a constitutional vision—that is, a substantive account of how governmental power should be exercised and individual rights protected in the American constitutional system.[77] Central to his liberal vision was a social and political commitment to providing economic security for all Americans. FDR would eventually propose an "economic bill of rights" as part of what Americans owe one another.[78]

FDR was livid about decisions like *Schechter Poultry, Carter Coal,* and others presumably to come given the principles reaffirmed in these rulings. In response, he surprised the country by advocating what came to be called the Court-Packing Plan.[79] He proposed, among other things, to have Congress add a Justice to the Supreme Court, up to a total membership of fifteen, for each Justice over the age of seventy who had served at least ten years and who did not

---

74   *See id.* at 209.

75   *Id.* at 210.

76   *See* U.S. GOV'T PRINTING OFFICE, OFFICIAL CONGRESSIONAL DIRECTORY, 75th Cong., 1st Sess. 3–130 (2d ed. 1937).

77   For discussions of the nature and functions of constitutional visions, see KEITH E. WHITTINGTON, POLITICAL FOUNDATIONS OF JUDICIAL SUPREMACY: THE PRESIDENCY, THE SUPREME COURT, AND CONSTITUTIONAL LEADERSHIP IN U.S. HISTORY 53–58 (2007); Neil S. Siegel, *"Equal Citizenship Stature": Justice Ginsburg's Constitutional Vision,* 43 NEW ENG. L. REV. 799, 801–12 (2009).

78   Franklin D. Roosevelt, United States President, Message to the Congress on the State of the Union (Jan. 11, 1944), *in* 1944–45 FRANKLIN D. ROOSEVELT. PUBLIC PAPERS AND ADDRESSES OF FRANKLIN D. ROOSEVELT 32 (1950).

79   *See* MARIAN C. MCKENNA, FRANKLIN ROOSEVELT AND THE GREAT CONSTITUTIONAL WAR: THE COURT-PACKING CRISIS OF 1937, at 351–356 (2002). For another good account of the Court-packing episode, see WILLIAM E. LEUCHTENBURG, THE SUPREME COURT REBORN: THE CONSTITUTIONAL REVOLUTION IN THE AGE OF ROOSEVELT 82–162 (1995).

retire within six months of his seventieth birthday.[80] Given the ages and tenures of the current Justices, FDR would immediately be able to make six appointments, thereby creating a pro-New Deal supermajority on the Court.

Even though FDR was very popular and the Democrats firmly controlled both houses of Congress, the plan proved intensely controversial. For example, the Senate Judiciary Committee Report characterized the Court-Packing Plan as "an invasion of judicial power such as has never before been attempted in this country," as "contrary to the spirit of the Constitution," and as "seek[ing] to do that which is unconstitutional."[81] Staunch New Dealers who shared FDR's frustrations with the Court's jurisprudence nonetheless concluded that packing it was the wrong way to address the problem.[82]

Yet some form of judicial discipline—if not FDR's very aggressive proposal—might have been approved had the Court not begun to change its decisionmaking (and had not one of the Court's conservatives, Justice Willis Van Devanter, agreed to retire at the end of the Court's term after Congress ensured that he would receive a generous pension).[83] As discussed below, the Court in 1937 issued major decisions breaking cleanly away from the earlier era. It happened because Justice Owen Roberts switched from voting with the prior majority to voting with what had been the dissent. To this day, scholars debate why Justice Roberts switched sides—whether he was responding to intense political pressure or whether he had independently changed his mind—but it became known as "the switch in time that saved nine."[84] As we will see in Chapter 9, the switch occurred simultaneously with the Court's overruling of economic substantive due process decisions that had long limited state economic regulations.

Soon the Court's make-up changed decisively. The four conservatives (Pierce Butler, James Clark McReynolds, George Sutherland, and Van Devanter), whom critics called the Four Horsemen of the Apocalypse, were replaced by New Dealers. By 1942, FDR had made eight consecutive appointments to the Court—all New Dealers—with a view to changing the Court's decisions. Using

---

[80]   PRESIDENT OF THE UNITED STATES, RECOMMENDATION TO REORGANIZE JUDICIAL BRANCH, H.R. Doc. No. 75–142 (1937).

[81]   S. COMM. ON THE JUDICIARY, REORGANIZATION OF THE FEDERAL JUDICIARY, S. Rep. No. 75–711, at 9, 11, 23 (1937). For analysis of the Senate report, see Curtis A. Bradley & Neil S. Siegel, *Historical Gloss, Constitutional Conventions, and the Judicial Separation of Powers*, 105 GEO. L.J. 255, 274–75, 279 (2017).

[82]   *See* Bradley & Siegel, *supra* note 81, at 274–83.

[83]   *See* FRIEDMAN, *supra* note 31, at 231.

[84]   For discussion of the historical dispute, see generally Daniel A. Farber, *Who Killed Lochner?*, 90 GEO. L.J. 985 (2002).

his power to nominate Justices, he accomplished the very doctrinal change that he had wanted to secure through Court-packing.

The Democrats completely controlled the federal government between 1932 and 1948, and they sought to transform constitutional doctrine through the appointments process (and not to accomplish other goals, such as rewarding loyal supporters). As a result, they were able to fill the courts with judges who supported the New Deal. These judges believed in broad federal power, and they changed constitutional law to reflect their beliefs. This is an example of Professor Jack Balkin and Sanford Levinson's theory of "partisan entrenchment," according to which the party that controls the White House (subject to a potential check from the Senate) can appoint new judges who share roughly similar views on questions of importance to the party.[85] Over time, this process can generate significant changes in constitutional doctrine.

V. From 1937 to the 1990s

We return now to the evolution of the Court's Commerce Clause jurisprudence. We begin with three pivotal decisions from 1937 to 1942 that define the scope of federal commerce power during this era. We then turn to the constitutional challenges to the Civil Rights Act of 1964, which illustrate the breadth of federal power during this period. We close this Part by taking a step back and discussing different possible approaches to the Commerce Clause given the robust deference that characterized post-1937 jurisprudence.

A. A New Era

The first case signaling a doctrinal transformation was *NLRB v. Jones & Laughlin Steel Corporation*, decided in 1937.[86] It involved a constitutional challenge to the National Labor Relations Act (called the NLRA or Wagner Act), which protected the rights of workers to unionize and bargain collectively, and created the National Labor Relations Board (NLRB) to enforce the law. The Court, in an opinion by Chief Justice Charles Evans Hughes, permitted Congress to use its commerce power to regulate production, deeming it "not determinative" that the employees of the steel corporation at issue "were engaged in production."[87] In addition, the Court seemed more interested in the magnitude (as opposed to the nature) of the effects on interstate commerce of "the stoppage of [respondent's manufacturing] operations by industrial strife."[88] That is, the Court

---

85   *See* Jack M. Balkin & Sanford Levinson, *Understanding the Constitutional Revolution*, 87 VA. L. REV. 1045, 1067 (2001).

86   301 U.S. 1 (1937).

87   *Id.* at 40.

88   *Id.* at 41; *see also* NLRB v. Friedman-Harry Marks Clothing Co., 301 U.S. 58 (1937) (upholding application of the NLRA to a clothing manufacturer).

distanced itself from the distinction between direct and indirect effects.[89]

Similarly, in *United States v. Darby*, in 1941, the Court considered a provision of the Fair Labor Standards Act of 1938 (FLSA) that prohibited the interstate shipment of goods produced in violation of the Act's minimum wage and maximum hours standards.[90] As an initial matter, the Court made clear that Congress's motivation for using the Commerce Clause was irrelevant; it could act with a moral motivation, such as opposition to certain labor practices that it deemed unfair.[91] The Court then upheld the Act's ban on interstate shipment of goods produced in violation of the wages and hours provisions, expressly overruling *Hammer v. Daggenhart*.[92] The Court thus allowed Congress to leverage its power to regulate interstate commerce in order to gain control over production. The Court also upheld a provision of the FLSA that directly required compliance with the minimum wage and maximum hours requirements of the Act; it invoked *Jones & Laughlin Steel Corporation* for the proposition that Congress can "regulate intrastate activities where they have a substantial effect on interstate commerce."[93] Abandoning the idea that the Constitution reserves a certain regulatory sphere to the states, the Court described the Tenth Amendment as "stat[ing] but a truism that all is retained which has not been surrendered."[94]

The following year, the Court decided *Wickard v. Filburn*, a case in which the Court upheld congressional regulation of agricultural production.[95] This decision, which sustained federal regulation of wheat grown by farmers for home consumption, has been described as pushing the outer limits of federal commerce power.[96] Farmers across the nation were producing substantially more wheat than consumers wanted to buy, which resulted in a low price for wheat in the interstate market. The Agricultural Adjustment Act of 1938 (AAA) authorized the Secretary of Agriculture to seek to raise the price of wheat in the market, which he did by setting a quota for wheat production and giving each wheat farmer an allotment. The

---

[89]   See *Jones & Laughlin Steel Corp.*, 301 U.S. at 40–43.

[90]   312 U.S. 100 (1941).

[91]   *Id.* at 114.

[92]   *See id.* at 116–17.

[93]   *Id.* at 119.

[94]   *Id.* at 124. *See* U.S. CONST. amend. X ("The powers not delegated to the United States by the Constitution, nor prohibited by it to the States, are reserved to the States respectively, or to the people.").

[95]   317 U.S. 111 (1942).

[96]   *See, e.g.*, United States v. Lopez, 514 U.S. 549, 560 (1995) (describing *Wickard* as "perhaps the most far reaching example of Commerce Clause authority over intrastate activity").

law was challenged by Roscoe Filburn, who owned a small farm in Ohio and who grew more than his allotted quantity; he said he intended to use the amount he produced in excess of his allotment for consumption by his family and livestock.

The Court stated that it was no longer following the distinctions between production and commerce and between direct and indirect effects. "[Q]uestions of the power of Congress," Justice Robert Jackson wrote for the Court, "are not to be decided by reference to any formula which would give controlling force to nomenclature such as 'production' and 'indirect' and foreclose consideration of the actual effects of the activity in question upon interstate commerce."[97] Moreover, even though growing food for one's own family and animals (not for sale) has struck many Americans then and now as local, the Court unanimously upheld the exercise of federal power. In explaining how wheat grown by Filburn could be viewed by Congress as having sufficient effects on interstate commerce, the Court relied upon both a demand side rationale and a supply side rationale.

On the demand side of the interstate market, the Court credited the government's explanation that wheat consumed on the farm by growers constituted more than twenty percent of the national demand for wheat.[98] If farmers like Filburn had not produced what they needed for personal use in excess of their allotment, they would have had to buy it on the market. By not buying such wheat, such producer-consumers depressed the price by cutting demand.[99] Although acknowledging that Filburn's "own contribution to the demand for wheat may be trivial by itself," the Court deemed this fact "not enough to remove him from the scope of federal regulation where, as here, his contribution, taken together with that of many others similarly situated, is far from trivial."[100] "The stimulation of commerce," the Court added, "is a use of the regulatory function quite as definitely as prohibitions or restrictions thereon."[101]

On the supply side, the Court concluded that Congress had a rational basis to fear diversion of allegedly home-consumed wheat into the market once the program proved effective and the price rose.[102] In other words, what farmers said they were doing with wheat they grew in excess of their allotments might end up differing

---

[97]   *Wickard*, 317 U.S. at 120.

[98]   *See id.* at 127.

[99]   *See id.*

[100]   *Id.* at 127–28.

[101]   *Id.* at 128.

[102]   *See id.* ("[B]eing in marketable condition such wheat overhangs the market, and, if induced by rising prices, tends to flow into the market and check price increases.").

from what they were actually doing, especially given imperfect enforcement.

Note two points about the breadth of the Court's reasoning. First, the Court was not requiring the federal government to actually prove the above effects on the market price of wheat; rather, it was sufficient for the government to show in litigation that Congress had a rational basis for concluding that such effects would result. Second, it was constitutionally irrelevant that Filburn's own impact on the price of wheat was trivial; the Court adopted the *aggregation principle*, which focuses on the cumulative effects on interstate commerce of the behavior of all similarly situated people. The Court's doctrine for the next half-century permitted Congress to regulate any activity that Congress could rationally believe had a substantial effect on interstate commerce in the aggregate. Although the Court today has crafted some exceptions to this principle, which we discuss later in this chapter, it still provides the primary constitutional justification for many federal statutes dealing with employment, financial markets, and the environment.

B.   The Constitutionality of the Civil Rights Act of 1964

An illustration of the breadth of federal commerce power during this era is the Court's disposition of constitutional challenges to the Civil Rights Act of 1964 (CRA). This law is one of the most important statutes ever passed by Congress because it broadly prohibited private racial discrimination in much of public life. For instance, Title VII, which prohibits various forms of discrimination in employment, is part of the CRA.

The Civil Rights Movement of the late 1950s and 1960s was one of the most important social movements in American history; it transformed American politics and led to what legal scholars call the nation's Second Reconstruction. During this time, Congress passed the first new civil rights laws since Reconstruction, which ended in 1876, after decades of failed efforts attributable to successful opposition by Southern members of Congress. Title II of the CRA prohibited racial discrimination and segregation in places of "public accommodation," such as privately owned hotels, restaurants, movie theaters, and sports arenas, "if [their] operations affect commerce." The law defined the "affect commerce" requirement (what lawyers call a jurisdictional trigger) more precisely—for example, hotels with more than five rooms, and restaurants offering service to interstate travelers or where a "substantial portion" of the food served "has moved in commerce."[103]

---

[103]   These provisions are reproduced in the Appendix to the Court's opinion in *Heart of Atlanta Motel, Inc. v. United States*, 379 U.S. 241 (1964).

When Congress considered banning racial discrimination in public accommodations in the early 1960s, it had to decide whether to rely primarily on the Commerce Clause or on its authority, under Section 5 of the Fourteenth Amendment, to "enforce" the equality right conferred in Section One of the amendment.[104] (We will study this "hook" for federal civil rights legislation in Chapter 13.) After much debate in Congress and within the administration of President John F. Kennedy about the soundest source of congressional authority for the statute, Congress elected to rely primarily on its authority to regulate interstate commerce, even though its motivation was moral opposition to racism, not facilitation of interstate commerce. (We will learn why Congress chose to emphasize the Commerce Clause in Chapter 13; the reason had to do not only with the *Darby* Court's licensing of moral motivations under the commerce power, but also with a Supreme Court decision from 1883 that prohibited Section 5 statutes regulating private action, as opposed to "state action.")[105]

Two test cases—decided the same day—were immediately filed challenging the power of Congress to pass the law under the Commerce Clause. The first was *Heart of Atlanta Motel, Inc. v. United States*, which involved an Atlanta motel that refused to accommodate African Americans.[106] It was accessible to interstate highways, had 216 rooms, and 75 percent of its guests came from out of state. The second case was *Katzenbach v. McClung*, which involved a family-owned restaurant named Ollie's Barbecue in Birmingham, Alabama, with a seating capacity of 220 located on a state highway eleven blocks from an interstate highway.[107] Of the roughly $150,000 in food procured by the restaurant in the previous year, almost half was meat from a local supplier who had procured it from outside the state. In both cases, the Court unanimously upheld application of the law under the commerce power.[108]

The Court had little difficulty concluding that Congress rationally could have concluded that racial discrimination in places of public accommodation affects interstate commerce. "[V]oluminous testimony" before Congress, the Court stated, "presents overwhelming evidence that discrimination by hotels and motels impedes interstate travel."[109] Racial discrimination by hotels and

---

[104]   U.S. CONST. amend. XIV, § 5.

[105]   The Civil Rights Cases, 109 U.S. 3 (1883).

[106]   379 U.S. 241 (1964).

[107]   379 U.S. 294 (1964).

[108]   The Court did not decide the validity of the law under Section 5 of the Fourteenth Amendment, but two Justices—William Douglas and Arthur Goldberg—wrote separately that they would have also sustained the law under Section 5.

[109]   *Heart of Atlanta Motel, Inc.*, 379 U.S. at 253.

motels meant, among other things, that African Americans and other racial minorities were less likely to travel interstate for work or vacation—both of which characteristically involve the purchase of good and services—because they could not be assured of a place to stay, of gas for their cars, and of food to eat.[110]

As for Ollie's Barbecue, the Court looked at the effects on interstate commerce of racial discrimination by restaurants generally. It again credited testimony before Congress, which "afforded ample basis for the conclusion that established restaurants in such areas sold less interstate goods because of the discrimination, that interstate travel was obstructed directly by it, that business in general suffered and that many new businesses refrained from establishing there as a result of it."[111] The Court did not care whether, given the intensity of white racism in certain parts of the country, particular restaurants would actually lose business if they were forced to desegregate; the Justices did not demand empirical proof regarding positive or negative impacts on the amount of interstate commerce. In the Court's view, the Constitution was satisfied because Congress rationally could have concluded that racial discrimination at restaurants or other places of public accommodation discouraged interstate travel or interstate commerce. Indeed, in *Daniel v. Paul*, in 1969, the Court held that the Civil Rights Act could validly be applied to a snack bar at a private park, thereby requiring the park to desegregate.[112]

Thus, it is fair to ask whether the Court was prepared to hold any conduct beyond the scope of federal commerce power. If not, it is also fair to ask whether the Court's test can be reconciled with the idea of a national government of limited, enumerated powers. If the Court went too far in one direction during the Republican Era, perhaps the Court went too far in the other direction during the post-New Deal period.

VI. The Current Era

The current constitutional law of the Commerce Clause dates to the 1990s. To understand contemporary doctrine, it is illuminating to begin with what preceded it: significant changes in constitutional politics during the 1980s.

---

[110] The *Negro Travelers' Green Book*, published from 1936 through 1966, listed businesses willing to offer gas, food, lodging, and other goods and services to African Americans traveling interstate. *See The Green Book*, NEW YORK PUBLIC LIBRARY DIGITAL COLLECTIONS, https://digitalcollections.nypl.org/collections/the-green-book#/?tab=about.

[111] Katzenbach v. McClung, 379 U.S. 294, 300 (1964).

[112] 395 U.S. 298 (1969).

A.   Changes in Constitutional Politics

National politics after 1937 revolved around liberalism and moderate conservative reactions to liberalism. This era ended with the election of Ronald Reagan as President in the pivotal election of 1980. The primary goal of the conservative political movement known as the "Reagan Revolution" was not seek to re-impose pre-New Deal understandings of constitutional law and politics; instead, it sought to reverse political, economic, social, and legal developments of the 1960s and 1970s. Like liberal Democrats before then, so-called Reagan Republicans formed a coalition of partially shared and partially conflicting interests and convictions. They included, among other groups, "establishment" Republicans, economic libertarians, social and religious conservatives, Cold War hawks on matters of national security, and, most relevant here, states' rights "federalists" (who, unlike the Federalists of the Founding Era, emphasized limits on federal power and a return of regulatory authority to the states).[113]

Just as FDR had articulated a constitutional vision and not just a list of policy proposals, so did Reagan. At the heart of Reagan's vision was a distrust of government regulations in general and regulation by the federal government in particular. In his First Inaugural Address in 1981, Reagan declared that "[i]n this present crisis, government is not the solution to our problem; government is the problem."[114] He also announced his "intention to curb the size and influence of the Federal establishment and to demand recognition of the distinction between the powers granted to the Federal Government and those reserved to the States or to the people."[115] "All of us need to be reminded," he said, echoing Maryland's argument in *McCulloch*, "that the Federal Government did not create the States; the States created the Federal Government."[116] Likewise, in his 1981 *Remarks in Atlanta, Georgia, at the Annual Convention of the National Conference of State Legislatures*, Reagan stated that his "administration is committed heart and soul to the broad principles of American federalism."[117]

---

[113]   *See* HOWARD GILLMAN, MARK A. GRABER, & KEITH E. WHITTINGTON, AMERICAN CONSTITUTIONALISM, VOLUME I: STRUCTURES OF GOVERNMENT 538 (2nd ed. 2017).

[114]   Ronald Reagan, First Inaugural Address (Jan. 20, 1981), The Avalon Project, Yale Law School, http://avalon.law.yale.edu/20th_century/reagan1.asp.

[115]   *Id.*

[116]   *Id.*

[117]   Ronald Reagan, *Remarks in Atlanta, Georgia, at the Annual Convention of the National Conference of State Legislatures* (July 30, 1981), The American Presidency Project, https://www.presidency.ucsb.edu/documents/remarks-atlanta-georgia-the-annual-convention-the-national-conference-state-legislatures.

In a variety of ways, Reagan Republicans unsettled a seemingly closed debate about the constitutional scope of federal powers. In addition to presidential rhetoric (as illustrated above), the Reagan Administration used taxing, spending, and regulatory policy; litigation aimed at persuading the Supreme Court to revisit past decisions that were contrary to the Reagan vision; and judicial appointments. Again like FDR before him, Reagan sought to nominate judges and Justices who shared his constitutional commitments on matters that were most important to him. So did his Vice President and successor, George H. W. Bush, who won the Presidency in 1988. Twelve years of Republican control of the Presidency (1980–1992) produced decisive change on the Supreme Court. Reagan appointed Sandra Day O'Connor (the first woman to serve on the Court) and Antonin Scalia, and he elevated William Rehnquist to Chief Justice. Reagan's nomination of the strong conservative Robert Bork was rejected by a Democratic Senate, but the Senate did confirm the moderate conservative Anthony Kennedy. The first President Bush successfully nominated Clarence Thomas, a very conservative jurist, as well as David Souter, who turned out to be more liberal than conservatives had hoped.

These labels are an oversimplification since there are different kinds of conservatives and liberals. In the context of constitutional disagreements over federalism, conservatives tend to emphasize judicially enforceable constitutional limits on federal power and so are called "federalists," whereas liberals tend to defend federal power and so are called "nationalists." This terminology can be confusing since the original Federalists in the Founding era were nationalists and the states' rights view was represented by Anti-Federalists.

With a new "federalist" majority consisting of Rehnquist, O'Connor, Scalia, Kennedy, and Thomas, the Court shifted back to a view of federalism as imposing judicially enforceable constitutional limits on congressional power. As we will now discuss, the Court narrowed the scope of the Commerce Clause somewhat, and it articulated a structural principle of federalism (symbolized by the Tenth Amendment) to further limit federal commerce power to some extent. Yet, much of the liberal legislation from the New Deal through the 1970s remained fundamentally untouched by this counter-reaction, a reflection of how much it had become part of the fabric of society. Once again, one can see how the American constitutional system typically works—how changes in constitutional politics produce, as well as resist, changes in constitutional law.

B. Changes in Commerce Clause Doctrine

From 1937 to 1995, the Court held no federal law to be beyond the scope of federal commerce power notwithstanding robust use of the Commerce Clause and other federal powers to create a modern regulatory state. In 1995, this period came to an abrupt end, when the Court handed down *United States v. Lopez*, which invalidated the federal Gun Free School Zones Act of 1990 (GFSZA) as beyond the scope of Congress's commerce power.[118] The law prohibited "any individual knowingly to possess a firearm at a place that the individual knows, or has reasonable cause to believe, is a school zone."[119] The statute defined a school zone as "in, or on the grounds of, a public, parochial or private school" or "within a distance of 1,000 feet from the grounds of a public, parochial or private school."[120] Afonso Lopez, a high school senior in San Antonio, Texas, was indicted under the GFSZA for carrying a handgun to his high school. He defended against his criminal prosecution by arguing that the law was beyond the scope of the Commerce Clause.

In his majority opinion, which was joined by Justices O'Connor, Scalia, Kennedy, and Thomas, Chief Justice Rehnquist began with "first principles. The Constitution creates a Federal Government of enumerated powers."[121] After canvassing the history of the Court's Commerce Clause decisions,[122] he identified three categories of activity that Congress is permitted to regulate using the Commerce Clause. First, he wrote, Congress can regulate the channels of interstate commerce—for example, highways and navigable waters.[123] Second, Rehnquist wrote, Congress can regulate the instrumentalities of interstate commerce (for example, railroads, vehicles, boats, and planes), which includes persons or things in interstate commerce.[124] Third, Rehnquist wrote, Congress can regulate activities that substantially affect interstate commerce.[125] *Lopez* fell within the third category, as have almost all of the cases decided by the Rehnquist or Roberts Court. This is no coincidence; the conservative Justices have been most concerned about the potential for statutes defended as falling within this category to obliterate the idea of a national government of limited, enumerated powers. For example, Chief Justice Rehnquist cited *Heart of Atlanta Motel, Inc. v. United States*,[126] which upheld the federal prohibition on racial discrimination by motels and hotels, as an example of a channels case,[127] but as we have seen, the Court in this decision

---

[118]   514 U.S. 549 (1995).

[119]   18 U.S.C. § 922(q)(1)(A).

[120]   18 U.S.C. § 921(a)(25).

[121]   *Lopez*, 514 U.S. at 552.

[122]   *See id.* at 553–58.

[123]   *See id.* at 558.

[124]   *See id.*

[125]   *See id.* at 558–59.

[126]   379 U.S. 241 (1964).

[127]   *See Lopez*, 514 U.S. at 558.

reasoned in terms of the effects of such discrimination on interstate commerce.

In defending the statute, the federal government argued that the presence of firearms in school zones substantially affect interstate commerce in two ways. First, the government contended, firearms in and around schools contribute to violent crimes in and around schools, and the costs of such crimes are spread around the country both by affecting the costs of insurance and by making it less likely that people will travel interstate to areas beset by gun violence.[128] Second, the government argued, guns and associated violence in schools affect the learning that occurs in schools, thereby impacting national economic productivity given the role of education in training people for participation in the modern American economy.[129]

Chief Justice Rehnquist rejected these arguments and struck down the statute. In supporting this conclusion, the Chief Justice did not actually refute the government's empirical assertions that guns near schools substantially affect interstate commerce in the aggregate. Instead, he arguably changed the subject in two ways. First, he stressed that the GFSZA "is a criminal statute that by its terms has nothing to do with 'commerce' or any sort of economic enterprise, however broadly one might define those terms."[130] In his view, the statute regulated noneconomic activity—specifically, possession of a handgun in a school zone. So the Court appeared to make a formal question of categorization—whether the activity regulated by Congress was economic in nature—dispositive of the ostensibly functional question of whether there were substantial effects on interstate commerce.

The Court indicated that it would apply this economic/noneconomic characterization to the general class of regulated activity at issue. The majority opinion embraced—and distinguished—*Wickard* by stating that gun possession in school zones, unlike the quota on wheat production challenged in *Wickard*, was "not an essential part of a larger regulation of economic activity, in which the regulatory scheme could be undercut unless the intrastate activity were regulated."[131] Chief Justice Rehnquist likely offered this clarification in order to account for all of the Court's post-1937 decisions and to avoid invalidating many modern federal laws.

The second way in which Chief Justice Rehnquist arguably changed the subject was by "paus[ing] to consider the implications of the Government's arguments," which were essentially that if

---

[128]   *See id.* at 563–64.

[129]   *See id.* at 564.

[130]   *Id.* at 561.

[131]   *Id.*

Congress may regulate gun possession in schools, then Congress may regulate anything.[132] Specifically, Rehnquist rejected the government's rationales because he could not "perceive [in them] any limitation on federal power, even in areas such as criminal law enforcement or education where States historically have been sovereign."[133] This response by the majority bears similarities to the Court's justifications for imposing constitutional limits on the scope of federal power during the Republican Era.

Likewise, Justice Kennedy, joined by Justice O'Connor, wrote in a concurring opinion that, "unlike the earlier cases to come before the Court here neither the actors nor their conduct has a commercial character, and neither the purposes nor the design of the statute has an evident commercial nexus."[134] While noting that "[i]n a sense any conduct in this interdependent world of ours has an ultimate commercial origin or consequence," he stressed that "we have not yet said the commerce power may reach so far."[135] Kennedy also deemed it constitutionally significant that "education is a traditional concern of the States."[136]

In contrast to the tone of the Kennedy concurrence, which emphasized how important a stable Commerce Clause jurisprudence was for the Court and the country,[137] Justice Thomas wrote a concurring opinion for himself alone in which he concluded that the majority in *Lopez* had not gone far enough.[138] As a textual and originalist matter, in Justice Thomas's view, "commerce" means "selling, buying, and bartering, as well as transporting for these purposes."[139] His view of the scope of the Commerce Clause is extremely restrictive; he rejects the substantial effects test in its entirety.[140]

There were three dissents in *Lopez*. Justice John Paul Stevens asserted that "[g]uns are both articles of commerce and articles that can be used to restrain commerce."[141] Justice Souter expressed the concern that the Court might be returning to the discredited and abandoned pre-1937 jurisprudence; he "look[ed] at history's sequence

---

[132]   *Id.* at 564.

[133]   *Id.*

[134]   *Id.* at 580 (Kennedy, J., concurring).

[135]   *Id.*

[136]   *Id.*

[137]   *See id.* at 574 ("[T]he Court as an institution and the legal system as a whole have an immense stake in the stability of our Commerce Clause jurisprudence as it has evolved to this point.").

[138]   *Id.* at 584 (Thomas, J., concurring).

[139]   *Id.* at 585.

[140]   *See supra* note 13 and accompanying text (discussing the trade theory).

[141]   *Id.* at 602 (Stevens, J., dissenting).

... to show how today's decision tugs the Court off course, leading it to suggest opportunities for further developments that would be at odds with the rule of restraint to which the Court still wisely states adherence."[142] Justice Stephen Breyer, joined by Justices Stevens, Souter, and Ruth Bader Ginsburg, authored the primary dissent. He marshaled empirical evidence that the presence of firearms in school zones substantially affects interstate commerce.[143] The strength of the Breyer dissent relative to the majority opinion was that it actually applied the substantial effects test and showed why it was satisfied. The relative weakness of the Breyer dissent was its unsupported assertion that not every federal law imaginable would pass this test.[144] Like the Solicitor General at oral argument, Justice Breyer did not offer examples of even hypothetical federal laws that would flunk this test.[145]

Five years later, the Court demonstrated that *Lopez* was not merely—or, at least, entirely[146]—symbolic. Congress passed the Federal Violence Against Women Act of 1994 (VAWA), among other reasons, to combat gender discrimination in the administration of state and local criminal justice systems. Unlike the GFSZA, VAWA contains extensive legislative findings; Congress found that gender-motivated violence across the country imposes billions of dollars in costs each year and restricts women's freedom of travel.[147] Reflecting Congress's concern that state police, prosecutors, judges, and juries were failing to take seriously crimes of violence against women (including domestic violence and sexual assaults), one provision of the law authorized victims of gender-motivated violence to sue their assailants for money damages in federal court.[148]

United States v. Morrison concerned the constitutionality of this civil damages provision; the question presented was whether the damages remedy fell within the scope of congressional authority under either the Commerce Clause or Section 5 of the Fourteenth

---

[142]   *Id.* at 604 (Souter, J., dissenting).

[143]   *See id.* at 618–24 (Breyer, J., dissenting).

[144]   *See id.* at 624.

[145]   For a discussion (with quotations) of this dynamic during the oral argument in *Lopez*, see Neil S. Siegel, *Four Constitutional Limits that the Minimum Coverage Provision Respects*, 27 CONST. COMMENT. 591, 593–94 (2011).

[146]   In late 1996, Congress enacted a new version of the GFSZA, with factual findings and a narrower scope. Now the law applies only if the firearm in question "has moved in or ... otherwise affects interstate or foreign commerce." 18 U.S.C. § 922(q)(2)(A) (2012). The Court has shown no interest in reviewing the constitutionality of this statute, even though in today's economy it is difficult to imagine a firearm or a component of a firearm that has not moved in interstate commerce.

[147]   *See* S. Rep. No. 103–138, at 41, 54 (1993).

[148]   42 U.S.C. § 13981.

Amendment.[149] The case arose when Christy Brzonkala sought money damages in federal court from two former football players at Virginia Polytechnic Institute, whom she alleged had raped her when she was a freshman. Neither football player was criminally prosecuted by Virginia authorities or ultimately punished by the university.[150]

Splitting five to four the same way as in *Lopez*, the Court invalidated the damages remedy as beyond the scope of federal power under both provisions.[151] In analyzing the Commerce Clause, Chief Justice Rehnquist again emphasized for the Court that Congress was regulating noneconomic activity traditionally regulated by the states: "Gender-motivated crimes of violence are not, in any sense of the phrase, economic activity."[152] Rehnquist declined to impose "a categorical rule against aggregating the effects of any noneconomic activity in order to decide these cases," but he nonetheless insisted that "thus far in our Nation's history our cases have upheld Commerce Clause regulation of intrastate activity only where that activity is economic in nature."[153]

The Court rejected the government's argument that violence against women substantially affects interstate commerce, despite a voluminous legislative history documenting Congress's judgment to this effect.[154] According to the Chief Justice, "Congress' findings are substantially weakened by the fact that they rely so heavily on a method of reasoning that we have already rejected as unworkable if we are to maintain the Constitution's enumeration of powers."[155] Specifically, such reasoning "seeks to follow the but-for causal chain from the initial occurrence of violent crime (the suppression of which has always been the prime object of the States' police power) to every attenuated effect upon interstate commerce."[156]

The Chief Justice warned that the government's reasoning, if accepted, "would allow Congress to regulate any crime as long as the nationwide, aggregated impact of that crime has substantial effects on employment, production, transit, or consumption."[157] This rationale could "be applied equally as well to family law and other

---

[149]   529 U.S. 598 (2000).

[150]   *See id.* at 602–04.

[151]   See *infra* Chapter 13 for discussion of the Court's holding that the provision at issue was beyond the scope of congressional power under Section Five of the Fourteenth Amendment.

[152]   *Morrison*, 529 U.S. at 613.

[153]   *Id.*

[154]   *See id.* at 614.

[155]   *Id.* at 615.

[156]   *Id.*

[157]   *Id.*

areas of traditional state regulation since the aggregate effect of marriage, divorce, and childrearing on the national economy is undoubtedly significant."[158] Again, the Court did not actually refute the government's empirical assertions. Instead, it denied "that Congress may regulate noneconomic, violent criminal conduct based solely on that conduct's aggregate effect on interstate commerce."[159] "The Constitution," Rehnquist insisted, "requires a distinction between what is truly national and what is truly local."[160]

In a concurring opinion, Justice Thomas again went further than the rest of the majority by rejecting the substantial effects test and calling upon the Court to "replace[ ] its existing Commerce Clause jurisprudence with a standard more consistent with the original understanding."[161] In a dissent joined by Justices Stevens, Ginsburg, and Breyer, Justice Souter emphasized the need for judicial deference to congressional findings regarding the effects of regulated activities on interstate commerce.[162] Here, he noted, Congress found that violence against women has a substantial effect on the American economy, and "the sufficiency of the evidence before Congress to provide a rational basis for the finding cannot seriously be questioned."[163]

The Court's next major Commerce Clause decision was *Gonzales v. Raich*, in 2005.[164] The case arose when California created a medical exception to its marijuana laws and the administration of President George W. Bush sought to prohibit the practice of prescribing marijuana for medicinal use, arguing that California's law was preempted by federal drug law, the Controlled Substances Act (CSA). Two patients, who were prescribed marijuana to alleviate their pain caused by severe medical problems, sued for an injunction prohibiting enforcement of the CSA against them and a declaration that it was unconstitutional as applied to them.[165]

The Court held by a vote of six to three that the Commerce Clause allows Congress to prohibit the local cultivation and use of marijuana in compliance with state law authorizing such use.[166] Justices Scalia and Kennedy joined the four dissenters from *Lopez* and *Morrison* to uphold the exercise of federal power in this case.

---

[158]   *Id.* at 615–16.

[159]   *Id.* at 617.

[160]   *Id.*

[161]   *Id.* at 627 (Thomas, J., concurring).

[162]   *See id.* at 628 (Souter, J., dissenting).

[163]   *Id.* at 634.

[164]   545 U.S. 1 (2005).

[165]   *See id.* at 5–8. Thus, *Raich* involved what lawyers call an "as-applied challenge," as opposed to the "facial challenge" at issue in *Lopez* and *Morrison*.

[166]   *See id.* at 22.

Writing for five Justices, Justice Stevens relied upon *Wickard*, which he read as "establish[ing] that Congress can regulate purely intrastate activity that is not itself 'commercial,' in that it is not produced for sale, if it concludes that failure to regulate that class of activity would undercut the regulation of the interstate market in that commodity."[167] Justice Stevens saw "striking" similarities between *Raich* and *Wickard*: Congress could have rationally concluded that leaving home-consumed wheat or marijuana outside the federal regulatory scheme would affect interstate price and market conditions, particularly through unlawful acts of diversion of the commodity into the market.[168]

Justice Scalia concurred in the judgment, relying upon the Necessary and Proper Clause instead of the Commerce Clause standing alone. In his view, "Congress may regulate even noneconomic local activity if that regulation is a necessary part of a more general regulation of interstate commerce."[169] As a practical matter, nothing turns on whether one adopts the majority's broad view of the commerce power, which obviates the need to rely upon the Necessary and Proper Clause, or Scalia's narrower view of the Commerce Clause, which caused him to invoke the Necessary and Proper Clause in support of federal power.

The six-Justice majority in *Raich* maintained continuity with the Court's account of *Wickard* in *Lopez* by applying its economic/noneconomic characterization to the general class of activity at issue.[170] Under the Court's doctrine, the general class of activity must be economic in order to fall within the scope of federal commerce power, but some particular instances within the class may be noneconomic. In other words, regulation may encompass activity that the Court deems noneconomic if Congress rationally could conclude that it is an essential part of a general class of activity that the Court deems economic. For example, production of marijuana or wheat generally is an economic activity and thus is subject to regulation by Congress under its commerce power. According to the Court, however, congressional regulation of this general activity can also cover marijuana or wheat grown and consumed at home, which may be noneconomic.

Justice O'Connor penned the main dissent, which was joined by Chief Justice Rehnquist and Justice Thomas. In her view, the Court was being excessively deferential to the federal government, which offered no actual proof of diversion or other substantial effects on

---

[167]   *Id.* at 18.

[168]   *Id.* at 18–19.

[169]   *Id.* at 37 (Scalia, J., concurring in the judgment).

[170]   *See id.*; *see id.* at 22 (majority opinion).

interstate commerce.[171] She also argued that California's regulatory regime (and similar regimes in other states) may well isolate activities related to medical marijuana from the illegal market.[172]

C. Applying Current Commerce Clause Doctrine

The brilliance of the Court's opinion in *Lopez* as a matter of legal craft is that its distinction between economic and noneconomic activity enabled it to limit the scope of the Commerce Clause without having to overrule any post-1937 precedents such as *Wickard* or to dismantle the modern regulatory state. In conformity with the specific outcomes of prior cases (although not their permissive doctrinal tests), the Court's modern Commerce Clause jurisprudence distinguishes situations in which Congress wants to regulate a general class of activity that the Court regards as economic (e.g., *Wickard* and *Raich*) from situations in which Congress wants to regulate a general class of activity that the Court regards as noneconomic (e.g., *Lopez* and *Morrison*).

Also counting in favor of the Court's distinction between economic and noneconomic activity is that it is potentially administrable by courts. It requires judges to distinguish conduct in and around markets from conduct outside of markets. Judges arguably can articulate this distinction in a rough-and-ready way even if legal scholars and economists might be skeptical of the distinction for reasons articulated below.

There are analytical problems, however, with applying the Court's distinction between economic and noneconomic activity. First, in order to determine whether the regulated activity is economic in nature, one first needs to determine what the regulated activity is. And the (at least partially) rhetorical act of characterizing the regulated activity can determine the outcome. For example, the Court in *Lopez* viewed the regulated activity as possessing a firearm in a school zone, but the activity could also plausibly be characterized as possessing a firearm near a sensitive workplace given all of the teachers, administrators, secretaries, janitors, etc., who are employed in schools. Meanwhile, in *Raich*, to the extent the case involved the federal ban on possession of marijuana, the regulated activity could be seen as noneconomic: the private possession and use of marijuana.

Second, it may not always be clear how one is to determine whether the regulated activity is economic or non-economic. For example, one could have a nice debate over whether marriage is an

---

[171]   *See id.* at 51–57 (O'Connor, J., joined by Rehnquist, C.J., and Thomas, J., dissenting).

[172]   *See id.* at 53, 55.

economic activity. The Court almost certainly would not allow Congress to use its commerce power to take the regulation of civil marriage away from the states, yet financial considerations are a reason why many people do or do not marry or divorce, and an individual's marital status can have significant tax and other financial consequences. And if marriage is noneconomic, what about payments for alimony or child support?

Third, determining the general class of regulated activity can pose significant difficulties. Unless the Court is prepared to defer to Congress's reasonable understanding of the general class of activity, as it did in *Wickard* and *Raich*, it is not clear how judges can determine in a non-resulted-oriented way the level of abstraction at which to define the class of activity.[173]

Indeed, one wonders whether the Court in these cases was determining the level of abstraction at which to define the general class of regulated activity based upon its sense of whether the problem being targeted by Congress was interstate in scope. Just as no state acting individually could succeed in raising the price of wheat on the interstate market, so Congress could (more than) rationally believe that medical marijuana grown and used in California would make it more difficult for neighboring states to enforce their drug laws given that medical marijuana is indistinguishable from recreational marijuana and Americans are free to move interstate.[174] By contrast, it was far less obvious that there was a collective action problem in *Lopez* given that how one state regulates guns in schools does not seem to affect how other states regulate guns in schools—except, perhaps, in a long-term, attenuated way. (By contrast, *Morrison* is a closer Commerce Clause case because of the evidence in the congressional record that gender-motivated violence was dissuading women from traveling interstate.)

On this interpretation, the Court's formal distinction between economic and noneconomic activity may actually be a proxy for the functional distinction between interstate and intrastate activity. Likewise, the Court's reference in *Lopez* to "a larger regulation of economic activity" could be translated as referring to "a larger regulation of interstate activity."[175] To be clear, the Court has never

---

[173]   Most recently, the Court did not defer to Congress's understanding of the general class of activity. See *NFIB v. Sebelius*, 567 U.S. 519 (2012), which is discussed in the next section.

[174]   As more states have partially or completely legalized marijuana use in recent years, conflicts between states over potential spillover effects have increased. *See, e.g.,* Joe Duggan, *Jon Bruning Files Lawsuit over Colorado's Legalization of Marijuana*, OMAHA WORLD-HERALD (Dec. 18, 2014), http://www.omaha.com/news/nebraska/jon-bruning-files-lawsuit-over-colorado-s-legalization-of-marijuana/article_89801fb6-86ef-11e4-b2e8-9bf0786ca418.html.

[175]   *See* BREST ET AL., *supra* note 26, at 723 (suggesting this substitution).

said as much, and the Court has rejected collective-action reasoning in two cases discussed below. But it is striking how similar are the outcomes of most of the recent Commerce Clause cases to what a functional federalism perspective would commend. Yet, there are exceptions, as we will see below.

D.   The Constitutionality of the "Individual Mandate"

The assertion that Congress lacked authority under the Commerce Clause to require financially able individuals to purchase health insurance was initially regarded as implausible in the judgment of most experts, including a good number of prominent legal conservatives. This was because Congress was regulating one-sixth of the American economy, which clearly qualified as "economic" under *Lopez* and *Morrison.* Over the course of only two years, however, professional judgments about the plausibility of the argument changed significantly and it ultimately attracted five votes on the Supreme Court. The Republican Party played a pivotal role in the expediting the processes of constitutional change, which often require decades of work by social movements.[176]

The Patient Protection and Affordable Care Act of 2010 (ACA) constituted "the biggest expansion of the social safety net in more than four decades, providing greater economic security to millions of poor and working-class families."[177] On par with Social Security, Medicare, and Medicaid, the ACA sought to ameliorate the problem of fifty million Americans who lacked health insurance[178]—and thus access to affordable healthcare—by achieving near-universal health insurance coverage. Barely passed, without a single Republican vote in Congress, the ACA triggered intense opposition, including a lawsuit by 26 states with Republican governors or attorneys general, several individuals, and a private business organization. Opponents focused on a key provision of the law, the minimum coverage provision, which they dubbed the "individual mandate." This provision required most Americans to purchase a minimum level of health insurance coverage required by the ACA; many of those who did not would have to pay the Internal Revenue Service a sum of

---

[176]   *See* Jack M. Balkin, *From Off the Wall to On the Wall: How the Mandate Challenge Went Mainstream*, THE ATLANTIC, June 4, 2012, https://www.theatlantic.com/national/archive/2012/06/from-off-the-wall-to-on-the-wall-how-the-mandate-challenge-went-mainstream/258040/.

[177]   THE STAFF OF THE WASHINGTON POST, LANDMARK: THE INSIDE STORY OF AMERICA'S NEW HEALTH-CARE LAW AND WHAT IT MEANS FOR US ALL 66–68 (2010).

[178]   According to the U.S. Census Bureau, around 19 percent of the nonelderly population, or roughly fifty million people, lacked health insurance in 2009. U.S. CENSUS BUREAU, U.S. DEP'T OF COMMERCE, INCOME, POVERTY, AND HEALTH INSURANCE COVERAGE IN THE UNITED STATES: 2009, at 23, Table 8.

money each year for foregoing insurance.[179] The plaintiffs argued first and foremost that this provision was beyond the scope of Congress's power under the Commerce Clause. In their view, the individual mandate did not "regulate" commerce;[180] rather, the mandate *required* commerce by compelling individuals to purchase a product (health insurance) from a third party (a health insurance company).[181]

In *NFIB v. Sebelius*, five Justices agreed with the opponents of the ACA that the Commerce Clause did not support the individual mandate.[182] Rejecting the Commerce Clause analysis offered by the federal government, Chief Justice John Roberts wrote that "[a]s expansive as our cases construing the scope of the commerce power have been, they all have one thing in common: They uniformly describe the power as reaching 'activity.' It is nearly impossible to avoid the word when quoting them."[183] He reasoned that the individual mandate "does not regulate existing commercial activity"; rather, it "compels individuals to *become* active in commerce by purchasing a product, on the ground that their failure to do so affects interstate commerce."[184] He then expressed concern about virtually unlimited federal power, a concern that he viewed as animating the distinction between regulating activity and inactivity: "Construing the Commerce Clause to permit Congress to regulate individuals precisely *because* they are doing nothing would open a new and potentially vast domain to congressional authority."[185]

Justice Ginsburg, joined by Justices Breyer, Sonia Sotomayor, and Elena Kagan, disagreed that the individual mandate regulated inactivity.[186] Ginsburg noted that "more than 60% of those without insurance visit a hospital or doctor's office each year," and that "[n]early 90% will within five years."[187] As a result, she continued, "[a]n uninsured's consumption of health care is . . . quite proximate: It is virtually certain to occur in the next five years and more likely

---

[179]   We speak about the individual mandate in the past tense because in 2018 a Republican Congress and President effectively repealed it. *See, e.g.*, Joel Dodge, *Can Obamacare Survive Without the Individual Mandate?*, NEW REPUBLIC (Jan. 3, 2018), https://newrepublic.com/article/146462/can-obamacare-survive-without-individual-mandate.

[180]   U.S. CONST. art. I, § 8, cl. 3.

[181]   *See, e.g.*, Randy E. Barnett, *Commandeering the People: Why the Individual Health Insurance Mandate is Unconstitutional*, 5 N.Y.U. J.L. & LIBERTY 581 (2010).

[182]   *See* 567 U.S. 519, 558 (2012) (opinion of Roberts, C.J.); *id.* at 657 (Scalia, Kennedy, Thomas, & Alito, JJ., dissenting).

[183]   *Id.* at 551 (opinion of Roberts, C.J.).

[184]   *Id.* at 552.

[185]   *Id.*

[186]   *See NFIB*, 567 U.S. at 589, 605–09 (Ginsburg, J., concurring in part, concurring in judgment in part, and dissenting in part).

[187]   *Id.* at 605.

than not to occur this year."[188] In order to pay for this consumption of health care, she reasoned, Americans either buy health insurance or they go without insurance and make a "decision to self-insure," which "is an economic act with the requisite connection to interstate commerce."[189] There was a sufficient connection to interstate commerce, in her view, because the inability of those without insurance "to pay for a significant portion" of the health care they consume each year "drives up market prices, foists costs on other consumers, and reduces market efficiency and stability."[190] She underscored Congress's estimation that the cost of providing uncompensated care to the uninsured in hospital emergency rooms " 'increases family [insurance] premiums by on average over $1,000 per year.' "[191]

The distinction developed in constitutional politics and embraced by the Court between activity and inactivity—like the distinction between acts and omissions in law more generally—is a tricky one. Inactivity can be re-described as activity (and vice versa) depending upon how broadly one defines the relevant market or extends the time horizon.[192] In *NFIB*, for example, the uninsured as a general class were at least temporarily inactive in the health insurance market but were likely active in the health care market. They may have been inactive in the health care market in the present moment but they were likely active if one projects one or five years into the future. The key question of constitutional law, therefore, is whether the Court is prepared to defer to reasonable judgments by Congress with respect to these issues of market definition and time horizon. In *Wickard* and *Raich*, the Court deferred to Congress's relatively broad definitions of the relevant market and time horizon: wheat produced for home consumption and marijuana produced and used for medicinal purposes in California were not currently being diverted to the interstate market, but the Court deferred to Congress's reasonable judgment about such diversion in the not-too-distant future. By contrast, five Justices in *NFIB* refused to defer to Congress's focus on the healthcare market (anticipated participation in which is why people purchase health insurance) and its regulatory concerns beyond the present moment.

There is another important way in which *Wickard* and *Raich* are in tension with *NFIB*. Whereas a functional analysis of collective action problems facing the states helps justify the outcomes in

---

[188]   *Id.* at 605–06.

[189]   *Id.* at 615; *see also id.* at 593–94, 603–04.

[190]   *Id.* at 603.

[191]   *Id.* at 593 (quoting 42 U.S.C. § 18091(2)(F) (2006 ed., Supp. IV)).

[192]   *See generally* Mark Kelman, *Interpretive Construction in the Substantive Criminal Law*, 33 STAN. L. REV. 591 (1981).

Wickard and *Raich*, collective action reasoning likely supports Justice Ginsburg's analysis in dissent in *NFIB*.[193] Ginsburg seems correct that "[s]tates cannot resolve the problem of the uninsured on their own" and "Congress's intervention was needed to overcome this collective-action impasse."[194] Only Massachusetts had tried to accomplish what the ACA sought to achieve at the time Congress passed the law, and Ginsburg quoted amicus briefs noting that emergency rooms in Massachusetts were serving thousands of uninsured, out-of-state residents, amounting to millions of dollars in costs each year.[195]

Accordingly, *NFIB* illustrates that there are limits on the extent to which the modern Court is prepared to endorse functional, collective action reasoning in the face of formal arguments for limiting federal power. So do the decisions articulating the anti-commandeering principle. We turn to them now.

E.   The Anti-Commandeering Principle

The modern Court has sought to impose additional federalism-based limits on federal regulation of state and local governments. After an initial attempt at doing so failed, the Court developed a different approach that has endured. These limits are sometimes described as being grounded in the Tenth Amendment.[196] The text of the Tenth Amendment, however, literally states what would be true even without the Tenth Amendment: the federal government is one of limited, enumerated powers, and the states are governments of general, plenary powers. Accordingly, the federalism-based limits discussed below are best understood to be grounded in the constitutional structure, not the text. They are thought to supplement the constitutional text in order to protect the regulatory autonomy of the states from certain forms of interference by the federal government.

The Court's first attempt came in its decision in *National League of Cities v. Usery*,[197] which was overruled less than a decade later after being distinguished into oblivion. Recall that in *United States v. Darby*, the Court upheld the minimum-wage and maximum-hours provisions of the federal Fair Labor Standards Act ("FLSA") as within

---

[193]   For development of this argument, see generally Neil S. Siegel, *Collective Action Federalism and the Minimum Coverage Provision*, 75 LAW & CONTEMP. PROBS. 29 (2012) (no. 3).

[194]   *NFIB*, 567 U.S. at 594, 595 (Ginsburg, J., concurring in part, concurring in judgment in part, and dissenting in part).

[195]   *Id.* at 595.

[196]   *See, e.g.*, ERWIN CHEMERINSKY, CONSTITUTIONAL LAW: PRINCIPLES AND POLICIES 332–40 (2015).

[197]   426 U.S. 833 (1976).

the scope of the Commerce Clause.[198] In *National League of Cities*, the Court held 5 to 4 that applying these FLSA provisions to employees of state and local governments, as opposed to the employees of privately owned companies, exceeded federal power. The Court reasoned that the statute "operate[d] to directly displace the States' freedom to structure integral operations in areas of traditional governmental functions."[199] The Court did not explain how to identify an "integral" or "traditional governmental functio[n]," and it unpersuasively distinguished *National League of Cities* in a series of subsequent decisions.[200]

The Court finally overruled *National League of Cities* in *Garcia v. San Antonio Metropolitan Transit Authority*, holding that the FLSA could constitutionally be applied to state and local governments.[201] Writing for himself and the four dissenters in *National League of Cities*, Justice Harry Blackmun "reject[ed], as unsound in principle and unworkable in practice, a rule of state immunity from federal regulation that turns on a judicial appraisal of whether a particular governmental function is 'integral' or 'traditional.'"[202] In addition, and more significantly, Blackmun wrote that the political process, not the courts, would protect the regulatory autonomy of the states going forward: "the principal and basic limit on the federal commerce power is that inherent in all congressional action—the built-in restraints that our system provides through state participation in federal governmental action. The political process ensures that laws that unduly burden the States will not be promulgated."[203] *Garcia*'s rejection of state immunity remains good

---

[198]   312 U.S. 100 (1941).

[199]   *Id.* at 852. Justice Harry Blackmun cast the decisive vote. He wrote ambiguously and ominously that the majority had adopted "a balancing approach [that] . . . does not outlaw federal power in areas such as environmental protection, where the federal interest is demonstrably greater and where state facility compliance with imposed federal standards would be essential." *Id.* at 856 (Blackmun, J., concurring).

[200]   *See, e.g.*, EEOC v. Wyoming, 460 U.S. 226 (1983) (rejecting a challenge to the application of the Age Discrimination in Employment Act (ADEA) to the states); Fed. Energy Regulatory Comm'n v. Mississippi, 456 U.S. 742 (1982) (rejecting a challenge to the Public Utilities Regulatory Policies Act of 1978, which required state utility commissions to consider FERC proposals). In each decision, the majority was composed of Justice Blackmun and the four dissenters in *National League of Cities*.

[201]   469 U.S. 528 (1985).

[202]   *Id.* at 546–47.

[203]   *Id.* at 556. For seminal contributions to the literature on the political safeguards of federalism, see generally JESSE CHOPER, JUDICIAL REVIEW AND THE NATIONAL POLITICAL PROCESS 171–259 (1980); Larry Kramer, *Understanding Federalism*, 47 VAND. L. REV. 1485 (1994); Andrzej Rapaczynski, *From Sovereignty to Process: The Jurisprudence of Federalism After Garcia*, 1985 SUP. CT. REV. 341; and, for the initial formulation, Herbert Wechsler, *The Political Safeguards of Federalism: The Role of the States in the Composition and Selection of the National Government*, 54 COLUM. L. REV. 543 (1954). For a critique of the claim that federalism values should be protected only in the political process, see generally Lynn A. Baker & Ernest A.

law; this holding is important because it makes clear that the federal government is permitted to regulate many state activities, just not through "commandeering," which we now consider.[204]

At issue in *New York v. United States*[205] was the validity of the federal Low-Level Radioactive Waste Policy Amendments Act of 1985, which required states to arrange for the safe disposal of radioactive waste produced within their borders. Governments, hospitals, research institutions, and industries throughout the country were generating the waste as a byproduct of producing various materials, devices, gear, and products used by Americans. But only three states (called "sited states") had disposal facilities, and they were tiring of serving as a dumping ground for the rest of the country. There was an obvious collective action problem facing the states ("NIMBY," as in *Comstock*, discussed in the previous chapter), and the federal law sought to resolve this problem.

The statute gave states monetary and access incentives to comply with its requirements, permitting the sited states to impose a surcharge on waste coming from other states and eventually to deny access to their disposal sites—moves that would otherwise violate the dormant commerce principle, discussed below. The most controversial part of the law, included to secure adequate regulatory action by the states, mandated that states would "take title" to any radioactive waste within their borders that was not appropriately disposed of by a certain date and would then "be liable for all damages directly or indirectly incurred."[206]

The Court affirmed Congress's clear power under the Commerce Clause to regulate the disposal of radioactive waste, as "[s]pace in radioactive waste disposal sites is frequently sold by residents of one State to residents of another" and so involves an "interstate market."[207] The Court also upheld the act's financial incentives as within Congress's power under the Commerce and Spending Clauses (discussed in the next chapter).[208] In addition, the Court sustained the law's access incentives as a conditional exercise of Congress's

---

Young, *Federalism and the Double Standard of Judicial Review*, 51 DUKE L.J. 75 (2001).

[204]   As covered in courses in Federal Courts, however, the Court has limited the impact of *Garcia* by holding that state sovereign immunity prohibits most lawsuits by private parties against states for money damages to remedy state violations of federal law. *See, e.g.*, Alden v. Maine, 527 U.S. 706 (1999). Other ways of holding states accountable remain available, however, especially suits by private parties to enjoin state officials from continuing to violate federal law. *See* Ex parte Young, 209 U.S. 123 (1908). This book does not cover this complex area of constitutional law.

[205]   505 U.S. 144 (1992).

[206]   *Id.* at 153.

[207]   *Id.* at 159–60.

[208]   *See id.* at 171–73.

commerce power. Congress, in other words, was permissibly giving states the choice between "regulat[ing] the disposal of radioactive waste according to federal standards by attaining local or regional self-sufficiency" and having "their residents who produce radioactive waste . . . be subject to federal regulation authorizing sited States and regions to deny access to their disposal sites."[209]

The Court held, however, that the "take title" provision was unconstitutional. Writing for a six-Justice majority, Justice O'Connor stated that this provision forced states to choose between "accepting ownership of waste" and "regulating according to the instructions of Congress."[210] Neither imposition was permissible, she concluded, because requiring states to accept ownership would unconstitutionally "commandeer" state governments, and mandating state regulation in accordance with Congress's instructions would unlawfully force states to implement federal statutes. Justice O'Connor declared that "[t]he Federal Government may not compel the States to enact or administer a federal regulatory program."[211]

The Court's constitutional concerns centered on the issue of political accountability. In the Court's view, Congress was requiring the states to regulate, yet the states (not the federal government) might be held politically accountable for the regulations if they proved unpopular. The Court reasoned that citizens affected by the regulations would see who was doing the regulating (i.e., states), not who had made the decision to order regulation in the first place (i.e., Congress).[212]

Despite holding that Congress may not force state legislatures to pass laws or require state administrative agencies to promulgate regulations, the Court emphasized that Congress had several regulatory alternatives to commandeering at its disposal. The Court stated that Congress could bypass state regulatory regimes entirely by establishing federal standards that all actors, public and private, must meet. Congress, in other words, could preempt state and local regulatory activity.[213] Moreover, the Court affirmed that Congress could condition federal funding of state and local government activities on their compliance with related regulatory requirements that Congress could not impose directly, a form of federal power that we discuss in the next chapter. Congress could thus induce states to clean up radioactive waste by placing conditions on related federal grants, even though Congress could not force states to clean up the

---

[209]   *Id.* at 174.

[210]   *Id.* at 175.

[211]   *Id.* at 188.

[212]   *See id.* at 168–69.

[213]   *See id.* at 168.

waste.[214] Finally, the Court declared that the Constitution allowed Congress to give states the choice between being commandeered and being preempted by federal law.[215]

The three dissenters in *New York* argued that the Court's distinction between commandeering states and regulating them along with private parties had no basis in logic, the text of the Constitution, the constitutional structure, the Court's precedent, or political reality. Logically, Justice Byron White wrote, "[a]n incursion on state sovereignty hardly seems more constitutionally acceptable if the federal statute that 'commands' specific action also applies to private parties. The alleged diminution in state authority over its own affairs is not any less because the federal mandate restricts the activities of private parties."[216] The text of the Constitution articulates no such distinction, he noted.[217] Justice Stevens added that the Constitution expanded federal power; it did not take away any powers that the national government possessed under the Articles of Confederation, including the power to commandeer states by requisitioning them for their fair share of tax revenue and troops.[218]

With respect to precedent, Justice White emphasized (among other things) that the Court was rejecting *Garcia*'s conclusion that federalism was to be protected through the political process, not judicial review.[219] Finally, he emphasized how effectively the political safeguards of federalism were functioning in this instance: the 1985 statute was a compromise between the sited states and unsited states like New York that Congress agreed to ratify, and now New York was harming sister states by trying to avoid fulfilling its end of the bargain after having reaped substantial benefits from it.[220]

The Justices fought their next battle over commandeering five years later. In *Printz v. United States*,[221] the question presented was whether the federal Brady Handgun Violence Prevention Act violated the anticommandeering principle by requiring state and local law enforcement officers to conduct background checks on would-be handgun buyers on an interim basis until a federal computer database was created. Writing for a five-Justice majority,

---

[214]   *See id.* at 166–67.

[215]   *See id.* at 174.

[216]   *Id.* at 201–02 (White, J., joined by Blackmun and Stevens, JJ., concurring in part and dissenting in part).

[217]   *See id.* at 207; *see also id.* at 211 (Stevens, J., concurring in part and dissenting in part).

[218]   *See id.* at 210 (Stevens, J., concurring in part and dissenting in part).

[219]   *See id.* at 205–06 (White, J., concurring in part and dissenting in part).

[220]   *See id.* at 189–99.

[221]   521 U.S. 898 (1997).

Justice Scalia declared the law unconstitutional, concluding that Congress was unlawfully commandeering state executive officers to enforce federal law. In the early years of the Republic and throughout American history, Justice Scalia observed, Congress had not engaged in such commandeering, an indication (in his view) that Congress thought the practice unconstitutional.[222] Turning from historical practice to the constitutional structure, he reaffirmed the view expressed by the Court in *New York* that the Constitution, unlike the Articles of Confederation, " 'confers upon Congress the power to regulate individuals, not states.' "[223] Finally, he relied "most conclusively in the present litigation" upon the Court's precedent and reaffirmed *New York*, concluding that "Congress cannot circumvent" its holding in *New York* by requiring state executive officials to enforce federal law.[224]

Justice Stevens dissented in an opinion that was joined by Justices Souter, Ginsburg, and Breyer. "When Congress exercises the powers delegated to it by the Constitution," he wrote, "it may impose affirmative obligations on executive and judicial officers of state and local governments as well as ordinary citizens."[225] He deemed this conclusion "firmly supported by the text of the Constitution, the early history of the Nation, decisions of this Court, and a correct understanding of the basic structure of the Federal Government."[226]

The Rehnquist Court next considered the scope of the anticommandeering principle in 2000. In *Reno v. Condon*,[227] the Justices unanimously *rejected* a Tenth Amendment challenge to a federal statute. At issue was the federal Driver's Privacy Protection Act ("DPPA"), which prohibited states from disclosing personal information gained by departments of motor vehicles ("DMVs"), including home addresses, phone numbers, and social security numbers. The Court unanimously reversed the judgment of the court of appeals, which had held that the DPPA unconstitutionally commanded states not to disclose the information. Writing for the Court, Chief Justice Rehnquist distinguished *New York* and *Printz*. He reasoned that, in *Condon*, Congress was not regulating private actors indirectly by commandeering the regulatory apparatus of the

---

[222] *See id.* at 905–18.

[223] *Id.* at 920 (quoting *New York*, 505 U.S. at 166).

[224] *Id.* at 925, 935. Justice Scalia also held that the provision at issue violated the separation of powers on the ground that requiring state and local law enforcement personnel to enforce federal law undermined unitary executive enforcement of federal law. *See id.* at 922–23. This conclusion is questionable given that logically it would render unconstitutional *voluntary* enforcement of federal law by state and local law enforcement personnel, a position nobody seems to hold.

[225] *Id.* at 939 (Stevens, J., dissenting).

[226] *Id.*

[227] 528 U.S. 141 (2000).

states; rather, Congress was regulating directly all entities that possess the driver's license information—states and private entities alike. Accordingly, the Court concluded, the DPPA did not trigger accountability concerns and fell outside the scope of the anticommandeering principle.[228]

The Court recently issued its first anticommandeering holding in almost two decades. *Murphy v. National Collegiate Athletic Association*[229] concerned the constitutionality of the Professional and Amateur Sports Protection Act of 1992 (or PASPA), which among other things banned most states from authorizing sports gambling. The law exempted Nevada, where sports betting has long been legal, along with sports lotteries in Delaware, Montana, and Oregon. Other states were given a year to opt in, but none acted in time. New Jersey acted 20 years later, passing a law in 2012 legalizing sports betting in the hope that allowing it would revive the state's struggling racetracks and casinos. The National Collegiate Athletic Association (NCAA) and the four major professional sports leagues sued, arguing that the 2012 New Jersey law violated PASPA and so was preempted. The lower federal courts agreed, prompting the New Jersey legislature to start over. In 2014, it passed a new law that rolled back existing bans on sports betting, at least as they applied to New Jersey casinos and racetracks. The NCAA and the pro leagues sued again, arguing that the new law also violated PASPA, and the court of appeals again ruled against the state.

The Supreme Court reversed, holding that PASPA's ban on state authorization of sports gambling violates the anti-commandeering principle. Justice Samuel Alito wrote the majority opinion, which was joined in full by the Chief Justice and Justices Kennedy, Thomas, Kagan, and Neil Gorsuch, and in part by Justice Breyer. (Notably, even some of the Court's liberal Justices now accept the anti-commandeering principle). Justice Alito wrote that the "anti-commandeering doctrine may sound arcane, but it is simply the expression of a fundamental structural decision incorporated into the Constitution"—namely, "the decision to withhold from Congress the power to issue orders directly to the States."[230] This, he said, is the problem with the provision of PASPA that bars states from authorizing sports gambling: it "unequivocally dictates what a state legislature may and may not do. . . . It is as if federal officers were installed in state legislative chambers and were armed with the authority to stop legislators from voting on any offending proposals."[231] Justice Alito concluded that whether to legalize sports

---

[228] *See id.* at 146–51.

[229] 138 S. Ct. 1461 (2018).

[230] *Id.* at 1475.

[231] *Id.* at 1478.

gambling "is a controversial subject" that "requires an important policy choice."[232] But this choice, he said, is not the Court's to make. "Congress can regulate sports gambling directly, but if it elects not to do so, each State is free to act on its own."[233]

In sum, in *New York*, *Printz*, and *NCAA*, the provision of federal law at issue was regulating activity that met the Court's definition of "economic." So the problem was not *whether* Congress was regulating economic activity that substantially affects interstate commerce in the aggregate (the *Lopez* test), but *how* Congress was regulating economic activity that substantially affects interstate commerce. That is, the constitutional problem had to do with the *means* employed by Congress to regulate interstate commerce. The anti-commandeering principle categorically prohibits the federal government from requiring state legislatures or executive officials to enact, to administer, or to enforce a federal regulatory program.[234] The anti-commandeering doctrine thus disables the federal government from using the states as regulators. It does not, however, prohibit the federal government from treating the states as regulated entities and preempting conflicting state laws, which is what *Garcia* permits.

Scholars, like the Justices, have vigorously debated the soundness of the Court's anti-commandeering principle.[235] In addition to the claims (noted above) about the original meaning and structure of the Constitution as well as a lack of historical practice of commandeering, the doctrine can also be defended functionally as maintaining clear lines of political accountability between the federal government and the states (as also noted above). Another argument in favor of the doctrine is that it preserves the regulatory autonomy of the states in areas not subject to preemptive federal regulation. An additional line of reasoning—this one from a law and economics perspective—maintains that the anti-commandeering principle helps

---

[232]   *Id.* at 1484.

[233]   *Id.* at 1484–85. Justice Ginsburg, joined by Justice Sotomayor, dissented. She did not explain her apparent conclusion that the central provision at issue was constitutional. She instead disputed the majority's decision to invalidate the entire statute rather than just this provision. *See id.* at 1488–90 (Ginsburg, J., dissenting). The relevant issue is one of "severability," and it turns on congressional intent and so statutory interpretation. It is covered in courses on Legislation.

[234]   State courts are a different matter. State judges can be required to entertain cases arising under federal law. *See* Testa v. Katt, 330 U.S. 386 (1947).

[235]   For academic treatments on both sides of the issue that offer many of the arguments presented in the following three paragraphs, see, for example, Evan H. Caminker, *State Sovereignty and Subordinacy: May Congress Commandeer State Officers to Implement Federal Law?*, 95 COLUM. L. REV. 1001 (1995); Vicki C. Jackson, *Federalism and the Uses and Limits of Law: Printz and Principle*, 111 HARV. L. REV. 2180 (1998); Saikrishna Bangalore Prakash, *Field Office Federalism*, 79 VA. L. REV. 1957 (1993); and Neil S. Siegel, *Commandeering and Its Alternatives: A Federalism Perspective*, 59 VAND. L. REV. 1629 (2006).

prevent "over-commandeering" by forcing Congress to internalize the full financial costs of commandeering the states. On this view, the principle forces cost internalization by requiring Congress to "purchase" the agreement of states to be commandeered through offers of related federal funds.

As articulated by the dissenting Justices in *New York* and *Printz*, criticisms of the anti-commandeering principle include a lack of textual basis for it and a more nationalist understanding of the Constitution's original meaning and structure. (A real difficulty for originalist argumentation on both sides of this issue is that the Founders never faced the precise question presented today because they never imagined that commandeering could prove effective in securing state compliance.) Additional criticisms are that the Court (1) overstates accountability concerns, given how easily citizens who care can learn which level of government is responsible for which regulations; (2) selectively enforces accountability values, given that federal preemption of conflicting state regulations and conditional federal spending also raise accountability concerns; and (3) wrongly focuses on accountability values, given that the Constitution's system of separation of powers and federalism inherently encourages blame-shifting in the service of protecting more important values, such as the prevention of dictatorship.

Critics also maintain that the anti-commandeering doctrine perversely encourages Congress to preempt state laws and thereby cut states out of the federal regulatory process entirely, which can make states worse off than if they had been commandeered and so had played a role in enforcing federal law—typically by exercising at least some enforcement discretion. In *New York*, for example, Congress could have simply banned the interstate shipment of the waste, forcing each state to build a disposal facility or lose a lot of businesses to sister states with disposal facilities. In addition, critics contend that concerns about whether Congress is internalizing the full financial costs of commandeering the states can be met by requiring Congress to pay the full costs; it is unnecessary overkill to give states a veto. Finally, critics underscore that the ability of Congress to commandeer state executive officials might be critically important in an emergency, such as a terrorist attack or a flu pandemic, yet the Court's doctrine imposes a categorical bar on commandeering, stronger protection than is generally given to constitutional rights for individuals. Indeed, complete categorical bars on governmental action are extraordinarily rare in U.S. constitutional law.

The constitutional politics of the anti-commandeering principle have changed in recent years, and critics of the doctrine appear to be fewer in number than they used to be. Although the debate initially seemed to pit conservative federalists against liberal nationalists, liberals have also wielded the anti-commandeering principle to resist exercises of federal power by conservative presidential administrations.[236] Recently, for example, liberals have invoked the principle in the debate over so-called "sanctuary cities"—that is, cities that refuse to cooperate with federal immigration officials who seek to vigorously enforce federal immigration laws.[237] Liberals have also the invoked anti-commandeering doctrine in resisting the federal government's efforts to enforce federal marijuana laws in states that have legalized the drug for either recreational or medicinal use.[238]

Some critics of the anti-commandeering principle, including one of us, initially described it as more symbolic than practically significant—as animated by concern that commandeering expresses disrespect for states—given (among other things) how rarely Congress has engaged in commandeering and all of the regulatory alternatives at Congress's disposal.[239] From the vantage point of the present, this characterization seems incorrect given the real-world impact of the above judicial decisions and political debates, and given how much more difficult it is for the federal government to put federal "boots on the ground," as opposed to relying upon state and local officials to enforce federal law. (The overwhelming majority of law enforcement officials in the United States work for state and local governments, not the federal government.[240]) As discussed in the next chapter, moreover, the Court in *NFIB* held for the first time in American history that a condition on the receipt of federal funds was unconstitutionally coercive, and it invoked the anti-commandeering principle to ground the constitutional limitation that it imposed on the use of conditional federal spending.[241] This result is hardly

---

[236] See, e.g., Ernest A. Young, *Welcome to the Dark Side: Liberals Rediscover Federalism in the Wake of the War on Terror*, 69 BROOK. L. REV. 1277 (2004).

[237] *See, e.g.,* Tal Kopan, *House Passes 'Kate's Law' and Bill Declaring War on Sanctuary Cities*, CNN (June 29, 2017, 6:30 PM), https://www.cnn.com/2017/06/29/politics/kates-law-sanctuary-cities-house-bill-immigration/index.html; Mark Joseph Stern, *Three Cheers for Federalism*, SLATE, May 14, 2018, https://slate.com/news-and-politics/2018/05/justice-alitos-opinion-on-sports-betting-shows-up-federalism-can-be-good-for-liberals.html.

[238] *See, e.g.,* Stern, *supra* note 237.

[239] *See, e.g.,* Siegel, *supra* note 235, at 1690; Elizabeth Anderson & Richard H. Pildes, *Expressive Theories of Law: A General Restatement*, 148 U. PENN. L. REV. 1503, 1559 (2000).

[240] *Compare* Brian A. Reaves, *Census of State and Local Law Enforcement Agencies, 2008*, Bureau Just. Stat. Bull., July 2011, at 1 (estimating that there are 765,000 full-time state and local law enforcement officials with general arrest powers), *with* Brian A. Reaves, *Federal Law Enforcement Officers, 2008*, Bureau Just. Stat. Bull., June 2012, at 1 (estimating that there are 120,000 full-time federal law enforcement officials with the authority to make arrests and carry firearms).

[241] *See* NFIB v. Sebelius, 567 U.S. 519, 576–78 (2012) (opinion of Roberts, C.J.).

symbolic; it has enabled the states to refuse to expand the federal Medicaid Program to help achieve the ACA's objective of near-universal health insurance coverage.

VII. The Dormant Commerce Principle

Unlike the Commerce Clause, which concerns the power of Congress to regulate interstate commerce, the dormant commerce principle is a judicially created doctrine that limits the power of state governments to regulate interstate commerce. (The name for the principle derives from the fact that it is implicated only when Congress's commerce power lies dormant.[242]) Courts usually invoke the dormant commerce principle to ensure a national free trade zone by prohibiting states from discriminating against interstate commerce or placing an undue burden on interstate commerce. Dormant commerce cases are typically ones in which a state regulation conveys a competitive advantage to in-state producers or users.

Although there are many doctrinal nuances, the Court often invalidates state laws that advantage in-state producers or users by impeding interstate commerce. State laws that discriminate against interstate commerce—whether facially, intentionally, or in effect—are virtually assured of being invalidated by the courts.[243] Laws that merely burden interstate commerce are much more likely to survive judicial review. Applying relatively deferential judicial scrutiny, courts will strike down such laws only if they conclude that the burdens on interstate commerce clearly exceed the public-regarding benefits of the law.[244]

The Court has inferred the existence of the dormant Commerce principle from the role played by state economic protectionism in inspiring the Constitutional Convention, as well as from the grant of legislative power to Congress in the Commerce Clause.[245] Although the idea that state and local governments are capable of violating the Commerce Clause is difficult to defend textually given that the clause is a grant of legislative authority to Congress, such a constitutional principle is more sound from a structural and consequentialist perspective. In international trade, economists regard tariffs as favoring domestic producers at the expense of foreign producers and

---

[242]   Chief Justice Marshall came up with the term in his opinion in *Willson v. Black-Bird Creek Marsh Co.*, 27 U.S. (2 Pet.) 245, 252 (1829).

[243]   *See, e.g.*, City of Philadelphia v. New Jersey, 437 U.S. 617 (1978) (invalidating a state law that facially discriminated against interstate commerce by prohibiting the importation of certain waste originating outside the state).

[244]   *See, e.g.*, South Carolina State Highway Dept. v. Barnwell Brothers, 303 U.S. 177 (1938) (upholding a non-discriminatory state law limiting truck size for reasons of safety and road conservation).

[245]   *See* U.S. CONST. art. I, § 8, cl. 3.

domestic consumers. Trade agreements restrict tariffs, and these tariff restrictions are accompanied by restrictions on regulations or taxes that discriminate against foreign goods. This analogy to international trade applies to the behavior of states in most dormant commerce cases. A collective problem is at the core of any regulation by a state that benefits its producers less than it harms out-of-state producers, out-of-state consumers, and in-state consumers.[246]

There are many examples in the Supreme Court's jurisprudence of these kinds of collective action problems.[247] We will not attempt a comprehensive or historical treatment of the doctrine; rather, we will offer an illustration. In *H.P. Hood & Sons, Inc. v. Du Mond*,[248] a New York law prevented a company from building an additional depot for receiving milk for interstate shipment. The effect of the law was to retain more milk for consumption in New York at the expense of consumers in Massachusetts. Justice Jackson wrote for the Court that "the established *interdependence* of the states only emphasizes the necessity of protecting interstate movement of goods against local burdens and repressions."[249] He continued:

> Our system, fostered by the Commerce Clause, is that every farmer and every craftsman shall be encouraged to produce by the certainty that he will have free access to every market in the Nation, that no home embargoes will withhold his exports, and no foreign state will by customs duties or regulations exclude them. Likewise, every consumer may look to the free competition from every producing area in the Nation to protect him from exploitation by any. Such was the vision of the Founders; such has been the doctrine of this Court which has given it reality.[250]

In general, collective action problems justify the Court's distinction in this case and others between state economic protectionism, which is almost always unconstitutional, and health and safety regulations, which are often permissible exercises of a state's police powers. States may not advantage their industries by imposing protectionist regulations, but states may disadvantage their industries in interstate competition by imposing higher health and safety standards.[251]

---

[246]   *See* Cooter & Siegel, *supra* note 24, at 166–68.

[247]   *See, e.g.*, Granholm v. Heald, 544 U.S. 460 (2005) (prohibiting New York and Michigan from discriminating against certain out-of-state wineries).

[248]   336 U.S. 525 (1949).

[249]   *Id.* at 538 (emphasis added)

[250]   *Id.* at 539.

[251]   *See, e.g., id.* at 533 ("This distinction between the power of the State to shelter its people from menaces to their health or safety and from fraud, even when

Judges and scholars have long debated the basic purpose of the dormant commerce principle. For example, some scholars have emphasized the "free trade" theory described above and others have stressed the value of "national unity."[252] The Court has at times suggested a *Carolene Products* political-process justification for the dormant commerce principle.[253] Experts—and some judges like Justices Scalia and Thomas—have also debated whether courts should enforce the principle at all given the lack of a textual basis for it.[254] They have further debated what its scope should be, assuming courts should enforce the principle at all.[255] Finally, they have debated the soundness of a judicially created exception to the principle: the market participant exception. According to this exception, states may favor their own businesses or residents when states act as market participants similar to private businesses or consumers, as opposed to sovereign regulators.[256]

There is not much of a debate about the soundness of the other exception to the dormant commerce principle: congressional approval. As we saw in *New York*, Congress may use its commerce power to license state conduct (such as prohibiting the importation of waste into the state for disposal) that would otherwise violate the dormant commerce principle. In this situation, the dormant commerce principle drops out because Congress's commerce power is

---

those dangers emanate from interstate commerce, and its lack of power to retard, burden or constrict the flow of such commerce for their economic advantage, is one deeply rooted in both our history and our law."); *id.* at 535 ("This Court consistently has rebuffed attempts of states to advance their own commercial interests by curtailing the movement of articles of commerce, either into or out of the state, while generally supporting their right to impose even burdensome regulations in the interest of local health and safety.").

[252] For seminal interpretations, see generally Earl M. Maltz, *How Much Regulation Is Too Much—An Examination of Commerce Clause Jurisprudence*, 50 GEO. WASH. L. REV. 47 (1981) (defending the free trade theory); Donald H. Regan, *The Supreme Court and State Protectionism: Making Sense of the Dormant Commerce Principle*, 84 MICH. L. REV. 1091 (1986) (emphasizing the value of national unity).

[253] *See* South Carolina Highway Dept. v. Barnwell Bros., Inc., 303 U.S. 177, 185 n.2 (1938) ("[W]hen the regulation is of such a character that its burden falls principally upon those without the state, legislative action is not likely to be subjected to those political restraints which are normally exerted on legislation where it affects adversely some interests within the state.").

[254] For example, Justice Thomas rejects the dormant commerce principle in its entirety. *See, e.g.*, South Dakota v. Wayfair, 138 S. Ct. 2080, 2100 (2018) (Thomas, J., concurring) (reiterating his rejection of the Court's "entire negative Commerce Clause jurisprudence").

[255] One middle-ground possibility would be to limit, but not eliminate, judicial discretion and intervention by enforcing the dormant commerce principle in cases of state discrimination against interstate commerce but not in cases of an asserted undue burden on interstate commerce. The Court has not embraced this approach.

[256] *See* Hughes v. Alexandra Scrap Corp., 426 U.S. 794 (1976) (introducing the market participant exception in upholding a Maryland program that favored in-state scrap processors over out-of-state scrap processors because the state had entered the market rather than regulated it).

no longer dormant. For the same reason, Congress may undo any decision by the Court enforcing the dormant commerce principle. This is an area of constitutional law in which Congress always has the last word. One can think of the Court as acting as Congress's delegate in enforcing a national free trade zone; Congress can revoke this delegation of authority in particular instances whenever it wants as long as its statutory revocation falls within the scope of the Commerce Clause.

Further Readings

JACK M. BALKIN, LIVING ORIGINALISM 138–82 (2011).

RANDY E BARNETT, RESTORING THE LOST CONSTITUTION: THE PRESUMPTION OF LIBERTY (2004).

Robert D. Cooter & Neil S. Siegel, *Collective Action Federalism: A General Theory of Article I, Section 8*, 63 STAN. L. REV. 115 (2010).

BARRY CUSHMAN, RETHINKING THE NEW DEAL COURT: THE STRUCTURE OF A CONSTITUTIONAL REVOLUTION (1998).

BARRY FRIEDMAN, THE WILL OF THE PEOPLE: HOW PUBLIC OPINION HAS INFLUENCED THE SUPREME COURT AND SHAPED THE MEANING OF THE CONSTITUTION (2009).

James Madison, *Vices of the Political System of the United States* (Apr. 1787), *at* NATIONAL ARCHIVES, FOUNDERS ONLINE, https://founders.archives.gov/documents/Madison/01-09-02-0187.

John F. Manning, *Foreword: The Means of Constitutional Power*, 128 HARV. L. REV. 1 (2014).

MARIAN C. MCKENNA, FRANKLIN ROOSEVELT AND THE GREAT CONSTITUTIONAL WAR: THE COURT-PACKING CRISIS OF 1937 (2002).

G. EDWARD WHITE, THE CONSTITUTION AND THE NEW DEAL (2000).

Chapter 6

TAXING AND SPENDING POWERS

We turn now from the Commerce Clause to another constitutional "hook" that Congress may rely upon to pass legislation. It is found in the first clause of Article I, Section 8, and provides in relevant part that "Congress shall have Power To lay and collect Taxes . . . to pay the Debts and provide for the common Defence and general Welfare of the United States."[1] This provision is called the Taxing Clause, the Taxing and Spending Clause, or the General Welfare Clause. Recall from Chapter 4 that under the Articles of Confederation, the federal government had no power to tax individuals directly and little money to spend because the states routinely failed to pay their fair share of contributions to the national treasury, opting instead to free ride off the contributions of sister states. Also recall that, to solve what was probably the most significant collective action failure during the 1780s—the problem of financing the national government—the Constitution empowers Congress to assess, levy, and collect taxes directly from individuals, bypassing the states. Greatly enhancing the taxing and spending powers of the federal government, the General Welfare Clause is listed first for a reason.

Today, the taxing and spending powers are two of the most important powers that Congress possesses. For example, the Court in *NFIB v. Sebelius*, the *Health Care Case*,[2] upheld the so-called individual mandate as a conditional tax, as we will soon see. The Court also held that Congress's expansion of Medicaid was coercive and thus beyond the scope of the conditional spending power.

We will examine three questions. First, for what purposes may Congress tax and spend? Second, what is the difference between a tax and a penalty for purposes of Congress's taxing power? Third, to what extent may Congress condition federal funds on the compliance by states with requirements that Congress would not be permitted to impose on them directly?

---

[1]   U.S. CONST. art. I, § 8, cl. 1. It is also worth noting that the Origination Clause requires tax bills to originate in the House of Representatives. *See* Art. I, § 7, cl. 1.

[2]   567 U.S. 519 (2012).

I.　The Purposes for Which Congress May Tax and Spend

After the Constitution was ratified, national politicians continued to debate the scope of federal power in Article I, Section 8, particularly the meaning of the reference in the initial clause to the "general Welfare." Because Congress seldom used its commerce power before the latter decades of the nineteenth century, and because presidential vetoes often prevented the constitutionality of spending bills from being litigated in court, the main participants in these debates tended to be presidents and members of Congress.

A.　The Constitutional Politics of the "General Welfare"

A major antebellum constitutional controversy concerned the extent to which the General Welfare Clause authorized Congress to spend money on "internal improvements" such as canals and roads. Members of the Federalist Party, who (as we have seen) were heavily influenced by Alexander Hamilton, defended robust congressional power under Clause 1 to spend for the "general Welfare" regardless of whether the expenditure could plausibly be viewed as carrying out another enumerated power in Section 8.[3] Federalists were opposed by Democratic Republicans such as James Madison, who had turned away from his earlier nationalism (as we saw in Chapter 4, in the debate over the Bank). Madison argued that Congress possessed no independent power to tax and spend in pursuit of the general welfare. Rather, Madison insisted, the phrase "general Welfare" is defined and limited by the specific grants of authority in Clauses 2 through 17 of Section 8.[4] On this view, the General Welfare Clause confers authority to tax and spend only for purposes indicated by the enumerated powers listed in Section 8. It is important to understand the difference between the two positions, because the choice between them has major implications for the constitutional scope of congressional power.

It was on constitutional grounds that President Madison, in 1817, rested his veto of Representative John C. Calhoun's Bonus Bill, which would have funded internal improvements, including roads and canals. Calhoun (at that time a nationalist, though later a fervent believer in state sovereignty) thought that it would advance the "general welfare" of the nation as a whole "to perfect the communication from Maine to Louisiana," "to connect all the great

---

　　[3]　*See* ALEXANDER HAMILTON, REPORT ON THE SUBJECT OF MANUFACTURES (1791), *reprinted in* 10 THE PAPERS OF ALEXANDER HAMILTON 230, 302–04 (Harold C. Syrett ed., 1966).

　　[4]　*See* THE FEDERALIST NO. 41 (James Madison); *see also* United States v. Butler, 297 U.S. 1, 65–66 (1936) (discussing Madison's restrictive view of the General Welfare Clause and Hamilton's expansive view).

commercial points on the Atlantic . . . with the Western States," and "to perfect the intercourse between the West and New Orleans."[5] Madison conceded the policy virtues of the proposal but vetoed it because he was "constrained by the insuperable difficulty I feel in reconciling the bill with the Constitution of the United States."[6] "[I]t does not appear," he reasoned, "that the power proposed to be exercised by the bill is among the enumerated powers, or that it falls by any just interpretation within the power to make laws necessary and proper for carrying into execution those or other powers vested by the Constitution in the Government of the United States."[7]

Likewise, Madison's successor, President James Monroe, vetoed a similar internal improvements bill on constitutional grounds in 1822,[8] and President Andrew Jackson voiced constitutional objections in vetoing the Maysville Road Bill in 1830.[9] Subsequent Democratic Presidents—specifically, Tyler, Polk, Pierce, and Buchanan—articulated increasingly narrow conceptions of congressional authority over internal improvements. "And thus on the eve of the Civil War," Professor David Currie writes, "Congress found itself unable even to remove obstructions to naturally navigable waters, which Andrew Jackson himself had conceded it not only could but ought to do."[10]

In the decades after the Civil War, the same constitutional qualms about federal spending extended to disaster relief, as it had before the war. There was substantial historical precedent for federal spending to help the victims of disasters.[11] But people disagreed about whether such spending was for the "general Welfare" as required by the Constitution, rather than for the particular welfare of those who benefited from the expenditures. For example, some congressional supporters of federal funding to aid the victims of an Ohio River flood in 1884 argued in effect that necessity trumped the Constitution.[12] Likewise, President Grover Cleveland signed certain disaster relief bills during his presidency, but in 1887 he vetoed on

---

[5] See PAUL BREST ET AL., PROCESSES OF CONSTITUTIONAL DECISIONMAKING: CASES AND MATERIALS 82 (6th ed. 2015) (quoting Calhoun).

[6] Id. at 83.

[7] Id.

[8] Id. at 84.

[9] See DAVID P. CURRIE, THE CONSTITUTION IN CONGRESS: DEMOCRATS AND WHIGS 1829–1861, at 10–12 (2005).

[10] Id. at 25.

[11] BREST ET AL., supra note 5, at 451 (discussing Michelle Dauber Landis, The Sympathetic State, 23 LAW & HIST. REV. 387, 403–06 (2005)).

[12] Id.

constitutional grounds a bill that would have provided relief to drought victims in Texas.[13]

B.   The Constitutional Law of the "General Welfare"

The Supreme Court did not weigh in on this longstanding political debate over the purposes for which Congress may tax and spend until 1936. In *United States v. Butler*,[14] the Court explicitly approved Hamilton's robust view of the scope of the taxing and spending powers as "the correct one," holding that Congress possesses broad authority to tax and spend for the general welfare, so long as Congress does not violate another constitutional provision.[15] Notably, the Court was unanimous on this question, with the conservatives joining the majority opinion and the liberals noting that this point was common ground.[16] The Court reaffirmed this holding in subsequent cases. In *Steward Machine Co. v. Davis*, the Court rejected a constitutional challenge to the federal unemployment compensation system created by the Social Security Act (SSA).[17] And in *Helvering v. Davis*, the Court sustained the constitutionality of the SSA's old age pension program, which had been funded exclusively by federal taxes.[18]

The Hamiltonian position remains the law to this day. It can be defended not only based upon longstanding precedent, but also on textual grounds: the General Welfare Clause is listed as a separate source of congressional power, and Madison's proposed limitation has no obvious basis in the constitutional text. In fact, if Madison were correct, the clause would serve no purpose, since every exercise of the taxing and spending powers would be necessary and proper to the exercise of another enumerated power. Moreover, the consequences of adopting Madison's position today would be so draconian that they would likely be deemed unacceptable by the American public. (Imagine the Supreme Court held that the federal government could not offer federal funds to help a state or local community rebuild after a natural disaster or terrorist attack.) On the other hand, the modern Court is so deferential to Congress's judgment that a particular instance of taxing or spending will promote the "general Welfare" that this language arguably imposes no judicially enforceable limitation upon Congress at all.[19]

---

[13]   *Id.* at 452–53.

[14]   297 U.S. 1, 66 (1936).

[15]   *Id.* at 66.

[16]   *See id.* at 80.

[17]   301 U.S. 548 (1937).

[18]   301 U.S. 619 (1937).

[19]   *See, e.g.*, South Dakota v. Dole, 483 U.S. 203, 218 n.2 (1987) ("The level of deference to the congressional decision is such that the Court has more recently questioned whether 'general welfare' is a judicially enforceable restriction at all.")

II. The Difference Between a Tax and a Penalty

In *McCulloch*, Chief Justice John Marshall wrote that "[t]he only security against the abuse of [the tax] power is found in the structure of the Government itself," for "[i]n imposing a tax, the legislature acts upon its constituents," who can hold their representatives accountable for the taxes they impose.[20] As applied to the federal government, this view holds that there are no judicially enforceable constitutional limits on Congress's power to tax. Yet it seems very unlikely that the modern Supreme Court, which has imposed some limits on Congress's use of the Commerce Clause (as we saw in the previous chapter), would allow these limits to be eviscerated by resort to the Taxing Clause. For example, imagine that in response to *United States v. Lopez*,[21] Congress imposed a "tax" of $25,000 each time that an individual carried a firearm in a school zone. It strains credulity to think that the Court would uphold such an exaction. It seems probable that the Court would view the so-called tax as a penalty and so beyond the scope of the Taxing Clause. In other words, some distinction between a tax and a penalty may be necessary to prevent circumvention by Congress of the constitutional limits on the Commerce Clause.

A second reason to insist upon a distinction between a tax and a penalty for purposes of Congress's taxing power has to do with the scope of the Taxing Clause itself. In order for the federal government to "collect" a federal tax "to pay the Debts and provide for the common Defence and general Welfare of the United States,"[22] the tax has to raise at least some revenue. Yet exactions that are so high that no one engages in the assessed conduct will not raise revenue. On this view, therefore, uses of the Taxing Clause must be consistent with at least some revenue raising by the federal government.

A.   The Distinction Before *NFIB*

Before the 1920s, the Court deferred to Congress's asserted uses of the Taxing Clause. Thus in *Veazie Bank v. Fenno*, the Court upheld a federal law that increased a tax on state bank notes from one percent to ten percent, even though the tax seemed likely to eliminate the state notes, thereby raising little or no revenue.[23] In response to the charge that the tax was "so excessive as to indicate a purpose on the part of Congress to destroy the franchise of the bank," the Court stated in part that courts "cannot prescribe to the legislative departments of the government limitations upon the exercise of its acknowledged powers. The power to tax may be exercised

---

[20]   17 U.S. 316, 428 (1819).

[21]   514 U.S. 549 (1995).

[22]   U.S. Const. art. I, § 8, cl. 1.

[23]   75 U.S. 533 (1869).

oppressively upon persons, but the responsibility of the legislature is not to the courts, but to the people by whom its members are elected."[24]

Similarly, in *McCrary v. United States*, the Court upheld a federal law that increased from two cents to ten cents the excise tax on oleomargarine that was colored yellow to make it look like butter.[25] (The tax on uncolored oleomargarine, which is white, remained one-quarter of a cent per pound.) The Court rejected the argument that the exaction was a penalty that would achieve the regulatory objective of preventing the production of yellow oleomargarine. Because "the taxing power conferred by the Constitution knows no limits except those expressly stated in that instrument, it must follow, if a tax be within the lawful power, the exertion of that power may not be judicially restrained because of the results to arise from its exercise."[26] The Court was unconcerned that the exaction would raise negligible revenue; it rejected "the proposition that where there is a lawful power to impose a tax its imposition may be treated as without the power because of the destructive effect of the exertion of the authority."[27]

Likewise, in *United States v. Doremus*, the Court upheld the Narcotic Drug Act of 1914, which both assessed individuals who dealt in narcotics and regulated their sale.[28] The exaction was only $1 per year, and Congress attached a detailed enforcement regime to it. Even though the exaction could not significantly change behavior or raise revenue, the Court wrote that "[i]f the legislation enacted has some reasonable relation to the [raising of revenue], it cannot be invalidated because of the supposed [regulatory] motives which induced it."[29]

The doctrine changed in the 1920s and 1930s, when (as we saw in the last chapter) the Court was imposing significant limits on the scope of Congress's power to regulate interstate commerce. Recall that in *Hammer v. Dagenhart*, the Court held that Congress may not use its commerce power to prohibit the shipment in interstate commerce of goods produced by child labor.[30] Congress responded with the Child Labor Tax Law, which provided that individuals employing child labor "shall pay for each taxable year, in addition to all other taxes imposed by law, an excise tax equivalent to 10 per

---

24   *Id.* at 548.

25   195 U.S. 27 (1904).

26   *Id.* at 59.

27   *Id.* at 56.

28   249 U.S. 86, 94–95 (1919).

29   *Id.* at 93.

30   247 U.S. 251, 276–77 (1918).

centum of the entire net profits received or accrued for such year from the sale or disposition of the product of such mine, quarry, mill, cannery, workshop, factory, or manufacturing establishment."[31] The law further authorized a federal inspection regime, interference with which was made subject to fine or imprisonment. The law exempted employers from liability for the exaction in cases of "a child employed or permitted to work under a mistake of fact as to the age of such child, and without intention to evade the tax."[32] (Lawyers call this mistake-of-fact exemption from the law a scienter requirement. Scienter means that the person did not have an innocent state of mind but was acting intentionally, knowingly, or recklessly.)

In *Bailey v. Drexel Furniture Company* (the *Child Labor Tax Case*), the Justices invalidated the law. Writing for the Court, Chief Justice William Howard Taft distinguished exactions that the Taxing Clause authorizes from penalties, which it does not authorize. He stated that taxes have "only that incidental restraint and regulation which a tax must inevitably involve[.]"[33] "Taxes," he elaborated, "are occasionally imposed in the discretion of the legislature on proper subjects with the primary motive of obtaining revenue from them and with the incidental motive of discouraging them by making their continuance onerous."[34] On this view, "[t]hey do not lose their character as taxes because of the incidental motive."[35] He insisted, however, that "there comes a time" when an exaction amounts to a penalty.[36] That time comes when, "in the extension of the penalizing features of the so-called tax . . . it loses its character as such and becomes a mere penalty with the characteristics of regulation and punishment."[37]

Turning to the child labor statute, Chief Justice Taft concluded that it "regulate[s] by the use of the so-called tax as a penalty" because it "provides a heavy exaction for a departure from a detailed and specified course of conduct in business," and because "[s]cienters [are] associated with penalties not with taxes."[38] The Chief Justice noted that the statute does not explicitly prohibit child labor, but "it does exhibit its intent practically to achieve [this] result by adopting the criteria of wrongdoing and imposing its principal consequence on

---

[31]   Child Labor Tax Case, 259 U.S. 20, 35 (1922).

[32]   *Id.*

[33]   *Id.* at 36.

[34]   *Id.* at 38.

[35]   *Id.*

[36]   *Id.*

[37]   *Id.* For a similar statement of the difference between a tax and a penalty, see *United States v. Butler*, 297 U.S. 1, 61 (1936).

[38]   *Child Labor Tax Case*, 259 U.S. at 36–37. Scienters are associated with penalties, not taxes, because Congress often wants to punish only those individuals who intentionally break the law.

those who transgress its standard."[39] The Chief Justice feared that recognizing such a penalty as a tax for constitutional purposes would end judicially enforceable limits on Congress's enumerated powers.[40] "[T]he so-called tax," he wrote, "is a penalty to coerce people of a State to act as Congress wishes them to act in respect of a matter completely the business of the state government under the Federal Constitution."[41]

Other decisions from this era similarly distinguished regulatory exactions, which the Court deemed to be penalties, from revenue-raising exactions, which the Court regarded as taxes. In *Hill v. Wallace*,[42] decided immediately after the *Child Labor Tax Case*, the Court invalidated a federal exaction on sales of grain for future delivery (grain future contracts). The "tax" was twenty cents a bushel, which would be imposed unless the contracts were made by or through a member of a board of trade recognized by the U.S. Department of Agriculture.[43] This exaction supplemented the existing federal tax of two cents on every hundred dollars in value of such sales.[44] The Court viewed this "most burdensome" exaction as a penalty and not a tax because its "manifest purpose" was "to compel boards of trade to comply with regulations, many of which have no relevancy to the collection of the tax at all."[45] According to the Court, "[t]he act is in essence and on its face a complete regulation of boards of trade, with a penalty of 20 cents a bushel on all 'futures' to coerce boards of trade and their members into compliance."[46] "When this purpose is declared in the title to the bill, and is so clear from the effect of the provisions of the bill itself," the Court reasoned, "it leaves no ground upon which the provisions we have been considering can be sustained as a valid exercise of the taxing power."[47]

---

[39]   *Id.* at 38; *see id.* at 37 ("[A] court must be blind not to see that the so-called tax is imposed to stop the employment of children within the age limits prescribed. Its prohibitory and regulatory effect and purpose are palpable. All others can see and understand this. How can we properly shut our minds to it?"); *id.* at 39 ("The case before us can not be distinguished from that of *Hammer v. Dagenhart*." (citation omitted)).

[40]   *See id.* at 38.

[41]   *Id.* at 39.

[42]   259 U.S. 44, 68 (1922).

[43]   *See id.* at 63. The other exception to imposition of the tax was "where the seller holds and owns the grain at the time of sale, or is the owner or renter of land on which the grain is to be grown, or is an association made of such owners or renters." *Id.*

[44]   *See id.*

[45]   *Id.* at 66.

[46]   *Id.*

[47]   *Id.* at 66–67.

In *United States v. Constantine*, the Court invalidated a federal exaction on liquor dealers who had violated state liquor laws.[48] In addition to the $25 excise tax that federal law already imposed on retail liquor dealers, the challenged provision imposed a "special excise tax" of $1000 on liquor dealers in business contrary to local law.[49] "If in reality a penalty," the Court wrote, "it cannot be converted into a tax by so naming it, and we must ascribe to it the character disclosed by its purpose and operation, regardless of name."[50] The Court ignored "the designation of the exaction," instead "viewing its substance and application."[51] (As we will see, the Court in *NFIB* much later performed this maneuver in reverse, finding a measure valid as a tax even though Congress labeled it a penalty.) Because the exaction was "highly exorbitant" relative to other federal taxes on liquor dealers, and because its imposition was conditioned on "the commission of a crime," the Court held that it "exhibits . . . an intent to prohibit and to punish violations of state law [and thus to] remove all semblance of a revenue act, and stamp the sum it exacts as a penalty."[52]

After the constitutional crisis of 1937, the Court did not formally overrule the *Child Labor Tax Case* and related decisions. The same is true of other pre-1937 precedents that have long since been abandoned, including *Lochner v. New York*, which we will discuss in Chapter 9.[53] Courts, commentators, and litigants have since disagreed about whether the Court's Taxing Clause doctrine from the 1920s and 1930s remains good law. One reason it is hard to be sure is that the laws in these cases would be upheld under the Commerce Clause today, leaving no need to distinguish between a tax and a penalty.

There is no question, however, that in the decades after 1937 the Court has sustained federal laws when interpreting the scope of the taxing power. Thus in *Sonzinsky v. United States*, the Court upheld as within the scope of the federal taxing power a $200 annual license tax on firearms dealers.[54] The Court appeared to rest on the ground

---

48   296 U.S. 287, 295–96 (1935).

49   *Id.* at 288–89.

50   *Id.* at 294; *accord* United States v. La Franca, 282 U.S. 568, 572 (1931) ("A tax is an enforced contribution to provide for the support of government; a penalty . . . is an exaction imposed by statute as punishment for an unlawful act. The two words are not interchangeable, one for the other.").

51   *Constantine*, 296 U.S. at 294.

52   *Id.* at 295. Justice Benjamin Cardozo, joined by Justices Louis Brandeis and Harlan Fiske Stone, dissented. "Not repression," Justice Cardozo stressed, "but payment commensurate with the gains is . . . the animating motive." *Id.* at 297 (Cardozo, J., dissenting).

53   198 U.S. 45, 53 (1905) (holding that the Fourteenth Amendment's Due Process Clause protects freedom of contract).

54   300 U.S. 506 (1937).

that exactions with regulatory effects are still taxes if they appear, both expressively and materially, to have been imposed pursuant to the taxing power. As to expression, the Court wrote:

> Every tax is in some measure regulatory. To some extent it interposes an economic impediment to the activity taxed as compared with others not taxed. But a tax is not any the less a tax because it has a regulatory effect, and it has long been established that an Act of Congress which on its face purports to be an exercise of the taxing power is not any the less so because the tax is burdensome or tends to restrict or suppress the thing taxed.[55]

The Court declared that "[i]nquiry into the hidden motives which may move Congress to exercise a power constitutionally conferred upon it is beyond the competency of courts."[56] As to materiality, it was enough for the Court that the tax "is productive of some revenue" and "operates as a tax."[57]

The Court deferred further to Congress in *United States v. Sanchez.*[58] The case involved a constitutional challenge to the Marihuana Tax Act, which imposed a tax of $100 per ounce on transferors of marijuana who make transfers to unregistered transferees without the order form required by federal law and without payment by the transferees of the tax.[59] Although it was "obvious" that the law "impos[ed] a severe burden on transfers to unregistered persons," the Court declared that an exaction is a tax even if it prevents the conduct and raises little or no revenue.[60] "It is beyond serious question," wrote the Court, "that a tax does not cease to be valid merely because it regulates, discourages, or even definitely deters the activities taxed."[61] (This is true, for example, of tariffs, which discourage purchase of the commodities in question.) Moreover, "the principle applies even though the revenue obtained is obviously negligible, or the revenue purpose of the tax may be secondary."[62] The Court also deemed it significant that the tax was "not conditioned upon the commission of a crime."[63] The Court thus rejected the claim that Congress had "levied a penalty, not a tax."[64]

---

[55]   *Id.* at 513 (citations omitted).

[56]   *Id.* at 513–14.

[57]   *Id.* at 514.

[58]   340 U.S. 42 (1950).

[59]   *See id.* at 44.

[60]   *Id.*

[61]   *Id.*

[62]   *Id.* (citations omitted).

[63]   *Id.* at 45.

[64]   *Id.* at 43.

Since *Sanchez*, the Court has repeatedly refused to invalidate exactions on the ground that Congress was using the Taxing Clause to regulate conduct. In *United States v. Kahriger*, the Court upheld a federal law imposing a wagering tax of $50 per year on bookmakers, requiring them to register with the Collector of Internal Revenue, and penalizing the failure to pay the tax and register.[65] "It is conceded that a federal excise tax does not cease to be valid merely because it discourages or deters the activities taxed," the Court wrote.[66] "Nor is the tax invalid because the revenue obtained is negligible."[67] The Court added that "[u]nless there are provisions extraneous to any tax need, courts are without authority to limit the exercise of the taxing power."[68] At the same time, the Court stressed that the exaction being challenged "produces revenue."[69]

None of the foregoing cases have been overruled, but many of them are inconsistent with one another. The general historical pattern has been that the Court has been most concerned to distinguish a tax from a penalty when it has been most concerned to impose constitutional limits on the scope of the Commerce Clause. Chief Justice Marshall in *McCulloch* and cases before the 1920s suggested that the Court would not be in the business of policing limits on the Taxing Clause. From the 1920s until the constitutional crisis of 1937, the Court constrained Congress's use of its taxing power by distinguishing exactions that have the primary purpose of raising revenue from exactions that have the primary purpose of regulating behavior. After 1937, the Court abandoned this distinction; it was enough for the Court that Congress said it was using the Taxing Clause, and the Court at times added that the exactions at issue raised at least some revenue, even if very little.

B. *NFIB*

The federalism challenge to the minimum coverage provision (or individual mandate) in *NFIB* provided the Court with its first occasion after *United States v. Lopez*[70] and *United States v. Morrison*[71] to revisit its view of the Taxing Clause. Because (as discussed in the prior two chapters) a majority of Justices concluded that the mandate was beyond the scope of the Commerce and

---

[65]   345 U.S. 22 (1953), *overruled on other grounds by* Marchetti v. United States, 390 U.S. 39, 41–42 (1968).

[66]   *Kahriger*, 345 U.S. at 28.

[67]   *Id.*

[68]   *Id.* at 31.

[69]   *Id.* In *Bob Jones University v. Simon*, the Court acknowledged its abandonment of the pre-1937 jurisprudence, which sought to distinguish between "regulatory and revenue-raising taxes." 416 U.S. 725, 741 n.12 (1974).

[70]   514 U.S. 549 (1995).

[71]   529 U.S. 598 (2000).

Necessary and Proper Clauses, the Court had to decide whether it was within the scope of the Taxing Clause.[72]

Writing for the Court, Chief Justice John Roberts upheld the ACA's minimum coverage provision and the associated payment for noncoverage (the "insurance mandate") as permissible exercises of Congress's taxing power notwithstanding the fact that the statute labeled the payment a "penalty."[73] He expressly rejected the argument emphasized by the four dissenting Justices that Congress's choice of label is controlling,[74] and he implicitly rejected the analysis of certain prior decisions that Congress's intent either to raise revenue or to regulate behavior is decisive:

> None of this is to say that the payment is not intended to affect individual conduct. Although the payment will raise considerable revenue, it is plainly designed to expand health insurance coverage. But taxes that seek to influence conduct are nothing new. Some of our earliest federal taxes sought to deter the purchase of imported manufactured goods in order to foster the growth of domestic industry.[75]

Chief Justice Roberts instead deemed dispositive the anticipated effect of an exaction on the conduct of the people potentially subject to it—especially whether it dampens this conduct, thereby raising revenue, or whether it prevents the conduct, thereby not raising revenue. This effect on behavior, he explained, is caused primarily by the material characteristics of the exaction and secondarily by its expressive form. Labeling the Court's inquiry a "functional approach," he emphasized two "practical characteristics" that distinguish a tax from a penalty for purposes of the Taxing clause: its level and whether there is a scienter requirement.[76] In the Court's view, a tax is an exaction at a moderate level that does not have a scienter requirement and is collected by the IRS:

> [T]he shared responsibility payment may for constitutional purposes be considered a tax, not a penalty: First, for most Americans the amount due will be far less than the price of insurance, and, by statute, it can never be

---

[72]   Chief Justice Roberts wrote that the minimum coverage provision "reads more naturally as command to buy insurance than as a tax," but he reached the taxing power question because a court has "a duty to construe a statute to save it, if fairly possible." *NFIB*, 567 U.S. at 574 (opinion of Roberts, C.J.). Lawyers call such a saving construction "constitutional avoidance."

[73]   *Id.* at 564 (opinion of the Court).

[74]   *Compare id. with id.* at 664–65 (Scalia, Kennedy, Thomas, & Alito, JJ., dissenting) ("[W]e have never—*never*—treated as a tax an exaction which faces up to the critical difference between a tax and a penalty, and explicitly denominates the exaction a 'penalty.'").

[75]   *Id.* at 567 (opinion of the Court).

[76]   *Id.* at 565, 573.

more. It may often be a reasonable financial decision to make the payment rather than purchase insurance, unlike the "prohibitory" financial punishment in *Drexel Furniture*. Second, the individual mandate contains no scienter requirement. Third, the payment is collected solely by the IRS through the normal means of taxation . . . .[77]

The Chief Justice thus stressed that a tax can tip into being a penalty when the burden becomes excessive and thus coercive, and that the minimum coverage provision is below this tipping point. Moreover, he connected the scienter requirement to the condemnation of an act as illegal.[78] Finally, he thought it pertinent that the payment will be collected by the IRS, "the agency that collects taxes," as opposed to an agency charged with punishing violations of the law.[79] On this last point, however, it seems unclear to us that why the identity of the enforcement agency bears on whether an exaction is a tax or a penalty.

Chief Justice Roberts explained that differences in the material characteristics of an exaction cause different effects on behavior. One such difference in effect is that a tax raises revenues, whereas a penalty does not necessarily do so. As the Chief Justice noted, "the essential feature of any tax" is that "[i]t produces at least some revenue for the Government," and the shared responsibility "payment is expected to raise about $4 billion per year by 2017."[80] Another difference in effect is that a tax dampens behavior without preventing it. These two effects are closely connected: taxes raise revenues *just because* they dampen behavior without preventing it.

The Court thus disagreed with liberal nationalists who reject any judicially enforceable limits on the Taxing Clause. This is no doubt because the Court is committed to the idea that courts have a role to play in maintaining a national government of limited, enumerated powers. The Court also disagreed with conservative federalists who argue that Congress may not escape political accountability by calling an exaction a "penalty" in the political arena and a "tax" in court.[81] The Court may have rejected this contention for any number of reasons: because the Democrats responsible for the ACA hardly escaped political accountability; because accountability

---

[77]   *Id.* at 566 (citations omitted).

[78]   *See id.* at 565–66.

[79]   *Id.* at 566 n.9.

[80]   *Id.* at 564.

[81]   *See, e.g.*, Randy E. Barnett, *Commandeering the People: Why the Individual Health Insurance Mandate is Unconstitutional*, 5 N.Y.U. J.L. & LIBERTY 581, 632 (2010) ("The public is acutely aware of tax increases. Rather than incur the political cost of imposing a general tax on the public using its tax powers, economic mandates allow Congress and the President to escape accountability for tax increases by compelling citizens to make payments directly to private companies.").

turns primarily on who must pay and how much they must pay, not on what Congress calls the payment; or because the Court is not accustomed to policing political accountability in the tax code, which is rife with efforts by members of Congress to avoid accountability. One example among many is the practice of burying tax breaks in the tax code instead of exposing them in the budget.[82]

By instead stressing the modest size of the exaction and the absence of a scienter requirement, the Court made clear that that there is a judicially enforceable non-coercion limitation on use of the Taxing Clause. The limit is crossed when Congress coerces people, which it may do when using the commerce power but not when using the taxing power. The Court did "not here decide the precise point at which an exaction becomes so punitive that the taxing power does not authorize it," even as it agreed with Justice Oliver Wendell Holmes that the "power to tax is not the power to destroy while this Court sits."[83] The best interpretation of the Court's opinion may be that to "destroy" is to prevent the conduct in question. On this view, an exaction changes from a tax to a penalty at the point where it prevents the conduct instead of dampening it.[84]

III. The Limits on Conditional Federal Spending

One way in which Congress uses its spending power is by giving money to the states without conditions attached. Another way is by attaching conditions to the receipt of federal funds, which is called conditional federal spending. We will focus here on the constitutional limits on conditional federal spending. The basic question is the extent to which Congress may condition federal funds on the agreement by states to comply with requirements that Congress may not constitutionally impose on them directly.

The problem of conditional grants extends well beyond the Spending Clause. For instance, a legislature may condition grant funding to individuals on their consent to conditions that would violate the Bill of Rights if the conditions took the form of regulatory mandates. Courts and commentators have had a great deal of trouble in distinguishing between conditions that are legitimately related to the grant and unconstitutional conditions. Drawing such a line in the

---

[82]   For development of these points, see Robert D. Cooter & Neil S. Siegel, *Not the Power to Destroy: An Effects Theory of the Tax Power*, 98 VA. L. REV. 1195, 1243–45 (2012).

[83]   *NFIB*, 567 U.S. at 573 (citations omitted).

[84]   For development of this approach, see generally Cooter & Siegel, *supra* note 82. This Article develops a theory of the Taxing Clause that the Court's opinion in *NFIB* appears to track. *See generally* Neal Kumar Katyal, *Foreword: Academic Influence on the Court*, 98 VA. L. REV. 1149 (2012).

context of federal funding to states also poses serious analytic problems.

According to governing Supreme Court doctrine, Congress may place strings on grants to states as long as four requirements are met. First, the conditions must be clearly stated, so that states understand what they are agreeing to do by accepting federal funds.[85] Second, the conditions must bear some relation to the purpose of the federal spending program at issue, a requirement called "relatedness" or "germaneness."[86] Third, the conditions may not violate independent constitutional limits on Congress's power, such as individual rights provisions in the Constitution.[87] Fourth, the conditions may not be coercive, a requirement called "non-coerciveness."[88]

We turn now to the two most important modern cases on conditional federal spending. The first, *South Dakota v. Dole*,[89] focused on the relatedness requirement. The second, *NFIB*, centered on the non-coerciveness requirement.

A. *Dole* and the Relatedness Requirement

The Court in *Dole* sustained broad congressional authority to attach strings to grants to state and local governments. In this case, federal law sought to establish a 21-year-old drinking age by denying 5 percent of federal highway funds to any state that declined to establish a 21-year-old drinking age. The Court assumed for purposes of its analysis that Congress lacked constitutional authority to establish a 21-year-old drinking age directly by using the Commerce Clause.[90] (This is a difficult question given Section 2 of the 21st Amendment, which gives states special authority to regulate alcohol.) Notwithstanding its assumption that Congress could not impose a 21-year-old drinking age directly, the Court held 7 to 2 that the condition was constitutional.

Writing for the Court, Chief Justice William Rehnquist stressed that the condition was clearly stated and related to the main purpose of the federal program giving highway money to the states: promoting "safe interstate travel."[91] He also noted briefly near the end of his majority opinion that the Court's "decisions have recognized that in some circumstances the financial inducement offered by Congress might be so coercive as to pass the point at which 'pressure turns into

---

[85]   *See* Pennhurst State School and Hospital v. Halderman, 451 U.S. 1, 17 & n.13 (1981).

[86]   *See* South Dakota v. Dole, 483 U.S. 203, 207–08 (1987).

[87]   *See id.* at 208.

[88]   *See* NFIB v. Sebelius, 567 U.S. 519 (2012).

[89]   483 U.S. 203 (1987).

[90]   *See id.* at 206.

[91]   *Id.* at 208.

compulsion.' "[92] But he dismissed any concern about coercion in this instance, calling 5 percent of federal highway funds "relatively mild encouragement."[93] He did not elaborate.

Justice Sandra Day O'Connor dissented, focusing on the relatedness requirement. She agreed with the Court's statement of this requirement but disagreed with its application. In her view, a minimum drinking age was not sufficiently related to the purpose of the federal program allocating highway funds because it was "far too over- and under-inclusive" with respect to the goal of highway safety.[94] As for over-inclusiveness, she observed that the condition prohibited drinking by individuals under the age of 21 in all circumstances, even though it was unreasonable to assume that all or most such individuals who drink alcohol are likely to drive afterward.[95] As for under-inclusiveness, she emphasized that people of all ages engage in drunk driving, so that a 21-year-old drinking age (as opposed to the 18-year-old drinking age that was used by some states) would not substantially improve highway safety.[96]

Whereas the majority applied deferential judicial scrutiny in examining the relationship between the condition and the purpose of the federal spending program, Justice O'Connor was more demanding. "When Congress appropriates money to build a highway," she wrote, "it is entitled to insist that the highway be a safe one."[97] "But," she added, "it is not entitled to insist as a condition of the use of highway funds that the State impose or change regulations in other areas of the State's social and economic life because of an attenuated or tangential relationship to highway use or safety."[98]

B. *NFIB* and Coercion

NFIB was the first time the Court held that a condition placed on federal grants to states was coercive and thus unconstitutional. This part of the case concerned the ACA's expansion of the federal Medicaid program. Before the ACA, the Medicaid program required states, as a condition attached to the receipt of federal Medicaid funds, to cover only certain categories of individuals: pregnant women, children, needy families, the blind, the elderly, and the disabled. There was no mandatory coverage for most childless adults, and states typically did not offer it.

---

[92] *Id.* at 211 (quoting *Steward Machine Co.*, 301 U.S. at 590).

[93] *Dole*, 483 U.S. at 211.

[94] *Id.* at 214 (O'Connor, J., dissenting).

[95] *See id.* at 214–15.

[96] *See id.* at 215.

[97] *Id.*

[98] *Id.*

The ACA's Medicaid provisions required states to expand their Medicaid programs by 2014 to cover all individuals under the age of 65 with incomes below 133 percent of the federal poverty line (FPL). The ACA provided that the federal government would pay 100 percent of the costs of covering these newly eligible individuals through 2016. In the following years, the federal payment level would gradually decrease to a minimum of 90 percent.

Critically, the ACA did not condition only the new Medicaid money made available under the ACA on the agreement by states to expand Medicaid coverage up to 133 percent of the FPL. Instead, the ACA gave the Secretary of Health and Human Services the discretion to withdraw *all* Medicaid funding from any state that did not sign on to the ACA's Medicaid expansion; this amounted to more than 10 percent of the average state's budget. The challengers in *NFIB* argued that if this condition was not coercive, then no condition was. Although no lower court agreed with the challengers on this point, the Supreme Court granted certiorari to decide the question.

The Justices fractured three ways in three opinions, concluding that the Medicaid expansion was unconstitutional by a vote of 7 to 2. In his controlling, plurality opinion, Chief Justice Roberts grounded the non-coerciveness requirement in the anti-commandeering principle and its concern with political accountability.[99] On this view, a conditional spending program becomes commandeering as a condition becomes coercive.

Roberts then concluded for himself and Justices Stephen Breyer and Elena Kagan that the condition at issue was coercive and therefore unconstitutional. He reasoned that Congress was conditioning continued receipt of a huge amount of federal money in an entrenched federal program (the pre-ACA Medicaid program) on the agreement by states to participate in a separate and independent program (the ACA's Medicaid expansion). "The threatened loss of over 10 percent of a State's overall budget," he reasoned, "is economic dragooning that leaves the States with no real option but to acquiesce in the Medicaid expansion."[100] "What Congress is not free to do," he added, "is to penalize States that choose not to participate in th[e] new program [under the Affordable Care Act] by taking away their existing Medicaid funding."[101] Attempting to invalidate the Medicaid expansion on relatively narrow grounds, the Chief Justice appeared to set forth three necessary conditions for a condition attached to federal funds to be coercive: (1) there must be a very large amount of federal money at stake; (2) the money must be part of an entrenched

---

[99]   *See NFIB*, 567 U.S. at 576–78 (opinion of Roberts, C.J.).

[100]   *Id.* at 582.

[101]   *Id.* at 585.

federal program, meaning that states have come to rely on continued receipt of the money; and (3) the program in which Congress is trying induce state participation must be distinct from the pre-existing, entrenched federal program.[102]

The Roberts opinion has the prudential virtue of not licensing courts to strike down many longstanding federal spending programs. Moreover, he did manage to breathe some substance into the Court's previous references to the possibility of coercion. But Roberts did not persuasively explain why, exactly, all three of the requirements he identified are necessary for coercion to exist. For example, it is not entirely clear why coercion exists when $X are at stake along with entrenchment and independent programs, but not when $3X alone are at stake. Nor did Roberts explain how to determine whether there were separate and independent programs, as opposed to an extension of a pre-existing program. It is also a challenge to figure out how coercion can ever exist when states have no constitutional entitlement at all to the continued receipt of any federal funds.

Justices Antonin Scalia, Anthony Kennedy, Clarence Thomas, and Samuel Alito agreed that the ACA's Medicaid expansion was coercive, but their reasoning was substantially broader. In their view, the condition was coercive because so much money was at stake that no state could reasonably decline Congress's offer. "[I]f States really have no choice other than to accept the package," they asserted, "the offer is coercive, and the conditions cannot be sustained under the spending power."[103] Making clear that their view of coercion was not limited to the strategic bundling of entrenched programs with independent programs, they further stated that Congress lacked the power to pass a hypothetical new law "offering each State a grant equal to the State's entire annual expenditures for primary and secondary education" with conditions comprehensively regulating the educational process.[104] These four Justices did not explain how the pre-ACA program was not also coercive for the same reason, nor did they explain how they would distinguish a coercive offer from the offer of a lifetime. It is questionable, as a matter of both contract law and conditional federal spending, that the more money a party is offered, the more the party is being coerced. (Imagine that your professor offered you $1,000,000 to be her research assistant this summer.)

Justice Ruth Bader Ginsburg, joined by Justice Sonia Sotomayor, dissented. She emphasized that states are not entitled to

---

[102]   For a lucid explication of this portion of the Roberts opinion, see generally Samuel R. Bagenstos, *The Anti-Leveraging Principle and the Spending Clause After NFIB*, 101 GEO. L.J. 861 (2013).

[103]   *NFIB*, 567 U.S. at 679 (Scalia, Kennedy, Thomas, & Alito, JJ., dissenting).

[104]   *Id.* at 680–81.

any federal funds, so that it would be clearly permissible for Congress to end the federal Medicaid program entirely and then to re-enact it with the ACA's Medicaid expansion folded into the re-enacted program. If Congress is permitted to do this in two steps, she rhetorically asked, why may it not do it in one?[105] She also disputed the Chief Justice's conclusion that there were two programs at issue, as opposed to an expansion of one.[106] In response to his assertion that, in covering Americans earning no more than 133 percent of the FPL, the Medicaid expansion (unlike pre-ACA Medicaid) does not "care for the neediest among us,"[107] Ginsburg asked "What makes that so?" and declared that "[s]ingle adults earning no more than $14,856 per year—133% of the current federal poverty level—surely rank among the Nation's poor."[108] (The sub-text of their dispute may have to do with longstanding debates between conservatives and liberals over the deserving versus the undeserving poor.[109])

Justice Ginsburg's dissent is best read as rejecting any non-coerciveness restraint on conditional federal spending based on two facts: the states have no constitutional entitlement to continued receipt of federal funds, and they always retain the legal choice to refuse Congress's offer. Her position is analytically clear, but it offers states no constitutional protection from possible federal coercion given their practical dependence upon federal funds.

Because the Roberts opinion is the narrowest in support of the judgment that the Medicaid expansion was unconstitutional, it states the governing law and so is the most important opinion going forward. Like many scholarly efforts to identify when conditions attached to a gratuitous benefit are coercive and so unconstitutional, whether in the context of conditional spending or individual rights,[110] the Chief Justice's analysis is not wholly successful. This is unsurprising: the problem of unconstitutional coercion is one of the most difficult in all of constitutional law. Indeed, this is a difficult

---

[105]   *See id.* at 624, 636–37 (Ginsburg, J., joined by Sotomayor, J., concurring in part, concurring in judgment in part, and dissenting in part).

[106]   *See id.* at 635–36.

[107]   *Id.* at 583 (opinion of Roberts, C.J.).

[108]   *Id.* at 635–36 (Ginsburg, J., concurring in part, concurring in judgment in part, and dissenting in part).

[109]   For a discussion, see generally Tomiko Brown Nagan, *Two Americas in Healthcare: Federalism and Wars over Poverty from the New Deal-Great Society to Obamacare*, 62 DRAKE L. REV. 981 (2014).

[110]   *See generally, e.g.*, Lynn A. Baker, *Conditional Federal Spending After Lopez*, 95 COLUM. L. REV. 1911 (1995); Mitchell N. Berman, *Coercion, Compulsion, and the Medicaid Expansion: A Study in the Doctrine of Unconstitutional Conditions*, 91 TEX. L. REV. 1283 (2013); Mitchell N. Berman, *Coercion Without Baselines: Unconstitutional Conditions in Three Dimensions*, 90 GEO. L.J. 1 (2001); Seth F. Kreimer, *Allocational Sanctions: The Problem of Negative Rights in a Positive State*, 132 U. PA. L. REV. 1293 (1984).

issue even in ordinary contract law, where distinguishing duress from hard bargaining is no easy task. The difficulty in persuasively distinguishing coercion from non-coercion may help explain why even a relatively federalist Court shied away from the issue until *NFIB*. It remains to be seen whether the Court will apply his test broadly or treat the Medicaid expansion as uniquely coercive.

Further Readings

Samuel R. Bagenstos, *The Anti-Leveraging Principle and the Spending Clause After* NFIB, 101 GEO. L.J. 861 (2013).

Mitchell N. Berman, *Coercion, Compulsion, and the Medicaid Expansion: A Study in the Doctrine of Unconstitutional Conditions*, 91 TEX. L. REV. 1283 (2013).

W. ELLIOT BROWNLEE, FEDERAL TAXATION IN AMERICA 16 (2d ed. 2004).

Robert D. Cooter & Neil S. Siegel, *Not the Power to Destroy: An Effects Theory of the Tax Power*, 98 VA. L. REV. 1195 (2012).

DAVID P. CURRIE, THE CONSTITUTION IN CONGRESS: DEMOCRATS AND WHIGS 1829–1861 (2005).

Michelle Dauber Landis, *The Sympathetic State*, 23 LAW & HIST. REV. 387 (2005).

Chapter 7

PRESIDENTIAL POWER

In this chapter, we switch our attention from Congress to the President. Whether or not the Framers foresaw this development (we tend to think not), the presidency has emerged as the focal point of American government and politics. There is broad agreement about the President's authority—in fact, duty as a general matter—to implement laws by passed by Congress.[1] But debate has raged for two centuries about the extent of presidential power beyond this core area of agreement. Perhaps never have the powers and immunities of the President been subject to more strenuous public debate than in this century, when intense and often partisan controversies have erupted over actions by a series of Presidents (George W. Bush, Barack Obama, and Donald Trump). For this reason, we believe it is important to discuss the subject in some depth.

I. The President's Constitutional Role

Americans are so focused on the presidency that many of them would be surprised to learn that the presidential form of government in the United States is in the minority among democratic systems internationally. Most democracies have a parliamentary system in which the head of government (usually called the prime minister) is chosen by the legislature. Some nations have a separate figure, often called the president, who serves a largely ceremonial function as head of state. In a two-party system, this parliamentary form of government guarantees that the executive and the legislature represent the same political party, minimizing conflict between the two branches. In a multiparty system, the situation is more complicated, since choosing the head of government requires forming a coalition, which in turn can require giving different parties a role in policymaking.

Commentators are divided about the merits of presidential and parliamentary systems. Critics of the presidential system argue that it invites impasses between the executive and the legislature, often tempting the executive to take unilateral action, while also leading to a "cult of personality" surrounding the president that is injurious to democratic politics.[2] Supporters of presidential government argue

---

[1]   *See* U.S. CONST. art. II, § 3 (providing that the President "shall take Care that the Laws be faithfully executed").

[2]   *See generally* Bruce Ackerman, *The New Separation of Powers*, 113 HARV. L. REV. 633 (2000). For a historical discussion of parliamentary critics of the presidential system beginning in the Nineteenth Century, see Thomas O. Sargentich, *The*

that it has many virtues, including more unified administration (as opposed to coalition governments), greater electoral accountability because the President provides a focal point for voters, and greater stability because frequent policy changes are blocked by disagreements between the legislature and executive.[3] Supporters of the presidential system also point to flaws in the parliamentary system, such as the possibility that party control will leave the prime minister unchecked and unaccountable.[4] Our system of government is clearly committed to the presidential model, but customary practice of the political branches and judicial review by courts has the potential to develop norms and design rules to ameliorate some of the potential flaws in this system while accentuating its strengths.

Compared to some other areas of constitutional law, any link between one's conception of presidential power and one's political party affiliation or ideology tends to be unstable. The reason is that partisan control of the White House switches hands on a regular basis, so the connection between the scope of presidential power and particular policy outcomes is unpredictable. Basically, the same theories that empower or constrain liberal presidents will similarly affect conservative ones. This may not prevent politicians from embracing whatever theory empowers their "side" at the moment or constrains the other party. But such inconsistency can be a real embarrassment for judges, and the unstable link between arguments and outcomes discourages the robust involvement of social movements or the general public that we see in other areas.

The constitutional text provides a fairly barebones sketch of presidential power. Article II is relatively brief—much shorter than Article I. Section 1 begins with a statement that "[t]he executive Power shall be vested in a President of the United States of America." As we will see, this Vesting Clause can be read either as a grant of authority or as merely descriptive of the President's role *vis-à-vis* the other branches. Section 1 continues with a lengthy description of election procedures. It concludes with the Presidential Oath Clause, prescribing a special oath for this office, in which the new President swears to "faithfully executive the Office of President of the United States, and to the best of my Ability, preserve, protect, and defend the Constitution of the United States."

Sections 2 and 3 lay out the powers of the President (or under the alternative interpretation, those powers not already included in

---

Limitations of the Parliamentary Critique of the Separation of Powers, 34 WM. & MARY L. REV. 680, 684–706 (1993).

[3]   *See generally* Steven G. Calabresi, *The Virtues of Presidential Government: Why Professor Ackerman is Wrong To Prefer the German to the U.S. Constitution,* 18 CONST. COMMENTARY 51 (2001).

[4]   *See* Sargentich, *supra* note 2, at 723–27.

the Vesting Clause). In terms of national security and foreign affairs, the President is made Commander-in-Chief of the military, given the power to make treaties with the advice and consent of the Senate, and given the authority to receive ambassadors. In terms of the internal operations of the government, the President can request written opinions from "principal officers," can appoint government officials, can issue pardons for "Offenses against the United States," can propose legislation, and is more generally directed "to take Care that the Laws be faithfully executed." (Article I, Section 7, also gives the President the power to veto legislation, subject to congressional override.) Since it is impossible for the government to investigate every possible violation of the law and bring enforcement proceedings, the executive branch has considerable discretion over enforcement decisions. One of the many unclear questions about presidential power is how to decide when enforcement discretion crosses the line into a failure to faithfully execute the laws.[5]

Finally, Section 4 says that the President and all other civil officers "shall be removed from Office on Impeachment for, and Conviction of, Treason, Bribery, or other high Crimes and Misdemeanors." The courts have never defined the scope of the grounds for impeachment, such as whether impeachment is limited to activities that violate criminal laws. (Most commentators believe that impeachment is not so limited.) Two Presidents (Andrew Johnson and Bill Clinton) have been impeached by the House, but neither was convicted by the constitutionally required 2/3 of the Senate (a very high hurdle). It is generally thought that Richard Nixon would have been impeached and convicted if he had not resigned first.

What Presidents do today is far more sweeping than Article II's list of powers might suggest. Domestically, the Office of the President rests atop a giant bureaucracy administering laws on subjects from immigration to environmental protection. Internationally, he controls ambassadors, the State Department, the Central Intelligence Agency (CIA), the National Security Agency (NSA), and other agencies of the world's most powerful country. He is Commander-in-Chief of the world's strongest military, with everything from Navy Seals to nuclear weapons at his command. Presidential responsibilities have become so large that the Office of the President now has several thousand employees.

As we will see, the President's powers are robust but not unlimited. Every recent President has been accused of usurpation of power by the political opposition. Courts have intervened when they

---

[5]   For discussion of this issue, see generally Patricia L. Bellia, *Faithful Execution and Enforcement Discretion*, 164 U. PA. L. REV. 1753 (2016).

have concluded that the President has transgressed legal limits. Congress, too, has attempted to curb the powers of the President, sometimes in ways that the Supreme Court has held unconstitutional.

As in the *Steel Seizure Case*, where the Court declared unconstitutional President Truman's seizure of the steel mills during the Korean War to keep them running in the face of a planned nationwide strike, the Court has recognized, but limited, presidential authority to act in domestic matters when Congress has not spoken.[6] Presidential authority over foreign affairs and the military are also ongoing controversies; probably every modern President has been accused of usurping congressional powers by the party out of power. With the tremendous growth in the size and power of the executive branch, the courts have increasingly found themselves arbitrating disputes about the boundaries between presidential and congressional authority over the appointment and tenure of government officials.

We will begin by considering theories of the presidency and the foundational case on presidential power, the *Steel Seizure Case*. We will then discuss the President's domestic powers as chief executive, before turning to his role in foreign and military affairs. Finally, we will discuss checks on the President.

II. The *Steel Seizure Case* and Theories of the Presidency

We ask some very basic questions in this section. How did the Framers think of the presidency during and just after the adoption of the Constitution? What assumptions did they make about how the separation of powers would operate, and to what extent have these assumptions held up? And what is the Supreme Court's general approach to questions of presidential power?

A. Presidential Power in the Founding Era

The discussion of the presidency at the Constitutional Convention was primarily focused on structural issues: whether to have a single head of the executive branch or divided control; how and by whom the President would be chosen; and how the President could be removed.[7] The presidency was also a bit of a side issue in the

---

[6]   *See* Youngstown Sheet & Tube Co. v. Sawyer, 343 U.S. 579, 637 (1952) (Jackson, J., concurring) ("When the President acts in the absence of either a congressional grant or denial of authority, he can only rely upon his own independent powers, but there is a zone of twilight in which he and Congress may have concurrent authority, or in which its distribution is uncertain.").

[7]   For a more detailed description of these portions of the debates, including key excerpts, see DANIEL A. FARBER & SUZANNA SHERRY, A HISTORY OF THE AMERICAN CONSTITUTION 115–63 (3d ed. 2013).

ratification debates, with much more attention being paid to the overall power and accountability of the federal government.

Nevertheless, there were some discussions of presidential power. The Anti-Federalists, who you will recall opposed ratification of the Constitution, were divided about the presidency, some thinking the President would be too strong and others too weak.[8] Some were worried that a weak president would be susceptible to "intrigues" by foreign powers.[9] One opponent worried that strong, ambitious Presidents would reduce members of Congress to "his sycophants and flatterers," while a weak President would be a "minion of the aristocrats, doing according to their will and pleasure, and confirming every law they think proper to make."[10]

On the pro-ratification side of the debate, the most notable contribution was by Hamilton, who then and always was a strong advocate of presidential power. In *Federalist No. 70*, Hamilton famously defended an energetic President:

> Energy in the Executive is a leading character in the definition of good government. It is essential to the protection of the community against foreign attacks; it is not less essential to the steady administration of the laws; to the protection of property against those irregular and highhanded combinations which sometimes interrupt the ordinary course of justice; to the security of liberty against the enterprises and assaults of ambition, of faction, and of anarchy.[11]

Hamilton explained the need for a single executive rather than a committee on the basis of this need for energetic government: "Decision, activity, secrecy, and dispatch will generally characterize the proceedings of one man in a much more eminent degree than the proceedings of any greater number; and in proportion as the number is increased, these qualities will be diminished."[12]

As a result of these disagreements, when Washington took office, it was unclear just how the power of the presidency would be implemented. Within a few years, a major dispute broke out about the scope of presidential power. Like many disputes to follow (such as the one over the national bank discussed in Chapter 4 and over

---

[8]   *See id.* at 306.

[9]   *Id.*

[10]   *Id.*

[11]   *Id.* at 307. The full text can be found at https://www.congress.gov/resources/display/content/The+Federalist+Papers#TheFederalistPapers-70.

[12]   *Id.*

the federal spending power in Chapter 6), this one found Hamilton on one side with Jefferson and Madison on the other.[13]

The dispute arose out of the delicate position in which the young nation was placed by war between France and England in the aftermath of the French Revolution. Everyone agreed that the United States, then a very weak power, needed to stay out of the conflict. In 1793, Washington issued the Neutrality Proclamation, which declared the nation to be a neutral party in the conflict and prohibited certain conduct by Americans, such as trade in contraband with either side. Despite the fact that Congress had never passed a statute criminalizing such behavior, the Proclamation announced that Americans would be subject to "punishment or forfeiture," including criminal prosecution, if they violated the rules governing neutrals under international law.[14] A public dispute arose over whether the President had the power to take this action.

Hamilton wrote a series of anonymous publications under the name "Pacificus" defending the President's action. He argued that the President is vested with broad powers beyond the explicit grants in Sections 2 and 3 of Article II, limited only by express constitutional language such as the clause giving the Senate a role in making treaties. He argued that the Vesting Clause of Article II gives the President powers beyond simply implementing the laws, and that these powers are merely illustrated in the rest of Article II. (This was the first appearance of what has come to be called the "unitary executive theory," which we discuss later in connection with the President's Appointments and Removal powers.) Since the nation's executive power was vested in the President, Hamilton reasoned, his authority to issue the Proclamation was unquestionable.[15] In addition, he argued that the President is responsible for executing the laws—not just domestic laws, but also "the Law of Nations" (as international law was then called).[16]

James Madison responded in another series of anonymous pamphlets under the name "Helvidius." He argued that executive authority must "presuppose the existence of laws to be executed," and these laws can be made only by the legislative branch.[17] He also accused Pacificus of deriving his vision of the President from the

---

[13]   For extensive background about the dispute, see generally Martin S. Flaherty, *The Story of the Neutrality Controversy: Struggling Over Presidential Power Outside the Courts, in* CHRISTOPHER H. SCHROEDER & CURTIS A. BRADLEY, PRESIDENTIAL POWER STORIES 21–52 (2009).

[14]   *Id.* at 25.

[15]   *See id.* at 35. Flaherty notes that this was only one of several arguments made by Hamilton on behalf of the Proclamation. *See id.*

[16]   *Id.* at 36.

[17]   *Id.* at 37–38.

powers of the English King, insisting that the Framers of the Constitution had rejected this vision of arbitrary executive power.[18]

The dispute between Hamilton and Madison over the powers of the President has endured until this day. Much of this dispute has taken place outside of the courts, particularly in the area of foreign policy, where courts are reluctant to intervene. Later in this chapter, we will devote considerable attention to the Supreme Court's rulings on key disputes that did make it into the courts.

B. Theoretical Perspectives

Madison explained the reasons for the separation of powers in a famous passage in *Federalist No. 51*:

> [T]he great security against a gradual concentration of the several powers in the same department, consists in giving to those who administer each department the necessary constitutional means and personal motives to resist encroachments of the others. . . . Ambition must be made to counteract ambition. The interest of the man must be connected with the constitutional rights of the place. It may be a reflection on human nature, that such devices should be necessary to control the abuses of government. But what is government itself, but the greatest of all reflections on human nature? If men were angels, no government would be necessary. If angels were to govern men, neither external nor internal controls on government would be necessary.[19]

Madison's vision has been contested in modern times, especially with respect to how Congress functions.[20] Elected officials may be much more interested in accomplishing their own goals, whether partisan or policy-oriented, than in defending the long-term strength of their institution.[21] Thus, under unified government, where Congress and the President are from the same party, Congress may have little interest in checking abuses by the executive branch or protecting its own prerogatives. The Framers did not anticipate the role of political parties in government, since the modern party system was only beginning to jell in England at the time. But political parties cut across the divisions of government so carefully created by the Framers, making possible unified action by party members in the

---

[18] *See id.* at 38.

[19] For the full text, see https://www.congress.gov/resources/display/content/The+Federalist+Papers#TheFederalistPapers-51.

[20] *See generally* Curtis A. Bradley & Trevor W. Morrison, *Historical Gloss and the Separation of Powers*, 126 HARV. L. REV. 411 (2012).

[21] *See generally* Daryl J. Levinson, *Foreword: Looking for Power in Public Law*, 130 HARV. L. REV. 33 (2016).

executive branch, Congress, and even state governments. Thus, institutions that were supposed to check each other may in fact be united by party allegiance.[22]

Thus, the empirical situation is more complex and in some ways quite different than what Madison imagined in *Federalist No. 51.* Yet, the constitutional framework developed by Madison and his colleagues remains intact. This leaves courts with the problem of applying separation of powers principles in a world in which governance can operate quite differently.

C.   The *Steel Seizure Case*

The leading case today on presidential power is *Youngstown Steel & Tube Co. v. Sawyer* (the *Steel Seizure Case*).[23] The case arose during the Korean War, when a labor dispute threatened to close American steel mills. President Harry Truman concluded that a strike would cripple the U.S. war effort. Consequently, he ordered the steel mills to be seized by the government. You may be picturing tanks and armed troops descending on the steel mills, but the seizure basically meant that notices were posted in the mills and that the government could set wages and prices. The steel companies continued to operate under protest and challenged the seizure as unconstitutional.

In the Supreme Court, the majority opinion was written by Justice Hugo Black. He observed that while two statutes did allow the President to seize property under certain circumstances, neither of them was applicable, and that Congress had provided other mechanisms for dealing with labor disputes.

He then turned to the potential sources of constitutional authorization for the seizure. Justice Black dismissed the argument that the seizure was an exercise of the President's power as commander-in-chief: "we cannot with faithfulness to our constitutional system hold that the Commander in Chief of the Armed Forces has the ultimate power as such to take possession of private property in order to keep labor disputes from stopping production. This is a job for the Nation's lawmakers, not for its military authorities."[24] Similarly, he was unwilling to rely on the President's executive power as a source of authority. "In the framework of the Constitution," he said, "the President's power to see that the laws are faithfully executed refutes the idea that he is to be

---

[22]   *See generally* Daryl J. Levinson & Richard H. Pildes, *Separation of Parties, Not Powers*, 119 HARV. L. REV. 1 (2006).

[23]   343 U.S. 579 (1952). For background on the case and an analysis of the opinions, see generally Patricia L. Bellia, *The Story of the Steel Seizure Case, in* SCHROEDER & BRADLEY, *supra* note 13, at 233–85.

[24]   *Steel Seizure*, 343 U.S. at 579.

a lawmaker."[25] Rather, Congress has the law-making power, and the Constitution "did not subject this law-making power of Congress to presidential or military supervision or control."[26] Finally, Justice Black found it irrelevant that previous Presidents had sometimes seized property without statutory authority in wartime or emergencies, for "even if this be true, Congress has not thereby lost its exclusive constitutional authority to make laws necessary and proper to carry out the powers vested by the Constitution 'in the Government of the United States, or in any Department or Officer thereof.' "[27] Because in his view the seizure lacked either congressional or constitutional authorization, Justice Black concluded that it was unconstitutional.

Although it was joined by four other Justices, the authoritativeness of Justice Black's majority opinion was undercut by the concurring opinions of these Justices, three of which deviated from his reasoning and considered the seizure invalid because it was at odds with congressional policy.[28] Instead of Justice Black's opinion, the more nuanced concurring opinion of Justice Robert Jackson has come to be seen as the authoritative statement of the law.[29] Justice Jackson's opinion is especially interesting because, as Attorney General for President Franklin Delano Roosevelt, he had endorsed strong executive action, including one seizure that the government cited in defense of the steel seizure.

Justice Jackson pooh-poohed the possibility of defining presidential power based on the original understanding. In his view, "[j]ust what our forefathers did envision, or would have envisioned had they foreseen modern conditions, must be divined from materials almost as enigmatic as the dreams Joseph was called upon to interpret for Pharaoh."[30] The lack of clear historical answers was not for lack of trying, he contended, for "[a] century and a half of partisan debate and scholarly speculation yields no net result but only supplies more or less apt quotations from respected sources on each side of any question."[31] Rather, he thought, it was important to view the issue of presidential power in the context of the working relationships between the branches of government, as they had struggled with the problems of governance over the years. Or, as put more eloquently by Justice Jackson, "[w]hile the Constitution diffuses power the better to secure liberty, it also contemplates that

---

[25]   *Id.* at 587.

[26]   *Id.* at 588.

[27]   *Id.* at 588–89.

[28]   *See* Belia, *supra* note 23, at 261.

[29]   *See id.* at 270–75.

[30]   *Steel Seizure*, 343 U.S. at 634 (Jackson, J., concurring).

[31]   *Id.* at 634–35.

practice will integrate the dispersed powers into a workable government. It enjoins upon its branches separateness but interdependence, autonomy but reciprocity."[32]

With this idea in mind, Justice Jackson divided issues of presidential power into three categories. In the first category, Congress has authorized the presidential action at issue, and the President's powers are at their maximum, because the President exercises the combined powers of both branches. In the second category, Congress is silent, but the President claims independent authority. Here, past practice can be important. According to Justice Jackson, "[w]hen the President acts in absence of either a congressional grant or denial of authority, he can only rely upon his own independent powers, but there is a zone of twilight in which he and Congress may have concurrent authority, or in which its distribution is uncertain."[33] Consequently, "congressional inertia, indifference or quiescence may sometimes, at least as a practical matter, enable, if not invite, measures on independent presidential responsibility."[34]

Justice Jackson found it difficult to prescribe rules for this category, believing that "any actual test of power is likely to depend on the imperatives of events and contemporary imponderables rather than on abstract theories of law."[35] In the third and final category, the President acts in the face of a congressional prohibition, and here "his power is at its lowest ebb."[36] The President's "claim to a power at once so conclusive and preclusive must be scrutinized with caution, for what is at stake is the equilibrium established by our constitutional system."[37]

Justice Jackson placed President Truman's steel seizure in the third category because Congress had not left property seizures as open territory, but had provided for its use in some circumstances that were not present. This left only the third category, in which presidential actions are subject to the most stringent scrutiny. He rejected the argument that the Vesting Clause gave the President unlimited powers: "The example of such unlimited executive power that must have most impressed the forefathers was the prerogative exercised by George III, and the description of its evils in the Declaration of Independence leads me to doubt that they were

---

[32] *Id.* at 635.
[33] *Id.* at 637.
[34] *Id.*
[35] *Id.*
[36] *Id.*
[37] *Id.* at 638.

creating their new Executive in his image."[38] Justice Jackson also thought the Commander-in-Chief Clause inapplicable, seeing "indications that the Constitution did not contemplate that the title Commander in Chief *of the Army and Navy* will constitute him also Commander in Chief of the country, its industries and its inhabitants."[39] Finally, Justice Jackson rejected the government's reliance on the Take Care Clause, which he viewed as extending presidential power as far as there is law to enforce, while the Due Process Clause means that government power extends no further than law exists to authorize it.[40] Finding no explicit grant of power to the President that might override congressional disapproval, Jackson held the seizure unconstitutional.

The *Steel Seizure Case* shows that exercises of presidential power are on strongest ground when they trace to some grant of authority, either in a specific clause in the Constitution or in a statute enacted by Congress. Relatedly, the case establishes what can be called the fundamental principle of congressional priority—that with few exceptions, the law maker (Congress) gets to control the law enforcer (the President).

The status of Justice Jackson's opinion as authoritative was cemented by *Dames & Moore v. Regan.*[41] Perhaps not coincidentally, this opinion was written by Justice William Rehnquist, who had been a law clerk for Justice Jackson during the term in which the *Steel Seizure Case* was decided.[42] *Dames & Moore* arose from the seizure of the American embassy in Tehran by Iranians. President Ronald Reagan negotiated an agreement for the release of the hostages, in return for which the United States agreed to release Iranian funds in America, suspend all legal actions in U.S. courts against the government of Iran, and refer all claims to an international tribunal. The major constitutional dispute involved the suspension of litigation in the U.S. courts. Although no statute directly authorized the suspension, the Court concluded that the case fell in Justice Jackson's first category, given a long practice of presidential settlement of private claims against foreign governments and congressional legislation implementing these settlements.

In practice, within the domestic sphere at least, presidential power nearly always stems solely from a grant of authority by Congress. If congressional authority is to exercise any constraint over the executive branch, Congress cannot be allowed to simply

---

[38] *Id.* at 641.

[39] *Id.* at 643–44.

[40] *Id.* at 646.

[41] 453 U.S. 654 (1981).

[42] *See* Belia, *supra* note 23, at 270.

surrender unlimited authority to the President. Under the nondelegation doctrine, a congressional grant of authority is valid only if it is governed by some "intelligible principle" setting its boundaries. This principle can be very broad. For instance, Justice Antonin Scalia's opinion for the Court in *Whitman v. American Trucking Associations, Inc.*,[43] upheld a statute giving the Environmental Protection Agency (EPA) the power to set air quality standards necessary to protect public health, even though the EPA must make many judgment calls about how much protection is required. To date, the Court has found a violation of the nondelegation doctrine in only two cases in its history, both dating from 1935.[44]

In the next two sections, we will consider how Presidents have executed their Article II powers, both in controlling the apparatus of government as the Chief Executive and in foreign affairs. We will then take a closer look at the checks on presidential power.

III. The President as Chief Executive

The President has several powers that provide legal authority over nearly all of the federal government's operations. He has broad power to nominate top-level federal officials and to appoint some others. While the Supreme Court has allowed some exceptions, it has tended to resist efforts to shift appointments authority to others. Although the appointments power is governed by Article II, the text says nothing explicitly about the President's power to remove officials. As we will see, however, the Supreme Court has implied a broad, but not unlimited, removal power.

The primary obligation of federal employees is to implement federal law. Their activities cover a very broad range, including managing federal lands, collecting taxes, investigating and prosecuting federal crimes, paying government benefits like Social Security, disbursing other funds, and issuing regulations. In addition to overseeing these activities, the President also represents the nation in the international sphere. The large majority of federal employees may never set eyes on the President. But the President's input into federal budget decisions and ability to hire and fire higher-

---

[43]   531 U.S. 457 (2001).

[44]   The two cases are *Panama Refining Co. v. Ryan*, 293 U.S. 388 (1935) (striking down a statute that gave the President complete discretion over whether to ban the shipment in interstate commerce of oil produced in violation of state law), and *A.L.A. Schechter Poultry Corp. v. United States*, 295 U.S. 495 (1935) (delegating to a private group the power to issue binding codes of conduct for an industry). The separate Commerce Clause challenge in the *Schechter Poultry* case was discussed in Chapter 5.

level officials provide leverage (albeit not completely effective control) over the rest of the federal government's sprawling operations.

The President takes an active role in these activities and has a large White House staff to implement presidential views. In the early days, Presidents had little or no staff, but the Executive Office of the President is now a bureaucracy in its own right, sitting above the formal bureaucracy. The White House vets appointments with support for the President's policies as one criterion. This allows the President to set policies and policy priorities for the administration. The President also does much to shape legislation, in part by methods set forth in the Constitution (such as the State of the Union Address and the veto power), but also by proposing new legislation and setting national reform agendas, not to mention twisting the arms of recalcitrant members of Congress. The President is also the face of the United States internationally.

In terms of control of the government, the power to hire and fire is perhaps the most important of the President's tools. We consider these powers below.

A.   The Appointments Power

The Appointments Clause takes up much of Article II, Section 2. It sets out three categories of appointments. First, with the advice and consent of the Senate, the President appoints "Ambassadors, other public Ministers and Consuls, [and] Judges of the supreme Court." Second, also subject to Senate approval, the President appoints "all other Officers of the United States, whose Appointments are not herein otherwise provided for, and which shall be established by Law." Third, Congress "may by Law vest the Appointment of such inferior Officers, as they think proper, in the President alone, in the Courts of Law, or in the Heads of Departments." The key distinction is between inferior officers, for which Congress can designate the person making the appointment, and principal officers (who are also called officers of the United States), for whom presidential nomination and Senate approval are required.

Another distinction, not explicit in the Constitution, is between "officers" and government employees. Obviously, it would make no sense to require that every file clerk and janitor employed by the federal government be appointed by the President or a cabinet officer, let alone to require Senate confirmation in the absence of legislation to the contrary.

This is a technical and somewhat arcane area of constitutional law, but it has significant implications for the scope of presidential control over the government and for the extent to which employees can be appointed through merit procedures like the Civil Service system. Besides involving a power struggle between Congress and the President over control of appointments, interpretation of the Appointments Clause also implicates disputes over which positions can be at least partially insulated from politics. There are really three key distinctions: between inferior and principal officers; between officers and employees, and between executive and legislative officers. A final issues involves the President's power to make appointments when the Senate is not in session.

The first key distinction is between principal officers, who require Presidential nomination and Senate approval, and inferior officers, who do not. In *Edmond v. United States*,[45] the Court was faced with the question whether a member of a military appeals court was a principal officer. The Court identified as the key factor whether an officer has a superior directing and supervising the officer's work. The Court held that members of the military court were inferior officers because their decisions could not become final without the permission of other executive officers.

In an earlier case, however, the Court had suggested a more flexible test. *Morrison v. Olson*[46] involved the constitutionality of a law permitting the appointment of independent counsels by the courts. (Recall that one of the options for appointing inferior officers is appointment by "the courts of law.") In holding that the independent counsels were inferior officers, the Court considered not only the degree of supervision but also the limited scope of the appointment (that is, investigations of only a particular event or official) and the removability of the prosecutor by the Attorney General. In a post-*Edmond* case, *Free Enterprise Foundation v. Public Company Accounting Oversight Board (PCAOB)*,[47] the Court again mentioned removability as well as supervision. Thus, it remains somewhat unclear whether the single-factor test of *Edmond* is controlling.

The second key distinction is between officers and employees. *Lucia v. Securities & Exchange Commission*[48] illustrates the legal standard. The Supreme Court cast doubt on laws that require administrative law judges to be appointed under the Civil Service system, which limits appointments to individuals passing through a merit-based test. Administrative law judges are officials in an administrative agency who conduct hearings on issues involving application of the law to specific facts, on issues such as whether a

---

[45]   520 U.S. 651 (1997).

[46]   487 U.S. 654 (1988).

[47]   561 U.S. 477 (2020). (PCAOB is often pronounced as "peekaboo.")

[48]   ___ U.S. ___, 138 S. Ct. 2044 (2018).

permit should be granted or (as in *Lucia*) whether an individual has violated the securities laws. The Court applied a two-part test: whether an official has a continuing government position or is temporary, and whether the official exercises significant legal authority involving the exercise of discretion. Even though the decisions of SEC judges do not become final without review by the Commission, the Court concluded that the judge's control over the conduct of the trial was enough to constitute significant legal authority. Hence, the appointment had to be made by the Commission itself (as head of the department) rather than being delegated to a staff member.

The final distinction is between executive branch and congressional officials. Congress can appoint its own officials, such as the head of the Congressional Budget Office, which is charged with estimating the budgetary impact of bills introduced in Congress. But the Appointments Clause provides no role for Congress in making executive branch appointments (apart from the Senate's power to give advice and consent for principal officers.) *Buckley v. Valeo*[49] applied the principle prohibiting congressional participation to strike down a law that gave the congressional leadership the power to appoint some members of the Federal Election Commission (FEC), which enforces laws relating to campaign contributions and expenditures.

The Recess Appointments Clause, located in the third clause of Article II, Section 2, authorizes presidential appointments when the Senate is in recess. It provides that "[t]he President shall have Power to fill up all Vacancies that may happen during the Recess of the Senate, by granting Commissions which shall expire at the End of their next Session." Although not their original purpose, these recess appointments have been an important fallback for Presidents when the Senate is blockading their appointments. The Senate has responded by attempting as much as possible to eliminate formal recesses. In *NLRB v. Noel Canning*,[50] President Barrack Obama had made appointments to an agency without Senate approval. The Senate had halted all official business and left for vacation, but left behind a Senator to hold brief "pro forma" sessions so as to avoid any recess. The Supreme Court held that these pro forma sessions were enough to prevent an actual recess, rendering invalid the President's efforts to make recess appointments, reasoning that the Senate is in session whenever it says it is, so long as Senate rules permit it to transact Senate business. The Court otherwise broadly interpreted the Recess Appointments Clause. Placing more weight on historical

---

[49]   424 U.S. 1 (1976).

[50]   134 S. Ct. 2550 (2014).

practice than on the ostensible plain meaning of the constitutional text, the Court held that the Clause authorizes the President to fill any existing vacancy during any recess of sufficient length, regardless of when the vacancy arose and regardless of whether the recess occurs during or between sessions of Congress.[51]

B.   The Implied Removal Power

The removal power has been far more contentious than the appointments power. The Constitution says nothing about the President's power to remove executive branch officials. One might infer from this silence that the matter is left to Congress to determine under the Necessary and Proper Clause. Alternatively, one might infer that the same procedures apply for removal as appointment, meaning that removal of a principal officer requires the consent of the Senate. The Supreme Court has not taken either of these approaches. Instead, the Court has held that the President has the implied power to remove executive branch officers, subject to some exceptions that we will discuss. There is considerable dispute about the original understanding and early government practice in this regard.[52]

Myers v. United States[53] is the foundational case. *Myers* involved the removal of a local postmaster by the Postmaster General, despite a statute requiring the advice and consent of the Senate for removals. The opinion of the Court was written by Chief Justice (and former President) William Howard Taft. The Court held that this statute was unconstitutional, upholding broad presidential power to remove executive branch officials. The Court reasoned that such power was necessary to preserve the unity and coordination of the executive branch and because in matters subject to presidential discretion, executive branch officials operate as the President's agents.

Myers used sweeping language regarding the removal power and the President's power to supervise the executive branch, but the holding is not quite as sweeping as it may seem. First, *Myers* did not disturb the holding of a previous decision that gave Congress the power to "limit and regulate removal of such inferior officers by heads of departments when it exercises its constitutional power to lodge the

---

[51]   For analysis of the interpretive relationship between historical political branch practice and the text of the Constitution in *Noel Canning*, see generally Curtis A. Bradley & Neil S. Siegel, *After Recess: Historical Practice, Textual Ambiguity, and Constitutional Adverse Possession*, 2014 SUP. CT. REV. 1. (2015).

[52]   *See generally* Lawrence Lessig & Cass R. Sunstein, *The President and the Administration*, 94 COLUM. L. REV. 1 (1994).

[53]   272 U.S. 52 (1926). For background on *Myers* and a defense of its holding, see generally Saikrishna Prakash, *The Story of* Myers *and Its Wayward Successors, in* SCHROEDER & BRADLEY, *supra* note 13, at_165–94.

power of appointment with them."[54] (In the *PCAOB* case, the Court limited this holding to cases in which the head of the department was subject to removal by the President.) Second, the Court recognized some exceptions to the President's power to supervise the executive branch. The Court noted that "there may be duties so peculiarly and specifically committed to the discretion of a particular officer as to raise a question whether the President may overrule or revise the officer's interpretation of his statutory duty in a particular instance."[55] The Court also noted that "there may be duties of a quasi judicial character imposed on executive officers and members of executive tribunals whose decisions after hearing affect interests of individuals, the discharge of which the President cannot in a particular case properly influence or control."[56] Even in these instances, however, the Court thought the President should be able to remove an officer based on a judgment that the "discretion regularly entrusted to that officer by statute has not been on the whole intelligently or wisely exercised."[57]

In its next encounter with the removal power, the Court gave further attention to the "quasi-judicial" category of officials. *Humphrey's Executor v. United States*[58] involved President Franklin Delano Roosevelt's removal of a member of the Federal Trade Commission (FTC). The FTC was established by Congress as an independent agency whose members are appointed by the President with the advice and consent of the Senate. The statute provides that these officials do not serve at the will of the President; rather, the President can remove these officials only for "inefficiency, neglect of duty, or malfeasance in office." (It is this statutory limitation on the President's removal power that makes the agency independent.) Conservative Justice George Sutherland wrote the opinion for a unanimous Court upholding the statute. Justice Sutherland's opinion limited *Myers* to purely executive officers, who do not exercise quasi-legislative or quasi-judicial powers. Members of the FTC were not purely executive in that they were charged with interpreting the broad language of the statute prohibiting unfair trade practices and they decided cases dealing with the conduct of individual companies.

The leading—and by far the most controversial—case regarding the removal power is *Morrison v. Olson*, which we discussed briefly

---

[54]   *Myers*, 272 U.S. at 127. The previous decision was *United States v. Perkins*, 116 U.S. 483, 483 (1886).

[55]   *Myers*, 272 U.S. at 135.

[56]   *Id.*

[57]   *Id.*

[58]   295 U.S. 602 (1935).

above in connection with the Appointments Clause.[59] A statute passed after Watergate established the position of independent counsel to pursue allegations of misconduct by high government officials, including the President. Congress was at great pains to eliminate political influence over the independent counsel. Apart from impeachment or the termination of the independent counsel's work, the independent counsel could be removed "only by the personal action of the Attorney General and only for good cause, physical disability, mental incapacity, or any other condition that substantially impairs the performance of such independent counsel's duties."[60]

Chief Justice Rehnquist's opinion for the Court abandoned the distinction between purely executive and quasi-legislative or quasi-judicial officials. Instead, his opinion upheld the "good cause" removal provision on broader grounds. He pointed out that the independent counsel is "an inferior officer under the Appointments Clause, with limited jurisdiction and tenure and lacking policymaking or significant administrative authority."[61] Chief Justice Rehnquist conceded that "the counsel exercises no small amount of discretion and judgment in deciding how to carry out his or her duties under the Act," but "we simply do not see how the President's need to control the exercise of that discretion is so central to the functioning of the Executive Branch as to require as a matter of constitutional law that the counsel be terminable at will by the President."[62] Nor did the Court think that the for-cause removal provision "impermissibly burdens the President's power to control or supervise the independent counsel, as an executive official, in the execution of his or her duties under the Act," since "the Executive, through the Attorney General, retains ample authority to assure that the counsel is competently performing his or her statutory responsibilities in a manner that comports with the provisions of the Act."[63]

Chief Justice Rehnquist also rejected a more general separation of powers challenge to the statute as a whole, including both the appointment and removal provisions.[64] The Court concluded that the statute did not involve the judicial branch in performing non-judicial functions in appointing the independent counsel or in determining

---

[59]   Background on the case can be found in Kevin M. Stack, *The Story of Morrison v. Olson: The Independent Counsel and Independent Agencies in Watergate's Wake*, *in* SCHROEDER & BRADLEY, *supra* note 13.

[60]   *Morrison*, 487 U.S. at 663.

[61]   *Id.* at 691.

[62]   *Id.* at 691–92.

[63]   *Id.* at 692.

[64]   *See id.* at 694–95.

the scope of the inquiry. Nor did the law aggrandize congressional power at the expense of the President, since Congress had no control over the appointment or removal of the independent counsel or the counsel's investigation.

Justice Scalia alone dissented. It would be something of an understatement to say that he emphatically rejected the majority's reasoning. He emphasized the general principle of separation of powers, saying that "[i]f to describe this case is not to decide it, the concept of a government of separate and coordinate powers no longer has meaning."[65] After quoting the Vesting Clause, he laid out what has come to be known as the theory of the unitary executive:

> This does not mean some of the executive power, but *all* of the executive power. It seems to me, therefore, that the decision of the Court of Appeals invalidating the present statute must be upheld on fundamental separation-of-powers principles if the following two questions are answered affirmatively: (1) Is the conduct of a criminal prosecution (and of an investigation to decide whether to prosecute) the exercise of purely executive power? (2) Does the statute deprive the President of the United States of exclusive control over the exercise of that power?[66]

To ask these questions was indeed to answer them, since prosecution is commonly considered a core executive function and the whole purpose of the statue was to limit presidential control over investigations of high officials. Of course, the majority did not agree that these were the right questions to ask.

Justice Scalia then disposed quickly of the removal issue:

> As far as I can discern from the Court's opinion, it is now open season upon the President's removal power for all executive officers, with not even the superficially principled restriction of *Humphrey's Executor* as cover. The Court essentially says to the President: "Trust us. We will make sure that you are able to accomplish your constitutional role." I think the Constitution gives the President—and the people—more protection than that.[67]

Morrison remains controversial to this day and is obviously unacceptable to adherents of the unitary executive theory. Arguably, the Court underestimated the extent to which the (since expired) independent counsel law undermined the functioning of the presidency. In Justice Scalia's view, however, this question is

---

[65]   *Id.* at 703–04 (Scalia, J., dissenting).

[66]   *Id.* at 705.

[67]   *Id.* at 726–27.

irrelevant, since he insisted that any interference with presidential control of the executive branch, however slight, would invalidate the statute.[68] Supporters of *Morrison* emphasize its vital importance in safeguarding congressional power to prevent the President from further entrenching himself in power by hobbling or terminating federal criminal investigations of the President or his campaign, aides, or associates. Regardless of who is right, *Morrison* remains the law.

C.   The Unitary Executive Theory and Its Critics

Justice Scalia's approach in *Morrison* illustrates the unitary executive theory, which holds that the President has inherent constitutional power to appoint any officer charged with executing the laws, to remove such officers at will, and to direct their decisions. In a nutshell, under this theory, every other executive officer is simply an alter ego of the President. This theory has been championed by conservatives like Justice Scalia in recent years, and not surprisingly has also found favor with Presidents of all political orientations. The theory can be seen as relying on three major arguments: the constitutional text, the original understanding, and subsequent practice.

Here, we will try to give a brief overview of the main arguments of the theory's advocates and critics. Hundreds of pages in law reviews have been devoted to this debate, and we do not purport to provide anything close to an in-depth analysis. Nor do we discuss the rounds of rebuttals and rejoinders from both sides that have developed around these main points.

Text. In terms of the text, the theory relies first and foremost on the Vesting Clause. Unitary executive theorists argue that this clause places the executive power in the President, not in some more diffuse body. This understanding of the Vesting Clause is reinforced by the Take Care Clause, which makes the President personally responsible for the execution of the laws.[69]

Critics of the unitary theory do not view the Vesting Clause as a substantive grant of power but rather as descriptive of the general nature of the office.[70] They note that other parts of Article II speak of duties or powers of other officers, implying that the President does not hold all executive power in his or her own hands. In the critics'

---

[68]   *See id.* at 708.

[69]   For discussion of the textual bases of the unitary executive theory, see Steven G. Calabresi & Saikrishna B. Prakash, *The President's Power to Execute the Laws*, 104 YALE L.J. 541, 579–99 (1994).

[70]   For the critics' view of the text, see Peter L. Strauss, *Overseer, or "The Decider"? The President in Administrative Law*, 75 GEO. WASH. L. REV. 696, 702–03 (2007).

view, the Take Care Clause requires the President to do his or her best to ensure that the laws are faithfully executed but does not imply that the President is responsible for all decisions made throughout the executive branch. And the Take Care Clause may actually impose limitations on the President's removal power, since removing a prosecutor just because the prosecutor is investigating the President's potential violation of federal criminal laws would seem to violate the obligation imposed by the Clause. Critics also point to other clauses that would seem superfluous if the President had complete control of the executive branch from the Vesting Clause, such as the power to require the heads of departments to give him their opinions in writing.[71] Furthermore, critics point out that the removal power is implied, not express, so there is no reason that exceptions could not also be implied. Finally, critics emphasize that the Necessary and Proper Clause gives Congress the power to pass not only laws necessary and proper to the exercise of its own powers, but also to the powers vested in the other branches of the federal government.

Original Understanding. Advocates of the unitary executive theory also point to a considerable body of evidence before and during the drafting and ratification of the Constitution.[72] Well-known political theorists such as John Locke and Montesquieu wrote of the importance of separating the legislative and executive powers to avoid tyranny. Some opponents of the Constitution advocated an executive council to restrain and counsel the President; supporters pointed to the need for a single head of the executive branch to obtain vigorous action as well as accountability. In addition, certain essays in the *Federalist Papers*, particularly *Federalist No. 70* (which we have discussed earlier), stress the need for an energetic executive. The ratification debates also contained expressions of the importance of the Take Care Clause to ensure the vigorous enforcement of federal law.

Critics of the unitary executive theory point to other historical evidence bearing on the role of the President.[73] Essentially, they view unitary theorists as cherry-picking statements that give a false picture of clarity and consensus rather than portraying the more complex and conflicted process of decisionmaking. Critics see considerable dispute and uncertainty at the Constitutional Convention about the meaning of the separation of powers. For

---

[71]   U.S. CONST. art. II, § 2, cl. 1.

[72]   *See* Calabresi & Prakash, *supra* note 69, at 603–35.

[73]   *See* Martin S. Flaherty, *The Most Dangerous Branch*, 105 YALE L.J. 1725, 1755–1810 (1996). For a thorough critique of the unitary executive theory, see generally Curtis A. Bradley & Martin S. Flaherty, *Executive Power Essentialism and Foreign Affairs*, 102 MICH. L. REV. 545 (2004).

instance, Madison proposed a Council of Revision that combined executive and judicial functions. Rather than reflecting a clear theoretical understanding of the separation of powers, debates turned on more functionalist considerations. During ratification, according to the critics, the supporters of the Constitution pointed to the need for unity at the top of the executive branch, but did not further argue that all officials must be at the beck and call of the chief executive in order to ensure effective government. Indeed, at the time of the Founding, a variety of public and private actors enforced federal law.

Historical Practice and Judicial Precedent. Advocates of the unitary executive theory rely on post-ratification historical practice to confirm their position.[74] Much of this history concerns actions and statements by early Presidents, who asserted the power to direct a variety of other executive branch officials. Congress was divided on the issue, but many members did believe that the President had the constitutional power to remove executive branch officers, though quite a few others disagreed.

Once again, critics contest the evidence.[75] They point to the laws establishing the Treasury Department and the Comptroller General as instances in which Congress took pains to establish the duties of offices independently of the President and in which Congress viewed these offices as enjoying a special relationship with its own activities. Madison seemed to think that officers performing more judicial functions should be shielded from removal. Although the statute establishing the Post Office originally provided that it would operate under the direction of the President, this language was removed almost immediately when the law was amended. Moreover, the Bank of the United States, which we discussed in Chapter 4, was considered a federal instrumentality but the President appointed only five directors and had the power to remove only these five.

As we observed earlier, none of these arguments and counter-arguments have gone uncontested. We do not expect the debate among legal scholars and historians to be settled any time soon. As for the Supreme Court, the closest that it has come to endorsing the unitary executive theory was in *Myers*. As we have seen, however, even in *Myers* there was some equivocation regarding quasi-judicial officers, and the Court acknowledged that the President does not have the constitutional power to fire inferior officers appointed by the heads of departments. Today's increasingly conservative Court may well embrace the unitary executive theory. But present doctrine has

---

[74] *See* Calabresi & Prakash, *supra* note 69, at 635–63. For more extensive treatment, see generally STEVEN G. CALABRESI & CHRISTOPHER S. YOO, THE UNITARY EXECUTIVE: PRESIDENTIAL POWER FROM WASHINGTON TO BUSH (2008).

[75] *See* Lessig & Sunstein, *supra* note 52, at 43–55.

yet to adopt it, and doing so would require the Court to overrule *Humphrey's Executor* and declare independent federal agencies unconstitutional. Overruling an 83-year-old precedent that provides a constitutional foundation for key parts of the modern administrative state would be no small judicial intervention.

More generally, the unitary executive theory is inconsistent with much of Twentieth Century political-branch practice. Modern practice includes not only a variety of independent federal agencies (for example, the FEC, the FTC, and the SEC, all mentioned above), but also civil service protections, inspectors general, a variety of for-cause removal restrictions in federal laws, and voluntary state enforcement of federal law. It is not clear how to reconcile such practice with the claim that the President must retain exclusive control over the exercise of federal executive power.

Modern practice also entails a President who wields great influence over the Department of Justice (DOJ), the Federal Bureau of Investigation (FBI), the Internal Revenue Service (IRS), the Central Intelligence Agency (CIA), and the National Security Agency (NSA), among other federal departments and agencies. No one at the time of the Founding or early Eighteenth Century imagined such a potent President, and it raises concerns about placing so much executive power in the hands of one individual, who the unitary executive theory would authorize to fire federal prosecutors at will just because they were investigating him (as in *Morrison*). Congress remains theoretically available to check the President, but nor did anyone early in American history imagine such a polarized and dysfunctional Congress as exists today.

IV. Foreign Affairs and Military Powers

As we will see, the President's powers are at their apex in the area of foreign affairs, including essentially everything outside our borders. But it is important to keep in mind that Congress also has important foreign affairs powers. The Senate must approve treaties and the appointment of ambassadors. Under Article I, Section 8, Congress is authorized to declare war and put in charge of raising armies and maintaining the Navy, including the power to make rules for their "Government and Regulation." The Commerce Clause gives Congress the power to regulate international commerce, not just commerce among the states. Congress also has power to punish "Offences against the Law of Nations." Congress can intervene using other powers, such as conducting oversight hearings and refusing to appropriate funds for some activity abroad that the President wants to pursue.

We saw in Chapter 3 that courts are wary of intervening in the area of foreign affairs, often invoking the political question doctrine as a barrier to jurisdiction. As a result of the rather circumspect judicial role, there is often no referee available to arbitrate disputes over the division of power between the President and Congress. Advocates on both side have, over the course of two centuries, evolved their own batteries of arguments based on the constitutional text and structure, evidence of the original understanding, whatever caselaw does exist, and historical practice, sometimes augmented by arguments about likely consequences. It is noteworthy, however, that both sides do feel compelled to make constitutional arguments rather than just relying on policy arguments or party loyalty. In this arena, constitutional politics plays a larger role than constitutional law, if by constitutional law we mean rulings by the courts.

A.　Inherent Foreign Affairs Powers

The Court spoke in sweeping terms about presidential power in the realm of foreign affairs in *United States v. Curtiss-Wright Export Corporation*.[76] The case grew out of a war in South America that had produced increasing bloodshed. Congress passed a law giving the President the power to ban exports of weapons to either side if doing so would help bring the war to a close. The President issued such a ban, and the defendant blatantly violated it, claiming it involved an unconstitutional delegation of power to the President. Although the *Steel Seizure Case* was still some years in the future, the Court rejected this argument on grounds that we can now see as referring to category one of Jackson's classification scheme. The Court emphasized the breadth of presidential power where Congress has authorized an action in the foreign sphere and where the President also has independent authority.

The language of the opinion went well beyond the facts of the case. The Court first stated that the foreign affairs power, unlike domestic legislative power, was already vested in the Union prior to the adoption of the Constitution as an aspect of national sovereignty.[77] The Court then argued that this inherent power was vested in the President:

> Not only, as we have shown, is the federal power over external affairs in origin and essential character different from that over internal affairs, but participation in the exercise of the power is significantly limited. In this vast external realm, with its important, complicated, delicate and manifold problems, the President alone has the power to speak or listen as a representative of the nation.[78]

---

[76]　299 U.S. 304 (1936).

[77]　*Id.* at 318.

[78]　*Id.* at 319.

In addition to this theoretical argument, the Court relied on practical considerations, such as the need for secrecy in the conduct of diplomacy and the President's access to confidential information.[79] "In short," the Court wrote, "we are here dealing not alone with an authority vested in the President by an exertion of legislative power, but with such an authority plus the very delicate, plenary and exclusive power of the President as the sole organ of the federal government in the field of international relations."[80]

The *Curtiss-Wright* theory of inherent foreign affairs powers, derived outside the power grants in the Constitution, has not been repeated in later opinions. This is perhaps because such a theory is in serious tension with the foundational idea of a national government of limited, enumerated powers. But lawyers for the executive branch never tire of quoting the language about presidential supremacy in foreign affairs.

Zivotovsky v. Kerry (*Zivotovsky II*)[81] exemplifies the approach taken in later decisions. The parents of a child who had been born in Jerusalem wanted his passport to identify this city as part of Israel. At the time, longstanding U.S. foreign policy was not to classify the city as part of any country so as to avoid taking sides in the conflict between Israelis and Palestinians, both of whom claim Jerusalem as their capitol. Notwithstanding this executive branch policy, Congress passed a statute allowing individuals born in Jerusalem to have Israel listed as the location of their birth. The Court viewed this as a "category three" situation under the *Steel Seizure Case*. Quoting this decision, the Court said that "[t]o succeed in this third category, the President's asserted power must be both 'exclusive' and 'conclusive' on the issue."[82]

The Court held that this was one of those rare instances in which the stringent category-three test was satisfied. It reasoned that Article II powers, such as the power to receive ambassadors, carry with them exclusive presidential control over the recognition of foreign governments, because recognition of a foreign government involves not only accepting the government as legitimate but also determining its boundaries. The Court further reasoned that passports are communications between the United States and foreign governments, and thus are also under presidential control. The Court thought these conclusions were confirmed by past practice, inasmuch as "the President since the founding has exercised this unilateral

---

[79]   *See id.*

[80]   *Id.* at 319–20.

[81]   576 U.S. ___, 135 S. Ct. 2076 (2015). *Zivotovsky I*, in which the Court held that the case was not covered by the political question doctrine, was discussed in Chapter 3.

[82]   *Id.* at 2084.

power to recognize new [nation] states—and the Court has endorsed the practice."[83] Interestingly, on this occasion, as in *Noel Canning* (discussed above), Justice Scalia argued for a narrower view of executive authority. "Recognition," he said, "is a type of legal act, not a type of statement."[84] In his view, it was "a leap worthy of the Mad Hatter to go from exclusive authority over making legal commitments about sovereignty to exclusive authority over making statements or issuing documents about national borders."[85] "The Court," he added, "may as well jump from power over issuing declaratory judgments to a monopoly on writing law-review articles."[86]

Medellín v. Texas[87] was an unusual defeat for the President in a foreign affairs case. The background of this case is complex. Under the Vienna Convention on Consular Relations, the United States and other countries have agreed to give each other's citizens the right to contact their countries' consuls (diplomatic representatives) when arrested. Some American states did not comply with this requirement. Mexico filed a case against the United States in the International Court of Justice (ICJ) in the Hague, which ruled that the United States was in violation and that certain individuals convicted without having been allowed to contact their consuls were entitled to reconsideration of their convictions, regardless of whether they had raised this objection at trial. One of these individuals then attempted to have his conviction vacated. The United States had agreed to submit to the jurisdiction of the ICJ in another treaty. The Supreme Court held that this second treaty was not self-executing, meaning that, until implemented through legislation, it could not be directly enforced by federal or state courts. Perhaps anticipating this problem, President George W. Bush had issued a memorandum stating that the United States "would 'discharge its international obligations' . . . 'by having State courts give effect to the decision.' "[88] The federal government argued that this memorandum was binding on state courts.

In an opinion by Chief Justice John Roberts, the Court rejected this assertion of presidential authority. Because a non-self-executing treaty is intended to have no domestic legal effect until implemented through legislation, a presidential edict to give it domestic legal effect falls into category 3 of the *Steel Seizure* trichotomy. Unlike the President's power to settle foreign claims, the Chief Justice wrote,

---

[83]   *Id.* at 2086.

[84]   *Id.* at 2121.

[85]   *Id.*

[86]   *Id.*

[87]   552 U.S. 491 (2008).

[88]   *Id.* at 503.

"the Government has not identified a single instance in which the President has attempted (or Congress has acquiesced in) a presidential directive issued to state courts, much less one that reaches deep into the heart of the State's police powers and compels state courts to reopen final criminal judgments and set aside neutrally applicable state laws."[89]

Medellín makes it clear that Justice Jackson's concurrence in the *Steel Seizure Case* is firmly established law. *Medellín* also reflects the Court's attentiveness to historical practice in this area, although the Court is always careful to note that past practice would not validate clearly unconstitutional conduct. Both of these aspects of the doctrine reflect a judicial recognition that disputes over the boundaries between Congress and the President are primarily resolved between these two branches through the political process.

B. Executive Agreements

Article II empowers the President to make treaties, but only with the consent of the Senate. Presidents make agreements with foreign countries all the time, however, without ever submitting them to the Senate for approval. The closest thing to a textual hook for this practice is the Compact Clause of Article I, Section 10. This Clause requires congressional consent for any state to "enter into any Agreement or Compact with another State, or with a foreign power." States are forbidden, however, from entering treaties with foreign powers by earlier language in Section 10. The implication is that an "Agreement or Compact" is different from a treaty, since states can enter into one but not the other. This does not necessarily mean that the President has the power to enter into these lesser agreements with foreign powers, but it does mean that if the President does so, Senate consent is not required. And given the President's leading role in foreign affairs and the states' minimal role, it would seem odd to say that states but not the President can enter some types of agreements with foreign countries.

United States v. Belmont[90] arose from President Franklin D. Roosevelt's decision to give diplomatic recognition to the Soviet Union in the 1930s. The Soviets had seized Russian corporations after the Russian Revolution, and an American bank held funds of these companies. Because the Soviet government had taken over the corporation, they demanded that the funds be paid to them. The Soviets agreed to assign their claims against these Americans to the U.S. government. The Court's opinion does not explain the purpose of this assignment, but it had the effect of keeping the Soviets out of

---

[89]   *Id.* at 532.

[90]   301 U.S. 324 (1937).

the U.S. courts, while also leaving the U.S. government holding money that the Soviets might want to use as an offset against their own debts to U.S. citizens and companies. This assignment was part of a larger effort to resolve all claims and counterclaims between the two countries. When the U.S. government sued the bank to recover some of the money that was allegedly owed to the corporation, the lower courts held that giving effect in this way to the Soviet seizure of private property violated state public policy.

In an opinion by Justice Sutherland, the Court emphasized the President's role as the sole international representative of the United States as well as the established practice of entering into executive agreements. As Justice Sutherland said, "an international compact, as this was, is not always a treaty which requires the participation of the Senate. There are many such compacts, of which a protocol, a modus vivendi, a postal convention, and agreements like that now under consideration are illustrations."[91] Consequently, the Court held that the executive agreement was valid and that any state policy to the contrary violated the Supremacy Clause.

United States v. Pink[92] arose from the same agreement. *Pink* involved a dispute between the federal government and the State of New York over the assets of a Russian insurance company that remained in the hands of New York insurance authorities after all outstanding insurance claims by U.S. citizens had been paid. The Court emphasized both the President's power to make such executive agreements and the dangers posed by state interference. For in this matter involving "an exclusive federal function," the Court reasoned, U.S. foreign policy might be thwarted if "state laws and policies did not yield before the exercise of the external powers of the United States"; indeed, the "nation as a whole would be held to answer if a State created difficulties with a foreign power."[93]

In *Dames & Moore v. Regan*,[94] discussed earlier, the Court upheld another executive agreement in the context of the Iranian hostage crisis arising out of the seizure of the U.S. embassy in Tehran in 1979. When President Ronald Reagan took office, he negotiated an agreement to free the hostages. In return, the U.S. agreed to terminate all attachmemts (i.e., court orders freezing assets) against Iranian government property such as its U.S. bank accounts, and to suspend all domestic legal actions by Americans against Iran, which would then be arbitrated by a special international tribunal. The Court upheld the agreement. It concluded that the termination of the

---

[91]   *Id.* at 330–31.

[92]   315 U.S. 203 (1942).

[93]   *Id.* at 232–33.

[94]   453 U.S. 654 (1981).

attachments had been directly authorized by Congress, placing it in category one of Justice Jackson's *Steel Seizure Case* trichotomy. Even though no statute authorized the suspension of the domestic lawsuits, the Court interpreted two statutes as signaling general approval of a broad presidential role in dealing with claims against foreign countries, and also found evidence of tacit congressional approval in a long history of claims settlement by Presidents. Thus, "in light of the fact that Congress may be considered to have consented to the President's action in suspending claims, we cannot say that action exceeded the President's powers."[95]

If executive agreements have the same legal force as treaties in preempting state law, you may wonder where the distinction lies and why Presidents ever bother submitting treaties to the Senate. As to the first question, there is no case law on the subject. The State Department has developed a set of criteria that it weighs in deciding whether Senate approval is required, based on factors such as past practice for similar agreements, the length of the agreement, and whether congressional implementation will be required.[96] But in practice this is likely to mean that the decision will be based either on a desire to give greater reassurance to other treaty signatories through the formality of Senate ratification, or on congressional pushback against the use of an executive agreement (and perhaps public opinion). Given that many agreements require at least some congressional implementation, if only in the form of funding, Presidents may be reluctant to use executive agreements if the Senate insists on playing its role in the treaty-making process.

There is a third form of international agreement that has been particularly common recently, the executive-congressional agreement. Such agreements are negotiated by the President but then enacted as statutes by Congress using one of its Article I powers, such as the power to regulate interstate or international commerce. Since many agreements do involve matters within Congress's legislative powers, this mechanism can potentially replace many Senate-confirmed treaties. It is unclear whether there are any matters reserved to the treaty power (excluding the House and requiring a Senate supermajority) or whether executive-congressional agreements can be revoked unilaterally by the President. We consider the validity of such unilateral revocations to be doubtful, given that Article I laws can be repealed only by a new exercise of the Article I lawmaking procedure.

---

[95]   *Id.* at 686.

[96]   *See* Oona A. Hathaway, *Treaties' End: The Past, Present, and Future of International Lawmaking in the United States*, 117 YALE L.J. 1236, 1250 (2008).

The President's legal power to terminate an executive agreement seems obvious: live by the sword of presidential prerogatives, die by the same sword. It is less clear whether the President can renounce a treaty unilaterally. This issue came before the Court in *Goldwater v. Carter*,[97] but only one Justice reached the merits and would have upheld the treaty abrogation in this particular case as incidental to the government's recognition of a different government as legitimate.[98] So in practice, the answer to this question has been given by constitutional politics rather than judge-made constitutional law, at least as of yet. Absent any judicial check, Presidents have generally felt free to revoke treaties. But using the treaty form, rather than an executive order, might provide greater assurance to other governments, partly because of the ambiguity over revocation and partly because ratification of a treaty is proof that it has widespread political support.

C.   The President as Commander in Chief

One of the most fraught issues in constitutional law is the President's ability to go to war or otherwise authorize the use of military force without the assent of Congress. The arguments in favor of the President are based on either the Vesting Clause or the Commander-in-Chief Clause. The primary argument for Congress is straightforward: Article I, Section 8, vests the power to declare war in Congress rather than the President. There is also the argument that one person should not be able to send American troops into battle, at least absent an emergency involving an attack on the United States or its citizens. Both sides invoke historical practice, debating the meaning and significance of past instances in which the President initiated hostilities. Lives are literally on the line in this situation, and the debate has been heated. But the courts have generally avoided deciding the issue, so we are mostly left with the passionate claims made on behalf of the President or Congress.

The Supreme Court did, however, uphold presidential war powers in the context of the Civil War in *The Prize Cases*.[99] (In case you were wondering about the name, a prize is a captured ship or goods.) After the South seceded and opened fire on Fort Sumter, Lincoln took a number of emergency actions, including a blockade of Southern ports. Under international law, a blockade was an act of war. Lincoln's action was challenged after several ships and their cargo were seized by the Navy. It was not until several months later that Congress was back in session and authorized the use of force against the Confederacy. The issue, then, was whether Lincoln had

---

[97]   444 U.S. 996 (1979).

[98]   *See id.* at 1007.

[99]   67 U.S. 635 (1863).

the authority to go to war without congressional action. A related issue, of less relevance today, was whether the conflict could qualify as a war even though, in the government's view, secession was illegal and the Southern states therefore remained part of the United States.

The Court upheld Lincoln's actions. First, the Court said, civil wars do not call for declarations of war. Rather, "[w]hen the party in rebellion occupy and hold in a hostile manner a certain portion of territory; have declared their independence; have cast off their allegiance; have organized armies; have commenced hostilities against their former sovereign, the world acknowledges them as belligerents, and the contest a war."[100] Second, the Court concluded, when faced with invasion or rebellion, the President must respond rather than waiting for congressional authorization: "the President is not only authorized but bound to resist force by force," and "he is bound to accept the challenge without waiting for any special legislative authority."[101] Finally, as to whether Southerners could be treated as enemies under the laws of war, rather than simply as criminals under domestic law, the Court wrote that they "have cast off their allegiance and made war on their Government, and are none the less enemies because they are traitors."[102]

The *Prize Cases* make it clear that the President can respond to attacks on the United States without awaiting congressional authorization, but the Court has provided little guidance about presidential power to use armed force under other circumstances. Congress attempted to fill the gap with legislation in the War Powers Resolution of 1973.[103] (This is a federal statute, not just a congressional resolution.) Without going too far into the details, we note that the Resolution is intended to avoid situations in which the President introduces U.S. troops in a conflict and leaves Congress the choice between funding the military intervention and the politically suicidal act of cutting off funding to an army in the field. Section 1543 requires the President to report to Congress when the Armed Forces are introduced into hostilities, "into situations where imminent involvement in hostilities is clearly indicated by the circumstances," or "into the territory, airspace, or waters of a foreign nation." Section 1544(b) requires the President to withdraw the Armed Forces sixty days after giving notice unless Congress authorizes the use of force. The statute also states Congress's view that the "constitutional powers of the President as Commander-in-Chief to introduce United States Armed Forces into hostilities, or into situations where

---

[100]   *Id.* at 666–67.

[101]   *Id.* at 668.

[102]   *Id.* at 674.

[103]   P.L. 93–148, *codified at* 50 U.S.C. § 1541 et. seq.

imminent involvement in hostilities is clearly indicated by the circumstances, are exercised only pursuant to (1) a declaration of war, (2) specific statutory authorization, or (3) a national emergency created by attack upon the United States, its territories or possessions, or its armed forces."[104] There is no definitive resolution of the constitutionality of these requirements, and their effectiveness is disputed, as is the extent to which Presidents have complied with them.

D.   Executive Power and Individual Rights

Tensions between presidential views of national security and civil liberties stretch back into American history. *Ex Parte Milligan*[105] involved military trials of civilians during the Civil War. During the war, the writ of habeas corpus was suspended, first by the President and then by Congress. (Habeas is a centuries-old procedure for challenging the legality of government detention). This suspension effectively cut off access to the courts to challenge the legality of detention or punishment. As a result, although many civilians were detained only temporarily, some were tried by the military for aiding the enemy or interfering with the war effort. Milligan was convicted by a military tribunal of aiding the enemy in Michigan, far from the battle lines or occupied territory. When the war ended, habeas was restored, and he sought relief in the courts. The Supreme Court held that military tribunals could be used only when the regular judicial system was not able to function.

Ex Parte Quirin[106] arose during World War II when the Germans landed saboteurs on the East Coast, one of whom had been born in the United States and was therefore a citizen (see the Citizenship Clause of Section 1 of the Fourteenth Amendment, discussed in Chapter 10). The saboteurs disposed of their uniforms (a violation of the laws of war) and then scattered. When they were captured, they were tried by a military tribunal. The Supreme Court upheld the convictions on the theory that trial by military tribunal (and hence without a jury) was legitimate for violation of the laws of war. The Court was under extremely heavy pressure to support the war effort at this point, and such pressure may have contributed to the decision, which upheld the convictions and resulted in the execution of the saboteurs before the Court issued its opinion in the case. Needless to say, this ordering of events constituted a gross departure from norms of appropriate judicial conduct that has not since been repeated. It is unclear whether *Quirin* is distinguishable from *Milligan*, although

---

[104]   *Id.* at § 1541(c).

[105]   71 U.S. 2 (1866).

[106]   317 U.S. 1 (1942).

Milligan was a civilian and the *Quirin* defendants were members of a foreign military.

Fast forward to the war on terror in the early 2000s. After the terrorist attacks of 9/11, President George W. Bush issued an order classifying the group behind the attack (Al Qaeda) and related groups as illegal combatants under the Geneva Conventions. (The President deemed these groups illegal on a number of grounds, including not wearing uniforms to allow them to be distinguished from civilians). He ordered their indefinite detention at the Naval Base in Guantanamo Bay, Cuba. Congress had passed a resolution authorizing the use of force against these terrorists and their allies. *Hamdi v. Rumsfeld*[107] involved an alleged illegal combatant who had been moved from Guantanamo Bay to a naval brig in South Carolina when the government discovered that he was a United States citizen. Thus, he was clearly within the jurisdiction of the federal courts at the time a habeas petition was filed on his behalf. The Court held that the congressional resolution authorized the President to indefinitely detain captured members of the terrorist groups in question without a normal criminal trial, but further held that the Due Process Clause entitled the detainee in this case to notice of the allegations against him and a hearing before a neutral decisionmaker in which he could contest the government's assertion that he was an illegal combatant.

Justice Sandra Day O'Connor wrote the controlling, plurality opinion for a group of four Justices. Her opinion held that the resolution authorizing the use of force authorized detention by implication. She reasoned that detention of captured enemy combatants "is so fundamental and accepted an incident to war as to be an exercise of the 'necessary and appropriate force' Congress has authorized the President to use."[108] But Justice O'Connor was at pains to emphasize that the detainee was entitled to due process:

> Striking the proper constitutional balance here is of great importance to the Nation during this period of ongoing combat. . . . It is during our most challenging and uncertain moments that our Nation's commitment to due process is most severely tested; and it is in those times that we must preserve our commitment at home to the principles for which we fight abroad.[109]

Recognizing that the interests of the government and of the individual were both very strong, Justice O'Connor devised a compromise under which military tribunals might be able to decide

---

[107]   542 U.S. 507 (2004).

[108]   *Id.* at 518.

[109]   *Id.* at 532.

detention cases, detainees were entitled to counsel, and the burden of proof might switch to the individual once the government put forward credible evidence that the individual was an illegal combatant.

The views of the other Justices were quite diverse. Justice David Souter, joined by Justice Ruth Bader Ginsburg, argued that detention was not authorized by Congress's authorization of the use of force and that the detention of citizens violated a law passed in the aftermath of World War II. Justice Scalia, joined by Justice John Paul Stevens, argued that a citizen held within the United States could be indefinitely detained only after a criminal trial, unless Congress suspended the writ of habeas corpus. Justice Clarence Thomas agreed that the detention was authorized but disagreed with the due process part of the Court's holding. In his view, Justice O'Connor's opinion underestimated "the breadth of the President's authority to detain enemy combatants, an authority that includes making virtually conclusive factual findings."[110]

Detention and trial are two separate issues, because a trial involves the potential imposition of punishment on individuals rather than merely holding them. In a subsequent decision involving the trial of Guantanamo detainees, the Court held that any actual trials for violation of the laws of war must comply under applicable statutes with the requirements of the Geneva Conventions and normal court martial procedures, and may not eliminate access to courts.[111] In another decision involving a challenge to the indefinite detention of the Guantanamo detainees, the Court held that Congress must allow access to the courts via habeas corpus or an equivalent process.[112]

The Court has been clear that even in areas such as foreign affairs and national security, presidential actions are subject to the Bill of Rights. Nevertheless, the President may have more leeway than other government actors, at least in the context of terrorism. For example, the Court was willing to allow detention hearings and trials of alleged terrorists to be conducted by military officials, but there is no precedent for allowing a state government to avoid the constitutional protections of the criminal process such as jury trials.

Trump v. Hawaii[113] seems to fit this pattern of substantial (but not unlimited) deference to presidential actions. The case involved an executive order all but eliminating entry into the United States by residents of certain countries. This executive order was the third in

---

[110]   *Id.* at 580 (Thomas, J., dissenting).

[111]   *See* Hamdan v. Rumsfeld, 548 U.S. 557 (2006).

[112]   *See* Boumediene v. Bush, 553 U.S. 723 (2008).

[113]   138 S. Ct. 2392 (2018).

a series of such orders issued by President Donald Trump. The initial order singled out a group of countries with majority Muslim populations and provided a sketchy justification. The final order contained a more fully developed justification, eliminated some countries in the initial order, and added two non-Muslim countries. All three orders cited as justifications poor security on the part of the countries involved and elevated risks to national security connected with visitors from these countries. The first and second orders were struck down by the lower federal courts as violations of either federal immigration law or the Establishment Clause, the latter based on a finding that they deliberately targeted members of a particular religion (Islam). The lower courts pointed for support to a series of public statements and tweets by Trump before and after his election and inauguration as President. For example, Trump had issued a "Statement on Preventing Muslim Immigration" that called for a "total and complete shutdown of Muslims entering the United States until our country's representatives can figure out what is going on."[114]

The Supreme Court upheld the last of the three immigration orders by a vote of 5 to 4. The majority opinion by Chief Justice Roberts reviewed previous decisions and concluded that "[t]he upshot of our cases in this context is clear: 'Any rule of constitutional law that would inhibit the flexibility' of the President 'to respond to changing world conditions should be adopted only with the greatest caution,' and our inquiry into matters of entry and national security is highly constrained."[115] The Court then adopted a very limited standard of review:

> For our purposes today, we assume that we may look behind the face of the Proclamation to the extent of applying rational basis review. That standard of review considers whether the entry policy is plausibly related to the Government's stated objective to protect the country and improve vetting processes. As a result, we may consider plaintiffs' extrinsic evidence, but will uphold the policy so long as it can reasonably be understood to result from a justification independent of unconstitutional grounds.[116]

After noting the deferential nature of rational basis review, the Court said that "[o]n the few occasions where we have [held that laws flunk this standard], a common thread has been that the laws at issue lack any purpose other than a "bare . . . desire to harm a politically

---

[114]   *Id.* at 2417.
[115]   *Id.* at 2419–20.
[116]   *Id.* at 2420.

unpopular group."[117] The President's order was "expressly premised on legitimate purposes: preventing entry of nationals who cannot be adequately vetted and inducing other nations to improve their practices. And the text of the order 'says nothing about religion.'"[118] Accordingly, the Court concluded that the executive order before it passed muster.

There were two dissents. Justice Stephen Breyer, joined by Justice Elena Kagan, wrote a relatively toned-down dissent, arguing that key portions of the evidence relied upon by the majority to show a legitimate purpose (namely, the availability of waivers and exemptions) were at least questionable and perhaps flimsy. Justice Sonia Sotomayor, joined by Justice Ginsburg, complained strenuously that the majority was able to uphold the President's order only "by ignoring the facts, misconstruing our legal precedent, and turning a blind eye to the pain and suffering the Proclamation inflicts upon countless families and individuals, many of whom are United States citizens."[119] Emphasizing what she viewed as overwhelming evidence of anti-Muslim bias on the part of the President, she compared the Court's ruling to its now-infamous ruling in *Korematsu v. United States*,[120] which upheld an order interning 110,000 people of Japanese ancestry—most of whom were U.S. citizens—in detention camps in World War II based on trumped-up national security claims and no individualized suspicion of espionage or sabotage.

Almost all commentators agree that *Korematsu* was one of the lowest points in Supreme Court history. The Court's opinion began on a high note, stating that "all legal restrictions which curtail the civil rights of a single racial group are immediately suspect."[121] The opinion continued that such restrictions must be subjected to "the most rigid scrutiny" by courts and that "[p]ressing public necessity may sometimes justify the existence of such restrictions" but that "racial antagonism never can."[122] In reality, however, the Court's review was extremely deferential to the government and failed to confront the ugly prejudices behind the order. It was enough for the Court that there was "evidence of disloyalty on the part of some," that "the military authorities considered that the need for action was great," and that "time was short."[123]

---

[117] *Id.* (quoting Department of Agriculture v. Moreno, 413 U.S. 528, 534 (1973)).

[118] *Id.* at 2421.

[119] *Id.* at 2433.

[120] 323 U.S. 214 (1944).

[121] *Id.* at 216.

[122] *Id.*

[123] *Id.* at 223–24. The only actual evidence of "disloyalty" cited by the Court was that "[a]pproximately five thousand American citizens of Japanese ancestry refused to

In dissent, Justice Frank Murphy protested in vain that the government's action "goes over 'the very brink of constitutional power' and falls into the ugly abyss of racism."[124] He pointed to a statement by the commanding general that referred to "all individuals of Japanese descent as 'subversive,' as belonging to 'an enemy race' whose 'racial strains are undiluted,' and as constituting 'over 112,000 potential enemies . . . at large today' along the Pacific Coast."[125] Justice Murphy contended that "the exclusion order necessarily must rely for its reasonableness upon the assumption that all persons of Japanese ancestry may have a dangerous tendency to commit sabotage and espionage and to aid our Japanese enemy in other ways. It is difficult to believe that reason, logic or experience could be marshalled in support of such an assumption."[126] Although Justice Murphy failed to persuade the majority, decades later a federal judge vacated Fred Korematsu's conviction because the government had concealed evidence directly undermining its claims.[127] Ultimately, Congress acknowledged the "grave injustice" of the internment and provided reparations to the individuals involved.[128]

Apparently stung by Justice Sotomayor's charge, the majority opinion explicitly repudiated *Korematsu*, declaring that it "was gravely wrong the day it was decided, has been overruled in the court of history, and—to be clear—'has no place in law under the Constitution.' "[129] The Court argued, however, that *Korematsu* was distinguishable. Justice Sotomayor was unpersuaded. "By blindly accepting the Government's misguided invitation to sanction a discriminatory policy motivated by animosity toward a disfavored

---

swear unqualified allegiance to the United States and to renounce allegiance to the Japanese Emperor, and several thousand evacuees requested repatriation to Japan." *Id.* at 219. As the Court admitted in the sentence preceding this one, this supposed display of disloyalty took place after Japanese citizens had been singled out for detention, which might put a damper on anyone's desire to publicly express loyalty or remain in the country. In any event, since this evidence did not exist at the time of the detention order, it is hard to see how it sheds light on whether the order had been based on genuine dangers to national security or instead on racist stereotypes. Notably, German and Italian Americans were not treated the way Japanese Americans were, even though the United States was also at war with Germany and Italy.

[124]   *Id.* at 233.

[125]   *Id.* at 236.

[126]   *Id.* at 235.

[127]   *See* Korematsu v. United States, 584 F. Supp. 1406, 1409 (N.D. Cal. 1984). Documents surfaced showing that the government had deliberately failed to disclose evidence to the Court that disproved the disloyalty claims. *See* Peter Irons, *Introduction, in* PETER IRONS, JUSTICE DELAYED: THE RECORD OF THE JAPANESE INTERNMENT CASES 5–6 (Peter Irons ed., 1989).

[128]   Civil Liberties Act of 1988 (Pub.L. 100–383, title I, Aug. 10, 1988, 102 Stat. 904, 50a U.S.C. § 1989b et seq.).

[129]   *Trump v. Hawaii*, 138 S. Ct. at 2433.

group," she said, "the Court redeploys the same dangerous logic underlying *Korematsu* and merely replaces one 'gravely wrong' decision with another."[130]

V. Checks on Presidential Power

The President, of course, does not head the only branch of government. In this section, we consider the methods used by the other two branches in their efforts to limit the President's discretion. Where the President relies on statutory authority for his actions, Congress can narrow or repeal this authority, although it may have to overcome a veto to do so. And we have already seen that the courts may interpret statutory language and overturn presidential actions on constitutional grounds. In this section, we examine some of the other options for restraining the President.

A. Congressional Appropriations and Investigations

Two congressional tools for exercising influence or control over the executive branch involve Congress's budgetary and investigative powers. The first tool, the power of the purse, is specifically set out in the Constitution. The Appropriations Clause provides that "[n]o Money shall be drawn from the Treasury but in Consequence of Law."[131] This requirement by itself is a significant restraint on the President, since every penny spent must somehow or another be tied to a specific appropriation statute. The requirement gives Congress the ability to "pull the plug" on nearly any presidential activity, if Congress has sufficient political will to do so, simply by refusing to appropriate funds to support the activity.

Oversight hearings are also a powerful means for Congress to influence administration officials. Hearings attract publicity and public attention to controversial actions and uncover misconduct. They can also be unpleasant experiences for powerful members of the executive branch, who must respond to pointed questions and, even worse, listen quietly to sharp criticism by members of Congress. Investigations can also produce information providing the basis for other congressional actions, such as statutory amendments to budget restrictions or, in rare cases, impeachment of executive branch officials.

The Constitution does not expressly provide Congress with the power to compel witnesses to testify in hearings. Nevertheless, the Supreme Court has held that this investigative power is inherent in Congress's legislative powers, pointing to a long history of such investigations:

---

[130]   *Id.* at 2488.

[131]   U.S. CONST. art. I, § 9, cl. 7.

[T]o secure needed information by such means has long been treated as an attribute of the power to legislate. It was so regarded in the British Parliament and in the colonial Legislatures before the American Revolution, and a like view has prevailed and been carried into effect in both houses of Congress and in most of the state Legislatures.[132]

In addition, the Court emphasized, congressional practice since 1798 "falls nothing short of a practical construction, long continued, of the constitutional provisions respecting their powers, and therefore should be taken as fixing the meaning of those provisions, if otherwise doubtful."[133] The Court concluded that that "the constitutional provisions which commit the legislative function to the two houses are intended to include this attribute to the end that the function may be effectively exercised."[134]

B. Legislative Control of Statutory Implementation

Because so much power has been delegated to the executive branch, Congress has made some efforts to regain control by inserting itself into the process. As we have discussed, appropriations and investigations provide one mechanism for influencing the system. The legislative veto provided another. Legislative vetoes were established by laws giving some legislative body—sometimes both Houses of Congress together, sometimes either one separately, and occasionally a committee—the ability to review and disapprove an administrative action.

The Supreme Court invalidated legislative vetoes in *Immigration and Naturalization Service v. Chadha*.[135] A deportation proceeding was undertaken against Jagdish Chadha for long-overstaying his visa. He conceded that he was deportable but asked the Attorney General to suspend his deportation. The statute that gave the Attorney General this power also empowered either house of Congress to pass a resolution overturning the suspension. For reasons that were unexplained, the House of Representatives did so in Chadha's case. Chief Justice Warren Burger's opinion for the Court dismissed the relevance of historical practice and instead viewed the case as a straightforward application of the constitutional text: Article I provides that a bill cannot become law until it has been passed by both houses of Congress and presented to the President for veto or signature, and the legislative veto in *Chadha* had not been

---

132   McGrain v. Daugherty, 273 U.S. 135, 161 (1927).
133   *Id.* at 174.
134   *Id.* at 175.
135   462 U.S. 919 (1983).

passed by both houses, nor was it ever presented to the President. Q.E.D, according to the Court.

The key to the Court's reasoning is the premise that the House's resolution overturning the suspension was a "law." The majority argued that the veto was indeed a type of legislation because it changed Chadha's legal status from eligible for suspension to ineligible and because it involved a determination of policy. But one might argue that the same law that made Chadha eligible also conditioned eligibility on the absence of a veto and that the veto was not a new law but merely a power reserved in the old one.

In dissent, Justice Byron White pointed out the existence of legislative vetoes in two hundred statutes, all of them presumably invalid after the Court's decision.[136] He argued that the legislative veto had "become a central means by which Congress secures the accountability of executive and independent agencies."[137] Without the option of the legislative veto, he urged, Congress was "faced with a Hobson's choice: either to refrain from delegating the necessary authority, leaving itself with a hopeless task of writing laws with the requisite specificity to cover endless special circumstances across the entire policy landscape, or in the alternative, to abdicate its law-making function to the executive branch and independent agencies."[138] Justice White regarded neither choice as satisfactory: refusing to delegate "leaves major national problems unresolved"; delegating without the legislative veto "risks unaccountable policymaking by those not elected to fill that role."[139] And "[i]f Congress may delegate lawmaking power to independent and executive agencies," he reasoned, "it is most difficult to understand Article I as forbidding Congress from also reserving a check on legislative power for itself."[140] From Justice White's perspective, if the goal of the separation of powers is to prevent any branch of government from acquiring too much power at the expense of the other branches, the legislative veto actually furthers this goal by giving Congress a check on the Attorney General's discretion.

The majority opinion in *Chadha* and the dissent exemplify two different forms of constitutional reasoning. The majority viewed its task as simply applying the rules laid down in the constitutional text to the legislative veto. The consequences of the decision were not relevant to the formal analysis. Justice White, on the other hand, applied a functional analysis, attempting to determine whether the

---

[136] *See id.* at 967.

[137] *Id.* at 967–68.

[138] *Id.* at 968.

[139] *Id.*

[140] *Id.* at 986.

legislative veto furthered the goals of accountability and effective government. These contrasting positions illustrate the distinction between formalist and functionalist analysis. Formalist analysis focuses on the language (that is, the form) of legal rules and seeks to apply them without regard to the consequences of alternative interpretations. Functionalist analysis focuses on the purposes underlying the rules and seeks to implement these purposes. In the realm of separation of powers, formalists are more apt to speak of the "separation of powers," while functionalists may instead focus on "checks and balances."

One feature of formalist rules is that they can be evaded by changes in form. Congress could have secured the same results as the legislative veto by providing that a suspension order would remain in effect only for a specified time unless Congress passed legislation making the order permanent. This legislation would then be presented to the President, who would routinely sign it since it confirmed the executive branch's own decision to grant suspension. Under this mechanism, either house of Congress could block the necessary legislation in an individual case, allowing the suspension to expire. This alternative approach would be a clumsier process, more prone to fail due to congressional inertia, than the one-house veto. The result might be fewer deportation suspensions because of the difficulty of getting Congress to take action. This alternative approach would, however, achieve the same allocation of power. Yet it would not be subject to challenge under *Chadha*, because it would involve both houses and presentment to the President. Upholding this alternative procedure risks elevating form over substance, but of course the whole point of formalism is that form matters.

Congress has attempted to use means other than the legislative veto to retain some control over statutory implementation. In *Bowsher v. Synar*,[141] Congress attempted to use one such technique in the context of budget control. In order to achieve a balanced budget, Congress established a special mechanism for imposing budget cuts. The mechanism was complex, but essentially two existing bodies would produce reports about the needed cuts. One of these bodies was in the executive branch, the other in the legislative. Based on these reports and his or her own independent judgment, the Comptroller General would make a judgment about what cuts would be imposed unless Congress fixed the deficit in some other way. The constitutional issue in the case related to the role of the Comptroller General. The Comptroller General is appointed by the President but removable by Congress. The Court held that the Comptroller General, in implementing this statute, was performing an executive

---

[141]   478 U.S. 714 (1986).

function and that such a function could not be performed by an official removable by Congress: "As *Chadha* makes clear, once Congress makes its choice in enacting legislation, its participation ends. Congress can thereafter control the execution of its enactment only indirectly—by passing new legislation."[142]

Bowsher, however, is actually an extension of *Chadha*, not a mere application of it. As Justice White pointed out in dissent in *Bowsher*, the Comptroller General could be removed only by a joint resolution of both Houses, which could be vetoed by the President.[143] Thus, there was no specific congressional action in *Bowsher* subject to the specific constitutional objections in *Chadha*—lack of bicameralism and presentment to the President. But *Bowsher* uses *Chadha* as the basis for a broader, structural argument. Indeed, under the *Bowsher* theory, the problem in *Chadha* was not that the veto involved the use of legislative power without the proper procedures, as the Court held there, but instead that it involved the use of executive power by Congress.

Metropolitan Washington Airports Authority v. Citizens for Abatement of Aircraft Noise, Inc.[144] involved congressional appointment rather than approval as a means to gaining leverage over decisions. The Airports Authority is a regional body that operates the airports in Washington, D.C. Certain actions by the Authority were subject to veto by a review board composed of designated members of Congress. The purpose of establishing the review board seems to have been to prevent too many flights from being moved from what is now called Reagan Airport to Dulles, which is much less convenient for members of Congress. The Court held the review board unconstitutional. While admitting that the board might seem to be a practical accommodation between competing interests, the Court feared that upholding the board would create a dangerous precedent. Given the breadth of congressional funding for state activities, the Court believed, "Congress could, if this Board of Review were valid, use similar expedients to enable its Members or its agents to retain control, outside the ordinary legislative process, of the activities of state grant recipients charged with executing virtually every aspect of national policy."[145]

The decisions we have discussed in this section express concern over Congress's use of legislation to aggrandize its own power at the expense of the executive branch. But the difference between aggrandizing power and attempting to maintain a balance of power

---

[142] *Id.* at 733–34.

[143] *Id.* at 764–72.

[144] 501 U.S. 252 (1991).

[145] *Id.* at 277.

may be in the eyes of the beholder. From a different perspective, these decisions, by invalidating Congress's efforts to check executive power, may have contributed to a long-term shift of power into the hands of the President.

C. Judicial Oversight

Like Congress, the judicial branch can also provide a check on the executive branch. It is now fairly routine for courts to review the actions of executive agencies to determine whether they have complied with the law in issuing regulations or in performing other administrative activities. Such cases provide the foundations for administrative law, which is the subject of a separate course in law school. There is little controversy over the ability of Congress to provide for litigation against administrators in their official capacities. ("Official capacity" means that any remedy requires them to perform only an official act.) Here, we focus on cases involving personal liability or penalties for official acts.

Are Presidents completely immune from the jurisdiction of the courts? The Supreme Court made it clear that the answer to this question is "no" in *United States v. Nixon*,[146] a decision that led to the President's resignation under threat of impeachment. The case arose from the Watergate scandal and involved allegations that the President had been part of a conspiracy to cover up the burglary of the opposing party's campaign headquarters. A special prosecutor was appointed by the Justice Department, and under the Department's regulations the appointee could be removed only for cause. The Court held that the special prosecutor was sufficiently independent of the President that an Article III controversy existed; this was not a case of the President essentially suing himself through his own agent. The issue before the Court arose from the grand jury's investigation of the cover-up.

The special prosecutor obtained a grand jury subpoena to obtain tapes that the President had surreptitiously made of his conversations regarding the break-in and the cover-up. The plan was for the judge in charge of the proceedings to then examine these materials *in camera* (i.e., without disclosure to anyone but the judge). The President refused to comply, claiming executive privilege, which he argued was an absolute privilege to withhold evidence relating to the executive branch. Justice Rehnquist did not participate, presumably because of some aspect of his own prior role in the Nixon Justice Department before becoming a Justice. The other eight Justices, in an opinion by Chief Justice Burger, rejected the President's claim of an absolute privilege. "Absent a claim of need to

---

[146]   418 U.S. 683 (1974).

protect military, diplomatic, or sensitive national security secrets," the Chief Justice said, "we find it difficult to accept the argument that even the very important interest in confidentiality of Presidential communications is significantly diminished by production of such material for in camera inspection with all the protection that a district court will be obliged to provide."[147] Moreover, he continued, "[t]he impediment that an absolute, unqualified privilege would place in the way of the primary constitutional duty of the Judicial Branch to do justice in criminal prosecutions would plainly conflict with the function of the courts under Art. III."[148]

The Court did, however, hold that a qualified privilege applied. On the one hand, Chief Justice Burger reasoned, the President's need for confidentiality "has all the values to which we accord deference for the privacy of all citizens and, added to those values, is the necessity for protection of the public interest in candid, objective, and even blunt or harsh opinions in Presidential decisionmaking."[149] On the other hand, he wrote, "[t]o ensure that justice is done, it is imperative to the function of courts that compulsory process be available for the production of evidence needed either by the prosecution or by the defense."[150] Balancing these interests, the Court settled on a qualified version of executive privilege. The burden was on the special prosecutor to demonstrate that the presidential material at issue was " 'essential to the justice of the (pending criminal) case.' "[151] In ordering the subpoena to produce the tapes, the trial judge had already made this determination.

Another issue of presidential immunity was presented in *Nixon v. Fitzgerald*.[152] In this case, the Court held that the President was absolutely immune from civil liability for conduct within the "outer perimeter" of his official duties. Cabinet officers, however, enjoy only qualified immunity, which does not cover conduct that was clearly forbidden by existing law. The case arose from the allegedly illegal firing of a government employee, which (according to the employee) was at the behest of the President in retaliation for congressional testimony. The Court said that, like "prosecutors and judges—for whom absolute immunity now is established—a President must concern himself with matters likely to 'arouse the most intense feelings.' "[153] But it is in these cases, the Court contended, that an

---

[147]   *Id.* at 706.

[148]   *Id.* at 707.

[149]   *Id.* at 708.

[150]   *Id.* at 709.

[151]   *Id.* at 713 (quoting United States v. Burr, 25 F. Cas. 187, 192 (C.C.D. Va. 1807)).

[152]   457 U.S. 731 (1982).

[153]   *Id.* at 752 (quoting Pierson v. Ray, 386 U.S. 547, 554 (1967)).

official's judgment must be unaffected by fear of personal consequences. In the Court's view, this concern is especially compelling in terms of the Presidency, an office "where the officeholder must make the most sensitive and far-reaching decisions entrusted to any official under our constitutional system."[154] In addition, the Court said, the prominence of the office makes it especially likely to prompt litigation against the President, and such litigation could distract from the performance of vital duties. Thus, the Court concluded, the President must enjoy absolute immunity from suit for official acts, unlike lower-level government officials, who receive only qualified immunity.

Justice White wrote the dissenting opinion, which was joined by Justices William Brennan, Thurgood Marshall, and Harry Blackmun. Justice White argued that providing the office of the presidency with absolute immunity "places the President above the law" and "is a reversion to the old notion that the King can do no wrong."[155] Justice White also raised the question of whether other legal actions against the President can be taken:

> Taken at face value, the Court's position that as a matter of constitutional law the President is absolutely immune should mean that he is immune not only from damages actions but also from suits for injunctive relief, criminal prosecutions and, indeed, from any kind of judicial process. But there is no contention that the President is immune from criminal prosecution in the courts under the criminal laws enacted by Congress or by the States for that matter. Nor would such a claim be credible.[156]

In Justice White's view, the majority was taking "a bizarre approach to the Constitution" given its position "that the assertion of a constitutional cause of action—the whole point of which is to assure that an officer does not transgress the constitutional limits on his authority—may offend separation-of-powers concerns."[157]

In *Clinton v. Jones*,[158] the issue was civil liability for sexual harassment prior to the time that the defendant became President. Distinguishing *Nixon v. Fitzgerald*, the Court held that Presidents are not immune from civil suits for non-official conduct prior to becoming President. The Court unanimously rejected President Bill Clinton's argument that the suit could not proceed until after he had left the presidency. The Court concluded, perhaps over-

---

[154]   *Id.*

[155]   *Id.* at 766.

[156]   *Id.* at 794.

[157]   *Id.*

[158]   520 U.S. 681 (1997).

optimistically, that the federal trial judge could manage the litigation so as to limit demands on the President's time and interference with his ability to conduct his duties. This litigation led to a report to Congress by an independent counsel (who had been appointed to pursue unrelated matters) recommending impeachment procedures based on alleged perjury in a deposition in the case. The House did vote to impeach the President, but the Senate did not convict.

Some key issues regarding checks on the President remain unresolved to this day. It is uncertain and debated by scholars whether impeachment/removal is the sole remedy for serious presidential misconduct and criminal prosecution must wait until the defendant is no longer President. The main argument for temporary criminal immunity is that criminal proceedings would interfere drastically with the performance of presidential duties. The primary argument on the other side is that no one should be above the law.

The scope of the impeachment power is also debated. The term "high crimes and misdemeanors" may sound like it requires violation of a criminal statute. But recent scholars have concluded that the House can impeach and the Senate can remove for abuse of authority, including violations of the Constitution, regardless of whether any criminal statute has been violated.[159] Because the issue is probably a nonjusticiable political question, the House and Senate would seem to have the final word. As a practical matter, it would be extraordinarily difficult in a polarized country to persuade the requisite 67 Senators to vote to remove a sitting President.

* * *

More than the other two branches, the office of the President is a work-in-progress—at least as a matter of practice, if not according to some constitutional theories. As we have seen, many of the constitutional issues surrounding the presidency have been contested for much of our history. Institutional practice seems to count for a lot in assessments of the constitutionality of presidential actions, especially when judicial decisions are few in number and narrow in scope. But the constitutional politics of the presidency will come to rest only when Presidents stop taking major controversial actions on vital national issues. This is another way of saying that we can expect the presidency to remain contested terrain for as long as the office endures.

---

[159]   *See generally* LAURENCE TRIBE & JOSHUA MATZ, TO END A PRESIDENCY: THE POWER OF IMPEACHMENT (2018); MICHAEL J. GERHARDT, IMPEACHMENT: WHAT EVERYONE NEEDS TO KNOW (2018); CASS R. SUNSTEIN, IMPEACHMENT: A CITIZEN'S GUIDE (2017).

Further Readings

Bruce Ackerman, *The New Separation of Powers*, 113 HARV. L. REV. 633 (2000).

David J. Barron & Martin S. Lederman, *The Commander in Chief at the Lowest Ebb—Framing the Problem, Doctrine, and Original Understanding*, 121 HARV. L. REV. 689 (2008).

Patricia L. Bellia, *Faithful Execution and Enforcement Discretion*, 164 U. PA. L. REV. 1753 (2016).

Curtis A. Bradley & Trevor W. Morrison, *Historical Gloss and the Separation of Powers*, 126 HARV. L. REV. 411 (2012).

Steven G. Calabresi, *The Virtues of Presidential Government: Why Professor Ackerman is Wrong To Prefer the German to the U.S. Constitution*, 18 CONST. COMMENT. 51 (2001).

Steven G. Calabresi & Saikrishna B. Prakash, *The President's Power to Execute the Laws*, 104 YALE L.J. 541 (1994).

Martin S. Flaherty, *The Most Dangerous Branch*, 105 YALE L.J. 1725 (1996).

Michael J. Gerhardt, IMPEACHMENT: WHAT EVERYONE NEEDS TO KNOW (2018).

Oona A. Hathaway, *Treaties' End: The Past, Present, and Future of International Lawmaking in the United States*, 117 YALE L.J. 1236 (2008).

Lawrence Lessig & Cass R. Sunstein, *The President and the Administration*, 94 COLUM. L. REV. 1 (1994).

Daryl J. Levinson, *Foreword: Looking for Power in Public Law*, 130 HARV. L. REV. 33 (2016).

FORREST MCDONALD, THE AMERICAN PRESIDENCY: AN INTELLECTUAL HISTORY (1994).

Victoria F. Nourse, *Toward A New Constitutional Anatomy*, 56 STAN. L. REV. 835 (2004).

Thomas O. Sargentich, *The Limitations of the Parliamentary Critique of the Separation of Powers*, 34 WM. & MARY L. REV. 680 (1993).

CHRISTOPHER H. SCHROEDER & CURTIS A. BRADLEY, PRESIDENTIAL POWER STORIES (2009).

Peter L. Strauss, *Overseer, or "The Decider"? The President in Administrative Law*, 75 GEO. WASH. L. REV. 696 (2007).

CASS R. SUNSTEIN, IMPEACHMENT: A CITIZEN'S GUIDE (2017).

LAURENCE TRIBE & JOSHUA MATZ, TO END A PRESIDENCY: THE POWER OF IMPEACHMENT (2018).

JOHN YOO, CRISIS AND COMMAND: A HISTORY OF EXECUTIVE POWER FROM GEORGE WASHINGTON TO GEORGE W. BUSH (2010).

Chapter 8

CONSTITUTIONAL RIGHTS
AND THE STATES

Beginning with this chapter, we turn the focus of this book from government structure to individual constitutional rights. As the Constitution was originally drafted and ratified, it had only a little to say about individual rights. Indeed, the question of individual rights barely figured in the Constitutional Convention, which was almost entirely concerned with the structural issues of creating a new government.

The origins of the Bill of Rights (the first ten amendments to the Constitution) was somewhat ironic, since the impetus came from the anti-Federalists, who opposed ratification of the Constitution. Although they would have preferred more limits on federal powers instead of rights provisions, their arguments about the dangers of a strong federal government resulted in the creation of the Bill of Rights.[1] The process leading to the Bill of Rights, which we discuss in Part I of this chapter, began a long process in which protection of rights eventually became as important a function of the U.S. Constitution and constitutional law as providing a framework of government.

Many people today are unaware that the Bill of Rights applied only to the federal government for much of American history; as far as the U.S. Constitution was concerned, states remained free to limit free speech or religion, establish official churches, take private property without providing just compensation, eliminate jury trials, and so forth, not to mention their freedom to discriminate on the basis of race. Indeed, nothing in the original Constitution challenged state laws recognizing slavery, and several constitutional provisions protected the institution.[2] These matters were left primarily to the states. This changed only due to a dramatic transformation in federalism following the Civil War.

Federalism featured heavily in the disputes leading up to the Civil War. In the decades before the Civil War, the single most explosive political and constitutional question facing the nation was

---

[1]   Often, in fact, references to the Bill of Rights have in mind only the first eight amendments, since the final two do not themselves protect specific constitutional rights.

[2]   *See, e.g.,* U.S. CONST. art. IV, § 2, cl. 3 (requiring fugitive slaves to be returned to their owners), art. I, § 9 & art. V (delaying any congressional action to end the international slave trade until at least 1808).

the scope of congressional power to regulate slavery in U.S. territories, out of which would come new states; the political branches managed the issue through a series of delicate political compromises. In the *Dred Scott* case, discussed in Chapter 10, the Supreme Court sought to end such political resolutions by holding that Congress lacked the constitutional power to ban slavery in U.S. territories and also that free blacks were barred from U.S. citizenship.[3] During secession, Southerners such as Jefferson Davis argued that the Constitution was a compact among states, from which they retained the right to withdraw.[4] Abraham Lincoln argued that, on the contrary, the United States was a nation, not a confederation.[5] Reconstruction brought with it other federalism issues, given that the states of the former Confederacy were under military occupation.

The crisis of federalism in the Civil War era led to the passage of the Thirteenth Amendment (abolishing slavery), the Fourteenth Amendment (establishing birthright citizenship and requiring states to comply with due process and equal protection), and the Fifteenth Amendment (prohibiting racial discrimination in voting). This chapter, as well as all of the chapters to come, discusses these amendments in detail.

It was not until a century later, however, during the Civil Rights era of the 1950s and 1960s, that the Supreme Court concluded that nearly all of the provisions of the Bill of Rights were "incorporated" in the Due Process Clause of the Fourteenth Amendment and therefore were applicable against the states. In so concluding, the Court completed a development that began in the late Nineteenth and early Twentieth Centuries.

In this chapter, we briefly trace this evolution. We then home in on one key aspect of the Fourteenth Amendment. Its language is addressed to action by the states. Thus, after "incorporation" of the First Amendment into the Fourteenth, the right of free speech was protected against both the federal government (under the First) and the states (under the Fourteenth). But it might surprise many students to know that their college or university has no federal constitutional obligation to respect free speech unless it is a state school.

The requirement of government action seems clear enough on its surface. But as we will see, the Supreme Court has found it difficult to define just when government involvement becomes too attenuated to trigger constitutional protections.

---

[3]   60 U.S. 393 (1857).

[4]   *See* DANIEL A. FARBER, LINCOLN'S CONSTITUTION 77–78, 82 (2003).

[5]   *Id.* at 79.

I. The Bill of Rights and Civil War Amendments

A. Individual Rights and the Original Constitution

From our point of view today, one of the most striking things about the proposed Constitution as it went out for ratification was its scant protection for individual rights. Sections 9 and 10 of Article I did (among other things) ban impairments of contracts, ex post facto laws (laws criminalizing or enhancing the punishment for conduct after the fact), and bills of attainder (laws punishing named individuals). Article III, Section 2, provides for a jury trial in criminal cases. And Article VI banned religious requirements for holding office.[6] But nothing in the Constitution prohibited government censorship, unreasonable searches, compelled self-incrimination, or other abuses of power.

The idea of a bill of rights had repeatedly surfaced during the Convention, only to be rebuffed.[7] On August 20, 1787, Charles Pickney of South Carolina submitted a proposal to the Committee of Detail, but it was never heard from again.[8] Pickney's proposal included freedom of the press and a ban on religious qualifications for office, but these proposals did not emerge from the Committee of Detail, which was in charge of drafting.

On September 14, Elbridge Gerry of Massachusetts unsuccessfully moved to insert a declaration that the "power of Congress does not extend to the Press."[9] It was unanimously defeated. He and Charles Pinckney moved "to insert a declaration 'that the liberty of the Press should be inviolably observed.' "[10] In opposition, Roger Sherman of Connecticut argued that "the power of Congress does not extend to the Press."[11] The motion was defeated, though by a narrower margin than before.[12]

---

[6]   In addition, rights protections of a sort were provided by two clauses of Article IV, Section 2: the Privileges and Immunities Clause, which prohibits certain forms of discrimination against out-of-state citizens, and the Fugitive Slave Clause, which required the return of slaves who escaped to other states, thereby protecting the "property rights" of their owners. These clauses could also be considered aspects of federalism, governing relationships between states, as opposed to individual rights provisions.

[7]   The relevant materials can be found in DANIEL A. FARBER & SUZANNA SHERRY, A HISTORY OF THE AMERICAN CONSTITUTION 336–37 (3d ed. 2013).

[8]   *See* ADRIENNE KOCH (INTRO.), NOTES OF DEBATES IN THE FEDERAL CONVENTION OF 1787 REPORTED BY JAMES MADISON 486 (rev. ed. 1984).

[9]   *Id.* at 640.

[10]   *Id.*

[11]   *Id.*

[12]   Massachusetts, Maryland, Virginia, and South Carolina voted for the proposal. *See id.*

In the last week of the Convention, George Mason of Virginia raised the matter again, saying that a Bill of Rights would "give great quiet to the people; and with the aid of the State declarations, a bill might be prepared in a few hours."[13] The motion failed, and the Constitution was sent out to the Continental Congress for transmission to the states with no bill of rights. Mason himself refused to sign the Constitution and carried the fight to the states in the battle over ratification.

The Convention might have done better to heed the objections. The absence of a bill of rights figured prominently in the debates over whether to ratify the Constitution. One of the leading opponents of the Constitution, who wrote anonymously under the name of "Brutus," made this objection most forcefully. In "all the constitutions of our own states," he said, "there is not one of them but what is founded on a declaration or bill of rights, or has certain express reservations of rights interwoven into the body of them."[14] He could not help but find it all "the more astonishing, that this grand security, to the rights of the people, is not to be found in this constitution."[15] In response, Federalists argued that a bill of rights was unnecessary in a government of limited powers and might be dangerous, because it would taken to imply that rights not listed were unprotected.[16]

Virginia and other key states ultimately ratified the Constitution, but they also sent Congress a list of proposed amendments. Virginia and New York gave some added emphasis to their suggestions by proposing that a new convention be called, and two other states (North Carolina and Rhode Island) continued to reject the Constitution in part because it lacked a Bill of Rights.[17]

In response to these efforts, James Madison raised the issue in Congress after the first month of its initial session. He had never been a strong believer in the utility of a Bill of Rights, but he had come around to the view that it would be better to supply one. Reflecting the spirit of compromise that prevented the Constitutional Convention from collapsing, Madison ultimately supported adding rights provisions to the original Constitution so as to "render it as acceptable to the whole people of the United States, as it has been found acceptable to a majority of them."[18]

When Madison brought forward the issue, there were immediate objections that he was wasting the House of Representatives'

---

[13]   *Id.* at 630.

[14]   *See* FARBER & SHERRY, *supra* note 7, at 339–40.

[15]   *Id.* at 340.

[16]   *See id.*

[17]   *See id.* at 343.

[18]   1 ANNALS OF CONG. 448–49 (1789).

valuable time.[19] It was suggested that more pressing matters, like establishing the federal judiciary and a tax system, needed attention. Some Anti-Federalists actually switched positions and resisted congressional consideration of a bill of rights, perhaps in the hope that a new convention might be called by disgruntled states.[20] When Madison returned a month later to present his proposals, he began by apologizing for being "accessory to the loss of a single moment of time by the House."[21]

Nevertheless, by now it was clear that the movement to add a bill of rights had momentum, and most of the discussion turned to the substance of the proposal. Although there were a number of changes, by and large Madison's original list of proposed amendments survived with only minor changes. The most important change was the elimination of Madison's proposal to protect free speech and religious freedom against the states, although Madison called it the "most valuable amendment in the whole list."[22] As a result, the Bill of Rights contained no protection against rights violations by states. Madison's prescience would go unrewarded in his lifetime.

B. The Reconstruction Amendments

It took a savage Civil War to extend federal constitutional protection to even the most basic of freedoms. The Thirteenth Amendment permanently outlawed slavery, thus completing the process begun by Lincoln's Emancipation Proclamation.[23] Despite the obvious reasons for abolishing slavery, the Thirteenth Amendment did not breeze through Congress. The amendment was debated in both Houses of Congress in the spring of 1864. It passed the Senate easily but failed to obtain the necessary two-thirds majority in the House. It then became an issue in the presidential campaign of 1864, with Lincoln vigorously backing it. After his victory, the amendment finally passed in the next session of the House.

The follow-up to the Thirteenth Amendment was the Civil Rights Act of 1866, which in turn was the prelude to the Fourteenth Amendment. Congress passed the statute after it became clear that Southern blacks required additional protections beyond the end of slavery.[24] Leading Confederates dominated the state governments

---

[19]   See FARBER & SHERRY, *supra* note 7, at 343.

[20]   *See id.* at 343–44.

[21]   *Id.* at 344.

[22]   *Id.* at 364.

[23]   For an overview of the history, see *id.* at 414–16.

[24]   The history is recounted in *id.* at 450–51 or in any history of the Reconstruction period. The best such history may be ERIC FONER, RECONSTRUCTION: AMERICA'S UNFINISHED REVOLUTION 1863–1877 (1988).

initially created in the South. Even more disturbing were the new "black codes" that Southern states enacted, which starkly limited the rights and autonomy of former slaves. These codes prohibited blacks from renting land, forcibly prevented them from breaching unfair labor contracts or leaving their masters' premises, and authorized the compulsory "hiring out" of black children and of blacks unable to pay vagrancy fines. The black codes were little more than attempts by the Southern states to re-impose slavery in a subtler form. Republicans were now convinced of the need for additional guarantees to protect blacks in the South. Republicans were also concerned about the treatment of white Union sympathizers in the South, whom Confederates subjected to widespread reprisals.

Senator Lyman Trumbull of Illinois, who chaired the Senate Judiciary Committee, introduced the Civil Rights bill in the Senate in early 1866. When the bill first came up for debate, Section 1 contained four provisions that set the stage for the later Fourteenth Amendment.[25] First, blacks were declared to be citizens of the United States. Second, the bill prohibited discrimination in civil rights or immunities among the inhabitants of any state or territory on account of race. Third, all inhabitants were to have the same rights as whites to contract, to sue, and to engage in various real estate and personal property transactions. Fourth, all inhabitants were to have equal access to legal remedies and were to be subject to the same punishments. The most important subsequent change took place in the House at the initiative of Representative John Bingham of Ohio.[26] He successfully moved to have the general prohibition on "discrimination in civil rights or immunities" struck from the bill because he believed that Congress lacked constitutional power to pass it under the enforcement clause (Section 2) of the Thirteenth Amendment. (We discuss the enforcement clauses of the Civil War Amendments in Chapter 13).

On March 27, President Andrew Johnson, who was a white supremacist and a Democrat who sympathized with the South, vetoed the Civil Rights bill. He contended that the matters covered by the bill were within the exclusive jurisdiction of the states, and that the bill was thus unconstitutional. The Senate overrode the presidential veto on April 6, and the House did the same on April 9.

The Civil Rights Act had attempted to provide statutory protection for certain fundamental rights in the South. Whether Congress really had the constitutional power to do so was subject to some dispute. In addition, legislation such as the Civil Rights Act was vulnerable to subsequent repeal by a Democratic Congress. If the

---

[25]   *See* FARBER & SHERRY, *supra* note 7, at 452.

[26]   *See id.*

Republicans lost their grip on national power, Democrats might repeal the legislation and leave blacks to the not-so-tender mercies of Southern whites. The Fourteenth Amendment was designed to address these issues.

Bingham was one of those politicians who doubted the constitutionality of the Civil Rights Act. Even before the House had taken up the Civil Rights bill, it considered a constitutional amendment that he had proposed. The amendment provided that "Congress shall have power to make all laws which shall be necessary and proper to secure to the citizens of each State all privileges and immunities of citizens in the several States, and to all persons in the several States equal protection in the rights of life, liberty, and property."[27] Congress had more pressing business, and Bingham's amendment temporarily went on the back burner.

As noted, the Civil Rights bill became law on April 9, 1866. Two weeks later, Representative Thaddeus Stevens of Pennsylvania, the leader of the Radicals, placed before the joint committee a new Reconstruction plan.[28] After some maneuvering in committee, Bingham successfully had the original language of the Stevens proposal replaced by his own formulation: "No state shall make or enforce any law which shall abridge the privileges or immunities of citizens of the United States; nor shall any state deprive any person of life, liberty or property without due process of law, nor deny to any person within its jurisdiction the equal protection of the laws."[29]

This language was similar to the language contained in Bingham's earlier proposal. The most significant difference was that the earlier proposal was phrased solely as a grant of congressional power whereas the new proposal was phrased as a limitation on state power. Bingham's language became Section 1 of the Fourteenth Amendment, while the idea of congressional enforcement power found its home in Section 5 of the Amendment.

The ratification process was far from painless, nor did it comply with any vision of disinterested deliberation. In Tennessee, the governor told the legislature that ratification was the price of readmission to the Union. Other Southern states refused to ratify until elections were held under military supervision, while in the North, rescissions of ratification by Ohio and New Jersey were ignored by Congress.[30]

---

[27]   *Id.* at 460–67.

[28]   *See* BENJAMIN B. KENDRICK, THE JOURNAL OF THE JOINT COMMITTEE OF FIFTEEN ON RECONSTRUCTION 83–84 (1914); CHARLES FAIRMAN, RECONSTRUCTION AND REUNION 1864–88, at 1282 (1971).

[29]   KENDRICK, *supra* note 28, at 87.

[30]   *See* FARBER & SHERRY, *supra* note 7, at 485–86.

The last of the Reconstruction Amendments, the Fifteenth Amendment, prohibited racial discrimination in voting, thereby overriding the power of states to define their own political communities. The road to passage of this amendment through Congress was tortuous and the final version was narrower than earlier proposals, which addressed voter qualifications and restrictions on holding office.[31] The amendment met with serious resistance in the Midwest, the border states, and the West, but was eventually ratified after a bitter political struggle.[32]

A modern reader might wonder why the Fifteenth Amendment was deemed necessary after ratification of the Equal Protection Clause of the Fourteenth Amendment, which (as will be detailed in Chapter 10) prohibits various kinds of racial discrimination by states. The answer is that constitutional interpreters at the time followed certain distinctions among civil, social, and political equality.[33] The Fourteenth Amendment was thought to be limited to guaranteeing civil equality, which included the rights to contract, sue, and own property. Voting, by contrast, was deemed to be a political right and so, in the minds of most supporters, beyond the protections of the Fourteenth Amendment. Social equality concerned the right to choose one's associates and was generally understood to be outside the protections of all the Civil War Amendments, which is why most members of the Reconstruction Congress did not think the Equal Protection Clause touched state laws requiring racial segregation in public schools or prohibiting inter-racial marriage. The precise boundaries among these three categories of equality rights were contested, but their general purpose was clear enough: both to expand, and to limit the expansion of, the rights being granted to the citizens who had been slaves. This distinction between civil and political rights may have seemed sensible at the time, but it does not correspond to the way people today think about rights.

The upshot was that certain guarantees of liberty and equality were extended to the states, but only after the bloodiest war in American history and enormous political effort. The remainder of this book is focused on these new guarantees, and particularly on the guarantees of due process and equal protection in the Fourteenth Amendment. In the following two sections of this chapter, we will focus on two fundamental issues about these guarantees. First, how do they relate to the guarantees in the Bill of Rights? And second, to

---

[31]   *See id.* at 491–508.

[32]   *See id.* at 509.

[33]   For discussions of these distinctions, see generally Mark Tushnet, *The Politics of Equality in Constitutional Law*, 74 J. AM. HIST. 884 (1987); RICHARD A. PRIMUS, THE AMERICAN LANGUAGE OF RIGHTS 154–56 (1999).

what extent do these protections extend beyond acts by state officials?

II. Incorporation

A. The (Near) Demise of the Privileges or Immunities Clause

The most obvious route for applying Bill of Rights protections to the states is through the Privileges of Immunities Clause of Section 1 of the Fourteenth Amendment. It provides that "[n]o State shall make or enforce any law which shall abridge the privileges or immunities of citizens of the United States." It seems reasonable to think that the rights listed in original Constitution and the Bill of Rights are among the privileges or immunities of U.S. citizenship. What else could this provision being referring to? Indeed, at least one of the sponsors of the Fourteenth Amendment had precisely this understanding. Senator Jacob Howard of Michigan, who introduced the bill in the Senate because the sponsor was ill, said that the clause included "the personal rights guaranteed and secured by the first eight amendments of the Constitution," which he then proceeded to list one after another.[34]

Yet, U.S. constitutional law ended up taking a much more circuitous path to a similar destination.[35] We begin the saga of incorporation, therefore, with the story of why the most obvious road was not taken. The answer lies in the *Slaughter-House Cases*.[36]

A Louisiana law banned slaughter houses within the New Orleans city limits but made an exception for the Crescent City Company, which was thereby essentially given a monopoly. In an opinion by Justice Samuel Miller, the Supreme Court rejected a broad-gauged attack on the statute brought by New Orleans butchers. One of the butchers' arguments was based on the Privileges or Immunities Clause of the Fourteenth Amendment, which they asserted protected their fundamental right to work at their trade. The Court held, however, that this clause protected only a very limited set of national privileges, such as the right of access to federal officials and the right to use navigable waters.

In limiting the Fourteenth Amendment "P or I Clause" to protecting a limited set of national rights, the Court stressed that the language of the Fourteenth Amendment says that no state shall abridge "the privileges or immunities *of citizens of the United States*"

---

[34]   FARBER & SHERRY, *supra* note 7, at 474.

[35]   In one respect, however, the Due Process Clause is broader than the Privileges or Immunities Clause: the former applies to "persons" and the latter only to "citizens."

[36]   83 U.S. 36 (1872).

(our emphasis). Justice Miller reasoned that state citizenship remained distinct from national citizenship under the first sentence of the Fourteenth Amendment, which made anyone born or naturalized in the United States a national citizen but added a residence requirement for state citizens. Justice Miller contrasted this language with the language found in the Privileges and Immunities Clause of Article IV, which refers to the privileges and immunities of citizens of a state. By implication, he argued, the two covered different ground. The Article IV clause had been held to protect nonresidents from discrimination affecting a broad range of significant interests, such as the right to own property or the right to protection by the government. The right to pursue a trade was probably within the range of interests protected by the Article IV clause, Justice Miller reasoned, but this clause applied only to discrimination against nonresidents. If the same interests were protected by the Fourteenth Amendment against state abridgement, he feared, the effect would be a massive transfer of power to the federal government and "would constitute this court a perpetual censor upon all legislation of the States, on the civil rights of their own citizens, with authority to nullify such as it did not approve as consistent with those rights, as they existed at the time of the adoption of this amendment."[37]

The four dissenters argued for a broad reading of the Privileges or Immunities Clause of the Fourteenth Amendment. In their view, what the Article IV clause did to protect citizens against discrimination by other states, "the fourteenth amendment does for the protection of every citizen of the United States against hostile and discriminating legislation against him in favor of others, whether they reside in the same or in different States."[38] In particular, the dissent said, "all pursuits, all professions, all avocations are open" to American citizens equally.[39] "The State may prescribe such regulations for every pursuit and calling of life as will promote the public health, secure the good order and advance the general prosperity of society, but when once prescribed, the pursuit or calling must be free to be followed by every citizen who is within the conditions designated, and will conform to the regulations."[40]

More important than whether the Fourteenth Amendment protected a right to pursue a chosen vocation was the fact that the majority opinion required a strained reading of the Privileges or Immunities Clause, limiting it to a narrow set of rights, which were already protected in other ways or not susceptible to violation by

---

[37] *Id.* at 78.
[38] *Id.* at 101.
[39] *Id.* at 110.
[40] *Id.*

state governments. The congressional debates over the Fourteenth Amendment actually referred to the Article IV clause as covering similar rights.[41] But the majority feared that giving the language its more natural interpretation would shift too much power to the federal government. The majority opinion reflected a conservative vision of both the meaning of the Reconstruction Amendments and the meaning of the Civil War.

Despite the alternate vision articulated by the dissent, the majority opinion proved enduring; its holding with respect to the Privileges or Immunities Clause was never revisited in later opinions. As a result, the Clause lost nearly all significance after the *Slaughter-House Cases* and has rarely appeared again in Supreme Court opinions.[42]

After the eclipse of the Privileges or Immunities Clause, the Due Process Clause gradually grew in importance. (Constitutional law tends to be path dependent; if one provision is read very narrowly, pressure may mount to read another provision more broadly.) By the time it decided *Mugler v. Kansas*[43] in 1887, the Court had concluded that due process protects more than fair procedure—that someone is deprived of their property without due process of *law* if the deprivation is based on an arbitrary legislative fiat. In reviewing the constitutionality of a state law prohibiting alcoholic beverages, the *Mugler* Court said that if "a statute purporting to have been enacted to protect the public health, the public morals, or the public safety, has no real or substantial relation to those objects, or is a palpable invasion of rights secured by the fundamental law, it is the duty of the courts to so adjudge, and thereby give effect to the constitution."[44] For present purposes, the key language in this quote is the reference to "a palpable invasion of rights secured by the fundamental law." This language provided an opening for importing the Bill of Rights protections into the Fourteenth Amendment's Due Process Clause.

B. The Incorporation Debates

The Court only slowly came around to the view that the Due Process Clause was a vehicle for imposing Bill of Rights limitations on the states. In *Twining v. New Jersey*,[45] for instance, the Court rejected the defendant's claim that the Fifth Amendment's privilege against self-incrimination applies in state criminal proceedings as a

---

41   *See* FARBER & SHERRY, *supra* note 7, at 471, 473–74.

42   The rare exception was *Saenz v. Roe*, 526 U.S. 489 (1999), holding that the Privileges or Immunities Clause prohibits states from distinguishing between their citizens based on their length of residency.

43   123 U.S. 623 (1887).

44   *Id.* at 626.

45   211 U.S. 78 (1908).

matter of due process. Nevertheless, the Court slowly moved toward incorporation. In taking stock of the situation in *Palko v. Connecticut*,[46] some fifty years after *Twining*, the Court noted that a number of rights had by this point been incorporated, such as freedom of speech, the free exercise of religion, and the right to counsel in felony cases.

Justice Benjamin Cardozo's opinion for the Court in *Palko* also attempted to articulate a test for what rights should and should not be incorporated in due process. The defendant had been acquitted of first-degree murder by a jury but found guilty of second-degree murder and given a life sentence. Connecticut law allowed the government to appeal acquittals with the permission of the trial judge. The state supreme court reversed the acquittal for first-degree murder, and after the second trial he was sentenced to death. In a federal case, such a retrial would have been considered double jeopardy and barred by the Fifth Amendment's Double Jeopardy Clause.[47] The question before the Court, then, was whether the prohibition on double jeopardy applied to the states via the Fourteenth Amendment's Due Process Clause.

Justice Cardozo noted that the right to a jury trial and indictment had been held by the Court not to be incorporated in due process, unlike some of the other rights noted above. Justice Cardozo then tried to articulate a standard for distinguishing what rights should be incorporated. The right to a jury trial and indictment may have "value and importance," he said, but "they are not of the very essence of a scheme of ordered liberty."[48] Thus, to abolish these rights is "not to violate a 'principle of justice so rooted in the traditions and conscience of our people as to be ranked as fundamental.' "[49] In his view, "[f]ew would be so narrow or provincial as to maintain that a fair and enlightened system of justice would be impossible without them."[50] Applying this test, Justice Cardozo concluded that the prohibition on the government's appealing jury verdicts did not rank as basic to ordered liberty.

After *Palko*, the Court struggled with the question of which rights qualified as fundamental under this test, while debate arose over whether *Palko* was the right approach. A key case in this development was *Adamson v. California*.[51] The issue was whether a jury could be told that the defendant's failure to testify might give

---

[46]   302 U.S. 319 (1937).

[47]   *See* U.S. CONST. amend. V ("No person shall . . . be subject for the same offense to be twice put in jeopardy of life or limb . . . . ").

[48]   *Palko*, 302 U.S. at 325.

[49]   *Id.* (quoting Snyder v. Mass., 291 U.S. 97, 105 (1934)).

[50]   *Id.*

[51]   332 U.S. 46 (1947).

rise to an inference of guilt. If this had been a federal criminal case, the defendant could not be penalized in this way for exercising her right against self-incrimination. The majority rejected the defendant's claim, relying on *Palko*'s embrace of what lawyers call "selective incorporation."

The case is notable, however, for the other opinions, not for the majority opinion. In dissent, Justice Hugo Black argued largely on originalist grounds that the entire Bill of Rights was incorporated by the Fourteenth Amendment.[52] He advocated for what lawyers call "total incorporation." Notably, Justice Black was one of the two most liberal members of the Court, and he fervently embraced originalism as a basis for his constitutional views before the rise of the modern conservative legal movement. He accused the Court of subverting the original intent of the Framers of the Fourteenth Amendment and substituting for the Bill of Rights its own view of what was just and fair. From today's perspective, much of Justice Black's rhetoric resonated with the rhetoric later used by Justice Antonin Scalia and other modern originalists, although to different ends.

Two of the other opinions in the case are worth noting. Justice Felix Frankfurter's concurring opinion offered a sturdy defense of *Palko*. He contested Black's historical evidence. In his view, the Due Process Clause "inescapably imposes upon this Court an exercise of judgment upon the whole course of the proceedings in order to ascertain whether they offend those canons of decency and fairness which express the notions of justice of English-speaking peoples."[53] Meanwhile, Justices Frank Murphy and Wiley Rutledge, who dissented, were prepared to go even farther than Justice Black in protecting defendants. They agreed that the Fourteenth Amendment incorporated the Bill of Rights, but they believed it might go farther than that. In their view, "[o]ccasions may arise where a proceeding falls so far short of conforming to fundamental standards of procedure as to warrant constitutional condemnation in terms of a lack of due process despite the absence of a specific provision in the Bill of Rights."[54]

Thus, the opinions present three separate positions: Justice Frankfurter's and the majority's view that the Court should use a common law method to decide which rights are fundamental; Justice Black's view that it should apply the entire Bill of Rights and stop there; and the Murphy/Rutledge view that it should do both.

---

[52]   *See id.* at 68 (Black, J., dissenting).

[53]   *Id.* at 67 (Frankfurter, J., concurring).

[54]   *Id.* at 124 (Murphy, J., dissenting).

C. Incorporation Today

Justice Black lost the battle but won the war. As of the beginning of this century, the Court had incorporated virtually all of the provisions of the Bill of Rights into the Fourteenth Amendment, with the most important exceptions being the right to indictment in criminal cases[55] and the Second Amendment. In *McDonald v. City of Chicago*, a sharply-divided Court eliminated one of these exceptions by holding that the Fourteenth Amendment incorporates the right to keep and bear arms.[56] Justice Samuel Alito's opinion for the Court saw no reason to distinguish the Second Amendment from other protections of the first Eight Amendments, almost all of which had been incorporated.

As in *Adamson*, the concurrence and dissent staked out positions in favor of either total incorporation or a fundamental rights approach. But the ideological roles were reversed. Justice Clarence Thomas, the most conservative member of the Court, agreed with the result but revived Justice Black's historical argument for total incorporation (but using the Privileges or Immunities Clause, not the Due Process Clause.)[57] Meanwhile, Justice John Paul Stevens, then the Court's most liberal member, argued against incorporation, taking something like the Frankfurter position. In Justice Stevens' view, "[w]hether an asserted substantive due process interest is explicitly named in one of the first eight Amendments to the Constitution or is not mentioned, the underlying inquiry is the same: [w]e must ask whether the interest is "comprised within the term liberty."[58]

Given that for all practical purposes the issue of incorporation is now settled, the reader is entitled to ask the reasons for recounting this history at some length. It remains important for at least three reasons. First, it illustrates how constitutional law evolves over long

---

[55] An indictment is one way to begin a prosecution, requiring the prosecutor's decision to be confirmed by a grand jury. Many states instead allow a prosecutor to begin a criminal case by filing an "information" in her own name. The other provisions that still have not been incorporated are the Third Amendment (prohibiting the quartering of soldiers in peacetime in people's homes); one clause of the Sixth Amendment (requiring jurors to be from the state and district where the crime was committed); the Seventh Amendment right to a jury in a civil case; and the Eighth Amendment right to be free from excessive fines (which the Supreme Court may incorporate in a pending case). Whether the Eighth Amendment right to bail has been incorporated was left somewhat unclear by *Schilb v. Kuebel*, 404 U.S. 357 (1971).

[56] 561 U.S. 742 (2010).

[57] *See id.* at 805 (Thomas, J., concurring). For an exploration of why the rest of the Court, including Justice Scalia, stuck with the Due Process Clause in *McDonald* notwithstanding strong originalist arguments for reviving the Privileges or Immunities Clause, see generally Neil S. Siegel, *Prudentialism in* McDonald v. City of Chicago, 6 DUKE J. CONST. L. & PUB. POL'Y 16 (2010).

[58] *McDonald*, 561 U.S. at 864–65 (Stevens, J., dissenting).

periods. At any one time, lawyers can largely rely on a stable body of precedents. These precedents, moreover, provide a matrix to which new decisions can adhere. Over time, however, this process of change can shift expectations drastically.

Second, the incorporation debate provides an apt case study for constitutional theorists. Although their purposes were very different, Justices Black and Thomas illustrate originalism at its most forceful. Justices Cardozo, Frankfurter, and Stevens provide strong examples of evolutionary theories in action. Their views perhaps resemble those of Professor David Strauss, the most oriented toward the common law method among the theorists we discussed in Chapter 3.

Third, while the incorporation debate is over, the debate over fundamental rights is far from over. Justice Black argued for total incorporation—a war he essentially, if not technically, won—and against recognition of any additional fundamental rights. Recall that Justice Murphy rejected the second part of Justice Black's vision. This debate is very much alive, as we will see in Chapter 12.

III. State Action Doctrine

Regardless of what rights the Fourteenth Amendment provides individuals, who has a duty to respect these rights? The Fourteenth Amendment says that "no state" shall deny rights of due process and equal protection. But to what extent does the government or a government official have to be involved in an action in order to trigger constitutional protection? (Note that, despite the name, the state action doctrine applies equally to all levels of government, from local to national.) In the great majority of cases, the answer is clear, because the decision has been made by a government official on the one hand, or because it is clearly just the decision of a private individual with no state involvement. But in the intermediate zone, whether to find "state action" and apply constitutional guarantees can be a very difficult question.

State action doctrine is not limited to discrimination cases, but in practice it has been closely linked to the ebb and flow of race relations. As we will see, it was initially deployed as part of the Supreme Court's effort to limit Reconstruction. It surfaced again in the Civil Rights Era, when the Court used an expansive conception of state action to expand racial equality. In the post-Civil Rights Era, the Court has been less prone to find state action. The end result has been an unusually confusing body of doctrine.

A. *The Civil Rights Cases*

The Civil Rights Cases[59] cemented the state action doctrine in place. There, the Court confronted the Civil Rights Act of 1875, which may be considered the last gasp of Reconstruction. As the leading historian of Reconstruction explains, "the interconnected issues of white supremacy, low taxes, and control of the black labor force set the tone for the Democratic campaigns of the mid-1870s," as a result of which "the Democrats solidified their hold on states already under their control and 'redeemed' new ones."[60] By 1875, "the political landscape had been transformed," and the Republicans knew they would retain control of Congress only during the lame duck session before the new Congress took office.[61] "With political violence having again erupted in many parts of the South," Republicans "devised a program to safeguard what remained of Reconstruction."[62] The 1875 Civil Rights Act was a key part of this effort. In passing the law, Congress relied upon is power, under Section 5 of the Fourteenth Amendment, to enforce the constitutional rights guaranteed in Section 1 of the Amendment.

Section 1 of the Act provided that "all persons within the jurisdiction of the United States shall be entitled to the full and equal enjoyment" of public accommodations such as inns and railroads, "subject only to the conditions and limitations established by law, and applicable alike to citizens of every race and color, regardless of any previous condition of servitude."[63] Violation was a misdemeanor and also entitled the victim to recover $500 in damages.[64]

In an opinion by Justice Joseph Bradley, the Court held the law unconstitutional. In the Court's view, "positive rights and privileges are undoubtedly secured by the Fourteenth Amendment; but they are secured by way of prohibition against State laws and State proceedings affecting those rights and privileges," and congressional statutes "must necessarily be predicated upon such supposed State laws or State proceedings, and be directed to the correction of their operation and effect."[65] According to Justice Bradley, it would be "absurd to affirm that, because the rights of life, liberty, and property (which include all civil rights that men have) are by the amendment sought to be protected against invasion on the part of the state without due process of law," Congress could legislate against denials

---

[59]   109 U.S. 3 (1883).

[60]   FONER, *supra* note 24, at 549.

[61]   *Id.* at 553.

[62]   *Id.*

[63]   *Civil Rights Cases*, 109 U.S. at 9.

[64]   *See id.*

[65]   *Id.* at 11–12.

of these rights by purely private actors like owners of inns, as opposed to state actors.[66] In the Court's view, civil rights protected by the Fourteenth Amendment "cannot be impaired by the wrongful acts of individuals, unsupported by State authority in the shape of laws, customs, or judicial or executive proceedings."[67] Unless a wrongful act is "sanctioned in some way by the State" or "done under State authority," the victim's rights "remain in full force, and may presumably be vindicated by resort to the laws of the State for redress.[68]

In a dissent for himself alone, the first Justice John Marshall Harlan protested in vain that the Reconstruction Amendments "have been so construed as to defeat the ends the people desired to accomplish."[69] Among other arguments, he contended that "[i]n every material sense applicable to the practical enforcement of the Fourteenth Amendment, railroad corporations, keepers of inns, and managers of places of public amusement are agents of the State, because they are charged with duties to the public, and are amenable, in respect of their public duties and functions, to governmental regulation."[70] If the Reconstruction Amendments were properly enforced, he said, "there cannot be, in this republic, any class of human beings in practical subjection to another class, with power in the latter to dole out to the former just such privileges as they may choose to grant."[71] But this was not the view of the majority, whose view has endured to this day, as we will see in Chapter 13.

B.   *Shelley v. Kramer* and the Civil Rights Era

The view that only state actors are capable of violating the Due Process and Equal Protection Clauses is now unquestioned. But the Court's position on what constitutes state action has varied over time. Beginning in the aftermath of World War II and extending through the Civil Right Era, the Court took an expansive view of what qualified as state action.

Shelley v. Kramer[72] signaled the start of this trend. It remains the best-known state action case and is studied in both Constitutional Law and Property courses. *Shelley* involved a state court injunction enforcing a racial covenant in a real estate deed—that is, a provision stating that the property could be owned only by whites. The Court began with two premises. The first, established by the *Civil Rights*

---

[66]   *Id.* at 13.

[67]   *Id.* at 25.

[68]   *Id.* at 25–26.

[69]   *Id.* at 33 (Harlan, J., dissenting).

[70]   *Id.* at 58–59.

[71]   *Id.* at 62.

[72]   334 U.S. 1 (1948).

Cases, was that the purely voluntary adherence to this covenant by property owners would not implicate the Fourteenth Amendment. The second, established by earlier Twentieth Century cases, was that a state or city mandating residential segregation would be invalid. But the constitutionality of judicial enforcement was an open question until *Shelley*.

The Court found that judicial enforcement of the racially restrictive covenant constituted state action. "These are not cases," Chief Justice Fred Vinson wrote for the Court, "in which the States have merely abstained from action, leaving private individuals free to impose such discriminations as they see fit."[73] Instead, he reasoned, "the States have made available to such individuals the full coercive power of government to deny to petitioners, on the grounds of race or color, the enjoyment of property rights in premises which petitioners are willing and financially able to acquire and which the grantors are willing to sell."[74] Thus, he wrote, "[t]he difference between judicial enforcement and nonenforcement of the restrictive covenants is the difference to petitioners between being denied rights of property available to other members of the community and being accorded full enjoyment of those rights on an equal footing."[75] After all, the Court observed, "freedom from discrimination by the States in the enjoyment of property rights was among the basic objectives sought to be effectuated by the framers of the Fourteenth Amendment."[76]

Shelley raises the question of whether any judicial decree that gives effect to a private decision would be state action. If so, a court could not, for instance, enforce a trespass law against a person who was refused permission to be on private property if the owner had a racial motive. Such a holding would go a long way toward constitutionalizing all of anti-discrimination law. But if *Shelley* does not go this far, where is one to draw the line? The Court did not say, and commentators have struggled with the question ever since.[77] Perhaps the racial covenants in *Shelley* are distinctive in the widespread nature of the practice as a basis for segregation, the coercive effect of the covenants on later property owners who did not originally sign them, and the extent to which enforcement of the covenants deviated from the normal rules of property law, which

---

[73]   *Id.* at 19.

[74]   *Id.*

[75]   *Id.*

[76]   *Id.* at 23.

[77]   *See generally, e.g.*, Mark Tushnet, *Shelley v. Kramer and Theories of Equality*, 33 N.Y. L. Sch. L. Rev. 383 (1988); Mark Rosen, *Was Shelly v. Kramer Incorrectly Decided?: Some New Answers*, 95 Cal. L. Rev. 451 (2007); Robert Glennon & John Nowak, *A Functional Analysis of the Fourteenth Amendment "State Action" Requirement*, 1976 Sup. Ct. Rev. 221.

disfavor restraints on the sale of property. Yet it is not clear that all of these considerations speak to the constitutional question at issue: whether there was state action.

Burton v. Wilmington Parking Authority[78] reflects the Court's willingness to interpret state action broadly in the Civil Rights Era. The Delaware courts had upheld the exclusion of a black customer from a private restaurant located in a municipal parking garage. The government had not participated in the restaurant's action. But the Supreme Court reversed, finding a symbiotic relationship between the city and the restaurant:

> Guests of the restaurant are afforded a convenient place to park their automobiles, even if they cannot enter the restaurant directly from the parking area. Similarly, its convenience for diners may well provide additional demand for the Authority's parking facilities. . . . Neither can it be ignored, especially in view of [the restaurant's] affirmative allegation that for it to serve Negroes would injure its business, that profits earned by discrimination not only contribute to, but also are indispensable elements in, the financial success of a governmental agency.[79]

The Court adopted a kind of totality-of-the-circumstances test. It disclaimed any intention of laying down a firm rule, saying "a multitude of relationships might appear to some to fall within the Amendment's embrace, but that, it must be remembered, can be determined only in the framework of the peculiar facts or circumstances present."[80]

In dissent, the second Justice John Marshall Harlan (the more conservative grandson of the first Justice Harlan), complained that "[t]he Court's opinion, by a process of first undiscriminatingly throwing together various factual bits and pieces and then undermining the resulting structure by an equally vague disclaimer, seems to me to leave completely at sea just what it is in this record that satisfies the requirement of 'state action.' "[81] Justice Harlan's lament retains its sting even today. State action doctrine remains a tangle of judicial rulings that often remains puzzling. After a look at current doctrine, we will offer some thoughts about its evolution in the more conservative era since the end of the liberal Warren Court.

---

[78]   365 U.S. 715 (1961).

[79]   *Id.* at 724.

[80]   *Id.* at 725–26.

[81]   *Id.* at 728–29 (Harlan, J., dissenting).

C. Modern State Action Doctrine

Despite the confusion within the doctrine, the modern Court is generally not eager to expand state action. Indeed, it is easier to compile a list of factors that do not suffice to establish state action than to explain cases that do find state action. First, the fact that an activity is licensed by the state does not turn its discriminatory policies into state action. In *Moose Lodge No. 107 v. Irvis*,[82] the Court held that a fraternal organization was free to discriminate even though it had a state liquor license, and in *Jackson v. Metropolitan Edison Company*,[83] the Court held that not even a state-granted monopoly was enough to create state action.

Second, the government's deliberate decision to allow a private action to take place does not constitute state action. In *Flagg Brothers v. Brooks*,[84] state law allowed the owner of a warehouse to sell goods stored there to satisfy the owner's bills. The Court reasoned that the state was merely stepping aside rather than involving itself in the warehouse's seizure of property without notice or hearing. Even more strikingly—and disturbingly—the Court held that the state could not be liable when a government social worker knew that a parent was physically abusing a child and did nothing.[85]

The Court seems to be most prone to find state action when when the decision involves an inherently governmental function or government officials are themselves involved in a decision. As an example of the governmental function test, the Court held the state responsible for the actions of a private doctor with whom it had contracted to treat prisoners.[86] The official involvement test is exemplified by *Lugar v. Edmondson Oil Company*,[87] in which the Court held that state action was present when a creditor obtained a prejudgment writ of attachment, which is an order freezing an asset while the litigation is proceeding. The county sheriff executed the writ and seized the debtor's property. State action may also be found when an otherwise neutral action seems designed to encourage private discrimination, as in the case of a state program providing free textbooks to private schools that practiced racial discrimination.[88]

Some of these threads came together in a series of cases involving peremptory challenges to potential jurors. Under American

---

[82]   407 U.S. 163 (1972).

[83]   419 U.S. 345 (1974).

[84]   436 U.S. 149 (1978).

[85]   Deshaney v. Winnebago County Social Services Dept., 489 U.S. 189 (1989).

[86]   *See* West v. Atkins, 487 U.S. 42 (1988).

[87]   457 U.S. 922 (1982).

[88]   *See* Norwood v. Harrison, 413 U.S. 455 (1973).

trial procedure, either side in a case can object to seating a particular juror "for cause," meaning there is reason to doubt the juror's impartiality. But each side also has a certain number of peremptory challenges, which do not require any justification and may be based on nothing more substantial than a hunch that a juror would be unfavorable to one's side. What happens when the motivation for using a peremptory is the race or gender of the juror, either of which may be thought by a lawyer to offer a clue as to how the juror might vote in a case? For example, prosecutors may believe that African American jurors are less likely than white jurors to vote in favor of capital punishment, and female jurors might be thought to be more sympathetic to female plaintiffs in sexual harassment cases.

The Court began with the easiest case, in which the peremptory challenge is made by the prosecutor in a criminal case. Since prosecutors are state officials, this use of a peremptory challenge fell easily within state action doctrine.[89] *Edmondston v. Leesville Concrete Company* presented a tougher question because it involved private parties using peremptory challenges.[90] The Court began by listing some relevant factors and calling for a context-specific inquiry:

> Although we have recognized that this aspect of the analysis is often a factbound inquiry, our cases disclose certain principles of general application. Our precedents establish that, in determining whether a particular action or course of conduct is governmental in character, it is relevant to examine the following: the extent to which the actor relies on governmental assistance and benefits, whether the actor is performing a traditional governmental function, and whether the injury caused is aggravated in a unique way by the incidents of governmental authority.[91]

Applying this approach, the Court concluded that the use of preemptory challenges does constitute state action. The key reason was that, "[w]ere it not for peremptory challenges, there would be no question that the entire process of determining who will serve on the jury constitutes state action"; the "fact that the government delegates some portion of this power to private litigants does not change the governmental character of the power exercised."[92]

Readers who are having trouble making sense of these cases should not feel alone: almost everyone has the same reaction. But

---

[89]   *See* Batson v. Kentucky, 476 U.S. 79 (1986).

[90]   500 U.S. 614 (1991).

[91]   *Id*. at 621–22.

[92]   *Id*. at 626. The Court extended this rule in *J.E.B. v. Alabama ex rel. T.B.*, 511 U.S. 127 (1994), holding that preemptory challenges based on gender are unconstitutional.

why has the Court had so much trouble articulating clear rules or even sensible, consistent standards? We think there are at least three reasons.

The first is that state action doctrine serves several different functions. It serves a separation of powers function by leaving regulation of private conduct mostly to Congress, often using the Commerce Clause. It also serves a federalism function, because those aspects of private action outside of congressional control are left to the states. And it serves a liberty function, by recognizing an area of personal autonomy that is not subject to constitutional constraint. Yet, at the same time, the power of the state in modern America is pervasive, and constitutional restraints that applied only to the actions of government employees would allow the government to quietly foster many practices that it could not engage in openly. Balancing these diverse interests may not lend itself to coherent doctrine.

A second reason for the confusion is that the Court has been loath to overrule its state-action precedents even though its approach has shifted over time as it has become more conservative. The Court's past anxiety to address private racial discrimination by constitutional means may seem less urgent now that Congress has taken action on many fronts, and state and local antidiscrimination law is more widespread than it used to be. Moreover, the substantive issues in cases have also shifted over time from racial discrimination to more subtle concerns, like whether private actors must provide hearings to employees or customers. Federal judicial action may seem less called-for in cases involving such issues.

The third and theoretically most fundamental reason is that determining whether the state is responsible for an action requires a baseline of the world without such action. Yet the state is always in the background somewhere. Its laws of property, contract, and tort are the basis for private activities, and in today's world the state is often a regulator or funder (either through contracts, subsidies, or tax benefits.) So the question is not whether private action is connected with the state; it is whether the state's involvement has risen beyond some kind of neutral baseline. Judges inevitably differ in how they picture this baseline.

For the practicing lawyer or judge—or law student—the doctrinal confusion precludes the possibility of relying on simple, clear-cut rules. In determining whether state action is present in a given situation, the best approach is probably to think about the broad categories of traditional public function, public-private symbiosis, and official involvement. At this point in the analysis, there is no substitute for comparing the facts of the case at hand with the facts of the key modern precedents, and trying to find a compelling analogy one way or the other.

We will return to the issue of state action in the final chapter of this book, which deals with congressional enforcement of civil rights. As indicated by the *Civil Rights Cases*, the doctrine can act as a restriction not only on the courts but also on Congress. But, as we will see, it is incorrect to say that Congress can never address private action using its authority to enforce the Reconstruction Amendments. In the meantime, we turn to a series of chapters about the scope of constitutional rights, particularly rights of due process and equal protection.

Further Readings

Richard Aynes, *On Misreading John Bingham and the Fourteenth Amendment*, 103 YALE L.J. 47 (1993).

Charles Fairman, *Does the Fourteenth Amendment Incorporate the Bill of Rights? The Original Understanding*, 2 STAN. L. REV. 5 (1949).

ERIC FONER, RECONSTRUCTION: AMERICA'S UNFINISHED REVOLUTION 1863–1877 (1988).

Robert Glennon & John Nowak, *A Functional Analysis of the Fourteenth Amendment "State Action" Requirement*, 1976 SUP. CT. REV. 221.

Jerold Israel, *Selective Incorporation Revisited*, 71 GEO. L.J. 253 (1982).

Mark Rosen, *Was* Shelly v. Kramer *Incorrectly Decided: Some New Answers,* 95 CAL. L. REV. 451 (2007).

David Strauss, *State Action After the Civil Rights Era*, 10 CONST. COMMENT. 409 (1993).

Mark Tushnet, Shelley v. Kramer *and Theories of Equality*, 33 N.Y. L. SCH. L. REV. 383 (1988).

Chapter 9

ECONOMIC REGULATION AND CONSTITUTIONAL RIGHTS

From the Nineteenth Century onward, constitutional protection of economic rights has been a major bone of contention. The history roughly parallels that of the Commerce Clause, with courts using what lawyers call "substantive due process" to strike down a variety of economic regulations until the New Deal, and then retreating almost entirely. Today, the Supreme Court has abandoned the use of the Due Process Clause and the Equal Protection Clause to invalidate economic regulations, although there are libertarian legal academics who have urged the courts to revitalize economic substantive due process. As we will see, however, an island of doctrinal protection still exists against regulations that are so severe that they may qualify as takings of private property.

This chapter also addresses the other aspect of due process, called procedural due process. This is the requirement that the government use fair procedures before depriving a person of life, liberty, or property. While economic regulations may have little to fear from review of their substance (unless they fall afoul of the Takings Clause), the procedures for applying these regulations may still receive careful scrutiny from the courts.

I. The Nineteenth Century and the *Lochner* Era

In this section, we will trace the history of the Court's review of economic regulations up to the "switch in time"—that is, the reversal in constitutional doctrine during the New Deal that was discussed in Chapter 5. This history provides the backdrop for the current doctrine in this area. What is more, this history is important to understanding constitutional disputes in other areas like abortion and same-sex marriage, where aggressive pre-New Deal judicial review of economic regulations is still invoked as a cautionary warning. Thus, the arguments made by Justices today about hot-button constitutional issues can be understood only in the context of the Court's rejection of the pre-New Deal legacy. Indeed, much of the constitutional theory discussed in Chapter 3 is designed to address the problem of whether and how modern substantive due process doctrine is distinguishable from the economic substantive due process of the past.

A. Pre-*Lochner*-Era Restrictions on Economic Regulation

At different times, the State of New York enacted one law restricting the hours that bakers could work and another law restricting the owners' use of designated historic buildings. Such statutes involve important economic interests. What federal constitutional restrictions apply to such economic regulations? This is an unexpectedly complicated question. The historic preservation law might run afoul of the Takings Clause, which we discuss at the end of this chapter. The bakery regulation could be challenged under two other constitutional provisions.

If the law regulating the hours of bakers were applied to rewrite existing labor-management contracts, it might violate the Contracts Clause of Article I, Section 10, which says that "[n]o State shall . . . pass any . . . Law impairing the Obligation of Contracts." This clause provided the primary constitutional protection against economic regulation before the Civil War.

The Contracts Clause was originally aimed at debtor-relief legislation passed by the states and was liberally applied in the early Nineteenth Century. Thus, in *Fletcher v. Peck*,[1] the Marshall Court refused to allow Georgia to rescind land grants that had been obtained by bribing the state legislature, because rescission would impair vested rights that the ultimate purchasers had acquired by contract. In the *Dartmouth College Case*,[2] the Court struck down a New Hampshire law changing the provisions of the college's state charter, which the Court viewed as a contract. The same principle was applied by the Marshall Court to limit state regulation of business corporations.

The Taney (pronounced "taw-ney") Court (1836–64) retreated from the Marshall Court's broad use of the Contracts Clause. In *Charles River Bridge v. Warren Bridge*,[3] the Court upheld the state's power to adopt new policies in derogation of a public charter granting a monopoly to a ferry company. Justice Joseph Story (a Marshall Court holdover) adamantly objected that the Court was sanctioning a violation of the Contracts Clause and undermining vested rights. But Chief Justice Roger Taney's opinion for the Court insisted that "contract" rights should not be needlessly constructed when they would derogate from the public interest. This was obviously a

---

[1]   10 U.S. 87 (1810).

[2]   17 U.S. 518 (1819).

[3]   36 U.S. 420 (1837).

different attitude toward state regulation of private property[4] than that adopted by the Marshall Court.[5]

In the late Nineteenth Century, the Court turned in another doctrinal direction, following the lead of some state courts. These state courts were interpreting the Due Process Clause of the Fourteenth Amendment to protect the liberty of private contracting and the sanctity of private property.[6] Some of the state court judges who viewed the Due Process Clause in economic terms—Judges David Brewer from Kansas and Rufus Peckham from New York— were later appointed to the U.S. Supreme Court. In the 1890s, they transformed American constitutional law under cover of the Due Process Clause. The primary innovation of the state cases in the 1880s[7] and of the Supreme Court cases in the 1890s was their recognition of a "liberty of contract" right in the Due Process Clause. This line of cases is exemplified by *Lochner v. New York*. We discuss this decision and some related rulings below.

B. *Lochner* and Related Cases

Substantive due process did not achieve a real foothold on the Supreme Court until almost the end of the Nineteenth Century. Perhaps it was no coincidence that progressive and populist reformers were gaining power in a number of states, to the alarm of conservatives.

In *Allgeyer v. Louisiana*,[8] the Court struck down a Louisiana law requiring all insurance on Louisiana property to be issued by insurers registered to do business in the state. The Court characterized the law as an infringement on the right of out-of-state brokers to pursue their livelihoods and subjected the law to close scrutiny, which it failed.

It was not immediately clear that this ruling had broader import for economic regulation. In contrast to *Allgeyer*, the Court in *Holden v. Hardy*[9] upheld a Utah statute limiting miners and smelter workers

---

[4]   This shift paralleled a movement toward utilitarianism by the courts. For instance, a broadly utilitarian justification for state regulation of private property is set forth in Chief Judge Lemuel Shaw's opinion in *Commonwealth v. Alger*, 61 Mass. 53 (1851).

[5]   We return later in this chapter to the Contracts Clause, providing a brief discussion of current doctrine. For present purposes, suffice it to say that the Clause is only sporadically invoked today, and even then, often unsuccessfully.

[6]   For instance, in *Bertholf v. O'Reilly*, 74 N.Y. 509, 511 (1878), the New York Court of Appeals recognized that the due process "right to liberty [includes] the right to exercise his faculties and to follow a lawful avocation for the support of life; the right to property [includes] the right to acquire possession and enjoy it in any way consistent with the equal rights of others."

[7]   *See, e.g.*, In re Jacobs, 98 N.Y. 98 (1885) (a leading case).

[8]   165 U.S. 578 (1897).

[9]   169 U.S. 366 (1898).

to eight-hour days. Over the dissent of Justices David Brewer and Rufus Peckham, the Court upheld the regulation as a valid health and safety measure for those working in such hazardous jobs. Between 1898 and 1905, the U.S. Supreme Court upheld a series of state laws limiting freedom of contract, sometimes relying upon an idea suggested in *Holden*—that placing an employer and employee on a more equal footing was itself a sufficient state interest to justify labor regulation.[10]

But *Lochner v. New York*[11] cast a new light on this doctrine and became the symbol of the entire period of judicial protection of economic rights. Lochner was convicted and fined $50 for making an employee in his bakery work more than sixty hours a week, a misdemeanor violation of state law. The statute also prohibited making employees work for more than ten hours a day. Lochner appealed, arguing that the law unconstitutionally burdened his freedom to contract with his employees. In his opinion for the Court, Justice Peckham began with the premise that the "general right to make a contract in relation to his business is part of the liberty of the individual protected by the 14th Amendment."[12] Justice Peckham conceded that this liberty is limited by the state's "police power"— that is, its power to protect the safety, health, morals, and general welfare of the public.[13] The question, then was whether the law was "a fair, reasonable, and appropriate exercise of the police power of the state, or . . . an unreasonable, unnecessary, and arbitrary interference with the right of the individual to his personal liberty, or to enter into those contracts in relation to labor which may seem to him appropriate or necessary for the support of himself and his family."[14] To pass scrutiny, the Court said, the law must have more than a remote bearing on public welfare: it must "have a more direct relation, as a means to an end, and the end itself must be appropriate and legitimate."[15]

The majority concluded that the law fell on the "unreasonable" side of the line because it served no legitimate police power purpose. First, the Court thought there was no basis for paternalistic intervention on behalf of the bakers. As the Court put it, there was no indication that bakers are "not equal in intelligence and capacity to men in other trades or manual occupations, or that they are not able to assert their rights and care for themselves without the protecting arm of the state, interfering with their independence of

---

[10]   *See, e.g.*, Knoxville Iron Co. v. Harbison, 183 U.S. 13 (1901).

[11]   198 U.S. 45 (1905).

[12]   *Id.* at 53.

[13]   *Id.*

[14]   *Id.* at 56.

[15]   *Id.* at 57.

judgment and of action."[16] Absent such a disability, the Court insisted, the state had no entitlement to interfere based on perceived unfairness of the bargaining process. Second, the Court said, "[t]o the common understanding the trade of a baker has never been regarded as an unhealthy one," and statistics did not show it to be an extraordinarily dangerous or unhealthy occupation.[17] In short, wrote Justice Peckham, "[t]he act is not, within any fair meaning of the term, a health law, but is an illegal interference with the rights of individuals, both employers and employees, to make contracts regarding labor upon such terms as they may think best, or which they may agree upon with the other parties to such contracts."[18]

Today, the majority opinion is given far less credence than the dissent of Justice Oliver Wendell Holmes, Jr. He accused the majority of reading its own vision of the economy into the Constitution. But, he said, "a Constitution is not intended to embody a particular economic theory, whether of paternalism and the organic relation of the citizen to the state or of laissez faire."[19] In his view, such a statute should not be struck down unless it is beyond the bounds of reason. Or, as he put it, "the word 'liberty,' in the 14th Amendment, is perverted" when used to overturn democratically enacted legislation, "unless it can be said that a rational and fair man necessarily would admit that the statute proposed would infringe fundamental principles as they have been understood by the traditions of our people and our law."[20] There was also a much lengthier dissent by the first Justice John Marshall Harlan, joined by two other Justices, arguing that the New York law was amply justified as a health measure.

The *Lochner*-era Court was never really able to escape from Justice Holmes's charge that it was privileging the free market and implementing its preferred economic policy, which was to secure a relatively unregulated economic sphere. Rightly or wrongly, this is how the *Lochner* era is commonly regarded today, although there are libertarian dissenters in the legal academy.[21] *Lochner* would remain good law for three decades. It collapsed when the Court's vision of economic liberty was decisively repudiated by the public.

---

[16]   *Id.* at 57.

[17]   *Id.* at 59.

[18]   *Id.* at 61.

[19]   *Id.* at 75.

[20]   *Id.* at 76.

[21]   *See generally, e.g.*, RANDY E. BARNETT, RESTORING THE LOST CONSTITUTION: THE PRESUMPTION OF LIBERTY (rev. ed. 2014); DAVID E. BERNSTEIN, REHABILITATING LOCHNER: DEFENDING INDIVIDUAL RIGHTS AGAINST PROGRESSIVE REFORM (2011).

II. Rational Basis Review and *Carolene Products*

A. The Death of Substantive Due Process

Lochner signaled judicial hostility (at both the state and federal level) to legislation enacted at the behest of labor unions. Most prominently, *Lochner* was the basis for subsequent judicial invalidation of state laws prohibiting "yellow dog contracts," whereby the employer would require a promise by employees that they would not join a union.[22] On the other hand, in *Muller v. Oregon*,[23] the Supreme Court refused to apply *Lochner* to strike down a law regulating the hours women could work, and in *Bunting v. Oregon*,[24] it upheld a state law generally restricting factory and mill workers to ten hour work days because it was presented with evidence of health problems. Any implication that *Bunting* overruled the *Lochner* approach was dispelled, however, in *Adkins v. Children's Hospital of the District of Columbia*,[25] which struck down a minimum wage law for female employees.

Lochner, as well as other cases that limited the authority of Congress and state legislatures, caused a constitutional crisis in the 1930s, when the Great Depression led to tremendous political pressure for more national and state economic regulation.[26] As we saw in Chapter 5, FDR's Court-packing plan may have had something to do with the "switch in time that saved nine." In any event, changes in the composition of the Court, coupled with the crushing economic realities of the time, led a majority of the Justices to abandon *Lochner*.

Nebbia v. New York,[27] a 5 to 4 decision that upheld a law regulating milk prices, was the first signal of a retreat from economic substantive due process.[28] Later cases decisively repudiated *Lochner*'s assumption that liberty is defined by freedom to operate at will within the limits of traditional contract and property law. In reaction to what it saw as the abuses of the *Lochner* era, the Court went far in the direction of deference to potentially protectionist economic regulation.

---

[22]   *See* Coppage v. Kansas, 236 U.S. 1 (1915); People v. Marcus, 185 N.Y. 257 (1906); *see also* Adair v. United States, 208 U.S. 161 (1908) (invalidating a federal law as beyond Congress's commerce power).

[23]   208 U.S. 412 (1908).

[24]   243 U.S. 426 (1917).

[25]   261 U.S. 525 (1923).

[26]   *See, e.g.*, Home Building & Loan Ass'n v. Blaisdell, 290 U.S. 398 (1934) (upholding a temporary moratorium on mortgage foreclosures).

[27]   291 U.S. 502 (1934).

[28]   *See generally* Daniel A. Farber, *Who Killed* Lochner?, 90 GEO. L.J. 985 (2002).

In *West Coast Hotel v. Parrish*,[29] the Court upheld a state law establishing a minimum wage for women, overruling *Adkins*. The majority opinion of Chief Justice Charles Evans Hughes in *West Coast Hotel* stated that "[t]he Constitution does not speak of freedom of contract. It speaks of liberty and prohibits the deprivation of liberty without due process of law. [Regulation] which is reasonable in relation to its subject and is adopted in the interests of the community is due process."[30] The opinion stressed that the legislature "was clearly entitled to consider the situation of women in employment, the fact that they are in the class receiving the least pay, that their bargaining power is relatively weak, and that they are the ready victims of those who would take advantage of their necessitous circumstances."[31] The Court noted that "[t]he adoption of similar requirements by many States evidences a deep-seated conviction both as to the presence of the evil and as to the means adopted to check it."[32] The Court continued, echoing Justice Holmes's *Lochner* dissent: "Legislative response to that conviction cannot be regarded as arbitrary or capricious, and that is all we have to decide. Even if the wisdom of the policy be regarded as debatable and its effects uncertain, still the legislature is entitled to its judgment."[33]

The *West Coast Hotel* Court also rejected *Lochner*'s assumption that contracts are freely made: "There is an additional and compelling consideration which recent economic experience has brought into a strong light. The exploitation of a class of workers who are in an unequal bargaining position with respect to bargaining power and are thus relatively defenseless against the denial of a living wage is not only detrimental to their health and well being but casts a direct burden for their support upon the community."[34] Where the *Lochner* Court saw free choices by workers and companies, the Court now credited the perspective of legislatures, which saw bargaining inequality and coercion.

When the Court abandoned any meaningful review of federal economic legislation under the commerce power in the post-World War II period (see Chapter 5), it also rejected meaningful review of economic regulation under the Due Process Clause. The Court's deference to legislators in this domain is illustrated by *Williamson v. Lee Optical*.[35] Although opticians (who are not medical doctors) are capable of measuring a lens and determining its prescription, an

---

29   300 U.S. 379 (1937).

30   *Id.* at 391.

31   *Id.* at 398.

32   *Id.* at 399.

33   *Id.*

34   *Id.*

35   348 U.S. 483 (1955).

Oklahoma statute prohibited them from duplicating or replacing lenses without a written prescription from an ophthalmologist or optometrist (who are doctors). A cynic (or, simply, a realist) might have thought that this was just an effort to secure extra business for two politically influential groups of professionals. Indeed, the Court conceded that the statute was perhaps "a needless, wasteful requirement in many cases" and that the law was "not in every respect logically consistent with its aims."[36] Nevertheless, the Court upheld the statute because it was up to the legislature to balance the costs and benefits of the legislation. The Court reasoned that the legislature *might* have concluded that forcing people to have their eyes checked when their glasses needed to be replaced was a way to improve eye care, and this *conceivable*, even if not actual, state interest was enough for the Court.

The scope of review in *Williamson* was minimal: "It is enough that there is an evil at hand for correction, and that it might be thought that the particular legislative measure was a rational way to correct it."[37] The Court continued that "[t]he day is gone when this Court uses the Due Process Clause . . . to strike down state laws, regulatory of business and industrial conditions, because they may be unwise, improvident, or out of harmony with a particular school of thought. . . . 'For protection against abuses by legislatures the people must resort to the polls, not to the courts.' "[38]

Under *Williamson*, the substantive due process test is whether it would be completely irrational for the legislature to think that an economic regulation advanced *some* permissible goal. This is a light burden to carry. It is not easy to imagine a law without some conceivable justification that an ingenious lawyer might concoct in the course of litigation.

B.   Equal Protection and Economic Regulation

Lawyers challenging a law might have more than one arrow in their quiver. Blocked by the Court's doctrine from using the Due Process Clause, lawyers might seek to raise similar issues under the Equal Protection Clause. We will be spending considerable time on both clauses in this and subsequent chapters, so it is important at the outset to understand how they are related but distinct.

To see the distinction between these two clauses, consider two possible arguments in the *Lochner* case. One argument is that the New York law violated the liberty of bakers and bakery owners, a due process argument. Another argument is that the law discriminated

---

[36]   *Id.* at 487.

[37]   *Id.* at 488.

[38]   *Id.* (citation omitted).

against them by treating them differently from other employees and employers, an equal protection argument.

Resort to the Equal Protection Clause proved unavailing for challengers of economic regulations because the Court also applied—and still applies—the rational basis test to assess equal protection challenges to such economic regulations. The classic case was *Railway Express Agency v. New York*,[39] which prohibited ads on the sides of vehicles unless they advertised the business of the vehicle owner.[40] The Court upheld the law against an equal protection challenge, speculating that the legislature might have thought that such ads were less likely to distract drivers, although no evidence was presented in support of this unlikely assertion. But for the Court to uphold a law under the *Railway Express* test, it seems necessary for the Justices to imagine only a hypothetical rationale.

A more recent example is *Federal Communications Commission v. Beach Communications, Inc.*[41] In this case, the Court upheld a federal statute requiring cable television systems to be franchised by local governmental authorities, but exempting systems serving only buildings owned by the same company. Briefly, a franchise is an agreement by the city authorizing the cable system and approving its contract terms with customers. Franchising is intended to ensure high quality service and reasonable prices. Once a system is installed, the company normally enjoys a monopoly because it makes no financial sense to install a second set of cables; franchising prevents the monopolist from charging customers excessive prices. As construed by the FCC, the franchise requirement applied not just to traditional cable systems but also to retransmission to other units in a building or building complex of signals received by a satellite.

Under the exemption, whether a system that linked multiple buildings had to obtain a franchise depended upon whether the buildings were separately or commonly owned or managed. There is no obvious reason for making this distinction given the purpose of the franchise requirement, but the Court upheld the statute based on two conceivable justifications: (1) the system was more likely to be small in the common-ownership setting, making a franchise application more burdensome, and (2) consumers could more easily negotiate with the single property owner or manager, making city approval less necessary.

---

[39]   336 U.S. 106 (1949).

[40]   Today, such a law would be subject to challenge as an infringement of free speech, but at the time the Court did not consider advertising to be protected by the First Amendment.

[41]   508 U.S. 307 (1993).

It is worth quoting the Court's language in *Beach Communications* reaffirming the severe limits of rational basis review:

> On rational-basis review, . . . those attacking the rationality of the legislative classification have the burden "to negative every conceivable basis which might support it." Moreover, because we never require a legislature to articulate its reasons for enacting a statute, it is entirely irrelevant for constitutional purposes whether the conceived reason for the challenged distinction actually motivated the legislature.[42]

Furthermore, the Court said, legislation requires drawing lines, so courts must tolerate the inevitable arbitrariness of a decision to draw the line in one place or a slightly different place.[43] To illustrate the Court's point, it makes sense to have 70 mph rather than 10 mph or 120 mph serve as a highway speed limit; but the choice among 68, 70, and 72 mph is necessarily arbitrary.

C.   Understanding the Retreat from *Lochner*

The abandonment of *Lochner* reflected a broader shift in the way Americans felt about unregulated markets. In an earlier age, it may have made some sense for people to think of market outcomes as reflecting merely a series of independent decisions by different firms and people, reflecting their individual resources and priorities. But in the Great Depression, millions of workers lost their jobs because of general economic conditions, not individualized decisions, and farmers found themselves going bankrupt at the same time that they had plenty of production. The conclusion many drew was that economic outcomes reflected impersonal economic forces as much as they did individual decisions. Thus, it became harder to maintain the idea that unregulated markets were the benchmark for free choice.

The Court's virtual abandonment of judicial review of economic regulation also fits nicely with the *Carolene Products* approach discussed in Chapter 3. This should be no surprise, since the famous footnote 4 of *Carolene Products* accompanied a sentence setting out the rational basis test.[44] Footnote 4 was intended precisely to explain

---

[42]   *Id.* at 315 (quoting Lehnhausen v. Lake Shore Auto Parts Co., 410 U.S. 356, 364 (1973)).

[43]   *Beach Communications*, 508 U.S. at 315–16.

[44]   The sentence reads:

[T]he existence of facts supporting the legislative judgment is to be presumed, for regulatory legislation affecting ordinary commercial transactions is not to be pronounced unconstitutional unless in the light of the facts made known or generally assumed it is of such a character as to preclude the assumption that it rests upon some rational basis within the knowledge and experience of the legislators.

why more stringent judicial review was valid in contexts other than economic regulation. *Carolene Products* involved a federal statute banning the interstate transportation of filled milk, which was skimmed milk to which coconut oil was added to make it creamier. Although this law may well have been designed simply to protect the dairy industry from non-dairy substitutes, the Court upheld it on the theory that natural dairy fats might be healthier.

Footnote 4 was well-geared to justify reduced judicial review for economic regulation compared to other types of legislation. There is no clause of the Constitution singling out business activities for special protection. Moreover, businesses often find ready audiences in the legislature, and they are by no means a "discrete and insular minority." So *Carolene Products* suggests little reason for judicial intervention. In addition, there is a fine line between determining the reasonableness of economic regulation and simply deciding whether the legislation is wise, so the Court is at risk of functioning as a kind of super-legislature.

Of course, there are counterarguments. For instance, one could argue that economic legislation often benefits small, wealthy, and politically connected special interests and harms broad, diffuse groups of consumers or workers, who will have a hard time organizing themselves to be heard. Thus, the democratic process is no panacea. In addition, at least in some contexts, it is clear that economic liberty has great importance to individuals, as in the case of licensing requirements that may entirely prevent a person from pursuing a chosen occupation. In addition, there are undoubtedly some well-intended but ill-considered regulations whose costs exceed their benefits. Thus, it could be argued, judicious intervention by courts would be beneficial—and preferable to effectively complete judicial abstention.

So far, however, the Court has shown no indication of rethinking its repudiation of meaningful review of economic regulation under the Due Process or Equal Protection Clauses. This may seem a little puzzling, given the emphasis by many conservatives on deregulation as a goal and the dominance of conservatives on the Court. It also strays from the Court's path under the Commerce Clause, since the Court has made at least mild efforts to rein in the commerce power. One might have expected that an increasingly conservative Court would make a similar move with respect to economic due process and equal protection.

We suggest three reasons that may have inhibited the Court from instituting more robust review of economic regulation under the

---

United States v. Carolene Products Co., 304 U.S. 144, 152 (1938).

Due Process and Equal Protection Clauses. First, the regulatory state has now become embedded in the economy in ways that would be difficult to dislodge, inasmuch as regulations have shaped business investments and operations for decades. Americans now take it for granted that the government can regulate wages and hours, discriminatory hiring, sexual harassment in the workplace, and workplace safety. The entrenched nature of many regulations may provide extra support for the normal tendency of judges to follow precedent. By now, it has been more than seventy years since *Nebbia*. Overturning such a large body of precedent would be professionally troubling for judges under any circumstances, but particularly so when legislation reflects and reinforces such widespread societal practices.

Second, the idea that the Due Process Clause limits the substance of regulation—"substantive due process"—was the basis for Supreme Court decisions protecting abortion and same-sex marriage. We will discuss this topic in Chapter 12, but suffice it to say for present purposes that their arguments have committed many conservative thinkers to rejecting any general power of the Court to review the reasonableness of legislation. Reinstituting serious review of economic regulation under the Due Process Clause would undercut conservative arguments against the abortion and gay rights rulings. (This is not a complete explanation, however, because liberals have rejected economic substantive due process while embracing the Court's modern substantive due process jurisprudence.)

Third, judicial conservatives have arguably used other clauses and doctrines to protect economic liberty, and so may feel less need to directly revive freedom of contract. Although the Court's free speech decisions are beyond the scope of this book, we note that progressive critics of the Court have called parts of its First Amendment jurisprudence the new *Lochner*.[45] In recent decisions, the Court has invoked the Free Speech Clause both to insulate businesses from what had long been thought of as ordinary economic regulations,[46] and to financially hobble public employee unions.[47]

Whatever the reasons, the Court has not chosen to resuscitate due process or equal protection limits on economic regulation. But the Court has limited certain regulations by giving some force to another clause of the Constitution. Thus, at least in a subcategory of cases, the Court has found a way to limit regulation to some extent

---

[45]   *See, e.g.*, Jedediah Purdy, *The Constitution v. Democracy*, HUFFINGTON POST (Dec. 19, 2011), https://www.huffingtonpost.com/jedediah-purdy/the-constitution-v-democr_b_1157628.html.

[46]   *See, e.g.*, Sorrell v. IMS Health Inc., 564 U.S. 552 (2011).

[47]   *See* Janus v. American Fed. of State, Cty., & Municipal Employees, Council 31, 138 S. Ct. 2448 (2018).

without resurrecting substantive due process. In addition to the Free Speech Clause, the Court has relied upon the Takings Clause. We turn to the Court's takings jurisprudence in the next section.

III. The Takings Clause

The Takings Clause of the Fifth Amendment provides: "nor shall private property be taken for public use, without just compensation." This clause applies most obviously to exercises of eminent domain, which occurs when the government takes land to use for building a highway, a military base, or some other facility. But as explained in the next section, the Court has also said for nearly a century that some regulations may be takings even though the owner retains title to the property and the government does not conduct any activities using the property. This "regulatory takings" doctrine thus provides a setting for active judicial review of certain economic regulations, even though the Due Process and Equal Protection Clauses are no longer available. The scope of regulatory takings is limited: it does not apply to employment law, pollution laws, health regulations, or other regulations that do not directly target property rights. One might analogize the regulatory takings doctrine, which provides an island of judicial protection against economic regulation, to the anti-commandeering doctrine, which provides an island of protection against the commerce power.

A.   Foundations of Regulatory Takings Doctrine

Regulatory taking law began with *Pennsylvania Coal Co. v. Mahon*,[48] which rewrote the law of eminent domain. Until *Pennsylvania Coal*, the Court had not treated governmental restrictions on the use of property as takings of property. Justice Holmes's opinion in *Pennsylvania Coal* was a milestone, but it did little to clarify the standards for such regulatory taking claims.

The holding seems clear enough at first sight. The suit had been brought by homeowners whose land was subsiding due to the collapse of a coalmine beneath it. They relied on a Pennsylvania statute required mining companies to provide support under populated areas in the form of pillars of coal or support beams. Justice Holmes held the law to be an unconstitutional taking of the coalmine's property. Justice Holmes announced a "general rule that, while property may be regulated to a certain extent, if regulation goes too far it will be recognized as a taking."[49] There are few cases in which the Court has made so large a change in doctrine with so little explanation.

---

[48]   260 U.S. 393 (1922).

[49]   *Id.* at 415.

Justice Holmes's opinion is enigmatic in key respects, including how much he was actually relying on the Takings Clause, as opposed to the Contracts Clause or some more general due process claim.[50] His analysis was ambiguous about exactly what "property" was allegedly taken. He wrote that in terms of the rights of the mining company in the case, the "extent of the taking is great" and "we should think it clear that the statute does not disclose a public interest sufficient to warrant so extensive a destruction of the [mining company's] constitutionally protected rights."[51] But the opinion did not specify exactly what right was being destroyed, or how to tell when a regulation "goes too far."

It was not until 1970s, in *Penn Central Transportation Co. v. City of New York*,[52] that the Court made an effort to create a single unified test. New York City designated a railroad station as a historic landmark and rejected both of the railroad's proposals to expand on the site, largely by building above the terminal.[53] When the city rejected the company's proposals, the company claimed the city had taken its property, with particular reference to the airspace above the building, which the railroad had planned to use.[54]

Justice William Brennan's opinion for the Court sought to synthesize the Court's regulatory takings decisions, which he characterized as engaging in "essentially ad hoc, factual inquiries."[55] He first observed that takings were more likely to be found if a regulation amounted to acquisitions of resources rather than merely prohibiting certain uses of land.[56] In cases outside this category, no taking would be found unless the government unduly impaired "interests that were sufficiently bound up with the reasonable expectations of the claimant" or had an insufficient connection to public safety or welfare.[57]

Inability to use the air space above the building would seemingly deprive it of any economic value, whereas it might have been quite valuable if construction were allowed. The Court, however, rejected the company's argument that the airspace was a distinct property interest that could be "taken" regardless of the rest of the property.[58]

---

[50]   *See id.* at 413.

[51]   *Id.* at 414.

[52]   438 U.S. 104 (1976). It may be an unfortunate twist of history that the *Penn Central* case was not actually about Penn Central Station, to the confusion of generations of students.

[53]   *See id.* at 107.

[54]   *See id.* at 118–19.

[55]   *Id.* at 124.

[56]   *See id.* at 128.

[57]   *Id.* at 124–25.

[58]   *Id.* at 130.

The Court held that " 'taking jurisprudence' does not divide a single parcel into discrete segments and attempt to determine whether rights in a particular segment have been entirely abrogated."[59]

Since *Penn Central*, the Supreme Court has employed a three-part approach in regulatory taking cases, depending on the nature of the regulation.[60] First, the Court finds a taking when the government mandates a physical intrusion on private property. The second category builds on *Penn Central*'s description of cases involving so-called "total takings,"[61] in which the government has eliminated all economically beneficial use of the property.[62] The third category covers all remaining cases. This default category is governed by the "*Penn Central* test," which examines whether the government regulation unduly interferes with reasonable, investment-backed expectations.

It is relatively rare for the government to lose a case when the *Penn Central* "reasonable expectations" test is applied. Thus, lawyers for property owners have invested a great deal of effort to fit cases into the two exceptional categories laid out by *Penn Central*: physical intrusions and complete destruction of property value. We discuss a few of the most important cases below.

B.   Physical Takings

One of the categories singled out by *Penn Central* involves regulations that result in a physical intrusion on the property.[63] In *Loretto v. Teleprompter Manhattan CATV Corporation*,[64] New York City had passed an ordinance requiring landlords to allow tenants to purchase cable TV and to allow the cable companies to install cable boxes in unused rooftop space. The Court held that a permanent physical intrusion, however small, is a taking. In the Court's view, by mandating such a permanent intrusion "the government does not

---

[59]   *Id.*

[60]   Eminent domain extends back through the Founding Era, and its roots in legal theory are even older, but regulatory takings doctrine is a relatively modern development. *See* Joseph L. Sax, *Takings and the Police Power*, 74 YALE L.J. 36, 38–60 (1964). One constant since Professor Sax wrote fifty years ago is that "the predominant characteristic of this area of law is a welter of confusing and apparently incompatible results." *Id.* at 37.

[61]   *Penn Central*, 438 U.S. at 127–28.

[62]   The Court has recognized an important exception, allowing an activity to be completely banned when it constitutes a common-law nuisance, which is a remedy for harm caused by someone's unreasonable use of his or her land. For discussion of this exception, see generally Richard Lazarus, *Putting the Correct "Spin" on Lucas*, 45 STAN. L. REV. 1411 (1993).

[63]   The "physical invasion versus use" distinction has received some justified criticism from various directions. *See, e.g.*, Steven J Eagle, *The Four-Factor* Penn Central *Test*, 118 PENN. ST. L. REV. 602, 627 (2014).

[64]   458 U.S. 419 (1982).

simply take a single 'strand' from the 'bundle' of property rights: it chops through the bundle, taking a slice of every strand."[65] The Court hastened to add that, so long as a regulation does not involve the permanent occupation of property by a third-party, "our holding today in no way alters the analysis governing the State's power to require landlords to comply with building codes and provide utility connections, mailboxes, smoke detectors, fire extinguishers, and the like in the common area of a building."[66]

In a series of decisions, the Court has extended the physical intrusion doctrine to cases in which the owner agrees to the intrusion in return for permission to develop the property.[67] In such cases, as a condition of approving a development permit, the government demands that the landowner make a concession such as providing free public access or requiring a transfer of property or money to the government. Because these concessions are a condition of obtaining a permit that the owner voluntarily sought, these "exactions" are not per se takings. The Court has, however, required such exactions to have a clear justification as a means to address problems created by the development project.

Thus, project conditions involving access requirements are subjected to heightened scrutiny, beyond the rational basis level applied to other government regulations. This requirement seems to be an application of the unconstitutional conditions doctrine mentioned in Chapter 6: since the government could not directly mandate the access (a physical intrusion), it can make access a condition only when doing so is germane to the overall development project. Even so, the unconstitutional conditions doctrine seems to be applied in this context with unusual vigor, for reasons that the Court has never fully explained.

The physical intrusion doctrine thus has real bite in the context of land-use and landlord-tenant regulations, although even there it is subject to limits. Outside of these domains, it has not had great effect.

C. Total Takings

The other category singled out under *Penn Central* involves what might be called property wipeouts, in which the property loses all value as a result of a regulation. In *Lucas v. South Carolina Coastal Commission*,[68] the Court held that such regulations were per

---

[65]   *Id.* at 435.

[66]   *Id.* at 440.

[67]   *See* Koontz v. St. Johns River Water Management Dist., 570 U.S. 595 (2013); Dolan v. City of Tigard, 512 U.S. 374 (1994); Nollan v. Cal. Coastal Comm'n, 483 U.S. 825 (1987).

[68]   505 U.S. 1003 (1992).

se takings, subject to only a narrow exception. A developer had purchased two residential lots on an island in 1986. Two years later, the state passed a beachfront management act, which prohibited new construction on the lots because they were in a high erosion zone.[69] The Court held that "when the owner of real property has been called upon to sacrifice *all* economically beneficial uses in the name of the common good, that is, to leave his property economically idle, he has suffered a taking."[70] Thus, while an owner deprived of 95 percent of the property's use might sometimes recover nothing, the owner deprived of 100 percent would recover completely, due to the bright-line nature of the rule.[71]

The Court's announcement of the total taking rule did not, however, dispose of the case given that earlier cases had upheld the power of the government to severely regulate property to protect the public.[72] The Court held that regulations eliminating all economic uses can be upheld only if they merely duplicate the result that the common law would have reached through its prohibitions on unreasonably harmful land uses.[73] Justice Antonin Scalia gave as examples the denial of a permit to engage in landfilling that would flood the lands of neighbors, and an order to remove a nuclear plant that is discovered to sit on an earthquake fault.[74] In a concurrence, Justice Anthony Kennedy argued that Justice Scalia was wrong to limit the permissible justifications to common law doctrines rather than also allowing consideration of how statutes might shape reasonable expectations.[75] Notably, the Scalia approach mirrors the special status that *Lochner* gave to the common law rights of property and contract.

Property owners often try to take advantage of the *Lucas* rule by arguing that a regulation eliminates a specific, recognized legal interest in the property, even though the owner continues to have other ownership interests. Since *Lucas*, the Supreme Court has been generally unreceptive to this argument, as it was in *Penn Central* when it declined to treat air rights as a separate property interest. Most recently, in *Murr v. Wisconsin*,[76] the Court held that an owner who owned two adjoining lots near a scenic river had to treat them as a single unit for purposes of determining the amount of diminution of value. What might have been a total taking of one of the lots due

---

69   *See id.* at 1008 & n.1.

70   *Id.* at 1019.

71   *See id.* at 1019–20 n.8.

72   *See id.* at 1022.

73   *See id.* at 1029.

74   *Id.*

75   *See id.* at 1035 (Kennedy, J., concurring in judgment).

76   137 S. Ct. 1933 (2017).

to development restrictions was relatively minor when the two lots were considered together.

Justice Kennedy wrote the majority opinion in *Murr*. With his departure, there may well be changes in takings law. But perusal of the dissents in *Murr* does not suggest that we are in store for a major doctrinal expansion. Chief Justice John Roberts wrote the primary dissent, which was joined by Justices Clarence Thomas and Samuel Alito.[77] Notably, while the Chief Justice disagreed with the majority's view that the two lots should be considered together, he did not dispute the majority's conclusion that no taking had occurred, and he otherwise seemed content with the current state of takings law and with the *Penn Central* test in particular.

Justice Thomas joined the Roberts dissent but also wrote separately. He noted what seems to be common ground—that prior to *Pennsylvania Coal*, "it was generally thought that the Takings Clause reached only a 'direct appropriation' of property . . . or the functional equivalent of a 'practical ouster of [the owner's] possession.' "[78] This is a direct quote from Justice Scalia's opinion in *Lucas*.[79] Justice Thomas then suggested, as he not infrequently does in constitutional cases, that "it would be desirable for us to take a fresh look at our regulatory takings jurisprudence, to see whether it can be grounded in the original public meaning of the Takings Clause of the Fifth Amendment or the Privileges or Immunities Clause of the Fourteenth Amendment."[80]

Recall that this chapter began with a discussion of the early history of the Contracts Clause. It is worth noting that this clause is now subject to something very much like the *Penn Central* test for takings. In *Sveen v. Mellon*,[81] the Court rejected a claim that the Contracts Clause was violated by retroactive application of a law that terminated the designation of a spouse as an insurance beneficiary when the couple got divorced. The idea behind the law was that

---

[77]   *See id.* at 1950 (Roberts, C.J., dissenting). The newly appointed Justice Neil Gorsuch did not participate.

[78]   *Id.* at 1957 (Thomas, J, dissenting). The consensus among historians seems to be that the Framers understood the Takings Clause to apply only to government expropriation, which is the seizure of property for use in a government project such as a new road or building. *See* John H. Hart, *Land Use Law in the Early Republic and the Original Meaning of the Takings Clause: Setting the Record Straight*, 1996 UTAH L. REV. 1099 (2000); William Michael Treanor, *The Original Understanding of the Takings Clause and the Political Process*, 95 COLUM, L. REV. 782 (1995). Police power regulations were not equivalent to takings of property for public use. *Id.* at 662.

[79]   *See Lucas*, 505 U.S. at 1014.

[80]   *Id.* Justice Thomas cited an article whose title conveys its thesis: Michael Rappaport, *Originalism and Regulatory Takings: Why the Fifth Amendment May Not Protect Against Regulatory Takings, But the Fourteenth Amendment May*, 15 SAN DIEGO L. REV. 729 (2008).

[81]   138 S. Ct. 1815 (2018).

policyholders might well no longer find their ex-spouses appealing beneficiaries but might not get around to making the change.

Eight Justices voted to uphold the law and endorsed a two-part test for Contracts Clause cases. The first step is to determine whether the state law substantially impairs a contractual relationship, taking into account "the extent to which the law undermines the contractual bargain, interferes with a party's reasonable expectations, and prevents the party from safeguarding or reinstating his rights."[82] At the second step, the Court asks "whether the state law is drawn in an 'appropriate' and 'reasonable' way to advance 'a significant and legitimate public purpose.' "[83] The Court found no substantial interference, since many or most policyholders would agree with the change, and those who disagreed were free to change their beneficiaries back to the ex-spouse. Only Justice Neil Gorsuch dissented, arguing that the Court's current approach should be open to reconsideration.[84] But he was unable to attract the vote of any other Justice.

Thus, as with the Takings Clause, cases under the Contracts Clause trigger something more than rational basis review. But the Court does not seem inclined to apply stringent review under either clause, except for regulations physically displacing the owner or wiping out property value. As the next section shows, the Court is more interventionist when the issue is what procedures the government must use when imposing economic regulation, rather than when the issue is its ability to regulate.

IV. Procedural Due Process

The Due Process Clauses of the Fifth and Fourteenth Amendments, whether or not they do anything else, provide for some kind of process before the government deprives a person of life, liberty, or property. These clauses clearly have *some* content. Accordingly, even if due process is given a purely procedural definition, it can still be an important source of protection against governmental abuse.

Suppose, for example, that a state university establishes a rule that the Dean can expel any student she believes guilty of cheating. The law would clearly survive rational basis review. Nevertheless, it is troubling that the application of this criterion seems to be left to the unchecked discretion of the Dean, with no guarantee that accused students will have a right to be heard. In such a situation, the absence of a hearing process before a neutral decisionmaker may

---

82   *Id.* at 1821–22.

83   *Id.* at 1822 (citation omitted).

84   *See id.* at 1826, 1828 (Gorsuch, J., dissenting).

violate procedural due process, even though no substantive constitutional right is involved.

Fair procedures have independent value, regardless of the fairness or reasonableness of the underlying legal requirements. In *Marshall v. Jerrico, Inc.*,[85] the Supreme Court explained some of the significant values at stake. It pointed to "two central concerns of procedural due process, the prevention of unjustified or mistaken deprivations and the promotion of participation and dialogue by affected individuals."[86] Requiring an impartial decisionmaker "helps to guarantee that life, liberty, or property will not be taken on the basis of an erroneous or distorted conception of the facts or the law. At the same time, it preserves both the appearance and reality of fairness."[87]

Consider the "two central concerns of procedural due process" identified in *Jerrico*. The first is utilitarian: government proceedings affecting individuals should be designed for accuracy. The second is non-consequentialist and is often called the "dignitary" or "intrinsic" value to due process—the idea that respect for individuals demands that they have the opportunity to be heard by a neutral decisionmaker under fair procedures. In other words, one concern relates to the actuality of justice, and the other involves the society's sense of justice.

The importance of procedural due process is illustrated by *Hamdi v. Rumsfeld*, a case also discussed in Chapter 7.[88] The Court held that the federal government could indefinitely detain a person, even a citizen, who was an enemy combatant, either as a participant in the terrorist organization Al Qaeda or a soldier in the Afghan Taliban. But the Court rejected the government's argument that no hearing before a neutral decisionmaker was necessary to test the factual accuracy of the government's determination that the individual in question was an enemy combatant. The Court held that this deprivation of physical liberty required due process, and that due process required the government to provide a hearing at least before a properly constituted military tribunal, if not a federal court.

Note, however, that no one was entitled to a hearing before Congress regarding whether to pass the law that the Court interpreted as allowing the detention. The Supreme Court has held that due process does not require a legislature or other lawmaking body to provide any special procedural protections. The idea is that

---

[85]   446 U.S. 238 (1980).

[86]   *Id.* at 240.

[87]   *Id.*

[88]   542 U.S. 507 (2004).

the lawmaking process provides all of the process that is due,[89] because individualized hearings are impractical in this setting. Courts rely on the democratic process, rather than hearings, to provide citizens a voice in lawmaking and to ensure the legitimacy of the statute or rule. Courts further rely on the availability of due process objections after a statute or rule is enacted by those adversely affected by the rule who contend that it does not apply to them.

The Due Process Clause does not define the terms "liberty" or "property," nor does it say what process is "due" in individual cases. For instance, it is unclear from the language of the clause whether the student who is expelled from a state college for cheating is entitled to a hearing. The "right" to attend school is not the kind of property recognized by the common law, but it does seem to be a weighty interest on which students heavily rely. And if the student *is* entitled to a hearing, it is unclear precisely what kind of hearing— for example, whether the student is entitled to be represented by a lawyer.

Prior to the 1960s, the Supreme Court tended to look to the common law for guidance in defining what constituted a "liberty" or "property" interest. If one of these interests was present, the Court ordinarily assumed that the "process" that was "due" included notice and an opportunity to be heard before the deprivation occurred.

The common law considered government benefits (public employment, welfare, and so on) mere privileges rather than rights. Thus, due process was not triggered when a public employee lost her job or a recipient of governmental benefits like welfare or social security was cut off from these funds—or a student was expelled from college. In essence, this approach allowed the government to grant the "privilege" subject to whatever conditions the government chose to impose, including revocation without any accompanying procedural protections. The absence of procedural protections in these circumstances seemed harsh, however, in light of the post-New Deal expansion in the role of government as employer, regulator, and provider of "social security" in the broad sense.

Goldberg v. Kelly[90] marked the end of the distinction between rights and privileges. Welfare recipients challenged the termination of their benefits without a prior evidentiary hearing. The Court ruled that the continued receipt of welfare benefits is a form of property whose deprivation triggers the protections of the Due Process Clause, because the benefits were a matter of statutory entitlement for

---

[89]   *See* Bi-Metallic Investment Co. v. State Board of Equalization, 239 U.S. 441 (1915) (holding that a state agency may increase the valuation of all taxable property in a jurisdiction without providing a hearing).

[90]   397 U.S. 254 (1970).

qualified individuals. As to the process that was due, the Court balanced the potential harm to the recipient against the government's interest in streamlining the process. On this basis, the Court held that welfare recipients were entitled to a trial-type hearing before their benefits were terminated.

Notably, *Goldberg v. Kelly* is based on the perception that new forms of legal entitlements have arisen on which people reasonably rely just as they did on traditional property interests, at least to the extent of deserving procedural protections. An originalist or conservative traditionalist might find this rationale, which is based on social transformation rather than historical usage, at least somewhat suspect, although it now has the support of many decades of judicial precedent.

Before further consideration of current doctrine, we flag an issue that many students find confusing: the interplay between federal and state law in procedural due process cases. When a state program does not involve any substantive constitutional right, the state has a virtually free hand over eligibility standards. Thus, for example, it is up to the state to decide the requirements for continuing in college, subject only to the rational basis test. So we have to look to *state law* to answer the following question: "What factual findings, if any, are necessary to determine continued eligibility for this benefit?"

The character of the inquiry changes, however, when we switch from the question of substantive standards to the question of procedure. To apply the Due Process Clause, we must make two further inquiries. First, is the interest in question, as defined by state law, classified as liberty or property for due process purposes? Second, assuming the answer to this question is yes, what process is due before the state can take away this interest? In answering both questions, *federal law* takes over, since interpreting the Due Process Clause is a question of federal constitutional law.

Building on the discussion of entitlements in *Goldberg v. Kelley*, the Court held in *Board of Regents v. Roth*[91] that an individual must have a "legitimate claim of entitlement" as a predicate for a claim that property has been taken under the Due Process Clause. In other words, there must be some legal limit on the government's discretion, providing a basis for an evidentiary hearing about whether the government has exceeded this limit. *Roth* involved an untenured teacher on a one-year contract whose contract was not renewed, although renewal was customary except in cases of misconduct or incompetence. Because the decision to renew was completely discretionary, the Court reasoned, it did not create any entitlement

---

[91]   408 U.S. 564 (1972).

that qualified as property under the Due Process Clause. Hence, no hearing was required.

Once a deprivation of life, liberty or property is found, a court must determine what process is due. The leading case on this question is *Matthews v. Eldridge*,[92] which calls for a balancing of the burden on the government of providing an additional procedure, the severity of the potential loss for the person in question, and the increased accuracy that the added procedure would provide. Notably, this test does not pay heed to the dignitary interest in fair procedures, only to their utilitarian benefits.

To summarize modern law across all of the domains surveyed in this chapter, the Constitution offers far less protection against intrusive economic regulation today than it did before the New Deal. The Court applies only a rational basis test, unless a regulation has the effect of taking a specific piece of property or substantially impairs an existing contract. Even in these cases, moreover, the government can generally prevail by showing that the regulation at issue is reasonable. But in terms of procedure, the government has less leeway, and courts may second-guess the government's choice of a streamlined process. Given that courts are experts on process but not on policy, this division of labor may make functional sense.

Further Readings

RANDY E. BARNETT, RESTORING THE LOST CONSTITUTION: THE PRESUMPTION OF LIBERTY (rev. ed. 2014).

DAVID E. BERNSTEIN, REHABILITATING LOCHNER: DEFENDING INDIVIDUAL RIGHTS AGAINST PROGRESSIVE REFORM (2011).

BARRY CUSHMAN, RETHINKING THE NEW DEAL COURT: THE STRUCTURE OF A CONSTITUTIONAL REVOLUTION (1998).

RICHARD EPSTEIN, TAKINGS: PRIVATE PROPERTY AND THE POWER OF EMINENT DOMAIN (1985).

Daniel A. Farber, Murr v. Wisconsin *and the Future of Takings Law*, 2017 SUP. CT. REV. 115.

Dalton Mott, *The Due Process Clause and Students: The Road to a Single Approach of Determining Property Interests in Education*, 65 U. KAN. L. REV. 651 (2017).

Gary D. Rowe, Lochner *Revisionism Revisited,* 24 LAW & SOC. INQUIRY 221 (1999).

Cass Sunstein, Lochner*'s Legacy*, 84 COLUM. L. REV. 1689 (1984).

---

[92]   424 U.S. 319 (1976).

Chapter 10

"THE EQUAL PROTECTION OF THE LAWS": RACE AND GENDER

In this chapter, we turn to issues of constitutional equality. In the United States, equality questions have long been debated in both constitutional politics and constitutional law primarily through claims on the Equal Protection Clause of Section 1 of the Fourteenth Amendment. It provides that no state shall "deny to any person within its jurisdiction the equal protection of the laws."[1]

The original Constitution contained several provisions that protected the institution of chattel slavery. The Civil War and the Thirteenth Amendment ended slavery, and conflicts over racial equality were central to the passage of the Fourteenth and Fifteenth Amendments. With few exceptions, it would take almost a century for the Supreme Court to begin using the Equal Protection Clause in earnest to protect the basic equality of African Americans; it acted in the 1950s and 1960s to further racially liberal views of civil rights.

In subsequent decades, an increasingly conservative constitutional politics on matters of race helped produce an increasingly conservative Court. The Court then used equal protection jurisprudence to advance racially conservative views on the subjects of disparate impact and affirmative action—although the issue of the constitutionality of affirmative action in higher education has produced an awkward compromise between racially liberal and racially conservative commitments. With respect to this issue, the views of the moderates on the Court—Justices Lewis Powell, Sandra Day O'Connor, and Anthony Kennedy—won out for decades, but we expect this to change in the years ahead as a result of conservative appointments to the Court.

At the time of the Founding and throughout most of American history, women were regarded as citizens, but they were largely excluded from economic, educational, and political life. According to the ideology of the "separate spheres," men were destined for the public realm of politics and breadwinning, while women were destined for the private realm of family and caregiving. Women worked in abolitionist organizations in the hope that they too would earn the right to vote with the end of slavery and the beginning of voting rights for African American men. But it did not work out this way in either the Reconstruction Congress or the post-Civil War

---

[1] U.S. CONST. amend. XIV, § 1.

Supreme Court. Women would not win a federal constitutional right to vote until ratification of the Nineteenth Amendment in 1920. It would not be until the rise of the women's movement of the late 1960s and 1970s that the Court would begin to take many—although by no means all—claims of gender discrimination seriously. Today, the Court generally polices sex classifications that reflect or reinforce the sex-role stereotypes of the separate spheres tradition, but significant exceptions arguably endure.

We focus here on issues of racial and gender equality because they have been central to debates over whom the Equal Protection Clause protects and how. For example, the modern social movement for gay rights, which has invoked both the Equal Protection Clause and the Due Process Clause, often analogizes the circumstances of sexual orientation minorities to African Americans and women. We delay examination of the constitutional politics and constitutional law of gay rights until Chapter 12 because we think it most advisable to proceed historically on this subject, and doing so requires knowledge of both the Court's equal protection jurisprudence and its modern substantive due process decisions, the latter of which we cover in the initial sections of Chapter 12.

I.   Race and the Constitution

In this initial section, we analyze constitutional questions of racial (in)equality. We proceed historically, beginning with slavery. We note with significant regret, however, that space limitations require us to present much of this important history in highly compressed fashion. In our suggestions for further reading at the end of this chapter, we identify in-depth historical treatments for interested readers.

A.   The Constitutional Law and Politics of Slavery

It may be impossible for Americans living today to fully comprehend the institution of chattel slavery, which was widely practiced in the American colonies before the American Revolution and then, after the separation from England, in Southern states until the end of the Civil War. Notwithstanding the inspiring words of the Declaration of Independence that "all men are created equal," the Constitution in significant ways protected slavery. The economies of the Southern states were built on this institution, so they would not have ratified the Constitution if they had believed that it would have eliminated, or significantly interfered with, slavery.

Some southern state delegates to the Philadelphia Convention of 1787 secured several provisions in the Constitution directly affecting slavery and protecting their interests. For example, the Fugitive Slave Clause protected the property rights of slaveowners by providing that escaped slaves who crossed state lines "shall be delivered up on Claim of the Party to whom such Service or Labor may be due."[2] The Three-Fifths Clause for representation allocated seats in the House of Representatives to the states according to their total population of free persons and three-fifths of their population of slaves.[3] Congress was also disabled from prohibiting "[t]he Migration or Importation of such Persons as any of the States now existing shall think proper to admit"—that is, new slaves—"prior to [1808]."[4] Article V prohibited constitutional amendments altering the importation provision until 1808; this is an extraordinarily rare instance of *entrenchment* in the original Constitution; many modern constitutions entrench much more than does the U.S. Constitution. Southern states also expected to benefit from the Constitution's grant of congressional power "[t]o provide for calling forth the Militia to . . . suppress Insurrections,"[5] including slave revolts. It is also noteworthy that the Constitution did not prohibit slavery anywhere in the country.

For several reasons, however, it would be going too far to assert that the original Constitution was simply pro-slavery. First, the Constitution did not *guarantee* slavery anywhere in the country. If, for example, a state abolished slavery, slaveowners who lived in the state had no federal constitutional basis to object. Second, the Constitution imposed no specific limits on congressional power to regulate slavery except temporarily in Article V. Third, the Constitution gave Congress the "Power to dispose of and make all needful Rules and Regulations respecting the Territory or other Property belonging to the United States."[6] This clause does not expressly mention slavery, but it could be interpreted—and subsequently was interpreted by Congress—to authorize Congress to prohibit slavery in federal territories that would eventually become states.

Slavery eventually became the subject of the most controversial debates about national power and constitutional rights during the first half of the Nineteenth Century. Two issues in particular were explosive. The first was federal power to pass fugitive slave laws, such as the Fugitive Slave Act of 1793, which permitted slaveholders to recover alleged runaways merely by obtaining a certificate from a local magistrate. The second issue was federal power to prohibit slavery in American territories. Regulation of slavery in the territories was perhaps the single most important political and

---

2   U.S. CONST. art. IV, § 2, cl. 3.

3   U.S. CONST. art. I, § 2, cl. 3.

4   U.S. CONST. art. I, § 9, cl. 1.

5   U.S. CONST. art. I, § 8, cl. 15.

6   U.S. CONST. art. IV, § 3, cl. 2.

constitutional question in the United States in the decades before the Civil War. Politically, most people thought that the congressional decision to prohibit or permit slavery in the territories would determine the balance of power in the Senate between free and slave states. This was because free territories became free states and vice versa.[7] These two issues implicated disagreements about both the constitutional scope of congressional power and the rights of slaveholders, slaves, or alleged slaves, primarily under the Fugitive Slave Clause and the Due Process Clause of the Fifth Amendment.

Throughout the first half of the Nineteenth Century, Congress addressed these constitutional questions *not* through a commitment to a certain set of constitutional principles, whether abolitionist or pro-slavery, but through a series of political compromises. For example, the Missouri Compromise of 1820 sought to maintain a permanent balance between slave and free states in the Union by permitting slavery in territories south of the 36°30' line (the southern border of Missouri) and banning slavery in the territories north of that line. This compromise fully vindicated no one's constitutional convictions.

During this period, the U.S. Supreme Court had a pro-slavery majority that was typically protective of the interests of slaveowners. A notorious example is *Prigg v. Pennsylvania*, decided in 1842.[8] As we have seen, the Constitution's Fugitive Slave Clause compelled the return of escaped ("fugitive") slaves. The Clause did not expressly address whether Congress had the constitutional power to regulate "rendition"—that is, the process by which escaped slaves were identified, captured, and returned. Nor did the Clause expressly address whether any such congressional power was exclusive of the authority of the states to regulate the rendition process. In *Prigg*, the Court sided entirely with pro-slavery forces. It first upheld as within the scope of congressional power the Fugitive Slave Act of 1793, which allowed masters to use self-help to recover slaves with a minimal legal hearing before returning them to their home states. Second, the *Prigg* Court held unconstitutional state "personal liberty" laws, which anti-slavery Northern states passed both to force masters to rely on state officials (rather than private slave catchers) to find and detain escaped slaves, and to confer upon alleged slaves extensive procedural protections in which they could prove their free status at a hearing in the state to which they had fled.

In 1850, Congress passed an even more slavery-protective Fugitive Slave Act as part of the Compromise of 1850. California was

---

[7]   For a discussion of the federalism issues that divided the country, see DANIEL A. FARBER, LINCOLN'S CONSTITUTION 44–91 (2003).

[8]   41 U.S. 539 (1842).

admitted as a free state and the Utah and New Mexico territories were organized without a rule on slavery. The 1850 Act authorized federal officials to recapture escaped slaves; authorized federal marshals to order "bystanders" to assist the recapture; and made helping escaped slaves a federal crime. Congress also empowered slaveowners to obtain from federal commissioners a certificate for a fugitive slave through a one-sided proceeding and compelled courts in sister states to accept the certificate as conclusive proof of fugitive status. President Millard Fillmore's Attorney General, John Crittenden, deemed the law valid in light of *Prigg*,[9] and the Court upheld it in 1858, in *Ableman v. Booth*.[10]

Two years earlier, the Court decided *Dred Scott v. Sandford*,[11] a case in which Dred Scott was suing for his freedom. He did not deny that he had been a slave; rather, he argued that he had been emancipated because he had resided, and had not merely sojourned, with his master in a free state and a free territory. This was the conventional legal distinction in free and slave states alike. Recall that the Missouri Compromise provided that slavery would not be permitted in territory acquired by the United States in the Louisiana Purchase, except for Missouri.

The question of whether Scott had been emancipated was a question of state law, not federal law. The case was in federal court because Scott invoked the diversity jurisdiction of the federal courts, which extends to suits between citizens of different states.[12]

The Supreme Court, by a vote of 7 to 2, issued two holdings. The lead opinion was by Chief Justice Roger Taney. First, the Court held that, in the eyes of the U.S. Constitution, neither slaves nor former slaves nor free blacks could become state citizens or U.S. citizens. Thus, Scott was not allowed to sue in the diversity jurisdiction of the federal courts; in other words, the federal courts lacked jurisdiction—that is, authority—to decide the case.

Second, notwithstanding his initial determination that the Court lacked jurisdiction, Chief Justice Taney proceeded to the merits and concluded that the Missouri Compromise was unconstitutional for two reasons. First, he concluded, congressional regulation of slavery in the territories was beyond the scope of the Territory Clause because this

---

[9]   *See* 5 Op. Att. Gen. 254 (Sept. 18, 1850).

[10]   62 U.S. 506 (1859).

[11]   60 U.S. 393 (1857). This is the conventional title of the case, but we have some qualms about following the convention. Cases are generally not named in terms of the first names of the parties—for instance, no one calls the case *Dred Scott v. John Sandford*. Use of the Scott's full name seems attributable to his status as a slave at one point. Although we object in principle to this convention, we follow it here to avoid confusion.

[12]   U.S. CONST. art. III, § 2, cl. 1.

clause was limited to territory in the possession of the United States at the time the Constitution was ratified. Second, he also concluded, slaves were property protected by the Due Process Clause of the Fifth Amendment, so that the Missouri Compromise unconstitutionally deprived slaveholders of their property. More broadly, according to Chief Justice Taney, Congress could not ban slavery in American territories, no matter that Congress had been doing just that for many decades. There is some dispute about just how many Justices adhered to various parts of the Chief Justice's opinion, but a majority was at least in general agreement with him. Much of his reasoning borrowed from arguments made by Southern constitutionalists, who had developed their own pro-slavery interpretation of the Constitution.

As for the constitutional politics surrounding the decision, the country would have abided the jurisdictional holding, but invalidation of the Missouri Compromise was deemed unacceptable. It meant that Congress was prohibited from regulating slavery in the territories and that the Republican Party platform was illegitimate because it was inconsistent with the Constitution. This holding is what made *Dred Scott* an earthshaking decision. It was the first time since *Marbury v. Madison* in 1803 that the Court declared a federal law unconstitutional. Many politicians had wanted the Court to settle the issue of slavery in the territories; politics had proven incapable of doing so despite many efforts for decades. These politicians, like the Justices, were delusional to think that a judicial decision could decisively resolve a question of such magnitude.

During the 1850s, pro-slavery forces got rid of the Missouri Compromise not only in the Supreme Court, but also in Congress, in the Kansas-Nebraska Act of 1854. They did so, however, at the enormous cost of destroying the Democratic Party as a national party and fueling the organization of the Republican Party—the first major party in American history united in opposition to slavery. Democratic Senator Stephen Douglas of Illinois sought to hold the Democratic Party together by touting "popular sovereignty," which was the idea that each territory could decide for itself whether to allow slavery.[13] This was an attempted "federalism solution" to the slavery problem. Southerners eventually were having none of it. "[N]o Douglas dodges," they declared.[14] With the Democratic Party divided in two— between northern and southern factions—the party was finished.

---

[13] *See* Stephen A. Douglas, *The Dividing Line Between Federal and Local Authority: Popular Sovereignty in the Territories*, HARPER'S MAGAZINE 529–30 (1859), https://harpers.org/sponsor/balvenie/stephen-douglas.1.html.

[14] *See* Robert W. Johannsen, *Stephen A. Douglas and the South*, 33 J. S. HIST. 26, 40 (1967) (quoting Douglas). For a discussion of Senator Douglas's aims and their ultimate rejection by pro-slavery interests, see Neil S. Siegel, *Federalism as a Way Station:* Windsor *as Exemplar of Doctrine in Motion*, 6 J. LEGAL ANALYSIS 87, 88, 93, 128–30, (2013).

Republican Abraham Lincoln won the Presidential Election of 1860 with only a single electoral vote from a state that allowed slavery. He, too, emphatically rejected Senator Douglas's federalism solution to the slavery issue in light of the political and moral gravity of the question. Because of the issue of slavery, Americans soon fought a brutal civil war that killed more Americans than died in all the rest of America's wars combined, roughly two percent of the total American population at the time.

Although the constitutional politics and law of slavery are long gone, this pre-Civil War history matters for numerous reasons. We will briefly discuss three of them. First, it is hard to identify an issue that is more central to American constitutionalism than chattel slavery. Without some appreciation of the institution and how it was utterly embedded into the governing doctrines of constitutional law—without some encouragement to think of what, exactly, "slavery" was— Americans are likely to fall short in thinking about what might be required, permitted, or prohibited to overcome it, both within constitutional politics and within constitutional law.[15] Second, an understanding of this history helps correct an unjustified optimism that the American constitutional system produces happy endings—that constitutional law never serves to legitimate evil. It is critical for lawyers to remind themselves that constitutional law can also serve as a vehicle for rationalizing evil.[16] We saw another example of this with the *Korematsu* case, which we discussed in Chapter 7. Third, an understanding of pre-Civil War constitutional history may encourage us to be more thoughtful about our own moral and constitutional blind spots. Just as we Americans today view the past in ways that previous generations did not view themselves, so Americans in the future will view us in ways that we do not view ourselves.

B.   Adoption of the Reconstruction Amendments

Between 1865 and 1870, three vitally important constitutional amendments were added to the Constitution. They are called the Reconstruction Amendments or the Civil War Amendments. Ratified in 1865, Section 1 of the Thirteenth Amendment prohibits slavery. As the 2012 movie *Lincoln* makes clear,[17] there was opposition to the Thirteenth Amendment within both political parties. For example, Senator Lazarus Powell (D-KY) expressed his opposition during the congressional debate over the Thirteenth Amendment in a way that is

---

[15]   *See* Sanford Levinson, *Why I Do Not Teach* Marbury *(Except to Eastern Europeans) and Why You Shouldn't Either*, 38 WAKE FOREST L. REV. 553, 560–62 (2003).

[16]   *See id.* at 562; *see generally* MARK A. GRABER, *DRED SCOTT* AND THE PROBLEM OF CONSTITUTIONAL EVIL (2006).

[17]   For a description, see the motion picture *Lincoln* (2012), https://www.imdb.com/title/tt0443272/.

especially revealing: "I desire the Union to be restored, restored as it was with the Constitution as it is."[18]

Section One of the Fourteenth Amendment, ratified in 1868, provides that all persons born or naturalized in the United States are citizens of the United States, thereby overruling the first holding of *Dred Scott*. Section One also provides that *no state* may abridge the privileges or immunities of citizens of the United States (the Privileges or Immunities Clause); deprive any person of life, liberty, or property without due process of law (the Due Process Clause); or deny to any person within its jurisdiction the equal protection of the laws (the Equal Protection Clause). Unlike the original Bill of Rights, which generally restricted only the federal government, the Due Process and Equal Protection Clauses of the Fourteenth Amendment are directed expressly at the states, not the federal government. As we discussed in detail in Chapter 8, they make states liable for violations of certain federal constitutional rights. This was the main structural achievement of the Reconstruction Amendments.

Ratified in 1870, Section One of the Fifteenth Amendment provides that the right of United States citizens to vote shall not be denied or abridged by the United States or by any state because of race, color, or previous condition of servitude. Given ratification of the Thirteenth Amendment, Republicans in Congress came to view the Fifteenth Amendment as important because Democrats in Southern states were denying former slaves the vote, even as these states were obtaining more representation in Congress now that the former slaves counted as 5/5, not 3/5, for purposes of congressional representation. Thus, without further amendment and security for black voting rights in the South, the Democratic Party would benefit politically from its own racism. It turned out, however, that Section One of the Fifteenth Amendment would not be enforced by the federal courts for many decades.

During Reconstruction, there were robust disagreements, both between and within the Republican and Democratic parties, over whether each of the Reconstruction Amendments was necessary; what each should say to the extent it was necessary; and what the meaning was of the constitutional language that was ultimately ratified.[19] The basic constitutional question in dispute was whether the Reconstruction Amendments should—and, in retrospect, did—fundamentally transform the constitutional order, or whether they should, and did,

---

[18]   *Congressional Globe*, 38th Cong., 1st Sess. (1864), 1483.

[19]   For accounts of the framing and ratification of the Reconstruction Amendments, see AKHIL REED AMAR, AMERICA'S CONSTITUTION: A BIOGRAPHY 349–401 (2005); JACK M. BALKIN, LIVING ORIGINALISM 183–255 (2011); DANIEL A. FARBER & SUZANNA SHERRY, A HISTORY OF THE AMERICAN CONSTITUTION 449–82 (3d ed. 2013); ALEXANDER TSESIS, THE THIRTEENTH AMENDMENT AND AMERICAN FREEDOM: A LEGAL HISTORY (2004).

maintain the old Constitution for the most part minus slavery, birthright citizenship for African Americans, and perhaps some limited measure of racial equality. To this day, Justices and commentators debate this basic question about the scope of the Civil War Amendments.

For example, Section One of the Fourteenth Amendment was a compromise between the different factions of the Republican Party in Congress. The question of the reach of Section One did not receive extensive attention in the House and Senate debates over the Fourteenth Amendment.[20] The phrase "equal protection of the laws," in particular, did not have a settled meaning. Much of the discussion was at a very abstract level. John Bingham, the primary drafter, explained that it was linked to the requirement of due process of law and meant "law in its highest sense, that law which is the perfection of human reason and which is impartial, equal exact justice."[21] This formulation was not particularly helpful in fleshing out the concept of equal protection. Moreover, when the Fourteenth Amendment was sent to the states for ratification, Section One also received little attention in the ensuing ratification proceedings. As a result, the meaning attached to "equal protection" at the time of adoption remains opaque. It is possible to draw inferences from the mentions of equal protection in the debates and from the historical setting, but these inferences remain controversial.

We do know that Congress rejected proposals that would have prohibited all forms of racial discrimination by state governments—that is, constitutional colorblindness. We know this from the fact that the Fourteenth Amendment was generally not thought to touch racial segregation in public schools, bans on inter-racial marriage, or racial discrimination in voting.[22] For example, the same Congress that wrote the Fourteenth Amendment allowed the public schools in the District of Columbia to be racially segregated.[23] Conversely, Congress passed race-conscious legislation that was designed to help former slaves and impoverished blacks whether or not they were recently freed slaves. For example, the Freedman's Bureau Acts authorized federal agents to give former slaves land, homes, jobs, and an education, and Congress gave money to poor black women and children.[24]

---

[20]   For a summary of the limited discussion of Section 1, see FARBER & SHERRY, *supra* note 19, at 460–78. Most of the debates on the Amendment centered on Sections 2 and 3, which are virtually forgotten today but related more directly to the issues of Reconstruction. See *id.* at 467.

[21]   *Id.* at 465.

[22]   *See, e.g.*, BALKIN, *supra* note 19, at 223.

[23]   *See, e.g.*, Steven G. Calabresi & Michael W. Perl, *Originalism and* Brown v. Board of Education, 2014 MICH. ST. L. REV. 429, 492–97 (2014).

[24]   *See, e.g.*, BALKIN, *supra* note 19, at 223 & n.20.

It is worth recalling from Chapter 8 how it could have been thought when the Fourteenth Amendment was written that the Equal Protection Clause prohibited racial discrimination by state governments in contracting, owning property, and accessing the courts, but not racial segregation in public schools or state bans on inter-racial marriage. The answer lies in the distinction between *civil* rights and *social* rights, or between *civil* equality and *social* equality. Racial segregation in public schools and bans on miscegenation were thought to fall within the realm of social equality.

It is also worth recalling why it was thought necessary for Section One of the Fifteenth Amendment to prohibit racial discrimination in voting by states when Section One of the Fourteenth Amendment already existed and prohibited states from denying African Americans equal protection. The answer lies in another distinction, between *civil* rights and *political* rights, or between *civil* equality and *political* equality. Voting was considered a political right. The Fourteenth Amendment was thought to protect only civil equality.

Lawmakers who debated constitutional equality in connection with the Fourteenth Amendment generally accepted mid-century conceptions distinguishing equality with respect to civil rights, social rights, and political rights.[25] Although the precise contours of these categories were unclear, they provided a general framework for thinking about the meaning of constitutional equality. Civil rights included the rights to own property, contract, sue, and testify in court. Social rights included the right to select one's associates, especially in marriage and education. Political rights included voting and, perhaps, jury service. Voting was viewed as a political privilege to be exercised by competent individuals, not a right of free people. These distinctions informed the congressional debate over, among other things, the Fourteenth Amendment. They also defined the debate between the majority and the dissent in *Strauder v. West Virginia*[26] and *Plessy v. Ferguson*,[27] as discussed below. Although the boundaries among the categories were contested, the basic purpose of these distinctions was clear enough: to expand *and* to limit constitutional guarantees of equality for African Americans. These distinctions ensured that the Civil War Amendments would go only so far, but no farther.

The Republican Party, not social movements or interest groups, was the primary force behind the Reconstruction Amendments, although the terrorism of the Ku Klux Klan may have helped move matters along. The Republican Party won every national election

---

[25]　*See generally* Mark Tushnet, *The Politics of Equality in Constitutional Law*, 74 J. AM. HIST. 884 (1987); *see also* BALKIN, *supra* note 19, at 221–26; RICHARD A. PRIMUS, THE AMERICAN LANGUAGE OF RIGHTS 154–56 (1999).

[26]　100 U.S. 303 (1880).

[27]　163 U.S. 537 (1896).

between 1860 and 1872, and party members were motivated by considerations of both principle and politics.[28] As already indicated, however, Republicans were divided about racial issues, although they were united in rejecting slavery and in fearing a return to political power of former secessionists. There were radical Republicans in Congress, such as Thaddeus Stevens (R-PA) and Charles Sumner (R-MA), but there were also moderate and conservative Republicans on matters of race.

Between the end of the Civil War in 1865 and the end of Reconstruction a decade later, the racial conservatives eventually won out in national politics. The South was always hostile to Reconstruction, and Northern elites tired of it. They came to prefer reconciliation with the South and the promotion of business enterprise to the pursuit of racial equality.[29]

The date of the end of Reconstruction is typically identified as 1876. Reconstruction ended as part of a compromise resolution of the disputed presidential election in 1876 between Rutherford Hayes and Samuel Tilden.[30] The Democrats essentially gave the Republicans the White House in exchange for the end of military rule in the South. (Note that, whereas today the Republican Party is the dominant political party in the American South, the Democratic Party was dominant in this region from the Civil War to the 1980s.)

C.   The Republican Era

If Reconstruction offered African Americans hope that the federal government would ensure them a real measure of racial equality in the United States, this hope was crushed during the "Republican Era," which spanned roughly from roughly 1877 until 1932. Once federal troops withdrew, Southern states enshrined a caste system in which the principle of white supremacy was enforced by preventing African Americans from voting, terrorizing them when deemed necessary, and maintaining an apartheid social order. Southern states adopted many laws discriminating against African Americans (called Jim Crow laws), including laws requiring racial segregation in public settings such as schools and places of public accommodation.

During the late 1870s and 1880s, Congress and Republican administrations offered African Americans some protection of their constitutional right to vote, but the laws were relatively weak and

---

[28]   *See* HOWARD GILLMAN, MARK A. GRABER, & KEITH E. WHITTINGTON, AMERICAN CONSTITUTIONALISM, VOLUME II: RIGHTS AND LIBERTIES 224 (2nd ed. 2017).

[29]   *See* BARRY FRIEDMAN, THE WILL OF THE PEOPLE: HOW PUBLIC OPINION HAS INFLUENCED THE SUPREME COURT AND SHAPED THE MEANING OF THE CONSTITUTION 145–49 (2009).

[30]   *See id.* at 148.

federal enforcement efforts were intermittent; there was no significant impact on voting by African Americans.[31] Moreover, as just noted, a bipartisan coalition of Republicans and Democrats formed in Congress. They were united by a concern to promote economic interests, not racial equality, so they defeated bills that would have strengthened voting rights for blacks, and they secured the repeal of several Reconstruction statutes that endeavored to advance racial equality in the South by requiring federal supervision of elections.[32] Political elites in the South were emboldened by these developments in Washington, D.C., and they held state constitutional conventions in the late 1890s in which they candidly declared their commitment to white supremacy.[33] As Professor Richard Pildes writes, "[t]he effect of these disenfranchising constitutions throughout the South, combined with statutory suffrage restrictions, was immediate and devastating."[34]

With rare exceptions, the Supreme Court during this period legitimated and strengthened Southern racism. The Court had been composed of racial conservatives during Reconstruction, and after Reconstruction it read the Fourteenth Amendment mostly to protect business interests, not the rights of African Americans. It would be a long time before the Court would understand the Reconstruction Amendments to protect the rights of African Americans beyond the category of "civil" rights.

One of the rare exceptions was the Court's 1879 decision in *Strauder v. West Virginia*,[35] which concerned a West Virginia law providing that only whites could serve on juries. The Court held that the West Virginia law amounted to racial discrimination in violation of the Equal Protection Clause. Rather than articulating a robust principle of racial equality, however, the Court emphasized that the Fourteenth Amendment guarantees African Americans all of the "civil rights" that are enjoyed by whites and that jury service was such a right. The Court said that the Fourteenth Amendment had the "purpose" of "securing to a race recently emancipated, a race that, through many generations, had been held in slavery, all the civil rights that the superior race enjoy."[36] The dissent responded that jury service was a political right akin to voting, and thus was not protected by the Fourteenth Amendment.[37]

---

[31]   GILLMAN ET AL., *supra* note 28, at 346.

[32]   *See id.*

[33]   *See* Richard H. Pildes, *Democracy, Anti-Democracy, and the Canon*, 17 CONST. COMMENT. 295, 301–04 (2000).

[34]   *Id.* at 303.

[35]   100 U.S. 303 (1879).

[36]   *Id.* at 306.

[37]   Justice Stephen Field relied upon the reasoning in his dissent in the companion case of *Ex parte Virginia*, 100 U.S. 339, 367–68 (1879) (Field, J., dissenting).

More typical were decisions such as *The Civil Rights Cases* in 1883,[38] which was discussed in Chapter 8 and will be analyzed again in Chapter 13. The majority in this case was concerned that, by prohibiting racial discrimination in places of public accommodation, Congress was seeking to require social equality and forced association between whites and blacks even though whites opposed it. Privately, Justice Joseph Bradley called this objective requiring "the slavery of whites."[39] In his solo dissent, the first Justice John Marshall Harlan expressed his view that equal access to public accommodations was a civil right, not a social right.[40]

Also typical of the Court's behavior during the Republican Era was its infamous decision in *Plessy v. Ferguson* in 1896.[41] The Court in this case upheld a Louisiana Jim Crow criminal law requiring racial segregation of passengers on railroad cars. Homer Plessy was 7/8 white, 1/8 black—meaning that he had one black great grandparent. In order to set up a test case, he refused to go to the black area of the train and was convicted for violating the Louisiana law. He challenged the constitutionality of his conviction. Writing for the Court, the ironically surnamed Justice Henry Billings Brown held that separate but equal accommodations for blacks and whites comply with equal protection principles. The Court reasoned that, on its face, the law treated everyone the same—the accommodations were separate but equal—which is all that civil equality demanded. Put differently, in the Court's view, racial segregation in railroad cars implicated social equality, not civil equality.

In addition, the Court stated that the social meaning of the law was not the imposition of a badge of inferiority on black people. According to the *Plessy* majority, the "underlying fallacy" in Plessy's argument was "the assumption that the enforced separation of the two races stamps the colored race with a badge of inferiority."[42] "If this be so," the Court infamously declared, "it is not by reason of anything found in the act, but solely because the colored race chooses to put that construction upon it."[43] In other words, if black people saw the law as reflecting and re-enforcing their inequality, it was only because they elected to see it this way. The racism was in their heads. This is not the only time in American history that African Americans would be told that racism was in their heads. Regarding this utterance from the *Plessy* Court, Professor Charles Black, in arguably the greatest ten pages ever

---

[38]　109 U.S. 3 (1883).

[39]　For Justice Bradley's private writing on the matter, see 7 CHARLES FAIRMAN, THE HISTORY OF THE SUPREME COURT OF THE UNITED STATES: RECONSTRUCTION AND REUNION, 1864–1888, PART TWO 564 (1987).

[40]　109 U.S. at 34–36, 48–52, 55–62 (Harlan, J., dissenting).

[41]　163 U.S. 537 (1896).

[42]　*Id.* at 551.

[43]　*Id.*

written in a law review, would later memorably opine that "[t]he curves of callousness and stupidity intersect at their respective maxima."[44]

Justice Harlan dissented and wrote a powerful opinion. As forecasted in his dissent in the *Civil Rights Cases*, he thought that *Plessy* implicated civil equality, not social equality. As far as Justice Harlan was concerned, it did not matter that everyone was treated the same on the face of the law. In his view, the Court was required to look "under the hood" (our words) and determine what was really going on. His dissent was suffused with frames of candor and transparency; he was calling out his colleagues for practicing willful blindness.[45] And when one looked under the hood, he insisted, one found that the dominant purpose, effect, and social meaning of the Louisiana law was to reinforce the inferiority of African Americans in the state—to impose "a badge of servitude" on them.[46] This was the point of using the law to stop the association, Harlan insisted. The point was to keep blacks away from whites, not to protect blacks from exposure to whites or to honor the wishes of most members of both races not to be seated near members of the other race.

Harlan vehemently rejected the majority's position using language that has since become famous—and arguably misunderstood:

> But in view of the constitution, in the eye of the law, there is in this country no superior, dominant, ruling class of citizens. There is no caste here. Our constitution is color-blind, and neither knows nor tolerates classes among citizens. In respect of civil rights, all citizens are equal before the law. The humblest is the peer of the most powerful. The law regards man as man, and takes no account of his surroundings or of his color when his civil rights as guaranteed by the supreme law of the law are involved.[47]

Modern conservatives—most notably, Justice Clarence Thomas— have interpreted Justice Harlan's statement as articulating a colorblind *anti-classification principle*, according to which the harm that the Equal Protect Clause presumptively protects against is the harm of state action that treats individuals disadvantageously on the basis of their race.[48] From this perspective, the Equal Protection

---

[44]   Charles L. Black, Jr., *The Lawfulness of the Segregation Decisions*, 69 YALE L.J. 421, 422 n.8 (1960).

[45]   *See Plessy*, 163 U.S. at 557, 562 (Harlan, J., dissenting).

[46]   *Id*. at 562.

[47]   *Id*. at 559.

[48]   *See, e.g.*, Parents Involved in Community Schools v. Seattle Sch. Dist. No. 1, 551 U.S. 701, 772 (2007) (Thomas, J., concurring).

Clause protects individuals, not groups, and it does not matter which racial groups are benefited or burdened by state action. There is no doubt that some of Justice Harlan's language lends itself to this interpretation (in particular, "[o]ur constitution is color-blind"; "all citizens are equal before the law"; "[t]he law regards man as man, and takes no account of his surroundings or of his color").

Other parts of Justice Harlan's language, however, better reflect a color-conscious *anti-subordination principle*, according to which the harm that the Equal Protection Clause presumptively protects against is the harm of state action that reflects or reinforces the inferior social status of historically excluded groups.[49] From this point of view, the Equal Protection Clause protects members of groups, not individuals, and it does matter which racial groups are benefited or burdened because they are not similarly situated in light of our nation's disgraceful history of racial subordination. Several of Justice Harlan's statements—specifically, "there is in this country no superior, dominant, ruling class of citizens"; "[t]here is no caste here"; "[t]he humblest is the peer of the most powerful"—emphasize the constitutional imperative of disestablishing a status hierarchy, a caste system. These social phenomena make sense only in group terms, not individualistic ones. The fact that Justice Harlan's statement of principle in *Plessy* vibrates back and forth between anti-classification and anti-subordination commitments suggests that it was not clear at the time of *Plessy* that these were potentially competing principles. This is no doubt because both principles condemn state-mandated racial segregation: it was an individual racial classification in the Louisiana law that subordinated African Americans.[50]

One last point about Justice Harlan's statement is worth underscoring. Twice in this one quotation he limited his constitutional commitment to the equality of African Americans to the category of "civil

---

[49]   For expressions of antisubordination understandings of equality, see Owen M. Fiss, *Groups and the Equal Protection Clause*, 5 PHIL. & PUB. AFF. 107 (1976); Catherine A. MacKinnon, *Difference and Dominance: On Sex Discrimination*, in FEMINISM UNMODIFIED: DISCOURSES ON LIFE AND LAW 32 (1987); Reva B. Siegel, *Equality Talk: Antisubordination and Anticlassification Values in Constitutional Struggles over Brown*, 117 HARV. L. REV. 1470 (2004); *see also* Jack M. Balkin & Reva B Siegel, *The American Civil Rights Tradition: Anticlassification or Antisubordination?*, 58 U. MIAMI L. REV. 9 (2003); Jill Elaine Hasday, *The Principle and Practice of Women's "Full Citizenship": A Case Study of Sex-Segregated Public Education*, 101 MICH. L. REV. 755 (2002).

[50]   The anti-classfication and anti-subordination principles are mediating principles of equality, so called because they mediate between the text of the Equal Protection Clause and outcomes in particular cases. *See* Reva B. Siegel, *From Colorblindness to Antibalkanization: An Emerging Ground of Decision in Race Equality Cases*, 120 YALE L.J. 1278, 1282 n.8 (2011) ("A mediating principle interprets a clause purposively to vindicate one particular understanding of the concept or value the clause expressly guarantees, here the equal protection of the laws.").

rights." He was not articulating a robust principle of racial equality. On the contrary, he voted to uphold racial segregation in public education (and worse) in *Cumming v. Richmond County Board of Education* just a few years later (in 1899).[51] He apparently did not view racial discrimination in public schools as implicating civil rights.

Part of the disagreement between the majority and the dissent in *Plessy* has to do with categorization (that is, civil versus social equality), and part of the disagreement has to do with the purpose and social meaning of the law. As to the latter disagreement, it is worth pausing to consider who is right and why. The evidence most relevant to answering this question overwhelmingly supports Justice Harlan's position, which reflected the arguments made by able counsel for Homer Plessy, Albion Tourgée, "a former Union soldier, judge, author, and renowned advocate for Black equality."[52] For starters, Plessy was categorized as black under Louisiana law even though he was 7/8 white. The "one drop of black blood" notion underlying the law's racial definitions regarded black skin as a cancer.[53] In addition, whites passed this law and supported it; African Americans opposed it.[54] Moreover, the statute had an exception permitting (presumably black) "nurses attending children of the other race"; apparently, strict racial separation was not required when the racial hierarchy could be established in other ways.[55] Finally, other aspects of Louisiana law at the time supported Justice Harlan's interpretation. For example, it was actionable humiliation under state tort law to call a white person a black person, but not the other way around.[56] All this evidence suggests that claims about the purpose or social meaning of a law need not be hopelessly subjective and impressionistic.

With the Court's emphatic support in *Plessy*, every aspect of public life in the American South was segregated by race. In addition to requiring racially segregated seating on trains and buses, Jim Crow laws required separate schools, separate restaurants, separate hotels,

---

[51]   175 U.S. 528 (1899).

[52]   Cheryl I. Harris, *The Story of* Plessy v. Ferguson*: The Death and Resurrection of Racial Formalism, in* CONSTITUTIONAL LAW STORIES 181, 202 (Michael C. Dorf ed., 2004).

[53]   *See id.* at 210.

[54]   *See id.* at 199–203.

[55]   *See id.* at 212.

[56]   *See* Black, *supra* note 44, at 427:

[I]t would be the most unneutral of principles, improvised *ad hoc*, to require that a court faced with the present problem refuse to note a plain fact about the society of the United States—the fact that the social meaning of segregation is the putting of the Negro in a position of walled-off inferiority— or the other equally plain fact that such treatment is hurtful to human beings. Southern courts, on the basis of just such a judgment, have held that the placing of a white person in a Negro railroad car is an actionable humiliation; must a court pretend not to know that the Negro's situation there is humiliating?

separate parks and other places of public amusement, separate hospitals, separate prisons, separate bathrooms, separate drinking fountains, and separate cemeteries.

From the perspective of racial equality, the only enduring bright side during the Republican Era, other than Justice Harlan's lone(ly) dissents in the *Civil Rights Cases* and *Plessy*, was the founding of the National Association for the Advancement of Colored People (NAACP) in 1909 by W. E. B. DuBois and other civil rights activists.[57] The NAACP became a politically and legally powerful force for racial equality in the United States by the end of the Republican Era—specifically, in the fights in the American South against the lynching of African Americans, the disenfranchisement of African Americans, and racial segregation.

D.   *Brown v. Board of Education*

To talk about *Brown v. Board of Education*[58] is to talk about one of the two or three most important U.S. Supreme Court decisions in American history. For example, in race cases today, the Justices debate the original meaning of *Brown*; they do not debate the original meaning of the Fourteenth Amendment. And if a theory of constitutional interpretation or an understanding of constitutional equality cannot account for *Brown*, commentators across the ideological spectrum today view this fact as a problem for the theory or understanding. They do not view it as a problem for *Brown*.

It was not always so. When it was decided, and for more than a decade after it was decided, *Brown* was *intensely* controversial. The Court's decision declared the unconstitutionality of the defining feature of the culture of an entire region of the country. *Brown* was assailed relentlessly as lawless, massively resisted in the South, and questioned pointedly and publicly by very prominent jurists and legal academics, including Judge Learned Hand and Professor Herbert Wechsler.[59] In short, the *Brown* Court made a bet with constitutional destiny, and in doing so it placed the legitimacy of the Court itself in question. The Court could have lost this bet. It was not inevitable that it ultimately would succeed in persuading the country of the unconstitutionality of government-mandated racial segregation.

The New Deal/Great Society Era, which spanned 1933 to 1968, witnessed dramatic changes in the constitutional status of African Americans in the United States. To a great extent, these changes were the consequence of changing partisan commitments, especially the

---

[57]   *See* NAACP, Nation's Premier Civil Rights Organization, https://www.naacp.org/nations-premier-civil-rights-organization/ (visited Oct. 20, 2018).

[58]   347 U.S. 483 (1954).

[59]   *See generally* LEARNED HAND, THE BILL OF RIGHTS: THE OLIVER WENDELL HOLMES LECTURES (Atheneum 1964) (1958); Herbert Wechsler, *Toward Neutral Principles of Constitutional Law*, 73 HARV. L. REV. 1 (1959).

commitments of the Democratic Party, which moved from being the party of slavery, Black Codes, and Jim Crow to joining the Republican Party in opposing apartheid. A combination of Democratic and Republican presidents appointed Justices who either joined or reaffirmed the Court's decision in *Brown*.

Scholars debate the causes of the racial progress that occurred during this era. These causes were numerous; like many significant societal changes, this one was over-determined. First was an increasingly influential civil rights movement, which succeeded in persuading elected officials to promote racial equality. The litigation arm of this movement was led by Charles Hamilton Houston, Thurgood Marshall, and other lawyers from the NAACP Legal Defense Fund.[60] They developed the litigation strategy that first asked courts to apply— and, eventually, to overrule—*Plessy*.

Another significant cause of racial progress was the protest movement organized by A. Philip Randolph and Martin Luther King, Jr., which succeeded in persuading elected officials to adopt anti-discrimination measures and which enhanced public support for such policies in Northern states. Perversely helpful in this regard was the horrific violence of southern responses to non-violent civil rights protests organized by Dr. King. His urging of peaceful protests was not only (in our view) the right thing to do from a moral perspective; it was also politically brilliant. The violence of the southern responses caused outrage among many racial moderates in the North and resulted in passage of the Civil Rights Act of 1964 and the Voting Rights Act of 1965, two of the most important statutes ever enacted by Congress.[61]

Other causes of racial progress included increasing recognitions of the immorality of racism, scientific demonstrations of the falseness of claims of white genetic superiority, and the strongly negative public reaction to the horrific racism of Nazi Germany, which created concerns about racial practices at home, particularly with African Americans fighting and dying for the United States in World War II.[62] There was also the Cold War imperative of expanding American influence abroad, which was thought to require ending apartheid at home.[63] Finally, the great migration north of African Americans, as well as increasing

---

[60] For an account of the litigation campaign, see generally RICHARD KLUGER, SIMPLE JUSTICE: THE HISTORY OF *BROWN V. BOARD OF EDUCATION* AND BLACK AMERICA'S STRUGGLE FOR EQUALITY (2nd ed. 2004).

[61] *See generally* MICHAEL J. KLARMAN, FROM JIM CROW TO CIVIL RIGHTS: THE SUPREME COURT AND THE STRUGGLE FOR RACIAL EQUALITY (2006); Michael J. Klarman, *How Brown Changed Race Relations: The Backlash Thesis*, 81 J. AM. HIST. 81 (1994).

[62] *See* Michael J. Klarman, Brown, *Racial Change, and the Civil Rights Movement*, 80 VA. L. REV. 7, 14 (1994).

[63] *See generally* Mary L. Dudziak, *Desegregation as a Cold War Imperative*, 41 STAN. L. REV. 61 (1988).

urbanization, mobility, and prosperity, increased the economic and political power of African Americans in northern states.[64]

We will focus on the first cause—the litigation campaign. In 1931, the famous Margold Report, written by attorney Nathan Ross Margold for the NAACP, advocated desegregation as the remedy for state failures to comply with *Plessy* by providing equal schools for students of color.[65] Houston, as well as his former student and young associate Thurgood Marshall, instead implemented an equalization strategy—that is, lawsuits aimed at persuading courts actually to apply *Plessy*, which after all purported to allow separate facilities only if they were equal. Notably, the first challenges to this apartheid social order were in the context of higher education, especially law schools. Marshall joked that he did not understand why segregationists were most violently opposed to the desegregation of elementary schools, as opposed to higher education where people actually have intercourse and marry, but he was happy to target racism where the resistance was least strong.

For example, in 1938, in *State of Missouri ex rel. Gaines v. Canada*,[66] a state law school did not admit African Americans, but the state offered to send African Americans out of state for a legal education. The Court held that this arrangement contravened *Plessy*'s requirement of separate but equal, which was a constitutional obligation that Missouri could not outsource to a sister state. Another example of the equalization strategy was *Sweat v. Painter* in 1950.[67] Texas created a law school for African Americans, but it was inferior in every measure to University of Texas at Austin Law School, which to this day remains one of the best in the nation. The Court emphasized the inequalities between the two schools in terms of both tangible factors (such as number of faculty and books in the library) and intangible factors (such as prestige and alumni connections). If intangible factors counted in the equality analysis under *Plessy*—and why not?—application of the doctrine of separate but equal would result in many judicial invalidations. Also in 1950, the Court in *McLaurin v. Oklahoma State Regents* prohibited racial segregation within a university once African Americans were ordered admitted to the school.[68] *Plessy* was a powerful weapon of desegregation in the hands of judges who were prepared to take its requirement of equality seriously.

Even so, when the NAACP turned its attention to the politically more sensitive issue of racial segregation in public primary and

---

[64]   *See* PAUL BREST ET AL., PROCESSES OF CONSTITUTIONAL DECISIONMAKING: CASES AND MATERIALS 1093 (6th ed. 2015).

[65]   *See* MARK V. TUSHNET, THE NAACP'S LEGAL STRATEGY AGAINST SEGREGATED EDUCATION, 1925–1950, at 20, 25–28 (1987); KLUGER, *supra* note 60, at 131–37.

[66]   305 U.S. 337 (1938).

[67]   339 U.S. 629 (1950).

[68]   339 U.S. 637 (1950).

secondary education, Marshall realized that he could spend the rest of life bringing equalization suits school district by school district. The NAACP did not have resources or the patience to proceed in this fashion.[69] Marshall eventually decided to ask courts not to apply *Plessy*, but to overrule it.

In 1952, the Supreme Court heard oral arguments in five cases— from South Carolina, Virginia, Delaware, the District of Columbia, and Kansas. *Brown* was the Kansas case. The Court was unable to come to agreement and, rather than issue a divided ruling, put the cases over for re-argument. At Justice Felix Frankfurter's urging, the Court asked the parties to brief a series of questions, which were in part about the intent of the Framers of the Fourteenth Amendment. The world did not know it at the time, but the Court was less interested in the original history and more interested in offering a plausible rationale for delay.[70]

Then, during the summer of 1953, Chief Justice Fred Vinson died unexpectedly. He had appeared to favor reaffirming *Plessy*, and Justice Frankfurter is reported to have told a law clerk that Vinson's death was "the first indication that I have ever had that there is a God."[71] Earl Warren—then the Republican Governor of California—became the new Chief Justice. The cases were re-argued in October. The Supreme Court released its decision on May 17, 1954. It was unanimous. According to Richard Kluger's *Simple Justice*, a wonderful, accessible history of the *Brown* litigation from the perspective of the long view of American history, the Court was initially divided over whether to overrule *Plessy*. Chief Justice Warren worked tirelessly to convince the dissenters that it was in the best interests of the country and the Court for the Justices to be unanimous in light of how controversial the decision would be. Justice Stanley Reed had wanted to reaffirm *Plessy* on the ground that overruling it would threaten the nation's progress in the area of race relations, but he was persuaded by the Chief Justice's rationale.[72]

The Court's opinion was short and accessible to the public, but as a matter of legal craft, it was potentially vulnerable in at least three ways. First, the Court framed the question presented as whether segregated schools are inherently unequal despite having equal resources, even though there were great material inequalities between the black and white schools in some of the cases. The Court mischaracterized the situation on the ground, albeit with the best of intentions. The core question was whether government-mandated or permitted racial segregation in public education violated the Equal Protection Clause under any circumstances. Also, like the NAACP at this point, the Court

---

[69]   See KLUGER, *supra* note 60, at 133–34, 255, 274, 293–94.

[70]   See *id.* at 618–19.

[71]   See *id.* at 659; BERNARD SCHWARZ, SUPER CHIEF 72 (1983).

[72]   See KLUGER, *supra* note 60, at 701–02.

did not want endless litigation over whether specific school districts had committed constitutional violations.[73] (As it turned out, however, there would be constant litigation over whether specific school districts had remedied their constitutional violations by achieving desegregation.)

Second, the Court deemed the original understanding of the Fourteenth Amendment "inconclusive,"[74] even though (as we have seen) the Congress that voted for the Fourteenth Amendment also voted to allow segregated schools in the District of Columbia, and even though most states in 1868 segregated their public schools.[75] The prevailing, although not unanimous, view among legal scholars and historians is that *Brown* is an embarrassment for originalism.[76] Moreover, if *Brown* is a tough case for originalists, then *Bolling v. Sharpe*,[77] involving racially segregated schools in the District of Columbia, is even tougher. It is difficult to explain how the original meaning of the Due Process Clause of the Fifth Amendment condemned racial segregation in public education when, as discussed above, it was ratified at a time when the Constitution protected the institution of chattel slavery in significant ways.

More importantly, it seems unlikely that the Court would have viewed itself as bound by the original understanding even if, in its judgment, the historical record had been clearer. Warren wrote that the Court "cannot turn the clock back to 1868 when the [Fourteenth] Amendment was adopted."[78] So maybe the Court's real point was that circumstances had changed—not only changes in facts, but also changes in social meanings and social values. Warren implied that the Framers of the Fourteenth Amendment could not have known modern needs and the modern importance of public education.[79]

Third, and most importantly, the Court may not have adequately justified its conclusion that even tangibly equal separate schools were unconstitutional. According to the Court, schools that were equal with regard to tangible factors were still unconstitutional because of the harmful effects of racial segregation—because segregation decreased the quality of education for African American schoolchildren. This was an empirical claim about causation, and the Court sought to substantiate it with cites to the educational and social psychological

---

[73]   *See id.* at 710.

[74]   *Brown*, 347 U.S. at 489.

[75]   *See* BREST ET AL., *supra* note 64, at 1109.

[76]   For a challenge to the orthodox view, see generally Michael W. McConnell, *Originalism and the Desegregation Decisions*, 81 VA. L. REV. 947 (1995).

[77]   347 U.S. 497 (1954).

[78]   *Brown*, 347 U.S. at 492.

[79]   *See id.* at 492–93.

literature—with a controversial footnote (number 11 in the U.S. Reports) citing certain social science research.

One problem with the Court's purported reliance on these social science studies is that the methodology of the studies was flawed, particularly the "doll studies."[80] Another problem is that the Court's reliance on these studies was more apparent than real. If the analysis had turned on effects, the Court would likely not have insisted that separate but equal is "*inherently* unequal."[81] If the analysis had turned on effects, the Court might have been more sympathetic to studies by academics or fact finding by lower courts purporting to show that desegregation harmed children of both races more than segregation harmed African American children. We know that it was not sympathetic to such "findings."

So despite what the Court said was the key question (the effects of racial segregation), perhaps *Brown* is better read as turning on Supreme Court's analysis of the dominant social meaning of state-mandated or state-permitted racial segregation in public education. The Court quoted the Kansas court's statement that racial segregation by law "is usually interpreted as denoting the inferiority" of black schoolchildren.[82] This is a claim about the social meaning of the segregation laws, which was to demean, stigmatize, and exclude black people—to reinforce their status as second-class citizens. On this view, racial segregation is inherently unequal just because it regards black people as inferior; it is irrelevant whether the segregation causes harmful effects such as impaired ability to learn.

If *Brown* was decided based on either the effects or the social meaning of racial segregation in public education, *Brown* is better understood as an anti-subordination decision, not an anti-classification decision. The *Brown* Court did not suggest that the constitutional problem lay in the fact that states were using racial classifications— were discriminating against individuals on the basis of race. *Brown* focused on black children, not schoolchildren.

Interestingly, however, the same cannot be said of *Bolling v. Sharpe*,[83] the companion case to *Brown* involving racial segregation in the District of Columbia, a federal enclave to which the Equal Protection Clause of the Fourteenth Amendment does not apply. In *Bolling*, Chief Justice Warren did write for a unanimous Court about the evils of racial

---

[80]   *See* Mark Yudof, *School Desegregation: Legal Realism, Reasoned Elaboration, and Social Science Research in the Supreme Court*, 42 LAW & CONTEMP. PROBS. 57, 70 (1978); KLUGER, *supra* note 60, at 710.

[81]   *Brown*, 347 U.S. at 495 (emphasis added).

[82]   *Id.* at 494.

[83]   347 U.S. 497 (1954).

classifications—about racial discrimination on the face of the law[84]—and cited *Korematsu v. United States*,[85] the 1944 decision in which the Court first articulated the idea of applying strict scrutiny to racial classifications (even though, as we saw in Chapter 7, the Court in *Korematsu* actually applied deferential review and infamously upheld the Japanese internment during World War II). Textually, *Korematsu* and *Bolling* were both based on the Due Process Clause of the Fifth Amendment, which may have caused Warren to think in terms of racial classifications in *Bolling* because the Court had already done so in *Korematsu*. (Technically, *Korematsu* involved national origin discrimination, but the modern Court treats race, ethnicity, and national origin the same for equal protection purposes: discrimination on the basis of any of these categories triggers strict scrutiny.)

Maybe the *Brown* Court did not decide between anti-classification and anti-subordination principles because they both condemned racial segregation in public education, just as they both condemned racial segregation in railroad cars in *Plessy*. Like the first Justice Harlan before him, Chief Justice Warren did not seem to register the potential tension between his reasoning in *Brown* and his reasoning in *Bolling*. This was because the choice between anti-classification and anti-subordination perspectives made no difference in either case. Both principles led to the same results: state-mandated racial segregation violates equal protection and the equality component of due process.. But the differences between anti-classification and anti-subordination views of equality have major implications for future controversies.

Even though the Court in *Brown* purported to limit the scope of its holding to public education, the Court soon invalidated laws mandating racial segregation in all public settings. It did so without writing opinions; it simply cited *Brown* in brief unsigned orders affirming lower court decisions invalidating racial segregation in various settings.[86] The way the Court proceeded remains controversial to this day. On one hand, judicial opinions and reason giving matter. If not reasons, what else do judges with life tenure owe the rest of us? In law, as in parenting, "because I said so" is not much of a reason. On the other hand, the Court's conduct can be defended as a statesmanlike effort to expand the scope of *Brown*'s holding without fanning the flames of public controversy by giving reasons that would no doubt further alienate white southerners.

---

[84]   *See id.* at 499.

[85]   323 U.S. 214 (1944).

[86]   *See, e.g.*, New Orleans City Park Improvement Ass'n v. Detiege, 358 U.S. 54 (1958) (mem.) (per curiam), *aff'g* 252 F.2d 122 (5th Cir. 1958); Mayor & City Council of Baltimore City v. Dawson, 350 U.S. 877 (1955) (mem.) (per curiam), *aff'g* 220 F.2d 386 (4th Cir. 1955); Gayle v. Browder, 352 U.S. 903 (1956) (mem.) (per curiam), *aff'g* 142 F. Supp. 707 (M.D. Ala. 1956).

The Court in *Brown* (also called *Brown I*), in 1954, did not implement a remedy. Instead, it put the case over for re-argument on the remedial question. In *Brown II*, the Court again did not prescribe a specific remedy; it ordered lower federal courts to fashion remedies "with all deliberate speed."[87] This formulation is controversial to this day. It can be defended as admirable moderation and statesmanship on the Court's part. It can be criticized for facilitating massive resistance to court-ordered desegregation throughout the South and ultimately proving self-defeating. Linda Brown, the named plaintiff in *Brown*, never attended a desegregated school.

Throughout the *Brown* litigation, the Court feared public reaction and its limited ability to ensure that judicial orders were followed. In many ways, the Court acted out of concern for popular acceptance of *Brown*—out of concern to establish the conditions of the Court's own public legitimacy.[88] The Court set the case for re-argument twice; expended great efforts to achieve unanimity; initially limited the holding to public education; expanded the scope of the holding without offering reasons; offered the "all deliberate speed" formulation on the remedial question; and put off deciding the constitutionality of Virginia's ban on inter-racial marriage in *Naim v. Naim*,[89] even though the Court likely lacked a basis in law for doing so.

History proved that the Court's concerns about compliance were justified. There was massive resistance to court-ordered school desegregation pursuant to *Brown*, particularly in the Deep South. One-hundred-and-one Southern Congressmen signed a resolution—the Southern Manifesto—condemning the decision.[90] One can think of the Manifesto as the de facto dissent in *Brown*: it made some non-frivolous arguments (at the time) based on the constitutional text, the original understanding, the constitutional structure, historical practice, judicial precedent, and tradition. In addition, Southern states claimed that they could interpose their sovereignty and block desegregation orders.[91] A county in Virginia directed its public schools to close rather than desegregate and was ordered to reopen by the Court in *Griffin v. County School Board of Prince Edward County*.[92] In 1957, in Little Rock, Arkansas, federal troops were called out by President Eisenhower to

---

[87]   349 U.S. 294, 301 (1955).

[88]   For an argument that judicial statesmanship counsels judges to take some account of the conditions of the their own public legitimacy, see generally Neil S. Siegel, *The Virtue of Judicial Statesmanship*, 86 TEX. L. REV. 959 (2008).

[89]   350 U.S. 985 (1956).

[90]   Declaration of Constitutional Principles (The Southern Manifesto), 102 CONG. REC. 4515–16, 84th Cong., 2nd Sess. (Mar. 12, 1956).

[91]   For discussion of Southern laws declaring "interposition" or "nullification," see Robert B. McKay, *"With All Deliberate Speed"—A Study of School Desegregation*, 31 N.Y.U. L. REV. 991, 1039–40 (1956).

[92]   377 U.S. 218 (1964).

protect from mob violence the African American students seeking to attend the white high school. President Eisenhower was no great fan of *Brown*, but like President Andrew Jackson before him, he was not prepared to tolerate outright defiance of federal authority by Southern states. Arkansas officials asked for an extension the following year. The Court emphatically said "no" in *Cooper v. Aaron*,[93] in an extraordinary opinion equating *Brown* with the supreme law of the land that was jointly signed by every one of the Justices.

There was little compliance with *Brown* by 1964, a full decade later. Statistics showed little desegregation. Compliance began in earnest when Congress finally intervened and prohibited racial discrimination in programs receiving federal financial assistance.[94] Congress also authorized the Justice Department to bring and intervene in suits seeking school desegregation,[95] amplifying the efforts of civil rights organizations, which had limited financial and human resources. Congress gained additional financial leverage over state and local governments by appropriating boatloads of federal dollars for school districts with "educationally disadvantaged" children.[96]

Federal courts did fashion remedies. In the decade after *Brown II*, the Court mostly took a hands-off approach, occasionally telling state officials what they could not do but not offering school districts and lower courts much guidance on how to purge their school systems of the enduring effects of segregation. Nonetheless, federal courts were successful in many places in achieving desegregation. A number of federal judges in the American South, such as South Carolina District Judge Julius Waties Waring, acted heroically, sometimes at great personal cost.[97] After 1965, the Court became substantially more aggressive in deciding desegregation cases. In 1968, in *Green v. County School Board of New Kent County*,[98] the Court finally declared that there had been entirely too much deliberation and not nearly enough speed.

But as the Court became more conservative on matters of race in the mid-1970s, 1980s, and 1990s, it increasingly ordered an end to court-

---

[93]   358 U.S. 1 (1958).

[94]   *See* Title VI of the Civil Rights Act of 1964, Pub. L. No. 88–352, § 601, 78 Stat. 241, 252 (1964) (codified at 42 U.S.C. § 2000d (2012)).

[95]   *See* Title IV of the Civil Rights Act of 1964, Pub. L. No. 88–352, § 401, 78 Stat. 241, 246 (1964) (codified at 42 U.S.C. § 2000c (2012)); Title IX of the Civil Rights Act of 1964, Pub. L. No. 88–352, § 901, 78 Stat. 241, 266 (1964) (codified at 42 U.S.C. § 2000h-2 (2012)).

[96]   *See* Elementary and Secondary Education Act of 1965, Pub. L. No. 89–10, 79 Stat. 27 (1965) (codified at 20 U.S.C. §§ 6301–7981 (2012 & Supp. V. 2017)).

[97]   *See* KLUGER, *supra* note 60, at 295–305, 357, 365–67, 749. *See generally* JACK BASS, UNLIKELY HEROES (1981) (documenting the federal judges—especially on the Fifth Circuit—who implemented *Brown* in six Southern states).

[98]   391 U.S. 430 (1968).

ordered desegregation remedies, including when lifting the orders would mean resegregation of the schools in light of segregated housing patterns.[99] Public schools today, as a general matter, are highly segregated based on race. Perhaps the current segregated state of public education in the United States shows that courts are very limited in their ability to bring about social change.[100] Or perhaps the current unfortunate situation shows that courts did not do nearly enough because they became racially more conservative and did not want to do more than they did.

If the Rehnquist Court hastened the end of court-ordered school desegregation, the Roberts Court has limited what communities can do voluntarily to create or maintain racially integrated public schools.[101] In *Parents Involved in Community Schools v. Seattle School District No. 1*,[102] the Court prohibited school districts from using racial classifications to make their schools less racially identifiable, except perhaps as a last resort. Chief Justice John Roberts, joined by Justices Antonin Scalia, Thomas, and Samuel Alito, wrote a robustly colorblind plurality opinion, which explicitly read *Brown* as an anti-classification decision. Justice Stephen Breyer, joined by Justices John Paul Stevens, David Souter, and Ruth Bader Ginsburg, wrote a robustly color-conscious dissenting opinion and expressly read *Brown* as an anti-subordination decision. Justice Kennedy wrote a controlling, solo concurrence that sought to stake out a middle ground between these two warring camps. He emphasized the several race-conscious ways in which school districts can pursue racially diverse schools without resorting to racial classifications, such as drawing attendance zones, siting schools, and recruiting faculty with race in mind. He said that racial classifications should be used only as a last resort, and only along with non-racial considerations. Fascinatingly, the Justices in this case debated the original meaning of *Brown*, not the original meaning of the Fourteenth Amendment. No Justice made an originalist argument in favor of his interpretation of the Equal Protection Clause.

---

[99]   *See, e.g.*, Bd. of Educ. of Oklahoma City v. Dowell, 498 U.S. 237 (1991); Freeman v. Pitts, 503 U.S. 467 (1992); Missouri v. Jenkins, 515 U.S. 70 (1995).

[100]   For the now-classic statement of the position that courts have limited ability to create change, see generally GERALD N. ROSENBERG, THE HOLLOW HOPE: CAN COURTS BRING ABOUT SOCIAL CHANGE? (1991).

[101]   For discussion of the goals and techniques of "voluntary integration plans" or "race-conscious student assignment plans," see generally Neil S. Siegel, *Race-Conscious Student Assignment Plans: Balkanization, Integration, and Individualized Consideration*, 56 DUKE L.J. 781 (2006).

[102]   551 U.S. 701 (2007).

E. The Emergence of the Suspect Classification Doctrine

As we have seen, *Brown* did not emphasize the harms of racial classifications or emphasize that race is a suspect classification and so triggers strict scrutiny, the most demanding test known to constitutional law. Under strict scrutiny the government has the burden of showing that the racial classification is narrowly tailored to advance a compelling governmental interest. The constitutional principle that race is a suspect classification—the so-called suspect classification doctrine—emerged in the decade-and-a-half after *Brown*. A fateful year in this regard was 1964, when Congress passed the Civil Rights Act; Lyndon Johnson, a racial liberal, was elected in a landslide; and the Court decided *McLaughlin v. Florida*.[103] The criminal statute at issue in this case punished inter-racial cohabitation more severely than intra-racial cohabitation. The Court held that the Florida statute violated the Equal Protection Clause because it used a racial classification, "which must be viewed in light of the historical fact that the central purpose of the Fourteenth Amendment was to eliminate racial discrimination emanating from official sources in the States."[104] As authority for the proposition that racial classifications trigger strict scrutiny, the Court cited *Korematsu*, *Brown*, and *Bolling*, among other decisions. The most important point for present purposes is that the Court was reinterpreting *Brown* as an anti-classification case.

Three years later, the Court further responded to the changed political circumstances in the country by finally deciding the constitutionality of Virginia's ban on inter-racial marriage. In *Loving v. Virginia*,[105] an appropriately named case if ever there was one, the Court invalidated the law, thereby putting the final nail in the coffin of the constitutional distinction between civil and social equality. In the equal protection portion of its decision in *Loving* (there was also a substantive due process/right to marry portion, as discussed in Chapter 12), the Court reasoned that the Virginia law used a racial classification and so had to survive strict scrutiny. It easily flunked strict scrutiny.

Indeed, given the state's illegitimate purpose of perpetuating white supremacy, the law flunked even modern rational basis scrutiny, which is extraordinarily difficult to do. The Court has consistently held that, under rational basis review, there is a strong presumption of constitutionality and the burden is on the challenger to show that the classification is not rationally related to a conceivable, legitimate state

---

[103]   379 U.S. 184 (1964).

[104]   *Id.* at 192.

[105]   388 U.S. 1 (1967).

interest.[106] As we saw in Chapter 9, the requirement of mere rationality permits a great deal of underinclusivness (meaning that the law does not regulate everyone who is similarly situated with respect to the purpose of the law) and overinclusiveness (meaning that the law regulates some people who are not similarly situated with respect to the purpose of the law). Moreover, the legitimate interest need only be conceivable (meaning that a government lawyer can make it up in litigation). Every classification that does not trigger heightened scrutiny (that is, strict scrutiny or intermediate scrutiny, discussed below), triggers rational basis review. At present, the only way a law can flunk rational basis review is if it is motivated by animus against members of a certain group.[107]

From an anti-classification perspective, it is important to be clear on why an anti-miscegenation statute denies equal protection given that it applies equally to all: whites cannot marry non-whites, and non-whites cannot marry whites. (The same question could be asked of the racial segregation laws at issue in *Plessy* and *Brown*.) Regardless of equal application, it is still a racial classification. Who one could marry depended on one's race—or the race of one's partner. The Court stressed the evils of racial classifications.

The Virginia law was also constitutionally problematic from an anti-subordination perspective. The purpose of the law was to express hostility to African Americans. The social meaning of the law was the inferiority of African Americans: African Americans (and other minorities) are deemed not good enough to marry whites, not the other way around. The Court twice referenced the doctrine of "White Supremacy,"[108] which reflects anti-subordination reasoning. As in *Plessy*, ample evidence supported the Court's interpretation. The classification was whites versus everyone else; members of other minority groups could marry one another. In addition, someone who was almost entirely white was deemed black if he or she had any black blood at all. Moreover, whites were responsible for having passed and maintained the law; its historical origins went back to the days of slavery.[109]

The fact that the Court in *Loving* used both anti-classification and anti-subordination reasoning suggests that there was not yet a

---

[106]   *See, e.g.*, Railway Express Agency, Inc. v. New York, 336 U.S. 106 (1949); Williamson v. Lee Optical, 348 U.S. 483 (1955); New Orleans v. Dukes, 427 U.S. 297 (1976); New York Transit Authority v. Beazer, 440 U.S. 568 (1979); U.S. Railroad Retirement Board v. Fitz, 449 U.S. 166 (1980); FCC v. Beach Communications, 508 U.S. 307 (1993).

[107]   *See* Romer v. Evans, 517 U.S. 620 (1996) (animus against gay people); Cleburne v. Cleburne Living Center, Inc., 473 U.S. 432 (1985) (animus against mentally disabled); United States Dep't of Agriculture v. Moreno, 413 U.S. 528 (1973) (animus against "hippies").

[108]   *Loving*, 388 U.S. at 7, 11.

[109]   *See id.* at 4–7.

consciousness of the distinction between the two. Still, *Loving* is the modern origin of the suspect classification doctrine for racial classifications. The Court in *McLaughlin* and *Loving* became drawn to talking in terms of the harms of racial classifications, as opposed to the harms of racial subordination, as a "cooler," less provocative way of talking about the unconstitutionality of practices of racial subordination.[110] Instead of emphasizing that state action had the purpose, effect, or social meaning of harming African Americans in particular, the Court could instead emphasize that the conduct at issue was unconstitutional because it treated individuals disadvantageously on the basis of the color of their skin, a harm that could be suffered more widely. "Over the years[!]," the Court wrote, "this Court has consistently repudiated '[d]istinctions between citizens solely because of their ancestry' as being 'odious to a free people whose institutions are founded upon the doctrine of equality.' "[111] "We have consistently[!] denied the constitutionality of measures which restrict the rights of citizens on account of race," the Court added.[112]

One last point about *Loving* is worthy of observation: the Supreme Court of Appeals of Virginia had invoked federalism in defending the constitutionality of the law. Specifically, the court argued that marriage is a traditional subject of state regulation and so should be left to the states to regulate under the Tenth Amendment.[113] *Loving* illustrates how the force of federalism arguments changes over time as views towards particular issues change. *Loving* became a key precedent in debates over the constitutionality of state prohibitions on same-sex marriage, which we will discuss in Chapter 12.

One last case is especially worthy of mention in this section. In *Palmore v. Sidoti*,[114] in 1984, the Court reviewed the constitutionality of the action of a Florida court, which divested a white mother of custody of her child just because she cohabitated with and later remarried a black man. The state court reasoned that, given societal prejudice against inter-racial couples, the child would be better off with the father. This was an easy case for a Court that was prepared to subject racial classifications to strict scrutiny. The Supreme Court reversed, emphasizing that, while private bias may be beyond the reach of the Constitution, the government may not validate such bias by invoking it as a justification for governmental decisionmaking. This so-called

---

[110]   Siegel, *supra* note 49, at 1476, 1497–1505.

[111]   *Loving*, 388 U.S. at 11 (quoting Hirabayashi v. United States, 320 U.S. 81 (1943)).

[112]   *Id.* at 11–12.

[113]   *See id.* at 7 ("The court also reasoned that marriage has traditionally been subject to state regulation without federal intervention, and, consequently, the regulation of marriage should be left to exclusive state control by the Tenth Amendment.").

[114]   466 U.S. 429 (1984).

Palmore principle applies broadly, although it is worth thinking about whether *Brown II* is entirely consistent with it.

Palmore reflects another constitutional principle that has long been established: laws (like those regulating child custody determinations by judges) that do not overtly classify on the basis of race may violate the Equal Protection Clause if they are administered in a race-dependent manner. *Yick Wo v. Hopkins*,[115] decided nearly a century earlier, also reflects this principle. In that case, the Court invalidated racially discriminatory denials of permits to operate laundries in wooden buildings. There was nothing facially discriminatory about the law regulating the issuance of permits. The problem was that government officials denied permits to more than 200 Chinese applicants and granted them to all but one non-Chinese applicants.

F.   Disparate Impact

We move now from developments in constitutional law during the late 1960s to pivotal developments in the Court's treatment of race cases during the mid-to-late-1970s. The potential conflict between anti-classification and anti-subordination perspectives first emerged in constitutional debates over the following question: when is a law that is facially neutral with respect to race treated as a racial classification? In other words, when do facially race-neutral laws entail discrimination on the basis of race? The question matters because only racial classifications trigger strict scrutiny; laws that are viewed as race-neutral trigger only rational basis review.

Many laws are facially race neutral—they do not mention race— but they have a racially discriminatory impact. For example, imagine a city has a test to become a firefighter that is heavily weighted in favor of a multiple-choice exam instead of a field performance exam. Further imagine that racial and ethnic minorities fail the test three times more often than whites, in contrast to the outcomes in other cities that use a differently weighted exam. Should the firefighter test be subjected to deferential, rational basis review? Or should it be treated as a racial classification subject to heightened judicial scrutiny? The key difference is whether the city should have to present convincing evidence to support its use of the test. Racially disparate impacts arise in many settings, including criminal sentencing and the administration of the death penalty.[116]

Doctrinally, the specific constitutional question is whether, when a law is facially neutral with respect to race, proving the existence of a racial classification also requires proof of a discriminatory purpose, or

---

[115]   118 U.S. 356 (1886).

[116]   *See, e.g.,* McCleskey v. Kemp, 481 U.S. 279 (1987) (involving racially discriminatory impact in the administration of the death penalty).

whether a racially disparate impact alone is sufficient. In 1976, in *Washington v. Davis*,[117] the Court held that if a law is facially race neutral and has a racially discriminatory impact, there must be proof of a discriminatory purpose in order to establish a racial classification. Discriminatory impact is not enough.

This holding is now clearly established constitutional law. But in declining to read a "disparate impact" standard into the Equal Protection Clause, the Court in *Davis* parted ways with many federal courts of appeals at the time, with its own interpretation of federal employment discrimination law,[118] and with its own focus on racially identifiable effects in desegregation cases such as *Green* and *Griffin*. But since racial groups are very differently situated in society, a great many laws have a disparate racial impact, and as suggested below, the Court may have doubted its ability or authority to engage in such large-scale restructuring of society.

In *Davis*, the District of Columbia required a test to become a police officer. Statistics showed that African Americans failed the test much more often than whites. The Court held that discriminatory impact was not enough to trigger heightened scrutiny; there also had to be proof of a racially discriminatory purpose. This ruling has had enormous implications. It means that even when governmental action has a dramatically negative impact on racial minorities, the government need not offer a race-neutral explanation for this impact. Rather, the government need meet only rational basis review. This severely limits equal protection challenges to government decisions regarding, for example, residential zoning, education, child care, child support, the operation of the criminal justice system, and—in the gender context, where (as we will see) the same rules apply—sexual assault and domestic violence. For example, if a jurisdiction fails to take claims of sexual assault or domestic violence as seriously as other violent crimes, an equal protection challenge will not lie absent proof of a discriminatory purpose by the government against female victims of sexual assault or domestic violence. It is very difficult to discover such evidence even when it exists, and it often does not.

Davis held that a discriminatory purpose is required to make out the existence of a racial classification, but it did not explain what a discriminatory purpose is. In American law, there are generally two different definitions of "purpose," depending on the area of law. In tort law, another core course during the first year of law school, the term " "intent" includes knowledge of the consequences of one's actions. In tort, one intends the consequences that would almost certainly result. This is the conception of "purpose" that Justice Stevens expressed in his concurrence in

---

[117]   426 U.S. 229 (1976).

[118]   Griggs v. Duke Power Co., 401 U.S. 424 (1971).

Davis.[119] By contrast, in criminal law (also a core first-year course), the term "purpose" or "intent" means a desire to bring about the relevant consequences. In the Model Penal Code, for example, a person acts "purposely" with respect to the result of her actions if the actor's "conscious object" is to cause such a result.[120]

Three years after *Davis*, the Court in *Personnel Administrator v. Feeney*[121] chose the more restrictive, criminal law definition. *Feeney* was a sex discrimination case involving a preference for veterans in the context of government employment, which had a significant disparate impact on women (few or whom are veterans). But the same principle applies with regard to claims of race discrimination. The Court held that intent requires more than knowledge of consequences; intent is based on the desire to bring about these consequences:

> "Discriminatory purpose" . . . implies more than intent as volition or intent as awareness of consequences. It implies that the decisionmaker . . . selected or reaffirmed a particular course of action at least in part "because of," not merely "in spite of," its adverse effects upon an identifiable group.[122]

Requiring a specific intent to harm, which remains the legal requirement today, makes it extraordinarily difficult for racial and ethnic minorities to prevail in equal protection cases involving discriminatory impacts.

The question raised by *Feeney* is why the Equal Protection Clause should require the most stringent test of purpose known to American law—namely, a specific intent to harm members of a racial group. The issue, in other words, is why a state actor's acting with full knowledge of the consequences of his actions to a historically disadvantaged group should not suffice to trigger a burden of justification from the government. Such knowledge, critics of the Court's doctrine argue, should be sufficient to raise a rebuttable presumption that the act is unlawful.

In *Village of Arlington Heights v. Metropolitan Housing Development Corporation*,[123] the Court offered guidance regarding what constitutes evidence of discriminatory purpose. First, the Court deemed relevant statistical proof so clear as to leave no other explanation. As

---

[119] *Davis*, 426 U.S. at 253 (Stevens, J., concurring) ("Frequently the most probative evidence of intent will be objective evidence of what actually happened rather than evidence describing the subjective state of mind of the actor. For normally the actor is presumed to have intended the natural consequences of his deeds.").

[120] M.P.C. § 2.02(2)(a)(i).

[121] 442 U.S. 256 (1979).

[122] *Id.* at 279 (citation and footnotes omitted).

[123] 429 U.S. 252 (1977).

examples, the Court used *Yick Wo* and *Gomillion v. Lightfoot*,[124] which involved the redrawing of legislative districts in absurdly misshaped ways to disenfranchise African Americans. But the Court in *Arlington Heights* indicated that such cases are rare, and are they ever! Second, the Court identified the historical background of a governmental decision—that is, governmental actions taken in a setting in which the racially discriminatory purpose is evident from the context. Imagine, for example, a government moved to privatize a public park just after a court ordered the government to desegregate the park. Third, the Court emphasized the legislative or administrative history of a law or regulation, which may reveal a racially discriminatory purpose. An example is *Hunter v. Underwood*.[125] The Court held in this 1985 case that a law excluding people with certain criminal convictions from voting was based on a racially discriminatory purpose, given the evidence in the legislative history. Three additional factors mentioned by the Court are the sequence of events leading up to the challenged decision; departures from the normal procedural sequence; and substantive departures in which the factors usually considered important by the decisionmaker strongly favor a decision contrary to the one reached.

The Court has acknowledged that there are often multiple purposes behind a challenged governmental action. In recognition of this fact, the Court in *Arlington Heights* established a complex burden-shifting framework. First, the challenger must show evidence of the type that we just discussed—that is, he or she must make out a *prima facie* case of racial discrimination. Specifically, the challenger must show that race was "a motivating factor in the decision."[126] If (but only if) the challenger makes such a showing, the burden then shifts to the government to show that it would have taken the same action anyway. The court then decides if the government would have taken the same action anyway. If the court decides that the answer is yes, then there is no discriminatory purpose. If the court decides that the answer is no, the court holds that there *is* a discriminatory purpose.[127]

If the court concludes that there is a discriminatory purpose, a racial classification exists and, technically, strict scrutiny is then applied. But in practice the law will always then be held unconstitutional. Strict scrutiny requires a compelling purpose and the reviewing court has already found that the purpose is, at least in significant part, to harm racial minorities, which by definition is not even legitimate, let alone compelling. If the court concludes that there is

---

[124]   364 U.S. 339 (1960).

[125]   471 U.S. 222 (1985).

[126]   *Arlington Heights*, 429 U.S. at 265–66.

[127]   This is the framework used when criminal defendants allege that prosecutors have struck potential jurors on the basis of race. *See* Batson v. Kentucky, 476 U.S. 79 (1986).

no discriminatory purpose, the court applies only rational basis review (and the government wins).

Commentators have debated whether a racially discriminatory impact ought to be enough to establish the existence of a racial classification. From an anti-classification perspective, the answer is no; a racially discriminatory purpose is part of the very definition of equal protection, as the Court emphasized in *Davis*.[128] On this formal view of equality, equal protection means no disparate treatment of similarly situated individuals by government. In addition to this argument from constitutional principle, race conservatives argue that too many laws would be vulnerable to challenge if a discriminatory impact were sufficient, and the courts would constantly be in the business of closely examining them. This defense of existing doctrine sounds in social policy and institutional concerns about the scope of judicial intervention. The Court in *Davis* voiced these concerns toward the end of the majority opinion.[129] (Critics call such concerns a fear of too much justice.) One can also defend the doctrine as vindicating values associated with judicial restraint and deference to democratic decisionmaking, as well as serving federalism values.

By contrast, from an anti-subordination perspective, discriminatory impact ought to be enough to establish a racial classification; a racially discriminatory impact that is not justified by weighty governmental interests constitutes part of the definition/understanding of equal protection. On this substantive view of equality, the key question is whether the government is reinforcing the inferior social status of historically subordinated groups, not whether government is intentionally treating individuals differently on the basis of race. The government can be reinforcing the inferior social status of historically subordinated groups even when it is not doing so intentionally. For race liberals, callous disregard of the racially identifiable consequences of governmental action ought to be enough to require the government to justify its actions. For example, Professor Reva Siegel has argued that requiring governments to justify actions that have a racially discriminatory impact would force them to acknowledge and justify the racial effects of their decisions and their harmful impacts on minority communities, rather than permitting courts to defer to their

---

[128]   *See Davis*, 426 U.S. at 239 ("The central purpose of the Equal Protection Clause of the Fourteenth Amendment is the prevention of official conduct discriminating on the basis of race.").

[129]   *See id.* at 248:

> A rule that a statute designed to serve neutral ends is nevertheless invalid, absent compelling justification, if in practice it benefits or burdens one race more than another would be far reaching and would raise serious questions about, and perhaps invalidate, a whole range of tax, welfare, public service, regulatory, and licensing statutes that may be more burdensome to the poor and to the average black than to the more affluent white.

judgments as ordinary, nondiscriminatory legislation, which easily survives rational basis review.[130]

In addition to this argument from constitutional principle, race liberals argue that it is typically very difficult to prove the existence of a discrimination purpose, even when one exists. They also argue that discriminatory impact may be at least the partial result of past racism, a problem that anti-subordination scholars call "structural discrimination."

Davis and *Feeney*, unlike *Brown* and *Loving*, illustrate that the anti-classification and anti-subordination principles are distinct perspectives. They compel different answers to the question of whether an unjustified racially disparate impact is constitutionally significant under the Equal Protection Clause.

G. Affirmative Action

The issue of affirmative action is a heated, controversial one, including among undergraduates and law students. Today, the term "affirmative action" refers to the use by government or private institutions of racial classifications to help members of certain racial and ethnic minority groups gain better access to programs or institutions with competitive selection processes that implicate conventional conceptions of merit.

The term "affirmative action" was first used by Democratic Presidents John F. Kennedy and Lyndon Johnson in executive orders that sought to eliminate the enduring effects of past racial discrimination.[131] Affirmative action was originally justified primarily on remedial grounds, not in terms of diversity or other rationales. The Republican Nixon Administration advocated affirmative action in the contexts of employment and government contracting. Matters became substantially more controversial, however, when the issue of affirmative action arose in the context of access to higher education.

The Court took a long and somewhat circuitous path to the doctrinal conclusion that all uses of racial classifications, including in affirmative action programs, trigger strict scrutiny. The Justices responsible for crafting this rule of law were mostly appointed (Sandra Day O'Connor, Antonin Scalia, Anthony Kennedy, and Clarence Thomas) or elevated to Chief Justice (William Rehnquist) during twelve straight years of Republican control of the White

---

[130]   *See generally* Reva B. Siegel, *Why Equal Protection No Longer Protects: The Evolving Forms of Status-Enforcing State Action*, 49 STAN. L. REV. 1111 (1997).

[131]   *See generally, e.g.,* James E. Jones, Jr., *The Origins of Affirmative Action*, 21 U.C. DAVIS L. REV. 383 (1988); Carl E. Brody, Jr., *A Historical Review of Affirmative Action and the Interpretation of Its Legislative Intent by the Supreme Court*, 29 AKRON L. REV. 291 (1996).

House. These Justices moved constitutional law in a racially conservative direction. The Court's decisions have arisen mostly in the contexts of government contracting and higher education.[132] The government contracting cases are *Fullilove v. Klutznick* (1980),[133] *City of Richmond v. J.A. Croson Company* (1988),[134] and *Adarand v. Peña* (1995).[135] The higher education cases are *Regents of the University of California v. Bakke* (1978),[136] *Grutter v. Bollinger* (2003),[137] *Gratz v. Bollinger* (2003),[138] and *Fisher v. University of Texas at Austin* (2013 and 2016).[139]

We will not march through each of these decisions, some of which are no longer good law (*Metro Broadcasting* and, in all likelihood, *Fullilove*), and others of which are likely to be revisited in the years ahead (the higher education decisions) now that Justice Brett Kavanaugh has replaced Justice Kennedy. Instead, we will first analyze the basic issue of affirmative action from anti-classification and anti-subordination perspectives. We will then focus on affirmative action in higher education, a context in which the race moderates on the Court have, for decades now, followed neither a strict anti-classification approach nor a strict anti-subordination approach, but rather a third perspective that seeks to carve out something resembling a middle ground.

From an anti-classification perspective, affirmative action is characteristically viewed as constitutionally suspect. To repeat, the anti-classification principle is premised on the belief that the Constitution protects individuals, not racial groups, and so bars racial classifications except as a remedy for specific unconstitutional

---

[132]   Two decisions arose in other settings. *See* Wygant v. Jackson Bd. of Educ., 476 U.S. 267 (1986) (holding that the Equal Protection Clause prohibits a school board from extending preferential protection against layoffs to employees who are racial minorities); Metro Broadcasting, Inc. v. FCC, 497 U.S. 547 (1990) (holding that intermediate scrutiny applies to federal affirmative action programs and upholding a federal affirmative action program that sought to enhance broadcast diversity).

[133]   448 U.S. 448 (1980) (upholding a federal program involving a ten percent set-aside for minority-owned businesses without a majority opinion on the level of scrutiny).

[134]   488 U.S. 469 (1989) (holding that strict scrutiny applies to affirmative action programs used by state and local governments and invalidating Richmond's thirty percent set-aside of public works money for minority-owned businesses).

[135]   515 U.S. 200 (1995) (overruling *Metro Broadcasting* and holding that strict scrutiny applies to all affirmative action programs regardless of the level of government responsible for the program). Justice O'Connor stressed the possibility that such programs could survive strict scrutiny—that strict scrutiny is not necessarily "fatal in fact." *Id.* at 237. Justice Scalia rejected this suggestion. *Id.* at 239 (Scalia, J., concurring in part and concurring in the judgment). Their disagreement made a difference in *Grutter*, which is discussed below.

[136]   438 U.S. 265 (1978).

[137]   539 U.S. 306 (2003).

[138]   539 U.S. 244 (2003).

[139]   579 U.S. ___, 136 S. Ct. 2198 (2016) (*Fisher II*); 570 U.S. 297 (2013) (*Fisher I*).

conduct. Race conservatives wield the anti-classification principle to insist upon applying strict scrutiny to all racial classifications. They would invalidate affirmative action programs on the ground that the law should not discriminate between individuals on the basis of race. Strikingly, originalism plays little or no role in constitutional arguments against affirmative action.

From an anti-subordination perspective, affirmative action is not generally viewed as constitutionally suspect. The anti-subordination principle identifies the racial stratification of American society and institutions, not racial classification, as the constitutional wrong and seeks to ameliorate the inequalities among racial and ethnic groups that have been caused by both race-based and race-salient policies. From an anti-subordination perspective, the relevant question is not whether government draws a racial classification on the face of the law, but rather what are the purposes, effects, and dominant social meanings of governmental conduct. Race liberals would apply intermediate scrutiny to affirmative action programs and would certainly allow (some might require) government to remedy practices that entrench historic inequalities among racial groups. So the general issue of affirmative action, like the issue of disparate impact liability and unlike the issue of racial segregation, renders it legible that these two conceptions of equality are only partially overlapping.

In addition, the general subject of affirmative action illustrates the under-determinacy of the anti-classification and anti-subordination principles. The overwhelming majority of anti-classification theorists, activists, and judges oppose affirmative action and the overwhelming majority of adherents to the anti-subordination principle defend affirmative action. But the two principles are not sufficiently determinate to simply compel a specific conclusion about the constitutionality of affirmative action, either in general or in particular situations. For example, one might defend affirmative action from an anti-classification perspective by emphasizing that what is, or is not, a racial classification is not self-identifying. More specifically, it is not obvious why using race as one of several selection criteria qualifies as a racial classification in a university admissions program but not in a criminal suspect description.[140]

Moreover, one might criticize affirmative action from an anti-subordination perspective, as Justice Thomas has. In his view, affirmative action has negative effects on its intended beneficiaries, and its dominant social meaning is to stigmatize racial and ethnic minorities by sending the message that they cannot compete

---

[140]   *See* Siegel, *supra* note 50, at 1360–65.

effectively without the help of government.[141] There are, of course, counterarguments to both this argument and the one in the prior paragraph; our point is only to illustrate that mediating principles of equality are not fully determinate, even though they are less indeterminate than the bare text of the Equal Protection Clause.

Historically and today, controversy over affirmative action has been most visible in the context of university admissions, perhaps because of the perception of high stakes and scarce resources. The Court has repeatedly said that the same level of scrutiny—strict—applies in the university setting as in others, but it is unlikely that this has been the case in practice. Like Justice Lewis Powell in *Bakke*,[142] the Court in *Grutter, Gratz, Fisher I,* and *Fisher II* declared that the use of racial classifications in an affirmative action admissions program triggers strict scrutiny because of the harms to individuals and the social divisiveness caused by racial classifications. In a case like *Loving*, however, strict scrutiny meant that there was a strong presumption of unconstitutionality, the government received no deference from the Court, and the use of race was unconstitutional. In the higher education cases, however, strict scrutiny has meant something quite different.

In *Bakke*, the race moderate Justice Powell articulated the "diversity" rationale for affirmative action; his decisive, solo opinion in this case is the origin of the diversity rationale in both constitutional politics and constitutional law. He rejected the argument of the California Regents that its affirmative action admissions program at U.C. Davis Medical School, which set aside sixteen spots in a class of one hundred for members of certain racial and ethnic minority groups, was justified as a remedy for past "societal discrimination."[143] But Justice Powell articulated another interest that he said survived strict scrutiny. In his view, universities had a compelling interest in taking the race and ethnicity of applicants into consideration in order to secure the educational benefits produced by a student body that is diverse along many dimensions, including race and ethnicity. In particular, Justice Powell focused on the "academic freedom" of universities to choose a student body that would ensure " 'wide exposure' to the ideas and

---

[141]   *See, e.g., Grutter*, 539 U.S. at 373 (Thomas, J., dissenting) ("When blacks take positions in the highest places of government, industry, or academia, it is an open question today whether their skin color played a part in their advancement. The question itself is the stigma . . . .").

[142]   *See Bakke*, 438 U.S. at 287–91 (opinion of Powell, J.). Justice Powell wrote for himself alone in *Bakke*. Four other Justices (William Brennan, Byron White, Thurgood Marshall, and Harry Blackmun) would have applied intermediate scrutiny and upheld the program. The remaining four Justices (Warren Burger, Potter Stewart, William Rehnquist, and John Paul Stevens) would have held that the program violated Title VI of the Civil Rights Act of 1964.

[143]   *Id.* at 307–10.

mores of students as diverse as this Nation of many peoples."[144] He thus developed a rationale for affirmative action in higher education that would allow universities to fulfill their "mission" of selecting "those students who will contribute the most to the 'robust exchange of ideas.' "[145]

Twenty-five years later, the Court in *Grutter*, in a majority opinion written by the race moderate Justice O'Connor, reaffirmed that the educational benefits of a diverse student body—including, especially, a racially and ethnically diverse student body—qualified as a compelling interest sufficient to survive strict scrutiny.[146] (Whether there are such benefits is a question that is debated by judges, legal scholars, and social scientists.) Unlike Justice Powell, however, who stressed the contribution of diversity to the robust exchange of ideas within the classroom, Justice O'Connor placed greater emphasis on racial and ethnic diversity in particular and its contribution to preparing students for work as professionals, citizens, and leaders in a multi-racial and multi-ethnic society.[147] For example, she wrote that elite law schools like the one at the University of Michigan train "our Nation's leaders," a cadre that possesses "legitimacy in the eyes of the citizenry" only insofar as "the path to leadership [is] visibly open to talented and qualified individuals of every race and ethnicity."[148]

Notably, in evaluating the program at issue, Justice O'Connor presumed "good faith" on the part of the University of Michigan Law School,[149] which seems inconsistent with a presumption of unconstitutionality. More specifically, the Court deferred to the University's judgment that racial and ethnic diversity was essential to its educational mission, and also deferred to the University's judgment that it required a "critical mass" of underrepresented minority students in order to further its mission.[150] It seems as if the

---

[144]   *Id.* at 312–13 (quoting Keyishian v. Board of Regents, 385 U.S. 589, 603 (1967)).

[145]   *Id.* at 313 (quoting *Keyishian*, 385 U.S. at 603).

[146]   In terms of what the University of Michigan Law School was actually seeking in *Grutter*, closer to the mark is an interest in a racially diverse and academically elite student body. Otherwise, the law school likely would not have needed to use racial classifications; it could have instead lowered the test scores and grade point averages required in order to obtain admission and then used a lottery system, as Justice Thomas emphasized in his dissent in *Grutter*. *See* 539 U.S. at 355–56 (Thomas, J., dissenting). The law school presumably did not take this approach because it did not want to compromise its academically elite status, and the Court insisted that it did not have to choose between these two goals. *See id.* at 340 (majority opinion).

[147]   *See id.* at 316, 330–33.

[148]   *Id.* at 332.

[149]   *Id.* at 329.

[150]   *See id.* at 329–30, 333.

Court applied strict-scrutiny-light—that is, a less exacting form of strict scrutiny than it applied in cases like *Loving*.

If this conclusion is correct—and commentators have debated the point—it follows either that the admissions programs at issue in *Bakke* and *Grutter* were likely unconstitutional under *Loving*-style strict scrutiny, or that *Loving*-style strict scrutiny is inappropriate for reasons that Justices Powell and O'Connor never articulated. Other Justices did articulate such a rationale in arguing for intermediate scrutiny when government acts to integrate members of traditionally excluded racial and ethnic groups into institutions from which they were historically excluded.[151] Perhaps Justice O'Connor did not simply and straightforwardly apply intermediate scrutiny because she had rejected it in multiple previous cases and she was unwilling or unable to explain why higher education is different from, say, government contracting. In *Croson*, for example, she wrote that "[c]lassifications based on race carry a danger of stigmatic harm. Unless they are strictly reserved for remedial settings, they may in fact promote notions of racial inferiority and lead to a politics of racial hostility."[152] In *Grutter*, she instead arguably changed the previously accepted understanding of strict scrutiny, as another race moderate, Justice Powell, had done before her.

Indeed, despite Justice O'Connor's rejection of using racial classifications to remedy societal discrimination against members of certain racial and ethnic minority groups, remedial logic appeared at several points in both the admissions program itself and her majority opinion in *Grutter* upholding it. As for the admissions program, the racial and ethnic minorities who benefited from it—African Americans, Latinos, and Native Americans—were both historically excluded from such opportunities and would not be represented in meaningful numbers without the existence of the program. Moreover, the differences in the number of members of each minority group admitted seemed to track the differences in their representation in the applicant pool much more closely than they tracked the differences that would be commended by the pursuit of diversity and "critical mass."[153] For example, from the perspective of achieving diversity and critical mass, it is not clear why the University would admit so many more African Americans than Native Americans (91 to 108 from 1995 through 2000 versus 13 to 19). The dissenters

---

[151] *See, e.g.*, Gratz v. Bollinger, 539 U.S. 244, 301 (Ginsburg, J., concurring) ("Actions designed to burden groups long denied full citizenship stature are not sensibly ranked with measures taken to hasten the day when entrenched discrimination and its aftereffects have been extirpated.").

[152] *Croson*, 488 U.S. at 493 (plurality opinion of O'Connor, J.).

[153] *See Grutter*, 539 U.S. at 381–86 (Rehnquist, C.J., dissenting).

emphasized this point in arguing that Michigan Law School was actually engaged in "race balancing," which is "patently unconstitutional."[154]

Turning to the majority opinion, Justice O'Connor referred to "a society, like our own, in which race unfortunately still matters."[155] She also emphasized "our Nation's struggle with racial inequality."[156] And she announced an expectation at the end of her majority opinion that affirmative action would no longer be necessary in another twenty-five years.[157] This does not necessarily make sense if the interest is diversity; it makes more sense if the interest is remedial, because remedies come to an end when the victim has been made whole. So perhaps the Court in *Grutter*, like Justice Powell in *Bakke*, was, to a greater extent than it was admitting, in effect applying intermediate scrutiny, permitting universities to remedy societal discrimination, and vindicating anti-subordination values.

Matters get even more curious when one turns from the compelling interest prong of strict scrutiny to the narrow tailoring prong. In order to survive strict scrutiny, a university's use of race not only must advance a compelling governmental interest, but also must be narrowly tailored to advance this interest. In *Grutter*, the Court quoted *Croson*: "The purpose of the narrow tailoring requirement is to ensure that 'the means chosen 'fit' th[e] compelling goal so closely that there is little or no possibility that the motive for the classification was illegitimate racial prejudice or stereotype.' "[158] The Court made clear that there are four components of a narrowly tailored affirmative action program: (1) affording candidates individualized consideration instead of imposing racial quotas; (2) avoiding the imposition of an undue burden on applicants who are not the intended beneficiaries of the affirmative action program; (3) considering race-neutral alternatives; and (4) imposing time limits.

In *Grutter* and the companion case of *Gratz*, which involved a challenge to the constitutionality of the University of Michigan undergraduate admissions program, the requirement of individualized consideration did the dispositive work. Although the Court allowed the University to pursue a race-conscious end (the educational benefits of racial and ethnic diversity), it did not allow the means used by the University to be straightforwardly race-conscious. Like Justice Powell in *Bakke*, who approved the use of race as a "plus" factor in evaluating the applications of members of certain

---

154   *Id.* at 386.

155   *Id.* at 333 (majority opinion).

156   *Id.* at 338.

157   *See id.* at 343.

158   *Id.* at 333 (quoting *Croson*, 488 U.S. at 493 (plurality opinion)).

minority groups but prohibited the use of racial set asides (also called quotas) for members of such groups, the Court permitted Michigan Law School to use race as a "plus" factor but prohibited the undergraduate college from assigning certain minority applicants twenty points (out of a total of one hundred required for admission) on the basis of their race or ethnicity.

The question that has divided courts and commentators is whether there is a difference in *reality* between these different uses of race, or whether it is mostly a potential difference in *appearance*. Justices Powell and O'Connor insisted that there was a difference in reality. Concurring in *Gratz*, Justice O'Connor emphasized the distinction between individualized consideration, in which race or ethnicity is one among a number of different kinds of diversity, and "a nonindividualized, mechanical" system, which was impermissible.[159] The difficulty with this position is that a quota can be a flexible range, not a set number, and anything a university can accomplish with a quota it can also do with a plus factor as long as the size of the plus is set with an eye towards what the racial and ethnic composition of the class should be.[160] Justice Powell in *Bakke* said that universities can pay "some attention to the numbers,"[161] and the Court in *Grutter* agreed.[162] There is not necessarily more "individualized consideration" in one case than the other. Perhaps the primary purpose of the narrow tailoring requirement in *Bakke*, *Grutter*, and *Gratz* was other than what the Court said it was.

Put differently, it seems unlikely that either the anti-classification principle or the anti-subordination principle can persuasively explain the differences in treatment accorded the program upheld in *Grutter* (i.e., use of race as a plus factor) and the program struck down in *Gratz* (i.e., use of twenty points for racial or ethnic minority status). The anti-classification principle presumptively condemns racial quotas, the use of race as a plus factor, and the awarding of twenty points. The anti-subordination principle presumptively allows all of them. So maybe a third mediating principle of equality is required to explain these decisions.

As noted, Justice Powell and O'Connor were race moderates. They both allowed and limited affirmative action in higher education in order to promote social cohesion—to prevent racial balkanization, which is a situation in which members of different racial and ethnic groups identify primarily as members of their own racial or ethnic

---

[159]   *Gratz*, 539 U.S. at 280 (O'Connor, J., concurring).

[160]   For a masterful discussion, see generally Paul J. Mishkin, *The Uses of Ambivalence: Reflections on the Supreme Court and the Constitutionality of Affirmative Action*, 131 U. PENN. L. REV. 907 (1983).

[161]   *Bakke*, 438 U.S. at 323 (opinion of Powell, J.).

[162]   *See Grutter*, 539 U.S. at 336.

groups and view members of other racial or ethnic groups with hostility and distrust.[163] Justice Powell and O'Connor sought a middle ground between the anti-classification and anti-subordination principles. They wanted to allow government to take race into account in order to redress vast racial and ethnic inequalities after hundreds of years of horrible mistreatment of members of minority groups. But they also feared that government may make matters worse, not better, if it uses race to help certain minorities in ways that unduly stimulate racial resentment in whites.

On this interpretation, Justices Powell and O'Connor followed what scholars have called the anti-balkanization principle: government may, if it chooses, act through the democratic process so as to ensure that members of no racial or ethnic group are so deeply marginalized as to feel like outsiders or non-participants in educational or economic life, so long as government seeks to reduce group marginalization "by means that do not unduly stimulate group resentment."[164] From an anti-balkanization perspective, differently designed affirmative action programs, even if they produce roughly the same net-operative results, may differentially affect pre-existing racial beliefs, both within a university community and in the broader society.

More specifically, the thought—or hope—may be that a quota or a set number of points may exacerbate racial resentment in whites in ways that a non-specified plus factor may not because the plus is less salient, less publicly visible. Applicants are considered together as part of the same applicant pool; race and ethnicity are represented as just two of numerous dimensions of diversity; and no particular numerical value is publicly associated with the plus.[165] The Court in *Grutter* and *Gratz*—that is, Justices O'Connor and Breyer, who were the only Justices in the majority in both cases—seemed concerned not just to determine the constitutionality of affirmative action in higher education, but to influence the form it would take so that it would have the best chance of surviving politically in a world in which the Court does not have the last word. It turned out, however, that voters in Michigan ended affirmative action by popular initiative anyway.[166]

---

[163]   For a discussion, see generally Siegel, *supra* note 101.

[164]   Siegel, *supra* note 50, at 1284.

[165]   For discussions, see Mishkin, *supra* note 160, at 927–29; Robert C. Post, *The Supreme Court, 2002 Term—Foreword: Fashioning the Legal Constitution: Culture, Courts, and Law*, 117 HARV. L. REV. 4, 74–76 (2003); Siegel, *supra* note 101, at 790–800.

[166]   The Supreme Court upheld the constitutionality of the ballot initiative in *Schuette v. Coalition to Defend Affirmative Action*, 572 U.S. 291 (2014), rejecting the argument that the initiative itself violated equal protection.

If this interpretation is correct—and again, commentators disagree—there is much that it is controversial about such behavior by pivotal Justices. Justices Powell and O'Connor stated that their analysis turned on individualized consideration, not the potential for differently designed programs to exacerbate racial balkanization, perhaps because of concerns that full judicial transparency would be self-undermining.[167] It is also controversial for the Court to have effectively decided that the constitutionality of an affirmative action admissions program turns on a lack of transparency by universities when transparency is a core virtue of the rule of law.

The composition of the Court changed significantly in 2006, when Justice O'Connor was replaced by Justice Samuel Alito (after Chief Justice Rehnquist had been replaced by Chief Justice Roberts). One consequence was that Justice Kennedy, who had dissented in *Grutter* on relatively narrow grounds, moved to the center seat on the Court (i.e., he became the median Justice) on questions of racial equality. In *Fisher I* and *Fisher II*, the Roberts Court considered the constitutionality of the affirmative action admissions program at the University of Texas at Austin, which was structured like a layer cake. Roughly eighty percent of the class was admitted through the Texas Top Ten Percent Law, which guaranteed admission to Texas students who graduated in roughly the top ten percent of their high school class. The remaining twenty percent of the entering class was admitted through a *Grutter*-type "holistic review" affirmative action program, which used race as a plus factor. Only the holistic review portion of the program was at issue in the *Fisher* litigation.

In *Fisher I*,[168] Justice Kennedy wrote an obvious compromise majority opinion for eight Justices (only Justice Ginsburg dissented). The Court held that, in upholding the holistic review component of the program, the Fifth Circuit did not apply strict scrutiny as required by *Grutter*, particularly regarding whether the program was narrowly tailored, and more particularly whether there were adequate race-neutral alternatives. This holding appeared to reflect the Court's increasing race conservatism, given that the requirement to consider race-neutral alternatives was not a demanding one in *Grutter*; the University of Texas had afforded individualized consideration as required by *Grutter*; and the University used racial classifications much less extensively than in *Grutter*.

On remand, the court of appeals again upheld the program. It reasoned in part that holistic review allows for consideration of a much wider range of elements of diversity, including within groups of applicants of a given race or ethnicity, than does the Top Ten

---

[167]   *See* Mishkin, *supra* note 160, at 928.

[168]   570 U.S. 297 (2013).

Percent Law, which considers only high school class rank.[169] When the Court granted review again, it was widely expected that it would reverse and strike down the holistic review part of the program.

This is not, however, what happened. In a majority opinion written by Justice Kennedy and joined by Justices Ginsburg, Breyer, and Sonia Sotomayor (Justice Elena Kagan was recused), the Court held by of vote of 4 to 3 that the University had met the narrow tailoring requirement of strict scrutiny.[170] This was the first time that Justice Kennedy had ever voted to uphold an affirmative action program, and his surprising vote and opinion triggered widespread speculation among commentators regarding why he had had an apparent change of heart toward the end of his tenure on the Court. Justice Kennedy reasoned that the University made very modest use of racial classifications, and that the Texas Top Ten Percent Law was neither race-neutral nor a sufficient alternative to holistic review and in fact conflicted with the objective of attaining a genuinely diverse student body. So by the end of his career, Justice Kennedy had become less of a race conservative and more of a race moderate like Justices Powell and O'Connor before him. *Grutter* and *Fisher I* were left in place.

Justice Alito, joined by Chief Justice Roberts and Justice Thomas (Justice Scalia had passed away and had not yet been replaced), dissented in *Fisher II* in an opinion that was two-and-a-half times longer than the majority opinion.[171] He also read his dissent from the bench, a sign of vigorous disagreement. Among other things, Justice Alito emphasized that the University's plan defied judicial review because the University had refused to define with specificity the interests that its use of race and ethnicity were supposed to serve. (The University presumably did not define critical mass with numerical precision because as soon as it did so, the Court's race conservatives would have voted to strike it down as a racial quota.) Justice Alito also argued that the program benefited affluent African American students at the expense of impoverished students and Asian American students, despite a long history of discrimination against Asian Americans. The asserted harm that affirmative action causes to Asian Americans is a major theme of pending litigation involving the admissions program at Harvard University.[172] With Justice Kennedy's retirement and replacement

---

[169]   758 F.3d 633, 653 (5th Cir. 2014).

[170]   579 U.S. ___, 136 S. Ct. 2198 (2016).

[171]   *See id.* at 2215–43 (Alito, J., dissenting).

[172]   *See, e.g.*, Anemona Hartocollis, *Does Harvard Admissions Discriminate? The Lawsuit on Affirmative Action, Explained*, N.Y. TIMES (Oct. 15, 2018), https://www.nytimes.com/2018/10/15/us/harvard-affirmative-action-asian-americans.html ("The plaintiffs accuse Harvard of effectively setting a restrictive quota for the number of Asian-American students its accepts, a claim the university denies.").

by Justice Kavanaugh, we expect the Court in the years ahead to invalidate affirmative action programs, including affirmative action admissions programs.

II. Gender and the Constitution

Our discussion of gender equality and the Constitution begins with history and then turns to modern social movements and equal protection doctrine. There was a long history of discrimination against, and subordination of, women in the United States that was tolerated under the Constitution. For most of American history, women in key respects were not part of "the People" for whom the Constitution purported to speak. The Supreme Court did not begin to understand the Equal Protection Clause to protect women until the 1970s, in response to the demands of the women's movement for gender equality in economic, educational, and political life. The modern Court has accepted the claims of the women's movement to a significant, albeit incomplete, extent.

A. History

During the early decades of the American republic under the Constitution, women were regarded as citizens, but they were not permitted to vote. Voting was generally limited to propertied white men on the ground that people should be permitted to vote only if they possess enough independence to exercise the franchise responsibly. Women thought to lack independent political judgment because their vote would be controlled by the people of property upon whom they depended for subsistence—namely, their husbands.[173]

The common law understood the relationship between husband and wife as falling within the realm of "domestic relations." According to the common law rules of coverture (or marital status), a husband was entitled to the labor of his wife, whether paid or uncompensated, as well as to most of the property that she brought into the marriage. A wife was required to obey her husband, and he was required to support her and represent her in the legal system. Wives were prohibited from suing in court or making contracts without the approval of their husbands. Husbands were legally liable for much of the conduct of their wives. The common law entertained the legal fiction of marital unity, so that a woman's legal existence was " 'suspended during marriage.' "[174]

During the Early National Era, which spanned 1791 to 1828, Americans became committed to the idea of "separate spheres" for men and women. The ideology of the separate spheres was the commitment

---

[173]   *See generally* Reva B. Siegel, *Collective Memory and the Nineteenth Amendment: Reasoning About "the Woman Question" in the Discourse of Sex Discrimination, in* HISTORY MEMORY, AND THE LAW 131–82 (Austin Sarat & Thomas R. Kearns eds., 1999).

[174]   BREST ET AL., *supra* note 64, at 186 (quoting 1 WILLIAM BLACKSTONE, COMMENTARIES 430 (1765)).

to a regime in which women were destined for work within the home (raising children and maintaining a household), while men were destined for the world of public affairs (educational, economic, and political life). Note the relationship between restrictions on voting and the position of women in the family and in society: possessing the right to vote meant possessing a superior status in one's family and thus society. Lacking the right to vote meant a subordinate status in a family and society. In other words, voting restrictions were regulations based upon social status.[175] This hierarchical regime co-existed with the ideology of liberty and equality associated with the American Revolution, which Abigail Adams would famously invoke in her correspondence on women's rights with her husband, John Adams, in 1776.[176] There was a conventional distinction between the public sphere of citizenship and commerce on the one hand, and the private sphere of domestic relations on the other. The ideology of the Revolution, including the declaration of "no taxation without representation," was thought to govern in the public realm only, which was a realm for men only. Women were said to be "virtually represented" by their fathers or husbands.[177] Notably, the British government had argued that the American colonists were virtually represented in Parliament, a contention that the colonists vigorously disputed.[178]

During the early to mid-1800s, married women increasingly began to earn rights under state law to own property and make contracts, partly in response to the first movements for women's rights, which culminated in the first women's rights convention at Seneca Falls, New York, in July 1848. The Declaration of Sentiments adopted by the convention,[179] as well as Elizabeth Cady Stanton's Keynote Address,[180] sought to secure for women the same equal political and economic rights that radical abolitionists were then seeking for African American men. Along similar lines, women's rights advocates worked in abolitionist

---

[175]   *See id.*

[176]   *See* FAMILIAR LETTERS OF JOHN ADAMS AND HIS WIFE ABIGAIL ADAMS, DURING THE REVOLUTION 148–150, 153–55, 168–70 (Charles Francis Adams ed., 1876) (reproducing a letter from Abigail to John of March 31, 1776, John's response of April 14, 1776, and Abigail's reply of May 7, 1776).

[177]   For a discussion of American men's persistent claims for virtual representation of women, see Reva B. Siegel, *She the People: The Nineteenth Amendment, Sex Equality, Federalism, and the Family*, 115 HARV. L. REV. 947, 991–93 (2002).

[178]   For discussion of the Crown's claims for virtual representation of the American colonists, see JACK P. GREENE, THE CONSTITUTIONAL ORIGINS OF THE AMERICAN REVOLUTION 67–72 (2011).

[179]   *See* Declaration of Sentiments and Resolutions, Women's Rights Convention, Held at Seneca Falls (July 19–20, 1848), THE ELIZABETH CADY STANTON & SUSAN B. ANTHONY PAPERS PROJECT, http://ecssba.rutgers.edu/docs/seneca.html.

[180]   Elizabeth Cady Stanton, Keynote Address, Seneca Falls Convention (July 19, 1848), https://www.greatamericandocuments.com/speeches/stanton-seneca-falls/.

organizations before the Civil War in the hope that voting rights for blacks would also mean voting rights for women.

Unfortunately, it did not work out this way in Congress. Reconstruction Republicans extended the franchise to blacks but not women, rejecting calls by such activists as Stanton and Susan B. Anthony for constitutional amendments endorsing not just racial equality, but also gender equality. They were told that "[t]his was the negro's hour."[181] Actually, the story is worse than that. The Civil War Amendments enshrined the first sex classification in the text of the Constitution.[182]

Nor was the post-Civil War Supreme Court receptive to claims of gender equality. After ratification of the Fourteenth Amendment and continuing for much of the next century, the Court permitted state action discriminating between men and women as rationally reflecting real, natural differences in the roles of men and women. In 1873, in *Bradwell v. Illinois*,[183] the Court rejected Myra Bradwell's claim that an Illinois law prohibiting women from practicing law violated the Fourteenth Amendment's Privileges or Immunities Clause. In a since-notorious concurrence, Justice Bradley read the Fourteenth Amendment in light of the common law of marital status and the ideology of separate spheres, and he invoked God as authority for the separate spheres tradition.[184] (A century later, Professor Ruth Bader Ginsburg would write of *Bradwell* in a brief that "the method of communication between the Creator and the jurist is never disclosed," and that " 'divine ordinance' has been a dominant theme in decisions justifying laws establishing sex-based classifications."[185]) Two years later, in *Minor v. Happersett*, the Court rejected Frances Minor's constitutional claim that the Privilege or Immunities Clause guaranteed women the right to vote.[186] The distinction between the public and private realms was invoked to justify prohibiting women from voting.

After the Supreme Court rejected their claims under the Fourteenth Amendment, the "suffragists"—so called because of their support for women's suffrage (voting)—sought an amendment to the

---

[181]   For a discussion, see GILLMAN ET AL., *supra* note 28, at 264–65 (quoting Editorial, *Women's Rights*, AMERICAN ANTI-SLAVERY STANDARD (Dec. 30, 1865)).

[182]   U.S. CONST. amend. XIV, § 2 (providing for a reduction in the number of representatives in any state that denies the right of "male inhabitants of such state" to vote in federal or state elections).

[183]   83 U.S. 130 (1873).

[184]   *See id.* at 141 (Bradley, J., concurring) ("The paramount destiny and mission of woman are to fulfil the noble and benign offices of wife and mother. This is the law of the Creator.").

[185]   Brief for the Petitioner at 39, Struck v. Sec'y of Def., 409 U.S. 1071 (1972) (No. 72–178), 1972 WL 135840.

[186]   88 U.S. 162 (1875).

U.S. Constitution. Suffragists understood that the subordinate status of women in the family was related to their lack of political and economic rights. They argued that in order to free women politically and economically, one had to end their inferior status in the family, a status that the law enforced.[187]

It was not until the beginning of the Twentieth Century that all of the state coverture rules were abolished and women, with the ratification of the Nineteenth Amendment in 1920, earned a federal constitutional right to vote after many decades of struggle. Before adoption of the amendment, western states, seeking to attract new residents from eastern states, offered voting rights for women as an incentive to move.[188] Support for women's suffrage (voting) grew as other Americans saw that the sky did not fall when women voted. (A similar federalism dynamic would unfold later in American history in the context of same-sex marriage, as we will discuss in Chapter 12.) President Woodrow Wilson's support, as well as the democracy rhetoric of World War I, proved pivotal in the end.[189] But the groundwork had been laid by robust practices of contestation and persuasion that spanned decades. The suffragists lost many battles before winning this particular war.

During the 1920s, some state and federal courts read the Nineteenth Amendment broadly as guaranteeing political equality for women that extended to holding public office and serving on juries.[190] But many other courts limited the Nineteenth Amendment to voting rights. By the 1930s, courts no longer viewed the Nineteenth Amendment as a constitutional source of equality rights for women, and courts routinely permitted sex classifications for the next several decades. For example, in 1948, in *Goesaert v. Cleary*,[191] the Court upheld as rational a Michigan law prohibiting women from being bartenders except in bars owned by their fathers or husbands. In 1961, in *Hoyt v. Florida*,[192] the Court upheld a Florida law allowing women (but not men) to opt out of jury service.

Feminists were undeterred. A women's movement was mobilizing, as veterans of the suffrage movement joined forces with women and men in the labor and civil rights movements, who themselves drew inspiration from the civil rights movement of the 1960s. Feminists succeeded first in the executive branch, and then in Congress. President

---

[187] For a discussion of the claims on both sides of the debate over women's suffrage, see generally Siegel, *supra* note 177.

[188] For a discussion, see AMAR, *supra* note 19, at 421–22.

[189] *See id.* at 424–25.

[190] *See* Siegel, *supra* note 173, at 158–59.

[191] 335 U.S. 464 (1948).

[192] 368 U.S. 57 (1961). *Hoyt* was not overruled until 1975, in *Taylor v. Louisiana*, 419 U.S. 522 (1975).

John F. Kennedy's Commission on the Status of Women, which began in 1961, convened feminists from around the nation to coordinate on legal and political strategies. Congress passed the Equal Pay Act of 1963, which required equal pay for equal work, and Congress also passed Title VII of the Civil Rights Act of 1964, which prohibited sex discrimination in employment. These laws committed the federal government to enforcing principles of sex equality.

In 1966, the National Organization for Women (NOW) was founded in an attempt to press the Equal Employment Opportunity Commission (EEOC), the federal agency charged with enforcing Title VII's bans on workplace discrimination, to enforce its ban on sex discrimination. (The EEOC at the time was focused on racial equality.) By the late 1960s, feminists who set their sights on the Constitution embraced a "dual strategy"[193]—both a more expansive interpretation of the Equal Protection Clause by the Supreme Court, and ratification of the Equal Rights Amendment (ERA), which would have provided that "[e]quality of rights under the law shall not be denied or abridged by the United States or by any State on account of sex." The ERA was supported by a significant majority of Americans, but it fell three states short of the thirty-eight required for ratification, in part because it became entangled in the debate over abortion, although Nevada ratified in 2017 and Illinois ratified in 2018.[194]

In response to the growing power of the women's movement in the 1970s, Congress easily passed the ERA in 1972 and sent it to the states for ratification. Congress also applied Title VII to the states; passed Title IX, which barred sex discrimination in educational programs receiving federal money; passed legislation banning sex discrimination in public- and private-sector transactions; and passed child-care legislation to alleviate conflicts between work and family.[195]

As Congress led, the Supreme Court in the 1970s began to follow. The Justices pointed to all of this legislation as they took steps toward declaring sex a "suspect" classification under the Equal Protection Clause. Notably, the Court lagged in this story much more than it led; it learned from the political branches and social movements. This story epitomizes how claims on the Constitution outside the courts (what this book calls constitutional politics) can eventually affect how the Constitution is interpreted inside the courts (what this book calls judge-made constitutional law).

---

[193]   *See* Serena Mayeri, *Constitutional Choices: Legal Feminism and the Historical Dynamics of Change*, 92 CALIF. L. REV. 755, 784–92 (2004).

[194]   *See* EQUAL RIGHTS AMENDMENT WEBSITE, http://www.equalrightsamendment. org. It is not clear at this point whether these recent ratifications count or whether the time for ratification expired years earlier.

[195]   *See* BREST ET AL., *supra* note 64, at 1381.

Something else about the constitutional politics of sex equality is noteworthy: partisan political divisions over gender roles did not exist before 1980. For example, Presidents Richard Nixon (a Republican), Gerald Ford (another Republican), and Jimmy Carter (a Democrat) all championed the ERA. It was after President Ronald Reagan's election in 1980—an election year in which the Democratic Party Platform strongly endorsed the ERA while the Republican Party Platform took no position—that the Democratic Party became seen as the party of choice for feminists and the Republican Party came to be viewed as the party of choice for more traditionalist women.

B. The Race-Sex Analogy

When they pursued constitutional litigation, feminists pushed the race-sex analogy. At a time when courts were taking racial discrimination seriously, feminists meant to persuade an overwhelmingly male judiciary that sex discrimination and race discrimination were similar forms of discrimination and warranted a similar judicial response. This was no easy task because courts at the time viewed sex discrimination as reasonably reflecting the different social roles of women and men. Pauli Murray, a hugely important African-American lawyer in the both the civil rights and women's movements, invoked the idea of "stereotypes" with which judges were already familiar in the context of the fight for racial equality. Murray argued that gender stereotypes, like racial stereotypes, harmed individuals within a given group by erasing meaningful differences between members of the group.[196]

Ruth Bader Ginsburg leveraged the race-sex analogy in constitutional litigation. As a young law professor and women's rights advocate, she was selected by the American Civil Liberties Union (ACLU) to write appellant Sally Reed's Supreme Court brief in *Reed v. Reed*,[197] the historic 1971 decision in which the Court first struck down a sex classification as violating equal protection. Ginsburg argued that sex discrimination was like the race discrimination that the Court had already invalidated under the Equal Protection Clause. She stressed the immutability and high visibility of an individual's sex; the irrelevance of sex to the ability of an individual to contribute to society; the historical stigmatization of women as an inferior class; and women's lack of political power to remedy the discrimination to which they had long been subject.[198] These were the four criteria of suspect-ness that the Court

---

[196] *See generally* Pauli Murray, *The Negro Woman's Stake in the Equal Rights Amendment*, 6 HARV. C.R.-C.L. L. REV. 253 (1971).

[197] 404 U.S. 71 (1971).

[198] Brief for Appellant, Reed v. Reed, 404 U.S. 71 (1971).

had invoked to explain why racial classifications trigger heightened judicial scrutiny while other classifications do not.[199]

Although there is much force to the race-sex analogy, there were (and are) also problems with reasoning from race in order to persuade courts to take seriously the subordination of women. Racism and sexism in America have traditionally employed different means to enforce a status hierarchy: segregation is not the same thing as role differentiation, and degradation/disdain is not the same thing as paternalism. Moreover, certain biological differences between men and women are real (even if their relevance has traditionally been vastly overstated), while asserted biological differences between people of different races almost never have any basis in science or medicine.

The race-sex analogy also does not capture the issue of intersectionality. This concept directs attention to the fact that various forms of discrimination may overlap and so differentially affect members of multiple traditionally excluded groups.[200] For example, African American women may be discriminated against for being both black and female, and so may be differently situated from both African American men and white women. The idea of intersectionality has been extended to illuminate the particular struggles for equality of members of a variety of different groups. For example, gay African American men may be differently situated in certain respects from both gay people generally and African Americans generally.

C. The Road to Intermediate Scrutiny

Today, it is clearly established constitutional law that sex classifications trigger intermediate scrutiny.[201] This means that sex classifications are presumptively unconstitutional, and the government bears the burden of showing that its use of such classifications is substantially related to an actual, important state interest. We will now consider how the Court decisions eventually produced this doctrinal conclusion.

---

[199]   Most controversial is whether women as a group are fairly characterized as politically powerless for equal protection purposes. On one hand, they constitute a numerical majority and can vote as a group if they so choose. On the other hand, a distinct minority of Americans in positions of power in economic, educational, and political life are women, and American culture—in which girls and boys are socialized—remains deeply gendered in ways that limit opportunities for women. To this day, women are expected to care for children and ill family members to an extent that men are not.

[200]   The seminal work is Kimberle Crenshaw, *Demarginalizing the Intersection of Race and Sex: A Black Feminist Critique of Antidiscrimination Doctrine*, Feminist Theory and Antiracist Politics, 1989 U. CHI. LEGAL FORUM 139 (1989).

[201]   *See, e.g.,* United States v. Virginia, 518 U.S. 515 (1996).

As noted above, the Court first invalidated a sex classification in 1971, in *Reed v. Reed*.[202] Idaho law preferred men over women as administrators of estates when two would-be administrators were just as closely related to the decedent (which was the main criterion for selection). The Court, while purporting to apply only rational basis review, held that this sex classification violated the Equal Protection Clause. It is not clear, however, why the law flunked rational basis review, which (to reiterate) is exceedingly deferential to the government. There had to be some way of breaking a tie between potential administrators, and flipping a coin would have been permissible; some elections are settled this way when there is a tie vote. Moreover, it might have been empirically true that men were more likely than women to have experience with finances, or, at least, the legislature might have thought so. The sex classification in *Reed* did not appear to be simply irrational; there must have been something else that was constitutionally problematic about it.

Two years later, these suspicions were validated by the Court's response to *Frontiero v. Richardson*,[203] in which four Justices concluded that sex classifications should trigger strict scrutiny. A provision of federal law provided that men in the military could automatically claim their wives as dependents, but women in the military could claim their husbands as dependents only upon proof that their husbands depended on them for more than one half of the husbands' financial support. Following then-Professor Ginsburg's lead, Justice William Brennan's plurality opinion emphasized the history of discrimination against women, the immutability of the sex characteristic, and its irrelevance to the ability of women to participate in society.[204] Justice Brennan also looked to Congress as authority for requiring strict scrutiny, which the sex classification obviously flunked.[205]

Given pervasive differences at the time in the roles of men and women in supporting dependents, the government had a point when it argued that the compensation scheme was rational and administratively convenient. The problem with the scheme, therefore, was not its irrationality, and administrative convenience qualifies as a sufficient governmental interest only under rational basis review. The problem, rather, was that the sex classification at issue reflected and reinforced the sex-role stereotypes of the separate spheres tradition by viewing men as breadwinners and women as caregivers. *Reed* and *Frontiero* reflect the broader constitutional principle that sex classifications based on traditional sex-role stereotypes violate the

---

[202] 404 U.S. 71 (1971).

[203] 411 U.S. 677 (1973).

[204] *See id.* at 684–87.

[205] *See id.* at 687–88.

Equal Protection Clause. This has come to be known as the anti-stereotyping principle.

Because Justice Brennan did not speak for a majority, the question of the level of scrutiny for sex classifications remained open after *Frontiero*. Three years later, in *Craig v. Boren*,[206] the Court expressly adopted intermediate scrutiny as the standard. *Craig* involved an Oklahoma law providing that women could buy 3.2 percent beer at age eighteen; men could not buy such beer until age twenty-one. The government offered statistics, invoked by then-Justice Rehnquist in his dissent, emphasizing the traffic-safety justification for the law: teenage men were more likely to drive dangerously and under the influence than teenage women.[207]

The Court agreed that traffic safety, which is obviously compromised by drinking and driving, is an important governmental interest under intermediate scrutiny. The Court's problem with the law was that the sex classification was not substantially related to this interest. It reasoned that only two percent of males had been arrested for driving under the influence; the prohibition extended to selling to young males, not to drinking by young males; and Oklahoma regarded 3.2 percent beer to be non-intoxicating. One might add that it was easy to circumvent the sex classification, since young women could simply have bought the beer for the young men with whom they socialized. Also, any argument from real physical differences between the sexes cuts in the opposite direction, given that men tend to weigh more than women and so generally have a higher tolerance for alcohol consumption.

Craig was one of a number of cases in which Ginsburg represented male plaintiffs who brought sex discrimination claims.[208] Some commentators have praised Ginsburg's choice of male plaintiffs as a smart litigation strategy, the idea being that male judges (they were almost entirely male in those days) were more sympathetic to male plaintiffs than to female plaintiffs. Other commentators have criticized Ginsburg's choice of male plaintiffs as reflecting a commitment to a sex-blind formal equality, as opposed to a more robust, substantive equality.[209] We are not persuaded by either interpretation. In our view, Ginsburg chose male plaintiffs primarily because she recognized that

---

[206]   429 U.S. 190 (1976).

[207]   *See id.* at 223 (Rehnquist, J., dissenting) ("One survey of arrest statistics assembled in 1973 indicated that males in the 18–20 age group were arrested for 'driving under the influence' almost 18 times as often as their female counterparts, and for 'drunkenness' in a ratio of almost 10 to 1.").

[208]   *See, e.g.,* Weinberger v. Wiesenfeld, 420 U.S. 636 (1975); Moritz v. Comm'r, 469 F.2d 466 (10th Cir. 1972).

[209]   *See, e.g.,* Judith Baer, *Advocate on the Court: Ruth Bader Ginsburg and the Limits of Formal Equality, in* REHNQUIST JUSTICE: UNDERSTANDING THE COURT DYNAMIC 216, 231 (Earl M. Maltz ed. 2003); David Cole, *Strategies of Difference: Litigating for Women's Rights in a Man's World*, 2 L. & INEQUALITY 33, 55 (1984).

women would be better able to occupy roles that were not traditional for them (i.e., breadwinning) only if men were also freed to occupy roles that were not traditional for them (i.e., caregiving).

From this perspective, *Craig* is arguably unfortunate not because of the male plaintiff, but because a case about purchasing beer turned out to be the one in which the Court announced heightened scrutiny for sex classifications. The ability of women to access alcohol at a slightly younger age than men does not obviously implicate traditional sex-role stereotypes about breadwinning and caregiving. Such a vehicle risked trivializing the stakes for women in educational, economic, and political life—and for men in family life. In any event, it is clearly established that intermediate scrutiny is the test, whether the classification discriminates against men or against women.

A better example of the Court's use of the anti-stereotyping principle is its 1982 decision in *Mississippi University for Women v. Hogan*.[210] In a majority opinion written by Justice O'Connor, the first female Justice, the Court invalidated a state law maintaining a nursing school for women only on the ground that the state was reinforcing the traditional understanding of nursing as women's work. The Court in *Hogan* not only reaffirmed intermediate scrutiny for all sex classifications, but also declared that sex classifications require an "exceedingly persuasive justification" in order to be upheld.[211]

Yet, the Court was arguably not always consistent in applying the anti-stereotyping principle. The year prior, in *Rostker v. Goldberg*,[212] the Court upheld male-only draft registration (which remains federal law to this day) based on the assumption that it is constitutional to have a male-only combat policy. The Court in *Rostker v. Goldberg* proclaimed deference to Congress, which is inconsistent with intermediate scrutiny. Moreover, the assumption that it is constitutional to have a male-only combat policy seems based on little other than a sex-role stereotype, although this policy was not challenged in the case. Alternatively, even if women did not serve in combat at that time (they do now), women could and did occupy many other positions in the military. It is not clear why the government was permitted not to register women to be drafted for these positions when it required men to register to be drafted potentially for all positions in the military. *Rostker* may reflect the Court's unwillingness to enforce the anti-stereotyping principle in the context of Congress's use of its powers to raise and support a military,[213] as opposed to a debatable attempt to apply this principle. If *Rostker* was wrongly decided (note, however, that it remains the law), an implication

---

[210]   458 U.S. 718 (1982).

[211]   *Id.* at 724 (internal quotation marks and citations omitted).

[212]   453 U.S. 57 (1981).

[213]   *See* U.S. CONST. art. I, § 8, cl. 12–13.

may be that sex equality requires not only equal rights, but also equal responsibilities of citizenship.

D.   The Meaning of Intermediate Scrutiny

Arguably the most important equal protection, sex discrimination decision is *United States v. Virginia*,[214] which was decided in 1996. The Court held 7 to 1 in this case (Justice Thomas was recused) that the Equal Protection Clause was violated by Virginia's categorical exclusion of women from the Virginia Military Institute, (VMI), a publicly funded institution of higher education. Writing for six of her colleagues, Justice Ginsburg (who had joined the Court three years earlier) reiterated that sex classifications trigger intermediate scrutiny. But she also stated, quoting *Mississippi University for Women*, that such classifications require " 'an exceedingly persuasive justification.' "[215] Chief Justice Rehnquist objected to this language in his concurrence in the judgement, arguing that it spoke to the difficulty of meeting the level of scrutiny but was not a statement of the level of scrutiny itself.[216] Justice Scalia, in his solo dissent, vehemently rejected the language, arguing that the Court's abandonment of intermediate scrutiny was the only reason why Virginia lost the case.[217] If, however, one is persuaded that VMI's admissions policy was grounded in traditional sex-role stereotypes (which fail intermediate scrutiny), it is not obvious how this disagreement over the level of scrutiny could have affected the outcome.

More important than whether the Court was applying intermediate scrutiny or strict scrutiny was how Justice Ginsburg interpreted intermediate scrutiny:

> "Inherent differences" between men and women, we have come to appreciate, remain cause for celebration, but not for denigration of the members of either sex or for artificial constraints on an individual's opportunity. Sex classifications may be used to compensate women "for particular economic disabilities [they have] suffered," to "promot[e] equal employment opportunity," to advance full development of the talent and capacities of our Nation's people. But such classifications may not be used, as they once were, to create or perpetuate the legal, social, and economic inferiority of women.[218]

Ginsburg restated intermediate scrutiny as anti-subordination. She made express connections to the ideology of the separate spheres.

---

[214]   518 U.S. 515 (1996).

[215]   *Id*. at 531 (quoting *Mississippi University for Women*, 458 U.S. at 724).

[216]   *See id*. at 559 (Rehnquist, C.J., concurring in judgment).

[217]   *See id*. at 566, 570–74 (Scalia, J., dissenting).

[218]   *Id*. at 533–34 (majority opinion) (citations and footnote omitted).

Virginia invoked two interests in defense of its male-only admissions policy—that single-sex education offered diversity in educational approaches, and that VMI's military-style "adversative" approach to education was inherently unsuited to women. Regarding the first asserted interest, Justice Ginsburg responded that diversity was not an actual interest pursued by the state; rather, it was made up for purposes of litigation. One can see in this response the difference that intermediate scrutiny makes. As for the second asserted interest, Justice Ginsburg responded that the notion of inherent differences between the sexes was a self-fulfilling prophecy grounded in sex-role stereotypes.

Moving from the liability phase of the litigation to the remedial phase, Virginia proposed not to permit women to apply to VMI, but to establish the Virginia Women's Institute for Leadership (VWIL) at Mary Baldwin College. VWIL would offer leadership training, emphasize cooperation, and build self-esteem rather than provide rigorous military training and education and subject cadets to physical rigor and mental stress. Justice Ginsburg responded for the Court by invoking *Sweatt* and declaring VWIL separate and unequal. From the Court's perspective, the VWIL remedy reflected and reinforced the very sex-role stereotypes that had caused the Court to rule against Virginia during the liability phase.

Justice Scalia penned a vehement, solo dissent, accusing the Court of having "shut[ ] down" VMI.[219] His central claim was that "[w]hen a practice [such as the all-male constitution of VMI] not expressly prohibited by the text of the Bill of Rights bears the endorsement of a long tradition of open, widespread, and unchallenged use that dates back to the beginning of the Republic, we have no proper basis for striking it down."[220] Notably, this is not an originalist argument; rather, it is an argument from objectively, deeply rooted tradition. As we will discuss in Chapter 12, one tends to encounter this modality of interpretation in modern substantive due process cases, not equal protection cases. Among the arguments in favor of Justice Scalia's approach are judicial restraint and federalism. Among the arguments against it is the difficulty of distinguishing seminal decisions like *Brown* and *Loving*.

At the end of her opinion for the Court, Justice Ginsburg offered a very different constitutional understanding. She wrote that "[a] prime part of the history of our Constitution . . . is the story of the extension of constitutional rights and protections to people once ignored and

---

[219]   *Id.* at 566 (Scalia, J., dissenting).

[220]   *Id.* at 568 (internal quotation marks omitted).

excluded."[221] So, in addition to implicating a debate over the level of scrutiny for sex classifications and the scope of the anti-stereotyping principle, *United States v. Virginia* triggered a debate within the Court about the role and authority of tradition and anti-tradition in constitutional law. Notably, Ginsburg did not ignore the relevance of history; on the contrary, she made anti-traditionalist arguments and invoked what scholars call "negative precedent,"[222] which are repudiated precedents that are invoked as mistakes that the Court should not repeat.[223]

Off the Court, there has been a debate about whether single-sex public education survives *United States v. Virginia*. We do not read this decision as prohibiting all single-sex public education, which as a practical matter continues to exist in the United States. But the answer is not entirely clear because the Court has not revisited the issue since 1996. Answers in particular cases may depend on whether the government is reflecting or reinforcing traditional sex-role stereotypes or is instead pursuing other, important educational objectives. Relevant questions likely include why the government is separating students based on gender, and what differences, if any, there are between the schools in terms of the number and quality of faculty, physical plant, course offerings, classroom environments, and extracurricular activities. Now that the composition of the Court has changed significantly, it is difficult to make predictions about how it would respond to a constitutional challenge to a gender-segregated school system. We suspect, however, that the current, more socially conservative Court would be more sympathetic to gender segregation than was the Court that decided *United States v. Virginia*.

E. Pregnancy as Justification for Different Treatment

We will now turn to some decisions that have purported to apply intermediate scrutiny to sex classifications. A key question is whether they apply the anti-stereotyping principle and simply recognize pregnancy as a real difference between the sexes that justifies different treatment, or whether (arguably like *Rostker*) they reflect limits on the extent to which the Court is prepared to police sex-role stereotypes. We will start with *Michael M. v. Superior Court of Sonoma County*,[224] which

---

[221]   *Id.* at 557 (majority opinion) (citing RICHARD B. MORRIS, THE FORGING OF THE UNION, 1781–1789, at 193 (1987)).

[222]   For a discussion, see generally Deborah A. Widiss, Note, *Re-Viewing History: The Use of the Past as Negative Precedent in* United States v. Virginia, 108 YALE L.J. 237 (1998).

[223]   *See, e.g., supra* note 218 and accompanying text. In this passage, Ginsburg invoked *Goesart v. Cleary*, 335 U.S. 464, 467 (1948), as negative precedent.

[224]   450 U.S. 464 (1981).

was decided in 1981, and then turn to *Nguyen v. INS*, which was decided two decades later.[225]

Michael M. concerned the constitutionality of a criminal law that allowed only men to be prosecuted for statutory rape. Even though intermediate scrutiny for sex classifications had been established five years earlier, the Court upheld the law, reasoning that it sought to reduce out-of-wedlock teen pregnancies, an important interest, by equalizing the risks of engaging in sex. One problem with the Court's analysis is that there was scant evidence in the record of the case that reducing out-of-wedlock teen pregnancies was the actual interest animating the legislature that passed the law. Another problem is that this rationale may not make much sense. Justice Stevens argued in dissent that, if one's goal is to reduce the amount of teen sex, it is irrational to immunize from criminal liability half of the people who engage in the conduct.[226] One might also ask whether the decision is consistent with the anti-stereotyping principle. There was evidence in the record that the law was based on stereotypes about male sexual aggression and female chastity, and the actual purpose is what is supposed to matter under intermediate scrutiny. Perhaps the sex classification might be justified if the victims of sexual assault were almost always girls who were victimized by older men. We know from the many priest sex abuse scandals, however, that boys are victims, too. We also know that women older than eighteen have been prosecuted for having sexual relationships with boys.

Notwithstanding the Court's statement and application of intermediate scrutiny in *United States v. Virginia*, the Court held 5 to 4 in *Nguyen v. INS* that sex classifications ostensibly benefiting women because of real biological differences between men and women are permissible.[227] The Court in *Nguyen* upheld a provision of federal immigration law that makes it easier for citizen mothers than citizen fathers to convey their citizenship to children born out-of-wedlock abroad. For citizen fathers only, a paternity decree was required before the child turned eighteen years of age.

Justice Kennedy's majority opinion emphasized two justifications for the facial sex classification. First, he argued that there is no doubt as to the identity of the mother because the mother must be present at birth, but there can be doubt as to the identity of the father because he need not be present at birth. Second, he contended that the mother, by virtue of having given birth, will necessarily have the opportunity to form an emotional attachment to the child, but the father may not have this opportunity because the father need not be present at birth.

---

[225]   533 U.S. 53 (2001).

[226]   *See Michael M.*, 450 U.S. at 499 (Stevens, J., dissenting).

[227]   533 U.S. 53 (2001).

The key question is whether these rationales survive intermediate scrutiny, or whether they really just reflect the Court's refusal to apply intermediate scrutiny notwithstanding the presence of traditional sex-role stereotypes. The Court did not inquire whether either of these justifications actually motivated the sex classification; there was little indication in the legislative history that they did. When the Court works to make up interests to justify a law, it is an indication that the Court is not actually applying intermediate scrutiny.

Moreover, even assuming both were actual interests, modern DNA testing render doubts about the identity of the father virtually nonexistent. As for the suggestion that DNA testing is still not perfect, we note that newborns are occasionally sent home with the wrong mothers. As for the second asserted interest, it is not clear why the opportunity to form an attachment qualifies as an important interest, particularly when no such attachment may materialize. The attachment itself may be important, but then the sex classification is not substantially related to the interest because the attachment may exist with the father as well (and may not exist with the mother). So, in order to avoid a serious tailoring problem, Justice Kennedy seriously watered down the significance of the governmental interest. This is the point of Justice O'Connor's analytically sharp dissent for four Justices,[228] which was joined by the other woman on the Court at the time (Justice Ginsburg). Justice Kennedy retained a majority for his position because Justice Stevens, one of the Court's liberals, joined the majority opinion.

Nyugen may be best understood as a decision based on deference to Congress in the area of immigration law, in which case it would have been better for purposes of doctrinal clarity and consistency for the Court to have said so. It may also have been a case in which the Court shared Congress's concerns about American men, including soldiers, unintentionally (and perhaps unknowingly) fathering children abroad. Finally, it may have been a case in which the majority saw real physical differences between the sexes or admirable differences in social roles, while the dissent saw traditional stereotypes about men and women. We do not think the Court was applying the anti-stereotyping principle so much as declining to do so.

To the extent anyone should be offended by the Court's endorsement of the sex classification at issue in *Nyugen*, it is worth thinking about who. Present fathers may have reason to be offended, because their roles in parenting are minimized. But as Professor Kristin Collins has argued, the law also burdens mothers with full responsibility for taking care of non-marital children by reflecting and re-enforcing the stereotype that men

---

[228]   *See id.* at 74–97 (O'Connor, J., dissenting).

cannot be expected or trusted to take care of their children.[229] For centuries, the law expected women, not men, to assume care and financial responsibility for children born out of wedlock.[230]

Justice Ginsburg invoked the work of Professor Collins in the Court's most recent equal protection, sex discrimination case. Like *Nyugen*, *Sessions v. Morales-Santana*[231] involved an equal protection challenge to a facial sex classification in federal law governing the acquisition of U.S. citizenship by a child born abroad, when one parent is a U.S. citizen and the other is not. And both cases concerned the imposition of more burdensome requirements on the citizen father than on the citizen mother. But whereas *Nyugen* concerned a more demanding proof-of-relationship requirement, *Morales-Santana* concerned an additional residency requirement for the unwed citizen father.

Morales-Santana involved a complicated statutory scheme. The main rule, which applies to married couples, requires a period of physical presence in the United States for the U.S.-citizen parent. The requirement was initially ten years' physical presence prior to the child's birth; currently, it is five years pre-birth. This main rule is rendered applicable to unwed U.S.-citizen fathers by another provision of immigration law. Congress ordered an exception, however, for unwed U.S.-citizen mothers. It allows an unwed mother to transmit her citizenship to a child born abroad if she lived in the United States for just one year before the child was born. Thus, unwed mothers require a shorter period of residence than unwed fathers (as well as married couples).

The case involved the son of an unwed citizen father, who would have qualified for citizenship if it had been his mother rather than his father who was a U.S. citizen. Because Justice Scalia's former seat had not yet been filled when the Court heard the case, eight Justices participated in its disposition. Six Justices agreed that there was an equal protection violation (the remaining two would not have decided the issue), but all eight concluded that the son was not entitled to citizenship because Congress could not have intended for unmarried parents to convey their citizenship more easily than married parents.

Drawing from the legislative history and legal scholarship, Justice Ginsburg wrote for the Court that federal immigration law's more favorable treatment for unmarried U.S.-citizen mothers rested

---

[229]   *See generally* Kristin Collins, *Illegitimate Borders:* Jus Sanguinis *Citizenship and the Legal Construction of Family, Race, and Nation*, 123 YALE L.J. 2134 (2014); *see also* Kristin Collins, Note, *When Fathers' Rights are Mothers' Duties: The Failure of Equal Protection in* Miller v. Albright, 109 YALE L.J. 1667 (2000).

[230]   *See generally* Serena Mayeri, *Marital Supremacy and the Constitution of the Non-Marital Family*, 103 CALIF. L. REV. 1277 (2015).

[231]   582 U.S. ___, 137 S. Ct. 1678 (2017).

on the centuries-old stereotype that an unmarried mother was "the child's natural and sole guardian."[232] She wrote that such "overbroad generalizations" harm women *and* men: they perpetuate stereotypes that require women "to continue to assume the role of primary family caregiver" while hurting men who "exercise responsibility for raising their children."[233]

According to Justice Ginsburg, the "unwed-mother-as-natural-guardian notion renders [the law's] gender-based residency rules understandable."[234] The administration of President Franklin Delano Roosevelt feared that a foreign-born child could turn out "more alien than American in character,"[235] reasoning that a citizen parent with ties to the United States of significant duration would combat the influence of the parent who was not a U.S. citizen but that unwed citizen fathers were unlikely to be involved in childrearing.[236]

The government offered two rationales for the sex classification, each of which the Court rejected. First, the government argued that it wanted to ensure that a child born overseas had a strong enough connection to the United States to obtain citizenship. But this government interest had no apparent connection to the sex of the parent who was a citizen. Second, the government argued that it wanted to ensure that a child born outside the United States to an unmarried U.S.-citizen parent would not be "stateless," lacking any citizenship at all. Justice Ginsburg observed that there is little reason to think Congress had this concern when it enacted the law or that the risk of statelessness disproportionately threatened children of unwed mothers.

F. Establishing a Sex Classification

Because sex classifications trigger intermediate scrutiny, which is substantially more demanding than rational basis review, the question of how one proves the existence of a sex classification is critical. The answer is the same as for racial classifications and was discussed earlier in this chapter. First, a sex classification may exist on the face of the law, as in *Reed, Frontiero, Craig, Hogan, Rostker, Virginia, Michael M., Nguyen,* and *Morales-Santana.* Second, for facially sex-neutral laws, there must be proof of a discriminatory purpose, meaning that the government acted the way it did at least in part *because of*, not merely in spite of, an adverse impact on women. As we have seen, the case

---

232   *Id.* at 1691.

233   *Id.* at 1692–93 (internal quotation marks omitted).

234   *Id.* at 1692.

235   *Id.*

236   *Id.*

establishing this proposition is *Personnel Administrator v. Feeney*,[237] which involved a veteran's preference for hiring by the government.

This is formalist legal doctrine, and one question it raises is whether and when pregnancy discrimination qualifies as sex discrimination. The practical stakes for women are high—far higher than whether members of one sex can buy certain beer before members of the other sex—because of longstanding, rampant discrimination in the workplace against pregnant women and mothers. This includes firing women just because they became pregnant; discrimination in access to parental and family leave; and discrimination in the provision of disability benefits.

The Court's key constitutional case on pregnancy discrimination was decided in 1974—after *Reed* and *Frontiero*, but before *Craig*.[238] In *Geduldig v. Aiello*,[239] California paid disability benefits for all disabilities experienced by employees except for disabilities related to normal pregnancy. The Court concluded that there was no sex classification because there was no disability regarding which men received benefits but women did not, and there was no disability regarding which women received benefits but men did not. The Court reasoned that there were two categories of people: pregnant women and non-pregnant persons. Because women were in both categories, the Court concluded, there was no sex discrimination.

The Court's reasoning may be sound from the perspective of formal equality. From the perspective of substantive equality, however, defining the classification as between pregnant and non-pregnant persons ignores the fact that only women are in the first category. Thus, the denial of disability benefits for normal pregnancy has a large, disproportionate impact on women. Put differently, the law's impact is on those capable of being pregnant (women), not on those incapable (men). In addition, pregnancy is *sex-linked*—differential capacity to become pregnant is physiologically what most distinguishes women and men—and pregnancy has long been invoked to subordinate women by excluding them from educational, economic, and political life. The provision, in other words, may have been shaped, at least in part, by gender bias even if it does not meet *Feeney*'s definition of discriminatory purpose, which is akin to malice.

It is worth pausing to inquire whether the California law reflected or reinforced traditional sex-role stereotypes about how a woman should

---

[237]   442 U.S. 256 (1979).

[238]   For discussion of the case that came close to being first, see generally Neil S. Siegel, *The Pregnant Captain, the Notorious REG, and the Vision of RBG: The Story of Struck v. Secretary of Defense, in* REPRODUCTIVE RIGHTS AND JUSTICE STORIES (Melissa Murray, Kate Shaw, & Reva B. Siegel eds., forthcoming 2019).

[239]   417 U.S. 484 (1974).

respond to a pregnancy, or whether it was simply a financial cost-savings measure. Whenever considerations of cost are invoked, a relevant question is why the government is seeking to save costs in a way that harms many women and not in other possible ways. As gender-equality advocates are quick to point out, denying female employees disability benefits for normal pregnancy may be less troubling if one believes that the appropriate female response to a pregnancy is to quit one's job, stay at home, and prepare to become a mother, in which case one would not receive any employment-related disability benefits anyway—and also would not need them given one's presumed dependence on a male wage-earner. Notably, California provided comprehensive coverage to male employees, including coverage for conditions that only men are capable of experiencing.

It is also worth comparing how the Court in *Geduldig* reasoned about the possibility of real physical differences between men and women with how the Court in *Nguyen* reasoned about this possibility. In *Nguyen*, the Court perceived real physical differences when they arguably did not exist, and the Court leveraged these asserted differences to explain why sex discrimination was justified. In *Geduldig*, by contrast, the Court ignored the presence of real physical differences when they clearly did exist, and the Court leveraged what it believed to be the absence of real physical differences to explain why sex discrimination did not exist at all.

If pregnancy discrimination is never sex discrimination, it would seem to follow that, as far as the Constitution is concerned, governments can fire women from public employment just because they become pregnant; bar pregnant women from enrolling in public educational facilities; and provide a medical-care program for employees that does not cover gynecological care. The legal reason why such questions do not tend to arise any more is because of the Pregnancy Discrimination Act of 1978 (PDA), which provides as a matter of federal statute what the Court in *Geduldig* declined to provide as a matter of constitutional law. The PDA defines pregnancy discrimination as sex discrimination. After four decades of PDA litigation, the norm is solidly entrenched in American society.

In 2003, the Court articulated an understanding of pregnancy discrimination that was more in line with the PDA than with *Geduldig*. In *Nevada Department of Human Resources v. Hibbs*,[240] the Court upheld the family-care leave provided by the Family and Medical Leave Act of 1993 (FMLA) as a valid exercise of Congress's power under Section Five of the Fourteenth Amendment to combat unconstitutional sex discrimination. The scope of Congress's Section Five power will be discussed in Chapter 13. Relevant here is the fact

---

[240]   538 U.S. 721 (2003).

that, in so holding, the Court appeared to suggest—in line with the PDA and despite *Geduldig*—that pregnancy discrimination can constitute unconstitutional sex discrimination. Endorsing Congress's concern about unjustified discrimination against women when they are " 'mothers or mothers-to-be' " (that is, pregnant),[241] the Court seemed to be implying that discrimination against pregnant women is tantamount to discrimination against women—that is, sex discrimination—and so is presumptively prohibited under the Equal Protection Clause.

Given the current composition of the Court, however, we do not expect it to overrule *Geduldig* any time soon. As noted in the above discussion of racial equality, Justice Alito replaced Justice O'Connor in 2006, and in 2012 the Court held in *Coleman v. Court of Appeals of Maryland*[242] that Section Five did not authorize the FMLA's medical (or self-care) leave provisions. In a vigorous dissent, Justice Ginsburg argued in part that the Court was ignoring the links between pregnancy and sex-stereotyping—that a pregnancy leave policy would cause employers to avoid hiring women of childbearing age, so Congress called it self-care leave instead in the hope that men would also take such leave. Justice Kennedy had invoked *Geduldig* in his dissent in *Hibbs*, and he wrote the majority opinion in *Coleman*. With his replacement by Justice Kavanaugh, we expect *Geduldig* to remain the law of the land.

* * *

We have focused in this chapter on race, ethnicity, national origin, and gender because of the historical and contemporary significance of these forms of discrimination and subordination in American constitutional politics and constitutional law. We have also focused on them because they are relevant to more recent social movements for constitutional equality. For example, the gay rights movement, which we discuss in Chapter 12, has drawn inspiration—and legal arguments—from the civil rights and women's movements.

We should, however, briefly mention two other categories of laws to which the Court has applied heightened scrutiny. The first involves laws discriminating against noncitizens. Constitutional law here is rather complex. State laws that discriminate against noncitizens lawfully in the United States are subject to strict scrutiny.[243] But federal laws are not covered by this rule,[244] nor are state laws dealing with "public functions." The Court has construed this category broadly to include

---

[241]   *Id.* at 736 (quoting Congress).

[242]   566 U.S. 30 (2012).

[243]   *See* Graham v. Richardson, 403 U.S. 365 (1971) (welfare benefits); In re Griffiths, 413 U.S. 717 (1973) (admission to the bar).

[244]   *See* Matthews v. Diaz, 426 U.S. 67 (1978).

police officers[245] and school teachers (on the ground that teachers impart civic values),[246] but not most low-level state employees.[247]

The second category involves laws discriminating against children of unmarried parents (who used to be called "illegitimate" and are now called "nonmarital" children.) Such laws are subject to intermediate scrutiny.[248] But the Court was receptive to arguments that some distinctions were required by the greater difficulty of proving paternity.[249] This justification seems obsolete in the era of DNA testing. But in any event, perhaps in part due to the Court's decisions, the stigma faced by nonmarital children has declined, along with discriminatory state laws.

The Court has resisted expanding heightened scrutiny to other equal protection categories. Race and gender remain by far the most important domains for equal protection analysis.

Further Readings

AKHIL REED AMAR, AMERICA'S CONSTITUTION: A BIOGRAPHY 349–401 (2005).

JACK M. BALKIN, LIVING ORIGINALISM 183–255 (2011).

Jack M. Balkin & Reva B Siegel, *The American Civil Rights Tradition: Anticlassification or Antisubordination?*, 58 U. MIAMI L. REV. 9 (2003).

Charles L. Black, Jr., *The Lawfulness of the Segregation Decisions*, 69 YALE L.J. 421 (1960).

Steven G. Calabresi & Michael W. Perl, *Originalism and* Brown v. Board of Education, 2014 MICH. ST. L. REV. 429 (2014).

Kristin Collins, *Illegitimate Borders:* Jus Sanguinis *Citizenship and the Legal Construction of Family, Race, and Nation*, 123 YALE L.J. 2134 (2014).

Kimberle Crenshaw, *Demarginalizing the Intersection of Race and Sex: A Black Feminist Critique of Antidiscrimination Doctrine, Feminist Theory and Antiracist Politics*, 1989 U. CHI. LEGAL FORUM 139 (1989).

DANIEL A. FARBER, LINCOLN'S CONSTITUTION 70–92 (2003).

---

[245] *See* Foley v. Connelie, 435 U.S. 291 (1978).

[246] *See* Ambach v. Norwick, 441 U.S. 68 (1978) (involving a state law barring aliens who declined to seek naturalization from teaching jobs).

[247] *See* Sugarman v. Dougall, 413 U.S. 634 (1973).

[248] *See* Clark v. Jeter, 486 U.S. 456 (1988); Levy v. Louisiana, 391 U.S. 68 (1968).

[249] For discussions of this governmental interest, see *Lalli v. Lalli*, 439 U.S. 259, 268 (1978); *Mathews v. Lucas*, 427 U.S. 495; and *Weber v. Aetna Casualty & Surety Company*, 406 U.S. 164 (1972).

DANIEL A. FARBER & SUZANNA SHERRY, A HISTORY OF THE AMERICAN CONSTITUTION 449–82 (3d ed. 2013).

Owen M. Fiss, *Groups and the Equal Protection Clause*, 5 PHIL. & PUB. AFF. 107 (1976).

Cheryl I. Harris, *The Story of* Plessy v. Ferguson*: The Death and Resurrection of Racial Formalism*, *in* CONSTITUTIONAL LAW STORIES 181, 202 (Michael C. Dorf ed., 2004).

MICHAEL J. KLARMAN, FROM JIM CROW TO CIVIL RIGHTS: THE SUPREME COURT AND THE STRUGGLE FOR RACIAL EQUALITY (2006).

RICHARD KLUGER, SIMPLE JUSTICE: THE HISTORY OF *BROWN V. BOARD OF EDUCATION* AND BLACK AMERICA'S STRUGGLE FOR EQUALITY (2nd ed. 2004).

Catherine A. MacKinnon, *Difference and Dominance: On Sex Discrimination*, *in* FEMINISM UNMODIFIED: DISCOURSES ON LIFE AND LAW 32 (1987).

Michael W. McConnell, *Originalism and the Desegregation Decisions*, 81 VA. L. REV. 947 (1995).

GERALD N. ROSENBERG, THE HOLLOW HOPE: CAN COURTS BRING ABOUT SOCIAL CHANGE? (1991).

Neil S. Siegel, *The Pregnant Captain, the Notorious REG, and the Vision of RBG: The Story of* Struck v. Secretary of Defense, *in* REPRODUCTIVE RIGHTS AND JUSTICE STORIES (Melissa Murray, Kate Shaw, & Reva B. Siegel eds., forthcoming 2019).

Reva B. Siegel, *Equality Talk: Antisubordination and Anticlassification Values in Constitutional Struggles over* Brown, 117 HARV. L. REV. 1470 (2004).

Reva B. Siegel, *From Colorblindness to Antibalkanization: An Emerging Ground of Decision in Race Equality Cases*, 120 YALE L.J. 1278 (2011).

Reva B. Siegel, *She the People: The Nineteenth Amendment, Sex Equality, Federalism, and the Family*, 115 HARV. L. REV. 947 (2002).

Reva B. Siegel, *Why Equal Protection No Longer Protects: The Evolving Forms of Status-Enforcing State Action*, 49 STAN. L. REV. 1111 (1997).

ALEXANDER TSESIS, THE THIRTEENTH AMENDMENT AND AMERICAN FREEDOM: A LEGAL HISTORY (2004).

MARK V. TUSHNET, THE NAACP'S LEGAL STRATEGY AGAINST SEGREGATED EDUCATION, 1925–1950 (1987).

Herbert Wechsler, *Toward Neutral Principles of Constitutional Law*, 73 HARV. L. REV. 1 (1959).

Chapter 11

FUNDAMENTAL RIGHTS PROTECTED UNDER EQUAL PROTECTION

Although the default standard of review under the Equal Protection Clause is the rational basis test, we have seen that certain classifications such as race and gender receive more stringent scrutiny. As we will examine in this chapter, some laws also receive elevated scrutiny because they regulate individual interests that the Court regards as particularly crucial. This is often called the fundamental rights prong of equal protection doctrine.

This prong of equal protection doctrine offers a kind of qualified, indirect strategy for protecting rights. As discussed in the next chapter, some legal rights are protected more directly: everyone is entitled to exercise those rights absent a particularly strong justification for government infringement of them. Under the indirect approach, by contrast, the government is not required to provide certain rights or benefits at all, but once it does so, it needs a strong justification for giving them to some and not others. Why is the indirect strategy available and sometimes more useful than the direct approach? There are at least two reasons.

One reason for the indirect strategy is that some rights may not lend themselves to direct protection. For instance, nothing in the Constitution requires that city mayors be elected rather than appointed by the governor or the city council. It therefore seems reasonable to leave the choice of how to pick mayors with state government or local voters. But if a state does provide for mayoral elections, it seems constitutionally problematic to give some people more votes than others. In situations like this, the direct strategy for rights protection does not apply, so equality arguments are at least available as a second-best approach.

A second reason for the indirect strategy may be the link between certain equality arguments and Footnote 4 of *Carolene Products*, which justifies heightened judicial review in part based on its capacity to ensure that the political process functions properly. In many of the cases in this chapter, the Supreme Court has used equal protection to guarantee that individuals have opportunities to address their grievances through their legislatures. It has also ensured that individuals can have their day in court when particularly important interests are at stake. The effect in both situations is to give voice to individuals whose interests might otherwise be ignored by officials. Thus, voting and access to the courts have been prime arenas for equality arguments. When participation is not a feasible alternative—for instance, for out-of-state residents who seek to live in the state—equality arguments are used to ensure that these individuals, who lack political representation, are treated equally with state citizens who possess such representation. This provides indirect political protection to those without representation, since to protect its own interests the state electorate is also forced to protect future newcomers. These doctrines fit within the vision of the judicial role under *Carolene Products*, which is to make government more responsive to individual interests that it might otherwise ignore.

We will focus on four examples of equal protection for fundamental rights. In three of these examples—reapportionment, access to ballots and courts, and interstate travel—the Court has been active in protecting equality. The fourth example, education, demonstrates the limits of the Court's willingness to identify fundamental rights for equal protection purposes. The Court was, however, willing to intervene in one extreme case.

I. Legislative Districting

Concerns about whether the Court was stepping too far into the "political thicket," as Justice Felix Frankfurter put it, have long surrounded its efforts to use the Equal Protection Clause to adjust voting rights.[1] Of course, the Fifteenth Amendment prohibits racial discrimination in voting, but it says nothing about other issues such as unequal voting power between different regions of a state. Prior to the 1960s, many state legislatures were severely malapportioned, with districts of vastly different populations. As cities and suburbs grew in population, election districts were not redrawn to reflect the population changes. The result was the creation of large disparities in legislative representation. For example, a rural district and an urban district might have the same number of legislators, even though the urban district had far more voters. The legislature might well end up giving far more weight to the views and needs of rural areas than those of cities and suburbs. The same malapportionment problem existed in congressional districts in states across the country.

In the 1960s, amidst concerns that urban voters had substantially less political voice than rural voters, the Supreme Court intervened in a series of cases by announcing its principle of "one person, one vote."[2] It then found itself immersed in issues of

---

[1]   Colegrove v. Greene, 328 U.S. 549, 556 (1946) (admonishing that "[c]ourts ought not to enter this political thicket" of legislative reapportionment).

[2]   *See, e.g.,* Gray v. Sanders, 372 U.S. 368, 381 (1963) ("The conception of political equality from the Declaration of Independence, to Lincoln's Gettysburg

racial gerrymandering and political gerrymandering. We discuss these issues below.

A. One Person, One Vote

Until 1962, when the Court decided *Baker v. Carr*,[3] legislative districting was considered a nonjusticiable political question and therefore outside the purview of the courts. As we discussed in Chapter 3, *Baker v. Carr* revamped the political question doctrine and held that courts have jurisdiction to decide whether districting violates the Equal Protection Clause. Rulings on the merits of redistricting cases in state and federal courts around the country soon followed.[4]

Reynolds v. Sims[5] is the foundational case. Alabama's 1901 state constitution required reapportionment of legislative districts after the U.S. census every ten years. But such a reapportionment never took place. By 1961, about one quarter of the voters resided in districts representing a majority of the legislature. The population of the largest county was forty times larger than that of the smallest county, but both had a single representative in the State Senate. In the Alabama House, one small county had a ratio of one representative per 6,200 residents, while a large urban county had a ratio of one representative per 90,400 residents.[6]

Chief Justice Earl Warren's opinion for the Court began with the premise that the "right to vote freely for the candidate of one's choice is of the essence of a democratic society, and any restrictions on that right strike at the heart of representative government."[7] He viewed it as obvious that a statute giving extra votes to individuals in one part of a state would violate equal protection, yet Alabama's districting in effect did the same thing. "To the extent that a citizen's right to vote is debased," the Chief Justice said, "he is that much less a citizen," so the "weight of a citizen's vote cannot be made to depend on where he lives."[8]

By analogy to the U.S. Senate, the state argued that it was defensible to give each of its counties a single seat in the legislature. The argument has intuitive appeal, given that the Framers

---

Address, to the Fifteenth, Seventeenth, and Nineteenth Amendments can mean only one thing—one person, one vote.").

[3]   369 U.S. 186 (1962).

[4]   For discussion of the mutually supportive relationship between the Supreme Court and lower courts in reapportionment litigation, see Neil S. Siegel, *Reciprocal Legitimation in the Federal Courts System*, 70 VAND. L. REV. 1183, 1206–11 (2017).

[5]   377 U.S. 533 (1964).

[6]   *See id.* at 545–46 (providing these figures).

[7]   *Id.* at 555.

[8]   *Id.* at 566–67.

apparently found it consistent with their ideas of democracy to give residents in small states equal votes with those of large states (a situation that has only become more extreme over the years). But Chief Justice Warren rejected the analogy on two grounds. First, when the Constitution was ratified, the states had previously enjoyed independent sovereignty, while counties are legally arms of the state government. And second, equal representation in the U.S. Senate was a pragmatic compromise necessary to achieve acceptance of the Constitution, not necessarily an arrangement that the Framers endorsed in principle.

Although the constitutional requirement articulated by the Court in *Reynolds* was equal representation, Chief Justice Warren permitted states some flexibility. For instance, he wrote that it might be feasible to use existing political subdivisions as a basis in apportionment, "so long as the resulting apportionment was one based substantially on population and the equal-population principle was not diluted in any significant way."[9]

The second Justice John Marshall Harlan was the only dissenter.[10] He argued forcefully that the Court's decision was inconsistent with the original understanding of the Fourteenth Amendment. Among its congressional supporters, he contended, the Amendment was not thought to apply at all to voting. The text of the reconstruction amendments supports his reading, for as noted in Chapters 8 and 10, if the Equal Protection Clause covered voting, it is hard to see why the Fifteenth Amendment would be necessary to prevent racial discrimination against black voters. Beyond the text, Justice Harlan amassed a considerable body of evidence to show that members of Congress who wanted to give the vote to Southern blacks understood full well that the Fourteenth Amendment did not do so.

In *Westberry* v. Sanders,[11] a parallel case involving apportionment of the U.S. House of Representatives, the Court considered the right of equal representation in this chamber. The case arose from Georgia, where some congressional districts had two or three times the population of others. Rather than looking to the Equal Protection Clause, the Court turned to another part of the Constitution. Article I, Section 2, provides that Representatives shall be chosen "by the People of the several States." Justice Hugo Black, writing for the Court, said that weighting votes more highly in some districts than others "would not only run counter to our fundamental ideas of democratic government, it would cast aside the principle of a

---

[9]   *Id.* at 570.

[10]   *Id.* at 589 (Harlan, J., dissenting). By this time, Justice Frankfurter was no longer on the Court.

[11]   376 U.S. 1 (1964).

House elected 'by the People,' a principle tenaciously fought for and established at the Constitutional Convention."[12]

In dissent, Justice Harlan argued that, "[w]hatever the dominant political philosophy at the Convention, one thing seems clear: it is in the last degree unlikely that most or even many of the delegates would have subscribed to the principle of 'one person, one vote.' "[13] For instance, he pointed out that the Three-Fifths Clause of the original Constitution[14] in effect gave additional votes to whites in states with large slave populations by counting slaves as three-fifths of a person for purposes of apportionment of the House.[15]

At a time when originalism was not especially well-regarded, Justice Harlan's dissents apparently made little impression on the majority. Instead, the majority was clearly more concerned with strengthening the democratic character of the state and federal governments than with the niceties of historical interpretation. The Court has not since questioned the validity of these holdings, which are now apparently considered bedrock precedent by the Justices.

These decisions left open some issues for later clarification. We discuss the three most important ones. First, how much deviation from equality is allowed? In both cases discussed above, the majority announced the principle of one-person, one-vote but allowed some room for deviations. How much is permitted?

Later cases have provided some guidance. In *Gaffney v. Cummings*,[16] the deviation from equality was below eight percent in one house of the Connecticut legislature and under two percent in the other; the Court considered these deviations too insignificant to require justification. As a rule of thumb, the Court said, deviations under ten percent seem generally acceptable in state elections, but larger deviations may be justified by a state policy of preserving political subdivisions.[17] In contrast, for the U.S. House, the Court has been very strict in enforcing mathematical equality, requiring justification for even a one-percent deviation.[18]

A second reapportionment issue deserves mention. The Court has exempted some elections for special purpose districts from the one-person, one-vote requirement. The exemption is aimed at districts that impact only a segment of the population, such as the

---

12   *Id.* at 8.
13   *Id.* at 30–31.
14   *See* U.S. CONST. art. I, § 2, cl. 3.
15   *Wesberry*, 376 U.S. at 26.
16   412 U.S. 735 (1973).
17   *See* Voinovich v. Quilter, 507 U.S. 146, 161 (1993).
18   *See* Karcher v. Daggett, 462 U.S. 725 (1983).

owners of water rights, rather than the general public.[19] The Court has reasoned that these organizations essentially exist to regulate affairs between a small group that do not affect the general public. For this reason, public representation is not required.

Third, in determining consistency with the requirement of "one person, one vote," do courts count the total populations of each legislative district, or do they count the total number of registered voters in each district? This question matters because the current count includes children and non-citizens living in a district, who are not entitled to vote. Excluding these people would disproportionately affect areas with high numbers of such individuals, which often include cities or concentrations of minority voters.

For the U.S. House, the answer is clear because the constitutional text references "the People," not registered voters.[20] But what about state legislative districts?

The Court had never squarely addressed this issue until recently, although states have overwhelmingly followed the same practice: they have taken the total number of people in their state and divided up this total by the number of seats in the legislature or local governing body, with the quotient dictating how many people (plus or minus a few) should be in each district. In *Evenwel v. Abbott*,[21] two Texas voters, supported by a host of conservative advocacy groups, argued that the Constitution requires voter equality, not population equality.

The Court unanimously disagreed. Writing for six Justices, Justice Ruth Bader Ginsburg held that a state or locality may draw its legislative districts based on total population; it need not base its districts on voter population. In so concluding, Justice Ginsburg relied upon the original understanding of the Constitution and the Fourteenth Amendment, Supreme Court precedent since the Court's declaration of the "one person, one vote" standard in 1964, and the historical practice of the states in their redistricting decisions. The Court did not decide whether states must use total population, although much of its reasoning seemed to suggest as much, which helps explain why Justice Samuel Alito concurred in the judgment

---

[19]   *See* Salyer Land Co. v. Tulare Lake Basin Water Storage Dist., 410 U.S. 719, 720 (1973).

[20]   *See supra* notes 11–12 and accompanying text (discussing reapportionment in the House).

[21]   578 U.S. ___, 136 S. Ct. 1120 (2016).

only, meaning that he agreed with the result but not the reasoning in the majority opinion.[22]

Given the extent of political polarization during the current period of American history, the issue is particularly important. A switch from total population to voter population would have meant a significant electoral advantage for the Republican Party. Voters tend to register and vote more often in districts that favor Republicans, compared to urban areas that favor Democrats and in which reside more people ineligible to vote: children, prisoners, ex-convicts, and non-citizens.

The foundational reapportionment decisions reflected a clash between different judicial philosophies. One emphasized judicial restraint and focused on the original understanding. The other sought in living constitutionalist fashion to vindicate the national commitment to majoritarian democracy, which has strengthened over the centuries following the Founding.[23] In the later cases just noted, the Court has retained this democratic commitment but with pragmatic adjustments to what it sees as the realities of modern governance.

From the perspective of the relationship between constitutional politics and constitutional law, what is most fascinating about this area is how quickly the country accepted the Court's reapportionment revolution. Justice Frankfurter had warned his colleagues for some fifteen years about the fraught political context of legislative reapportionment and the need for the Court to stay out of it lest judicial legitimacy be imperiled.[24] And *Reynolds v. Sims* did ignite a political firestorm that included various threatened responses, including a proposed constitutional amendment that would have partially reversed the result in the case. The proposal fell just short of passage by the Senate in 1965, however, and all other efforts to reverse the decision likewise failed. Moreover, all of these efforts failed swiftly. What the Court's assertiveness lacked in

---

[22]   *See id.* at 1142 (Alito, J., concurring in judgment). Justice Thomas also concurred in the judgment only, but he rejected the principle of one person, one vote in its entirety. *See id.* at 1133 (Thomas, J., concurring in judgment).

[23]   Consider, for example, all of the amendments that expanded voting rights during the Nineteenth and Twentieth Centuries. *See* U.S. CONST. amends. XV, XVII, XIX, XXIII, XXIV, XXVI.

[24]   *See supra* note 1 and accompanying text (quoting *Colegrove*); *Baker*, 369 U.S. at 267 (Frankfurter, J., dissenting) ("The Court's authority—possessed of neither the purse nor the sword—ultimately rests on sustained public confidence in its moral sanction. Such feeling must be nourished by the Court's complete detachment, in fact and in appearance, from political entanglements and by abstention from injecting itself into the clash of political forces in political settlements.").

originalist warrant it made up for in intuitive appeal: the idea of "one person, one vote" just made sense to most Americans.[25]

Although it is not clear whether it has any lasting doctrinal significance, we would be remiss if we closed this section without mentioning *Bush v. Gore*,[26] a case that helped determine the outcome of a presidential election. This was not a one-person, one-vote case, but the majority opinion did reflect a similar concern that votes count equally despite being cast in different geographic areas. And the case did very quickly place the Court in the middle of the political thicket, although the extent of the long-term impact on public perception of the Court is unclear.

The 2000 election was a statistical tie, with the result turning on the vote count in Florida, where George W. Bush had a razor-thin margin of 1800 votes out of nearly six million cast—a margin that was smaller than the error rate of the voting machines used in much of the state. The state courts ordered a manual recount of the punch-card ballots, which the Supreme Court halted with a stay. The Court then declared the recount invalid because it allowed county canvassing boards in different districts to apply their own subjective standards. The Court held that such a recount violated equal protection because it might have been practical to establish more objective standards (although the Court did not allow a recount with more objective standards to take place). The Court's holding was carefully limited: "The recount process, in its features here described, is inconsistent with the minimum procedures necessary to protect the fundamental right of each voter in the special instance of a statewide recount under the authority of a single state judicial officer."[27] The five conservatives on the Court joined this opinion (all were Republican appointees), while all the liberals dissented (two were Democratic appointees and two were Republican appointees). Reaction to the decision at the time, and even today, often remains sharply divided along partisan lines, which may suggest that the high stakes involved have influenced legal judgments on and off the Court. *Bush v. Gore* may seem like ancient history to current law students, but we remember it well; for one of us, it was the defining experience of his last year in law school.

---

[25] Another fascinating question is whether the Court's reapportionment revolution would be accepted today if the Court were just beginning to intervene. Now, unlike then, geography has taken on a partisan flavor, with predominantly "blue" urban areas in most parts of the country and primarily "red" rural areas.

[26] 531 U.S. 98 (2001).

[27] *Id.* at 109.

B.   Racial Discrimination and Racial Gerrymandering

The Court's encounters with racial discrimination and voting rights have a mixed and long history that we can only touch upon here. A few examples will have to do. These decisions are covered in detail in law school courses on voting rights and election law.

The Court took an inauspicious turn in *Giles v. Harris*.[28] The Alabama Constitution provided that persons registered to vote before 1903 remained electors permanently (with some narrow exceptions), while after this date severe tests came into play that would exclude most black voters. Without reaching the merits of the case, the Court held that it was powerless to remedy what the complaint alleged to be a conspiracy of the state's public officials and white residents. Read most charitably—which the opinion may or may not deserve— Justice Oliver Wendell Holmes, a wounded Civil War veteran, implied for the Court that correcting the situation required the use of the kind of military force available to the executive branch but not to a court. For this reason, the Court dismissed the case notwithstanding the complaint's allegation of a pervasive and willful violation of Section 1 of the Fifteenth Amendment, which prohibits racial discrimination in voting. This was not one of the Court's prouder days in American history.

Fortunately, the Court did not take a consistent attitude of ignoring black disenfranchisement. You may have heard the phrase "grandfather clause," which is now used broadly for any exemption based on past conduct. The phrase comes from *Guinn v. United States*.[29] In 1910, Oklahoma adopted a new state constitution that imposed a literacy test on voters but exempted those whose grandfathers had been eligible to vote in 1865 (which included only whites). The Court struck down this provision, seeing no possible nondiscriminatory reason for setting the date before the passage of the Fifteenth Amendment.

Thwarted on this front, states adopted other methods of disenfranchising blacks. For instance, under solid Democratic control, Texas used primaries run by the state government to select political candidates, and the state passed a law allowing only whites to vote in the Democratic primary.[30] After the Court struck down this law, in 1932, the Texas Democratic party itself adopted the same rule, which the Court again invalidated because the primary was an integral part of the election process.[31] Democrats then formed a voluntary association containing all white voters called the Jaybirds,

---

[28]   189 U.S. 475 (1903).

[29]   238 U.S. 347 (1915).

[30]   *See* Nixon v. Herndon, 273 U.S. 536 (1927).

[31]   *See* Smith v. Allwright, 321 U.S. 649 (1944).

which ran its own primary outside of the state process. In practice, at least in some parts of the state, the winners of the Jaybird primary invariably were nominated in the "official" primary and then went on to win the general election. Although there was no majority opinion, the Court held that these elections, too, violated the Fifteenth Amendment.[32] As we will discuss in Chapter 13, it proved impossible for the courts to keep up with the ever-shifting efforts to disenfranchise blacks in states across the South, and Congress ultimately responded with the Voting Rights Act of 1965.

Even when blacks were able to register and vote, states adopted more subtle techniques, using redistricting to minimize the political impact of black voters. The two basic approaches are called "cracking" and "packing." In the case of cracking, members of disfavored groups are split up among multiple districts, ensuring that they will be too small a minority in each one to exercise political influence. In the case of packing, members of the group are packed into a single district, ensuring them one representative but preventing them from influencing elections in districts where they might otherwise help sway elections. Which gerrymandering technique is most effective depends on the distribution of voters, the ease or difficulty of forming coalitions with other voters, and the legal constraints on redistricting (such as one-person, one-vote). The same techniques can also be used in reverse to increase minority representation.

There is again a rich body of case law on racial gerrymandering that we can discuss only briefly here. The leading case is *Mobile v. Bolden*,[33] which requires proof of discriminatory intent as the basis for a Fifteenth Amendment claim, not merely proof that the effect was to diminish minority voting power. Applying the intent test has turned out to be a complex undertaking. Race can sometimes be an excellent proxy for party affiliation, especially in much of the South. Since reapportionment has traditionally been conducted by state legislators who seek re-election, voters' party affiliation is inevitably likely to enter into consideration. In addition, the legislative process is complicated and discussions among legislators are not always public, so untangling the motivation(s) behind legislation can be difficult.

The Court has sometimes looked to what it considered to be objective criteria as evidence of intent. *Shaw v. Reno*[34] involved a North Carolina redistricting plan that was adopted under pressure from the U.S. Justice Department, which contended that a previous

---

[32]   *See* Terry v. Adams, 345 U.S. 461 (1953). Today, *Terry* and *Smith v. Allwright* are generally classified under the "public function" exception to the state action requirement, which is discussed in Chapter 8.

[33]   446 U.S. 55 (1980).

[34]   509 U.S. 630 (1993).

plan violated the Voting Rights Act. (This statute is discussed in detail in Chapter 13). The state adopted a new plan that was designed to increase minority representation, and this plan was in turn challenged by white voters. The plan created some weirdly shaped districts, including one district that in some places connected different black communities with narrow corridors barely wider than the interstate highway they tracked. In an opinion by Justice Sandra Day O'Connor, the Court held in a 5-to-4 ideological split that apportionment plans based on race were subject to strict scrutiny. Admittedly, Justice O'Connor said, it may be difficult to establish the race-based nature of a plan. But in this case, she said, the districting map spoke for itself. Even apart from their significance as evidence of intent, she wrote, contorted districts are objectionable for another reason. According to Justice O'Connor, "reapportionment is one area in which appearances do matter."[35] When districting lumps together people who do not necessarily have anything in common other than their race, she reasoned, it "bears an uncomfortable resemblance to political apartheid," reinforcing "the perception that regardless of other differences, all members of the same racial group . . . think alike, share the same political interests, and will prefer the same candidates at the polls."[36] She found this to be an impermissible racial stereotype.

Like *Shaw v. Reno*, *Miller v. Johnson*[37] involved a challenge by white voters to a reapportionment plan adopted in response to demands by the U.S. Department of Justice. The Court, again splitting 5 to 4 along ideological lines, rejected the state's argument that bizarrely shaped districts are an essential argument of a racial gerrymandering claim. Rather, the Court said, "[t]he plaintiff's burden is to show, either through circumstantial evidence of a district's shape and demographics or more direct evidence going to legislative purpose, that race was the predominant factor motivating the legislature's decision to place a significant number of voters within or without a particular district."[38]

The Court seems to have settled on a near-unanimous view that, unless a state has a compelling justification, it may not draw districts designed to increase minority representation. In *Cooper v. Harris*,[39] Justice Elena Kagan's opinion for the Court embraced this test and

---

[35]   *Id.* at 647. As discussed in Chapter 10, the Court's decisionmaking in the area of affirmative action in higher education, including Justice O'Connor's majority opinion in *Grutter v. Bollinger* and concurring opinion in *Gratz v. Bollinger*, can also be interpreted as standing for the proposition that appearances matter.

[36]   *Id.*

[37]   515 U.S. 900 (1995).

[38]   *Id.* at 916.

[39]   581 U.S. ___, 137 S. Ct. 1455 (2017).

rejected the state's attempted justification. The state had argued that a majority-black district was needed because blacks would otherwise lack the ability to influence elections (a "vote dilution" claim). But the Court found that whites did not vote as a bloc in this area, making it possible for blacks to form coalitions with whites to elect representatives even when blacks were a minority. Interestingly, while the liberal members of the Court and Justice Clarence Thomas joined the majority, three more conservative members of the Court (Justice Alito, Chief Justice John Roberts, and Justice Anthony Kennedy) dissented. They argued that the plaintiffs had failed to show that the main purpose of the districting was racial (that is, electing a black representative) rather than political (that is, packing Democratic black voters into a single district).

In another 2017 redistricting case, *Bethune-Hill v. Virginia State Board of Elections*,[40] the Court upheld the creation of a 55 percent black district by a vote of 7 to 1. Although the Court concluded that race was the dominant motive for creating the district, it accepted the state's vote-dilution rationale based on the facts of the case. At the time the plan was adopted, the Court reasoned, failure to address the vote-dilution problem would probably have been a violation of the federal Voting Rights Act. The need to comply with the statute provided a compelling interest. While upholding this district, the Court clarified that a racial gerrymander can exist even when states follow traditional districting principles if voters have still been predominantly sorted into districts by race. Furthermore, the Court said, a reviewing court must broadly analyze each district as a whole, rather than just the parts of each district that deviate from traditional redistricting criteria.

Most of the cases discussed above involved claims of racial discrimination brought by whites, not members of a racial minority group. Part of the reason is that such claims can be brought instead under the Voting Rights Act, which was amended after *Bolden* to cover both discriminatory intent and discriminatory effect. After this statutory amendment, minority plaintiffs have largely switched from equal protection claims to statutory claims in racial gerrymandering cases, because it is easier to prove discriminatory effect than it is to prove discriminatory intent. Minority plaintiffs may also suspect that the increasingly conservative Supreme Court will not prove a favorable forum for their efforts to prove discriminatory intent on the part of Republican state legislators.

---

[40]   580 U.S. ___, 137 S. Ct. 788 (2017).

C. Political Gerrymandering

Bizarrely shaped districts that pack members of the same group together need not based on race. A legislative majority that seeks to maintain power can use similar techniques to limit the voting strength of the opposing political party. The Court has yet to decide whether courts have the authority to resolve such cases. The problem facing the Court is that it has no great option. On one hand, legislative redistricting is inherently political. If the Court applied a "dominant motive" test of the kind used in racial gerrymandering cases, lower courts might strike down many legislative apportionments. The immediate result would be that many elections would be placed under court-ordered plans, moving reapportionment out of the democratic process. Alternatively, states would be forced to switch to nonpartisan redistricting commissions, a drastic change from longstanding practice in all but a few states.

On the other hand, declaring all partisan gerrymander claims nonjusticiable is problematic because modern computer technology enables the party in control of the legislature to produce partisan gerrymanders that nearly turn on its head the basic principle of representative government that the people choose their representatives, not the other way around. In what sense is a system democratic if the party that receives, say, 40 percent of the statewide vote earns, say, 60 percent of the seats in the state legislature? From a *Caroline Products* perspective, it seems constitutionally problematic for a party to entrench itself in power in this way. Thus, the conundrum is for the Court to find some meaningful but limited way of determining when a politically motivated redistricting goes too far, assuming such a way exists.

The Court first encountered the issue of political gerrymandering in *Davis v. Bandemer*.[41] The Republican-controlled Indiana legislature had redistricted after the 1980 census, resulting in serious under-representation of Democrats compared to the popular vote. The most striking disparities were in the state House, where the Democrats won nearly 52 percent of the popular vote but only 43 percent of the seats. The legislature had set up multi-member districts in two counties, where the Democrats won 43 percent of the vote but only three out of 21 seats (about 15 percent of the seats up for election). A majority of the Court agreed that the issue of political gerrymandering was justiciable and not a political question. Justice O'Connor (joined by Chief Justice Warren Burger and then-Justice William Rehnquist) dissented on this point.

---

[41]   478 U.S. 109 (1986).

Although the members of the majority agreed that political gerrymandering is a justiciable issue, they fragmented on the merits of the case. Justice Byron White, writing for four Justices, argued that political considerations were inevitable in redistricting by legislatures. The test, Justice White argued, was whether "the electoral system is arranged in a manner that will consistently degrade a voter's or group's influence on the political process as a whole."[42] Justice White did not find this test to be satisfied in this case. For Justice Lewis Powell, joined by Justice John Paul Stevens, the key factors in establishing a political gerrymander were an intent to exclude the other party from power combined with contorted districts and the systematic failure to follow existing political boundaries by combining areas from different (and often remote) cities and counties. Based on these factors, Justice Powell concluded that the district court had properly invalidated the redistricting plan.

The Court returned to the issue eighteen years later in *Vieth v. Jubelirer*.[43] The Court's most conservative members joined an opinion for four Justices by Justice Antonin Scalia arguing that political gerrymandering presents a political question because of the lack of any judicially manageable standards. (Note, however, that they did not have enough votes to overrule *Davis v. Bandemer*'s contrary holding, which presumably remains good law.) The four liberal Justices (Stevens, David Souter, Ginsburg, and Stephen Breyer) dissented and proposed several standards for adjudicating such cases.

The fifth vote to dismiss the case was cast by Justice Kennedy, but he was not prepared to agree that political gerrymandering cases invariably present political questions. He kept the door open in a long and somewhat tortuous sentence:

> While agreeing with the plurality that the complaint the appellants filed in the District Court must be dismissed, and while understanding that great caution is necessary when approaching this subject, I would not foreclose all possibility of judicial relief if some limited and precise rationale were found to correct an established violation of the Constitution in some redistricting cases.[44]

And there the matter has rested until 2018, when the Court appeared poised to resolve two political gerrymandering cases before it, but instead unanimously disposed of both of them on grounds that

---

42   *Id.* at 132 (plurality opinion).

43   541 U.S. 267 (2004).

44   *Id.* at 306 (Kennedy, J., concurring in judgment).

did not address the merits.[45] Then Justice Kennedy left the Court. Perhaps there is now a conservative majority to hold political gerrymandering nonjusticiable. But in the meantime, there are a number of ideas for identifying unconstitutional political gerrymanders. For instance, in a case remanded by the Court for reconsideration of standing, the lower court had adopted, as part of its analysis, a mathematical measure called "the efficiency gap," which is based on disparities in the number of votes wasted by each party in safe districts.[46] Wasted votes are either votes for a party that lost the district or votes for a party that exceed the number of votes the party requires to win the district.

As scholars have observed, "[t]he Court's tendency when confronted with the difficult question of whether to supervise an area of democratic politics is to vacillate between confessions of judicial impotence" and "professions of institutional confidence that it is uniquely suited to take on the pressing democratic problem" facing the nation.[47] At present, particularly in light of recent appointments to the Court, it appears that political gerrymandering may remain on the "confession of judicial impotence" side of this divide, although perhaps one should take such confessions with a grain of salt given the Court's striking institutional self-confidence in other areas of constitutional law.

Voters in a number of states have not waited for the Supreme Court to act. Agreeing with the Court's view that legislative redistricting is inherently political, voter initiatives in such states have cut through these complexities by creating redistricting commissions outside the legislature. Although no constitutional issues are presented by the use of these commissions for redistricting state legislatures, they were challenged as applied to congressional redistricting. In *Arizona State Legislature v. Arizona Independent Redistricting Commission*,[48] the Court rejected this challenge in a 5 to 4 decision in which Justice Kennedy joined the Court's liberal

---

[45]   *See* Gill v. Whitford, 585 U.S. ___, 138 S. Ct. 1916 (2018) (holding that Wisconsin Democratic voters who rested their equal protection claim of unconstitutional partisan gerrymandering on statewide injury have failed to establish Article III standing); Benisek v. Lamone, 585 U.S. ___, 138 S. Ct. 1942 (2018) (per curiam) (holding that, because the balance of equities and the public interest tilt against granting the motion for a preliminary injunction made by Republican voters claiming that a Maryland congressional district was gerrymandered to retaliate against them for their political views, the district court did not abuse its discretion in denying the motion).

[46]   Whitford v. Gill, 218 F. Supp. 3d 837 (W.D. Wis. 2016), *vacated and remanded*, 138 S. Ct. 1916 (2018). This approach derives from a law review article. *See generally* Nicholas O. Stephanopoulos & Eric M. McGhee, *Partisan Gerrymandering and the Efficiency Gap*, 82 U. CHI. L. REV. 831 (2015).

[47]   Guy-Uriel E. Charles & Luis Fuentes-Rohwer, Reynolds *Reconsidered*, 67 ALA. L. REV. 485, 487 (2015).

[48]   576 U.S. ___, 135 S. Ct. 2652 (2015).

members. Arizona voters had passed an initiative establishing an independent redistricting commission. The Arizona legislature sued in order to reclaim its traditional control over congressional redistricting, relying on the Elections Clause of Article I, Section 4.

The Elections Clause provides that "[t]he Times, Places and Manner of holding Elections for Senators and Representatives, shall be prescribed in each State by the Legislature thereof; but the Congress may at any time by Law make or alter such Regulations." The Arizona legislature claimed that this clause reserved to it control of congressional elections, subject only to control by Congress. Although the dissenters agreed that this was the plain meaning of the text, the majority rejected this argument, arguing that the reference to "the Legislature thereof" in this clause included any body in which the state chose to repose legislative power, in this case the people of the state, who had delegated their power to the commission. In short, Justice Ginsburg said in her opinion for the Court, "[w]e resist reading the Elections Clause to single out federal elections as the one area in which States may not use citizen initiatives as an alternative legislative process."[49] Thus, at least in states where voters have the option of wresting control over redistricting from the state legislature (and assuming a reconstituted Court does not revisit the issue), political gerrymandering can be addressed even if the Supreme Court remains unwilling to do so itself.

II. Access to Redress

The Court has used equal protection outside of the redistricting context to assure individuals the ability to access the courts, to access the ballot, and to vote, regardless of wealth. It may be unlikely that the current Court would have created these doctrines, but so far there is no sign of a desire to jettison them.

A. Access to Courts

Over sixty years ago, the Court ruled in *Griffin v. Illinois*[50] that an indigent defendant was entitled to a free transcript of his trial so that he could file an appeal. To understand this case, it is important to bear in mind some generally forgotten history. For a long time after the Constitution was ratified, convicted defendants did not have an automatic right to appeal under state or federal procedures. For this reason, appeals have not been considered part of due process. This view seems completely out of step with contemporary norms and practices, but the Court has not reconsidered it. Thus, the defendant in *Griffin* could not argue that he had a constitutional right to appeal

---

49   *Id.* at 2673.

50   351 U.S. 12 (1956).

his conviction; rather, he could argue only that he had as much of a right to appeal as more affluent defendants enjoyed.

The plurality in *Griffin* considered the effective denial of an appeal to indigents to be a violation of equal protection. The dissent said that the state had not created the defendants' poverty and had no affirmative obligation to assist them. The swing voter was Justice Frankfurter, who agreed with the plurality that if the state "has a general policy of allowing criminal appeals, it cannot make lack of means an effective bar to the exercise of this opportunity."[51] In *Douglas v. California*,[52] the Court extended *Griffin* by holding that the state must provide counsel to indigent defendants at least for their initial appeal. Despite the growing conservative bent of the Court, *Griffin* was reaffirmed as recently as 2005, in *Halbert v. Michigan*.[53]

There are limits, however, on how far the Court has been willing to extend *Griffin*. In many states, as in the federal system, the first level of appellate courts must consider any appeal filed with them, but further review by the highest court is at the discretion of this court. In *Ross v. Moffitt*,[54] the Court held that indigent defendants are not entitled to counsel for further, discretionary appeals. It reasoned that having counsel for the first mandatory review was necessary to provide defendants with a sufficient opportunity to challenge their convictions.

Even so, *Douglas* and *Griffin* illustrate how effective an equality strategy can be in protecting a right. Since there is no due process right to appeal a criminal conviction, a state might be tempted to abolish the right for some group of defendants disfavored by the legislature—say, those convicted of sex crimes. But the state would have a hard time justifying this distinction under an equality challenge. Thus, if the state wanted to limit criminal appeals, it might have to do so for *all* defendants. But such a move would be politically unthinkable, if only because criminal charges against legislators themselves, their family members, and major political donors are not unheard of. Because of the political impossibility of abolishing all appeals, the appeal rights of disfavored defendants are also protected.

Criminal procedure has been heavily constitutionalized—such as by the famous *Miranda* warnings—so perhaps it is more noteworthy that there are similar holdings relating to civil cases. In

---

[51]   *Id.* at 24 (Frankfurter, J., concurring in judgment).

[52]   372 U.S. 353 (1963).

[53]   545 U.S. 605 (2005) (invalidating a Michigan law that denied appointed counsel to defendants appealing guilty pleas).

[54]   417 U.S. 600 (1974).

Boddie v. Connecticut,[55] Justice Harlan wrote for the Court, establishing the right of indigents to file divorce cases even if they cannot pay required court fees and costs. *Boddie* was distinguished as involving fundamental marital interests, which are discussed in Chapter 12, in two later cases dealing with filing fees for bankruptcy and for judicial review of welfare denials.[56] Perhaps because of the increasingly conservative constitutional politics that ultimately produced subsequent appointments to the Court, *Boddie* has not ushered in an era in which free public aid for civil cases is constitutionally required.

Boddie has, however, retained its vitality in cases dealing with family-related issues. In *Little v. Streater,*[57] the Court unanimously held that the defendant in a paternity case was entitled to free blood tests. In *M.L.B. v. S.E.J.,*[58] the Court considered the case of a woman whose custody of her children had been terminated by the state trial court. Like the defendant in *Griffin*, she was unable to pay the filing fee to appeal. Surveying the prior cases, Justice Ginsburg's majority opinion noted that "this Court has not extended *Griffin* to the broad array of civil cases."[59] "But tellingly," she wrote, "the Court has consistently set apart from the mine run of cases those involving state controls or intrusions on family relationships."[60] And "[i]n that domain," she said, "to guard against undue official intrusion, the Court has examined closely and contextually the importance of the governmental interest advanced in defense of the intrusion."[61]

One final point about this line of cases is worth noting. A distinction is often drawn between negative rights to be left alone by the state and positive rights to state assistance. The First Amendment, for example, establishes a negative right protecting speakers from government sanctions, but not a positive right of would-be speakers to government support so that they may speak more effectively. In the United States, federal constitutional rights are generally of the negative type. But in many states and many other countries, constitutions also protect positive rights, such as the right to a clean environment, which imposes a constitutional obligation on the government to keep the environment clean. These rights require affirmative actions by the government in order to vindicate the right.

---

[55] 401 U.S. 371 (1971).

[56] *See* Ortwein v. Schwab, 410 U.S. 656 (1973); United States v. Kras, 409 U.S. 434 (1973).

[57] 452 U.S. 1 (1981).

[58] 519 U.S. 102 (1996).

[59] *Id.* at 116.

[60] *Id.*

[61] *Id.*

The rights discussed in this section straddle the line between negative and positive rights. On one hand, they are triggered only when a court takes some action against a person or where the state has forced recourse to the courts as the only way of settling a dispute, as in the requirement of a court decree to obtain a divorce. In either situation, the state is responsible for creating the situation that produces the need for individuals to exercise these rights. In this respect, they are like negative rights. On the other hand, it is not enough for the state to leave indigent people free to find their own lawyer or pay for their own trial transcript; instead, the state must provide financial assistance. This requirement of affirmative state aid is akin to a positive right—a very limited right to welfare.

B.   Access to the Ballot

Just as nondiscretionary criminal appeals cannot be denied to the indigent, neither can ballot access. In *Harper v. Virginia State Board of Elections*,[62] the Court concluded that "a State violates the Equal Protection Clause of the Fourteenth Amendment whenever it makes the affluence of the voter or payment of any fee an electoral standard," inasmuch as "[v]oter qualifications have no relation to wealth nor to paying or not paying this or any other tax."[63] Using similar reasoning, the Court struck down a state law that limited voting in school board elections to those owning property in the district or having children in district schools.[64] The Court stressed the "need for exacting judicial scrutiny of statutes distributing the franchise."[65]

In the context of access to the ballot by political candidates, the Court has applied a sliding scale, depending on the severity of the access barrier. In *Anderson v. Celebrezze*,[66] the Court considered an Ohio statute requiring candidates who are not affiliated with a political party to file seven months before the election. The Court articulated a balancing test taking into account the severity of the burden on candidates, the state's interest in the access requirement, and the closeness of the fit between the interest and the restriction. Applying this test, the Court held the restriction unconstitutional. The Court's approach creates a sliding scale, where judicial review can range from mild to rigorous depending upon the severity of a law's impact on candidates.

---

[62]   383 U.S. 663 (1966).

[63]   *Id.* at 666.

[64]   *See* Kramer v. Union Free Sch. Dist. No. 15, 395 U.S. 621 (1969).

[65]   *Id.* at 628.

[66]   460 U.S. 780 (1983).

A polarizing current issue involves voter identification requirements. *Crawford v. Marion County Election Board*[67] arose relatively early on in the partisan fights over such requirements. The case involved a law requiring voters to present government-issued photo identification in order to vote. Republicans legislators argue that voter identification laws prevent voter fraud. Democratic legislators note the lack of credible evidence of in-person voter fraud after much investigation and view such laws as suppressing the vote of citizens likely to vote Democratic. The six Justices in *Crawford* who voted to uphold the law were split into groups of three. One group, in an opinion by Justice Stevens, applied the *Anderson* test but concluded that the identification requirement was justified, at least in terms of a facial attack on the statute. (A facial attacks seeks to strike down a statute entirely, as opposed to an as-applied attack, which claims that the law is unconstitutional only as applied to the conduct of the challengers.) The other group of three Justices in the majority, in an opinion by Justice Scalia, found that no further justification was needed for such a "minimal" and clearly reasonable burden on the ability to vote.[68] He argued that the same requirement applied to all voters—namely, supplying a photo ID that the state made available for free; any disparate impact on some voters was irrelevant for equal protection purposes.[69] In a strongly worded dissent, Justice Souter argued that "the onus of the Indiana law is illegitimate just because it correlates with no state interest so well as it does with the object of deterring poorer residents from exercising the franchise."[70] Notably, of the Court's liberals, only Justice Stevens was in the majority, and he subsequently voiced doubts about whether the record in the case contained all of the information he required in reaching what he called a "fairly unfortunate decision."[71]

III. The Right to Travel

It seems obvious that, if the United States is to be considered a nation, as opposed to an alliance among separate nations, citizens must have the constitutional right to cross interstate borders without needing visas or submitting to passport checks by states. Yet finding a constitutional hook for this proposition has not proved easy.

---

[67]   553 U.S. 181 (2008).

[68]   *Id.* at 181 (Scalia, J., concurring in judgment).

[69]   *See id.* at 207–09.

[70]   *Id.* at 237 (Souter, J., dissenting).

[71]   Robert Barnes, *Stevens Says Supreme Court Decision on Voter ID Was Correct, But Maybe Not Right*, WASH. POST, May 15, 2016, https://www.washington post.com/politics/courts_law/stevens-says-supreme-court-decision-on-voter-id-was-correct-but-maybe-not-right/2016/05/15/9683c51c-193f-11e6-9e16-2e5a123aac62_story.html?noredirect=on&utm_term=.d40ea94ad1c8.

The Constitution has several provisions and structural principles bearing on movement between states. The Commerce Clause allows Congress to insist upon the free movement of goods, labor, and capital between states. And as also discussed in Chapter 5, the dormant commerce doctrine prohibits state regulations that discriminate against interstate commerce or place an undue burden on it, subject to some exceptions. But it is not clear whether interstate commerce includes people moving into a state to settle. The Privileges and Immunities Clause, the first clause of Article IV, Section 2, provides that "[t]he Citizens of each State shall be entitled to all Privileges and Immunities of Citizens in the several States." This clause prohibits at least some forms of discrimination against nonresidents. This provision is limited to basic interests like employment, as opposed to instance of access to recreational opportunities.[72] (Readers who attend public universities will know that paying in-state tuition is not considered one of these fundamental interests.) Yet there is nothing in the text of these provisions, or elsewhere in the Constitution, guaranteeing the simple right to enter a state or establish residence there in the first place. Even so, before the Civil War the Court had already protected the right to travel despite the lack of an obvious textual hook.[73]

Shapiro v. Thompson[74] is the leading modern case on the right to travel. The case involved several states that required a year of residency before the states would provide welfare and related benefits to families with dependent children. The plaintiffs were all individuals who had been denied benefits because they had lived in their states less than a year. The Court found it obvious that the provisions at issue were intended to prevent indigent individuals from moving to these states, and indeed, that they were well calculated to do so. As the Court put it, the "indigent who desires to migrate, resettle, find a new job, and start a new life will doubtless hesitate if he knows that he must risk making the move without the possibility of falling back on state welfare assistance during his first year of residence, when his need may be most acute."[75] The Court viewed the case as posing an equal protection problem. The statutes clearly classified applicants for benefits into two groups: those who had lived there for more than a year, and those with shorter periods of residence. The majority agreed with the lower court's ruling that this classification violated the Equal Protection Clause.

In assessing the relevant state interests, the Court applied strict scrutiny. Some of the statutes may have been designed to prevent the

---

72   *See* Baldwin v. Fish & Game Comm'n of Mont., 436 U.S. 371 (1978).

73   *See* the Passenger Cases, 48 U.S. 283 (1849).

74   394 U.S. 618 (1969).

75   *Id.* at 629.

indigent from moving into the state at all. The Court deemed this purpose clearly impermissible given the constitutional right to travel, which prevents states from isolating themselves from travelers from other states. A narrower motivation was to prevent individuals from moving into a state to take advantage of the state's benefits, because they might become long-term drains on the community. The Court also rejected this justification, saying that "a State may no more try to fence out those indigents who seek higher welfare benefits than it may try to fence out indigents generally."[76] The Court added that it did "not perceive why a mother who is seeking to make a new life for herself and her children should be regarded as less deserving because she considers, among others factors, the level of a State's public assistance."[77]

After *Shapiro*, the Court issued a series of rulings on durational residency requirements in state laws. The opinions are not always easy to reconcile. For instance, in *Memorial Hospital v. Maricopa County*,[78] the Court struck down a state law requiring a year of residency before an indigent could receive free nonemergency hospitalization at a county hospital. Yet a year earlier, the Court had upheld another one-year residency requirement in *Sosna v. Iowa*,[79] in this case for filing for divorce. The Court did not consider it unreasonable to expect someone to wait for a year to get a divorce. The majority thought that "[a] State such as Iowa may quite reasonably decide that it does not wish to become a divorce mill for unhappy spouses who have lived there as short a time as appellant had when she commenced her action in the state court after having long resided elsewhere."[80] One important factor in these cases may have been whether the residency requirement was reasonably aimed at determining whether people seeking a benefit really had moved there, as opposed to sojourned there to obtain a benefit such as permissive divorce laws.

A more recent case, *Saenz v. Roe*,[81] applied a novel approach rather than the usual equal protection analysis in durational residency cases. Apparently in an effort to prevent people from moving to the state to take advantage of higher welfare benefits, California provided benefits at the same level as the applicant's prior state for the first year of California residency. Thus, individuals coming from states with lower benefits were no worse off than if they had stayed in the previous state, but they received lower benefits

---

[76]   *Id.* at 631.

[77]   *Id.* at 632.

[78]   415 U.S. 250 (1976).

[79]   419 U.S. 393 (1975).

[80]   *Id.* at 407.

[81]   526 U.S. 489 (1999).

than long-time residents. California argued that this statute was distinguishable from the laws at issue in *Shapiro v. Thompson* because California merely failed to reward indigent newcomers rather than penalizing them. The Court avoided this argument by eschewing the Equal Protection Clause as the basis for its analysis. Instead, the Court invoked the long-dormant Privileges or Immunities Clause of Section 1 of the Fourteenth Amendment, holding that the right to move to a state and be treated like all other residents is one of the privileges or immunities of U.S. citizenship.[82]

As you may recall from Chapter 8, *The Slaughter-House Cases* seemed to strip any significance from this clause of the Constitution. Justice Stevens found a loophole, however, in the majority opinion in *The Slaughter-House Cases*. He quoted it to the effect that one of the privileges conferred by this Clause "is that a citizen of the United States can, of his own volition, become a citizen of any State of the Union by a *bonâ fide* residence therein, with the same rights as other citizens of that State."[83] Thus, Justice Stevens did not have to directly challenge the *Slaughter-House Cases*. Nevertheless, given the clause's marginal position in modern constitutional doctrine, the Court's use of the Privileges or Immunity Clauses is noteworthy. Perhaps it is a sign that the clause is not quite so dead as many have assumed. On the other hand, there have been no further developments over the ensuing two decades, and the Court in *McDonald v. City of Chicago*[84] declined an invitation to use the Privileges or Immunities Clause instead of the Due Process Clause to incorporate the Second Amendment.[85]

IV. Education

One of the basic functions of modern government is public education. This is a quintessential positive right, which enjoys no direct recognition in the U.S. Constitution. But an equality strategy might be available as a way of strengthening access to education, particularly among the poor, who are especially dependent on state-provided education.

Unequal access to education is a subject that the Supreme Court has addressed twice, declining to view education as a fundamental

---

[82]   For a review of the case law and discussion of the *Saenz* Court's novel approach, see generally Stacey E. Winick, *A New Chapter in Constitutional Law:* Saenz v. Roe *and the Revival of the Fourteenth Amendment's Privileges or Immunities Clause*, 10 HOFSTRA L. REV. 9 (1999).

[83]   *Roe*, 526 U.S. at 503 (*quoting* The Slaughter-House Cases, 16 Wall. 36, 80 (1872)).

[84]   561 U.S. 742 (2010).

[85]   For a discussion of why the Court likely proceeded this way in *McDonald*, see generally Neil S. Siegel, *Prudentialism in* McDonald v. City of Chicago, 6 DUKE J. CONST. L. & PUB. POL'Y 16 (2010).

right in the first case but nevertheless giving it some protection in a later one. These cases provide a fitting conclusion to our discussion of equal protection, because they involve both the fundamental rights prong of equal protection doctrine discussed in this chapter and the protected classes prong of equal protection doctrine analyzed in Chapter 10.

As we saw in Section III of this chapter, the Court has struck down barriers that unnecessarily prevent the indigent from enjoying a fundamental right. But the Court has steadfastly refused to classify the poor as a protected class. For instance, in *Dandridge v. Williams*,[86] the Court upheld a cap on welfare benefits based on family size, which severely disadvantaged children in large families. The Court worried that subjecting laws disadvantaging the poor to strict scrutiny would call into question a host of laws and would effectively require close judicial scrutiny of many economic regulations.

Education in most states varies depending on the district in which a person resides. The reason is that school districts traditionally have relied on local property taxes, so that affluent school districts could afford better schools than poorer ones. As we discuss later, many state constitutions have provisions guaranteeing citizens a public education, but there is no similar provision in the U.S. Constitution. Thus, federal challenges to these educational inequalities were based on equal protection.

The equal protection issue came before the Supreme Court in a fateful Texas case, *San Antonio Independent School District v. Rodriguez*.[87] *Rodriguez* was a class action brought by children in the Edgewood School District challenging the Texas system of school finance. The San Antonio School District was originally a defendant, but after the claim against it was dismissed, it switched sides and became a plaintiff. Edgewood was a low-income residential district with nearly a 96 percent minority population. With property taxes along with state and federal funding, it spent $356 annually per student. In contrast, Alamo Heights, a largely white, more affluent district, spent $594 per student, or 66 percent more.[88]

The Court ruled 5 to 4 in favor of the defendants, with the newly solidified conservative majority outvoting liberal holdovers from the Warren Court. Justice Powell, who had served as a member of the school board of Richmond, Virginia, wrote the opinion of the Court.

---

[86]   397 U.S. 471 (1970).

[87]   411 U.S. 1 (1973).

[88]   *See id.* at 4–9.

He applied rational basis scrutiny, rejecting the arguments that either a suspect class or a fundamental right was involved.

Regarding the potential presence of a suspect class, Justice Powell distinguished earlier cases that had given heightened scrutiny to certain classifications involving the poor, such as the ballot and court access decisions that we discussed earlier. He characterized these cases as limited to a specific type of deprivation. "The individuals, or groups of individuals, who constituted the class discriminated against in our prior cases," he wrote, "shared two distinguishing characteristics: because of their impecunity they were completely unable to pay for some desired benefit, and as a consequence, they sustained an absolute deprivation of a meaningful opportunity to enjoy that benefit."[89] He also reasoned that residents of districts with small assessed property values could not be considered a suspect class because this group was too amorphous to qualify, in that there is a spectrum of districts on this dimension rather than a dichotomy and their residents are also diverse. For instance, a district might have a poorer population but high revenue from property taxes due to commercial or industrial property.

Justice Powell than turned to whether public education is a fundamental right. "It is not the province of this Court," he said, "to create substantive constitutional rights in the name of guaranteeing equal protection of the laws."[90] The plaintiffs argued, however, that there were special reasons for constitutional recognition of education "because it is essential to the effective exercise of First Amendment freedoms and to intelligent utilization of the right to vote."[91]

Justice Powell offered two responses to this argument. First, he wrote, "we have never presumed to possess either the ability or the authority to guarantee to the citizenry the most effective speech or the most informed electoral choice."[92] Second, he added alternatively, "[e]ven if it were conceded that some identifiable quantum of education is a constitutionally protected prerequisite to the meaningful exercise of either right, we have no indication that the present levels of educational expenditures in Texas provide an education that falls short."[93]

Having dismissed the arguments for heightened scrutiny, Justice Powell argued that the Texas scheme easily passed rational basis review. For one thing, he noted, tax policy is a complex technical area, which judges are ill-suited to assess; the same is even more true

---

[89]   *Id.* at 20.

[90]   *Id.* at 33.

[91]   *Id.* at 35.

[92]   *Id.* at 36.

[93]   *Id.* at 36–37.

for educational policy. For another thing, Justice Powell had major federalism—and, perhaps, prudential—concerns: "it would be difficult to imagine a case having a greater potential impact on our federal system than the one now before us, in which we are urged to abrogate systems of financing public education presently in existence in virtually every State."[94]

Justice White wrote the lead dissent. He viewed the majority's opinion as a tragic mistake. In his view, "the right of every American to an equal start in life, so far as the provision of a state service as important as education is concerned, is far too vital to permit state discrimination on grounds as tenuous as those presented by this record."[95] Quoting *Brown v. Board of Education*, he expressed his disappointment with the decision: "I, for one, am unsatisfied with the hope of an ultimate 'political' solution sometime in the indefinite future while, in the meantime, countless children unjustifiably receive inferior educations that may affect their 'hearts and minds in a way unlikely ever to be undone.' "[96] If the majority was worried in part about the potentially dramatic political consequences of judicial intervention, the dissent was concerned in part about the human consequences of staying the judicial hand.

Rodriguez nearly closed the door of the federal courthouse to most educational reform litigation, but not quite. As indicated by some of the language quoted above, Justice Powell's opinion did leave some wiggle room for a future case dealing with a more sharply defined and disenfranchised group and a more absolute deprivation of educational rights.[97] In *Plyler v. Doe*,[98] just such a case presented itself to the Court. *Plyler* involved a Texas law that denied state funding to children who were not lawfully admitted to the United States and that authorized local school districts to exclude them from school entirely.

Justice William Brennan's opinion for the Court began by establishing a premise of continued significance today—for example, in debates over immigration. He rejected the argument that a person whose presence in the country is unlawful falls outside the protection of the Constitution. The Equal Protection Clause applies "to any person within [a state's] jurisdiction." Justice Brennan rejected the argument that the reference to state jurisdiction excluded individuals unlawfully present in a state. In his view, "[t]o permit a State to employ the phrase 'within its jurisdiction' in order to identify

---

94   *Id.* at 44.

95   *Id.* at 71 (White, J., dissenting).

96   *Id.* at 71–72 (quoting Brown v. Board of Education, 347 U.S. 483, 494 (1954)).

97   *See Rodriguqez*, 411 U.S. at 36–37.

98   457 U.S. 202 (1982).

subclasses of persons whom it would define as beyond its jurisdiction, thereby relieving itself of the obligation to assure that its laws are designed and applied equally to those persons, would undermine the principal purpose for which the Equal Protection Clause was incorporated in the Fourteenth Amendment."[99]

In assessing the equal protection claim, Justice Brennan noted that the long-term presence of undocumented aliens "raises the specter of a permanent caste of undocumented resident aliens, encouraged by some to remain here as a source of cheap labor, but nevertheless denied the benefits that our society makes available to citizens and lawful residents."[100] Unlike their parents, Justice Brennan said, these children were not responsible for their own presence in the country. He found it "difficult to conceive of a rational justification for penalizing these children for their presence within the United States."[101]

Turning to the individual interest at stake, Justice Brennan conceded that education is not a fundamental right, but he insisted that it had a distinctive status, pointing to it importance "in maintaining our basic institutions, and the lasting impact of its deprivation on the life of the child."[102] Further, he said, "denial of education to some isolated group of children poses an affront to one of the goals of the Equal Protection Clause: the abolition of governmental barriers presenting unreasonable obstacles to advancement on the basis of individual merit."[103]

Justice Brennan acknowledged that "[u]ndocumented aliens cannot be treated as a suspect class because their presence in this country in violation of federal law is not a 'constitutional irrelevancy.' "[104] "Nor," he said, "is education a fundamental right; a State need not justify by compelling necessity every variation in the manner in which education is provided to its population."[105] But given the interests at stake, he argued, the Texas statute "can hardly be considered rational unless it furthers some substantial goal of the State."[106] After an examination of the asserted justifications given by the state, he concluded that the law failed this test.

Justice Powell, the author of *Rodriguez*, provided the critical fifth vote. He analogized to cases giving heightened review to statutes

---

99   *Id.* at 213.

100   *Id.* at 218–19.

101   *Id.* at 220.

102   *Id.* at 221.

103   *Id.* at 221–22.

104   *Id.* at 223.

105   *Id.*

106   *Id.* at 224.

discriminating against children born outside of marriage, a condition attributable to their parents rather than themselves. Here, he found the discrimination more objectionable, if anything, because the children involved "have been singled out for a lifelong penalty and stigma" by a law "that threatens the creation of an underclass of future citizens and residents."[107]

The dissent by Chief Justice Burger took the majority to task for the ad hoc nature of its reasoning. In the end, he complained, "we are told little more than that the level of scrutiny employed to strike down the Texas law applies only when illegal alien children are deprived of a public education. If ever a court was guilty of an unabashedly result-oriented approach, this case is a prime example."[108] It seemed to the dissent as if the majority had combined half a suspect-class argument and half a fundamental-rights argument to somehow produce a winning constitutional claim.

The Rehnquist Court limited *Plyler* in *Kadrmas v. Dickinson Public Schools*.[109] This case involved a Nebraska law authorizing school districts to charge families a fee to bus students to school. The law applied only to school districts that had chosen not to consolidate with neighboring districts. The apparent purpose was to encourage school district consolidation. The Court held that the rational basis test applied and read *Plyler* narrowly:

> We have not extended [*Plyler*] beyond the "unique circumstances" that provoked its "unique confluence of theories and rationales." Nor do we think that the case before us today is governed by the holding in *Plyler*. Unlike the children in that case, [the plaintiff] has not been penalized by the government for illegal conduct by her parents. . . . Nor do we see any reason to suppose that this user fee will "promot[e] the creation and perpetuation of a subclass of illiterates within our boundaries, surely adding to the problems and costs of unemployment, welfare, and crime."[110]

It is, at the very least, unclear whether *Plyler* would command a majority today—or at any point during the existences of the Rehnquist and Roberts Courts. Under current political conditions, *Plyler* may be more relevant for what it has say about the constitutional rights of undocumented aliens than for its holding on education. In the meantime, the federal courts seem to have exited from any constitutional engagement with educational inequality

---

[107] *Id.* at 238–39 (Powell, J., concurring).

[108] *Id.* at 244 (Burger, C.J., dissenting).

[109] 487 U.S. 450 (1988).

[110] *Id.* at 459 (quoting the concurring and dissenting opinions in *Plyler*).

notwithstanding (in our view as educators, at least) the magnitude of the problem and the federal constitutional rights and purposes that are advanced by a good basic education.

Although the federal courts have played only a small role in educational equality, many state courts have been less reluctant to enter the political fray. This fact provides us an opportunity to explain the role of state constitutional law in the U.S. legal system.

It is important to understand that every state has its own constitution; state governments exist in virtue of these state constitutions. Under the Supremacy Clause of Article VI, of course, state constitutions are not permitted to violate federal law. Thus, state constitutions cannot validly authorize a state to violate federally guaranteed rights or to invade areas of exclusive federal authority. But these federal constitutional limitations leave open a very wide domain of state activity consistent with federal law. States are entirely free to place parts of this domain off-limits by providing rights in their constitutions that go beyond the ones in the federal constitution. Many state constitutions have done so—for example, they have language mandating that state governments provide public education. Such provisions have provided a basis for litigation attacking the kinds of funding inequalities involved in *Rodriguez.*

Indeed, the Texas Supreme Court considered this issue in a case brought by the Edgewood School District, the same district involved in *Rodriguez* itself. In *Edgewood Independent School District v. Kirby,*[111] the state supreme court held that the Texas school system violated the Texas Constitution. The court described the inequalities of the system in stark terms, pointing to a 700 to 1 ratio in the amount of assessed property between the richest and the poorest district. The court observed that the "300,000 students in the lowest-wealth schools have less than 3% of the state's property wealth to support their education while the 300,000 students in the highest-wealth schools have over 25% of the state's property wealth."[112] The court concluded that this degree of inequity violated the mandate of the Texas Constitution that the legislature must "establish and make suitable provision for the support and maintenance of an efficient system of public free schools."[113] As this case illustrates, state courts interpreting state constitutions may protect rights that are not

---

[111]   777 S.W.2d 391 (Tex. 1989).

[112]   *Id.* at 392. The protracted subsequent litigation seeking to implement the Texas constitutional requirement is summarized in *Morath v. The Texas Taxpayer & Student Fairness Coalition,* 490 S.W.3d 826 (Tex. 2016), in which the court held that state constitutional requirements had finally been satisfied.

[113]   TEXAS CONST. art. VII, § 1.

protected—either at all or as much—by federal courts enforcing the U.S. Constitution.[114]

Rodriguez indicates that there are clear limits on the Court's willingness to protect fundamental rights under the Equal Protection Clause. Yet within these boundaries, which were set by a liberal Court that has long since ceased to exist, the Court's work is not particularly controversial: for example, there is no political pressure to overrule *Reynolds v. Sims* or *Shapiro v. Thompson*. In the next chapter, we will examine the far more controversial protection of fundamental rights under the Due Process Clause. The issues in this area of law remain front-page news and are highlighted in many a political campaign and Supreme Court confirmation process.

Further Readings

Richard Briffault, Bush v. Gore *as an Equal Protection Case*, 29 FSU L. REV. 325 (2002).

Guy-Uriel E. Charles & Luis Fuentes-Rohwer, Reynolds *Reconsidered*, 67 ALA. L. REV. 485 (2015).

RICHARD L. HASEN, THE SUPREME COURT AND ELECTION LAW: JUDGING EQUALITY FROM *BAKER V. CARR* TO *BUSH V. GORE* (2003).

Richard M. Hills, Jr., *Poverty, Residency, and Federalism: States' Duty of Impartiality Toward Newcomers*, 1999 SUP. CT. REV. 277, 278 (1999).

Samuel Issacharoff, *Gerrymandering and Political Cartels*, 116 HARV. L. REV. 593 (2002).

CHARLES J. OGLETREE JR., KIMBERLY JENKINS ROBINSON, & JAMES E. RYAN (EDS.), THE ENDURING LEGACY OF *RODRIGUEZ*: CREATING NEW PATHWAYS TO EQUAL EDUCATIONAL OPPORTUNITY (2015).

J. DOUGLAS SMITH, ON DEMOCRACY'S DOORSTEP: THE INSIDE STORY OF HOW THE SUPREME COURT BROUGHT "ONE PERSON, ONE VOTE" TO THE UNITED STATES (2014).

Nicholas O. Stephanopoulos & Eric M. McGhee, *Partisan Gerrymandering and the Efficiency Gap*, 82 U. CHI. L. REV. 831 (2015).

---

[114] State constitutional litigation over school funding has at times threatened to produce constitutional crises, with the political branches of a state's government threatening to defy judicial rulings that require equitable funding of public education in the state. For a discussion of such a situation in Kansas, see Siegel, *supra* note 4, at 1228–30.

Chapter 12

FUNDAMENTAL RIGHTS: SUBSTANTIVE DUE PROCESS

Chapter 12 brings us to perhaps the most controversial area of current constitutional doctrine. Building on a handful of earlier decisions dealing with family autonomy and procreation, the Supreme Court began in the 1960s and 1970s to provide protection for the reproductive rights of contraception and abortion. The Court's abortion decisions eventually helped trigger a revolt led by religious conservatives. This led to a moderation of judicial doctrine in a jurisprudential compromise that failed to satisfy critics and past supporters alike. The Court then participated in a national debate about same-sex intimacy and same-sex marriage, issues on which public views changed very rapidly in the early Twenty-First Century. And other questions, such as physician-assisted suicide, have been subject to social controversy, although the Court so far has avoided any dramatic interventions. Social movements, based on feminism and gay rights on the one hand and conservative religious views on the other hand, have played a pervasive role in these developments,[1] as did the political party realignment of the last third of the Twentieth Century.[2]

Our starting point is a series of cases stretching back to the 1920s, in which the Court gave special protection to issues relating to the family. In the 1960s, the Court moved into what was then a somewhat controversial issue, contraception, although its intervention was generally accepted by the public, if not by some constitutional law scholars. In the 1970s, the Court moved into what would become much more controversial territory in a landmark case that placed sharp constitutional limitations on laws restricting access to abortion. Later in the century and into the current one, the Court again found itself in the middle of a sustained social conflict, this time over gay rights. We close our discussion by examining the Court's relatively hands-off approach to another fraught issue, assisted suicide.

Doctrinally, the law in this area can be seen as an outgrowth of the incorporation debate discussed in Chapter 8. Incorporation of most of the Bill of Rights into the Due Process Clause of the

---

[1]   For a general discussion, see William N. Eskridge, Jr., *Some Effects of Identity-Based Social Movements on Constitutional Law in the Twentieth Century*, 100 MICH. L. REV. 2962 (2002).

[2]   This point is developed in Linda Greenhouse & Reva B. Siegel, *Before (and After) Roe v. Wade: New Questions About Backlash*, 120 YALE L.J. 2028 (2012).

Fourteenth Amendment did not merely subject the states to the discrete rights listed in the first eight amendments. Despite the demise of *Lochner*, incorporation made it clear that the Court continued to view the Due Process Clause as embodying substantive rights, not merely a guarantee of fair procedures. Incorporation, in other words, is a form of substantive due process. Some Justices insisted that incorporation exhausted the substantive content of the Due Process Clause. As we will see, however, this has never been the majority view on the Court.

Another doctrinal point to watch for is the interplay between liberty rights and equality values in these cases. A few of the cases that we will discuss are explicitly founded on the Equal Protection Clause. More often, the Court relies textually upon the Due Process Clause but enforces equality values in addition to liberty values. Part of the reason for this overlap is that the laws involved in these cases involve discrete groups such as women or gays. Another part of the reason is that the Court's modern, classification-based equal protection jurisprudence imposes a variety of doctrinal impediments to the straightforward expression of substantive, anti-subordination values, as we saw in Chapter 10; the Court's substantive due process jurisprudence lacks these impediments.

I.   Family Autonomy and Marriage

The existence of families is not mentioned in the Constitution or its amendments. Yet, families in some form are a universal human institution of deep personal and societal importance. In general, the Court has left issues of family law to the states. But from time to time the Court has found occasion to explicate the fundamental constitutional status of the family and marriage.

A.   Parental Rights and Family Relationships

In *Meyer v. Nebraska*,[3] a Nebraska law prohibited teaching children in any public or private school in any language but English before the eighth grade. The defendant, who taught German, was convicted of violating the law. The goal of the law was to ensure that the children of immigrants fully learned English rather than their parents' language, in order to ensure their assimilation into American society. Citing precedents from the *Slaughter-House Cases* through *Lochner*, the Court said that the term "liberty" in the Due Process Clause "denotes not merely freedom from bodily restraint but also the right of the individual . . . to marry, establish a home and bring up children," and "generally to enjoy those privileges long recognized at common law as essential to the orderly pursuit of

---

[3]   262 U.S. 390 (1923).

happiness by free men."[4] Hence, the defendant's right "to teach and the right of parents to engage him so to instruct their children, we think, are within the liberty of the amendment."[5] Note the Court's reliance on freedom of contract (between the parents and teacher), the basis for *Lochner*, which is not surprising given that the author of the opinion, Justice James McReynolds, was the most reactionary member of the Court.

The Court did not find a sufficient basis for infringing on this liberty. True, the Court said, "the state may do much, go very far, indeed, in order to improve the quality of its citizens, physically, mentally and morally," yet "the individual has certain fundamental rights which must be respected."[6] The Constitution's protection "extends to all, to those who speak other languages as well as to those born with English on the tongue."[7] Justices Oliver Wendell Holmes (who had dissented in *Lochner*), and Justice George Sutherland, one of the more conservative members of the Court, dissented without opinion.

Following *Meyer*, the Court in *Pierce v. Society of Sisters*[8] ruled that a state could not require all children to attend public schools. The law was challenged by a religious school and a military school. Applying *Meyer*, Justice McReynolds, again writing for the Court, deemed *Meyer* controlling. The brief opinion took a slightly different turn, however, with less emphasis on freedom of contract and more on individual autonomy. As Justice McReynolds wrote, the "fundamental theory of liberty upon which all governments in this Union repose excludes any general power of the state to standardize its children by forcing them to accept instruction from public teachers only."[9] For "[t]he child is not the mere creature of the state; those who nurture him and direct his destiny have the right, coupled with the high duty, to recognize and prepare him for additional obligations."[10]

Today, *Pierce* and *Meyer* could be defended on First Amendment grounds, but as written they hover between general *Lochner*-era skepticism of government regulation and a more modern attitude that certain personal and familial matters enjoy special protection from government interference.

---

4   *Id.* at 399.

5   *Id.* at 400.

6   *Id.* at 401.

7   *Id.*

8   268 U.S. 510 (1925).

9   *Id.* at 535.

10   *Id.*

Two more recent cases also dealt with family relationships. The first case, *Moore v. City of East Cleveland*,[11] involved a grandmother who could not lawfully live with her grandchildren because of a local zoning ordinance; there were five votes to hold this restriction unconstitutional but no majority opinion. The second case, *Michael H. v. Gerald D.*,[12] involved a biological father's claim to parental rights over a child who was conceived while the mother was married to another man. Under California law, a baby born during a marriage was presumed to be the child of the husband and wife; only they could rebut the presumption and only under limited circumstances. The plurality opinion was written by Justice Antonin Scalia, who found no basis in American tradition narrowly conceived for recognizing the parental rights of a biological father under such circumstances. Justices Sandra Day O'Connor and Anthony Kennedy joined Justice Scalia's opinion, but with the caveat that Justice Scalia's tradition-based approach did not provide the exclusive avenue for establishing fundamental rights.

B. Marriage

Loving v. Virginia[13] is best remembered as an equal protection case, but its alternative holding was based on substantive due process. Recall from Chapter 10 that this case involved a ban on inter-racial marriage. Besides condemning the law as blatantly discriminatory, the Court also held that it deprived the couple of liberty without due process. As the Court said, "[t]he freedom to marry has long been recognized as one of the vital personal rights essential to the orderly pursuit of happiness by free men."[14] The Court held that the ban on inter-racial marriage violated this right:

> Marriage is one of the "basic civil rights of man," fundamental to our very existence and survival. . . . To deny this fundamental freedom on so unsupportable a basis as the racial classifications embodied in these statutes, classifications so directly subversive of the principle of equality at the heart of the Fourteenth Amendment, is surely to deprive all the State's citizens of liberty without due process of law.[15]

Notably, the Court so held even after observing that bans on inter-racial marriage went back to the days of slavery, so they could hardly be said to be foreign to American history and tradition.

---

[11]   431 U.S. 494 (1977).

[12]   491 U.S. 110 (1989).

[13]   388 U.S. 1 (1967).

[14]   *Id.* at 12.

[15]   *Id.*

In *Zablocki v. Redhail*,[16] the Court struck down a Wisconsin law preventing remarriage by people with unpaid child support obligations from previous marriages. Reaffirming that marriage is a fundamental right, the Court said that a statute significantly interfering with this right "cannot be upheld unless it is supported by sufficiently important state interests and is closely tailored to effectuate only those interests."[17] The Court found the fit between the statute and the state's interest in assuring child support too weak to satisfy this test. The Court reasoned that the law was underinclusive because it did not prevent the errant parent from entering into other kinds of debts and overinclusive since remarriage might actually improve the parent's financial position and ability to pay support.

Prior to the debate over same-sex marriage, the most recent of this line of marriage cases was *Turner v. Safley*,[18] which involved a ban on prisoners marrying other prisoners or people from the "civilian" population unless the prison superintendent found compelling circumstances. Because of the prison context, a lower level of scrutiny applied: the government needed to show only that the marriage ban was reasonably related to a legitimate penological objective. In her opinion for the Court, Justice O'Connor was unimpressed by the state's purported security and rehabilitation arguments, particularly because the "proposed marriages of all female inmates were scrutinized carefully even before adoption of the current regulation—only one was approved at Renz [one prison] from 1979–1983, whereas the marriages of male inmates during the same period were routinely approved."[19] This portion of O'Connor's opinion represented the unanimous views of the Justices; the dissenters objected only to a separate holding regarding limits on prisoner's correspondence.

From the perspective of the present, these cases shared a commonality that was simply taken for granted at the time: they all involved restrictions on the right of heterosexuals to marry. We return at the end of this chapter to the topic of marriage in connection with our discussion of gay rights.

II. Reproductive Rights

If parental rights are protected, what about the right to become a parent or not to do so? The cases in this section involve issues of state-mandated sterilization, bans on contraceptives, and bans or restrictions on abortion.

---

[16]   434 U.S. 374 (1978).

[17]   *Id.* at 388.

[18]   482 U.S. 78 (1997).

[19]   *Id.* at 99.

A. Sterilization

A century ago and continuing into the 1930s, state legislatures embraced the notion that compulsory sterilization was an appropriate strategy to rid American society of "defective people." Although today the idea is repulsive to the vast majority of Americans, for many people prior to World War II it was seen as a progressive reform. Numerous laws were passed providing for sterilization of inmates of mental hospitals, prisoners, and others considered defective such as drug addicts, but the laws were vigorously enforced only in California and Virginia.[20]

In *Buck v. Bell*,[21] the Court gave its imprimatur to the practice. Justice Holmes' opinion for the Court upheld a Virginia statute establishing a process for the sterilization of intellectually disabled persons in state institutions. The statute was based on the assumptions that intellectual disability is inheritable; that reproduction by such adults is against society's interests; and that some of these people, if sterilized, could be discharged from state institutions and become self-supporting contributors to society. The state invoked the statute against Carrie Buck, an institutionalized woman. According to findings made by the state trial court, Buck was intellectually disabled, as were both her mother and her child born out of wedlock. Buck argued that the statute was unconstitutional because it intruded on her bodily integrity in violation of substantive due process and that, in applying only to institutionalized persons, the statute was so under-inclusive as to violate equal protection.

Justice Holmes dismissed both arguments. Finding a sufficient state interest in promoting the public welfare to justify the statute under substantive due process, Justice Holmes relied upon *Jacobson v. Massachusetts*,[22] which upheld a state law requiring people to submit to vaccination against infectious disease. Justice Holmes said:

> It is better for all the world, if instead of waiting to execute degenerate offspring for crime, or to let them starve for their imbecility, society can prevent those who are manifestly unfit from continuing their kind. The principle that sustains compulsory vaccination is broad enough to cover cutting the Fallopian tubes.[23]

---

[20] *See* Stephen Jay Gould, *Carrie Buck's Daughter*, 2 CONST. COMM. 331, 332 (1985).

[21] 274 U.S. 200 (1927).

[22] 197 U.S. 11 (1905).

[23] 274 U.S. at 207.

Justice Holmes then added a sentence, since infamous, that further captured his disdain toward Buck and others: "Three generations of imbeciles are enough."[24]

Turning to Buck's second contention, Justice Holmes dismissed the Equal Protection Clause as "the usual last resort of constitutional arguments" and said "the answer is that the law does all that is needed when it does all that it can, indicates a policy, applies it to all within the lines, and seeks to bring within the lines all similarly situated so far and so fast as its means allow."[25]

Buck v. Bell has not endured, either morally or legally. Within a few decades, attitudes had changed. *Skinner v. Oklahoma ex rel. Williamson*[26] was decided during World War II. Jack Skinner was convicted once for stealing chickens and twice for armed robbery. While serving his sentence for the third offense, Oklahoma passed a law providing for the sterilization of habitual criminals, defined as those with three convictions for certain crimes. For instance, the Oklahoma law classified robbery as one such crime, but not embezzlement, even though the two carried the same sentences. Justice William O. Douglas, writing for the Court, held these distinctions unacceptable as a matter of equal protection. Justice Douglas rejected the argument that the rational basis test should apply to "legislation which involves one of the basic civil rights of man," for "[m]arriage and procreation are fundamental to the very existence and survival of the race."[27] Instead of rational basis review, he said, "[s]trict scrutiny of the classification which a State makes in a sterilization law is essential, lest unwittingly or otherwise invidious discriminations are made against groups or types of individuals in violation of the constitutional guaranty of just and equal laws."[28] Indeed, "[w]hen the law lays an unequal hand on those who have committed intrinsically the same quality of offense and sterilizes one and not the other, it has made as invidious a discrimination as if it had selected a particular race or nationality for oppressive treatment."[29]

Skinner had been convicted and sentenced to sterilization in 1930s Oklahoma, when legislators, prosecutors, and ordinary people were anxious about the perpetuation of so-called "degenerates." But as the case made its way up the appellate system, eugenics policy encountered increased skepticism. Scientists in the 1930s cast doubt

---

[24]   *Id.*

[25]   *Id.* at 208.

[26]   316 U.S. 535 (1942).

[27]   *Id.* at 541.

[28]   *Id.*

[29]   *Id.*

on these theories, and national policymakers by the end of the decade were acutely aware of the similarities between American and Nazi eugenics. By the time the case reached the Supreme Court, scientific experts, elite lawyers, and national policymakers had set their minds against sterilization and other eugenics policies. The Court's reference to discrimination against disfavored groups and to racial discrimination carried particular force in light of the Nazi regime with which the country was at war. In a concurring opinion, Justice Robert Jackson, who would later be the U.S. Chief of Counsel at the Nuremberg war-crime trials, added that "[t]here are limits to the extent to which a legislatively represented majority may conduct biological experiments at the expense of the dignity and personality and natural powers of a minority—even those who have been guilty of what the majority define as crimes."[30]

Unfortunately, practices of involuntary sterilization survived the Court's decision in *Skinner*. In her study of such practices in the United States from 1950 to 1980, historian Rebecca Kluchin documents, among other things, how "[f]orced sterilization practices changed and spread in the late 1960s and early 1970s through newly established federal family planning programs."[31] "Increasingly," she finds, "poor women of color entered hospitals for labor and delivery where the neo-eugenic physicians who treated them forced them to undergo tubal ligation. Black women remained the targets of such physicians in the South, while women of color in other regions came under increasing scrutiny."[32] North Carolina was especially aggressive: "[b]etween 1929 and 1974, the state authorized the sterilization of nearly 7,600 people under the state's 1929 sterilization law and subsequent North Carolina Eugenics Board program."[33] In 2013, the legislature passed a statute establishing a $10 million public fund for reparations to sterilization victims.[34] Notwithstanding this sobering history of not protecting vulnerable individuals from coerced sterilization, we cannot imagine a scenario today in which the U.S. Supreme Court would uphold mandatory sterilization.

B. Contraception

Even as the government experimented with forced sterilization, it seemed anxious to prevent many other forms of birth control, especially those that were most effective for women. Contraception

---

[30]   *Id.* at 546 (Jackson, J., concurring).

[31]   REBECCA M. KLUCHIN, FIT TO BE TIED: STERILIZATION AND REPRODUCTIVE RIGHTS IN AMERICA 1950–1980, at 7 (2011).

[32]   *Id.; see id.* at 94–113 (corroborating these claims).

[33]   Alfred L. Brophy & Elizabeth Troutman, *The Eugenics Movement in North Carolina*, 94 N.C. L. REV. 1871, 1877 (2016).

[34]   *See id.* at 1938.

was first banned under federal and state law not in the Founding era, but in the decade after the Civil War.[35] The 1873 federal Comstock Act was premised on the view that it was obscene to separate sex and procreation.[36] Soon after, many states passed laws modeled on the Comstock Act criminalizing contraception and abortion.[37]

Like the federal law, Connecticut's ban on contraception drew no formal distinctions by sex; rather, it prohibited "[a]ny person" from "us[ing] any drug, medicinal article or instrument for the purpose of preventing conception."[38] Even so, contemporaries understood the judgments about nonprocreative sex in the federal and state laws through Victorian mores concerning gender roles. The Comstock Act, for example, was enacted a year after Justice Joseph Bradley explained that "[t]he constitution of the family organization, which is founded in the divine ordinance, as well as in the nature of things, indicates the domestic sphere as that which properly belongs to the domain and functions of womanhood."[39] Doctors reasoned that women who enjoyed sex while endeavoring to avoid its natural procreative consequences engaged in "physiological sin"—and predicted that they would suffer health harms as a result.[40] Press coverage of the Comstock Act focused on women who were prosecuted for defying the ban.[41]

The new bans on contraception applied to all at a time when men and women were held to different standards in matters of sex and parenting. Men were allowed to breach prevailing sexual norms in

---

[35]   Six of the first seven paragraphs in this section draw from Neil S. Siegel & Reva B. Siegel, Griswold *at 50: Contraception as a Sex Equality Right*, 124 YALE L.J. F. 349 (2015).

[36]   *See* Comstock Act ch. 258, 17 Stat. 598, 599 (1873) (repealed 1909) (prohibiting as "obscene" any person from selling or distributing in U.S. mail articles used "for the prevention of conception," or for "causing unlawful abortion," or sending information concerning these practices).

[37]   *See* Carol Flora Brooks, *The Early History of the Anti-Contraceptive Laws in Massachusetts and Connecticut*, 18 AM. Q. 3, 4 (1966) (observing that "anti-contraceptive laws were passed in 24 states as part of obscenity statutes, and obscenity laws in 22 other states came to be used as anti-contraceptive laws because of federal statutes and interpretation").

[38]   *See* Griswold v. Connecticut, 381 U.S. 479, 480 (1965) (quoting CONN. GEN. STAT. § 53–32 (1958)).

[39]   Bradwell v. Illinois, 83 U.S. 130, 141 (1872) (Bradley, J., concurring). This opinion is discussed further in Chapter 10.

[40]   *See* Reva B. Siegel, *Reasoning from the Body: A Historical Perspective on Abortion Regulation and Questions of Equal Protection*, 44 STAN. L. REV. 261, 292–96 (1992) (tracing usage of "physiological sin" and quoting doctors on sins and health harms of preventing pregnancy).

[41]   *See* Ana C. Garner, *Wicked or Warranted?*, JOURNALISM STUD., Jan. 2, 2014, at 6–9.

ways that women were not, and women were expected to assume parenting responsibilities in ways that men were not.[42]

By World War I, the federal government and most states had made it a crime to distribute articles of contraception, and almost half the states criminalized a doctor's providing contraceptive information to patients.[43] Prohibition of birth control bore harshly on women, and feminists such as Emma Goldman and Margaret Sanger objected that these laws not only threatened women's health but also deprived them of life choices that most men took for granted.[44] The state went after both women, deporting Goldman and arresting Sanger, her sister, and her husband. New York closed Sanger's birth control clinic in 1916, and she appealed the conviction to the U.S. Supreme Court.[45] Her attorney argued that the state had no more power to compel a woman to have a baby than an individual had power to compel her to have sex.[46] The Court dismissed her appeal on the ground that it raised no substantial federal question.[47] Notwithstanding the Court's indifference, Sanger and her organization engaged in a relentless and ultimately successful campaign against state and federal anti-contraception laws.[48] The effort to legalize contraceptives failed in Massachusetts and Connecticut, however, due to their high Catholic populations.[49]

Still, Connecticut and many other jurisdictions relaxed enforcement of Comstock laws in ways that reflected the role-based judgments about men and women discussed above. During World War I, the U.S. military concluded that providing condoms to men significantly lowered the rates of sexually transmitted diseases and authorized the use of condoms for preventing disease.[50] Following the federal government's lead, the Massachusetts high court crafted an exception to the state's ban on contraception permitting use of

---

[42]   For example, for centuries, the law expected women, not men, to assume care and financial responsibility for children born out of wedlock. *See generally* Serena Mayeri, *Marital Supremacy and the Constitution of the Non-Marital Family*, 103 CALIF. L. REV. 1277 (2015).

[43]   *See* Eskridge, *supra* note 1, at 2117. For further historical background, see generally JANET FARRELL BRODIE, CONTRACEPTION AND ABORTION IN NINETEENTH-CENTURY AMERICA (1994); THOMAS DIENES, LAW, POLITICS, AND BIRTH CONTROL (1974).

[44]   *See* Eskridge, *supra* note 1, at 2118.

[45]   *See id.* at 2118.

[46]   *See id.* In the days before the Court had discretion to deny certiorari, this was a standard way to dispose of appeals.

[47]   Sanger v. People, 251 U.S. 537 (1919) (per curiam).

[48]   *See* Eskridge, *supra* note 1, at 2120–21.

[49]   *See id.*

[50]   *See* ANDEA TONE, DEVICES AND DESIRES: A HISTORY OF CONTRACEPTIVES IN AMERICA 106–07 (2002).

condoms to prevent the spread of venereal disease.[51] The court recognized an implied exception to the ban that would protect men's health, even though two years earlier the court had reasoned that the ban was absolute and prohibited the sale of contraceptives to married women on a physician's prescription to preserve their lives or health.[52]

Gendered assumptions about sex and parenting also shaped the enforcement of Connecticut's ban on contraception. By the mid-twentieth century, it was widely understood that one could buy certain contraceptives in drug stores in Connecticut. The state deemed the threat of venereal disease sufficiently compelling to make a health exception to its law banning contraception. This exception allowed pharmacies to sell condoms under the auspices of "disease prevention" as well as certain products for "feminine hygiene" that might have contraceptive properties.[53] Yet like Massachusetts, the Connecticut Supreme Court rejected a health exception to the ban that would allow doctors to prescribe contraception for women physically unable to tolerate pregnancy or childbirth.[54] The court advised women with a medical need for contraception that they should simply abstain from sex,[55] but did not advise men to protect themselves from the risk of venereal disease in this fashion. Instead, the state allowed men to buy condoms on demand in the state's drug stores, while making no effort to ensure that men (particularly married men) actually were using condoms to prevent disease, as opposed to conception.[56]

Connecticut's crafting of a health exception for men, but not for women, led to a second inequality in the state's enforcement of its ban on contraception. Connecticut enforced the ban so as to allow men easy access to the most effective form of contraception for men (condoms), but to deny women access to the most effective forms of contraception for women (diaphragms or the pill). Thus, contraception bans raise equality concerns for women, in additional to liberty concerns. The Supreme Court, however, could not see these equality concerns when it eventually decided the fate of Connecticut's law. Equality concerns would not significantly enter the Court's

---

[51]   *See* Commonwealth v. Corbett, 307 Mass. 7, 8 (1940).

[52]   *See* Commonwealth v. Gardner, 300 Mass. 372 (1938).

[53]   Connecticut seemed to follow the Massachusetts Supreme Court's interpretation of its similarly restrictive statute. *See* Tileston v. Ullman, 129 Conn. 84, 91 (1942) (citing *Corbett*, 307 Mass. at 8, with apparent approval).

[54]   *See* State v. Nelson, 126 Conn. 412, 417 (1940); *Tileston*, 129 Conn. 84 (affirming *Nelson*); Buxton v. Ullman, 147 Conn. 48 (1959) (affirming *Nelson* and *Tileston*).

[55]   *See Tileston*, 129 Conn. at 92.

[56]   *See, e.g.*, Mary Dudziak, *Just Say No: Birth Control in the Connecticut Supreme Court Before* Griswold v. Connecticut, 75 IOWA L. REV. 915, 926–27 (1989).

substantive due process jurisprudence until 1992, as discussed below.

The Connecticut statute criminalizing birth control came before the Supreme Court as early as 1943. In *Tileston v. Ullman*,[57] a physician argued that the statute prevented him from providing birth-control advice to patients whose health would be threatened by pregnancy and birth. The Court refused to address whether the statute violated the Fourteenth Amendment because, it said unanimously, the doctor did not have standing to sue: he had alleged no injury to himself caused by the statute, and he could not get into court merely by asserting harm to his patients.

Not quite two decades after *Tileston*, a new lawsuit was brought that avoided the standing problem. Sanger's clinic, now called Planned Parenthood, worked with a law professor at Yale to bring a challenge to the law.[58] In *Poe v. Ullman*,[59] the plaintiffs included married women who claimed a medical need for birth-control advice because pregnancy would endanger her health, but could not receive it because of the statute. The Court again ducked the issue, this time concluding that the lawsuit was not "ripe." Essentially, a bare majority (five Justices) thought there was no real-world controversy. Apparently, only one prosecution for violation of the statute had been brought since its adoption in 1879, and in that case the prosecutor eventually refused to proceed. As noted above, certain contraceptives, especially condoms, were readily available in Connecticut drug stores, notwithstanding the statute. As Justice Felix Frankfurter explained for four Justices, "[t]he undeviating policy of nullification by Connecticut of its anti-contraceptive laws throughout all the long years that they have been on the statute books bespeaks more than prosecutorial paralysis."[60] Justice William Brennan, who provided the crucial fifth vote to dismiss the appeals in the case, stated that he was not convinced that plaintiffs "as individuals are truly caught in an inescapable dilemma."[61]

The dissenters marked out ground for the future. Justice Douglas said that the regulation "reaches into the intimacies of the marriage relationship"; full enforcement of the law would "reach the point where search warrants issued and officers appeared in bedrooms to find out what went on."[62] The second Justice John Marshall Harlan (another dissenter) took a different tack, in an

---

[57]   318 U.S. 44 (1943) (per curiam).

[58]   *See* Eskridge, *supra* note 1, at 2121.

[59]   367 U.S. 497 (1961).

[60]   *Id.* at 500.

[61]   *Id.* at 509.

[62]   *Id.* at 519–20 (Douglas, J., dissenting).

opinion that would resonate with later Courts and Justices such as O'Connor and Kennedy. Justice Harlan argued that a statute making it a criminal offense for married couples to use contraceptives was an intolerable and unjustifiable invasion of privacy in the conduct of the most intimate concerns of an individual's personal life.[63] In his view, the Due Process Clause was not limited to the specific rights set forth in the first eight amendments. "Due process," he argued, "has not been reduced to any formula; its content cannot be determined by reference to any code." Rather, he emphasized, "[t]he best that can be said is that through the course of this Court's decisions it has represented the balance which our Nation, built upon postulates of respect for the liberty of the individual, has struck between that liberty and the demands of organized society."[64] He continued, using language that has endured:

> If the supplying of content to this Constitutional concept has of necessity been a rational process, it certainly has not been one where judges have felt free to roam where unguided speculation might take them. The balance of which I speak is the balance struck by this country, having regard to what history teaches are the traditions from which it developed as well as the traditions from which it broke. That tradition is a living thing.[65]

The consensus on the constitutional issue between Justices Douglas (a liberal) and Harlan (a conservative) is noteworthy—the two spanned the ideological spectrum on the Warren Court.

The Court finally decided the constitutionality of the Connecticut law in *Griswold v. Connecticut*.[66] Estelle Griswold was Executive Director of the Planned Parenthood League of Connecticut. Another appellant, Lee Buxton, was a professor at the Yale Medical School who served as Medical Director for Planned Parenthood at its Center in New Haven. They provided individualized birth control advice to women. No statute prohibited the sale of birth control devices. But as noted above, it was a crime under the 1879 Connecticut law to use "any drug, medicinal article or instrument for the purpose of preventing conception," and they were charged as accessories to this offense.

Justice Douglas wrote the opinion of the Court. As in his dissent in *Poe v. Ullman*, he emphasized that this was no routine state regulation: "We do not sit as a super-legislature to determine the wisdom, need, and propriety of laws that touch economic problems,

---

[63] *Id.* at 539 (Harlan, J., dissenting).

[64] *Id.* at 542.

[65] *Id.*

[66] 381 U.S. 479 (1965).

business affairs, or social conditions. This law, however, operates directly on an intimate relation of husband and wife and their physician's role in one aspect of that relation."[67] After discussing some cases in which the Court had protected rights outside the strict bounds of the Bill of Rights, Justice Douglas drew a broader conclusion that the "specific guarantees in the Bill of Rights have penumbras, formed by emanations from those guarantees that help give them life and substance."[68] This line of argument seems to have been intended to deflect criticism that the Court was simply imposing its own view of good policy, as in *Lochner*, although his theory was not met with much respect by legal commentators. The idea of penumbras—the fringes of shadows—from emanations of constitutional provisions seemed tenuous as a basis for a constitutional ruling.

In his effort to support this theory, Justice Douglas pointed to the privacy interests protected by freedom of association under the First Amendment, the Third Amendment right again quartering of soldiers, the Fourth Amendment's protection against unreasonable searches, the Fifth Amendment's prohibition on compelled self-incrimination, and the Ninth Amendment's protection of unenumerated rights. Justice Douglas concluded that the penumbras of these rights embraced the privacy right at issue in the case:

> We deal with a right of privacy older than the Bill of Rights—older than our political parties, older than our school system. Marriage is a coming together for better or for worse, hopefully enduring, and intimate to the degree of being sacred. It is an association that promotes a way of life, not causes; a harmony in living, not political faiths; a bilateral loyalty, not commercial or social projects. Yet it is an association for as noble a purpose as any involved in our prior decisions.[69]

In a concurring opinion for three Justices, Justice Arthur Goldberg emphasized the relevance of the Ninth Amendment as a protection for unenumerated rights. But this possible textual basis for privacy rights has never found favor with the Court. Rather, this amendment is an interpretive guide, instructing the reader not to infer from the fact that certain rights are listed that they are the only ones protected.

It is an interesting reflection of how the relationship between judicial ideology and interpretive methodology can change that Justice Harlan, one of the Court's leading conservatives in the 1960s,

---

[67]   *Id.* at 482.

[68]   *Id.* at 484.

[69]   *Id.*

was sometimes open to the idea of a living Constitution, as evidenced by his reliance on evolving traditions in his *Ulman* dissent. Moreover, in his *Griswold* dissent, Justice Hugo Black, one of the Court's leading liberals, forcefully attacked the concept of a living constitution:

> The idea is that the Constitution must be changed from time to time and that this Court is charged with a duty to make those changes. . . . The Constitution makers knew the need for change and provided for it [in the Amendment process]. That method of change was good for our Fathers, and being somewhat old fashioned, I must add it is good enough for me.[70]

Justice Black was both a self-described textualist like the much later Justice Scalia and a staunch liberal. Justice Black found nothing in the text of the Constitution prohibiting the Connecticut law. The other dissenter, Justice Potter Stewart, scoffed at the idea of a constitutional right to privacy:

> What provision of the Constitution, then, does make this state law invalid? The Court says it is the right of privacy "created by several fundamental constitutional guarantees." With all deference, I can find no such general right of privacy in the Bill of Rights, in any other part of the Constitution, or in any case ever before decided by this Court.[71]

Although the Court in *Griswold* grounded the contraception right in the privacy of the marriage relationship, just seven years later, in *Eisenstadt v. Baird*,[72] the Court struck down a law prohibiting the sale of contraceptives to unmarried individuals. The majority opinion, written by Justice Brennan, purported to apply rational basis equal protection analysis.[73] According to Justice Brennan, the state surely could not have meant to make the threat of unwanted pregnancy a punishment for non-marital sex, although deterrence of non-marital sex may well have been the actual purpose. Having refused to consider the statute's most probable purpose, the

---

[70]   *Id.* at 522 (Black, J., dissenting).

[71]   *Id.* at 530 (Stewart, J., dissenting). For a conservative attack on *Griswold*, see generally Robert H. Bork, *Neutral Principles and Some First Amendment Problems*, 47 IND. L.J. 1 (1971).

[72]   405 U.S. 438 (1972).

[73]   The Court cited the recently decided case of *Reed v. Reed*, 404 U.S. 71 (1971). As discussed in Chapter 10, *Reed* was the first time that the Court invalidated a sex classification under the Equal Protection Clause. The Court's equal protection analysis in *Eisenstadt* may suggest a dawning recognition that contraception bans undermine gender equality.

Court then examined a variety of alternative rationales for the statute, unsurprisingly finding them to be unconvincing.

Regarding the expansion of privacy doctrine beyond *Griswold*'s focus on the marriage relationship, the Court said in *Eisenstadt* that, "[i]f the right of privacy means anything, it is the right of the individual, married or single, to be free from unwarranted governmental intrusion into matters so fundamentally affecting a person as the decision whether to bear or beget a child."[74] Although *Griswold* articulated the privacy right in terms of family (and specifically marriage), *Eisenstadt* rearticulated privacy in terms of the individual's central life choices. This reframing was important in the later cases involving abortion and the regulation of contraceptive access by minors. Indeed, *Roe v. Wade* had already arrived at the Court and been argued once when Justice Brennan wrote this language.[75]

In a later contraception case, *Carey v. Population Services International*,[76] the Court considered the sale of contraceptives to minors. Justice Brennan's plurality opinion concluded that restrictions on such sales infringed minors' right to privacy. Three concurring Justices made it clear that they did not believe minors had a constitutional right to be sexually active, but instead that denying them access to birth control was an inappropriate means of deterring sexual activity. Concurring, Justice John Paul Stevens remarked that "[i]t is as though a State decided to dramatize its disapproval of motorcycles by forbidding the use of safety helmets."[77] Dissenting alone, Justice William Rehnquist observed tartly that if the men who struggled to establish the Constitution or the Reconstruction Amendments "could have lived to know that their efforts had enshrined in the Constitution the right of commercial vendors of contraceptives to peddle them to unmarried minors, [it] is not difficult to imagine their reaction."[78]

C.   *Roe v. Wade* and Strict Scrutiny

Roe v. Wade[79] is probably the most controversial Supreme Court decision of the past fifty years. It is also the best known: if Americans are asked to name a Supreme Court case, they are most likely to pick *Roe* (naming *Roe* is eight times more likely than naming *Brown v.*

---

[74]   *Eisenstadt*, 405 U.S. at 442.

[75]   *See* LINDA GREENHOUSE, BECOMING JUSTICE BLACKMUN: HARRY BLACKMUN'S SUPREME COURT JOURNEY 80–86 (2006).

[76]   431 U.S. 678 (1977).

[77]   *Id.* at 715 (Stevens, J., concurring in part and concurring in judgment).

[78]   *Id.* at 717 (Rehnquist, J., dissenting).

[79]   410 U.S. 113 (1973).

Board of Education).[80] At the time it was decided, *Roe* seemed far less controversial than it has become today. In 1972, a survey showed that nearly two-thirds of Americans (including sixty-eight percent of Republicans and a majority of Catholics) agreed that "abortion should be a decision between a woman and her physicians."[81]

The moving force behind the *Roe* litigation was recent law school graduate and feminist Sarah Waddington.[82] She brought suit on behalf of a pregnant woman to challenge a Texas law that made it a criminal offense to procure or provide an abortion except when the pregnancy would endanger the woman's life. Waddington had been inspired by a student law review note laying out a constitutional argument, based on *Griswold*, against abortion restrictions.[83]

Justice Harry Blackmun began his opinion for the Court by acknowledging "awareness of the sensitive and emotional nature of the abortion controversy, of the vigorous opposing views, even among physicians, and of the deep and seemingly absolute convictions that the subject inspires."[84] After disposing of some justiciability issues, the Court turned to a detailed examination of the historic attitudes toward abortion. Its review of this history led the Court to the conclusions that laws penalizing abortion prior to the eighteenth week of pregnancy were a product of the nineteenth century and were based in large part on safety concerns, and that there had been a recent trend toward liberalizing abortion laws.[85]

With this background in mind, the Court began its legal analysis. Pointing to cases like *Pierce, Meyers,* and *Griswold,* the Court found it to be well-settled law that the Constitution protects a right of privacy encompassing "personal rights that can be deemed 'fundamental' or 'implicit in the concept of ordered liberty.' "[86] This language was taken from *Palko v. Connecticut,* a case regarding the incorporation doctrine that we discussed in Chapter 8. The Court then concluded in a brief paragraph that the right to privacy encompassed the abortion decision. In the Court's view, "[t]his right of privacy, whether it be founded in the Fourteenth Amendment's concept of personal liberty and restrictions upon state action, as we feel it is, or, as the District Court determined, in the Ninth

---

[80]   *See* Greenhouse & Siegel, *supra* note 2, at 2030.

[81]   *Id.* at 2031.

[82]   *See* Lucinda M. Finley, *Contested Ground: The Story of* Roe v. Wade *and its Impact on American Society* 233, 353, *in* CONSTITUTIONAL LAW STORIES (Michael C. Dorf ed., 2d ed. 2009).

[83]   *See id.*

[84]   *Roe,* 410 U.S. at 116. For an illuminating account of the opinion writing process, see GREENHOUSE, *supra* note 75, at 72–101.

[85]   *See Roe,* 410 U.S. at 140–41.

[86]   *Id.* at 152.

Amendment's reservation of rights to the people, is broad enough to encompass a woman's decision whether or not to terminate her pregnancy."[87] Justice Blackmun also emphasized the harmful impacts of abortion restrictions on women's lives:

> The detriment that the State would impose upon the pregnant woman by denying this choice altogether is apparent. Specific and direct harm medically diagnosable even in early pregnancy may be involved. Maternity, or additional offspring, may force upon the woman a distressful life and future. Psychological harm may be imminent. . . . All these are factors the woman and her responsible physician necessarily will consider in consultation.[88]

The Court rejected the argument that abortion was immune from state regulation, while also rejecting the state's claims that Fourteenth Amendment personhood began at conception and that the state had a compelling interest in preserving fetal life from this moment. Rather, the Court staked out what must have seemed at the time like a compromise position, allowing increasing restrictions on abortion as pregnancy progressed.

The Court identified two state interests that potentially justified government regulations of abortion: an interest in preserving fetal life that grew in significance as the fetus developed during pregnancy and an interest in protecting the pregnant woman's health. The Court determined that the interest in protecting the fetus became compelling in the third trimester of pregnancy, at which point the fetus "presumably has the capability of meaningful life outside the mother's womb."[89] The Court further determined that the interest in protecting maternal health began in the second trimester, when the risk of abortion began to exceed the risk of carrying a child to term.

Based on its assessment of these interests, the Court provided a three-stage standard governing the constitutionality of abortion regulations. During the first trimester of pregnancy, the state was not entitled to interfere with the abortion decision made by a woman and her doctor. In the second trimester, the state could regulate the abortion decision only to protect maternal health. In the third trimester, the state could ban all abortions except those necessary to protect maternal health or life.[90]

---

[87]   *Id.* at 153.

[88]   *Id.*

[89]   *Id.* at 163.

[90]   *See id.* at 164–66.

Only two Justices dissented. Writing in the companion case from Georgia to explain his views in both cases, Justice Byron White argued that "[t]he Court simply fashions and announces a new constitutional right for pregnant women and, with scarcely any reason or authority for its action, invests that right with sufficient substance to override most existing state abortion statutes."[91] Justice (later Chief Justice) Rehnquist argued that the right to an abortion could not be considered so rooted in tradition as to rank as fundamental, given "[t]he fact that a majority of the States, reflecting after all the majority sentiment in those States, have had restrictions on abortions for at least a century" and that abortion remained a controversial issue.[92] He would have applied rational basis review and thought it obvious that abortion restrictions like those in Texas survived such deferential scrutiny.[93]

Justice Rehnquist also raised larger jurisprudential concerns. As in *Lochner*, he wrote, "the adoption of the compelling state interest standard will inevitably require this Court to examine the legislative policies and pass on the wisdom of these policies in the very process of deciding whether a particular state interest put forward may or may not be 'compelling.' "[94] Indeed, he said, "[t]he decision here to break pregnancy into three distinct terms and to outline the permissible restrictions the State may impose in each one, for example, partakes more of judicial legislation than it does of a determination of the intent of the drafters of the Fourteenth Amendment."[95]

Rather than being seen as a fundamental rights case, *Roe* might have been approached by the Court as an equality case.[96] After all, it is only women who can become pregnant, and only women who will be forced to carry a pregnancy to term absent abortion. Moreover, given the long-gendered organization of American society, in which women were expected to perform the lion's share of childcare responsibilities and workers were assumed not to have such responsibilities, control over whether and when to become mothers is related to women's ability to plan their lives and to participate in educational, economic, and political life on terms equal with men.

---

[91]   Doe v. Bolton, 410 U.S. 179, 221–22 (1973) (White, J., dissenting).

[92]   *Roe*, 410 U.S. at 174 (Rehnquist, J., dissenting).

[93]   Justice Rehnquist did, however, argue that "[i]f the Texas statute were to prohibit an abortion even where the mother's life is in jeopardy, I have little doubt that such a statute would lack a rational relation to a valid state objective." *Id.* at 173.

[94]   *Roe*, 410 U.S. at 174. A leading liberal constitutional law scholar echoed this critique of *Roe. See generally* John Hart Ely, *The Wages of Crying Wolf: A Comment on* Roe v. Wade, 82 YALE L.J. 920 (1973).

[95]   *Roe,* 410 U.S. at 174.

[96]   *See generally* Ruth Bader Ginsburg, *Some Thoughts on Autonomy and Equality in Relation to Roe v. Wade*, 63 N.C. L. REV. 375 (1985).

Amicus briefs submitted to the Court forcefully made equality arguments.[97] At the time, however, the Court was not ready to hear them. As explained in Chapter 10, the constitutional law of sex discrimination may have been too underdeveloped to make this legal theory appealing to the Justices. The Court had invalidated a sex classification for the first time in American history only two years earlier,[98] and the same year as *Roe*, Justice Brennan was unable to muster a majority to hold that laws discriminating on the basis of sex were subject to strict scrutiny.[99] In contrast, the fundamental rights argument garnered a solid 7 to 2 majority in *Roe*, perhaps in part because the Court characterized it as a right possessed by the pregnant woman's physician.[100]

Roe v. Wade involved one of the most restrictive abortion laws in the country because it did not include an exception for non-life-threatening health risks. In a companion case, *Doe v. Bolton*,[101] the Court struck down a more permissive Georgia law, which allowed abortion subject to some procedural restrictions under several circumstances: when continued pregnancy would endanger a pregnant woman's life or injure her health, the fetus would likely be born with a serious defect, or the pregnancy resulted from rape. The lower court had struck down the limitation of lawful abortions to these three categories, but had upheld procedural requirements that two other doctors agree with the treating physician on the need for an abortion and that the abortion be performed in a hospital. The Court struck down these additional requirements as medically unnecessary and inconsistent with *Roe*.

The women's rights movement during the late 1960s and 1970s, along with other social and political changes, including Republican Party mobilization, helped trigger a "pro-life" countermovement seeking to preserve traditional ideas about the family and the origins of human life.[102] Pro-life advocates persuaded state legislatures to adopt numerous measures to make abortions more difficult for women, including rules against abortions for minors without parental consent or for wives without their husbands' consent;

---

[97]   *See* LINDA GREENHOUSE & REVA B. SIEGEL, BEFORE *ROE V. WADE*: VOICES THAT SHAPED THE ABORTION DEBATE BEFORE THE SUPREME COURT'S RULING 324–37 (2012), https://documents.law.yale.edu/sites/default/files/beforeroe2nded_1.pdf.

[98]   *See* Reed v. Reed, 404 U.S. 71 (1971).

[99]   *See* Frontiero v. Richardson, 411 U.S. 677 (1973).

[100]   *See Roe*, 410 U.S. at 164 ("For the stage prior to approximately the end of the first trimester, the abortion decision and its effectuation must be left to the medical judgment of the pregnant woman's attending physician.").

[101]   410 U.S. 179 (1973).

[102]   *See generally* DALLAS BLANCHARD, THE ANTI-ABORTION MOVEMENT AND THE RISE OF THE RELIGIOUS RIGHT: FROM POLITE TO FIERY PROTEST (1994) (examining the institutional history and ideology of the pro-life movement).

requirements that women be given state-specified information meant to discourage abortion and be forced to wait for a period of time before they could have abortions; refusals to fund abortions in state Medicaid and employee health insurance programs; and prohibitions on abortions at municipal hospitals.[103]

There has been a continuing scholarly debate over whether *Roe* sparked a backlash against abortion liberalization, which might otherwise have continued in the state legislatures.[104] The conventional wisdom is that *Roe* caused the backlash, but there are reasons to question this conclusion. The Catholic Church had begun to mobilize strong opposition to state liberalization legislation prior to *Roe*, and Republican strategists had identified abortion as a wedge issue that might split Catholics and social conservatives from the Democratic Party.[105] During the 1960s and 1970s, evangelical Protestants supported abortion liberalization; this began to shift only in the late 1970s, well after *Roe*.[106] We suspect that the debate over what caused the backlash will not be settled soon. Whatever the cause(s), legislatures soon began to enact a wave of anti-abortion legislation.

In the wake of *Roe*, the Court invalidated most of the new restrictions. In *Planned Parenthood v. Danforth*,[107] the Court invalidated requirements of parental consent for minors and spousal consent for wives. Reaffirming the individualist rather than family nature of the privacy right declared in *Eisenstadt* and *Roe*, Justice Blackmun's opinion for the Court ruled that parents and husbands cannot have vetoes over a right personal to the pregnant woman or teen.

In *Bellotti v. Baird*,[108] the Court invalidated a parental consent law as an "undue burden" on the minor's right to choose. The Court hinted, however, that such a law would be acceptable if it gave minors the option of seeking a judge's approval instead. Justice Lewis Powell's plurality opinion in *Bellotti* recognized "the peculiar vulnerability of children; their inability to make critical decisions in an informed, mature manner; and the importance of the parental role in child rearing."[109] In dictum, Justice Powell opined that states could require parents to consent so long as there was a "judicial bypass" procedure available for the minor to invoke in lieu of a parental

---

[103] For a review of the post-*Roe* legislation and litigation, see Eskridge, *supra* note 1, at 2144–49.

[104] *See* Finley, *supra* note 82, at 379.

[105] *See* Greenhouse & Siegel, *supra* note 2, at 2032–33.

[106] *See id.* at 2263–66.

[107] 428 U.S. 52 (1976).

[108] 443 U.S. 622 (1979).

[109] *See id.* at 634.

dialogue. Under the bypass procedure, a minor can obtain an abortion without parental consent if the court concludes that it is in her best interests or that she is mature enough to decide for herself. Thus, it was no great surprise when the Court in *Planned Parenthood v. Ashcroft*[110] upheld a state law requiring a minor to obtain either parental consent or judicial approval of her choice to abort.

In *Akron v. Akron Center for Reproductive Health*,[111] the Court struck down a requirement that dilatation-and-evacuation abortions be performed in hospitals, because the ban imposed a heavy and medically unnecessary burden on women's access in clinics to a relatively inexpensive, otherwise accessible, safe abortion procedure. The Court also invalidated the government's blanket determination that *all* minors under the age of 15 are too immature to make the abortion decision or that an abortion can never be in the minor's best interests without parental approval. The *Akron* Court objected that the statute did not provide any opportunity for case-by-case evaluations of the maturity of pregnant minors. The Court was similarly unsympathetic to an "informed consent" requirement. By requiring the attending physician to give the woman a lengthy and inflexible list of information, and by imposing a twenty-four-hour waiting period, the state had placed a burden on abortions that was not reasonably related to health or safety. The Court struck down a similar informed consent law in *Thornburgh v. American College of Obstetricians and Gynecologists*.[112]

Perhaps the post-*Roe* case going the farthest in protecting abortion rights was *Colautti v. Franklin*,[113] which involved a Pennsylvania statute requiring doctors to determine fetal viability before performing abortions. The Court held the statute to be unconstitutionally vague, largely because it was unclear how much evidence of viability was required.

For poor women, the rights granted in theory by *Roe* were not necessarily available in practice. In *Maher v. Roe*[114] and *Harris v. McRae*,[115] the Court held that the government has no affirmative obligation to pay for abortions even if pays for childbirth, despite the lower cost of abortion. The Court in *Maher* found no violation of the fundamental right to abortion because the government was imposing

---

[110]   462 U.S. 476 (1983). *See also H.L. v. Matheson*, 450 U.S. 398 (1981) (approving a law requiring that parents be notified whenever possible). Note that this case involved a notice requirement, not a consent requirement as in *Bellotti*, and the Court concluded that this difference eliminated the necessity of a judicial bypass.

[111]   462 U.S. 416 (1983).

[112]   476 U.S. 747 (1986).

[113]   439 U.S. 379 (1979).

[114]   432 U.S. 464 (1977).

[115]   448 U.S. 297 (1980).

no "unduly burdensome interference" with the freedom to decide whether to terminate the pregnancy. In response to the equal protection challenge, the Court applied only the rational basis test, reasoning that the poor are not a suspect class and the Court had already determined that no fundamental right was infringed. A rational basis was present, the Court concluded, because of the government's legitimate (although not always, according to *Roe*, compelling) interest in protecting the potential life of the fetus. The Court's abortion funding decisions reflect the great extent to which the U.S. Constitution protects "negative" rights, not "positive" rights. As discussed in Chapter 11, constitutional rights in the United States almost always prevent the government from acting in ways that unjustifiably interfere with them; constitutional rights almost never oblige the government to act in ways that affirmatively facilitate their exercise.

The Reagan Administration mounted a sustained constitutional attack on *Roe*. In *Akron* and *Thornburgh*, the Solicitor General urged the Court to abandon *Roe*'s "rigid" trimester framework and adopt *Maher*'s "undue burden" approach. Three Justices—including newly appointed Justice O'Connor—dissented from the invalidation of an informed consent law in *Akron*, and they were joined by Chief Justice Warren Burger in *Thornburgh*. The retirement of Justice Powell in 1987 cost the Court a fairly loyal adherent to *Roe*. Although President Ronald Reagan's nomination of Judge Robert Bork—who rejected *Griswold* and the right to privacy—was defeated, his substitute, Anthony Kennedy, a devout Roman Catholic, was not considered a friend of *Roe*. By now, only three members of the original seven-Justice *Roe* majority were still on the Court.[116] In the next case we discuss, Missouri asked the Court to overrule *Roe*—a petition joined by dozens of *amici* and by the U.S. Solicitor General. The Reagan Administration argued to the Court that *Roe* created a fundamental right unsupported by constitutional text, original intent, or American tradition; denigrated the state's interest in potential human life without any legal or moral basis; and engaged in judicial activism in the teeth of popular demands for regulation of this controversial activity.[117]

Webster v. Reproductive Health Services[118] involved a Missouri law requiring doctors to determine fetal viability before performing an abortion after the twentieth week of pregnancy. The plurality opinion, written by Chief Justice Rehnquist, purported to decline to revisit *Roe*'s holding that abortion enjoys some constitutional protection, and it did concede that abortion involves a "liberty

---

[116]   *See* Eskridge, *supra* note 1, at 2149.

[117]   *See id.*

[118]   492 U.S. 490 (1989).

interest protected by the Due Process Clause."[119] The plurality opinion then contended that the trimester system should be rejected. Applying an unspecified level of review that amounted to rational basis scrutiny (which would have effectively overruled *Roe*), the plurality opinion concluded: "The Missouri testing requirement here is reasonably designed to ensure that abortions are not performed where the fetus is viable—an end which all concede is legitimate— and that is sufficient to sustain its constitutionality."[120] Interestingly, in light of later developments, Justice Kennedy joined Rehnquist's opinion. Justice O'Connor concurred on the ground that Missouri law did not impose an "undue burden" and in any event was consistent with the Court's previous decisions. Her support for *Roe*, however, remained unclear.

In an angry concurrence, Justice Scalia berated the other members of the majority for refusing to overrule *Roe* outright: "The outcome of today's case will doubtless be heralded as a triumph of judicial statesmanship. It is not that, unless it is statesmanlike needlessly to prolong this Court's self-awarded sovereignty over a field where it has little proper business since the answer to most of the cruel questions posed are political and not juridical."[121] In a dismissive criticism that may well have alienated Justice O'Connor from his position, Justice Scalia also said that her reliance on judicial restraint as a reason not to reconsider *Roe* "cannot be taken seriously."[122]

The dissenters were a coalition of moderates and liberals: Justice Blackmun, the Nixon appointee who wrote *Roe*, Justice Stevens, who had been considered a moderate conservative when appointed by President Gerald Ford (but who eventually became one of the Court's most liberal members), and the two Warren Court survivors, Justices Brennan and Thurgood Marshall. They argued that the Court's ruling was inconsistent with *Roe*.

Hodgson v. Minnesota[123] was the next opportunity for the Court to reconsider *Roe*. Minnesota required the notification of both parents (one of eight states to do so) and had virtually no exceptions except for an alternate procedure for judicial bypass, as required by *Ashcroft*. On the basis of extensive evidence, the trial judge found that the paternal notification requirement was a prohibitive barrier for many minors even with a judicial bypass and invalidated the

---

[119]   *Id.* at 520.

[120]   *Id.*

[121]   *Id.* at 532 (Scalia, J., concurring in part and concurring in judgment).

[122]   *Id.*

[123]   497 U.S. 417 (1990).

notice requirement.[124] The Supreme Court reversed. Justice Kennedy's controlling opinion simply applied *Ashcroft* and the other precedents upholding parental notification and consent requirements that allowed a judicial bypass.[125] He did not disagree with the lower court's findings of fact but he considered them, essentially, irrelevant. In a concurrence, Justice O'Connor maintained that the two-parent notification requirement standing alone was in fact an undue burden on a minor's right to abortion but agreed with the Court that the availability of the judicial bypass procedure saved the statute. In retrospect, Justice O'Connor's repeated invocation of the undue burden standard was deeply significant.

When President George H.W. Bush appointed Justices David Souter and Clarence Thomas to replace Justices Brennan and Marshall, the future of *Roe* looked even dimmer. There then appeared to be at least five votes to overrule *Roe* (Rehnquist, White, Scalia, Kennedy, and Thomas), and possibly six (Souter). When *Planned Parenthood of Southeastern Pennsylvania v. Casey*[126] was argued, the Solicitor General for the George H.W. Bush Administration and the State of Pennsylvania both asked the Court to overrule *Roe*. Planned Parenthood, which challenged the state restrictions on abortion at issue, asked the Court to overrule *Roe* if it was no longer willing to give the right to privacy real bite. The Court responded with a compromise formulation, which we consider below.

D. *Casey* and the Undue Burden Test

Among other abortion restrictions, which the Court upheld, *Casey* involved a Pennsylvania statute requiring a twenty-four hour waiting period before a woman could obtain an abortion, spousal notification before a woman could obtain an abortion, and parental notification with a judicial bypass before a minor could obtain an abortion. Given the changes in the Court's membership, there was reason to expect that the Court might overrule *Roe* rather than simply decide the constitutionality of these provisions. This is not how the Court responded.

Unusually, the lead opinion in the case was authored jointly, written not by one Justice but by three: Justices Kennedy, O'Connor, and Souter. All were relatively recent Republican appointees (two by Reagan, one by the senior President Bush). The joint opinion authored by these three Justices affirmed *Roe*'s holding that the right

---

[124]   *See id.* at 438–39.

[125]   Confusingly, Justice Stevens wrote the opinion of the Court on most issues, but Justice Kennedy's dissenting opinion was controlling on this issue because Justice O'Connor's separate opinion gave him five votes, although she joined Justice Stevens on other issues, making his the majority opinion on those issues.

[126]   505 U.S. 833 (1992).

to an abortion before fetal viability is constitutionally protected but rejected *Roe*'s three-part framework and strict scrutiny standard in favor of the undue burden test. Justices Blackmun and Stevens (earlier Republican appointees) agreed that the right to abortion is protected but would have continued to apply strict scrutiny and struck down other provisions of the law. The remaining Justices would have overruled *Roe* entirely and upheld the whole law under the rational basis test.

In upholding the core holding of *Roe*, the joint opinion rested in part on its understanding of the scope of constitutional liberty and on *stare decisis* (respect for precedent). In its discussion of liberty, the joint opinion relied heavily upon (and quoted extensively) Justice Harlan's opinion in *Poe v. Ullman*, which we discussed earlier.[127] Based on precedents such as the contraception decisions and *Roe* itself, the joint opinion identified a protected zone relating to family and certain intimate personal matters:

> These matters, involving the most intimate and personal choices a person may make in a lifetime, choices central to personal dignity and autonomy, are central to the liberty protected by the Fourteenth Amendment. At the heart of liberty is the right to define one's own concept of existence, of meaning, of the universe, and of the mystery of human life. Beliefs about these matters could not define the attributes of personhood were they formed under compulsion of the State.[128]

The joint opinion then observed that "the liberty of the woman is at stake in a sense unique to the human condition and so unique to the law. The mother who carries a child to full term is subject to anxieties, to physical constraints, to pain that only she must bear."[129] The opinion added that prior rulings protecting access to contraception supported protecting other personal decisions relating to reproduction.

This analysis of liberty was buttressed by a strong appeal to the force of precedent. The joint opinion found special reason to respect precedent for a foundational opinion such as *Roe*. It stressed several factors. First, "for two decades of economic and social developments, people have organized intimate relationships and made choices that define their views of themselves and their places in society, in reliance on the availability of abortion in the event that contraception should fail."[130] Second, "subsequent constitutional developments

---

[127]   *See id.* at 848–51.

[128]   *Id.* at 851.

[129]   *Id.* at 852.

[130]   *Id.* at 856.

have neither disturbed, nor do they threaten to diminish, the scope of recognized protection accorded to the liberty relating to intimate relationships, the family, and decisions about whether or not to beget or bear a child."[131] Furthermore, if "the woman's interest in deciding whether to bear and beget a child had not been recognized as in *Roe*, the State might as readily restrict a woman's right to choose to carry a pregnancy to term as to terminate it, to further asserted state interests in population control, or eugenics, for example."[132] Third, the joint opinion declared that overruling *Roe* would undermine the Court's institutional legitimacy. When the Court has taken a position on a deeply divisive societal issue, as it did in *Brown v. Board of Education* and in *Roe*, the joined opinion reasoned, "only the most convincing justification under accepted standards of precedent could suffice to demonstrate that a later decision overruling the first was anything but a surrender to political pressure."[133] Whether or not this sentence states a convincing normative position (and whether or not declaring it publicly was self-undermining), it clearly reflects the determination of these Justices not to serve as merely a tool of the very political forces that were partly responsible for their presence on the Court.

Based on a these arguments, the joint opinion upheld the core holding of *Roe* that the Constitution protects a woman's right to end a pregnancy before viability. But the joint opinion rejected the trimester approach as too rigid, because "[o]nly where state regulation imposes an undue burden on a woman's ability to make this decision does the power of the State reach into the heart of the liberty protected by the Due Process Clause."[134] The joint opinion explained that "a finding of an undue burden is a shorthand for the conclusion that a state regulation has the purpose or effect of placing a substantial obstacle in the path of a woman seeking an abortion of a nonviable fetus."[135] Applying this test, the joint opinion upheld the provisions of the Pennsylvania law, with the exception of the requirement of spousal notification. It held this requirement to be an undue burden, observing that "there are millions of women in this country who are the victims of regular physical and psychological abuse at the hands of their husbands," and that these women may have "very good reasons for not wishing to inform their husbands of their decision to obtain an abortion."[136]

---

[131]　*Id.* at 857.

[132]　*Id.* at 859.

[133]　*Id.* at 867.

[134]　*Id.* at 874.

[135]　*Id.* at 877.

[136]　*Id.* at 893.

It may seem puzzling that the same plurality would uphold a 24-hour waiting period and strike down a spousal notification provision: both can make it substantially more difficult for women in vulnerable situations to obtain an abortion. For example, the waiting period could require a single mother to miss work, secure child care, and travel long distances to and from an abortion clinic on two occasions, not one. The plurality's actions may seem somewhat less puzzling, however, once one realizes that equality values, in addition to liberty values, threaded through the joint opinion in *Casey*.[137] Equality values helped identify the kinds of restrictions on abortion that impose an undue burden. As the joint opinion applied the test, abortion restrictions that deny women's equality impose an undue burden on women's fundamental right to decide whether to become a mother. On this interpretation, the Court struck down the spousal notification provision because the majority viewed it as reinforcing the traditional hierarchical relationship between husband and wife. Just as the common law of marital status (called coverture, and discussed in Chapter 10) gave husbands absolute dominion over their wives' property, so "[a] State may not give to a man the kind of dominion over his wife that parents exercise over their children."[138]

In other ways as well, the Court drew upon equality values in order to make sense of the substance of the abortion right. At the very instant when the Court reaffirmed the abortion right, it explained that a woman's "suffering is too intimate and personal for the State to insist, without more, upon its own vision of the woman's role, however dominant that vision has been in the course of our history and our culture."[139] This emphasis on the role autonomy of the pregnant woman reflects the influence of the equal protection sex discrimination cases (discussed in Chapter 10), which prohibit the government from imposing stereotypical roles on women. Likewise, in the stare decisis passages of *Casey*, the Court emphasized, as a reason to reaffirm *Roe*, that "[t]he ability of women to participate equally in the economic and social life of the Nation has been facilitated by their ability to control their reproductive lives."[140]

Chief Justice Rehnquist, Justice White, Justice Scalia, and Justice Thomas argued that *Roe* should be overruled in its entirety. Rehnquist's dissent on behalf of this group reiterated his arguments in *Webster* for applying the rational basis test and upholding the statute. Justice Scalia, also speaking for the group, was more biting in his attack on the majority. "The emptiness of the 'reasoned

---

[137] This paragraph and the next one draw from Neil S. Siegel & Reva B. Siegel, *Equality Arguments for Abortion Rights*, 60 UCLA L. REV. DISCOURSE 160 (2013).

[138] *Casey*, 505 U.S. at 898.

[139] *Id.* at 852.

[140] *Id.* at 856.

judgment' that produced *Roe*," he said, "is displayed in plain view by the fact that . . . the best the Court can do to explain how it is that the word 'liberty' must be thought to include the right to destroy human fetuses is to rattle off a collection of adjectives that simply decorate a value judgment and conceal a political choice."[141] These same adjectives, he added, "might be applied, for example, to homosexual sodomy, polygamy, adult incest, and suicide, all of which are equally "intimate" and "deep[ly] personal" decisions involving "personal autonomy and bodily integrity," and all of which can constitutionally be proscribed. . . . It is not reasoned judgment that supports the Court's decision, only personal predilection."[142]

E. Beyond *Casey*

The Court's post-*Casey* cases have applied the undue burden test. In the post-*Casey* era, opponents of abortion attempted to chip away at abortion rights by incrementally imposing greater restrictions. *Stenberg v. Carhart*[143] involved Nebraska's ban on a controversial method of abortion that opponents call "partial birth abortion," defined as a procedure in which the doctor "partially delivers vaginally a living unborn child before killing the unborn child." The statute defined this phrase to mean "intentionally delivering into the vagina a living unborn child, or a substantial portion thereof, for the purpose of performing a procedure that the [physician] knows will kill the unborn child and does kill the unborn child."[144] Thus, the statute prohibited an abortion procedure, not abortion per se, and banned this procedure both pre- and post-viability. The statute was aimed at a procedure called "dilation and extraction" (D&X), pursuant to which the fetus is withdrawn intact during the later stages of pregnancy before fetal viability. Many doctors believe that this procedure is safer for women with certain medical conditions.

Abortions after the first trimester are relatively rare, and this procedure was used in only a small number of cases. Banning the procedure would push women toward alternate and perhaps less safe procedures more often than it would prevent abortions. Thus, bans on the procedure would have little or no impact on abortion rates. Nevertheless, "partial birth abortion" made an appealing target for two reasons. First, as the label indicates, attacking this procedure was a way of connecting abortion with infanticide. Second, descriptions of the procedure can be disturbing, making abortion advocates seem less sympathetic and fostering political support for

---

[141]   *Id.* at 893–94 (Scalia, J., dissenting).

[142]   *Id.*

[143]   530 U.S. 914 (2000).

[144]   *Id.* at 922.

the bans. Given that this form of procedure was only marginally different than the alternatives, banning D&X could be a stepping stone toward banning second-trimester abortions entirely.

In a majority opinion written by Justice Stephen Breyer and joined by Justices Stevens, O'Connor, Souter, and Ruth Bader Ginsburg, the Court struck down the statute. (All except Justice Souter also wrote concurring opinions.) First, the majority concluded that the statute could not constitutionally be applied even post-viability. The majority invoked the language that *Casey* had quoted from *Roe*: any regulation of abortion, whether pre- or post-viability, must allow abortions "necessary, in appropriate medical judgment, for the preservation of the life or health of the mother," and the statutory ban contained no such exception. Relying upon the district court's finding that in some circumstances the D&X procedure is the safest, the Court rejected the state's argument that no exception was required because other safe abortion procedures were available.

Second, the Court held that the statute imposed an undue burden on a woman's ability to choose an abortion because it was unconstitutionally vague. The Court reasoned the wording of the ban appeared to reach beyond the D&X procedure to criminalize the most common procedure for pre-viability, second-trimester abortions, the "dilation and evacuation" (D&E) procedure, pursuant to which at least some fetal tissue is removed by surgical instruments.

In a lengthy and emotional dissent, Justice Kennedy, joined by Chief Justice Rehnquist, argued that the state intended to prohibit only the D&X procedure and should be allowed to make the moral decision that killing the fetus when it is substantially outside the womb (D&X) is more gruesome and horrifying—more like infanticide—than killing it when it is in the womb. Justice Kennedy further contended that the D&X procedure is highly controversial even within the medical community and that restricting pregnant women to the D&E procedure would deprive none of them of a safe abortion. The state, he concluded, should be able to take sides on a disputed medical question. Justice Kennedy's dissent reads like he thought the other members of the *Casey* plurality had betrayed the compromise that he had enabled them to craft in *Casey*.

Justice Thomas, joined by Chief Justice Rehnquist and Justice Scalia, also dissented, contending that the statutory text reached only the D&X procedure and should be so interpreted to avoid deciding the second constitutional question reached by the majority. As for the need for an exception to protect the health of the mother, Justice Thomas argued that the Court should distinguish between a situation in which a woman seeks an abortion because her pregnancy genuinely risks her health and a situation in which she elects abortion for whatever other reason and simply prefers one procedure over another. The "health exception" of *Casey* should apply only to the former situation, he contended. He was concerned about the health exception swallowing the rule.

Justice Scalia also dissented, lumping the case together with *Roe* and *Casey* as "policy-judgment[s]-couched as law"[145] and expressing hope that someday the invalidation of this "humane law"[146] barring "[t]he method of killing a human child . . . so horrible that the most clinical description of it evokes a shudder of revulsion" will be "assigned its rightful place in the history of this court's jurisprudence beside *Korematsu* and *Dred Scott*."[147]

Between 2000 and 2007, the medical evidence regarding advisability of using the D&X procedure in certain situations had not changed, but two other changes did occur. First, Congress responded to *Stenberg* by passing the Partial-Birth Abortion Ban Act of 2003, which defined the D&X procedure more precisely than the Nebraska law had and prohibited it nationwide without including a health exception on the face of the law. Second, and more importantly, the Court's composition changed decisively in 2006, when Justice Samuel Alito replaced Justice O'Connor.

In 2007, in *Gonzales v. Carhart*,[148] the Court rejected a facial challenge to the federal law by a vote of 5 to 4. Justice Kennedy wrote the opinion of the Court. Justice Kennedy concluded that the law had neither the intent nor the effect of imposing an undue burden. In terms of intent, he viewed the law as expressing the government's legitimate interest in showing respect for human life: "The government may use its voice and its regulatory authority to show its profound respect for the life within the woman."[149] Justice Kennedy also noted that "Congress was concerned . . . with the effects on the medical community and on its reputation caused by the practice of partial-birth abortion."[150] Thus, he concluded, the purpose of the law was not to impose an undue burden. Nor, according to Justice Kennedy, did the ban have the effect of imposing an undue burden. The most commonly used method of abortion (D&E) remained available, he reasoned, and he found documented medical uncertainty about whether the D&X procedure was sometimes safer than the alternatives. The Court held that Congress was not foreclosed by this uncertainty from acting to preserve respect for

---

145   *Id.* at 954 (Scalia, J., dissenting).

146   *Id.*

147   *Id.* at 953.

148   550 U.S. 124 (2007).

149   *Id.* at 157.

150   *Id.*

human life; it sufficed under *Casey* for a pregnant woman to be able to bring an as-applied challenge to the law if her doctor believed that the banned procedure would be safest for her. Justice Kennedy also expressed concern about women being consumed by regret after having abortions,[151] a concern that Justice Ginsburg dismissed as an "anti-abortion shibboleth."[152]

Justice Ginsburg penned an uncharacteristically vehement dissent on behalf of the four liberal Justices. She deemed the Court's decision "alarming" because it both "tolerates, indeed applauds, federal intervention to ban nationwide a procedure found necessary and proper in certain cases by the American College of Obstetricians and Gynecologists (ACOG)," and blurs "the line, firmly drawn in *Casey*, between pre-viability and post-viability abortions."[153] "And, for the first time since *Roe*," she observed, "the Court blesses a prohibition with no exception safeguarding a woman's health."[154] In her view, the newly reconstituted Court was overruling *Stenberg* without admitting it and refusing to take *Casey* seriously as law.

The Court's most recent abortion decision as of this writing was also Justice Kennedy's last. Rather than involving fetal-protective restrictions on abortion, *Whole Woman's Health v. Hellerstedt*[155] involved two provisions of Texas law that the state sought to justify on woman-protective grounds—that is, as protecting women's health. One provision required a doctor performing or inducing an abortion to have admitting privileges at a hospital within thirty miles of the location in which the doctor performed the abortion. The second provision required abortion facilities to meet the same standards as ambulatory surgical centers. The district court found that there had been forty abortion facilities in Texas prior to the passage of this law, which dropped by almost one half after the law went into effect, leaving facilities only in a few cities. Fewer than ten facilities would be left if the law were fully enforced. This is because it is extremely difficult for doctors performing abortions to obtain admitting privileges (abortion is so safe that such doctors admit very few patients), and it is very expensive to transform abortion clinics into ambulatory surgical centers (prohibitively so for many clinics). The district court also found that the requirement of admitting privileges would greatly increase the distances women would need to travel to obtain abortions, so that more than a million women of childbearing

---

[151]   *See id.* at 160.

[152]   *Id.* at 183–84 (Ginsburg, J., dissenting).

[153]   *Id.* at 170–71.

[154]   *Id.* at 171.

[155]   579 U.S. ___, 136 S. Ct. 2292 (2016).

age would be over 100 miles from the nearest facility, with 750,000 women over 250 miles away.[156]

The court of appeals had applied a two-stage test, first determining whether the burden on women was large enough to qualify as undue, and then separately whether the law advanced any health interest.[157] The court applied rational basis review to the second question, deferring to the legislature's assertion that the provisions at issue would protect women's health. Based on this test, the court of appeals upheld the application of the law to most of the affected facilities, ruling for instance that there was no undue burden in El Paso because women there could go to clinics in New Mexico.[158] The fundamental issue before the Supreme Court was whether this approach was correct, or whether the burden and health benefits of the law had to be compared and independently evaluated by the courts to determine whether the burden was undue.

In a majority opinion written by Justice Breyer and joined by Justice Kennedy, the Court rejected the approach of the court of appeals and insisted upon an independent comparison of burdens and benefits, rather than considering them separately and deferentially. Under *Casey*, Justice Breyer wrote, courts must consider "the burdens a law imposes on abortion access together with the benefits those laws confer."[159] Applying this test, the Court found that the medical benefits of the Texas law were at best slight, and were far outweighed by the burdens on women seeking abortions: "[I]n the face of no threat to women's health, Texas seeks to force women to travel long distances to get abortions in crammed-to-capacity superfacilities," where they "are less likely to get the kind of individualized attention, serious conversation, and emotional support that doctors at less taxed facilities may have offered."[160] The primary dissent, written by Justice Alito and joined by Chief Justice John Roberts and Justice Thomas, contested the district court's findings and raised procedural objections to the lawsuit. In a separate, solo dissent, Justice Thomas lambasted the Court's abortion rulings as a whole.

Assuming the continuing validity of *Casey*, the Court's decision in *Whole Woman's Health* makes sense in our view. *Casey* was a compromise, permitting states to attempt to *persuade* women not to have abortions, but prohibiting states from *preventing* women from

---

[156]   For the district court's findings, see *id*. at 2301–03.

[157]   *Id*. at 2309.

[158]   *Id*. at 2304.

[159]   *Id*. at 2309.

[160]   *Id*. at 2308.

having abortions.[161] If *Whole Woman's Health* had come out the other way, all a legislature would need to do to accomplish otherwise-impermissible prevention is relabel its actual interest in protecting fetal life as an interest in protecting women's health.[162] The Court's decision in *Whole Woman's Health* precludes such circumvention of *Casey.* Whether *Casey* should remain the law, however, is deeply contested.

With Justice Kennedy's departure from the Court in 2018, the future of *Roe* and *Casey* looks unpromising. Whether or not these decisions are overruled outright, it is likely that the Court's reconstituted conservative majority will uphold laws resulting in the closing of abortion clinics, bans on medication abortions (such as the "morning after" pill), and a wide variety of fetal-protective measures—for example, longer waiting periods, requirements to submit to an ultrasound, requirements to view sonograms, and pre-viability bans on abortion based upon such rationales as alleged fetal pain or detection of a fetal heartbeat. If this occurs, it will make the right to abortion increasingly theoretical to economically vulnerable women in states with hostile legislatures. Affluent adult women will be able to obtain abortions in other states or countries, while younger or poor women will be unable to do so. Depending on the national political climate, federal anti-abortion legislation is also conceivable, as it was in *Gonzales v. Carhart.*

III. Gay Rights and the Constitution

Abortion may be nearly matched in its level of controversy by constitutional questions falling under the general heading of gay rights. As much as any other development analyzed in this book, the litigation discussed in this section was the product of a social movement.[163] The growth of this movement was accompanied by a remarkable transformation of social attitudes. In 1993, when the first state court ruling in favor of same-sex marriage was issued, the public was opposed by a three-to-one margin.[164] No state allowed such marriages. In contrast, by the time of *Griswold,* all but two states allowed the sale of contraceptives to married couples.[165]

---

[161]   Interestingly, as discussed in Chapter 6, the Chief Justice's tax power analysis in *NFIB v. Sebelius,* 567 U.S. 519 (2012), also articulates a distinction between persuasion and prevention.

[162]   *See generally* Linda Greenhouse & Reva B. Siegel, Casey *and the Clinic Closings: When "Protecting Health" Obstructs Choice,* 125 YALE L.J. 1428 (2016).

[163]   *See generally* MICHAEL J. KLARMAN, FROM THE CLOSET TO THE ALTAR: COURTS, BACKLASH, AND THE STRUGGLE FOR SAME-SEX MARRIAGE (2013).

[164]   *See id.* at xiii.

[165]   *See id.* at xix.

A.   Sodomy Laws

Support for the gay rights movement had little traction until the 1960s, when advocacy efforts began to expand quickly.[166] One turning point was the eruption of the "Stonewall Riots" after police raided a gay bar in New York.[167] These riots are typically thought of as the start of the modern gay rights movement. During the 1970s, about half the states repealed their sodomy laws prohibiting anal or oral sex.[168] But even in 1987, over three-fourths of Americans thought same-sex intimacy was always wrong.[169]

The attack on sodomy laws reached the Supreme Court for the first time in *Bowers v. Hardwick.*[170] Michael Hardwick had been charged with violating a Georgia statute criminalizing sodomy by having sex with another adult male in the bedroom of Hardwick's home.[171] Justice White delivered the opinion of the Court, rejecting what he dismissively described as Hardwick's claim of "a fundamental right to engage in homosexual sodomy."[172] He observed that "[i]n 1868, when the Fourteenth Amendment was ratified, all but 5 of the 37 States in the Union had criminal sodomy laws. In fact, until 1961, all 50 States outlawed sodomy, and today, 24 States and the District of Columbia continue to provide criminal penalties for sodomy performed in private and between consenting adults."[173] Given these facts, White said, "to claim that a right to engage in such conduct is 'deeply rooted in this Nation's history and tradition' or 'implicit in the concept of ordered liberty' is, at best, facetious."[174]

Justice Powell concurred but suggested that the statute's twenty-year sentence might violate the Eighth Amendment. He had initially voted to invalidate the law but changed his mind (and changed his mind again after he retired, saying he had voted the wrong way). In the course of his deliberations, he told his law clerk that he had never met a gay person; it turns out that the law clerk to

---

[166]   *See id.* at 11.

[167]   *See id.* at 16–17.

[168]   *See id.* at 23.

[169]   *See id.* at 35.

[170]   478 U.S. 186 (1986). The Court had turned down many previous opportunities to consider issues of gay rights. *See* Eskridge, *supra* note 1, at 2178.

[171]   Georgia Code Ann. § 16–6–2 (1984) provided, in pertinent part, as follows:

(a)   A person commits the offense of sodomy when he performs or submits to any sexual act involving the sex organs of one person and the mouth or anus of another. . . .

(b)   A person convicted of the offense of sodomy shall be punished by imprisonment for not less than one nor more than 20 years. . . .

[172]   *Hardwick*, 478 U.S. at 191.

[173]   *Id.* at 193–94.

[174]   *Id.*

whom he was speaking was gay.[175] In contrast, when one of us clerked at the Court during the October 2003 Term, there were clerks who were openly gay, and their sexual orientation was not regarded as a big deal.

In dissent, Justice Blackmun maintained that "[o]nly the most willful blindness could obscure the fact that sexual intimacy is 'a sensitive, key relationship of human existence, central to family life, community welfare, and the development of human personality.' "[176] For this reason, he said, "[t]he fact that individuals define themselves in a significant way through their intimate sexual relationships with others suggests . . . that much of the richness of a relationship will come from the freedom an individual has to choose the form and nature of these intensely personal bonds."[177]

Justice Stevens also dissented on the ground that the statute banned certain sexual acts regardless of gender, and the state had failed to justify a policy of applying the statute only to same-sex acts. He contended that the liberty "that animated the development of the law in cases like *Griswold*, *Eisenstadt*, and *Carey* surely embraces the right to engage in nonreproductive, sexual conduct that others may consider offensive or immoral."[178] In his view, expressing moral opposition to conduct does not by itself qualify as a legitimate state interest that would justify banning the conduct.

In the years after *Bowers*, ferment over gay rights continued. Berkeley, California, became the first jurisdiction to enact a domestic partnership measure.[179] The gay rights movement prompted a powerful backlash, resulting in efforts to roll back ordinances passed in some cities banning discrimination on the basis of sexual orientation.[180]

Romer v. Evans,[181] decided a decade after *Bowers*, suggested that the Court's attitude toward gay rights was shifting. After several Colorado cities had passed ordinances banning discrimination on the basis of sexual orientation, Colorado voters passed a referendum measure prohibiting the state and cities from making sexual orientation or conduct the basis for a discrimination claim absent a further amendment to the state constitution. This state constitutional amendment was part of a larger countermovement

---

[175]   *See* KLARMAN, *supra* note 163, at 37.

[176]   *Bowers*, 478 U.S. at 205 (Blackmun, J., dissenting) (quoting Paris Adult Theatre I v. Slaton, 413 U.S. 49, 63 (1973)).

[177]   *Id.*

[178]   *Id.* at 218 (Stevens, J., dissenting).

[179]   *See* KLARMAN, *supra* note 163, at 56.

[180]   *See id.* at 41.

[181]   517 U.S. 620 (1996).

invoking family values and opposing gay rights.[182] Justice Kennedy wrote the opinion of the Court. Although the state characterized the referendum measure as merely placing gays and lesbians on the same plane as others who do not enjoy protected status, Justice Kennedy saw the amendment very differently:

> Homosexuals, by state decree, are put in a solitary class with respect to transactions and relations in both the private and governmental spheres. The amendment withdraws from homosexuals, but no others, specific legal protection from the injuries caused by discrimination, and it forbids reinstatement of these laws and policies.[183]

Justice Kennedy also suggested that the referendum measure might deprive gays and lesbians of general protections against arbitrary treatment, such as civil service rules.[184] In any event, Justice Kennedy emphasized that the referendum measure made it impossible for gays and lesbians to gain protection against discrimination except through a constitutional amendment, "protections taken for granted by most people either because they already have them or do not need them; these are protections against exclusion from an almost limitless number of transactions and endeavors that constitute ordinary civic life in a free society."[185]

Once the Court had characterized the referendum measure in these terms, the holding in the case was inevitable. In Justice Kennedy's view, the ordinance was unprecedented in placing such a broad disability, applying to so many aspects of life, on a defined class of people, and "its sheer breadth is so discontinuous with the reasons offered for it that the amendment seems inexplicable by anything but animus toward the class it affects."[186] The state had attempted to justify the ordinance as protecting the freedom of association of those with objections to homosexuality and conserving state resources to fight other forms of discrimination. But Justice Kennedy responded that "breadth of the amendment is so far removed from these particular justifications that we find it impossible to credit them."[187] Accordingly, the Court held that Amendment 2 failed even rational basis review and violated equal protection.

Many commentators have viewed *Romer* as applying heightened scrutiny without saying so. Saying so would have committed the Court to striking down the federal ban on gays in the military and

---

[182]   *See* Eskridge, *supra* note 1, at 2179–80.

[183]   *Romer*, 517 U.S. at 627.

[184]   *See id.* at 630.

[185]   *Id.* at 631.

[186]   *Id.* at 632.

[187]   *Id.* at 635.

prohibitions on same-sex marriage, among other forms of discrimination against gay people, in the very year in which Democratic President Bill Clinton signed the federal Defense of Marriage Act (DOMA) into law in order to avoid having the issue of gay rights become a "wedge issue" in an election year. DOMA is discussed below; among other things, it defined marriage for all purposes under federal law as limited to opposite-sex couples.

Justice Scalia dissented in *Romer*, joined by Chief Justice Rehnquist and Justice Thomas. In Scalia's view, the referendum measure "is not the manifestation of a " 'bare . . . desire to harm' " homosexuals, but is rather a modest attempt by seemingly tolerant Coloradans to preserve traditional sexual mores against the efforts of a politically powerful minority to revise those mores through use of the laws."[188] Justice Scalia recast the Court's argument in sweeping terms, saying that "[t]he central thesis of the Court's reasoning is that any group is denied equal protection when, to obtain advantage (or, presumably, to avoid disadvantage), it must have recourse to a more general and hence more difficult level of political decisionmaking than others."[189] This argument he found ridiculous: "The world has never heard of such a principle, which is why the Court's opinion is so long on emotive utterance and so short on relevant legal citation."[190] As for the Court's claim of animus, he said, "one could consider certain conduct reprehensible—murder, for example, or polygamy, or cruelty to animals—and could exhibit even 'animus' toward such conduct."[191]

Although they dealt with different issues, there was an obvious tension between *Bowers*, which held that the state could criminalize same-sex intimacy based on moral opposition to it, and *Romer*, which recast moral opposition as animus and condemned animus against those engaging in the conduct. Thus, the Court's decision in *Romer* called the continued vitality of *Bowers* into question. Public opinion was also shifting, with a large majority of Americans by 2003 favoring legalization of same-sex intimacy.[192]

Seven years after *Romer*, the Court in *Lawrence v. Texas*[193] overruled *Bowers*. Justice Kennedy, who wrote the opinion of the Court, noted the connection between the *Bowers* issue and *Romer*,

---

[188]   *Id.* at 636 (Scalia, J., dissenting).

[189]   *Id.* at 639.

[190]   *Id.*

[191]   *Id.* at 644.

[192]   *See* Klarman, *supra* note 163, at 86.

[193]   539 U.S. 558 (2003). For commentary on *Lawrence*, see generally Pamela Karlan, *Loving* Lawrence, 102 MICH. L. REV. 1447 (2004); Laurence Tribe, Lawrence v. Texas: *The "Fundamental Right" That Dares Not Speak Its Name*, 117 HARV. L. REV. 4 (2003).

writing that "[w]hen homosexual conduct is made criminal by the law of the State, that declaration in and of itself is an invitation to subject homosexual persons to discrimination both in the public and in the private spheres."[194] Justice Kennedy criticized *Bowers* for distorting both the history of prohibitions on homosexuality and modern attitudes, concluding that Justice Stevens had been correct in his *Bowers* dissent:

> The petitioners are entitled to respect for their private lives. The State cannot demean their existence or control their destiny by making their private sexual conduct a crime. Their right to liberty under the Due Process Clause gives them the full right to engage in their conduct without intervention of the government.[195]

Justice Kennedy invoked equality as well as liberty, writing for the Court that "[e]quality of treatment and the due process right to demand respect for conduct protected by the substantive guarantee of liberty are linked in important respects, and a decision on the latter point advances both interests."[196] These passages illustrate how equality values, in addition to liberty values, animated Justice Kennedy's interpretation of the Due Process Clause in *Lawrence*, as they did in *Casey*. Concerns about demeaning, disrespecting, and stigmatizing gay people pervade the Court's interpretation of the Due Process Clause in *Lawrence*. The Court even wrote that the very "continuance" of *Bowers* "as precedent demeans the lives of homosexual persons."[197]

Because the Court purported to apply rational basis review, it left itself room to maneuver in the future. In particular, it did not commit itself to any position regarding same-sex marriage. Thus, the Court was free to consider how the country reacted to *Lawrence* and whether public support for same-sex marriage would grow.[198]

Justice Scalia authored another impassioned dissent. He thought *Bowers* was well rooted in traditional jurisprudence:

> State laws against bigamy, same-sex marriage, adult incest, prostitution, masturbation, adultery, fornication, bestiality, and obscenity are likewise sustainable only in light of *Bowers'* validation of laws based on moral

---

[194]   *Id.* at 575.

[195]   *Id.* at 578.

[196]   *Id.* at 575.

[197]   *Id.*

[198]   *See* Robert C. Post, *Foreword: Fashioning the Legal Constitution: Culture, Courts, and Law*, 117 HARV. L. REV. 4, 11 (2003) (arguing that "*Lawrence* is best interpreted as an opening bid in a conversation between the Court and the American public").

choices. . . . The impossibility of distinguishing homosexuality from other traditional "morals" offenses is precisely why *Bowers* rejected the rational-basis challenge.[199]

Where the majority saw a deprivation of liberty and discrimination, Scalia saw an expression of traditional morality: "Many Americans do not want persons who openly engage in homosexual conduct as partners in their business, as scoutmasters for their children, as teachers in their children's schools, or as boarders in their home. They view this as protecting themselves and their families from a lifestyle that they believe to be immoral and destructive."[200] Justice Scalia ended with a warning that the Court's decision would lead inexorably to a constitutional right to same sex marriage, in part because it was illogical to limit marriage to opposite-sex couples on procreation grounds given that "the sterile and the elderly are allowed to marry."[201]

B. *Obergefell* and Beyond

Justice Scalia's prediction was ultimately proven right (and gay rights advocates invoked the sharp analysis in his *Lawrence* dissent to move matters along), but not for another dozen years.[202] It was not until 2015 that the Court recognized the right to same sex marriage, in *Obergefell v. Hodges*.[203] In the meantime, the countermovement against gay rights continued, and by 2012 thirty-six states had adopted statutes or constitutional amendments declaring the illegality of same-sex marriage. Support for same-sex marriage grew substantially from 2009–2012,[204] but the intensity of opposition also grew. Among the public, opponents tended to feel more passionately about the issue than most supporters, and all but one Southern state passed constitutional amendments limiting marriage to a man and a woman.[205] In political terms, according to one prominent legal historian, same-sex marriage was a "godsend to religious conservatives and Republicans" because of the issue's power to motivate conservative voters.[206]

Two years before *Obergefell,* an intervening, transitional case took a substantial step toward protecting same-sex marriage. *United*

---

[199]   *Id.* at 590 (Scalia, J., dissenting).

[200]   *Id.* at 602.

[201]   *Id.* at 605. Justice Scalia thus wrote a "sky is falling" dissent, as opposed to a "damage control" dissent.

[202]   *See* Eskridge, *supra* note 1, at 2187.

[203]   576 U.S. ___, 135 S. Ct. 2584 (2015).

[204]   *See* Klarman, *supra* note 163, at 196–97.

[205]   *See id.* at 173, 193.

[206]   *Id.* at 183.

States v. Windsor[207] involved a federal statute passed in 1996—the Defense of Marriage Act (DOMA)—that defined marriage for federal law purposes as including only marriages between a man and a woman, even if same-sex couples were lawfully married under the law of their state of residence. Edith Windsor and Thea Spyer were married in Ontario, Canada, and the marriage was recognized as valid by the State of New York, where they lived. Spyer died and left her estate to Windsor. The issue before the Court was whether Windsor qualified for a marital estate tax exemption under federal law, which she would have received except for DOMA. The procedural posture of the case was unusual and provoked controversy. Under President Barack Obama, the Justice Department had concluded that the statute was unconstitutional and refused to defend it in litigation, but the Administration continued enforcing it until or unless it was invalidated by the courts, out of respect for the Congress that passed it and for the courts that would then be able to determine its constitutionality.[208] A group of members of Congress was allowed to intervene to defend the law.[209]

Justice Kennedy's opinion for the Court struck down the statute, holding that it violated the Due Process Clause of the Fifth Amendment. His perhaps intentionally ambiguous opinion had a federalism aspect, stressing that "the Federal Government, through our history, has deferred to state-law policy decisions with respect to domestic relations."[210] The apparent implication of this part of his opinion was that states could decide for themselves whether to allow same-sex marriage, as Chief Justice Roberts emphasized in his "damage control" dissent. But on our reading, the heart of the opinion, as in *Romer* and *Lawrence*, was that DOMA was motivated by anti-gay animus—and, more generally, that it had the purpose, effect, and dominant social meaning of demeaning the dignity and reinforcing the inequality of married same-sex couples and their children: "The history of DOMA's enactment and its own text demonstrate that interference with the equal dignity of same-sex marriages, a dignity conferred by the States in the exercise of their sovereign power, was more than an incidental effect of the federal statute. It was its essence."[211] The apparent implication of this part of his opinion was that states could not decide for themselves whether to allow same-sex marriage.

In dissent, Justice Scalia bitterly rebuffed the Court's finding of animus, castigating the Court for "formally declaring anyone opposed

---

[207]   570 U.S. 744 (2013).
[208]   *See id.* at 755.
[209]   *See id.*
[210]   *Id.* at 767.
[211]   *Id.* at 770.

to same-sex marriage an enemy of human decency."[212] Perhaps
Justice Kennedy came to appreciate this critique. In any event, his
next opinion, in *Obergefell*, attempted to take a different tack,
although Justice Scalia was left no happier that his prediction in
Windsor about what the Court would do next was born out.

One of us wrote in the wake of *Windsor* that Justice Kennedy
used analytically gratuitous federalism reasoning and rhetoric as a
"way station" along a route whose ultimate destination was a
constitutional right to same-sex marriage. By sending mixed
messages, but also a stronger message about the equal dignity of
same-sex couples and their children and the unacceptability of
humiliating them, Justice Kennedy was attempting to persuade—but
not yet to require—federal judges to invalidate state prohibitions on
same-sex marriage.[213] This is what almost all of them did after
Windsor. Wielding the individual rights (as opposed to the
federalism) interpretation of *Windsor* as authority, federal courts
moved much more quickly than the *Windsor* majority had likely
anticipated.

Obergefell involved referendums in Michigan, Kentucky, Ohio,
and Tennessee that had approved state constitutional amendments
defining marriage as a union between a man and a woman. These
amendments were challenged by same-sex couples as a denial of their
rights to marry and to have their out-of-state marriages, which were
valid where performed, recognized in these states.[214] Justice
Kennedy's opinion for the Court focused on the harmfulness of the
ban on same-sex marriage rather than on anti-gay animus.
Admittedly, Justice Kennedy wrote, "[t]he limitation of marriage to
opposite-sex couples may long have seemed natural and just."[215] But
"its inconsistency with the central meaning of the fundamental right
to marry is now manifest," and "[w]ith that knowledge must come the
recognition that laws excluding same-sex couples from the marriage
right impose stigma and injury of the kind prohibited by our basic
charter."[216] By focusing on the scope of the fundamental right to
marry, as opposed to discrimination on the basis of sexual orientation
or sex, Justice Kennedy's opinion emphasized liberty, protected
through the Due Process Clause. In considering whether the
tradition of respect for marriage should be understood to encompass
same-sex relationships, Kennedy laid out the reasons why marriage
has value to couples, to any children they choose to have, and to

---

[212] *Id.* at 800 (Scalia, J., dissenting).

[213] *See generally* Neil S. Siegel, *Federalism as a Way Station:* Windsor *as
Exemplar of Doctrine in Motion*, 6 J. LEGAL ANALYSIS 87 (2014).

[214] *See Obergefell*, 135 S. Ct. at 2593.

[215] *Id.* at 2602.

[216] *Id.*

society. He found that each of these reasons applied equally to same-sex and opposite-sex couples.

Although emphasizing constitutional liberty, Justice Kennedy added some equality reasoning near the end of his opinion. He noted the long history of discrimination against gay people in this country, and he reaffirmed that discrimination with respect to access to the fundamental right to marry warrants strict scrutiny under the Equal Protection Clause.[217] (This path to heightened scrutiny, which is limited to marriage, is distinct from a holding—which to date the Court has not issued—subjecting discrimination on the basis of sexual orientation to heightened scrutiny.) Drawing from the extensive judicial record that had been built up for years, the Court found no evidence that recognition of same-sex marriage as within the scope of the right to marry would harm either the institution of marriage or children raised by same-sex couples. The last paragraph of Justice Kennedy's opinion encapsulates his perspective:

> It would misunderstand these men and women to say they disrespect the idea of marriage. Their plea is that they do respect it, respect it so deeply that they seek to find its fulfillment for themselves. Their hope is not to be condemned to live in loneliness, excluded from one of civilization's oldest institutions. They ask for equal dignity in the eyes of the law. The Constitution grants them that right.[218]

There were several dissents. Writing for himself and Justices Thomas and Scalia, Chief Justice Roberts stressed judicial restraint. "The purpose of insisting that implied fundamental rights have roots in the history and tradition of our people," he wrote, "is to ensure that when unelected judges strike down democratically enacted laws, they do so based on something more than their own beliefs."[219] The Chief Justice called for a "more modest and restrained" view of the judicial role, one "more skeptical that the legal abilities of judges also reflect insight into moral and philosophical issues," and one "more sensitive to the fact that judges are unelected and unaccountable, and that the legitimacy of their power depends on confining it to the exercise of legal judgment."[220]

Writing only for himself and Justice Thomas, Justice Scalia lambasted the Court's opinion, going even beyond his usual level of rhetoric. He argued that "a system of government that makes the People subordinate to a committee of nine unelected lawyers does not

---

[217]   *See id.* at 2604–05.

[218]   *Id.* at 2608.

[219]   *Id.* at 2622–23 (Roberts, C.J., dissenting).

[220]   *Id.* at 2626.

deserve to be called a democracy."[221] Going even further, he said he was astounded by "the hubris reflected in today's judicial Putsch,"[222] and in a more *ad hominem* comment, that the majority opinion "is couched in a style that is as pretentious as its content is egotistic."[223] On an even more caustic note, he wrote that "[i]f, even as the price to be paid for a fifth vote, I ever joined an opinion for the Court that began: 'The Constitution promises liberty to all within its reach, a liberty that includes certain specific rights that allow persons, within a lawful realm, to define and express their identity,' I would hide my head in a bag. The Supreme Court of the United States has descended from the disciplined legal reasoning of John Marshall and Joseph Story to the mystical aphorisms of the fortune cookie."[224]

Justice Alito also wrote a dissent, which was joined by Justices Thomas and Scalia. He accepted that his "colleagues in the majority sincerely see in the Constitution a vision of liberty that happens to coincide with their own," but this very sincerity, he thought, "evidences . . . the deep and perhaps irremediable corruption of our legal culture's conception of constitutional interpretation."[225]

One reason why the majority and the dissents seemed to be talking past each other was that they framed the issue differently. For the majority, marriage is defined as a type of personal decision and chosen connection between two people, from which same-sex couples were excluded. There was plenty of precedent for scrutinizing exclusions from marriage, as we saw at the beginning of this chapter. For the dissenters, marriage is defined as involving a man and a woman; same-sex couples were seeking to radically expand the institution into new territory. Thus, where one side saw an existing exclusion, the other side saw a demand for expansion. Naturally, the two sides were unable to understand each other.

A recurrent theme in the dissenting opinions, mentioned by the majority as well, was the situation of individuals with sincere religious objections to recognition of same-sex marriages. This general issue seems likely to increasingly occupy the Court's attention.

The first of what may become a longer line of cases on this issue was *Masterpiece Cakeshop v. Colorado Civil Rights Commission.*[226]

---

[221] *Id.* at 2629 (Scalia, J., dissenting).

[222] *Id.*

[223] *Id.* at 2630.

[224] *Id.* at 2630 n. 22.

[225] *Id.* at 2643 (Alito, J., dissenting). Despite the dissents, *Obergefell* has found some conservative support. For an originalist defense of the holding, see generally Steven G. Calabresi & Hannah M. Begley, *Originalism and Same-Sex Marriage*, 70 U. MIAMI L. REV. 648 (2016).

[226] 584 U.S. ___, 138 S. Ct. 1719 (2018).

The owner of a cakeshop refused to make a wedding cake for a gay couple, contending that his custom decorations would amount to an endorsement of their marriage. He was found to have discriminated on the basis of sexual orientation, in violation of the state's civil rights law. In challenging this finding of discrimination, the owner's primary argument was based on the Free Speech Clause of the First Amendment. His legal theory was that his cake decorating was expressive activity and that the state anti-discrimination law had the effect of making him express a position against his will. If the Court were to accept this argument, the implications for sexual orientation minorities would be serious given the number of other businesspeople who might also be constitutionally entitled to deny service to them.

Justice Kennedy appeared to be looking for an off-ramp, however, and the Court decided *Masterpiece Cakeshop* narrowly on the basis of the Free Exercise Clause, finding evidence in the record from which it surprisingly discerned unconstitutional hostility toward the baker's religious views. Justice Kennedy's opinion for the Court strove to maintain a balance between the competing interests at stake.[227] Although the baker won the case, Justice Kennedy observed that any decision in his favor "would have to be sufficiently constrained, lest all purveyors of goods and services who object to gay marriages for moral and religious reasons in effect be allowed to put up signs saying 'no goods or services will be sold if they will be used for gay marriages,'" a result that would "impose a serious stigma on gay persons."[228]

With Justice Kennedy's departure from the Court, the balance he was seeking in *Masterpiece Cakeshop* may move heavily toward religious claimants and against same-sex couples. From different perspectives, this could be seen as a surrender to bigotry or a vindication of religious freedom. The large number of married same-sex couples that now exist, however, may inhibit the Court from overruling *Obergefell*, despite Justice Kennedy's retirement. Still, a differently constituted Court could well define the marriage right narrowly and permit discrimination against gay people in related contexts such as adoption.

IV. Privacy Rights at the End of Life

The issues we have discussed in this chapter revolve around the family, reproduction, and sexuality. These topics have indeed been the focus of the Court's attention. But on several occasions, it has also

---

[227] For background on the Free Exercise Clause, see the discussion of *Employment Division v. Smith*, 494 U.S. 872 (1990), in Chapter 13 and DANIEL A. FARBER, THE FIRST AMENDMENT: CONCEPTS AND INSIGHTS (4th ed. 2014).

[228] *Masterpiece Cakeshop*, 138 S. Ct. at 1728–29.

examined the application of privacy concepts in a very different context: individuals facing the end of life.

A. Refusals of Medical Treatment

Cruzan v. Director, Missouri Department of Health[229] involved a young woman in a persistent vegetative state (similar to a permanent coma). She had suffered brain damage in a car crash. Her parents sought to end her life by discontinuing hydration and nutrition via a feeding tube (to which her then-husband had consented). They argued that there was a fundamental constitutional right, protected under the liberty provision of the Due Process Clause, to end one's life under these circumstances. Under state law, however, they had the burden of proving by clear and convincing evidence that their daughter would have wanted to die if she found herself in these circumstances. They sued, claiming that this standard of proof was too high and that the state should defer to their judgment as her closest family members.

Chief Justice Rehnquist's opinion for the Court began by reviewing state court decisions dealing with similar questions and Supreme Court cases supporting "the recognition of a general liberty interest in refusing medical treatment."[230] "But," he wrote, "determining that a person has a 'liberty interest' under the Due Process Clause does not end the inquiry; 'whether respondent's constitutional rights have been violated must be determined by balancing his liberty interests against the relevant state interests.' "[231] On the other side of the balance, the Chief Justice identified the state's general interest in preserving human life and its more particular interest in preventing people's lives from being terminated when they would not have wanted this outcome. Balancing these interests, he held that the state's scheme was constitutionally warranted.

The swing voter in this case was Justice O'Connor, who wrote a concurring opinion. (The Court's four more liberal Justices dissented). Justice O'Connor explained why she agreed "that a protected liberty interest in refusing unwanted medical treatment may be inferred from our prior decisions, and that the refusal of artificially delivered food and water is encompassed within that liberty interest."[232] Justice Scalia also wrote separately to make clear his view that no liberty interest was involved because the law had never recognized a legal right to commit suicide.[233] But he was

---

[229]   497 U.S. 261 (1990).

[230]   *Id.* at 278.

[231]   *Id.* at 270 (quoting Youngberg v. Romeo, 457 U.S. 307, 321 (1982)).

[232]   *Id.* at 287 (O'Connor, J., concurring).

[233]   *Id.* at 293 (Scalia, J., concurring).

outnumbered. Even though Chief Justice Rehnquist's opinion may be read as somewhat equivocal as to whether it actually recognized a liberty interest or did so only for the sake of argument, Justice O'Connor's vote plus the four dissenters made a clear majority of the Court opposed to Justice Scalia.

B. Physician-Assisted Suicide

Seven years later, the Court faced two more cases dealing with the right to die. These cases led to a confusing welter of opinions. In *Washington v. Glucksberg*,[234] three terminally ill patients, four physicians, and a nonprofit organization brought an action for a declaratory judgment that a statute banning assisted suicide violated the Due Process Clause. Chief Justice Rehnquist wrote the majority opinion, which was joined by Justices O'Connor, Scalia, Kennedy, and Thomas. Based on an examination of history and current law, the Chief Justice concluded that "our laws have consistently condemned, and continue to prohibit, assisting suicide. Despite changes in medical technology and notwithstanding an increased emphasis on the importance of end-of-life decisionmaking, we have not retreated from this prohibition."[235] Most importantly, he insisted that the only unenumerated rights protected under the liberty provision of the Due Process Clause are ones that are deeply rooted in American history and tradition. This has come to be known as the "*Glucksberg* test" in substantive due process cases; Chief Justice Roberts emphasized it in his dissent in *Obergefell*, and Justice Kennedy expressly rejected it in his majority opinion in *Obergefell*.

A companion case, *Vacco v. Quill*,[236] was an equal protection attack on New York's ban on assisted suicide. New York gave terminally patients the right to refuse further treatment, and the plaintiffs claimed that it was irrational to distinguish between assisted suicide (illegal) and refusal of treatment (legal). The Court disagreed, finding that this distinction between acts and omissions was widespread in many states and that the distinction between causing something through affirmative action and doing so through passive inaction was deeply embedded in the law.

Five Justices—O'Connor, Stevens, Souter, Ginsburg, and Breyer—wrote separately in these 1997 cases to reserve a number of questions. In particular, Justice O'Connor emphasized that the case did not present the issue of whether a "patient who is suffering from a terminal illness and who is experiencing great pain can obtain medication, from qualified physicians, to alleviate this suffering,

---

[234]   521 U.S. 702 (1997).

[235]   *Id.* at 719.

[236]   521 U.S. 793 (1997).

even to the point of causing unconsciousness and hastening death."[237] The other concurrences all seemed to agree that this issue was still open. One medical observer suggested that, in effect, by endorsing potentially lethal sedation of terminal patients (which is normally accompanied by the withholding of hydration and nutrition), the Court rejected assisted suicide only to embrace euthanasia.[238] From the perspective of constitutional law, it is noteworthy that at least five Justices viewed this issue as open; the implication is that there were not actually five votes for the *Glucksberg* test in *Glucksberg* itself.

One intriguing aspect of this case was the handling of precedent. Chief Justice Rehnquist sidestepped any criticism of *Roe* or *Casey* (perhaps to retain the votes of Justices Kennedy and O'Connor). He also conspicuously avoided any reliance on *Bowers*, which had yet to be overruled at the time. The concurring Justices also seemed to feel no need to deal with this precedent.

The Court has been largely content to allow the states to deal with the difficult issues posed by end-of-life decisions. These decisions sometimes lead to highly publicized conflicts between individuals or families and healthcare providers or government officials. But by-and-large, the states seem to have managed to deal with the issue with far less turmoil than in the areas of abortion or gay rights. Perhaps one reason is that these are dilemmas that everyone in society will face sooner or later. Another is that many issues are worked out by individuals, their families, and their health-care providers without legal intervention.

The cases in this chapter embody several of the themes we discussed in Chapter 1. There is no question that constitutional politics has helped shape constitutional law in this area, as conservative Republicans increasingly made judicial appointments. But as the *Casey* joint opinion illustrates, the Court's decisions are not just a passive reflection of political forces. And these decisions have both responded to societal changes and influenced them, sometimes by encouraging proponents of its decisions and sometimes by energizing opponents of its rulings. These cases also illustrate some of the sharp jurisprudential divisions on the Court—primarily, between Justices who view certain constitutional rights as fixed by history, and Justices who view them as evolving in response to changes in facts and values.

In this half of the book, we have focused on individual rights. In the next chapter, our last, we come full circle with a topic that

---

[237]   *Glucksberg*, 521 U.S. at 736–37 (O'Connor, J., concurring).

[238]   *See generally* David Orentlicher, *The Supreme Court and Physician-Assisted Suicide*, 337 N. ENG. J. MED. 1236 (1997).

combines individual rights with the structural issues covered in the first half of the book. There, too, social movements and counter-movements have helped shape the law.

Further Readings

Robert H. Bork, *Neutral Principles and Some First Amendment Problems*, 47 IND. L.J. 1 (1971).

Steven G. Calabresi & Hannah M. Begley, *Originalism and Same-Sex Marriage*, 70 U. MIAMI L. REV. 648 (2016).

John Hart Ely, *The Wages of Crying Wolf: A Comment on* Roe v. Wade, 82 YALE L.J. 920 (1973).

William N. Eskridge, Jr., *Some Effects of Identity-Based Social Movements on Constitutional Law in the Twentieth Century*, 100 MICH . L. REV. 2962 (2002).

Lucinda M. Finley, *Contested Ground: The Story of* Roe v. Wade *and its Impact on American Society* 233, *in* CONSTITUTIONAL LAW STORIES (Michael C. Dorf ed., 2d ed. 2009).

Ruth Bader Ginsburg, *Some Thoughts on Autonomy and Equality in Relation to* Roe v. Wade, 63 N.C. L. REV. 375 (1985).

LINDA GREENHOUSE, BECOMING JUSTICE BLACKMUN: HARRY BLACKMUN'S SUPREME COURT JOURNEY (2006).

LINDA GREENHOUSE & REVA B. SIEGEL, BEFORE *ROE V. WADE*: VOICES THAT SHAPED THE ABORTION DEBATE BEFORE THE SUPREME COURT'S RULING (2012), https://documents.law.yale.edu/sites/default/files/beforeroe2nded_1.pdf.

Linda Greenhouse & Reva B. Siegel, *Before (and After)* Roe v. Wade*: New Questions About Backlash*, 120 YALE L.J. 2028 (2012).

Pamela Karlan, *Loving* Lawrence, 102 HARV. L. REV. 1447 (2004).

MICHAEL J. KLARMAN, FROM THE CLOSET TO THE ALTAR: COURTS, BACKLASH, AND THE STRUGGLE FOR SAME-SEX MARRIAGE (2013).

REBECCA M. KLUCHIN, FIT TO BE TIED: STERILIZATION AND REPRODUCTIVE RIGHTS IN AMERICA 1950–1980 (2011).

Neil S. Siegel, *Federalism as a Way Station:* Windsor *as Exemplar of Doctrine in Motion*, 6 J. LEGAL ANALYSIS 87 (2014).

Neil S. Siegel & Reva B. Siegel, *Equality Arguments for Abortion Rights*, 60 UCLA L. REV. DISCOURSE 160 (2013).

Neil S. Siegel & Reva B. Siegel, Griswold *at 50: Contraception as a Sex Equality Right*, 124 YALE L.J. F. (2015).

Reva B. Siegel, *Reasoning from the Body: An Historical Perspective on Abortion Regulation and Questions of Equal Protection*, 44 STAN. L. REV. 261 (1992).

Laurence H. Tribe, Lawrence v. Texas*: The "Fundamental Right" That Dare Not Speak Its Name*, 117 HARV. L. REV. 1893 (2004).

Chapter 13

WHERE STRUCTURE MEET RIGHTS: THE RECONSTRUCTION POWERS

Article I, Section 8—the home of the Commerce Clause—is not the only set of provisions granting Congress legislative powers. Decades after the original Constitution was ratified, new sources of congressional authority were provided by the Civil War Amendments, also called the Reconstruction Amendments. As we have seen, three vitally important amendments were added in the aftermath of the Civil War; in many ways, they laid the groundwork for a new constitutional order. As we have seen, Section One of each amendment establishes substantive rights. The Thirteenth Amendment prohibits slavery. Section One of the Fourteenth Amendment provides that all persons born or naturalized in the United States are citizens of the United States (the Citizenship Clause), thereby overruling *Dred Scott*.[1] As discussed in Chapter 8, Section One also contains the Privileges or Immunities Clause, the Due Process Clause, and the Equal Protection Clause. The Fifteenth Amendment prohibits the federal and state governments from limiting voting on the basis of race. Collectively, these amendments secure certain human rights within the United States—sometimes explicitly singling out violations by government, sometimes not.

These amendments are self-executing, meaning that Section One of each amendment prohibits certain practices even absent implementing legislation by Congress. But each amendment also provides, in an enforcement clause at the end, that Congress shall have the power to enforce the provisions of the amendment "by appropriate legislation."[2] Thus, each amendment authorizes Congress to enact civil rights legislation. These are potential "hooks" for congressional regulation, and we call them Congress's reconstruction powers.

Note the contrast between the structural logic animating much of Article I, Section 8, and the structural logic animating the enforcement clauses. Whereas Section 8 creates federal control in policy areas where states are hampered by collective action problems, the enforcement clauses confer federal power to regulate when, for

---

1   Dred Scott v. Sandford, 60 U.S. 393 (1857).

2   These enforcement clauses are located in Section 2 of the Thirteenth Amendment, Section 5 of the Fourteenth Amendment, and Section 2 of the Fifteenth Amendment.

internal reasons, states fail to protect certain key rights.[3] The practical significance of the Civil War and Reconstruction for the constitutional structure was to lay the groundwork for federal enforcement of civil rights in the face of state and local hostility or indifference. It took almost a century for Congress to begin using its reconstruction powers in earnest—and, as we saw in Chapter 5, to also use its commerce power in the service of civil rights.

As we shall see in this chapter, there continues to be a major debate about what exactly the enforcement clauses mean and thus how far they allow Congress to go in protecting citizens from their own state governments. As explained in Chapter 8, for example, Congress passed the Fourteenth Amendment in large part because of concerns about whether the Civil Rights Act of 1866 was within the scope of Section Two of the Thirteenth Amendment. In particular, there was no consensus about whether the Act's requirement that persons of color enjoy the same rights and liberties "for the security of persons and property as is enjoyed by white citizens" was an appropriate way of enforcing the prohibition on slavery in Section 1 of the Thirteenth Amendment.

The Warren Court, at the height of the Civil Rights Era, took a broad view of the enforcement clauses. Closer to the present, the Rehnquist and Roberts Courts imposed limits not only on the scope of Congress's powers in Article I, Section 8, but also on the scope of congressional power under Section 5 of the Fourteenth Amendment and Section 2 of the Fifteenth Amendment. The Roberts Court did so most recently in *Shelby County v. Holder*, a voting rights decision that has fundamentally altered the political dynamics in many states, as we will discuss at the end of this chapter.[4]

There are two primary constitutional questions regarding the scope of Congress's power under the enforcement clauses of the Civil War Amendments. First, may Congress target private behavior using the enforcement clauses, or may it target only government actions—so-called "state action"? The Commerce Clause, as we saw in Chapter 5, allows Congress to regulate both state governments and private actors. What about the Reconstruction powers?

Second, what is the nature of Congress's power under the Civil War Amendments? Is Congress limited to remedying or preventing what the Supreme Court has independently identified as a constitutional violation, or does Congress have its own authority to interpret Section 1 of each amendment? In other words, when Congress seeks to prohibit a state law or practice as violating

---

[3]   *See* Neil S. Siegel, *Collective Action Federalism and Its Discontents*, 91 TEX. L. REV. 1937, 1948 (2013).

[4]   570 U.S. 529 (2013).

Congress's understanding of Section 1 of the Civil War Amendments, how should courts respond if Congress's understanding differs from the Supreme Court's? At stake here are separation of powers issues about authority to interpret the Constitution as well as federalism issues about federal control displacing state regulation.

We will consider each question in turn in the context of the Thirteenth and Fourteenth Amendments, after which we turn to the Court's Fifteenth Amendment jurisprudence, including its decision in *Shelby County*.

As with other areas of constitutional law, it is impossible to separate the evolution of legal doctrine in this one from the ebb and flow of constitutional politics. The Reconstruction era was followed by a long period of "normalization" under which Southern states were given broad power to limit the rights of blacks. The Civil Rights era of the 1950s and 1960s resulted in a resurgence of federal power, but it was followed by a period of conservative reaction favorable to states' rights and skeptical of claims of widespread entrenched discrimination. But the Supreme Court's rulings were not merely passive reflections of their political context. Instead, the Court has also helped to shape the political atmosphere. The post-Civil War Court significantly limited the reach of congressional power to enforce the Civil War Amendments, and in the modern era the Court first championed federal authority to protect minority voting rights and later concluded that vigorous legal protection was no longer needed.

I.   May Congress Regulate Private Conduct?

The initial question is whether Congress may use its reconstruction powers to regulate certain forms of private action, or whether it is limited to situations involving unconstitutional behavior by government officials. The answer under current doctrine is that it depends on the power in question. We begin with past law, parts of which have been overruled and parts of which have been reaffirmed.

A.   *The Civil Rights Cases*

The key historical precedent is the *Civil Rights Cases*, decided in 1883 and introduced in Chapter 8.[5] In this case, the Supreme Court, in a majority opinion authored by Justice Joseph Bradley, strictly limited Congress's power to use the enforcements clauses of the Civil War Amendments to control private behavior. The Civil Rights Act of 1875, enacted at the end of Reconstruction, prohibited private racial discrimination by hotels, restaurants, transportation

---

[5]   109 U.S. 3 (1883).

services, and other public accommodations. By a vote of 8 to 1, the Court held that the Act was beyond the scope of the enforcement clauses of the Thirteenth and Fourteenth Amendments.

Regarding the Thirteenth Amendment, the Court recognized that Section 1 prohibits private conduct; it prohibits any person from owning a slave. But, the Court reasoned that Congress may ensure only an end to slavery; it may not seek to eliminate private racial discrimination:

> It would be running the slavery argument into the ground to make it apply to every act of discrimination which a person may see fit to make as to the guests he will entertain, or as to the people he will take into his coach or cab or car, or admit to his concert or theatre, or deal with in other matters of intercourse or business.[6]

Regarding the Fourteenth Amendment, the Court held broadly that, because only state actors are capable of violating Section 1 of the amendment, Congress may not use Section 5 to target private behavior. In the Court's view, the rights protected by Section 1 "cannot be impaired by the wrongful acts of individuals, unsupported by State authority in the shape of laws, customs, or judicial or executive proceedings."[7] The Court reasoned, in other words, that regulating private racial discrimination is not a valid means of enforcing the rights protected in Section 1 of the amendment because private actors are not capable of violating Section 1 in the absence of involvement by the state.

The first Justice John Marshall Harlan filed a vehement dissent for himself alone, as he would later do in *Plessy v. Ferguson*.[8] In his view, the Court was severely and inappropriately limiting the impact and promise of the Civil War Amendments through what amounted to "a subtle and ingenious verbal criticism."[9] With respect to the Thirteenth Amendment, he reasoned that Congress may use Section 2 not only to prohibit slavery, but also to destroy its "badges and incidents," and that the acts of private racial discrimination covered by the Act were badges or incidents of slavery.[10]

With respect to the Fourteenth Amendment, Justice Harlan rejected the majority's assertion that Section 1 of the amendment prohibits only state action. Focusing attention on the affirmative grant of citizenship in Section 1, he argued that Congress may use its

---

6   *Id.* at 24–25.
7   *Id.* at 17.
8   163 U.S. 537 (1896).
9   *Civil Rights Cases*, 109 U.S. at 26 (Harlan, J., dissenting).
10   *Id.* at 35–36.

power under Section 5 to enforce the Citizenship Clause, and that threats to the civil rights that accompany the citizenship of African Americans can come from acts of private racial discrimination as well as from racial discrimination by state actors.[11] In the alternative, he added that "[i]n every material sense applicable to the practical enforcement of the Fourteenth Amendment, railroad corporations, keepers of inns, and managers of places of public amusement are agents of the State, because they are charged with duties to the public, and are amenable, in respect of their public duties and functions, to governmental regulation."[12]

The *Civil Rights Cases* served as an obstacle to the passage of federal legislation criminalizing lynching, which was repeatedly put before Congress over the course of the Twentieth Century but never passed. An argument against the constitutionality of such legislation was that the Ku Klux Klan and other similarly minded terrorist groups were private actors, not state actors. Indeed, even before the *Civil Rights Cases*, the Court had already made it more difficult for Congress to address such terrorist behavior. In *United States v. Cruikshank*,[13] a white mob had attacked freed blacks, and participants were charged with depriving the victims of their rights to vote, assemble, and bear arms.[14] The Court threw out these charges on the ground that only state officials could deprive individuals of these rights. Moreover, in *United States v. Harris*,[15] decided the same year as the *Civil Rights Cases*, the Court overturned the criminal convictions of members of a lynch mob in Tennessee under the Ku Klux Klan Act, which (as its names suggests) was designed to combat the efforts of the Klan and other mobs to deprive African Americans of the equal protection of the laws.[16] The Court reasoned that Congress lacked any authority to criminalize private conspiracies under Section 5 of the Fourteenth Amendment.

---

[11]   *See id.* at 44–57. For development of Justice Harlan's position, see Akhil Reed Amar, *Intratextualism*, 112 HARV. L. REV. 747, 821–27 (1999).

[12]   *Civil Rights Cases*, 109 U.S. at 58–59 (Harlan, J., dissenting).

[13]   92 U.S. 542 (1876).

[14]   Section 6 of the Enforcement Act of 1870 made it a felony for "two or more persons [to] band or conspire together, or go in disguise upon the public highway, or upon the premises of another . . . to injure, oppress, threaten, or intimidate any citizen, with intent to prevent or hinder his free exercise and enjoyment of any right or privilege granted or secured to him by the constitution or laws of the United States."

[15]   106 U.S. 629 (1883).

[16]   Constituting Section 2 of the Civil Rights Act of 1871, the Ku Klux Klan Act imposed both criminal and civil liability upon "two or more persons [who] conspire or go in disguise on a highway or on the premises of another for the purpose of depriving any person or class of persons of the equal protection of the laws or of equal privileges and immunities under the laws."

The *Civil Rights Cases* is also why, as discussed in Chapter 5, Congress relied mainly on the Commerce Clause, not Section 5 of the Fourteenth Amendment, when it finally overcame Southern filibusters and passed the Civil Rights Act of 1964. This was the first major piece of civil rights legislation enacted by Congress since the Civil Rights Act of 1875.

B.   Current Law

The Thirteenth Amendment holding in the *Civil Rights Cases* remained the law for another eighty years—up until the 1960s. During the Civil Rights Movement of the 1960s, the Court adopted the view of Justice Harlan's dissent in the *Civil Rights Cases* and allowed Congress to use Section 2 of the Thirteenth Amendment to prohibit private racial discrimination in selling and leasing property,[17] as well as in private contracting.[18] The Court reaffirmed these rulings in 1989.[19] Thus, today Congress may prohibit many acts of private racial discrimination using Section 2 of the Thirteenth Amendment, although presumably not all such acts (such as deciding whom to admit to one's home). The theory behind these cases is that in passing the Thirteenth Amendment, Congress realized that slavery and its incidents could be imposed by private coercion, not just through state laws or acts of government officials, and so the Court has given Congress broad power to define the "badges and incidents" of slavery in using its Thirteenth Amendment reconstruction power.

By contrast, the Fourteenth Amendment holding of the *Civil Rights Cases* remains governing law. In *United States v. Morrison*,[20] in 2000, the Rehnquist Court reaffirmed the Fourteenth Amendment holding of the *Civil Rights Cases*. *Morrison*, as we discussed in Chapter 5, involved the constitutionality of Section 13981 of the Violence Against Women Act of 1994 (VAWA), which empowered victims of gender-motivated violence to sue their assailants in federal court for money damages. In *Morrison* itself, a young woman sued two Virginia Tech football players, whom she alleged had raped and brutalized her. By the same 5 to 4 vote as in *United States v. Lopez*,[21] the case in which the Court invalidated the Gun-Free School Zones Act of 1990, the Court in *Morrison* held VAWA's private civil damages remedy beyond the scope of both the Commerce Clause and Section 5 of the Fourteenth Amendment. (Section 2 of the Thirteenth

---

[17]   *See* Jones v. Alfred H. Mayer Co., 392 U.S. 409 (1968).

[18]   *See* Runyon v. McCrary, 427 U.S. 160 (1976).

[19]   *See* Patterson v. McLean Credit Union, 491 U.S. 164 (1989).

[20]   529 U.S. 598 (2000).

[21]   514 U.S. 549 (1995).

Amendment was not a possibility because the statute did not seek to remedy racial discrimination.)

Here we focus on the constitutional rationale for the statute under Section 5 of the Fourteenth Amendment. In passing VAWA, Congress compiled extensive evidence that state and local government officials—including police, prosecutors, judges, and juries—were systematically dismissive of allegations by women of criminal acts of violence against them. This concern potentially implicates the Fourteenth Amendment because, as we saw in Chapter 10, the Supreme Court has held since the 1970s that governmental discrimination against women presumptively violates the Equal Protection Clause of Section 1 of the Fourteenth Amendment.

Writing for the majority, Chief Justice William Rehnquist did not dispute Congress's findings that state actors had engaged in unconstitutional discrimination against women in state and local criminal justice systems. If anything, he went out of his way to stress that Congress had made "voluminous" findings of a constitutional problem.[22] He nonetheless invalidated Section 13981 as beyond the scope of congressional power under Section 5 of the Fourteenth Amendment, invoking what he called the "time-honored principle that the Fourteenth Amendment, by its very terms, prohibits only state action."[23] Citing the *Civil Rights Cases* approvingly, he reasoned that VAWA's remedy was beyond the scope of Section 5 because it was directed only at private actors (the football players), not at the Commonwealth of Virginia or its officials.

Justices David Souter and Stephen Breyer each filed dissents that focused on the Commerce Clause issue in the case.[24] Justice Breyer did tentatively express doubts about the Court's Section 5 holding. But he ultimately did not reach the question and this portion of his opinion was joined only by Justice John Paul Stevens.[25]

The Court's reasoning in *Morrison* can be critiqued on relatively narrow grounds and on relatively broad grounds. According to the narrow critique, which Justice Breyer expressed, even if Congress may target only state action when relying upon Section 5 of the Fourteenth Amendment, Congress was targeting state action with VAWA's civil-damages remedy—namely, sex discrimination in the administration of state criminal justice systems. On this view of

---

[22]   *Morrison*, 529 U.S. at 620.

[23]   *Id.* at 621.

[24]   *See id.* at 628 (Souter, J., joined by Stevens, Ginsburg, and Breyer, JJ., dissenting); *id.* at 655 (Breyer, J., joined in full by Stevens, J., and in part by Souter & Ginsburg, JJ., dissenting).

[25]   *See id.* at 664–66.

Section 5, an "appropriate" constitutional remedy provided by Congress need not run against a state actor just because the constitutional violator needs to be a state actor. Remedies are supposed to help make a victim whole (or, at least, less un-whole), and this one does that.

The broader critique rejects the Court's premise that Congress may target only state action when using its Section 5 power. On this view, Congress may target private gender discrimination under Section 5 because Section 1 is not limited to state action, and Section 1 is not limited to state action because of the presence of the Citizenship Clause, as Justice Harlan emphasized in the *Civil Rights Cases*. Just as the modern Court allows Congress to use Section 2 of the Thirteenth Amendment to target the badges and incidents of slavery in addition to slavery itself, so (on this view) the Court should allow Congress to use Section 5 to protect badges and incidents of citizenship and not just citizenship itself.[26] Although it may not be entirely clear what is—and is not—a badge and incident of citizenship, being denied a social invitation to someone's home would obviously not qualify, but protection against gender-motivated violence by public and private actors alike likely *would* qualify. It is difficult to regard women as full and equal citizens if their own state and local government officials do not take seriously private crimes of violence against them.

Notwithstanding such criticisms, the Court's reaffirmation, and arguably extension, of the *Civil Rights Cases* in *Morrison* remains governing law. In considering whether Congress has authority under Section 5 to pass a statute, one must always consider whether Congress is regulating state actors or private actors.

II. What Is the Nature of Section 5 of the Fourteenth Amendment?

Even when Congress is targeting only state actors, there is still the question of the nature of Congress's power under the enforcement clauses of the Civil War Amendments. Specifically, is Congress limited to remedying or preventing violations of constitutional rights that have been recognized by the Supreme Court, or may Congress act on its independent interpretation of the Constitution? There are two major views on this issue. The first reflects a Congress-centered, nationalist view and is associated with the liberal Warren Court. It is exemplified by the Court's 1966 decision in *Katzenbach v. Morgan*.[27] The second reflects a Court-centered, states' rights view and is associated with the conservative Rehnquist and Roberts

---

[26]   *See* Amar, *supra* note 11, at 824–26.

[27]   384 U.S. 641 (1966).

Courts. It is exemplified by the Court's 1997 decision in *City of Boerne v. Flores*.[28] We now consider each position in turn.

A.   The Nationalist View

As noted above, between 1875 and 1964, Congress passed no major civil rights statutes. Beginning in the 1960s, however, Congress finally got in the game by passing a number of immensely significant pieces of civil rights legislation, including the Civil Rights Act of 1964 and the Voting Rights Act of 1965. These new federal laws were challenged on constitutional grounds, and so the Supreme Court decided several important cases regarding the scope of Congress's powers under the Thirteenth, Fourteenth, and Fifteenth Amendments. There are a number of cases, and the legal questions they raise are varied and difficult. Law school courses on civil rights, voting rights, and election law cover the cases in depth. We will focus on one such case commonly covered in Constitutional Law courses— *Katzenbach v. Morgan*—and one recurring issue: the roles of Congress and the Court in interpreting and enforcing the Civil War Amendments.

Morgan concerned the constitutionality of Section 4(e) of the Voting Rights Act of 1965. Section 4(e) provided that no person who has completed the 6th grade in a Puerto Rican school, where instruction is in Spanish (and where, by the way, children are U.S. citizens), may be denied the right to vote due to failing an English literacy requirement. (Critically, the Supreme Court had recently upheld an English literacy requirement for voting as permitted by the Equal Protection Clause of Section 1 of the Fourteenth Amendment.[29]) Accordingly, Section 4(e) prohibited a practice of the State of New York that the Court had upheld as constitutional. The issue in *Morgan* was whether Congress may use Section 5 of the Fourteenth Amendment to enact such substantive civil rights legislation.

The Court gave an affirmative answer to this question, and it did so on alternative grounds. First, the Court reasoned that "§ 4 (e) may be viewed as a measure to secure for the Puerto Rican community residing in New York nondiscriminatory treatment by government—both in the imposition of voting qualifications and the provision or administration of governmental services, such as public schools, public housing and law enforcement."[30] In other words, the Court thought Congress could have determined that giving Puerto Ricans the ability to vote would enable them to eliminate unconstitutional discrimination against them. This theory views

---

28   521 U.S. 507 (1997).

29   *See* Lassiter v. Northampton County Bd. of Elections, 360 U.S. 45 (1959).

30   *See Morgan*, 384 U.S. at 652.

Section 4(e) remedially—that is, as a statutory remedy for discrimination in the provision of public services that the Supreme Court itself deems unconstitutional.

Second, the Court reasoned that Section 4(e) could be viewed as embodying Congress's judgment that disenfranchising individuals protected by Section 4(e) itself constitutes unconstitutional discrimination. "The result is no different," the Court said, "if we confine our inquiry to the question whether § 4 (e) was merely legislation aimed at the elimination of an invidious discrimination in establishing voter qualifications."[31] On this view, Congress may independently interpret the Constitution and conclude that a literacy requirement violates the Equal Protection Clause, even though the Supreme Court had concluded otherwise. Under this alternative theory, Congress makes a substantive constitutional interpretation not previously or subsequently made by the Court. This interpretation involves a choice of constitutional values of the kind implicated in adjudication involving interpretation of the Equal Protection Clause.

The Court in *Morgan* allowed space for Congress to exercise independent constitutional judgment by expressly invoking the *McCulloch* standard of deferential judicial review.[32] Congress, the Court said, need only have "a basis" for its determination that giving certain Puerto Ricans the vote would prevent or remedy violations of the Equal Protection Clause.[33] If, as the Necessary and Proper Clause seems to indicate,[34] *McCulloch* provides the correct test for judges to apply in assessing the constitutionality of congressional uses of all of its reconstruction powers (as it is for Section 2 of the Thirteenth Amendment under current law), then the scope of congressional power is very broad. Before the Civil War, the Court never invalidated an act of Congress as flunking the *McCulloch* standard, nor had the Court done so between 1937 and 1966, when *Morgan* was decided.[35] In this regard, it is noteworthy that the enforcement clauses, which all reference "appropriate legislation" by Congress, echo *McCulloch*'s famous line: "Let the end be legitimate . . . and all means which are *appropriate* . . . are constitutional."[36]

The second Justice John Marshall Harlan dissented in *Morgan*, emphasizing themes that sounded in both the separation of powers

---

[31]   *Id.* at 653–54.

[32]   *See id.* at 651.

[33]   *Id.* at 656.

[34]   The Necessary and Proper Clause applies to "all other Powers vested by this Constitution in the Government of the United States." U.S. CONST. art. I, § 8, cl. 18.

[35]   *See* PAUL BREST ET AL., PROCESSES OF CONSTITUTIONAL DECISIONMAKING: CASES AND MATERIALS 680–81 (6th ed. 2015).

[36]   McCulloch v. Maryland, 17 U.S. 316, 421 (1819).

and federalism. First, he objected that the Court was licensing Congress to undermine the Court's interpretive role, which in his view was to determine the meaning of the Fourteenth Amendment. "The question here is not whether the statute is appropriate remedial legislation to cure an established violation of a constitutional command," he wrote, "but whether there has in fact been an infringement of that constitutional command, that is, whether a particular state practice or, as here, a statute is so arbitrary or irrational as to offend the command of the Equal Protection Clause of the Fourteenth Amendment."[37] "That question is one for the judicial branch ultimately to determine," he reasoned, because if "the rule [were] otherwise, Congress would be able to qualify this Court's constitutional decisions under the Fourteenth and Fifteenth Amendments, let alone those under other provisions of the Constitution, by resorting to congressional power under the Necessary and Proper Clause."[38] Because "[i]n effect the Court reads § 5 of the Fourteenth Amendment as giving Congress the power to define the *substantive* scope of the Amendment," Justice Harlan did "not see why Congress should not be able as well to exercise its § 5 'discretion' by enacting statutes so as in effect to dilute equal protection and due process decisions of this Court."[39] The Court responded that Congress's power can permissibly operate only in an expansionary direction—that the Court's protection of rights imposes a constitutional floor below which Congress is not permitted to go.[40] This is called the "ratchet" argument, because ratchets characteristically work in one direction.

Second, and turning to federalism, Justice Harlan observed that the Court's very broad interpretation of the scope of Section 5 would allow Congress to regulate many matters that fall within "the primary legislative competence of the States," including the voter eligibility requirement at issue in the case.[41] "To hold, on this record, that § 4 (e) overrides the New York literacy requirement," he wrote, "seems to me tantamount to allowing the Fourteenth Amendment to swallow the State's constitutionally ordained primary authority in this field."[42]

---

[37]   *Morgan*, 384 U.S. at 667 (Harlan, J., dissenting).

[38]   *Id.* at 667–68.

[39]   *Id.* at 668.

[40]   *Id.* at 651 n.10 (majority opinion).

[41]   *Id.* at 670 (Harlan, J., dissenting).

[42]   *Id.* at 671.

B.   The States' Rights View[43]

Just as Reagan and Bush I appointees narrowed the scope of the Commerce Clause, so they also narrowed the scope of congressional power under Section 5 beginning with *City of Boerne v. Flores* in 1997.[44] The case involved a Texas church that was prohibited from building a new facility because its building was classified as a historic landmark. The church sued under a federal statute that is much in the news in recent years, the Religious Freedom Restoration Act of 1993 (RFRA, pronounced "rif-ra"). The city defended against the suit by challenging the power of Congress to enact RFRA under Section 5 of the Fourteenth Amendment.

It is important to understand at the outset why this was a Fourteenth Amendment case at all, given that the free exercise of religion is expressly protected by the First Amendment, not the Fourteenth. As we saw in Chapter 8, the Court has held that the Free Exercise Clause is incorporated into the Due Process Clause of Section 1 of the Fourteenth Amendment, so that it limits state and local governments in addition to the federal government.

Congress enacted RFRA in response to the Court's 1990 decision in *Employment Division v. Smith*.[45] Justice Antonin Scalia's opinion for the Court in this case had significantly changed the law of the Free Exercise Clause by holding that neutral laws of general applicability trigger only deferential, rational basis review. Recall that, under rational basis review, the challenger bears the near-impossible burden of showing that the law in question is not rationally related to a conceivable, legitimate governmental interest. A neutral law does not intentionally target a religious group or practice. A generally applicable law is one that applies broadly, not just to religious groups. An example of a neutral law of general applicability is a law banning animal cruelty that was passed out of concern about cruelty to animals. An example of a non-neutral law is a law banning animal cruelty that was passed out of hostility to the ritual animal sacrifices of a particular religious sect.[46] Such non-neutral laws trigger strict scrutiny under the Free Exercise Clause, which is the most demanding test known to constitutional law. Recall that, under strict scrutiny, the government has the burden of

---

[43]   The states' rights view is sometimes called the federalist view. We resist doing so because, as we saw in the opening chapters of this book, historically the Federalists were nationalists who supported broad federal power. The states' rights view seems more similar in its concerns to the Anti-Federalist position.

[44]   521 U.S. 507 (1997).

[45]   494 U.S. 872 (1990).

[46]   *See* Church of the Lukumi Babalu Aye v. City of Hialeah, 508 U.S. 520 (1993) (invalidating such a law on the ground that it targeted a particular religious group).

Sec. II

WHAT IS THE NATURE OF SECTION 5 OF THE
FOURTEENTH AMENDMENT?

439

showing that the law in question is narrowly tailored to advance a compelling governmental interest.

Before *Smith*, the Court's free exercise doctrine formally provided that laws that burden an individual's free exercise of religion trigger strict scrutiny even if they are not intended to burden free exercise, although the frequency with which the Court upheld governmental action suggested that the Court was not applying true strict scrutiny. Regardless, the pre-*Smith* law clearly was not rational basis review for neutral laws of general applicability, and RFRA provides that all laws that substantially burden a person's free exercise of religion trigger strict scrutiny.[47] In other words, and most relevant for present purposes, RFRA provides substantially more protection for a person's free exercise of religion than does the Court's post-*Smith* free exercise jurisprudence.

In *City of Boerne*, the Court held RFRA beyond the scope of Section 5 of the Fourteenth Amendment, so that it could not constitutionally be applied to state and local governments. The Court's objection to RFRA was not the absence of state action, as in the *Civil Rights Cases* and *Morrison*; there was clear state action in the city's denial of a permit to the church because of the city's neutral and generally applicable law providing for historic preservation. Writing for the Court, Justice Anthony Kennedy instead reasoned that Congress, when acting under Section 5, may not create new constitutional rights or expand the scope of such rights. Rather, he insisted, Congress may only prevent or remedy violations of constitutional rights that have been recognized by the Court, and the statutory remedies that Congress provides must be "congruent and proportional"—that is, properly tailored—to the judicially enforced constitutional right at issue. Here is the key language from the majority opinion, which we seek to clarify using brackets:

> While the line between measures that remedy or prevent unconstitutional actions and measures that make a substantive change in the governing law is not easy to discern, and Congress must have wide latitude in determining where it lies, the distinction exists and must be observed. There must be a congruence and proportionality between the injury to be prevented or remedied [that is, the violations of the constitutional right recognized by the Court] and the means adopted to that end [that is, the statutory rights created by Congress]. Lacking

---

47 Specifically, RFRA prohibits the "[g]overnment" from "substantially burden[ing]" a person's exercise of religion even if the burden results from a neutral law of general applicability unless the government can show that the burden "(1) is in furtherance of a compelling governmental interest; and (2) is the least restrictive means of furthering that compelling governmental interest."

such a connection, legislation may become substantive in operation and effect. History and our case law support drawing the distinction, one apparent from the text of the Amendment.[48]

Note the new doctrinal test for the permissibility of Section 5 legislation. Rather than continuing to apply *McCulloch* deference to Congress in Section 5 cases, as in *Morgan* and under Section 2 of the Thirteenth Amendment, the Court announced the congruence and proportionality test. It is clearly not rational basis review, but how much more demanding it is was not clear in *City of Boerne*. Later cases fleshed it out (not altogether coherently), as the Court initially held a flurry of other provisions of federal law beyond the scope of Section 5,[49] still others within the scope of Section 5,[50] and, more recently, another outside the scope of Section 5.[51] These cases are covered in Federal Courts, as is the reason why they are Section 5 cases as opposed to Commerce Clause cases; it has to do with the Court's doctrine concerning when Congress is permitted to override the states' sovereign immunity from suit by private litigants.

Rather than discuss these cases, we will focus on the Court's application of the congruence and proportionality test in *City of Boerne* itself. Why did the Court find a lack of congruence and proportionality between the constitutional free exercise right recognized by the Court and the statutory free exercise remedy provided by Congress? Whereas the Court's free exercise doctrine called for rational basis review given the city's mere application of its neutral and generally applicable historic preservation law, RFRA called for strict scrutiny. The Court noted that it might be permissible for Congress to provide greater protection for free exercise than the Court's doctrine does if Congress compiled evidence of widespread

---

[48]   *City of Boerne*, 521 U.S. at 519–20.

[49]   *See* Fla. Prepaid Postsecondary Educ. Expense Bd. v. College Savings Bank, 527 U.S. 627 (1999) (holding that a statute authorizing patent-infringement suits against states was beyond the scope of Section 5); College Savings Bank v. Fla. Prepaid Postsecondary Educ. Expense Bd. 527 U.S. 666 (1999) (holding that a trademark law subjecting states to suits for false and misleading advertising was beyond the scope of scope of Section 5); Kimel v. Fla. Bd. of Regents, 528 U.S. 62 (2000) (holding that the Age Discrimination in Employment Act of 1967 was beyond the scope of Section 5); Bd. of Trustees of Univ. of Ala. v. Garrett, 531 U.S. 356 (2001) (holding that Title I of the Americans with Disabilities Act of 1990 (ADA) was beyond the scope of Section 5).

[50]   *See* Nevada Dept. of Hum. Res. v. Hibbs, 538 U.S. 721 (2003) (holding that the family-care leave provision of the Family and Medical Leave Act of 1993 (FMLA) was within the scope of Section 5); Tennessee v. Lane, 541 U.S. 509 (2004) (holding that, as it applies to the class of cases implicating the fundamental right of access to the courts, Title II of the ADA was within the scope of Section 5); United States v. Georgia, 546 U.S. 151 (2006) (holding unanimously that insofar as Title II of the ADA creates a private cause of action for damages against states for unconstitutional conduct, Title II was within the scope of Section 5).

[51]   *See* Coleman v. Md. Ct. of Appeals, 566 U.S. 30 (2012) (holding that the self-care leave provision of the FMLA was beyond the scope of Section 5).

violations of the Free Exercise Clause under the Court's governing doctrine; sometimes it is warranted for Congress to go beyond what the Court protects in order to prevent or remedy violations of judicially recognized rights.[52] For example, it can be very difficult to prove intentional hostility toward religion in a judicial proceeding; if Congress found widespread evidence of such hostility, RFRA (which does not require proof of intentional hostility) might be a permissible way of remedying or preventing constitutional violations. But the Congress that passed RFRA did not find that there were widespread violations of the Free Exercise Clause as the Court understood the clause. Instead, Congress simply disagreed with *Smith* and sought to act on its own vision of free exercise. Although the congruence and proportionality test can be difficult to apply in many cases, *City of Boerne* was an easy case. Those who disagree with the outcome in this case likely disagree with the test itself.

Notably, Justice Kennedy invoked *Marbury* four times in his majority opinion, and he delivered what appeared to be a civics lecture at the end of the opinion. "Our national experience teaches that the Constitution is preserved best when each part of the government respects both the Constitution and the proper actions and determinations of the other branches,"[53] he wrote. "When the Court has interpreted the Constitution," he continued, "it has acted within the province of the Judicial Branch, which embraces the duty to say what the law is."[54] "RFRA was designed to control cases and controversies, such as the one before us," he concluded, "but as the provisions of the federal statute here invoked are beyond congressional authority, it is this Court's precedent, not RFRA, which must control."[55]

In passing RFRA, Congress was not shy about its desire to "overrule" *Smith*. The Court's response to the case—in stark contrast to the Warren Court's response to the VRA provision at issue in *Morgan*—indicates that the Court perceived Congress to be threatening its interpretive supremacy. This separation of powers concern was widely shared among the Justices in *City of Boerne*; Justices Stevens and Ruth Bader Ginsburg were in the majority, and Justices Sandra Day O'Connor, Souter, and Breyer dissented on free exercise grounds. None of them challenged the Court's new test for the validity of Section 5 legislation. Had they dissented on the Section

---

[52] *See City of Boerne*, 521 U.S. at 530 ("The appropriateness of remedial measures must be considered in light of the evil presented. Strong measures appropriate to address one harm may be an unwarranted response to another, lesser one.").

[53] *Id.* at 535–36.

[54] *Id.* at 536.

[55] *Id.*

5 issue, they might have asked what, exactly, is the *Marbury* problem with allowing Congress to interpret the Fourteenth Amendment on its own when using Section 5 so long as it does not dilute rights protected by the Court under Section 1.

It was only in the subsequent cases noted above, when the Court's application of the congruence and proportionality test seemed to have more to do with limiting federal power than with protecting judicial supremacy, that the Court fractured along states' rights-nationalist lines for the most part. The more expansive the scope of Congress's Section 5 power, the more Congress may regulate matters that otherwise would be left to the states, such as the local land use regulation at issue in *City of Boerne*. The two sides of the Court—and, perhaps, the country—seem to be animated by competing conceptions of the American ethos, including competing understandings of the meaning of the Civil War and the implications of Reconstruction for the relationship between the federal government and the states. In a sense (thankfully, a non-violent one), Americans are still fighting this war.

In recent years, RFRA has been back in the news. In *Burwell v. Hobby Lobby Stores, Inc.*,[56] the Court held 5 to 4 in an ideological split that, as applied to closely held, for-profit corporations whose owners have religious objections, federal regulations requiring employers to provide their female employees with no-cost access to contraception violate RFRA. This may seem puzzling: why is RFRA is still around after *City of Boerne*? The answer is that the Court did not strike down RFRA entirely; rather it held the law beyond the scope of Section 5 of the Fourteenth Amendment, so that it may not be applied to states and local governments (many of which now have their own state-law versions of RFRA). RFRA still applies to the federal government itself, which is the government that had imposed the contraception coverage requirement pursuant to the ACA.

Hobby Lobby illustrates how much the constitutional politics of religious liberty have changed since the days of *Smith*. Conservatives used to be skeptical of many free exercise claims, which often were brought by adherents of minority religions seeking narrow exemptions from generally applicable laws. Today, conservatives tend to be enthusiastic about RFRA claims, which typically are brought by evangelical Christians seeking potentially broad exemptions from generally applicable legal requirements. Liberals, for their part, are substantially more concerned today than they used to be about the impacts of granting religious exemptions on third parties, such as the thousands of female employees whose contraceptive access was potentially at issue in *Hobby Lobby*.

---

[56]   573 U.S. ___, 134 S. Ct. 2751 (2014).

III. Enforcement of the Fifteenth Amendment

Section 2 of the Fifteenth Amendment raises the same basic question as does Section 5 of the Fourteenth Amendment: May Congress act only to remedy or prevent state conduct that the Supreme Court would regard as violating Section 1's ban on racial discrimination in voting, or may Congress pass Section 2 statutes that reflect its independent interpretative judgment about which sorts of state conduct violate Section 1?

The Voting Rights Act of 1965 (VRA) is one of the most important civil rights statutes ever passed by Congress. The VRA was enacted to address entrenched racial discrimination in voting, which the Court in *South Carolina v. Katzenbach* in 1966 called "an insidious and pervasive evil which had been perpetuated in certain parts of our country through unremitting and ingenious defiance of the Constitution."[57]

The VRA was an outgrowth of increasing protests and efforts to register black voters in the South. Two phases of these efforts are probably best remembered today. In 1964, a group of civil rights organizations announced a "Freedom Summer," recruiting college students and others to educate and register Southern black voters for the 1964 presidential election.[58] Three young civil rights workers disappeared outside a small town in Mississippi; they had been murdered by whites, including a deputy sheriff.[59] Then, in 1965, a civil rights march in Selma, Alabama, was met by state troopers on a bridge; when the marchers attempted to cross the bridge they were attacked and beaten by the troopers, a scene broadcast on national television.[60]

As we discussed in Chapter 11, since the end of Reconstruction, Southern states had placed a series of statutory barriers to limit black voting, ensuring that African Americans would play no significant role in electoral politics. Among other things, the VRA was designed to solve the problem of jurisdictions continuously finding ever-more ingenious ways of denying African Americans the vote after earlier methods of disenfranchisement were adjudicated unconstitutional. This is called the "whack-a-mole" problem since every time one strategy of vote denial was knocked down, another popped up. The VRA proved spectacularly successful in

---

[57]   383 U.S. 301, 309 (1966).

[58]   *See* JUAN WILLIAMS: EYES ON THE PRIZE: AMERICA'S CIVIL RIGHTS YEARS, 1954–1965, at 228–29 (1987).

[59]   *See id.* at 234–35.

[60]   *See id.* at 269–73.

accomplishing its goal of reducing incidents of unconstitutional racial discrimination in voting by state and local governments.

We now describe key sections of the VRA. In the discussion throughout this section, it is critical to bear in mind whether we are referring to a section of the VRA or a section of the Fifteenth Amendment.

Section 2 of the VRA bans any "standard, practice, or procedure" that "results in a denial or abridgement of the right of any citizen . . . to vote on account of race or color." This section applies nationwide and is permanent. It allows for essential but onerous case-by-case adjudication of alleged voting rights violations.

Section 5 of the statute requires certain states and sub-divisions of states (mainly but not entirely in the South) to obtain permission (called "preclearance") from the federal government before changing any of their voting rules, whether such changes involve moving a polling place or imposing a voter-ID or other eligibility requirement. By adding the preclearance requirement to the pre-existing regime of case-by-case adjudication of claims alleging racial discrimination in voting, the VRA sought to place the burden on jurisdictions with a history of racial discrimination to show that any voting change would not make worse off the minority voters protected by the law. Although the preclearance section intruded on state lawmaking in an extraordinary fashion, the preclearance requirement proved very effective in solving the whack-a-mole problem.

Section 4(b) of the VRA provided a "coverage formula" for determining the "covered jurisdictions" to which Section 5 applied. Section 4(b) defined these covered jurisdictions as states or political sub-divisions of states that used tests or devices as prerequisites to voting and had low voter registration or turnout in the 1960s and early 1970s. The "bail out" provision of the VRA (currently Section 4(a)) allows for the release of a covered jurisdiction—that is, a jurisdiction subject to preclearance under Section 5—from the preclearance requirement if the jurisdiction maintains a clean record for a certain number of years.

Just as nationalists and advocates of states' rights have historically had different understandings of the scope of congressional power under Section 5 of the Fourteenth Amendment, so they have had diverging views of the scope of congressional power under Section 2 of the Fifteenth Amendment—although the states' rights view of the Fifteenth Amendment was late in emerging on the Supreme Court. We now consider each position in turn. As before, we proceed chronologically and end with the states' rights view, which is governing law.

A.   The Nationalist View

In *South Carolina v. Katzenbach*,[61] the Court upheld various provisions of the VRA as a valid exercise of Congress's power under Section 2 of the Fifteenth Amendment. For example, one provision suspended literacy tests and similar voting qualifications. The Court upheld this provision, even though the Court in *Lassiter* had held that literacy tests were not *per se* unconstitutional. The Court characterized Congress's enforcement power in very broad terms, stating that the Court would apply *McCulloch* deference to Section 2 legislation.[62] In addition, the Court rejected the objection that different states were being treated differently (because not all of them were required to comply with the VRA provisions at issue) by emphasizing that "[t]he doctrine of the equality of States, invoked by South Carolina, does not bar this approach, for that doctrine applies only to the terms upon which States are admitted to the Union, and not to the remedies for local evils which have subsequently appeared."[63]

At the same time, the Court emphasized that the VRA provisions at issue were remedies for proven violations of the Fifteenth Amendment. For example, the Court clarified that, *Lassiter* notwithstanding, Section 2 of the Amendment authorized Congress to prohibit literacy tests if its own fact-finding showed that they were being used with a racially discriminatory purpose and so violated Section 1 as the Court understood Section 1.[64]

Still, *McCulloch* deference makes it very difficult to distinguish genuinely remedial statutes from laws that reflect Congress's own interpretation of Section 1 of the Fifteenth Amendment. For example, in a subsequent case, *City of Rome v. United States*,[65] the Court held that the the preclearance section of the VRA was valid Section 2 legislation even though it imposed liability for voting changes that are discriminatory in effect, as opposed to on purpose:

> [W]e hold that the Act's ban on electoral changes that are discriminatory in effect is an appropriate method of promoting the purposes of the Fifteenth Amendment, even if it is assumed that § 1 of the Amendment prohibits only intentional discrimination in voting. Congress could rationally have concluded that, because electoral changes by jurisdictions with a demonstrable history of intentional racial discrimination in voting create the risk of purposeful

---

61   383 U.S. 301 (1966).

62   *See id.* at 326–27.

63   *Id.* at 328–29.

64   *See id.* at 333–34.

65   446 U.S. 156 (1980).

discrimination, it was proper to prohibit changes that have a discriminatory impact.[66]

Accordingly, the Fifteenth Amendment story during the Warren and Burger Court eras was similar to the Thirteenth and Fourteenth Amendment stories during this time period. Regarding all three amendments, the Court adopted an expansive, nationalist perspective in interpreting the scope of Congress's reconstruction powers.

All of these Fifteenth Amendment decisions, however, were handed down before the Rehnquist Court in *City of Boerne* ramped up the level of scrutiny that the Court would apply to legislation passed under Section 5 of the Fourteenth Amendment. One question after *City of Boerne* was whether the Court would continue to defer to Congress in cases involving Section 2 of the Fifteenth Amendment, or whether it would also apply the Fourteenth Amendment congruence and proportionality test to the Fifteenth Amendment. In 1999, in *Lopez v. Monterey County*,[67] the Rehnquist Court continued to defer to Congress by firmly rejecting a statutory and constitutional challenge to a particular application of the preclearance section of the VRA.[68] Justice O'Connor, a leading proponent of limited federal power on the Rehnquist Court, wrote the majority opinion, which was joined in full by Justice Scalia. Only Justice Clarence Thomas dissented. The Roberts Court would take a very different view of congressional power only ten years later.

B. The States' Rights View

Over the decades, Congress reauthorized the VRA's preclearance requirement and coverage formula several times. In 2006, Congress reauthorized the VRA for an additional 25 years by a near-unanimous vote, and President George W. Bush signed it into law. But the vote in Congress masked partisan disagreement over whether the VRA continued to be necessary. Many congressional Republicans were substantially less enthusiastic about reauthorization than were most Democrats, but such Republicans felt pressured to vote in favor given the iconic status of the VRA.[69]

---

[66]   *Id.* at 177 (footnote omitted).

[67]   525 U.S. 266 (1999).

[68]   *See id.* at 269 (holding that the VRA's "preclearance requirements apply to measures mandated by a noncovered State to the extent that these measures will effect a voting change in a covered county").

[69]   For a good discussion of the path of the VRA legislation in Congress, see Nathaniel Persily, *The Promise and Pitfalls of the New Voting Rights Act,* 117 YALE L.J. 174, 179–92 (2007).

The coverage formula in Section 4(b) was not changed because it was not politically feasible for members to agree on a new one.[70]

Shortly after the VRA's reauthorization in 2006, a Texas utility district sought to "bail out" from the Act's preclearance requirement in Section 5 of the Act and, alternatively, challenged the constitutionality of the preclearance requirement. To reiterate, the VRA's "bail out" provision allows the release of a "political subdivision" from the Act's preclearance requirements if it meets certain conditions.

In *Northwest Austin Municipal Utility District Number One v. Holder*,[71] the Roberts Court, in an obvious compromise, practiced constitutional avoidance—that is, avoided deciding whether the preclearance section of the VRA was constitutional—by resolving the case on statutory grounds. In a majority opinion written by Chief Justice John Roberts, the Court engaged in creative statutory interpretation and held 8 to 1 that the utility district was entitled to bail out from the VRA's preclearance requirement. But in so disposing of the case, the Court expressed serious doubts about the continued constitutionality of the preclearance requirement under Section 2 of the Fifteenth Amendment. Chief Justice Roberts wrote that "[t]he Act . . . differentiates between the States, despite our historic tradition that all the States enjoy 'equal sovereignty,'" and that "a departure from the fundamental principle of equal sovereignty requires a showing that a statute's disparate geographic coverage is sufficiently related to the problem that it targets."[72] Emphasizing that "[t]he Act's preclearance requirements and its coverage formula raise serious constitutional questions,"[73] the Chief Justice in effect sent a clear message to Congress that the Court would invalidate the preclearance requirement if Congress did not update the coverage formula to reflect what contemporary evidence indicated was the distribution of voting rights violations.

Congress predictably did not respond, and the Court acted four years later. In *Shelby County v. Holder*,[74] Shelby County, which is located in the covered jurisdiction of Alabama, sued the Attorney General of the United States in federal court in Washington, D.C., seeking facial invalidation of the VRA's coverage formula and preclearance requirement. The district court upheld the provisions and the U.S. Court of Appeals for the D.C. Circuit affirmed. After surveying the evidence in the record, the D.C. Circuit accepted

---

[70]   *See id.* at 208–11.

[71]   557 U.S. 193 (2009).

[72]   *Id.* at 203 (citations omitted).

[73]   *Id.* at 204.

[74]   570 U.S. 529 (2013).

Congress's conclusion that case-by-case litigation remained inadequate in covered jurisdictions to protect minority voting rights; the preclearance requirement therefore remained necessary; and the coverage formula remained constitutional.

When the case moved to the Supreme Court, it was widely expected that the Court would decide whether the preclearance requirement remained within the scope of congressional power under Section 2 of the Fifteenth Amendment. In light of *Northwest Austin*, it was also widely expected that the Court would invalidate the preclearance requirement by a vote of five to four. The Supreme Court did fracture five to four along ideological lines. But instead of invalidating the preclearance requirement as beyond the scope of Section 2 of the Fifteenth Amendment, the Court held that the coverage formula was unconstitutional, so that it could no longer be used as a basis for subjecting jurisdictions to preclearance. In theory, this left Congress free to resurrect preclearance by enacting a new coverage formula, although this was not a realistic political option.

Chief Justice Roberts wrote the majority opinion. He began with *Northwest Austin*'s conclusions that the VRA "must be justified by current needs" and that "a departure from the fundamental principle of equal state sovereignty requires a showing that a statute's disparate geographic coverage is sufficiently related to the problem that it targets."[75] He wrote that the VRA sharply departs from these guiding principles by requiring states to "beseech" the federal government for permission to enact voting laws that they would otherwise be constitutionally entitled to pass on their own.[76] And despite the tradition of equal state sovereignty, he continued, the VRA applies to only nine states and additional counties in some other states.[77]

In 1966, the Chief Justice wrote, these departures from the principle of equal state sovereignty were justified by the " 'blight of racial discrimination in voting' " that had " 'infected the electoral process in parts of our country for nearly a century.' "[78] Then, he wrote, the coverage formulate "made sense" because the VRA was limited to areas where Congress found " 'evidence of actual voting discrimination,' " and the covered jurisdictions "shared two characteristics: 'the use of tests and devices for voter registration, and a voting rate in the 1964 presidential election at least 12 points below the national average.' "[79]

---

[75]   *Id.* at 542 (quoting *Northwest Austin*, 557 U.S. at 203).

[76]   *Shelby County*, 570 U.S. at 544.

[77]   *See id.*

[78]   *Id.* at 545 (quoting *Katzenbach*, 383 U.S. at 308).

[79]   *Shelby County*, 570 U.S. at 546 (quoting *Katzenbach*, 383 U.S. at 330).

But a half century later, Roberts insisted, "things have changed dramatically."[80] Largely because of the VRA, he conceded, " 'voter turnout and registration rates' " in covered jurisdictions " 'now approach parity,' " " '[b]latantly discriminatory evasions of federal decrees are rare,' " and " 'minority candidates hold office at unprecedented levels.' "[81] What is more, he observed, the tests and devices that had prevented African Americans from voting have been prohibited nationwide for more than 40 years.[82] Notwithstanding all of these changes, he emphasized, the VRA has not eased the preclearance requirement's restrictions or narrowed the scope of the coverage formula. For these reasons, the Court invalidated the coverage formula, making clear that it viewed "the principle of equal state sovereignty" as a structural principle of constitutional law. The Court left the preclearance requirement in place, but as noted above, it does no work as long as Congress does not enact a new coverage formula because the Court's invalidation of the existing formula means that no jurisdictions are subject to the preclearance requirement.

Justice Ginsburg wrote a vehement dissent. "In the Court's view," she wrote, "the very success of Section 5 [the preclearance section] demands its dormancy."[83] She likened the Court's approach to "throwing away your umbrella in a rainstorm because you are not getting wet."[84] (The majority presumably believed its approach was like closing one's umbrella when it stops raining.) Justice Ginsburg emphasized that Congress "determined based on a voluminous record that the scourge of discrimination was not yet extirpated."[85] Examining the record compiled by Congress at substantially greater length than did the majority, she noted, for example, that covered jurisdictions contain less than 25 percent of the nation's population but 56 percent of successful challenges under Section 2 of the VRA since 1982.[86]

Justice Ginsburg also examined the evidence regarding Alabama in particular. Most distressing, in all likelihood, was a recent FBI investigation that offered a window into the continued existence of racial discrimination in Alabama politics. "Recording devices worn by state legislators cooperating with the FBI's investigation captured conversations between members of the state

---

[80]   *Shelby County*, 570 U.S. at 547.

[81]   *Id.* (quoting *Northwest Austin*, 557 U.S. at 202).

[82]   *Shelby County*, 570 U.S. at 547.

[83]   *Id.* at 559 (Ginsburg, J., joined by Breyer, Sotomayor, & Kagan, JJ., dissenting).

[84]   *Id.* at 590.

[85]   *Id.* at 559.

[86]   *See id.* at 577.

legislature and their political allies," Justice Ginsburg explained, and "[t]he recorded conversations are shocking."[87] In particular, "[m]embers of the state Senate derisively refer to African-Americans as 'Aborigines' and talk openly of their aim to quash a particular gambling-related referendum because the referendum, if placed on the ballot, might increase African-American voter turnout . . . . (legislators and their allies expressed concern that if the referendum were placed on the ballot, '[e]very black, every illiterate' would be 'bused [to the polls] on HUD financed buses')."[88]

Justice Ginsburg emphasized that "[t]hese conversations occurred not in the 1870's, or even in the 1960's, they took place in 2010."[89] She further observed that the judge presiding over the criminal trial in which these recorded statements were introduced described them as " 'compelling evidence that political exclusion through racism remains a real and enduring problem' in Alabama."[90] The judge added that racist views " 'remain regrettably entrenched in the high echelons of state government.' "[91]

The issue for Justice Ginsburg was "who decides whether, as currently operative, [preclearance] remains justifiable, this Court, or a Congress charged with the obligation to enforce the post-Civil War Amendments 'by appropriate legislation.' "[92] She observed that Congress had concluded overwhelmingly that the preclearance requirement should continue to "facilitate completion of the impressive gains thus far made" and "guard against backsliding."[93] In her view, "[t]hose assessments were well within Congress' province to make and should elicit this Court's unstinting approbation."[94] She also noted that the Court purported to invalidate only the coverage formula, but that the preclearance requirement is "immobilized" without it.[95] She concluded that "the Court errs egregiously by overriding Congress' decision."[96]

Shelby County v. Holder might be considered the end of what has been called the "Second Reconstruction" of the Civil Rights Era. It promises to have profound practical consequences. Shortly after

---

[87] *Id.* at 584.

[88] *Id.* (citation omitted).

[89] *Id.*

[90] *Id.* (quoting United States v. McGregor, 824 F. Supp. 2d 1339, 1347 (M.D. Ala. 2011)).

[91] *Shelby County*, 570 U.S. at 585 (Ginsburg, J., dissenting) (quoting *McGregor*, 824 F. Supp. 2d at 1347).

[92] *Shelby County*, 570 U.S. at 559 (Ginsburg, J., dissenting) (footnote omitted).

[93] *Id.* at 559–60.

[94] *Id.* at 560.

[95] *Id.* at 559 n.1.

[96] *Id.* at 594.

the decision, for example, Texas declared that it would begin enforcing a voter identification requirement (which requires citizens to show a specified form of identification in order to vote) after previously having been denied preclearance to do so because such laws disproportionately prevent racial minorities from voting.[97] Similarly, just after the decision, North Carolina passed a series of voting restrictions, including a voter ID requirement; it would not have been able to do so had the VRA's preclearance regime remained in effect.[98] Republicans tend to view voter ID laws as preventing voter fraud. Democrats point to the paucity of credible evidence of in-person voter fraud and tend to view such laws as suppressing the vote of citizens likely to vote Democratic. Both sides agree, however, that the consequences of *Shelby County* are great indeed.

As for both sides of the Court, it seems to us that each has some explaining to do. In our view, the majority did not persuasively explain what justified the Court in transplanting the idea of equal state sovereignty from the context of admitting states to the Union to the context of the Fifteenth Amendment, notwithstanding the fact that the Court in *South Carolina v. Katzenbach* expressly limited the idea to the context of admitting states to the union (and it was not consistently followed even in this context).[99] Notably, the principle of equal state sovereignty is nowhere stated in the constitutional text, and the presence of explicit uniformity guarantees in some clauses might be thought to create the inference that uniformity is not otherwise required.[100]

The dissenters did not persuasively explain why, a few years earlier, they had joined the Court's opinion in *Northwest Austin*, which announced the relevance of the idea of equal state sovereignty to the constitutionality of the VRA and voiced grave concerns about the VRA's constitutionality. Nor did Justice Ginsburg explain how her dissent in *Shelby County*, which emphasized deference to Congress, was consistent with her vote in *City of Boerne*, which rejected rational basis review of legislation passed under Section 5 of the Fourteenth Amendment in favor of some form of heightened scrutiny.

Shelby County illustrates that standards of scrutiny are often destiny in cases involving the constitutionality of laws passed

---

[97]   *See, e.g.*, Matt Ford, *The Entirely Preventable Battles Raging Over Voting Rights*, THE ATLANTIC, Apr. 14, 2017, https://www.theatlantic.com/politics/archive/2017/04/shelby-county-v-holder-voting-rights-supreme-court/522867/.

[98]   *See, e.g., id.*

[99]   *See supra* note 63 and accompanying text (quoting *South Carolina v. Katzenbach*).

[100]   *See, e.g.*, U.S. CONST. art. I, § 8, cl. 1 (specifying that "all Duties, Imposts and Excises shall be uniform throughout the United States").

pursuant to Congress's reconstruction powers. Chief Justice Roberts seems correct that Congress would not have come up with the coverage formula in the 2006 Act if it were starting over and just assessing the locations and frequency of voting rights violations in the early years of the 21st Century. The record compiled by Congress and stressed by Justice Ginsburg explains why covered jurisdictions should remain covered much better than it justifies the coverage of these jurisdictions but not others that might also have bad records in 2006.[101] Congress did not craft a new formula because, as noted above, it would have been politically impossible to do so given partisan polarization, and the Court either did not know about, or did not deem relevant, the limits of political possibility in Congress.

Because of the evidentiary problems in the record compiled by Congress, the extent of judicial deference determined the outcome. Equal state sovereignty seems like a higher level of scrutiny than the congruence and proportionality test of *City of Boerne*. Justice Ginsburg, by contrast, emphasized the reasons for rational basis review. If the proper standard is rational basis review, as it is under Section 2 of the Thirteenth Amendment, then—and probably only then—the Court should have upheld the coverage formula notwithstanding its under-inclusiveness in contemporary America. Thus, as in many other contexts, the standard of review was critical.

As we have seen throughout this book, constitutional law involves an interactive process involving both the Supreme Court and societal actors who make claims on the Constitution within constitutional politics. So, too, in *Shelby County*. The majority built on a body of doctrine restricting federal power to enforce civil rights going back to *City of Boerne*. This doctrine had, for the most part, grown and strengthened over time. Its growth, and the Court's extension of the doctrine in *Shelby County*, drew from a perspective on constitutional law that was greatly enhanced by a series of presidential elections and Supreme Court appointments. In turn, the Court's decision will help shape the political process in the future.

Our goal here and throughout the book has been to show how constitutional law is neither entirely autonomous of political forces nor simply a passive reflection of them. We hope the result has been to clearly present the key concepts and insights that illuminate constitutional doctrine while placing the doctrine within its broader historical and theoretical context. We do not know what the Constitution's third century will bring in the way of doctrinal change, but we are confident that this interaction between constitutional law and constitutional politics will continue.

---

[101]   *See* Persily, *supra* note 69, at 195.

Further Readings

Akhil Reed Amar, *Intratextualism*, 112 HARV. L. REV. 747 (1999).

Jack M. Balkin, *The Reconstruction Power*, 85 N.Y.U. L. REV. 1801 (2010).

Michael W. McConnell, *Institutions and Interpretation: A Critique of* City of Boerne v. Flores, 111 HARV. L. REV. 153 (1997).

Nathaniel Persily, *The Promise and Pitfalls of the New Voting Rights Act*, 117 YALE L.J. 174 (2007).

Robert C. Post & Reva B. Siegel, *Legislative Constitutionalism and Section Five Power: Policentric Interpretation of the Family and Medical Leave Act*, 112 YALE L.J. 1943 (2003).

Robert C. Post & Reva B. Siegel, *Protecting the Constitution from the People: Juricentric Restrictions on Section Five Power*, 78 IND. L.J. 1 (2003).

Appendix

THE CONSTITUTION OF THE UNITED STATES

PREAMBLE

We the People of the United States, in Order to form a more perfect Union, establish Justice, insure domestic Tranquility, provide for the common defence, promote the general Welfare, and secure the Blessings of Liberty to ourselves and our Posterity, do ordain and establish this Constitution for the United States of America.

ARTICLE I

Section 1. All legislative Powers herein granted shall be vested in a Congress of the United States, which shall consist of a Senate and House of Representatives.

Section 2. [1] The House of Representatives shall be composed of Members chosen every second Year by the People of the several States, and the Electors in each State shall have the Qualifications requisite for Electors of the most numerous Branch of the State Legislature.

[2] No Person shall be a Representative who shall not have attained to the Age of twenty five Years, and been seven Years a Citizen of the United States, and who shall not, when elected, be an Inhabitant of that State in which he shall be chosen.

[3] Representatives and direct Taxes shall be apportioned among the several States which may be included within this Union, according to their respective Numbers, which shall be determined by adding to the whole Number of free Persons, including those bound to Service for a Term of Years, and excluding Indians not taxed, three fifths of all other Persons. The actual Enumeration shall be made within three Years after the first Meeting of the Congress of the United States, and within every subsequent Term of ten Years, in such Manner as they shall by Law direct. The Number of Representatives shall not exceed one for every thirty Thousand, but each State shall have at Least one Representative; and until such enumeration shall be made, the State of New Hampshire shall be entitled to chuse three, Massachusetts eight, Rhode Island and Providence Plantations one, Connecticut five, New York six, New Jersey four, Pennsylvania eight, Delaware one, Maryland six,

455

Virginia ten, North Carolina five, South Carolina five, and Georgia three.

[4] When vacancies happen in the Representation from any State, the Executive Authority thereof shall issue Writs of Election to fill such Vacancies

[5] The House of Representatives shall chuse their Speaker and other Officers; and shall have the sole Power of Impeachment.

Section 3. [1] The Senate of the United States shall be composed of two Senators from each State, chosen by the Legislature thereof, for six Years; and each Senator shall have one Vote.

[2] Immediately after they shall be assembled in Consequence of the first Election, they shall be divided as equally as may be into three Classes. The Seats of the Senators of the first Class shall be vacated at the Expiration of the second Year, of the second Class at the Expiration of the fourth Year, and of the third Class at the Expiration of the sixth Year, so that one third may be chosen every second Year; and if Vacancies happen by Resignation, or otherwise, during the Recess of the Legislature of any State, the Executive thereof may make temporary Appointments until the next Meeting of the Legislature, which shall then fill such Vacancies.

[3] No Person shall be a Senator who shall not have attained to the Age of thirty Years, and been nine Years a Citizen of the United States, and who shall not, when elected, be an Inhabitant of that State for which he shall be chosen.

[4] The Vice President of the United States shall be President of the Senate, but shall have no Vote, unless they be equally divided.

[5] The Senate shall chuse their other Officers, and also a President pro tempore, in the Absence of the Vice President, or when he shall exercise the Office of President of the United States.

[6] The Senate shall have the sole Power to try all Impeachments. When sitting for that Purpose, they shall be on Oath or Affirmation. When the President of the United States is tried, the Chief Justice shall preside: And no Person shall be convicted without the Concurrence of two thirds of the Members present.

[7] Judgment in Cases of Impeachment shall not extend further than to removal from Office, and disqualification to hold and enjoy any Office of honor, Trust, or Profit under the United States: but the Party convicted shall nevertheless be liable and subject to Indictment, Trial, Judgment, and Punishment, according to Law.

Section 4. [1] The Times, Places and Manner of holding Elections for Senators and Representatives, shall be prescribed in each State by the Legislature thereof; but the Congress may at any time by Law make or alter such Regulations, except as to the Places of chusing Senators.

[2] The Congress shall assemble at least once in every Year, and such Meeting shall be on the first Monday in December, unless they shall by Law appoint a different Day.

Section 5. [1] Each House shall be the Judge of the Elections, Returns, and Qualifications of its own Members, and a Majority of each shall constitute a Quorum to do Business; but a smaller Number may adjourn from day to day, and may be authorized to compel the Attendance of absent Members, in such Manner, and under such Penalties as each House may provide.

[2] Each House may determine the Rules of its Proceedings, punish its Members for disorderly Behaviour, and, with the Concurrence of two thirds, expel a Member.

[3] Each House shall keep a Journal of its Proceedings, and from time to time publish the same, excepting such Parts as may in their Judgment require Secrecy; and the Yeas and Nays of the Members of either House on any question shall, at the Desire of one fifth of those Present, be entered on the Journal.

[4] Neither House, during the Session of Congress, shall without the Consent of the other, adjourn for more than three days, nor to any other Place than that in which the two Houses shall be sitting.

Section 6. [1] The Senators and Representatives shall receive a Compensation for their Services, to be ascertained by Law, and paid out of the Treasury of the United States. They shall in all Cases, except Treason, Felony, and Breach of the Peace, be privileged from Arrest during their Attendance at the Session of their respective Houses, and in going to and returning from the same; and for any Speech or Debate in either House, they shall not be questioned in any other Place.

[2] No Senator or Representative shall, during the Time for which he was elected, be appointed to any civil Office under the Authority of the United States, which shall have been created, or the Emoluments whereof shall have been encreased during such time; and no Person holding any Office under the United States, shall be a Member of either House during his Continuance in Office.

Section 7. [1] All Bills for raising Revenue shall originate in the House of Representatives; but the Senate may propose or concur with Amendments as on other Bills.

[2] Every Bill which shall have passed the House of Representatives and the Senate, shall, before it become a Law, be

presented to the President of the United States; If he approve he shall sign it, but if not he shall return it, with his Objections to that House in which it shall have originated, who shall enter the Objections at large on their Journal, and proceed to reconsider it. If after such Reconsideration two thirds of that House shall agree to pass the Bill, it shall be sent, together with the Objections, to the other House, by which it shall likewise be reconsidered, and if approved by two thirds of that House, it shall become a Law. But in all such Cases the Votes of both Houses shall be determined by Yeas and Nays, and the Names of the Persons voting for and against the Bill shall be entered on the Journal of each House respectively. If any Bill shall not be returned by the President within ten Days (Sundays excepted) after it shall have been presented to him, the Same shall be a Law, in like Manner as if he had signed it, unless the Congress by their Adjournment prevent its Return, in which Case it shall not be a Law.

[3] Every Order, Resolution, or Vote to which the Concurrence of the Senate and House of Representatives may be necessary (except on a question of Adjournment) shall be presented to the President of the United States; and before the Same shall take Effect, shall be approved by him, or being disapproved by him, shall be repassed by two thirds of the Senate and House of Representatives, according to the Rules and Limitations prescribed in the Case of a Bill.

Section 8. [1] The Congress shall have Power To lay and collect Taxes, Duties, Imposts and Excises, to pay the Debts and provide for the common Defence and general Welfare of the United States; but all Duties, Imposts and Excises shall be uniform throughout the United States;

[2] To borrow Money on the credit of the United States;

[3] To regulate Commerce with foreign Nations, and among the several States, and with the Indian Tribes;

[4] To establish an uniform Rule of Naturalization, and uniform Laws on the subject of Bankruptcies throughout the United States;

[5] To coin Money, regulate the Value thereof, and of foreign Coin, and fix the Standard of Weights and Measures;

[6] To provide for the Punishment of counterfeiting the Securities and current Coin of the United States;

[7] To establish Post Offices and Post Roads;

[8] To promote the Progress of Science and useful Arts, by securing for limited Times to Authors and Inventors the exclusive Right to their respective Writings and Discoveries;

[9]   To constitute Tribunals inferior to the supreme Court;

[10] To define and punish Piracies and Felonies committed on the high Seas, and Offences against the Law of Nations;

[11] To declare War, grant Letters of Marque and Reprisal, and make Rules concerning Captures on Land and Water;

[12] To raise and support Armies, but no Appropriation of Money to that Use shall be for a longer Term than two Years;

[13] To provide and maintain a Navy;

[14] To make Rules for the Government and Regulation of the land and naval Forces;

[15] To provide for calling forth the Militia to execute the Laws of the Union, suppress Insurrections and repel Invasions;

[16] To provide for organizing, arming, and disciplining, the Militia, and for governing such Part of them as may be employed in the Service of the United States, reserving to the States respectively, the Appointment of the Officers, and the Authority of training the Militia according to the discipline prescribed by Congress;

[17] To exercise exclusive Legislation in all Cases whatsoever, over such District (not exceeding ten Miles square) as may, by Cession of particular States and the Acceptance of Congress, become the Seat of the Government of the United States, and to exercise like Authority over all Places purchased by the Consent of the Legislature of the State in which the Same shall be, for the Erection of Forts, Magazines, Arsenals, dock-Yards, and other needful Buildings;— And

[18] To make all Laws which shall be necessary and proper for carrying into Execution the foregoing Powers, and all other Powers vested by this Constitution in the Government of the United States, or in any Department or Officer thereof.

Section 9. [1] The Migration or Importation of such Persons as any of the States now existing shall think proper to admit, shall not be prohibited by the Congress prior to the Year one thousand eight hundred and eight, but a Tax or duty may be imposed on such Importation, not exceeding ten dollars for each Person.

[2]   The Privilege of the Writ of Habeas Corpus shall not be suspended, unless when in Cases of Rebellion or Invasion the public Safety may require it.

[3]   No Bill of Attainder or ex post facto Law shall be passed.

[4]   No Capitation, or other direct, Tax shall be laid, unless in Proportion to the Census or Enumeration herein before directed to be taken.

[5]   No Tax or Duty shall be laid on Articles exported from any State.

[6]   No Preference shall be given by any Regulation of Commerce or Revenue to the Ports of one State over those of another: nor shall Vessels bound to, or from, one State, be obliged to enter, clear, or pay Duties in another.

[7]   No Money shall be drawn from the Treasury, but in Consequence of Appropriations made by Law; and a regular Statement and Account of the Receipts and Expenditures of all public Money shall be published from time to time.

[8]   No Title of Nobility shall be granted by the United States: And no Person holding any Office of Profit or Trust under them, shall, without the Consent of the Congress, accept of any present, Emolument, Office, or Title, of any kind whatever, from any King, Prince, or foreign State.

Section 10. [1] No State shall enter into any Treaty, Alliance, or Confederation; grant Letters of Marque and Reprisal; coin Money; emit Bills of Credit; make any Thing but gold and silver Coin a Tender in Payment of Debts; pass any Bill of Attainder, ex post facto Law, or Law impairing the Obligation of Contracts, or grant any Title of Nobility.

[2]   No State shall, without the Consent of the Congress, lay any Imposts or Duties on Imports or Exports, except what may be absolutely necessary for executing its inspection Laws: and the net Produce of all Duties and Imposts, laid by any State on Imports or Exports, shall be for the Use of the Treasury of the United States; and all such Laws shall be subject to the Revision and Controul of the Congress.

[3]   No State shall, without the Consent of Congress, lay any Duty of Tonnage, keep Troops, or Ships of War in time of Peace, enter into any Agreement or Compact with another State, or with a foreign Power, or engage in War, unless actually invaded, or in such imminent Danger as will not admit of delay.

ARTICLE II

Section 1. [1] The executive Power shall be vested in a President of the United States of America. He shall hold his Office during the Term of four Years, and, together with the Vice President, chosen for the same Term, be elected, as follows:

[2] Each State shall appoint, in such Manner as the Legislature thereof may direct, a Number of Electors, equal to the whole Number of Senators and Representatives to which the State may be entitled in the Congress: but no Senator or Representative, or Person holding an Office of Trust or Profit under the United States, shall be appointed an Elector.

[3] The electors shall meet in their respective States, and vote by ballot for two Persons, of whom one at least shall not be an Inhabitant of the same State with themselves. And they shall make a List of all the Persons voted for, and of the Number of Votes for each; which List they shall sign and certify, and transmit sealed to the Seat of the Government of the United States, directed to the President of the Senate. The President of the Senate shall, in the Presence of the Senate and House of Representatives, open all the Certificates, and the Votes shall then be counted. The Person having the greatest Number of Votes shall be the President, if such Number be a Majority of the whole Number of Electors appointed; and if there be more than one who have such Majority, and have an equal Number of Votes, then the House of Representatives shall immediately chuse by Ballot one of them for President; and if no Person have a Majority, then from the five highest on the List the said House shall in like Manner chuse the President. But in chusing the President, the Votes shall be taken by States, the Representation from each State having one Vote; A quorum for this Purpose shall consist of a Member or Members from two thirds of the States, and a Majority of all the States shall be necessary to a Choice. In every Case, after the Choice of the President, the Person having the greatest Number of Votes of the Electors shall be the Vice President. But if there should remain two or more who have equal Votes, the Senate shall chuse from them by Ballot the Vice-President.

[4] The Congress may determine the Time of chusing the Electors, and the Day on which they shall give their Votes; which Day shall be the same throughout the United States.

[5] No Person except a natural born Citizen, or a Citizen of the United States, at the time of the Adoption of this Constitution, shall be eligible to the Office of President; neither shall any Person be eligible to that Office who shall not have attained to the Age of thirty five Years, and been fourteen Years a Resident within the United States.

[6] In Case of the Removal of the President from Office, or of his Death, Resignation, or Inability to discharge the Powers and Duties of the said Office, the Same shall devolve on the Vice President, and the Congress may by Law provide for the Case of Removal, Death, Resignation or Inability, both of the President and

Vice President, declaring what Officer shall then act as President, and such Officer shall act accordingly, until the Disability be removed, or a President shall be elected.

[7] The President shall, at stated Times, receive for his Services, a Compensation, which shall neither be encreased nor diminished during the Period for which he shall have been elected, and he shall not receive within that Period any other Emolument from the United States, or any of them.

[8] Before he enter on the Execution of his Office, he shall take the following Oath or Affirmation: "I do solemnly swear (or affirm) that I will faithfully execute the Office of President of the United States, and will to the best of my Ability, preserve, protect and defend the Constitution of the United States."

Section 2. [1] The President shall be Commander in Chief of the Army and Navy of the United States, and of the Militia of the several States, when called into the actual Service of the United States; he may require the Opinion, in writing, of the principal Officer in each of the executive Departments, upon any Subject relating to the Duties of their respective Offices, and he shall have Power to grant Reprieves and Pardons for Offenses against the United States, except in Cases of Impeachment.

[2] He shall have Power, by and with the Advice and Consent of the Senate, to make Treaties, provided two thirds of the Senators present concur; and he shall nominate, and by and with the Advice and Consent of the Senate, shall appoint Ambassadors, other public Ministers and Consuls, Judges of the supreme Court, and all other Officers of the United States, whose Appointments are not herein otherwise provided for, and which shall be established by Law: but the Congress may by Law vest the Appointment of such inferior Officers, as they think proper, in the President alone, in the Courts of Law, or in the Heads of Departments.

[3] The President shall have Power to fill up all Vacancies that may happen during the Recess of the Senate, by granting Commissions which shall expire at the End of their next Session.

Section 3. He shall from time to time give to the Congress Information of the State of the Union, and recommend to their Consideration such Measures as he shall judge necessary and expedient; he may, on extraordinary Occasions, convene both Houses, or either of them, and in Case of Disagreement between them, with Respect to the Time of Adjournment, he may adjourn them to such Time as he shall think proper; he shall receive Ambassadors and other public Ministers; he shall take Care that the

Laws be faithfully executed, and shall Commission all the Officers of the United States.

Section 4. The President, Vice President and all civil Officers of the United States, shall be removed from Office on Impeachment for, and Conviction of, Treason, Bribery, or other high Crimes and Misdemeanors.

ARTICLE III

Section 1. The judicial Power of the United States, shall be vested in one supreme Court, and in such inferior Courts as the Congress may from time to time ordain and establish. The Judges, both of the supreme and inferior Courts, shall hold their Offices during good Behaviour, and shall, at stated Times, receive for their Services, a Compensation, which shall not be diminished during their Continuance in Office.

Section 2. [1] The judicial Power shall extend to all Cases, in Law and Equity, arising under this Constitution, the Laws of the United States, and Treaties made, or which shall be made, under their Authority;—to all Cases affecting Ambassadors, other public Ministers and Consuls;—to all Cases of admiralty and maritime Jurisdiction;—to Controversies to which the United States shall be a Party;—to Controversies between two or more States;—between a State and Citizens of another State;—between Citizens of different States;—between Citizens of the same State claiming Lands under Grants of different States, and between a State, or the Citizens thereof, and foreign States, Citizens or Subjects.

[2] In all Cases affecting Ambassadors, other public Ministers and Consuls, and those in which a State shall be Party, the supreme Court shall have original Jurisdiction. In all the other Cases before mentioned, the supreme Court shall have appellate Jurisdiction, both as to Law and Fact, with such Exceptions, and under such Regulations as the Congress shall make.

[3] The Trial of all Crimes, except in Cases of Impeachment, shall be by Jury; and such Trial shall be held in the State where the said Crimes shall have been committed; but when not committed within any State, the Trial shall be at such Place or Places as the Congress may by Law have directed.

Section 3. [1] Treason against the United States, shall consist only in levying War against them, or in adhering to their Enemies, giving them Aid and Comfort. No Person shall be convicted of Treason unless on the Testimony of two Witnesses to the same overt Act, or on Confession in open Court.

[2]   The Congress shall have Power to declare the Punishment of Treason, but no Attainder of Treason shall work Corruption of Blood, or Forfeiture except during the Life of the Person attainted.

ARTICLE IV

Section 1. Full Faith and Credit shall be given in each State to the public Acts, Records, and judicial Proceedings of every other State. And the Congress may by general Laws prescribe the Manner in which such Acts, Records and Proceedings shall be proved, and the Effect thereof.

Section 2. [1] The Citizens of each State shall be entitled to all Privileges and Immunities of Citizens in the several States.

[2]   A person charged in any State with Treason, Felony, or other Crime, who shall flee from Justice, and be found in another State, shall on Demand of the executive Authority of the State from which he fled, be delivered up, to be removed to the State having Jurisdiction of the Crime.

[3]   No Person held to Service or Labour in one State, under the Laws thereof, escaping into another, shall, in Consequence of any Law or Regulation therein, be discharged from such Service or Labour, but shall be delivered up on Claim of the Party to whom such Service or Labour may be due.

Section 3. [1] New States may be admitted by the Congress into this Union; but no new State shall be formed or erected within the Jurisdiction of any other State; nor any State be formed by the Junction of two or more States, or Parts of States, without the Consent of the Legislatures of the States concerned as well as of the Congress.

[2]   The Congress shall have Power to dispose of and make all needful Rules and Regulations respecting the Territory or other Property belonging to the United States; and nothing in this Constitution shall be so construed as to Prejudice any Claims of the United States, or of any particular State.

Section 4. The United States shall guarantee to every State in this Union a Republican Form of Government, and shall protect each of them against Invasion; and on Application of the Legislature, or of the Executive (when the Legislature cannot be convened) against domestic Violence.

ARTICLE V

The Congress, whenever two thirds of both Houses shall deem it necessary, shall propose Amendments to this Constitution, or on the Application of the Legislatures of two thirds of the several States, shall call a Convention for proposing Amendments, which, in either

Case, shall be valid to all Intents and Purposes, as Part of this Constitution, when ratified by the Legislatures of three fourths of the several States, or by Conventions in three fourths thereof, as the one or the other Mode of Ratification may be proposed by the Congress; Provided that no Amendment which may be made prior to the Year One thousand eight hundred and eight shall in any Manner affect the first and fourth Clauses in the Ninth Section of the first Article; and that no State, without its Consent, shall be deprived of its equal Suffrage in the Senate.

ARTICLE VI

[1] All Debts contracted and Engagements entered into, before the Adoption of this Constitution, shall be as valid against the United States under this Constitution, as under the Confederation.

[2] This Constitution, and the Laws of the United States which shall be made in Pursuance thereof; and all Treaties made, or which shall be made, under the Authority of the United States, shall be the supreme Law of the Land; and the Judges in every State shall be bound thereby, any Thing in the Constitution or Laws of any State to the Contrary notwithstanding.

[3] The Senators and Representatives before mentioned, and the Members of the several State Legislatures, and all executive and judicial Officers, both of the United States and of the several States, shall be bound by Oath or Affirmation, to support this Constitution; but no religious Test shall ever be required as a Qualification to any Office or public Trust under the United States.

ARTICLE VII

The Ratification of the Conventions of nine States, shall be sufficient for the Establishment of this Constitution between the States so ratifying the Same.

ARTICLES IN ADDITION TO, AND AMENDMENT OF, THE CONSTITUTION OF THE UNITED STATES OF AMERICA, PROPOSED BY CONGRESS, AND RATIFIED BY THE LEGISLATURES OF THE SEVERAL STATES, PURSUANT TO THE FIFTH ARTICLE OF THE ORIGINAL CONSTITUTION.

AMENDMENT I [1791]

Congress shall make no law respecting an establishment of religion, or prohibiting the free exercise thereof; or abridging the freedom of speech, or of the press; or the right of the people peaceably to assemble, and to petition the Government for a redress of grievances.

Amendment II [1791]

A well regulated Militia, being necessary to the security of a free State, the right of the people to keep and bear Arms, shall not be infringed.

Amendment III [1791]

No Soldier shall, in time of peace be quartered in any house, without the consent of the Owner, nor in time of war, but in a manner to be prescribed by law.

Amendment IV [1791]

The right of the people to be secure in their persons, houses, papers, and effects, against unreasonable searches and seizures, shall not be violated, and no Warrants shall issue, but upon probable cause, supported by Oath or affirmation, and particularly describing the place to be searched, and the persons or things to be seized.

Amendment V [1791]

No person shall be held to answer for a capital, or otherwise infamous crime, unless on a presentment or indictment of a Grand Jury, except in cases arising in the land or naval forces, or in the Militia, when in actual service in time of War or public danger; nor shall any person be subject for the same offence to be twice put in jeopardy of life or limb; nor shall be compelled in any criminal case to be a witness against himself, nor be deprived of life, liberty, or property, without due process of law; nor shall private property be taken for public use, without just compensation.

Amendment VI [1791]

In all criminal prosecutions, the accused shall enjoy the right to a speedy and public trial, by an impartial jury of the State and district wherein the crime shall have been committed, which district shall have been previously ascertained by law, and to be informed of the nature and cause of the accusation; to be confronted with the witnesses against him; to have compulsory process for obtaining witnesses in his favor, and to have the Assistance of Counsel for his defence.

Amendment VII [1791]

In Suits at common law, where the value in controversy shall exceed twenty dollars, the right of trial by jury shall be preserved, and no fact tried by a jury, shall be otherwise re-examined in any Court of the United States, than according to the rules of the common law.

Amendment VIII [1791]

Excessive bail shall not be required, nor excessive fines imposed, nor cruel and unusual punishments inflicted.

Amendment IX [1791]

The enumeration in the Constitution, of certain rights, shall not be construed to deny or disparage others retained by the people.

Amendment X [1791]

The powers not delegated to the United States by the Constitution, nor prohibited by it to the States, are reserved to the States respectively, or to the people.

Amendment XI [1798]

The Judicial power of the United States shall not be construed to extend to any suit in law or equity, commenced or prosecuted against one of the United States by Citizens of another State, or by Citizens or Subjects of any Foreign State.

Amendment XII [1804]

The Electors shall meet in their respective states and vote by ballot for President and Vice-President, one of whom, at least, shall not be an inhabitant of the same state with themselves; they shall name in their ballots the person voted for as President, and in distinct ballots the person voted for as Vice-President, and they shall make distinct lists of all persons voted for as President, and of all persons voted for as Vice-President, and of the number of votes for each, which lists they shall sign and certify, and transmit sealed to the seat of the government of the United States, directed to the President of the Senate;—The President of the Senate shall, in the presence of the Senate and House of Representatives, open all the certificates and the votes shall then be counted;—The person having the greatest number of votes for President, shall be the President, if such number be a majority of the whole number of Electors appointed; and if no person have such majority, then from the persons having the highest numbers not exceeding three on the list of those voted for as President, the House of Representatives shall choose immediately, by ballot, the President. But in choosing the President, the votes shall be taken by states, the representation from each state having one vote; a quorum for this purpose shall consist of a member or members from two-thirds of the states, and a majority of all the states shall be necessary to a choice. And if the House of Representatives shall not choose a President whenever the right of choice shall devolve upon them, before the fourth day of March next following, then the Vice-President shall act as President, as in the case of the death or other constitutional disability of the President.

The person having the greatest number of votes as Vice-President, shall be the Vice-President, if such number be a majority of the whole number of Electors appointed, and if no person have a majority, then from the two highest numbers on the list, the Senate shall choose the Vice-President; a quorum for the purpose shall consist of two-thirds of the whole number of Senators, and a majority of the whole number shall be necessary to a choice. But no person constitutionally ineligible to the office of President shall be eligible to that of Vice-President of the United States.

AMENDMENT XIII [1865]

Section 1. Neither slavery nor involuntary servitude, except as a punishment for crime whereof the party shall have been duly convicted, shall exist within the United States, or any place subject to their jurisdiction.

Section 2. Congress shall have power to enforce this article by appropriate legislation.

AMENDMENT XIV [1868]

Section 1. All persons born or naturalized in the United States, and subject to the jurisdiction thereof, are citizens of the United States and of the State wherein they reside. No State shall make or enforce any law which shall abridge the privileges or immunities of citizens of the United States; nor shall any State deprive any person of life, liberty, or property, without due process of law; nor deny to any person within its jurisdiction the equal protection of the laws.

Section 2. Representatives shall be apportioned among the several States according to their respective numbers, counting the whole number of persons in each State, excluding Indians not taxed. But when the right to vote at any election for the choice of electors for President and Vice President of the United States, Representatives in Congress, the Executive and Judicial officers of a State, or the members of the Legislature thereof, is denied to any of the male inhabitants of such State, being twenty-one years of age, and citizens of the United States, or in any way abridged, except for participation in rebellion, or other crime, the basis of representation therein shall be reduced in the proportion which the number of such male citizens shall bear to the whole number of male citizens twenty-one years of age in such State.

Section 3. No person shall be a Senator or Representative in Congress, or elector of President and Vice President, or hold any office, civil or military, under the United States, or under any State, who, having previously taken an oath, as a member of Congress, or as an officer of the United States, or as a member of any State legislature, or as an executive or judicial officer of any State, to support the Constitution of the United States, shall have engaged in insurrection or rebellion against the same, or given aid or comfort to the enemies thereof. But Congress may by a vote of two-thirds of each House, remove such disability.

Section 4. The validity of the public debt of the United States, authorized by law, including debts incurred for payment of pensions and bounties for services in suppressing insurrection or rebellion, shall not be questioned. But neither the United States nor any State shall assume or pay any debt or obligation incurred in aid of insurrection or rebellion against the United States, or any claim for the loss or emancipation of any slave; but all such debts, obligations and claims shall be held illegal and void.

Section 5. The Congress shall have power to enforce, by appropriate legislation, the provisions of this article.

AMENDMENT XV [1870]

Section 1. The right of citizens of the United States to vote shall not be denied or abridged by the United States or by any State on account of race, color, or previous condition of servitude.

Section 2. The Congress shall have power to enforce this article by appropriate legislation.

AMENDMENT XVI [1913]

The Congress shall have power to lay and collect taxes on incomes, from whatever source derived, without apportionment among the several States, and without regard to any census or enumeration.

AMENDMENT XVII [1913]

[1]   The Senate of the United States shall be composed of two Senators from each State, elected by the people thereof, for six years; and each Senator shall have one vote. The electors in each State shall have the qualifications requisite for electors of the most numerous branch of the State legislatures.

[2]   When vacancies happen in the representation of any State in the Senate, the executive authority of such State shall issue writs of election to fill such vacancies: *Provided,* That the legislature of any State may empower the executive thereof to make temporary appointments until the people fill the vacancies by election as the legislature may direct.

[3]   This amendment shall not be so construed as to affect the election or term of any Senator chosen before it becomes valid as part of the Constitution.

AMENDMENT XVIII [1919]

Section 1. After one year from the ratification of this article the manufacture, sale, or transportation of intoxicating liquors within, the importation thereof into, or the exportation thereof from the United States and all territory subject to the jurisdiction thereof for beverage purposes is hereby prohibited.

Section 2. The Congress and the several States shall have concurrent power to enforce this article by appropriate legislation.

Section 3. This article shall be inoperative unless it shall have been ratified as an amendment to the Constitution by the legislatures of the several States, as provided in the Constitution, within seven years from the date of the submission hereof to the States by the Congress.

AMENDMENT XIX [1920]

[1] The right of citizens of the United States to vote shall not be denied or abridged by the United States or by any State on account of sex.

[2] Congress shall have power to enforce this article by appropriate legislation.

AMENDMENT XX [1933]

Section 1. The terms of the President and Vice President shall end at noon on the 20th day of January, and the terms of Senators and Representatives at noon on the 3d day of January, of the years in which such terms would have ended if this article had not been ratified; and the terms of their successors shall then begin.

Section 2. The Congress shall assemble at least once in every year, and such meeting shall begin at noon on the 3d day of January, unless they shall by law appoint a different day.

Section 3. If, at the time fixed for the beginning of the term of the President, the President elect shall have died, the Vice President elect shall become President. If a President shall not have been chosen before the time fixed for the beginning of his term, or if the President elect shall have failed to qualify, then the Vice President elect shall act as President until a President shall have qualified; and the Congress may by law provide for the case wherein neither a President elect nor a Vice President elect shall have qualified, declaring who shall then act as President, or the manner in which one who is to act shall be selected, and such person shall act accordingly until a President or Vice President shall have qualified.

Section 4. The Congress may by law provide for the case of the death of any of the persons from whom the House of Representatives may choose a President whenever the right of choice shall have devolved upon them, and for the case of the death of any of the persons from whom the Senate may choose a Vice President whenever the right of choice shall have devolved upon them.

Section 5. Sections 1 and 2 shall take effect on the 15th day of October following the ratification of this article.

Section 6. This article shall be inoperative unless it shall have been ratified as an amendment to the Constitution by the legislatures of three-fourths of the several States within seven years from the date of its submission.

AMENDMENT XXI [1933]

Section 1. The eighteenth article of amendment to the Constitution of the United States is hereby repealed.

Section 2. The transportation or importation into any State, Territory, or possession of the United States for delivery or use therein of intoxicating liquors, in violation of the laws thereof, is hereby prohibited.

Section 3. This article shall be inoperative unless it shall have been ratified as an amendment to the Constitution by conventions in the several States, as provided in the Constitution, within seven years from the date of the submission hereof to the States by the Congress.

AMENDMENT XXII [1951]

Section 1. No person shall be elected to the office of the President more than twice, and no person who has held the office of President, or acted as President, for more than two years of a term to which some other person was elected President shall be elected to the office of the President more than once. But this Article shall not apply to any person holding the office of President when this Article was proposed by the Congress, and shall not prevent any person who may be holding the office of President, or acting as President, during the term within which this Article becomes operative from holding the office of President or acting as President during the remainder of such term.

Section 2. This article shall be inoperative unless it shall have been ratified as an amendment to the Constitution by the legislatures of three-fourths of the several States within seven years from the date of its submission to the States by the Congress.

Amendment XXIII [1961]

Section 1. The District constituting the seat of Government of the United States shall appoint in such manner as the Congress may direct:

A number of electors of President and Vice President equal to the whole number of Senators and Representatives in Congress to which the District would be entitled if it were a State, but in no event more than the least populous State; they shall be in addition to those appointed by the States, but they shall be considered, for the purposes of the election of President and Vice President, to be electors appointed by a State; and they shall meet in the District and perform such duties as provided by the twelfth article of amendment.

Section 2. The Congress shall have power to enforce this article by appropriate legislation.

Amendment XXIV [1964]

Section 1. The right of citizens of the United States to vote in any primary or other election for President or Vice President, for electors for President or Vice President, or for Senator or Representative in Congress, shall not be denied or abridged by the United States or any State by reason of failure to pay any poll tax or other tax.

Section 2. The Congress shall have power to enforce this article by appropriate legislation.

Amendment XXV [1967]

Section 1. In case of the removal of the President from office or of his death or resignation, the Vice President shall become President.

Section 2. Whenever there is a vacancy in the office of the Vice President, the President shall nominate a Vice President who shall take office upon confirmation by a majority vote of both Houses of Congress.

Section 3. Whenever the President transmits to the President pro tempore of the Senate and the Speaker of the House of Representatives his written declaration that he is unable to discharge the powers and duties of his office, and until he transmits to them a written declaration to the contrary, such powers and duties shall be discharged by the Vice President as Acting President.

Section 4. Whenever the Vice President and a majority of either the principal officers of the executive departments or of such other body as Congress may by law provide, transmit to the President pro tempore of the Senate and the Speaker of the House of

Representatives their written declaration that the President is unable to discharge the powers and duties of his office, the Vice President shall immediately assume the powers and duties of the office as Acting President.

Thereafter, when the President transmits to the President pro tempore of the Senate and the Speaker of the House of Representatives his written declaration that no inability exists, he shall resume the powers and duties of his office unless the Vice President and a majority of either the principal officers of the executive department or of such other body as Congress may by law provide, transmit within four days to the President pro tempore of the Senate and the Speaker of the House of Representatives their written declaration that the President is unable to discharge the powers and duties of his office. Thereupon Congress shall decide the issue, assembling within forty-eight hours for that purpose if not in session. If the Congress, within twenty-one days after receipt of the latter written declaration, or, if Congress is not in session, within twenty-one days after Congress is required to assemble, determines by two-thirds vote of both Houses that the President is unable to discharge the powers and duties of his office, the Vice President shall continue to discharge the same as Acting President; otherwise, the President shall resume the powers and duties of his office.

AMENDMENT XXVI [1971]

Section 1. The right of citizens of the United States, who are eighteen years of age or older, to vote shall not be denied or abridged by the United States or by any State on account of age.

Section 2. The Congress shall have power to enforce this article by appropriate legislation.

AMENDMENT XXVII [1992]

No law, varying the compensation for the services of the Senators and Representatives, shall take effect, until an election of Representatives shall have intervened.

TABLE OF CASES

A.L.A. Schechter Poultry Corp. v. United States, 194
Abbott Laboratories v. Gardner, 56
Ableman v. Booth, 283
Adair v. United States, 260
Adamson v. California, 242
Adarand v. Peña, 314
Adkins v. Children's Hospital of the District of Columbia, 260
Akron v. Akron Center for Reproductive Health, 398
Alden v. Maine, 151
Alger, Commonwealth v., 257
Allen v. Wright, 51
Allgeyer v. Louisiana, 257
Ambach v. Norwick, 344
Anderson v. Celebrezze, 365
Arizona State Legislature v. Arizona Independent Redistricting Commission, 361
Arlington Heights, Village of v. Metropolitan Housing Development Corporation, 310
Bailey v. Drexel Furniture Company (Child Labor Tax Case), 169
Baker v. Carr, 46, 349
Baldwin v. Fish & Game Comm'n of, Mont., 367
Batson v. Kentucky, 251, 311
Bellotti v. Baird, 397
Belmont, United States v., 209
Benisek v. Lamone, 361
Bertholf v. O'Reilly, 257
Bethune-Hill v. Virginia State Board of Elections, 358
Bi-Metallic Investment Co. v. State Board of Equalization, 275
Board of Educ. of Oklahoma City v. Dowell, 304
Board of Regents v. Roth, 276
Board of Trustees of Univ. of Ala. v. Garrett, 440
Bob Jones University v. Simon, 173
Boddie v. Connecticut, 364
Boerne, City of v. Flores, 92, 435, 438
Bolling v. Sharpe, 299, 300
Boumediene v. Bush, 36, 216

Bowers v. Hardwick, 411
Bowsher v. Synar, 223
Bradwell v. Illinois, 326, 385
Breedlove v. Suttles, 40
Brown v. Board of Education, 30, 295, 372
Buck v. Bell, 382
Buckley v. Valeo, 197
Bunting v. Oregon, 260
Burr, United States v., 226
Burton v. Wilmington Parking Authority, 249
Burwell v. Hobby Lobby Stores, Inc., 442
Bush v. Gore, 354
Butler, United States v., 164, 166
Buxton v. Ullman, 387
Calder v. Bull, 17
Caminetti v. United States, 122
Carey v. Population Services International, 392
Carolene Products Co., United States v., 62, 99
Carter v. Carter Coal Company, 119
Champion v. Ames, 121
Charles River Bridge v. Warren Bridge, 256
Chisholm v. Georgia, 40
Church of the Lukumi Babalu Aye v. City of Hialeah, 438
Civil Rights Cases, 133, 246, 291, 429
Clapper v. Amnesty International, 53, 54
Cleburne v. Cleburne Living Center, Inc., 306
Clinton v. Jones, 227
Cohens v. Virginia, 100
Colautti v. Franklin, 398
Colegrove v. Greene, 14, 348
Coleman v. Court of Appeals of Maryland, 343, 440
College Savings Bank v. Fla. Prepaid Postsecondary Educ. Expense Bd., 440
Comstock, United States v., 102
Constantine, United States v., 171
Cooley v. Board of Wardens, 112
Cooper v. Aaron, 303
Cooper v. Harris, 357

Coppage v. Kansas, 260
Corbett, Commonwealth v., 387
Craig v. Boren, 332
Crawford v. Marion County
  Election Board, 366
Cruikshank, United States v.,
  431
Cruzan v. Director, 422
Cumming v. Richmond County
  Board of Education, 294
Curtiss-Wright Export
  Corporation, United States v.,
  206
Dames & Moore v. Regan, 193,
  210
Dandridge v. Williams, 370
Daniel v. Paul, 134
Darby, United States v., 130, 150
Dartmouth College Case, 256
Davis v. Bandemer, 48, 359
Davis, Helvering v., 166
Department of Agriculture v.
  Moreno, 218
Deshaney v. Winnebago County
  Social Services Dept., 250
District of Columbia v. Heller, 2,
  65
Doe v. Bolton, 395, 396
Dolan v. City of Tigard, 270
Doremus, United States v., 168
Douglas v. United States, 363
Dred Scott v. Sandford, 29, 40,
  232, 283, 427
E.C. Knight Company, United
  States v., 118
Edgewood Independent School
  District v. Kirby, 375
Edmondston v. Leesville
  Concrete Company, 251
Edmond v. United States, 196
EEOC v. Wyoming, 150
Eisenstadt v. Bair, 391
Employment Division v. Smith,
  421, 438
Evenwel v. Abbott, 352
FCC v. Beach Communications,
  263, 306
Federal Election Commission v.
  Akins, 53
Federal Energy Regulatory
  Comm'n v. Mississippi, 150
Fisher v. University of Texas at
  Austin (Fisher I), 314, 322
Fisher v. University of Texas at
  Austin (Fisher II), 314
Flagg Brothers v. Brooks, 250
Fletcher v. Peck, 256

Florida Prepaid Postsecondary
  Educ. Expense Bd. v. College
  Savings Bank, 440
Foley v. Connelie, 344
Free Enterprise Foundation v.
  Public Company Accounting
  Oversight Board [PCAOB], 196
Freeman v. Pitts, 304
Friends of the Earth, Inc. et al. v.
  Laidlaw Environmental
  Services, Inc., 53
Frontiero v. Richardson, 331, 396
Fullilove v. Klutznick, 314
Gaffney v. Cummings, 351
Gardner, Commonwealth v., 387
Gayle v. Browder, 301
Geduldig v. Aiello, 341
Georgia, United States v., 440
Gibbons v. Ogden, 79, 107, 110
Giles v. Harris, 355
Gill v. Whitford, 361
Goesaert v. Cleary, 327, 336
Goldberg v. Kelly, 275, 276
Goldwater v. Carter, 212
Gomillion v. Lightfoot, 311
Gonzales v. Carhart, 407
Gonzales v. Raich, 142
Graham v. Richardson, 343
Granholm v. Heald, 99, 160
Gratz v. Bollinger, 314, 318
Gray v. Sanders, 15, 348
Green v. County School Board of
  New Kent County, 303
Griffin v. County School Board of
  Prince Edward County, 302
Griffin v. Illinois, 362
Griffiths, In re, 343
Griggs v. Duke Power Co., 309
Griswold v. Connecticut, 385, 389
Grutter v. Bollinger, 314
H.L. v. Matheson, 398
H.P. Hood & Sons, Inc. v. Du
  Mond, 160
Halbert v. Michigan, 363
Hamdan v. Rumsfeld, 216
Hamdi v. Rumsfeld, 215, 274
Hammer v. Dagenhart, 119, 123,
  168
Harper v. Virginia State Board of
  Elections, 365
Harris v. McRae, 398
Harris, United States v., 431
Heart of Atlanta Motel, Inc. v.
  United States, 132, 133, 137
Hill v. Wallace, 170
Hirabayashi v. United States,
  307
Hodgson v. Minnesota, 400

Holden v. Hardy, 257

Hollingsworth v. Perry, 54

Home Building & Loan Ass'n v. Blaisdell, 260

Houston, E. & W. Tex. Ry. Co. v. United States, 124

Hoyt v. Florida, 327

Hughes v. Alexandra Scrap Corp., 161

Humphrey's Executor v. United States, 199

Hunter v. Underwood, 311

Hylton v. United States, 17

Immigration and Naturalization Service v. Chadha, 221

J.E.B. v. Alabama, 251

Jackson v. Metropolitan Edison Company, 250

Jacobs, In re, 257

Jacobson v. Massachusetts, 382

Jones v. Alfred H. Mayer Co., 432

Kadrmas v. Dickinson Public Schools, 374

Kahriger, United States v., 173

Karcher v. Daggett, 351

Katzenbach v. McClung, 133

Katzenbach v. Morgan, 434

Kebodeaux, United States v., 105

Keyishian v. Board of Regents, 317

Kimel v. Fla. Bd. of Regents, 440

Knoxville Iron Co. v. Harbison, 258

Koonts v. St. Johns River Water Management Dist., 270

Korematsu v. United States, 218, 219, 301

Kramer v. Union Free Sch. Dist. No. 15, 365

Kras, United States v., 364

La Franca, United States v., 171

La Vengeance, United States, v., 17

Lalli v. Lalli, 344

Lassiter v. Northampton County Bd. of Elections, 435

Lawrence v. Texas, 414

Lehnhausen v. Lake Shore Auto Parts Co., 264

Levy v. Louisiana, 344

Lexmark International, Inc. v. Static Control Components, Inc., 58

Little v. Streater, 364

Lochner v. New York, 108, 115, 171, 258

Lopez v. Monterey County, 446

Lopez, United States v., 112, 130, 137, 432

Loretto v. Teleprompter Manhattan CATV Corporation, 269

Loving v. Virginia, 305, 380

Lucas v. South Carolina Coastal Commission, 270

Lucia v. Securities & Exchange Commission, 196

Lugar v. Edmondson Oil Company, 250

Lujan v. Defenders of Wildlife, 49, 51

Luther v. Borden, 46

M.L.B. v. S.E.J., 364

Maher v. Roe, 398

Marbury v. Madison, 17, 18, 23

Marcus, People v., 260

Marshall v. Jerrico, Inc., 274

Martin v. Hunter's Lessee, 29, 100

Massachusetts v. EPA, 53, 54, 55

Masterpiece Cakeshop v. Colorado Civil Rights Commission, 420

Mathews v. Lucas, 344

Matthews v. Diaz, 343

Matthews v. Eldridge, 277

Mayor & City Council of Baltimore City v. Dawson, 301

McCleskey v. Kemp, 308

McCrary v. United States, 168

McCulloch v. Maryland, 25, 80, 81, 436

McDonald v. City of Chicago, 2, 244

McGrain v. Daugherty, 221

McGregor, United States v., 450

McIntyre v. Ohio Elections Comm'n, 69

McLaughlin v. Florida, 305

McLaurin v. Oklahoma State Regents, 297

Medellín v. Texas, 208

Memorial Hospital v. Maricopa County, 368

Metro Broadcasting, Inc. v. FCC, 314

Metropolitan Washington Airports Authority v. Citizens for Abatement of Aircraft Noise, Inc., 224

Meyer v. Nebraska, 378

Michael H. v. Gerald D., 380

Michael M. v. Superior Court of Sonoma County, 336

Miller v. Johnson, 357

Milligan, Ex Parte, 214
Minor v. Happersett, 326
Mississippi University for
  Women v. Hogan, 333
Missouri v. Jenkins, 304
Missouri, State of, ex rel. Gaines
  v. Canada, 297
Mobile v. Bolden, 356
Moore v. City of East Cleveland,
  380
Moose Lodge No. 107 v. Irvis,
  250
Morath v. The Texas Taxpayer &
  Student Fairness Coalition,
  375
Moritz v. Comm'r, 332
Morrison v. Olson, 4, 196
Morrison, United States v., 141,
  432
Mugler v. Kansas, 241
Muller v. Oregon, 260
Murphy v. National Collegiate
  Athletic Association, 155
Murr v. Wisconsin, 271
Myers v. United States, 198
Naim v. Naim, 302
National League of Cities in
  Garcia v. San Antonio
  Metropolitan Transit
  Authority, 150
National League of Cities v.
  Usery, 149
Nebbia v. New York, 260
Nelson, State v., 387
Nevada Department of Human
  Resources v. Hibbs, 342, 440
New Orleans City Park
  Improvement Ass'n v. Detiege,
  301
New Orleans v. Dukes, 306
New York Transit Authority v.
  Beazer, 306
New York v. United States, 151
NFIB v. Sebelius, 6, 81, 103, 145,
  147, 163, 177, 410
Nguyen v. INS, 337
Nixon v. Fitzgerald, 226, 227
Nixon v. Herndon, 355
Nixon v. United States, 39, 48
Nixon, United States v., 4, 225
NLRB v. Friedman-Harry Marks
  Clothing Co., 129
NLRB v. Jones & Laughlin Steel
  Corporation, 129
NLRB v. Noel Canning, 197
Nollan v. Cal. Coastal Comm'n,
  270

Northwest Austin Municipal
  Utility District Number One v.
  Holder, 447
Norwood v. Harrison, 250
Obergefell v. Hodges, 3, 416
Ortwein v. Schwab, 364
Osborn v. Bank of the United
  States, 99
Palko v. Connecticut, 242
Palmore v. Sidoti, 307
Panama Refining Co. v. Ryan,
  194
Parents Involved in Community
  Schools v. Seattle Sch. Dist.
  No. 1, 292, 304
Paris Adult Theatre I v. Slaton,
  412
Passenger Cases, 367
Patchak v. Zinke, 37
Patterson v. McLean Credit
  Union, 432
Penhandle Oil Co. v. Mississippi
  ex rel. Knox, 97
Penn Central Transportation Co.
  v. City of New York, 268
Pennhurst State School and
  Hospital v. Halderman, 177
Pennsylvania Coal Co v. Mahon,
  267
Perkins, United States v., 199
Personnel Administrator v.
  Feeney, 310, 341
Philadelphia, City of v. New
  Jersey, 159
Pierce v. Society of Sister, 379
Pierson v. Ray, 226
Pink, United States v., 210
Planned Parenthood of Se. Pa. v.
  Casey, 4, 401
Planned Parenthood v. Ashcroft,
  398
Planned Parenthood v. Danforth,
  397
Plessy v. Ferguson, 288, 291
Plyler v. Doe, 372
Poe v. Ullman, 388
Pollock v. Farmers' Loan and
  Trust Company, 40
Powell v. McCormick, 47
Prigg v. Pennsylvania, 282
Printz v. United States, 153
Prize Cases, The, 212
Quirin, Ex parte, 214
Railway Express Agency v. New
  York, 263, 306
Reed v. Reed, 329, 331, 396
Regents of the University of
  California v. Bakke, 314

Reno v. Condon, 154
Reynolds v. Sims, 349
Richmond, City of v. J.A. Croson Company, 314
Roe v. Wade, 3, 58, 392
Rome, City of v. United States, 445
Romer v. Evans, 306, 412
Ross v. Moffitt, 363
Rostker v. Goldberg, 333
Runyon v. McCrary, 432
Sabri v. United States, 102
Saenz v. Roe, 241, 368
Salyer Land Co. v. Tulare Lake Basin Water Storage Dist., 352
San Antonio Independent School District v. Rodriguez, 370
Sanchez, United States v., 172
Sanger v. People, 386
Schechter Poultry Corporation v. United States, 123
Schilb v. Kuebel, 244
Schuette v. Coalition to Defend Affirmative Action, 321
Sessions v. Morales-Santana, 339
Shapiro v. Thompson, 367
Shaw v. Reno, 356
Shelby County v. Holder, 428, 447
Shelley v. Kramer, 247
Sierra Club v. Morton, 50
Skinner v. Oklahoma ex rel. Williamson, 383
Slaughter House Cases, 239, 369
Smith v. Allwright, 355, 356
Sonzinsky v. United States, 171
Sosna v. Iowa, 368
South Carolina State Highway Dept. v. Barnwell Brothers, 159, 161
South Carolina v. Katzenbach, 443, 445
South Carolina v. United States, 69
South Dakota v. Dole, 166, 177
South Dakota v. Wayfair, 161
Spokeo, Inc. v. Robins, 55
Stafford v. Wallace, 122
Stenberg v. Carhart, 405
Steward Machine Co. v. Davis, 166
Strauder v. West Virginia, 288, 290
Struck v. Sec'y of, Def., 326
Stuart v. Laird, 20
Sugarman v. Dougall, 344
Sveen v. Mellon, 272
Sweat v. Painter, 297

Taylor v. Louisiana, 327
Tennessee v. Lane, 440
Terry v. Adams, 356
Testa v. Katt, 156
Thornburgh v. American College of Obstetricians and Gynecologists, 398
Tileston v. Ullman, 387, 388
Trump v. Hawaii, 216, 219
Turner v. Safle, 381
Twining v. New Jersey, 241
United States Dep't of Agriculture v. Moreno, 306
United States Railroad Retirement Board v. Fitz, 306
Vacco v. Quill, 423
Veazie Bank v. Fenno, 167, 173
Vieth v. Jubelirer, 48, 360
Virginia, Ex parte, 290
Virginia, United States v., 330, 334, 336, 337
Voinovich v. Quilter, 351
Washington v. Davis, 309
Washington v. Glucksberg, 423
Weber v. Aetna Casualty & Surety Company, 344
Webster v. Reproductive Health Services, 399
Weinberger v. Wiesenfeld, 332
West Coast Hotel v. Parrish, 261
West v. Atkins, 250
Westberry v. Sanders, 350
Whitford v. Gill, 361
Whitman v. American Trucking Associations, Inc., 194
Whole Woman's Health v. Hellerstedt, 408
Wickard v. Filburn, 130
Williamson v. Lee Optical, 261, 306
Willson v. Black-Bird Creek Marsh Co., 115, 159
Windsor, United States v., 417
Wygant v. Jackson Bd. of Educ., 314
Yick Wo v. Hopkins, 308
Young, Ex parte, 151
Youngberg v. Romeo, 422
Youngstown Sheet & Tube Co. v. Sawyer, 13, 28, 186, 190
Zablocki v. Redhail, 381
Zivotofsky v. Clinton, 47
Zivotovsky v. Kerry (Zivotovsky II), 207

INDEX

References are to Pages

ABORTION
Fundamental Rights, this index

ADVISORY OPINIONS, 43, 45

AFFORDABLE CARE ACT LITIGATION
Interstate Commerce Clause, 146
Necessary and Proper Clause, 104
Taxes and penalties distinguished, 174
Taxing and spending powers, 163

APPOINTMENTS OF SUPREME COURT JUSTICES
Confirmation procedure, 5, 33
Political influences, 4

BILL OF RIGHTS
Generally, 231 et seq.
Federal government, original limitation to
Generally, 231
See also Incorporation Doctrine, this index
Historical background, 13
Individual rights protections, development of, 233
Ratification discussions, 234
State Action Doctrine, this index

CHECKS AND BALANCES
Formalist and functionalist analyses distinguished, 223
Judicial review as supporting mechanism, 28

COLLECTIVE ACTION PROBLEMS
Articles of Confederation era, 81
Commerce Clause as remediation tool, 114, 145
Constitutional law remedy, 84

COMMANDEERING
Anti-commandeering principle, constitutional politics, 157
Commerce Clause, 149
Preemption distinguished, 152, 156

COMMERCE CLAUSE
Interstate Commerce Clause, this index

CONGRESSIONAL POWERS
Advice and consent of Senate as to appointments, 195
Concurrent presidential power, 186
Courts, regulation of
Court Packing Plan, this index
Judicial Power, this index
Economic Regulation, this index
Enumerated and implicit powers of Congress, 79
Foreign affairs, 205 et seq.
Interstate Commerce Clause, this index
Military matters, 205 et seq.
Necessary and Proper Clause, this index
Nondelegation doctrine, 194
Political parties, development effects, 189
Presidential power limitations
Congressional appropriations and investigations, 220
Legislative control of statutory implementation, 221
Presidential power tensions, 193
Reconstruction powers
Generally, 427 et seq.
See also Reconstruction Amendments, this index
Taxing and Spending Powers, this index

CONSTITUTIONAL POLITICS
Generally, 2, 328
Affirmative action, 316
Affordable Care Act challenges, 104
Anti-commandeering principle, 157
Commerce Clause litigation, 116, 135
Congressional powers created by Reconstruction Amendments, 429
Court-packing plan, 33
Equality questions, 279
Executive agreements, 212
Foreign affairs powers, 206
Fundamental rights, substantive due process, 424
Gender discrimination, 328
General Welfare Clause authority, 164
Judge-made constitutional law disciplined by, 3, 30
Judicial review and, 17, 29

Litigation, regulation of courts
　　through, 40
Missouri Compromise, 284
Necessary and Proper Clause
　　litigation, 80, 85, 99
Presidential rhetoric, regulation of
　　courts through, 40
Racial and gender equality, 343
Reconstruction Amendments creation
　　of congressional powers, 429
Religious liberty issues, 442
Sex equality, 328
Social movement advocacy,
　　regulation of courts through, 40
Supreme Court jurisprudence as
　　tracking, 5

CONSTRUCTION OF
**　　CONSTITUTIONAL**
**　　PROVISIONS**
Interpretation of Constitution, this
　　index

CONTRACEPTION
Fundamental Rights, this index

COUNTER-MAJORITARIAN
**　　DIFFICULTY**
Generally, 71
Carolene Products vs originalism
　　interpretation theories, 65
Interpretation theories, 60

COURT PACKING PLAN
Generally, 127, 260
Constitutional politics, 33
Switch in time that saved nine, 128

DEPARTMENTALISTS, 27, 101

DICTUM, 23, 59

DISCRIMINATION
Racial and Gender Equality, this
　　index
Sexual orientation, 412

DORMANT COMMERCE
**　　CLAUSE**
Interstate Commerce Clause, this
　　index

ECONOMIC REGULATION
Generally, 255 et seq.
Carolene Products judicial review
　　limitations, 264
Contract rights protections, 256
Due process, substantive and
　　procedural, 255
Equal protection challenges, 262
Historical background, 14
Interpretation theories, 62
Judicial review limitations, 264

Lochner Era
　　Generally, 255
　　Retreat from Lochner, 264
New Deal Era, 260
Nineteenth century decisions, 255
Procedural due process limitations,
　　273
Rational basis review, 260
Substantive due process protections
　　Applications, 257
　　Retreat from, 260
Supreme Court principles,
　　development of, 255
Takings Clause as judicial review
　　mechanism, 267

EXECUTIVE POWER
Presidential Power, this index

FEDERALISM, FEDERAL
**　　POWERS, AND FEDERAL**
**　　SUPREMACY**
Generally, 79
Anti-commandeering principle, 149
Articles of Confederation era, 81
Collective action federalism, 114, 145
Commerce Clause applications
　　testing, 109
Crisis of federalism in Civil War era,
　　232
Enumerated vs general powers, state
　　governments distinguished, 79
Implicit and enumerated powers of
　　Congress, 79
Necessary and Proper Clause, this
　　index
Preemption, 111
State governments distinguished,
　　enumerated vs general powers,
　　79
States' Rights, this index
Tenth Amendment limitations
　　Generally, 79
　　Necessary and Proper Clause
　　　　tensions, 84
Tenth Amendment tensions, 307

FUNDAMENTAL RIGHTS
　　Generally, 347 et seq.
Abortion
　　Generally, 392
　　Fundamental nature of, 395
　　Government funding, 398
　　Informed consent issues, 399
　　Liberty interest, 399
　　Medical procedure laws
　　　　restrictions, 408
　　Partial-Birth Abortion Ban Act,
　　　　407
　　Politicalization of issue, 393,
　　　　396

Precedent observance in
  subsequent decisions, 403
Privacy, 393
Procedural restrictions, 396
Standard of review, 402
Trimester framework
    Generally, 394
    Undue burden test
      distinguished, 399,
      403
  Undue burden test
    Generally, 399, 401
    Medical procedure laws
      restrictions, 408
    Trimester framework
      distinguished, 399,
      403
Constitutional politics influencing,
  424
Contraception
  Religious Freedom Restoration
    Act of 1993, 438
  Substantive due process, 384
Direct and indirect protections, 347
Equal protection
    Generally, 347 et seq.
    Historical background, 14
    Indigents, access to ballot, 365
    Indigents, access to courts, 362
    Interstate travel rights, 366
    Legislative districting, 348
    Political gerrymandering, 359
    Public education rights, 369
    Racial gerrymandering, 355
    Redistricting disputes, 348
    Voting rights, 365
    Welfare benefit rights, 370
Family autonomy rights, 378
Gay rights, 410
Indigents, access to ballot, 365
Indigents, access to courts, 362
Interstate travel rights, 366
Legislative districting, 348
Marriage rights, 380
Parental rights, 378
Political gerrymandering, 359
Privacy rights
    Abortion, 393
    Contraception, 389
    End of life, 421
Public education rights, 369
Racial gerrymandering, 355
Redistricting disputes, 348
Reproductive rights
    Generally, 381 et seq.
    Gendered assumptions, 387 et
      seq.
Same sex marriage, 416
Sexual orientation discrimination,
  412
Sodomy laws, 411

Sterilization, 382
Substantive due process
    Generally, 377
    Abortion rights, above
    Constitutional politics
      influencing, 424
    Contraception, 384
    Family autonomy rights, 378
    Gay rights, 410
    Historical background, 15
    Marriage rights, 380
    Parental rights, 378
    Privacy rights at the end of life,
      421
    Reproductive rights
        Generally, 381 et
          seq.
        Gendered assumptions,
          387 et seq.
    Same sex marriage, 416
    Sexual orientation
      discrimination, 412
    Sodomy laws, 411
    Sterilization, 382
Voting rights, 365
Welfare benefit rights, 370

GENDER EQUALITY
Racial and Gender Equality, this
  index

GENERAL WELFARE CLAUSE
Taxing and Spending Powers, this
  index

GOVERNMENTAL POWERS
Enumerated vs general powers,
    states and federal governments
    distinguished, 79
Individual rights balancing, 15
New Deal Era challenges, 127
Original limitations, 25

INCORPORATION DOCTRINE
    Generally, 239 et seq.
    See also Bill of Rights, this
      index
Development, 13, 232, 241
Judicial review as mechanism of, 30
Modern jurisprudence, 244
Privileges or Immunities Clause, 239
Slaughter-House Cases limiting, 239
State Action Doctrine, this index

**INDEPENDENT COUNSEL
  APPOINTMENTS,** 196, 200

INDIVIDUAL RIGHTS
    See also Bill of Rights, this
      index; Fundamental
      Rights, this index
Executive power tensions, 214

Governmental powers balancing, 15
Original Constitution, 231

**INTERPRETATION OF
CONSTITUTION**
Carolene Products approach
            Generally, 62
            Counter-majoritarian difficulty,
            65
            Evolutionary theories
                distinguished, 70
            Originalism distinguished, 64
Clear, determinate rules, 60
Common-law constitutionalism, 72,
    76
Consequentialist arguments, 8
Counter-majoritarian difficulty, 60
Dead hand problems
            Generally, 60
            Evolutionary theories, 70
Departmentalists, 27, 101
Dialogic theories, 76
Diversity of evolutionary theories, 70
Eclectic approaches, 76
Economic regulations, 62
Ethos arguments, 8
Evolutionary theories
            Generally, 70 et seq.
            Carolene Products
                distinguished, 70
            Common law development
                parallels, 72
            Court-focused theories, 72
            Dead hand problem, 70
            Diversity of, 70
            Inevitability of constitutional
                evolution, 72
            Originalism distinguished, 67
            Public-focused theories, 74
Historical governmental practice
    arguments, 7, 9
Inevitability of constitutional
    evolution, 72
Judicial discretion applicable, 5
Living constitutionalism
            Generally, 3
            Originalism compared, 67, 69
            Proponents, 9
Modalities of interpretation, 7
Necessary and Proper Clause, strict
    vs liberal constructions, 88
Originalism
            Generally, 3, 64
            Arguments for and against, 65
            Brown decision, explaining, 299
            Carolene Products perspective
                distinguished, 64
            Counter-majoritarian difficulty,
            65
            Evolutionary theories
                distinguished, 67

First- and second-generation
    originalists, 64
Living constitutionalism
    compared, 67, 69
New originalism, 69
Original intent arguments, 7
Original intent vs original
    meaning as foundation,
    66, 67
Precedent tensions, 74, 299
Precedential interpretations
    distinguished, 8
Popular constitutionalism, 76
Precedential arguments
            Generally, 7
            Originalist interpretations
                distinguished, 8
            Political and judicial precedent
                distinguished, 9
Presumption of constitutionality, 62
Prudential arguments, 8
Purposive arguments
            Generally, 8
            Structural arguments
                distinguished, 8
Stare decisis, 61
Statutory interpretation
    distinguished, 111
Strict vs liberal constructions of
    Necessary and Proper Clause,
    88
Structural arguments
            Generally, 7
            Purposive arguments
                distinguished, 8

**INTERSTATE COMMERCE
CLAUSE**
            Generally, 107 et seq.
Affordable Care Act litigation, 146
Agricultural Adjustment Act, 130
Anti-commandeering principle, 149
Brady Handgun Violence Prevention
    Act, 153
Child labor laws, 121
Civil Rights Act of 1964, 132
Collective action problems
    remediation, 114, 145
Constitutional politics, 135
Current Commerce Clause doctrine,
    134, 144
Dangerous goods, 122
Direct and indirect effects on
    interstate commerce, 122, 124
Dormant commerce analysis of state
    laws, 112, 159
Driver's Privacy Protection Act, 154
Economic changes and constitutional
    politics, 116
Economic vs noneconomic activity
    distinctions, 144

Failure of commerce jurisprudence
during Republican Era, 125
Fair Labor Standards Act
Generally, 130
Public employees, applicability
to, 149
Federalism, Commerce Clause
applications testing, 109
Gun Free School Zones Act, 137
Historical background, 12, 108, 115
Intra vs interstate commerce, 122
Lochner Era, 115
Low-Level Radioactive Waste Policy
Amendments Act, 151
Modern applications, 115
National Labor Relations Act, 129
New Deal Era, crisis of, 12, 119, 126
Preemption issues, 111
Production and commerce
distinguished, 118, 124
Professional and Amateur Sports
Protection Act of 1992, 155
Reagan Republicans, 135
Republican Era
Generally, 115
Failure of commerce
jurisprudence during, 125
Intra vs interstate commerce,
122
Limitations, 123
Scope of protected commerce, 112,
118
Slave states' concerns, 115
State marijuana laws, 142
Stream of commerce analysis, 122,
125
Tenth Amendment tensions, 107
Value pluralism, 110
Violence Against Women Act of 1994,
140

JUDICIAL POWER
Generally, 17 et seq.
See also Judicial Review, this
index
Constitutional amendment,
regulation of courts through, 39
Court Packing Plan, this index
Executive officer duties, quasi-
judicial character of, 199
Impeachment of federal judges, 38
Independent counsel appointments,
196, 200
Judiciary Act of 1789, 19, 31
Judiciary Act of 1801
Enactment, 19
Repeal, 20
Jurisdiction of Supreme Court, this
index
Justiciability Doctrines, this index
Litigation, regulation of courts
through, 40

Nomination and confirmation of
federal judges, 37
Presidential power, judicial oversight
limiting, 225
Presidential rhetoric, regulation of
courts through, 40
Regulation of courts
Generally, 31 et seq.
Appointments of Justices,
political aspects, 5, 33
Constitutional amendment, 39
Impeachment of federal judges,
38
Litigation, regulation through,
40
New Deal, Court-packing
controversy, 33
Nomination and confirmation
of federal judges, 37
Presidential rhetoric, 40
Social movement advocacy, 40
Size of Supreme Court, congressional
regulation
Generally, 31, 127
See also Court Packing Plan,
this index
Social movement advocacy,
regulation of courts through, 40
Subject matter jurisdiction of
Supreme Court, 21

JUDICIAL REVIEW
Generally, 17 et seq.
See also Judicial Power, this
index
Advisory opinions limitation, 43, 45
Arguments supporting, 24
Avoidance, constitutional, 23, 29
Burden of proof, 61
Checks and balances principle
supporting, 28
Countermajoritarian difficulties, 2
Deferential approach to, 61
Economic regulation, *Carolene
Products* judicial review
limitations, 264
Formalist and functionalist analysis
distinguished, 222
Functional arguments for, 27
Historical background, 17
Implementing judicial review, 43 et
seq.
Incorporation doctrine development,
30
Interpretation of Constitution, this
index
Jurisdictional limits, 43
Justiciability doctrines limiting
Generally, 44
See also Justiciability
Doctrines, this index
Limitations, 43 et seq.

Origin of doctrine, 11
Political judgment as prudential
  element, 30
Presumption of constitutionality, 62
Prudential limitations, 59
Separation of powers principle
  supporting, 28
Standard of review
  Abortion rights, 402
  Carolene Products standard,
    62, 260, 347
  Equal Protection Clause
    claims, 347
  Racial and Gender Equality,
    this index
  Sexual orientation
    discrimination, 413
Supremacy Clause arguments for, 26
Takings Clause as judicial review
  mechanism, 267
Vertical vs horizontal, 26, 29

**JURISDICTION OF SUPREME
  COURT**
Appellate and original jurisdiction
  distinguished, 23, 35
Congressional control of federal
  courts' jurisdiction, 34, 36
Judicial review, jurisdictional limits,
  43
Subject matter jurisdiction, 21, 25

JUSTICIABILITY DOCTRINES
Generally, 44 et seq.
Advisory opinions, 43, 45
Cases or controversies, 44
Development, 11
Injury-in-fact component of standing
  test, 50
Judicial review limitations, 44 et seq.
Mootness
  Generally, 55
  Capable of repetition yet
    evading review, 58
Nexus theories of standing, 52
Political question doctrine, 45
Prudential extensions of justiciability
  doctrines, 56, 59
Ripeness, 55
Standing to seek relief, 48
Three-part standing test, 49, 51
Value-laden nature of standing
  questions, 59

LEGISLATIVE POWER
Congressional Powers, this index

MEDICAID
Abortion funding, 398
Taxing and spending powers, 163,
  178

**NECESSARY AND PROPER
  CLAUSE**
Generally, 80, 85 et seq.
Affordable Care Act litigation, 104
Modern applications, 102
National bank disputes
  First bank bill, 85
  Second bank bill, 90
  Supreme Court resolution, 90
Necessary vs proper activities, 105
Scope of Clause, 85
Separation of powers issues, 85
Strict vs liberal constructions, 88
Supremacy Clause as maxim of
  political law, 92
Tenth Amendment tensions, 84, 94

ORIGINALISM
Interpretation of Constitution, this
  index

**POLITICS AFFECTING
  CONSTITUTIONAL LAW**
Constitutional Politics, this index
Senate advice and consent to
  appointments, 4, 195

**POPULAR
  CONSTITUTIONALISM, 76**

PRECEDENT
Force of, 4, 7
Negative precedent, 336
Originalism tensions, 74, 299
Supreme Court reliance on
  Generally, 8
  Abortion cases, 403

PREEMPTION
Commandeering principle
  distinguished, 152, 156
Commerce Clause powers, 111
Marijuana laws, 142
Sports betting laws, 155

PRESIDENTIAL POWER
Generally, 183 et seq.
Advice and consent of Senate as to
  appointments, 4, 195
Broad powers beyond the explicit
  grants, 188
Checks on, 220
Chief executive, President as, 194
Commander-in-Chief powers, 190,
  212
Concurrent Congressional power, 186
Congressional appropriations and
  investigations limiting, 220
Congressional power tensions, 193
Constitutional role of President, 183
Courts, regulation of. See Judicial
  Power, this index

Executive agreements and treaties, 209
Foreign affairs, 205 et seq.
Founding era tensions, 186
Historical background, 12
Immunity, presidential, 225
Implied removal power, 198
Independent counsel appointments, 196, 200
Individual rights tensions, 214
Inherent foreign affairs powers, 206
Japanese internment order, 218
Judicial oversight limiting, 225
Legislation shaping, 195
Legislative control of statutory implementation limiting, 221
Limitations, 185
Military matters
    Generally, 205 et seq.
    Commander-in-Chief status, 190, 212
Neutrality Proclamation, 188
Parliamentary systems distinguished, 183
Political parties development effects, 189
Privilege, executive, 225
Quasi-judicial character of executive officer duties, 199
Regulation of courts. See Judicial Power, this index
Separation of powers, theoretical perspectives on, 189
Steel Seizure Case, 186
Theoretical perspectives on separation of powers, 189
Treaties and executive agreements, 209
Unitary executive theory, 202
War on terrorism, 216
War powers, 190

PRIVACY
Fundamental Rights, this index

RACIAL AND GENDER EQUALITY
Generally, 279 et seq.
Affirmative action, 313 et seq.
Discriminatory application of neutral statutes, 308
Disparate impact, 308
Education
    Gender discrimination, 334, 336
    Racial discrimination, 295
Equal Protection Clause jurisprudence, development of, 279
Gender discrimination
    Generally, 324 et seq.
    Civil Rights Act of 1964, 328

Constitutional politics considerations, 328
Coverture laws, 324, 327
Education, 334, 336
Equal Rights Amendment, 328
Establishing a sex classification, 340
Inherent differences issues
    Generally, 334
    Pregnancy, 336
Political power of women as group, 330
Race-sex analogy, feminists', 329
Reconstruction Amendments, 326
Reproduction rights, gendered assumptions, 387
Separate spheres era, 279, 324
Standard of review, 330
Stereotyping, 331
Suffrage, 324
Women's rights movements, 325
National origin discrimination, 301
Race-sex analogy, feminists', 329
Racial discrimination
    Generally, 280 et seq.
    Affirmative action, 313 et seq.
    Anti-classification and anti-subordination principles, 293, 301
    Badges of inferiority, 291
    Black codes era, 236
    Colorblind anti-classification principle, 292
    Desegregation cases
        Generally, 295
        Enforcement, 302
    Discriminatory application of neutral statutes, 308
    Disparate impact cases, 308
    Education, 295, 302
    Japanese internment policy, 301
    Jim Crow laws, 289
    Political and civil rights distinctions, 288
    Pre-Civil War history, 285
    Reconstruction Amendments, 285
    Republican Era, 289
    Separate but equal principle, 291
    Slavery era, 280
    Social and civil rights distinctions, 288
    Standard of review, 305
    Supreme Court composition issues affecting decisions, 314, 322

Suspect classification doctrine, 305
Voting rights, racial gerrymandering, 355
Reconstruction Amendments, racial discrimination jurisprudence development, 285
Sexual orientation discrimination, substantive due process challenges, 412
Standard of review
 Gender discrimination challenges, 330, 333
 Racial discrimination challenges, 305
 Suspect classifications, 305

RECONSTRUCTION AMENDMENTS
Generally, 235
Black codes era, 236
Civil Rights Act of 1866, 236
Congressional powers created by
 Generally, 427 et seq.
 Civil Rights Act of 1875, 429
 Civil Rights Act of 1964, 435
 Constitutional politics, 429
 Development, 428
 Fifteenth Amendment enforcement, 443 et seq.
 Fourteenth Amendment enforcement, 430, 432 et seq.
 Nature of power granted, 428
 Religious Freedom Restoration Act of 1993, 438
 State action issues, 428
 States' rights view
  Fifteenth Amendment, 446
  Fourteenth Amendment, 438
 Thirteenth Amendment enforcement, 430, 432
 Voting Rights Act of 1965, 435
Development of congressional powers created by, 428
Gender discrimination, 326
Racial discrimination jurisprudence development, 285
State action doctrine limitations on enforcement, 247

SAME SEX MARRIAGE, 416

SEPARATION OF POWERS
Advisory opinions as violating, 45
Formalist and functionalist analyses distinguished, 223
Judicial review as supporting mechanism, 28

Necessary and Proper Clause effects, 85
Standing doctrine and, 49
State action doctrine, 252
Theoretical perspectives, 189

SEXUAL ORIENTATION DISCRIMINATION, 412

SIZE OF SUPREME COURT
See also Court Packing Plan, this index
Congressional control, 31, 127

SLAVERY
Generally, 280
Commerce Clause authority, slave states' concerns, 115
Federalism issues preceding Civil War, 231
Missouri Compromise, 284
Racial and Gender Equality, this index
Reconstruction Amendments, this index
Supreme Court composition pre-war, slave state representation, 32

SPENDING POWER
Taxing and Spending Powers, this index

STANDARD OF REVIEW
Judicial Review, this index
Racial and Gender Equality, this index

STANDING
Justiciability Doctrines, this index

STARE DECISIS, 61

STATE ACTION DOCTRINE
Generally, 245 et seq.
Civil rights cases, 246, 253
Congressional powers created by
 Reconstruction Amendments, 428
Fifteenth Amendment enforcement, 443 et seq.
Fourteenth Amendment enforcement, 430, 432 et seq.
Individual acts, state sanctioning of, 247
Judicial enforcement availability, 248
Racial covenants in real estate deeds, 247
Reconstruction Amendments
 Congressional powers created by, 428
 Enforcement, 247
Separation of powers function, 252

Supreme Court development, 247
Thirteenth Amendment enforcement,
    430, 432

STATES' RIGHTS
Commerce Clause, Tenth
    Amendment tensions, 107
Congressional powers created by
    Reconstruction Amendments
    Fifteenth Amendment, 446
    Fourteenth Amendment, 438
    Thirteenth Amendment, 430,
        432
Federal government distinguished,
    enumerated vs general powers,
    79
Federalism, Federal Powers, and
    Federal Supremacy, this index
Historical background, 12
Judicial review, vertical vs
    horizontal, 26, 29
Slavery, this index
Tenth Amendment limitations on
    federal powers
        Generally, 79
        Commerce Clause tensions, 107
        Federalism tensions, 307
        Necessary and Proper Clause
            tensions, 84, 94

SUPREMACY CLAUSE
    Generally, 92
Federalism, Federal Powers, and
    Federal Supremacy, this index
Vertical judicial review, 26

TAKINGS CLAUSE, 267

**TAXING AND SPENDING
    POWERS**
        Generally, 163 et seq.
Affordable Care Act Litigation, 163
Coercive spending offers, 180
Conditional federal spending, limits
    on, 176
Disaster relief, 165
General Welfare Clause
        Generally, 163
        Constitutional law of, 166
        Constitutional politics of, 164
Historical background, 12
Internal improvements, 165
Medicaid expansion, 163, 178
Penalties and taxes distinguished,
    167
Purposes limitations, 164
Taxes and penalties distinguished,
    167

TENTH AMENDMENT
States' Rights, this index

VALUE PLURALISM, 110

VOTING
Fundamental Rights, this index
Reconstruction Amendments, this
    index